SOUTH BRIDGE
CATALOGUED
R. Economics
Economics
MEADE
Meade
23299

TO BE
DISPOSED
BY
AUTHORITY

D0260656
5405600627213

THE THEORY OF

INTERNATIONAL ECONOMIC POLICY

VOLUME TWO

TRADE AND WELFARE

The Royal Institute of International Affairs is an unofficial and non-political body founded in 1920 *to encourage and facilitate the scientific study of international questions. The Institute, as such, is precluded by the terms of its Royal Charter from expressing an opinion on any aspect of international affairs. Any opinions expressed in this publication are not, therefore, those of the Institute.*

THE THEORY OF
INTERNATIONAL ECONOMIC POLICY
VOLUME TWO

TRADE AND WELFARE

BY

J. E. MEADE

Professor of Commerce, University of London

Issued under the auspices of the
Royal Institute of International Affairs

OXFORD UNIVERSITY PRESS
LONDON NEW YORK TORONTO
1955

Oxford University Press, Amen House, London, E.C.4
GLASGOW NEW YORK TORONTO MELBOURNE WELLINGTON
BOMBAY CALCUTTA MADRAS KARACHI CAPE TOWN IBADAN
Geoffrey Cumberlege, Publisher to the University

PRINTED IN GREAT BRITAIN

Preface

THIS is the second volume of a theory of international economic policy. The first volume, published in 1951, dealt with three important problems of international economic policy. The first and basic problem there discussed was the maintenance of equilibrium in international balances of payments. Secondly, it was an essential feature of Volume I to look for balance-of-payments policies which were compatible with the maintenance of full employment domestically within each trading country; overall internal and external balance were to be combined. Thirdly, special attention was directed to the circumstances in which internal and external balance could be maintained without recourse to direct controls over trade, payments, or factor movements; in so far as such direct controls can be avoided purely as balance-of-payments instruments, the way is clear to discuss their merits and demerits on other grounds. In fact, such a discussion is the subject-matter of this second volume.

Accordingly, in the present volume we shall proceed upon the assumption that internal and external balance are continually maintained by methods of price adjustment; that is to say, without special recourse to import restrictions or other direct controls. In this volume we turn to a consideration of the other arguments—what may be broadly termed the 'welfare' arguments—in favour of direct controls. Assuming there to be full employment of resources and equilibrium in international balances of payments, we now raise the question whether economic welfare can be increased by direct controls over international movements of commodities or of factors of production. Are there cases in which some direct intervention in international markets is desirable in order to promote a more efficient use of the world's resources or in order to improve the distribution of income?

It had been my intention when I embarked upon this second volume to take over what is often called the 'new welfare economics' and merely to apply it to international economic problems. This intention was foreshadowed to some extent in Volume I, particularly in Chapter XXIV of that volume. Indeed, a first draft of the greater part of the present volume was written on that basis. But then, as is explained in Part I of the present volume, it seemed impossible adequately to incorporate either questions concerning the distribution of income or questions of what will be called the 'second-best'. The first draft of this volume was accordingly scrapped and rewritten on more old-fashioned 'utilitarian' lines. For these reasons Part I of the present volume has become a long essay on the general theory of economic welfare without any special reference to international economic problems. The general theory developed in Part I is then applied to the special case of international trade in Parts II, III, and IV.

The preparation of this preparatory essay on the theory of economic welfare has been much influenced by many recent works on this subject, and in particular by the writings of J. R. Hicks, N. Kaldor, T. de Scitovszky, I. M. D. Little, M. W. Reder, and A. P. Lerner.[1] For example, the problem discussed in Chapter V of this volume is very largely that of the 'compensation' principle enunciated by N. Kaldor modified by the 'bribery' condition enunciated by T. Scitovszky. But in influencing the selection of the method of analysis which has finally been used in this volume, there is one work which has been of predominant importance, namely J. M. Fleming's article 'On Making the Best of Balance of Payments Restrictions on Imports'. This article has been fully but, it is hoped, frankly plagiarized and perhaps slightly developed in Chapter XXXIV of the present volume. The problem discussed in that chapter was left over unsettled from Chapter XXXI of Volume I, and J. M. Fleming's article which deals with exactly the same problem has in my view provided the theoretically correct solution. But in providing the answer to that particular problem it outlined a method of analysis which has been used extensively throughout the present volume; in particular it lies at the back of the treatment of what are called problems of the 'second-best' in Chapter VII of the present volume.

But the perplexing and disturbing question which still remains is whether the whole enterprise is a waste of time or not. Such doubts may arise on two quite separate grounds. First, can 'economic welfare' be in any real sense defined and measured as an ultimate objective of economic policy, or is it a mere will-o'-the-wisp? Second, is there, in any case, any use in a general theory of economic policy as opposed to the application of economic analysis to some specific *ad hoc* problems of policy? The second of these two doubts applies equally well to Volume I of this work as to the present volume. But the first of these two doubts applies only to the present volume which may, therefore, be regarded as doubly suspect.

As far as the possibility of a meaningful theory of economic welfare is concerned, common sense comes to the rescue. If one man is starving but smothered with an excess of warm clothing while his neighbour is sick from overfeeding but shivering naked in the cold, common sense suggests that an economic policy which enabled them to exchange

[1] See N. Kaldor's 'Welfare Propositions of Economics and Interpersonal Comparisons of Utility'; J. R. Hicks' 'The Foundations of Welfare Economics'; T. de Scitovszky's 'A Note on Welfare Propositions in Economics.' I. M. D. Little, *A Critique of Welfare Economics*, M. W. Reder, *Studies in the Theory of Welfare Economics*, and A. P. Lerner, *The Economics of Control*.

clothing and food would in some real sense increase economic welfare. Moreover, if a rich alderman replete from a city dinner should meet a starving beggar and give him the crust of his dinner roll (which he has conveniently brought in his pocket with him), only an excess of philosophy will produce the remark that there is no basis for the judgement that the alderman will feel the loss of the crumbs less than the beggar will feel their gain. No doubt these are both extreme examples—and the foreign reader who is unfamiliar with modern social and economic developments in the United Kingdom is warned that neither of them is very realistic in present conditions in this country. But the theory of economic welfare which is developed and applied in this volume is merely a carrying to its logical conclusion of propositions of these two kinds. In its broad outlines it is certainly relevant and realistic, though some of its refinements may be of little use other than as an intellectual exercise.

The simplest form of any such theory of economic welfare is to argue 'as if' there were an entity 'economic welfare' which is made up of the sum of the separate (but not necessarily independent) 'economic welfares' of each member of the community; and this is the hypothesis adopted throughout this volume. In my view this presents a simple tool of analysis which corresponds sufficiently closely to what most people would regard—at least in a non-totalitarian State—as a sensible meaning of economic welfare, and which enables most if not all of the main questions of policy to be posed. At least this would appear to be the case, as long as the analysis is confined to problems affecting a given set of individual members of the community. Common sense may begin to boggle when, as is done in Chapter VI of this volume, the logic of the principle is carried still further, and a comparison is made between the actual economic welfare of existing members of a population and the potential economic welfare of unborn members of that population. But after due deliberation I decided to let Chapter VI stand for two reasons: first, because it is perhaps only fair to display the ultimate implications of one's methods and assumptions rather than to suppress those cases in which they appear least persuasive; but, second, because, in spite of the rather extravagant flavour which Chapter VI may leave on some palates, in my personal view the analysis does draw attention to some of the realistically most important issues in demographic policies.

The other main question, namely whether in any case the construction of a general theory of economic policy is possible or worth while, applies to the whole conception of these two volumes. The case against this method has been put forcibly by H. G. Johnson in a review of Volume I of this work entitled 'The Taxonomic Approach to Economic Policy'. This review, as is shown later in this preface, has been a chief factor in moderating certain claims for the method which I should have previously made and which I would now regard as excessive. But Mr. Johnson's complete condemnation of the method seems to me to be misplaced.

To condemn taxonomy is to condemn all general economic theory and not only a general theory of economic policy. In what, for example, does the theory of demand consist except in such statements as the following? 'When the price of a product falls, more of it will be bought —except in those cases in which it is so "inferior" in character but so important in the consumer's budget that less of it is bought.' Or, 'if as a result of a fall in the price of a commodity the amount bought goes up more than in proportion to the fall in the price, then the total amount spent on the product will increase, whereas if the amount bought goes up less than in proportion to the fall in the price, then the total amount spent on the product will fall'. And so on. The theory of demand consists of mental exercises in the implications of these different possibilities: and the application of the theory of demand to a particular market consists in observing the facts so as to see into which of these categories the particular example falls. Personally, I fail to see any fundamental advantage in refusing to do any preliminary general exercises, but in insisting on working out separately for each particular issue all the relevant general questions to be raised. On the contrary, there would seem to be grave danger that some possibilities will in that case be overlooked which a more systematic preliminary consideration of logical alternatives would have brought to the surface.

Nevertheless, partly as a result of my own experience in taxonomic theorizing, partly as a direct result of criticisms made of Volume I of this work, and partly through reading Milton Friedman's essay on taxonomy [1] as an indirect result of these criticisms, I would now make less extravagant claims for this approach than I would have been inclined to do when I embarked on this work seven years ago. Taxonomy plus a modicum of awareness of, and experience in, affairs of the real world would probably be able to take one a very long way if one had only to deal with what in the present volume are called the 'utopian' solutions of problems in economic policy. In those circumstances the number of categories of possible cases about which one could not make fairly reliable realistic assumptions would be limited. Some very important doubtful cases would remain. An outstanding example of this would be the vital issue of fact mentioned in connexion with Volume I, namely whether the price elasticities of demand for imports in international trade are in general sufficiently large to enable balances of payments to be kept in equilibrium by means of price adjustments. But when allowance is made for the necessity for making what are called in the present volume choices between 'second-best' policies—when, that

[1] See Milton Friedman's 'Lange on Price Flexibility and Employment'.

is to say, it is necessary to allow for the fact that one 'imperfection' in policy may be positively desirable in order to offset the evil effects of some other and inevitable 'imperfection' of policy or of institutions—then the number of possible relevant categories of cases becomes so large that detailed factual study of each separate case becomes much more important.

When it comes to making these particular applications of policy, it is necessary to assess the quantitative importance of very many different factors. I am very doubtful whether in the present stage of development of the subject much help can be expected in this task from refined econometric methods of measurement. The quantitative relationships are so many in number, so complicated in their relationships, and so unlikely to remain constant for any considerable length of time or to be the same in different countries. The conclusion would seem to be a rather discouraging one. The best course would seem to be to undertake general taxonomic analysis as an exercise in looking for important factors and important relationships, and then to turn to the study of particular problems, making what use one can of such quantitative and other factual information as can be gleaned from the present development of econometric studies, from case studies, and from the feel of the market. Perhaps for a long time economic policy in the final count must remain much more of an art than of a science.

In the preparation of the present volume extensive use has been made of the work of other writers on international economic problems. The general works on the theory of international trade by Haberler, Viner, Harrod, Ohlin, Mosak, Stolper and Samuelson, de Scitovszky, and Lerner, which are mentioned in the preface to Volume I of this work, have been of equal help in the preparation of the present volume. I fear that I may have borrowed particular ideas from colleagues in the following chapters without realizing my indebtedness. If so, I hope they will excuse me. But authors to whom I am consciously indebted for particular ideas in this volume are as follows. My treatment in Chapter VI of the optimum level of savings is essentially based upon F. P. Ramsay's 'A Mathematical Theory of Saving'. Chapters XX–XXIII owe much to A. P. Lerner's 'Factor Prices and International Trade' and to P. A. Samuelson's two articles on 'International Factor-Price Equalisation'. Chapter XXV is based largely on J. M. Buchanan's 'Federalism and Fiscal Equity' and A. D. Scott's 'A Note on Grants in Federal Countries', and on the controversy between these two authors on 'Federal Grants and Resource Allocation'. Chapters XVII and XVIII contain ideas taken from Lloyd A. Metzler's 'Tariffs, the Terms of Trade, and the Distribution of National Income'. Appendix IV is based on ideas in Alfred Weber's *The Theory of Location of Industries*. Chapter XXXII owes a very great deal to J. Viner, *The Customs Union Issue*.

An important pitfall in Chapter XVII was avoided by reading the admirable taxonomic classification of possible cases contained in H. G. Johnson's 'Optimum Tariffs and Retaliation'. As has already been mentioned, Chapter XXXIV is based almost wholly on J. M. Fleming's 'On Making the Best of Balance of Payments Restrictions on Imports'.

In form this Volume II is the mixture as before. A great deal of the verbal argument is based upon geometric and simple algebraic models. The geometry has already been published in my *A Geometry of International Trade*. The algebraic models, for the clumsiness of which I would once more apologize to any mathematician who may see them, are published as a special mathematical supplement to this volume. In the main volume I have once more made extensive use of arithmetical examples. Experience convinces me that there is a considerable class of readers for whom such a method is really helpful. But I have tried to minimize the tedium which they may cause to other readers by putting many of them, together with other bits of geometry or algebra, in appendices at the end of the main volume. The volume can be read as a whole without any reference to these appendices or to the mathematical supplement.

I would like to thank Mr. L. F. Manneke and Mr. J. Veverka for their work in preparing the index for this volume. Once more I must express my sincere gratitude to Professor Lionel Robbins, who read my manuscript and made important suggestions for its improvement, and to the Royal Institute of International Affairs who, by means of a continued grant from the Rockefeller Foundation, have sponsored the second half of this study in the Theory of International Economic Policy.

J. E. MEADE

London School of Economics
and Political Science

June 1954

Contents

PART IV. MULTILATERAL TRADE

APPENDICES

List of Tables

PART I. THE THEORY OF ECONOMIC WELFARE

PART I. THE THEORY OF ECONOMIC WELFARE

CHAPTER I

INTRODUCTION

In the first volume of this work we discussed the problems involved in reconciling domestic policies for the maintenance of full employment with the preservation of equilibrium in international balances of payments. Accordingly, throughout this volume we shall assume that economic resources are fully employed and that international balances of payment are in equilibrium.

But the full utilization of economic resources is by no means the only condition which is necessary in order to raise standards of living as high as possible. It is, of course, a very important condition. If resources of men, machinery, and other useful economic factors are being left in idleness, then it should be possible by bringing them into employment to produce more goods and services of every kind so that, with an efficient system of distribution, every citizen could be simultaneously better off than before. But it does not follow that, merely because resources are more or less fully employed, it will be impossible to raise standards of living still further. It is necessary also to ensure that resources are used to the best purpose. This volume will be devoted to international problems concerning the best use, as opposed to the full use, of economic resources.

In the previous volume we concentrated upon those aspects of economic analysis which were most useful for an understanding of governmental policies; and we shall continue this emphasis upon problems of economic policy. But the subject-matter will, of course, be different. In the former volume we discussed the domestic fiscal and monetary policies (for example, rates of taxation and rates of interest) needed to maintain full employment and considered the other measures of governmental policy (for example, the control of imports and the variation of exchange rates) which would be necessary to maintain simultaneously an equilibrium in the balance of external payments. In this volume we shall be considering once more the use of many of the same instruments of governmental policy. For example, a large part of this volume will be devoted to a consideration of policies of protection; but in this case we shall be considering the arguments for limiting imports by tariffs or by quantitative import restrictions or other commercial-policy devices, not in order to achieve full employment without disturbing the balance of payments, but in order to obtain a more effective use of a given amount of economic resources.

In order to form a final judgement on questions of economic policy it is, of course, necessary to combine the considerations of Volumes I and II. An example will make this clear. Suppose that we were to reach the conclusion in the present volume that, in some relevant sense, the most efficient use of the world's economic resources would be achieved in the absence of all commercial-policy barriers to international trade. This in itself would constitute an important argument in favour of using instruments other than import restrictions for the maintenance of equilibrium in the balance of payments. In the terminology of Volume I, it would constitute a strong reason for preferring price-adjustment mechanisms (such as exchange-rate variations) to direct controls (such as import restrictions) for dealing with balance-of-payments problems, even though the latter were in some respects more effective or more reliable purely as balance-of-payments instruments.[1] From time to time in the following pages we shall refer explicitly to this consideration, and shall refer to the problem of reconciling the policies which are most likely to produce the best use of resources with the policies which are most likely to lead to the full use of resources. But for the most part the reader will be left to himself to make his own final choice of policies in view of the considerations raised in the former volume as well as those raised in this volume.

We shall not in fact reach the conclusion in this volume that there are no circumstances at all in which trade controls of one form or another may lead to a better use of the world's resources. Our purpose will be to discuss and to define in some detail those precise circumstances in which trade controls may be desirable from this point of view. It will be left to the reader to decide for himself, in the light of the analysis of Volume I, whether there is a case for a still further movement away from the free-trade position on the purely balance-of-payments considerations discussed in Volume I.

We have then to consider what are the conditions which, apart from the full use of resources, are necessary in order to achieve the highest possible standards of living. This branch of economic analysis is often known as the 'economics of welfare'. In Part I of this volume we shall undertake a general discussion of the theory of economic welfare before applying it to problems of international trade in Parts II, III, and IV. Part I will have to be of considerable length because the existing general theory of the subject is not in a form which is altogether suitable for our present purpose.

In the chapters which follow, for reasons which will be discussed

[1] See Chapters XXII and XXIII of Volume I.

later, we shall adopt very largely the old-fashioned utilitarian criterion of considering the total economic welfare of the community as made up of the sum of economic welfares of all its individual citizens; and we shall attempt to judge all acts of policy from the point of view of their effects upon this total sum.

Such will be our definition of the economic criterion: the maximization of the sum of individual economic welfares. But it is important to realize that the statesman cannot confine himself to this economic criterion, even when it is so defined—as ours is—that it allows for effects upon the distribution as well as for effects upon the size of the community's income. There are other social and political criteria of which we need mention only two: freedom and equality.

Thus the removal of a number of direct controls over economic activities will often add to the freedom of action of the individual citizens. As we shall see in what follows, it will also often raise standards of living and increase economic welfare. But it is not always so. In what follows we shall frequently find cases in which some measures of State intervention in the economic system might lead to an increase of economic welfare. In these cases there is some conflict between the economic criterion of raising standards of living and the political criterion of individual freedom.

Or consider the choice between equality and economic welfare. Citizen A has an income of 200 and citizen B of 400. A policy which involved transferring 100 from B to A would increase equality; and it would probably also increase economic welfare since an additional 100 to A who has only 200 is likely to mean more than it does to B whose income is 400. A with 300 plus B with 300 adds up to more equality and to more economic welfare than A with 200 plus B with 400. But suppose now that the measures for the equal redistribution of income (for example, the taking away in taxation of all incomes above the average level and the supplementation out of the State budget of all personal incomes below the average level) remove a great part of the incentives to earn income. We might then have a choice between A with 100 plus B with 100 or A with 200 plus B with 400. The first would add up to more equality than the second; but the second would add up to more economic welfare than the first, since in the second case both A and B have larger incomes than in the first case.

Thus a more equal distribution of income may be required as a means of raising economic welfare, and that is the context in which we shall discuss it in the rest of this volume. But beyond a point there may be a conflict between more equality and more economic welfare. Measures which increase equality still further may reduce total economic welfare. Now some people may hold that equality in itself is not worth anything; it is valuable only in so far as it is a means for making the available income give the greatest result in economic welfare. To such there will be no conflict between the ends of economic welfare and equality. But to those who value equality in itself, who consider that a society is more desirable if it lacks class distinctions between rich and poor, there may well be a conflict between equality and welfare.

In cases such as these where economic welfare conflicts with freedom or with equality or with some other recognized social end, some political decision is required in order to decide how much of the one should be sacrificed for how much of the other. Such decisions are not in themselves primarily economic, even though they may be—and usually are—involved in deciding upon acts of economic policy.

In what follows we shall be concerned only with economic welfare, not with the other social ends of freedom, equality, and the like. But in considering what governmental policies may be adopted even for this limited purpose of raising economic welfare, there are three important cross-classifications of policies to be remembered. We shall refer to these three bases of choice between policies in the following terms:

(1) *Marginal* as contrasted with *Structural* adjustments.

(2) Considerations of *Efficiency* as compared with considerations of *Equity*.

(3) *Utopian* as compared with *Second-best* types of policy.

It may be useful to say something about each of these major considerations before we embark upon the analysis itself.

(1) *Marginal versus structural adjustments.* When we are considering, for example, the level of an import duty which is levied by a particular government upon the imports of a particular product, there are two types of question which we may pose. We may ask ourselves: 'Would a small reduction in this duty—from, say, 200 per cent *ad valorem* to 195 per cent *ad valorem*—be a movement in the right direction or not?' Or we may pose the quite different question: 'Would the total elimination of this duty—i.e. its reduction from 200 per cent to zero—improve economic welfare?' Questions of the former type we shall call 'marginal' problems and those of the latter type 'structural' problems.

In fact, it is much easier to find answers to marginal than to structural problems. It is difficult enough to decide whether it is in the interests of the efficiency of the world's resources that the scale of a particular industry should be somewhat increased in this country and somewhat reduced in another country. But we shall hope to find criteria which it may not be totally impossible to apply for the answer of such problems. It is quite another matter to find an answer to questions involving vast structural changes, such as whether world welfare would be improved by the installation of industry on a considerable scale in a country which previously had produced only agricultural products. Such a vast structural change might so completely alter many of the surrounding economic conditions that it is almost impossible to say in advance what the results would be.

A simple analogy may help to make the distinction clear. A man wishes to get to the highest point on a range of hills. If, starting wherever he happens to be, he always walks uphill, he will reach the summit of the particular hill on which he happens to stand. Even in a dense fog his senses will enable him to know whether he is walking uphill or downhill. But he may not be climbing the highest hill in the range, and in a dense fog it will be impossible and even in clear weather very difficult for him with his own unaided senses to determine which is the highest hill which he ought to be climbing. Some more elaborate instruments will be necessary for this purpose. A government may perhaps hope, by the means which we shall develop, to know whether in slightly raising a duty it is increasing or decreasing welfare. It will be a totally different problem for it to decide whether the great structural changes which would follow on a huge programme of economic development with large structural changes in its commercial policy will leave it better or worse off. Nevertheless, whatever hill one has chosen—whether it be the right one or not—one will always get higher by walking uphill; though it may be difficult to be sure whether the correct structure has been chosen, it is nevertheless important and useful to know the marginal rules for making the best of a given structure.

(2) *Efficiency versus equity*. We may say that an economic policy has led to an inefficient economic situation (or, more briefly, that an economic policy is an inefficient one) when a change in that policy would make it *possible* for one citizen to be made better off without any other citizen being worse off. But this is not at all the same thing as saying that the change in the policy would *actually* make the one citizen better off without making any other citizen worse off. It might, in fact, also involve a redistribution of welfare between the various citizens so that the one citizen was made a great deal better off while some other citizen was made slightly worse off, all other citizens remaining as they were. If it had this effect, the desirability of the change in policy would clearly be less certain than if it left no citizen worse off than before.

A simple illustration will serve to make the issue clear. Suppose that the reduction of very high rates of tax on high incomes from profits together with a corresponding reduction of expenditure on certain social services would so improve the economic incentives of entrepreneurs throughout the economy that more of every single product would be produced. Clearly, in the new situation everyone *could* be better off; every single citizen *could* have more of every single commodity to consume. But the result might, in fact, be that while all profit-makers and even most wage-earners were better off some few of the poorest members of the community might be worse off. The new situation could be called a more efficient one; but in view of its effect upon the distribution of incomes, it might nevertheless be judged an undesirable change. In what follows we shall talk of an economic system being more or less efficient according as it approaches more or less nearly to a situation in which it is impossible to make any one citizen better off without making someone else worse off; and we shall talk of the distribution of income as being more or less equitable according as it approaches more nearly to a pattern in which it is impossible to increase the sum of individual economic welfares merely by transferring income from one citizen to another.

One of the major tasks of the theory of economic welfare is to disentangle these efficiency and equity aspects of changes in policy. The criterion of economic efficiency is in one sense clearly more objective than that of economic equity. Theoretically, at least, it is possible to inquire objectively whether each individual citizen would prefer one situation to another, and a change in policy is an efficient one if it enables some citizens to move into a preferred situation without causing any others to move into a less preferred situation. But when a change involves making someone better off and somebody else worse off, clearly some outside subjective decision must be taken as to whether the increased welfare of the former outweighs the decreased welfare of the latter.

(3) *Utopian versus second-best solutions.* When we consider a particular act of policy—for example, the removal of a duty on the import of a particular product—we can consider it on either of two basic conditions. We can assume that this policy only is subject to revision, all other policies remaining unchanged—for example, all other import duties remaining at their existing level. Or we can assume that a simultaneous revision of all existing policies is being undertaken—in our example, that the abolition of all other import duties is also under consideration. Now there may be a much stronger case for the removal of one import duty (say, an import duty on Australian wheat) if import duties on other products (say, on Canadian wheat) are also removed. When we ask whether it would be a good thing to alter one particular policy, we shall say that we are applying a utopian criterion if we assume that all other policies are of an optimum nature, and we shall say that we are applying a second-best criterion if we assume that all other policies continue to be just what they happen to be at the moment. As we shall see in the sequel, the application of the second-best criterion may lead to results which are very different from those reached by the application of a utopian criterion.

In the remaining chapters of this Part we shall undertake a general analysis of the theory of economic welfare, bearing in mind the three main considerations outlined above. In the following Parts we shall apply this analysis to the problems of international economic policy. In making this application of the criteria of economic welfare to problems of international economic policy, it is possible to take either a national or a cosmopolitan point of view. That is to say, in a world made up of countries A, B, C, D, etc., one can take as one's criterion for economic policy either the sum of the welfares of the citizens of A, the citizens of B, C, D, etc., counting for nothing, or the sum of the welfares of all the world citizens, each person in each country counting equally. The basic outlook of this volume will be the cosmopolitan one, although the argument will be so presented that the nationalist should also be able to derive from it the analysis which is appropriate to his own case.[1]

[1] See Chapter IX and Figure LI of my *A Geometry of International Trade* for a geometrical representation of the difference between the nationalist and the cosmopolitan criteria for economic welfare.

CHAPTER II

DIVERGENCES BETWEEN MARGINAL SOCIAL VALUES AND COSTS

(1) *Values and Costs*

BEFORE we turn to a more detailed consideration of the actual conditions which must be fulfilled in order to raise standards of living to the highest possible level, there is one preliminary matter to be discussed. It concerns a problem which, as we shall see, is continually coming up for discussion in the following chapters.

In a free-enterprise economy activity consists in a great number of independent decisions on the part of independent economic agents to use certain economic resources or factors of production to produce certain results. Common sense suggests that such free agents are more likely to decide to do what is in the interests of society if the rewards which they are offered in each activity correspond to the value to society of the additional product which they would produce in each line of activity. We shall submit this common-sensical conclusion to more rigid analysis in subsequent chapters. But this chapter is devoted to a consideration of the factors which in a more or less free economy will determine the relation between rewards and products.

Suppose that someone decides to put into employment a previously unemployed unit of a given economic resource (e.g. one more unit of labour) in producing a particular commodity or group of commodities. For example, a farmer takes on one more farm-labourer to increase his production of wheat. The result will be a certain net increase in the products produced in the community. This net increase we shall call the *marginal social net product* of labour employed on this farm.

We speak of the *marginal* product of labour because we are not at present dealing with large structural changes but only with the small extra product which would be produced as a result of employing a small additional amount of labour; and it is to be distinguished from the *average* product of labour which would express the total output of the product divided by the total labour force employed, i.e. in our case the total output of wheat divided by the total number of farm-workers employed on the farm.

We speak of the *social* product of labour because we are considering the additional production which accrues to the whole society and not merely the additional output which accrues to the particular farmer employing the additional labour. This latter is called the *private* product of labour. An example may help to make the distinction clear. Suppose that our farmer employs the additional labour to drain his land

and thereby to increase his output of wheat. This drainage may affect the moisture of his neighbour's land and may thus improve or worsen his neighbour's crop. The marginal *social* product is the total increase in the output of both farmers' crops resulting from the labour employed by the first farmer; and the marginal *private* product is the change in the output of the first farmer's farm alone, which is all that the first farmer will have in mind when he considers the profitability of employing the additional labour.

Finally, we speak of the *net* product of labour and not of the *gross* product of labour in order to emphasize the fact that we are considering only the net maintainable increase in output. An example will again help to make the distinction clear. By taking on more labour to farm his land more intensively a farmer can increase his output of wheat. But this more intensive farming may gradually diminish the fertility of the land, unless steps are taken to restore it. The *net* product of labour is the increase in the output of wheat which can be achieved by taking on more labour when a sufficient part of that labour is employed not directly to produce more wheat here and now but indirectly to take such steps as are necessary to maintain the fertility of the land unimpaired.

Now let us give the name 'marginal cost of a factor' to the amount of additional money income which in any given situation the owner of a factor of production would have to receive in order to find it just worth while providing another unit of that factor for employment by a particular employer. A man is working 6 hours a day for a particular employer, and is receiving and enjoying a certain money income. In order to be willing to work a 7th hour each day for that employer, he must in these conditions receive an additional income of $1 a day from that employer so as to offset the loss of leisure and the additional strain of the work which would be involved if he worked harder or to offset the loss of income involved if he transferred his labour from some other employer. If he could thereby add more than $1 to his daily income, he would willingly work the additional hour. If he could add less than $1 to his income, he will not be willing to work the additional hour. In this case the marginal cost to him of an hour's work per day is $1.

Let us, similarly, give the name 'marginal value of a product' to the amount of additional money expenditure on a product which in any given situation the consumer of a product would be willing to pay out in order to receive one more unit of the commodity for consumption. A man is consuming 6 cigarettes a day and is spending the rest of his income on other goods and services. In order to smoke a 7th cigarette each day he would be willing to pay out on cigarettes an additional $0·1 a day, with a corresponding reduction of his consumption of something else. If he can acquire a 7th cigarette each day for an additional expenditure of less than \$0·1 a day on cigarettes, he will willingly purchase the greater quantity. If he had to pay out more than \$0·1 a day for the additional cigarette, he would forgo the additional consumption of this product. The marginal value to him of a cigarette a day is \$0·1.

Now there are certain forces at work in a competitive situation tending to equate the marginal value of the marginal social net product of a factor to the marginal cost of that factor. By a competitive situation we mean one in which no individual buyer or seller of any factor or of any product can by his own action influence the market price of the thing which is being bought or sold. In these conditions the following propositions will all be true.

(1) Since the seller of the factor, say labour, cannot influence the wage or price paid for labour by selling more or less of it, the wage rate or price of labour will measure the amount which he can add to his income by selling another unit of his labour. He will therefore work up to the point at which the marginal cost of his labour is equal to the price of labour.

(2) Since the individual employer of the labour cannot affect the price of labour by employing more or less labour, he will add to his costs by employing another unit of labour the price or wage rate of that labour. Since the employer also cannot affect the price received for his product by putting more or less of it on the market, he will by employing one more unit of labour add to his receipts the price of the marginal product of labour. He will maximize his profit by taking on more labour so long as what he thereby adds to his costs is less than what he thereby adds to his receipts. He will therefore employ more and more labour until the wage rate or price of labour is equal to the price of the marginal product of labour.

(3) Since the individual consumer of the product cannot affect the price of the product by buying more or less of it, the price of the product will measure the additional expenditure which he has to make in order to acquire one more unit of the product. He will therefore consume more and more of the product until the marginal value of the product is equal to the price of the product.

Since the marginal cost of the factor will equal the price of the factor (proposition 1), and since the price of the factor will equal the price of the marginal net product of the factor (proposition 2), and since the marginal value of the product will equal the price of the product (proposition 3), it follows that the marginal cost of the factor will equal the marginal value of the marginal net product of the factor.

In the actual world there are likely to be important divergences between the marginal cost of a factor of production and the marginal value of its marginal social net product. The reasons for such divergences may be classified under four main heads, and it will be the purpose of the rest of this chapter briefly to discuss each of these four main causes of divergence.

The first cause is the absence of perfectly competitive conditions in the economic system. When it is possible for a seller of a factor, or of a product, to affect the price of what he sells by selling more or less of it, it will no longer be true that he adds to his receipts by selling one more unit the current price of whatever he is selling. Similarly, when a buyer can influence the price of what he is buying by buying more or less of it, he no longer adds to his expenditure by buying one more unit merely the current market price of what he is buying. Any one of the three propositions on p. 12 may be falsified for this reason.

The second cause is the existence of what we shall call external economies and diseconomies which, in the terminology used on pp. 10–11, means that there is a divergence between the social and the private net product of a factor, i.e. between what the extra factor produces for the benefit of society and what it produces for the enjoyment of its employer.

The third cause is the existence of governmental or other institutional interventions in the market which prevent the operation of the competitive forces described above from leading automatically to the removal of a divergence between marginal costs of factors and the marginal values of their marginal products because the possibility of small adjustments at the margin is removed. Either no changes in quantities bought or sold are allowed or else only large structural changes are permitted.

A fourth and obvious possible cause of divergence between marginal values and costs is the existence of taxes and subsidies. Taxes will cause the price received by the ultimate factor of production to be lower than the price paid by the final consumer of the product. Subsidies will have the opposite effect. In either case there may be a consequential divergence between marginal costs and marginal values.

So far we have spoken entirely in terms of a divergence between the marginal cost of a factor and the marginal value of its marginal social net product. We could express exactly the same real facts in terms of a divergence between the marginal value of a product and the marginal social net cost of its marginal factor content. Suppose that the employment of 1 more unit of labour on a farm will add 10 more units of wheat net to the farm's output. Then we can say that the marginal net product of labour on that farm is 10 units of wheat. But in these circumstances to add 1 more unit of wheat to the farm's output would require 1/10 more units of labour in employment. We could, therefore, describe the same situation by saying that the marginal factor content of a unit of wheat is 1/10 of a unit of labour.

Suppose now that in these circumstances the marginal value of the marginal social net product of a unit of labour was $10, because the

10 units of additional wheat produced measured the marginal *social* as well as the *private* net product of the unit of labour and a unit of wheat had a marginal value of $1 to the consumers of it; but suppose that at the same time the marginal cost of the unit of labour was only $5. Then we could say that there was a 100 per cent rate of divergence between the marginal cost of the factor ($5) and the marginal value of its marginal social net product ($10). But we could describe exactly the same conditions by saying that the marginal value of an additional unit of output was $1, but that the marginal cost of its marginal factor content was only $0·5 (namely 1/10 of a unit of additional labour employed at a wage rate of $5 per unit of labour). We could describe this situation as one in which there was a 100 per cent divergence between the marginal value of the product ($1) and the cost of the marginal social net factor content ($0·5) of the marginal unit of the product.

In what follows in the rest of this volume we shall use these methods of expression quite indifferently. Sometimes we shall consider a unit of a factor, what is its cost, what it produces for society, and the value of what it produces for society. In this case we shall be considering the relationship between the value of the marginal social net product of a unit of a factor and the marginal cost of a unit of that factor. At other times we shall start at the other end with a unit of a product, what is its marginal value to consumers, what additional amount of labour or of other factors is required by society to produce it, and what is the marginal cost of that amount of the factor which is socially necessary for its production. In this case we shall be considering the relationship between the marginal value of a unit of a product and the marginal cost of its marginal social net factor content.

Before we leave this discussion of the terms which we shall be using in this volume there are two implications of this terminology which it is useful to make clear.

First, marginal values and marginal costs are measured simply in money terms in any given market situation. Thus the marginal cost of a unit of labour is simply the amount of additional money income which, in any given market situation, the worker would have to receive to make it just worth his while providing an additional unit of effort in that occupation. The marginal value of a product to a consumer is simply the additional amount of money which, in any given market situation, he would be willing to spend on that product in order to have one more unit of that product to consume. Suppose then that the marginal value of the marginal social net product of a factor is equal to the marginal cost of that factor. This implies merely that the amount of money which consumers would be just willing to give up in order to add to their consumption the additional supplies available to society is just equal to the amount of additional money income which would just make it worth while for the factor to produce those supplies. It does not imply that in any more fundamental sense the real sacrifice of the factor in making the additional effort is equivalent to the additional real enjoyment of the consumers of the products. If an additional unit of money in some fundamental sense meant more to the worker (because being poverty-stricken he was already working overtime to avoid starvation) than to the consumer of the additional product (because he was very wealthy and would hardly notice the addition to his real consumption), the whole transaction might reduce welfare. If the worker could have more leisure at the expense not of his own consumption but of this additional consumption of the millionaire consumers, there might in some fundamental sense be a better balance between effort and consumption. It will be one of our most important but difficult tasks to take account of this sort of consideration.

Second, we have so far applied this concept of a divergence between marginal values and marginal costs to the total outcome of a whole series of transactions in which an employer employs more labour, produces more product, and sells the greater output. But the concept can be applied to any individual transaction, whether it be the sale of labour to an employer, the sale of a raw material from one producer to another, the sale of a finished product by a producer to a trader, or the purchase of a finished product by a final consumer from a trader. In each case we could say that the marginal cost to the seller was measured by the net addition to his money receipts which, in any given market situation, would just make it worth while to the seller to part with what he sells, and that the marginal value to the buyer was measured by the net addition to his money expenditure which it would just be worth his while making in order to obtain what he buys. If the transaction is one which carries with it an external economy (i.e. increases the supplies available to others by some external repercussion which is not accounted for in the private transaction), then we can either add the marginal value of these extra external supplies to their consumers to the marginal value of the private transaction, call this the marginal social value of the transaction, and talk about the divergence between marginal social value and marginal cost; or, alternatively, we can deduct the saving of cost to the people who would otherwise have had to produce these extra supplies from the marginal cost of the private transaction, call this the marginal social cost of the transaction, and talk about the divergence between marginal value and marginal social cost. When we have no need to specify which of these methods we are adopting, we shall talk simply of divergences between marginal social values and costs.

2. *Monopoly and Monopsony*

The first cause of divergence between marginal social values and costs is the absence of perfect competition in the market in which the transaction is taking place.

We will say that a monopolistic element exists in a market whenever the individual seller of the factor or product in the market can exercise an appreciable effect upon the price received for the factor or product by altering the scale of his own individual sales. When there is a large number of independent sellers selling a standardized factor or product on a well-organized market, no individual seller imagines that he will appreciably reduce the market price of the factor or product by increasing his own, relatively insignificant, part of the supply; nor does he believe that he alone can raise the price obtained for the factor or product by restricting his individual sales. At the other extreme, however, a single monopolistic seller who commands the whole market will take carefully into account the effect which he will have in spoiling his market and depressing the price if he puts too much upon the market.

In a similar way, we will say that there is some monopsonistic element in a market whenever the individual buyer of a factor or product can exercise an appreciable effect upon the price of the factor or product in question by altering the scale of his own individual purchases. Again, if there are a large number of independent buyers operating in a well-organized market for a more or less standardized factor or product, no single buyer will be able to affect the market price by varying the scale of his own relatively insignificant purchases. But if there is a single large buyer who dominates the whole market, he may be very careful not to raise his demand too high for fear of raising the price of the factor or product against himself.

TABLE I

MONOPOLY AND MONOPSONY

1. *A Monopolistic Market*

Quantity sold (*a*)	Price received (*b*)	Total receipts (*c*)	Marginal receipt (*d*)
	$	$	$
99	10·00	990	—
100	9·95	995	5

2. *A Monopsonistic Market*

Quantity bought (*a*)	Price paid (*b*)	Total payment (*c*)	Marginal payment (*d*)
	$	$	$
99	10·00	990	—
100	10·05	1,005	15

The arithmetical example which is given in Table I may help to make these relationships clear. Suppose, as in the top half of the table, that the individual seller of a factor or of a product has some monopolistic influence over the market for what he is selling. When he increases his sales from 99 to 100 units (column *a*) the price which he receives falls from \$10 to \$9·95 (column *b*). Then his total receipts for the sale of the factor or product increase from 99 units at \$10 each or \$990 to 100 units at \$9·95 each or \$995 (column *c*). He thus adds to his receipts for the sale of the 100th unit \$5, or the difference between his total receipts of \$990 and \$995. This we will call the marginal receipts from the 100th unit (column *d*).

This individual seller will be in equilibrium only if his marginal cost of providing the 100th unit is equal to the \$5 marginal receipts from the sale of the product. For we have defined his marginal cost as being the amount of money which he would have to add to his income to make it just worth his while to supply the additional unit, and his marginal receipts of \$5 is what he does in fact add to his money receipts by selling this unit.

If, however, the individual buyers of the factor or product are fully competitive, each individual one of them by purchasing another unit will add to his expenditure simply the current price of a unit of the factor or product. Each of the buyers will then purchase until the marginal value to him of the factor or product is equal to its market price. For the purchasers to be in equilibrium in the position shown in the top half of Table I the marginal value of the 100th unit must be equal to the price of \$9·95.

Thus in these conditions the marginal cost will be equal to the marginal revenue of \$5 and the marginal value will be equal to the market price of \$9·95, and there will thus be a divergence of 98 per cent $\left(\text{i.e. } \frac{\$9{\cdot}95 - \$5}{\$5}\right)$ between marginal values and costs due to the element of monopoly among the sellers.

A similar divergence between marginal costs and values can be seen to occur when a monopsonistic element exists among the buyers of the commodity. This is shown in the bottom half of Table I. Suppose that the individual buyer has some monopsonistic power in the market over the price of what he buys. When he increases the amount bought from 99 to 100 units (column *a*) he drives up the price from \$10 to \$10·05 a unit (column *b*) so that his total payment goes up from \$990 to \$1,005 (column *c*) or by \$15 (column *d*). We will call this additional payment due to buying one more unit the 'marginal payment' for the factor or product in question.

The buyer will go on buying only up to the point at which the marginal value of the product to him is equal to the marginal payment which he has to make to get the last unit, which in our example is \$15 for the 100th unit bought. The sellers, on the other hand, if they are fully competitive, will each add to his receipts by selling one more unit the full market price of the factor or product sold, namely \$10·05 for the 100th unit. Thus, if the market is in equilibrium at the purchase and sale of 100 units, the marginal cost to the sellers will be \$10·05 and the marginal value to the buyers \$15, which represents a rate of divergence of almost 50 per cent $\left(\frac{\$15 - \$10{\cdot}05}{\$10{\cdot}05}\right)$ between marginal cost and value.

Now such elements of monopoly or of monopsony may exist in the markets for products or for factors. If therefore we consider the relation between the marginal value of the marginal social net product of labour and the marginal cost of labour, a divergence between the two may exist for either of four reasons:

(1) There may exist an element of monopoly on the workers' side in the sale of their labour, so that their marginal receipts fall below the price of a unit of labour with the result that the price paid by the employers for the labour exceeds the marginal cost of the labour.

(2) There may exist an element of monopsony on the employers' side in the purchase of labour, so that the marginal payment for labour exceeds the price of a unit of labour, in which case the marginal value of the labour to employers will exceed the price of labour.

(3) There may exist an element of monopoly on the part of the entrepreneurs who produce and sell the product, so that the price of the product exceeds the marginal receipts from the product and therefore exceeds the marginal cost of the product to the producers.

(4) There may exist an element of monopsony on the part of the buyers of the product, so that the marginal payment for the product and therefore the marginal value of the product exceeds the price of the product.

The final divergence between the marginal value of the marginal product and the cost of the factor will be the cumulative outcome of all four elements of divergence.

3. *External Economies and Diseconomies*

In the preceding discussion of monopoly and monopsony we have in effect been considering divergences between marginal *private* values and marginal *private* costs. We have not allowed for any external economies or diseconomies which cause the social product of a factor to diverge from its private product (or, in the alternative terminology, cause the social factor-content of a product to diverge from its private factor-content). But when any economic agent takes a decision some part of the real cost of his action may directly fall upon some other economic agent, or some part of the real benefit arising from his action may directly accrue to some other economic agent, quite apart from the effect of his action on the prices of products and of factors considered above under the headings of monopoly and monopsony. We shall say that in the first case there is an 'external diseconomy' and in the second case that there is an 'external economy'; for in the first case the economic agent who is taking the decision causes some diseconomy for which he does not himself pay, i.e. which is 'external' to his own business, and in the second case he causes some economy which accrues to someone 'external' to his business.

We have already given (pp. 10–11) an example of an external economy. The farmer who takes on labour to drain his land and who thereby incidentally improves the fertility of his neighbour's land has undertaken an action to which an external economy is attached. If the same action of the same farmer had drained moisture from his neighbour's land and thereby had made it less fertile, this would have been a case of an external diseconomy.

Any type of economic act may involve such external economies and diseconomies. The following are merely some examples where acts of employment, production, or consumption carry with them such external effects.

(i) *An external economy associated with employment.* The employment of a larger number of skilled engineering operatives may increase the interest in mechanical matters of other people in the district and thus set up a psychological atmosphere which encourages the growth of skill in industry. These men in effect produce for society not only the output of the particular firm in which they are employed; they also contribute indirectly towards the efficiency of other firms. There is an external economy attached to their employment. In this case the external economy is attached to the employment of the skilled workers and not to the production of the firm's output. It may be that the firm could have increased its production to the same extent by the alternative method of employing more unskilled workers together with more automatic machinery, and that this would not have disseminated knowledge of and interest in mechanical matters to the same extent. In this case it is the *employment* of skilled workers and not the mere act of *production* which gives rise to the external economy.

(ii) *An external diseconomy associated with employment.* Suppose that a firm employs more coal to produce a larger output. The additional use of coal produces smoke in the district which dirties the houses and clothing of those in the neighbourhood and raises costs of house cleaning and laundry. If the same output were produced by the firm with the use of electricity instead of coal, there would be no such smoke nuisance. If the extra cost of cleaning and laundry does not fall on the firm using the coal, there will be an external diseconomy due to the use of coal.

(iii) *An external economy associated with production.* Suppose that the growing of a larger number of trees in a certain area improves the climate for farmers in that area, and that this is the case whatever are the methods of production employed by those responsible for the afforestation scheme. Here is an external economy attaching to the production of timber.

(iv) *An external diseconomy associated with production.* Suppose that the production of a particular product, such as the tanning of leather, will inevitably cause a horrible stench in the locality in which it is conducted, and that the firm undertaking this production does not have to bear the cost of this inconvenience to others. Here is an external diseconomy attaching to this line of production.

(v) *An external economy associated with consumption.* The wearing of decorative clothes by an individual consumer of clothing may give pleasure to other persons, a pleasure for which no payment is made to the wearer. Here is an external economy associated with an act of consumption.

(vi) *An external diseconomy associated with consumption.* The use of an ill-designed and noisy motor-car may distress others in a way in which a well-designed and quiet vehicle would not. Here is an external diseconomy associated with an act of consumption.

The above list is not an exhaustive catalogue of types of divergence between private and social net products. Any economic act may be accompanied by some such divergence, and there are important acts which are only with difficulty called acts of employment, production, or consumption. For example, a man may decide to abstain from enjoying consumption goods and services now, save his money, and invest it in some security which will return the capital sum together with interest at some time in the future. But there is a given probability that he will die before that time comes; and if he does so, his heirs will reap where he has sown. Mortality thus brings it about that there is some element of external economy which necessarily attaches to the act of saving.

Not only are the three categories of employment, production, and consumption which are used in the above examples incomplete; for certain purposes they may be much too broad, and a narrower and more detailed classification may be needed. Let us take an example. The introduction of a firm employing a particular type of process which will give the men working on it a new insight into some type of mechanical process may lead to an important external economy due to the general dissemination of useful technical knowledge, if the new firm is placed in a locality in which there is a large population of already reasonably skilled mechanics. But it might have no such effect if it were placed in a countryside in which there was only a sparse agricultural population. This would be an example of an external economy attaching to a particular productive process in a particular locality. Thus there may in certain cases be important external economies associated with the concentration of industries close to each other, a possibility which has important implications when we come to consider the use of commercial policy in international trade for the purpose of influencing the growth of particular industries in particular countries.

On the other hand, in some cases even the broad categories of employment, production, and consumption used for the above examples may be unnecessarily narrow. If the wearing of well-designed clothes gives pleasure to people other than the wearer and the wearing of ill-designed clothes gives general displeasure, it may seem immaterial whether we say that these external effects are associated with the production or the consumption of clothes. If all the clothes which are produced are consumed, it will not matter much whether we say that it is the act of production or the act of consumption which gives the social pleasure or pain. But suppose that there is international trade in clothing and that we are interested in the welfare of only one of the trading nations. Consumption is no longer necessarily equal to production, and we are at once interested in the distinction between external effects which are associated with production and those which are associated with consumption. It is the wearing or consumption of well-designed clothes in our country, even if they are imported, and not their production for export, which provides the social pleasure in the community with which we are concerned.

Clearly where external economies and diseconomies are important there will be another reason why the value of the marginal *social* net product of a factor may diverge from the marginal cost of that factor, since competition will tend only to equate the marginal cost of the factor to the marginal *private* net product of the factor. Or in the alternative terminology we may say that where there are important external economies or diseconomies there will be a further reason for divergence between the marginal value and the marginal cost of the marginal *social* net factor content of the product, since competition will tend only to equate the marginal value of a product to the marginal cost of the marginal *private* net factor content of the product.

4. *Institutional Regulations*

There may be governmental or other institutional regulations which directly prevent the marginal adjustments which factors of production, producers, traders, and consumers must make in a competitive situation in order to remove divergences between marginal values and costs.

The most obvious of these are the direct controls of the government over economic activity.

Suppose, for example, that there is a governmental control which prevents a particular employer from employing a greater amount of a particular factor of production than is allocated to him under some official plan. The price at which the employer can purchase the factor may be appreciably below the price at which he can sell the marginal product of that factor. As we have shown, the competitive process would then, subject to the other qualifications mentioned in this chapter, tend to expand employment and output until this divergence had disappeared, since individual employers would find it profitable to attempt to employ more and more of the factor so long as this divergence remained. In the competitive process the divergence would finally be closed because (i) the combined efforts of all competing employers to employ more of the factor would drive up the price of that factor, (ii) the combined effort of all the producers in putting more of the product on to the market would reduce the price of the product, and (iii) the employment of more of that factor by each individual employer would reduce the marginal net product of the factor. But if the process of competitive bidding for the scarce factor were directly prevented by a quantitative allocation of the factor to the various employers, these forces tending to equate the price paid to the factor to the price received for its marginal net product would be interrupted.

A similar result might occur if there were a governmental control of the prices of the factor of production which, by government fiat, kept the price to be paid to the factor at a level below the competitive market level. In this case employers might well have an incentive to employ more than the total available supply of the factor. But if it was illegal to bid up the price of the factor, the only result might be that some employers would simply remain short of the factor of production. In this case the reward paid to the factor will remain below the value of its marginal product.

Exactly similar situations may occur in the markets for finished products. A rationing scheme may be introduced in order to ensure that each citizen obtains a fair share of some product. In such a case, even though the price charged to the consumer is below the marginal value to him of the product, there will be no competitive forces tending to remove this divergence. It is illegal for the consumer to compete for more supplies and thus to drive up the price charged. If the price chargeable to the consumer is controlled without a rationing scheme, some consumers might wish to purchase more at the current price because it was lower than the marginal value of the product to them. But the price control would make it illegal for them to bid up the price; there would be queues and shop shortages of the product; and for some consumers at least the marginal value would remain above the marginal cost.

But in addition to quantitative governmental controls of this kind, there are also some institutional quantitative arrangements of this kind which are not due to governmental controls but to the extreme inconvenience or administrative cost in permitting marginal adjustments in a competitive economy. The most notable example of this sort of institutional rigidity is the fact that most individual workers are not in fact free to determine how many hours they will work. A factory must be so organized that there is for each worker, say, an eight-hour shift each day. Now to one worker with heavy family responsibilities, expensive tastes, and little love of leisure the marginal cost of an extra hour's work may be considerably below the value to him of the additional wage he could obtain from another hour's work. To another worker with no family responsibilities, who has no desire to drink or smoke but prizes leisure highly, the marginal cost of effort may be much greater than the price offered for the last unit of work. To the former marginal value exceeds marginal cost; to the latter marginal cost exceeds marginal value. But neither of them can adjust their effort at the margin, and each must work eight hours a day or not at all.

Nor is the rigidity in the labour market confined to the total amount of work which each worker must do. It also affects the distribution of his work among different occupations. A consumer can say that out of his total expenditure of $100 he chooses to spend $86 on food and $14 on clothing, or $85 on food and $15 on clothing. A worker cannot normally say that, working, say, 40 hours a week, he chooses to devote 32 hours to working on the land and 8 hours to minding a loom in a factory. It is not possible normally so to organize things that a worker can work 4 days a week at one job and 1 day a week at another. If he moves from one job to another, he must normally move all his labour. While at the margin a worker might like to work a bit more on the land and a little less in a factory, he will never have this marginal choice. This means that for him the marginal value of working on the land might exceed the marginal cost for him of supplying the work on the land (i.e. of forgoing his wage in the factory); but nevertheless he may not transfer a unit of his work, because he can transfer only the whole of his work from the factory to the farm. And this might not be attractive to him.

5. *Taxes and Subsidies*

Fiscal arrangements may themselves be an important cause of divergences between marginal values and costs. Suppose that a man employs some economic resource in order to undertake some particular line of production. If a governmental authority removes by an indirect tax or other levy some part of the price which consumers offer for the product, then the employer of the economic resource commands for his own benefit only a part of the product's marginal value to the consumer.

The price received by the producer is lowered relatively to the price paid by the consumer. Conversely, a subsidy imposed for one reason or another will raise the price received by the producer above the price paid by the consumer. Direct taxation (or subsidization) of a factor's income will have a similar effect. The factor will be able to keep for its own private use only a part of (or more than) the price paid by the consumer for the factor's product. Whether indirect taxation withholds a part of the price paid by the consumer or whether direct taxation withholds a part of the price received by a factor for its effort in producing the product, the result is to this extent the same: it will cause a divergence between the marginal value of the product and the marginal cost of the factor-content of that product.

Such fiscal arrangements, introduced—for example—to raise revenue for the finance of such public expenditures as defence, education, police, etc., may thus be the cause of divergences between marginal values and costs, though in the next chapter we shall consider types of tax and subsidy which are introduced for the express purpose of removing divergences which would otherwise exist.

6. *The Rate of Divergence: a Numerical Example*

When an economic agent exerts an additional unit of effort a certain net additional product is produced for society. By the marginal value of the marginal social net product we mean the amount of money which in current circumstances the consumers of this net additional product would have been willing to give up to obtain that product. By the marginal cost of the factor we mean the amount of money which the provider of the additional effort would have to receive to make him just willing to undertake that additional effort. Suppose that the marginal value of the marginal social net product to the consumers was \$55 and that the marginal cost of the factor was \$10, then we shall say that there was a rate of divergence of 450 per cent $\left(\text{i.e. } \frac{\$55 - \$10}{\$10}\right)$ between the marginal value of the marginal social net product and the marginal cost of the factor. For short, we shall often call this simply the 'rate of divergence'.

As a method of summarizing the analysis of this chapter we will give one numerical example of the way in which this rate of divergence might be built up.

(i) Suppose that the provider of the additional effort was liable to a $33\frac{1}{3}$ per cent income tax on his additional earnings. Then he would have to be able to earn a gross marginal revenue from his work of \$15 in order to keep a net marginal revenue of \$10 to recompense him for the \$10 marginal cost of his effort.

(ii) Suppose that there is an element of monopoly in the sale of his effort. Then he may add only \$15 to his pre-tax income by selling one more unit of effort even though the gross wage rate is \$30, because by selling more of his effort he may spoil the market for the effort which he is already selling. Or, while the gross wage rate is \$15, his employer may have to make a marginal payment for employing him of \$30 because by employing the last unit of effort he may somewhat raise the price he was previously paying for all the other units of effort. In either case the marginal payment for the effort would be \$30 to the employer although the gross marginal revenue from the effort was only \$15 to the worker.

(iii) Suppose there were a sales tax of $33\frac{1}{3}$ per cent on the product of the labour. Then the marginal cost to the employer, including the tax payable on the labour's product as well as the marginal payment for the additional labour, would be \$40.

(iv) The employers might have an element of monopoly power in the sale of the product, so that they would receive a marginal revenue of \$40 from the sale of the marginal private net product when the price of the product charged to the consumers was \$50. Or the buyers of the product might have an element of monopsony such that they would have to make a marginal payment of \$50 for the marginal private net product even though its market price was only \$40. In either case the marginal payment made by the consumers (which will measure the value to them of the marginal private net product) will be \$50 although the marginal revenue to the sellers (which must be sufficient to cover the marginal cost to them of its production) will be only \$40.

(v) So far we have allowed only for the private net product. If the private production carried with it an additional social product equal to 10 per cent of the private product, then the value of the marginal social net product would be \$55.

We have done this sum in terms of a factor and its marginal product. Exactly the same example could be calculated in terms of a product and its marginal factor content. Suppose we start with a unit of product having a marginal value to consumers of \$10, so that consumers would be prepared to make a marginal payment of \$10 for it. Then because of the element of monopoly among producers or of monopsony among buyers (point iv above), this would represent a marginal revenue to producers of only \$8. Because of the sales tax on the product (point iii), this would represent a tax-free marginal revenue from the sale of the product of only \$6. Because of the element of monopoly or monopsony in the market for the hire of the factor (point ii), the \$6 marginal payment which the employer would be prepared to make for the additional labour necessary to produce the unit of product would represent only a marginal revenue of \$3 to the worker himself. Because of the income tax which he has to pay (point i), this would represent only a \$2 net marginal reward for him. But we have still not allowed for the external economies. From point v it is clear that we are assuming that the cost of only $\frac{10}{11}$ of the labour employed on any private production should really be calculated against that production, since for every 10 units of private product there are 11 units of social product. The marginal cost of the marginal *social* (as opposed to *private*) net factor content is, therefore, not \$2, but $\$2 \times \frac{10}{11}$. The rate of divergence between marginal value and marginal cost of the marginal social net factor content is therefore $\frac{\$10 - \$2 \times \frac{10}{11}}{\$2 \times \frac{10}{11}}$ or, once more, 450 per cent.

We can therefore talk of a rate of divergence between marginal social values and costs in connexion with any particular transaction, the divergence being due to a monopolistic or monopsonistic element, to a tax or subsidy or other governmental intervention, or to an external economy or diseconomy. In a series of transactions in which some intermediate product passes from hand to hand between the original factor of production and the final consumer, these rates of divergence must be accumulated in the way illustrated in the preceding numerical example. In that case there was (i) a 50 per cent rate of divergence between the net and the gross earnings of the factor due to the $33\frac{1}{3}$ per cent rate of income tax;[1] (ii) a 100 per cent rate of divergence between the sale and the purchase of the factor due to an element of monopoly or monopsony in the labour market; (iii) a $33\frac{1}{3}$ per cent rate of divergence between the production and sale of the product due to a sales tax; (iv) a 25 per cent rate of divergence between marginal value and cost in the market for the product because of an element of monopoly or monopsony in that market; and (v) finally, a 10 per cent divergence, due to an external economy, between the private and social net product.

Thus there were successive divergences of 50 per cent, 100 per cent, $33\frac{1}{3}$ per cent, 25 per cent, and 10 per cent. These can be accumulated into a total rate of divergence between the marginal value to the final consumer and the marginal cost to the original factor by the formula

$$\left(1 + \frac{50}{100}\right)\left(1 + \frac{100}{100}\right)\left(1 + \frac{33 \cdot 3}{100}\right)\left(1 + \frac{25}{100}\right)\left(1 + \frac{10}{100}\right) - 1$$

which gives the final result of a total divergence of 450 per cent. If we wish to find the rate of divergence between any two points in a series of transactions, we must accumulate the relevant intermediate rates of divergence in this manner.

[1] With a $33\frac{1}{3}$ per cent rate of tax, a gross earning of \$15 is reduced to a net earning of \$10. In this case, as we have defined the terms, there is a rate of divergence of $\frac{\$15 - \$10}{\$10}$ or 50 per cent.

CHAPTER III

DOMESTIC POLICIES FOR THE ELIMINATION OF DIVERGENCES

1. *Forms of Policy*

THIS volume is concerned with International Economic Policy; and it would, therefore, be out of place to consider in any detail the vast range of issues which are raised in the choice of domestic policies to eliminate or control the divergences between marginal values and costs which have been described in the last chapter.

But as we shall see in subsequent Parts of this volume, the choice between different international economic policies will often depend essentially upon the extent to which domestic divergences between marginal values and costs have been removed within the trading countries. In order to proceed we must, therefore, have at the back of our minds some idea of the sort of considerations of domestic policy which are involved when in the later chapters of this volume we glibly assume that the national government of one of our trading countries takes action to remove or control some specified domestic divergence between marginal values and costs. This chapter will, however, be nothing more than, as it were, a list of contents for a volume on The Theory of Domestic Economic Policy.

The first type of divergence which we discussed in the last chapter was due to elements of monopoly or monopsony in the market concerned. In order to understand the types of action which might be taken to counteract divergences of this type, it is first of all necessary briefly to enumerate the different reasons which may give rise to a monopolistic or monopsonistic situation. The reasons which, in the modern world, lead to the formation and successful maintenance of important monopolistic or monopsonistic elements may be grouped under three headings.

(i) *Governmental support.* The government may itself set up a monopoly for the production of, or trade in, some important commodity, such as the governmental monopolies in the production and sale of tobacco in certain countries. But apart from outright State monopolies in certain socialized or nationalized activities, the government can give support or protection to private monopolies. Thus a government may restrict in some way the number of persons who may enter a given trade or occupation, thereby giving those individuals the power to maintain a monopolistic organization without fear of outside competition; or the government may give legal sanction to the activities of a marketing board which restricts the amount of a particular commodity which can be sold or bought.

(ii) *Unified ownership of a factor of production or a right to produce.* In some cases the whole or a large part of the available supply of some natural resource may fall into the control of a single concern or of a monopolistic organization. In this case the persons concerned may be able to exploit their monopolistic position without fear of new outside competition. Similarly, the ownership of patent rights may endow a particular producer with the sole right to use a particular process or to produce a particular product.

(iii) *Indivisibilities of factors and the size of the market.* A frequent cause of some element of monopolistic or monopsonistic power is due to the facts that a productive or trading concern must for technical reasons be of a certain size in order to produce or to trade efficiently, and that the size of the market to be served is not large enough to make room for a large number of competing concerns of this technically efficient size.

The most striking instances of this factor are sufficiently obvious. A railway system to act efficiently must be of a certain size. Normally it would be obviously uneconomical to have even two separate systems providing rail transport between two localities; much less would it be sensible to envisage a really large number of independent competing concerns. And if there is only one railway system connecting two towns, those in charge of it will clearly be able to influence the price offered for railway services by providing them in greater or in smaller volume.

But this cause of monopolistic or monopsonistic elements in various markets is more widespread than is at first sight obvious. A monopolistic element will exist even though the technical size of the individual productive unit is, in some absolute sense, small, if at the same time the market for its product is small. Markets are never perfect, and there are at least two important causes of market imperfection which may often lead to monopolistic or monopsonistic elements.

First, there may be some real differences between the output of different producers of what is, broadly speaking, the same product; and these differences may be exaggerated in consumers' imaginations by the advertising campaigns of individual producers who attempt to bind individual buyers to their own particular brands. In these cases an individual producer can influence the price obtained for his product by putting more or less of it on the market; he can retain his most faithful customers even though he raises his price, and he will not be able to tempt customers away from his rivals without an appreciable cut in the price at which he sells his product.

Second, transport costs may protect particular markets. Where the cost of transporting the product is great, producers are likely to be found near their customers. In a large city there is not normally one quarter of the town where barber's shops are to be found; the cost and inconvenience of transporting the customer to the barber or the barber to the customer results in a dispersion of barbers about the city. In such cases each producer has a market of customers near him which is protected by transport costs. If he is to produce and to sell more, he must cut his price in order either to offset the additional transport costs of invading the markets of other producers in other localities or in order to persuade customers in his own small localized monopoly market to purchase more of this commodity. Where transport costs of the product are high relatively to the other costs of production there is, *ceteris paribus*, likely to exist some monopolistic element in markets.

As we have already observed, this is not the appropriate place to discuss in detail the policies which may be adopted to prevent or correct these effects of monopolistic or monopsonistic powers. Here we shall merely enumerate the possibilities which would, however, require exhaustive treatment in any Theory of Domestic Economic Policy.

(i) The first obvious policy is for the State to remove all those State regulations which in the interests of so-called orderly marketing are often introduced in order to restrict competition, for example, by restricting by licence the number of producers or the total output in a particular industry.

(ii) Changes in the legal framework in which industry and trade are conducted may make it more difficult to form a buyers' or sellers' monopoly and to hinder the entry of new competitors into any market.

(iii) Measures may be taken to give buyers and sellers better information about the qualities of various products and the prices at which substitutes are available, thereby making markets more nearly perfect and reducing all forms of irrational tie between individual buyers and sellers.

(iv) Maximum prices may be fixed for things which a monopolist sells, thereby removing his incentive to restrict supplies merely in order to raise the price of the product which he is selling; and minimum prices may be fixed for things which a monopsonist buys, thereby removing his incentive to restrict his purchases merely in order to depress the price of the thing which he is buying.

(v) Concerns may be socialized or brought under direct public control of such a kind that they are no longer operated in order to maximize profits (which requires the equating of the marginal payment for a factor to the marginal revenue from the sale of its marginal private net product), but are operated instead with the express purpose of making the marginal value of the marginal social net product equal to the marginal cost of the factor concerned.

It is not our intention here to discuss the various conditions in which these different policies may be appropriate means for reducing monopolistic and monopsonistic elements. In discussing a number of international problems we shall, however, be obliged to refer to the problem of the national control of domestic monopolies. Whether or not such national controls can be successfully instituted may greatly affect the propriety of various international economic policies.

We must turn next to a consideration of the sort of action which national governments might take in order to control such divergences between marginal social values and costs as are due to the existence of external economies and diseconomies. It may be possible to affect such divergences by the introduction of direct governmental controls. For example, an external diseconomy due to the fact that a factory which emits a large volume of smoke does not itself have to bear the cost of the nuisance which this causes to residents in the neighbourhood might be counterbalanced in whole or in part by smoke-abatement laws governing the types of fuel which may be used. Or zoning regulations which prevent factories from being built in residential areas or dwelling-houses in national parks may be used to control activities in the case of which there are important external economies.

Theoretically, if it is desired to remove a divergence between marginal values and costs, a more sensitive and refined instrument than such direct prohibitions or regulations might be provided by the fiscal weapon. If, to continue with the example quoted above, a factory could be taxed on the amount of smoke which it caused in the neighbourhood on a scale equal to the marginal cost of the smoke nuisance to the residents of the area, the divergence would be removed; and the factory would be left to decide for itself how most cheaply to abate the smoke nuisance or whether the gain to its own efficiency of continuing as before was not in fact worth the extra cost to the residents as measured by the tax. Similarly, in the case of an external economy an economic agent may theoretically be subsidized by an amount equal to the marginal value to consumers of the additional benefits which his action brings with them.

There may, of course, be very considerable administrative difficulties in levying a tax or paying a subsidy on just those acts which carry with them external economies or diseconomies. Even more important, there may be enormous difficulties in determining and then evaluating the innumerable external economies and diseconomies which may be associated with a vast range of economic acts. All that can be done is to deal with the most obvious external effects by the least costly administrative device. In what follows we shall frequently talk of external economies or diseconomies being offset by subsidies or taxes; but this must be interpreted as doing no more than refer to the ideal position, to which in fact government policy will never achieve anything more than a very rough approximation.

Divergences between marginal values and costs which are due to institutional rigidities may be very intractable. For example, it may not be at all easy to give to different men who have different evaluations of leisure and of earnings from work the ability to work different hours so that each may equate the marginal value of real income with the marginal cost of the work which it entails. It is possible, as Professor Lerner has suggested,[1] that something might be done if thought were given to the organization of different factories working shifts of different lengths, so that those who preferred short hours and low earnings could go to the one while those who preferred long hours and high earnings could seek employment in the other. But it seems clear that a number of institutional rigidities are inevitable.

In the case of divergences due to governmental regulations or to taxes and subsidies imposed by governments, the formal answer to the question how to remove divergences is obvious—namely, the removal of the regulations or taxes and subsidies which cause the divergence in the first place. But while the formal answer is clear, taxation itself involves perhaps the most difficult and intractable of all the problems raised by any attempt to equate marginal values and costs.

The reason for this is that taxes and subsidies cannot be used solely for the purpose of equating marginal values and costs in transactions which would otherwise be marked by a divergence. Taxation of one form or another is needed for at least four other major purposes.

(i) First, public revenue is needed in order to finance the State expenditure on communal needs which can be satisfied most economically only by communal expenditure. Into this category there falls expenditure on such matters as defence, police, justice, and some would add also much expenditure on health, education, public amenities, and the like. In any case, to be at all realistic we must assume that each national government will have to raise a considerable net revenue for these purposes. In this volume we need say no more on this most important topic.

(ii) We have already pointed out that taxes and subsidies may themselves be used as a means of removing or offsetting divergences between marginal social values and costs which might otherwise exist. Now it may well be that to obey this rule of fiscal policy throughout the economy would involve the State in a large additional net expenditure on subsidies of this kind—for example, the subsidies needed to offset external economies might outweigh the taxes required to offset external diseconomies. It would then be necessary to raise a tax revenue in order to finance the balance of the subsidies. We shall devote the next part of this chapter to this problem.

(iii) We have so far said little or nothing about the problems of economic equity. As soon as policies are considered for improving the

[1] See A. P. Lerner, *The Economics of Control* (New York, Macmillan, 1944). Chapter 9, p. 104.

distribution of income in an economy, the obvious suggestion will arise to tax the rich and to use the money to provide benefits of one kind or another for the poor. Economic equity may therefore provide another reason for taxing one section of the community and for subsidizing another. We shall devote a large part of Chapter V to a discussion of this subject.

(iv) Finally, as we shall show in Chapter VI, private citizens may save out of their current incomes much less than it is in the interests of society that they should save. In order to bring the community's savings more nearly up to the optimum level, the State may need to raise revenue in excess of its current expenditure and to use the public savings which the budgetary surplus represents to supplement the inadequate flow of private savings on to the capital market.

2. *The Adding-Up Problem and the Raising of Revenue*

A fiscal problem which involves the raising of a net amount of revenue from general taxation in order to be able to pay subsidies to remove particular divergences between marginal social values and costs may arise either in the case of the control of monopoly and monopsony or in the case of the control of external economies and diseconomies.

The third cause leading to monopolistic conditions, which we examined on p. 28, was the indivisibility of factors of production in relation to the total market for the product. A monopolistic situation which is due to the technical indivisibility of an instrument of production is very likely to raise this fiscal problem of taxation and subsidization.

The essential problem is due to the fact that in such a situation there may be 'increasing or decreasing returns to scale' instead of the normal situation of 'constant returns to scale'. We shall say that there are constant returns to scale when a 10 per cent increase in every factor of production—10 per cent more labour, 10 per cent more land, 10 per cent more capital, and so on—would lead to a 10 per cent increase in total output. We shall say that there are increasing (or decreasing) returns to scale when a 10 per cent increase in every factor would lead to a more than (or less than) 10 per cent increase in total output.

We can regard constant returns to scale as the normal case. When every productive resource is, say, doubled in amount, we might naturally expect to find the total output also doubled. But returns to scale are not necessarily constant when there are important indivisibilities of productive resources. Let us take the case of a railway line between A and B as an example. It is impossible to build the line between A and B at all unless the whole equipment of embankments, cuttings, tunnels, and rails for at least a single line of track is installed. This is a large indivisible unit of equipment. At some point of traffic density it may become necessary to lay a double track between A and B in order to cope with more traffic. At this point it is no use adding the double track for a small part of the way; it must be done for the whole stretch of line. Here is a second large indivisible capital investment.

Consider first of all the operation of the railway line when it is first built and when the demand for transport between A and B is not sufficient to allow it to be at all fully used. If the managers of such a railway were for some reason or another given a further 10 per cent of all factors of production—labour, capital, and materials—to use, they would be able to carry more than 10 per cent more traffic. There would be no need to extend the actual fixed equipment of the track which could still easily carry more traffic. The 10 per cent additional capital could therefore be used to increase the rolling stock by more than 10 per cent [1] since none of it would be needed to increase the track. In this case there would be increasing returns to scale; with a 10 per cent increase in all factors of production, output would be increased by more than 10 per cent; the very fact that production was on a larger absolute scale would increase the average return or product per unit of factors employed.

But consider next the operation of the railway when the traffic has grown to such a density that the single track is becoming overcrowded. So many trains are running that more and more elaborate signalling systems are required in order to enable still more to be run; the wear and tear of the track is so heavy that it has become frequently necessary to stop the use of portions of the line for repair and maintenance, thus adding to the congestion on the line. In such circumstances, if the managers have 10 per cent more resources of all kinds to use, they will be unable to increase the output by as much as 10 per cent. In order to run more traffic on the line so heavy an investment in new signalling equipment may be necessary that the total investment of capital required to increase the carrying capacity by 10 per cent might be considerably in excess of 10 per cent of the existing capital equipment, even when there is 10 per cent more labour and other resources to work with the increased capital. Yet because of the indivisibility of the capital investment in the track it may not yet be worth while laying a double instead of a single track between A and B. There may already be too much traffic to enable a single track to be operated as efficiently as possible, but not nearly enough traffic to justify a second track. In such a case a 10 per cent increase in all resources will enable the managers to

[1] Since the amount of labour co-operating with the rolling stock is to be increased by only 10 per cent, the rolling stock might have to take rather a different form—e.g. more powerful locomotives—so that a 10 per cent increase in labour could with instruments which were not only 10 per cent more in quantity but also of better quality, increase the output by more than 10 per cent.

provide some more carrying capacity, but not as much as 10 per cent more. The concern will be showing decreasing returns to scale; because of the indivisibility of the capital equipment in the track a mere increase in the absolute scale of operations will cause a diminution in the average return to, or product of, the factors employed.

In every firm, i.e. independent productive unit, there is always at least one element of indivisibility, namely, the unit of management. However small the firm, there must be at least one man to take decisions and to manage the affair; however large, there cannot be more than one centre of final control. For this reason, in any single firm returns are likely to be increasing to scale at first (when the firm is too small to enable one indivisible unit of management to be fully used), to reach a maximum at the optimum size of the firm, and thereafter to start decreasing to scale (when the firm is too large to enable the single unit of control to manage it efficiently). In a fully competitive industry in which there are a large number of separate firms this consideration will not cause increasing or decreasing returns to scale for the industry as a whole because the size of the industry can always increase or decrease by, say, 10 per cent through an increase or decrease by 10 per cent in the number of firms of the optimum size. But in an industry (like railway transport) where there is room only for one or at the most two independent firms, returns are liable to increase or decrease to scale for the industry as a whole, because a 10 per cent increase or decrease in output cannot be accompanied by a 10 per cent increase or decrease in the number of firms of the optimum size. In such cases returns are liable to increase or decrease as the scale of output varies because of the technical indivisibility of certain instruments of production used in the particular firms in the industry.

When there are increasing or decreasing returns to scale, certain very important relationships result between the prices of factors and their marginal products. We can establish the propositions that if there are constant returns to scale then the payment of a price to each factor which is just equal to the value of its marginal net product will absorb the whole of the product of the concern; that if there are increasing returns to scale, then the payment of a price to each factor equal to the value of its marginal product would absorb more than the whole of the product of the concern; and that if there are decreasing returns to scale, then the payment of a price to each factor equal to the value of its marginal product would absorb less than the whole of the product of the concern.

These propositions are illustrated in Table II. We start in situation I with 100 units of labour and 100 units of capital producing 100 units of output (column *a* of Table II). We proceed from this situation to situation II in which there are still 100 units of labour but 101 units of capital. The unit increase in the amount of capital, labour remaining constant, has caused the output to increase from 100 to 100¼ units (column *b*). Thus in column *d* we show the marginal product of capital as ¼ of a unit since a comparison of situations I and II shows that an increase of 1 unit in the amount of capital employed will cause an increase of ¼ of a unit in the output.

TABLE II

The Adding-Up Problem

	Amounts in situations I	II	III	Marginal products	Total output needed to pay to each factor a price equal to its marginal product
	(*a*)	(*b*)	(*c*)	(*d*)	(*e*)
Labour	100	100	101	¾ (i) 1¾ (ii) ¼ (iii)	75 (i) 175 (ii) 25 (iii)
Capital	100	101	101	¼	25
Output	100	100¼	101 (i) 102 (ii) 100½ (iii)	—	—
				Total	100 (i) 200 (ii) 50 (iii)

Case (i)—Constant Returns to Scale.
Case (ii)—Increasing Returns to Scale.
Case (iii)—Decreasing Returns to Scale.

We now (situation III in column *c*) allow the amount of labour also to increase by 1 unit. As between situations I and III the amount of capital has increased by 1 per cent and the amount of labour has increased by 1 per cent as well. If there are constant returns to scale, total output will also have increased by 1 per cent, i.e. from 100 to 101; and this is shown as case i in column *c*. If there are increasing returns to scale, output will have increased by more than this, for example by 2 per cent from 100 to 102, as is shown in case ii in column *c*. On the other hand, if there are decreasing returns to scale, output will have increased by less than 1 per cent, say, by only $\frac{1}{2}$ of 1 per cent, as is shown in case iii in column *c*.

By a comparison of situations II and III we can now derive the marginal product of labour. As between these two situations the amount of capital employed has remained constant at 101 but the amount of labour employed has risen by 1 unit from 100 to 101. The increase in output between situations II and III is, therefore, equal to the marginal product of labour. In case i (constant returns) it is $\frac{3}{4}$ of a unit (from $100\frac{1}{4}$ to 101); in case ii (increasing returns) it is $1\frac{3}{4}$ of a unit (from $100\frac{1}{4}$ to 102); and in case iii (decreasing returns) it is $\frac{1}{4}$ of a unit (from $100\frac{1}{4}$ to $100\frac{1}{2}$). These marginal products of labour are shown in column *d*.

In column *e* we can now calculate what is required to pay the factors employed in situation I prices equal to their marginal products. As far as capital is concerned, 100 units are employed (column *a*) and the marginal product of capital is $\frac{1}{4}$ (column *d*), so that to pay each of the 100 units of capital a price equal to the value of its marginal product would require $100 \times \frac{1}{4}$ or 25 units of output (column *e*).

In the case of labour the amount required will depend upon whether we are dealing with constant, increasing, or decreasing returns. In these three cases the marginal product of labour is $\frac{3}{4}$, $1\frac{3}{4}$, or $\frac{1}{4}$ units of output respectively (column *d*). In order to pay each of the 100 units of labour (column *a*) a price equal to its marginal product will, therefore, require $100 \times \frac{3}{4}$ (or 75), $100 \times 1\frac{3}{4}$ (or 175), or $100 \times \frac{1}{4}$ (or 25) units of output respectively (column *e*).

Adding together the amounts as shown in column *e* which are necessary to pay to both labour and capital prices equal to their marginal products, we see that the total amounts to 100, 200, or 50 units of output according as we are assuming constant, increasing, or decreasing returns to scale. But the total output of situation I is only 100 units. Thus we have illustrated our proposition that the total output will be equal to, less than, or greater than the total required to pay each factor a price equal to its marginal product according as there are constant, increasing, or decreasing returns to scale.

It is important in this analysis to distinguish carefully between what we may call constant, increasing, or decreasing returns to scale at the margin and constant, increasing, or decreasing returns to scale over a large structural change in output. Or, to express the same point in different words, we must distinguish between *marginal* economies (or diseconomies) of large-scale production and *structural* economies (or diseconomies) of large-scale production.

In the analysis which we have just developed on the basis of Table II we have reached the conclusion that the total output will be less than (or more than) sufficient to pay to each factor a reward equal to the value of its marginal net product according as there are *marginal* economies (or diseconomies) of large-scale production. Our argument was based essentially upon an analysis of what happens to total output when there are small *marginal* changes first in the employment of capital and then in the employment of labour.

But the degree to which there are *marginal* economies or diseconomies of large-scale production in any given industry when it is of any given size does not, of course, have any direct connexion with the degree to which there may be *structural* economies or diseconomies of large-scale production in the same industry when its size alters by a large structural amount. This is very easily illustrated from the case of the railway line to which we have just referred. If the railway happens to be of the size at which the indivisible capital equipment of tracks, embankments, tunnels, etc., is just but only just fully utilized, it will, as we have seen, be operating at a point at which there are no marginal economies or diseconomies of large-scale production. But this is not at all incompatible with the fact that if the railway grew by a large structural change from a very small and therefore very uneconomic affair to a large concern of the optimum size which we have just described, its output per unit of factors employed would have greatly increased. When it was very small and inefficient it would have been subject to marginal economies of large-scale production and its total output would have been insufficient to pay to each factor of production employed a reward equal to the value of its marginal product; over the structural change of growth from a small and inefficient to a large and efficient concern it would have enjoyed structural economies of large-scale production; but at its new efficient size there would be no marginal economies or diseconomies of scale and the output produced would be just sufficient to pay to each factor employed a reward equal to the value of its marginal product.

The analysis which is illustrated in Table II also serves to demonstrate one other conclusion which will be of importance in future arguments in this volume. In cases in which there are constant returns to scale the marginal product of any one factor is not affected by the scale of total output but only by the ratio between the amount of that factor employed and the amount of other factors employed. Consider the figures in Table III. The left-hand half of the table merely reproduces the figures which were used in Table II to illustrate the case of constant

TABLE III

Marginal Products and Constant Returns to Scale

	Situations					
	I	II	III	IV	V	VI
Labour	101	100	101	200	200	202
Capital	100	101	101	200	200	202
Output	100	100¼	101	200	200½	202

returns to scale. The right-hand half of the table merely reproduces the figures used in the left-hand half, after doubling every figure. If there are constant returns to scale over this structural change, this is a legitimate process; to employ twice as many men and twice as many acres of land will lead to the production of twice as great an output. As before, by comparing situations I and II we see that the marginal product of capital is $\frac{1}{4}$ of a unit of product; the increase of capital by one unit from 100 to 101 causes an increase of output of $\frac{1}{4}$ of a unit. But by comparing situations IV and V it can be seen that with the scale of operations twice as large the marginal product of capital remains $\frac{1}{4}$ of a unit of output; the increase of capital by 2 units from 200 to 202 raises output by $\frac{1}{2}$ a unit. Similarly, a comparison of situations II and III shows that the marginal product of labour is $\frac{3}{4}$ of a unit of output, since an increase in the amount of labour by 1 unit from 100 to 101 raises output by $\frac{3}{4}$ of a unit; and at the same time a comparison of situations V and VI shows that the marginal product of labour remains unchanged at $\frac{3}{4}$ of a unit of output even though the scale of production has doubled, since an increase in the amount of labour by 2 units from 200 to 202 raises output by $1\frac{1}{2}$ units.

Thus if there are constant returns to scale, the marginal products of labour and capital do not depend at all upon the scale of employment and production. They depend solely upon the ratio between the amount of labour and the amount of capital employed. If the ratio of capital to labour employed rises, the marginal product of capital will fall and that of labour will rise. The marginal product of capital will fall because when capital is plentiful and labour is scarce all the most productive uses for capital as a means of raising output per head will already have been undertaken: a new supply of capital will now have relatively unimportant effects upon output. Similarly, when labour is scarce and capital plentiful, it will make a great difference to output to have more labour to employ and the marginal product of labour will be high.

Let us return now to the conclusion which we reached on p. 36, namely that an industry will produce a total output which will be less than, or greater than, sufficient to pay to each factor of production a reward equal to the value of its marginal product according as there are marginal economies or diseconomies of large-scale production in that industry.

This means that industries with marginal economies of large-scale production must be subsidized and industries with marginal diseconomies of large-scale production must be taxed if prices are to be paid to factors of production equal to the value of their marginal social net products in the various industries. Otherwise the former industries would not earn sufficient and the latter would earn more than sufficient to enable them to do so.

These facts have obvious implications for the control of monopolies. Clearly no fiscal problem is involved in anti-monopoly action of the kind mentioned in methods i, ii, and iii on p. 29. Where the causes of monopoly are such that governmental action designed to organize the market in a more competitive manner is sufficient to cope with the problem, because there are no important indivisibilities demanding on technical grounds a monopolistic organization of the market, the fiscal problem does not arise. But suppose an attempt is made to control a monopoly by setting a maximum price for the product and a minimum price for the factors of production so as to equate marginal values to marginal costs by removing the ability of the producer monopolistically to raise the price of his product by putting less on the market or monopsonistically to reduce the price paid to the factors by restricting the scope of employment for him. (See method iv on p. 29.) If the monopoly is a technical one due to an important indivisibility and if the concern is still in its increasing-returns phase, then the result will be to bankrupt the concern, unless it is simultaneously being subsidized out of general revenue. For its total output will not be sufficient to pay to each factor a reward equal to its marginal product. Or if the concern were in its decreasing-returns phase, the result would be to leave it with a monopoly profit in spite of the price control.

A similar problem would arise if an attempt were made to deal with such a monopoly by nationalizing it and instructing its new managers directly to pay prices to the factors equal to the value of their marginal products. (See method v on p. 29.) If the concern were in its increasing-returns phase, it would have to be run at a loss and subsidized out of the general tax revenue of the State; if it were in its decreasing-returns phase, it would make a net profit which could be paid into the central government budget and used to finance part of the general expenditures of the State.

A very similar problem arises when we consider the fiscal problems involved in the control of external economies and diseconomies. There are some forms of external economy and diseconomy the control of which would not impose any net fiscal burden on (or provide any net fiscal relief to) the government's budget. There are other forms of external economy and diseconomy the control of which would involve just such a net fiscal problem. We shall call the former type of external economy or diseconomy a case of 'unpaid factors' and the latter type a case of 'atmosphere-creation'. Both of these types of external economy or diseconomy may occur in fully competitive conditions. Neither of them is a phenomenon of monopoly; but the latter type raises the same adding-up problem as the indivisibilities of factors which we discussed above.

Let us start by considering external economies or diseconomies due to *unpaid factors*. There are cases where an external economy in one part of the economic system is exactly matched by a corresponding external diseconomy in another part of the system. To take an example, suppose that in a given region farmers are growing apples and keeping bees to produce honey. Suppose, further, that the bees feed on the apple-blossom. Now if any particular farmer keeps more bees, his bees will feed more intensively on the apple-blossom in the neighbourhood, and there will be less food available for his neighbours' bees. There is an external diseconomy associated with the keeping of bees. But in this case there is an exactly equivalent external economy associated with the production of apples. If any farmer grows more apples, he will produce more blossom; he will thus improve the feeding of his neighbours' bees and will increase their output of honey. His act will carry with it an external economy.

In this case, if we consider society as a whole, there are no economies or diseconomies of large-scale production and no adding-up problem. If the apple-farmers apply 10 per cent more labour, land, and capital to apple-farming, they will increase the output of apples by 10 per cent; but they will also provide more food for the bees. On the other hand, the bee-keepers will not increase the output of honey by 10 per cent by increasing the amount of land, labour, and capital applied to bee-keeping by 10 per cent unless at the same time the apple-farmers also increase their output and so the food of the bees by 10 per cent. Thus there are constant returns to scale for both industries taken together: if the amounts of land, labour, and capital employed both in apple-farming and bee-keeping are doubled, the output of both apples and honey will be doubled. But if the amount of land, labour, and capital are doubled in bee-keeping alone, the output of honey will be less than doubled; whereas, if the amount of land, labour, and capital in apple-farming are doubled, the output of apples will be doubled and, in addition, some contribution will be made to the output of honey.

We call this a case of an unpaid factor because the situation is due simply and solely to the fact that the apple-farmer cannot charge each individual bee-keeper for the bees' food which the former produces for the latter. If this charge could be made, every factor would earn the value of its marginal social net product. But as it is, the apple-farmer provides to the bee-keeper some of his factors free of charge. The apple-farmer is paid less than the value of his marginal social net product and the bee-keeper receives exactly so much more than the value of his marginal social net product. On the principle illustrated in Table II (p. 35), since there are constant returns to scale for all the factors in both industries taken together, the total product of apples and honey is just sufficient to pay all factors a reward equal to the value of their marginal social net product. All that is required is a tax on bee-keepers to pay an exactly equal subsidy to apple-farmers.

It is of the nature of an unpaid factor that—administrative difficulties apart—the divergence between marginal social values and costs could be removed merely by a tax imposed on those whose private product exceeds their social product which will raise just the correct amount of revenue to subsidize those whose social product exceeds their private product.

We can turn now to the second type of external economies or diseconomies, namely, the *creation of atmosphere*, whose significant feature is the existence of an external economy which is not matched by an exactly equivalent external diseconomy in some other part of the economic system. An example may help to make this clear. Suppose that the greater afforestation schemes which are associated with increased timber production in a particular region increase the rainfall and so improve the atmosphere for wheat growing in that region. There will clearly be an external economy in the production of timber, since this will indirectly help to increase the output of wheat, just as the production of apples in our previous example indirectly increased the output of honey. But in the former case there was also an external diseconomy in the production of honey since each bee-keeper by increasing the number of his bees took food away (without paying) from his neighbour's bees. But in our present case the increased rainfall due to greater afforestation may well help every wheat-farmer without any one wheat-farmer by increasing his output of wheat taking rainfall away from his competitors.

For this reason we must draw a distinction between a 'factor of production' and a physical or social 'atmosphere' affecting production. We may take the rainfall in a district as a typical example of atmosphere. The rainfall may be deficient in the sense that a higher rainfall would increase the farmers' output, but nevertheless what rainfall there is will be available to all farms in the district regardless of their number. Thus if in the district in question the amount of land, labour, and capital devoted to, say, wheat-farming were to be increased by 10 per cent, the output of wheat would also be increased by 10 per cent even if the rainfall were to remain constant. This is quite different from the case of a factor of production for which no payment is made; in our previous example, a 10 per cent increase in the output of apples (and so in the supply of apple-blossom) would be necessary, in addition to a 10 per cent increase in the amount of land, labour, and capital devoted to bee-keeping, if the output of honey is to be increased by 10 per cent. In these examples, rainfall is an 'atmosphere' for wheat-farming; but apple-blossom is an unpaid 'factor of production' for bee-keeping.

Thus, both a factor of production and an atmosphere are conditions which affect output. But an atmosphere is a fixed condition of production which remains unchanged for each producer in the industry in question without anyone else doing anything about it, however large or small—within limits—is the scale of operations of the industry. On the other hand, a factor of production is an aid to production which is fixed in amount and which is therefore available on a smaller scale to each producer in the industry if the number of producers increases, unless someone does something to increase the total supply of the factor.

The external economies due to unpaid factors which we examined above are concerned with factors of production for which the individual producer pays nothing. But there are also external economies and diseconomies which are due to the fact that the activities of one producer or one group of producers provide an atmosphere which is favourable or unfavourable to the activities of another producer or group of producers. We have given as an example of this the case in which afforestation schemes in one locality increase the rainfall in that district and this is favourable to the production of wheat in that district. In this case the production of timber creates an atmosphere favourable to the production of wheat.

In such cases there is what we have called an 'adding-up problem' for society as a whole. There may be constant returns to the factors of production employed in either industry alone. That is to say, a 10 per cent increase in the amounts of land, labour, and capital employed in producing wheat might, in any given atmosphere, result in a 10 per cent increase in the output of wheat. And a 10 per cent increase in the amount of land, labour, and capital employed in producing timber might, apart from its effect in changing the atmosphere for wheat-farmers, cause a 10 per cent increase in the output of timber. It follows that a 10 per cent increase in the amount of land, labour, and capital employed both in the timber industry and in wheat-farming will increase the output of timber by 10 per cent and the output of wheat by more than 10 per cent (because of the improvement in the atmosphere for wheat-producers). To society as a whole there are increasing returns to scale; and thus, on the principle illustrated in Table II (p. 35), to pay every factor a reward equal to the value of its marginal social net product will account for more than the total output of the two industries; revenue will have to be raised from outside sources by general taxation if subsidies are to be paid to the timber-growers to bring their rewards up to the value of their marginal social net products inclusive of the favourable effect upon wheat output of an increase in the scale of their activities.

Thus there are very many types of external economy and diseconomy in production. An unpaid factor in one industry may be either the actual output of the other industry (for example, apples may provide food for bees), or a particular use of factors in the other industry (for example, the employment of factors on drainage operations in one farm may affect a neighbour's output). In the case of a creation of atmosphere it may be the output of one industry which creates an atmosphere for the output of another industry (for example, the output of timber may affect the rainfall and so the output of wheat) or it may be the employment of a factor of production in one industry which creates an atmosphere favourable or unfavourable to the efficiency of a particular factor in another industry (for example, the employment of skilled labour in one industry may indirectly communicate know-how to, and so raise the efficiency of, labour in another industry). Or it might be the output of one industry which increased indirectly the efficiency of a particular factor in another industry, or the employment of a particular factor in one industry which affected generally the output of another industry. And in considering the external effects of firm or industry A on firm or industry B and vice versa, it must be remembered that any combination of these different kinds of external economies or diseconomies which A exercises on B may be combined with any combination of such effects of B upon A. Clearly the forms of repercussion are very numerous indeed and they cannot be considered at all exhaustively here.[1]

3. *A Classification of Industries*

It may help to clarify the points made in this and the preceding chapter to point out that for the purpose of understanding the relations which will exist between marginal social values and costs there are three distinct principles of classification. The resulting classification is illustrated in Table IV.

(i) Row 1 of Table IV states that in any industry there may or may not be a monopolistic or monopsonistic situation in which the individual consumer, entrepreneur, or factor can affect the price of what he sells or buys by varying the scale of his operations. If there is such a monopolistic or monopsonistic situation, there will be a divergence between marginal private values and costs.

(ii) Row 2 of the table expresses the fact that the total market for the product of the industry may or may not leave room for a large number of competing productive units of a technically efficient size. This depends upon the degree to which the factors of production are capable of being divided into small independent units without loss of efficiency. If the factors are not sufficiently divisible, then there will be room in the market for only one or two productive units and there will necessarily be a monopolistic situation. Rows 1 and 2 leave us, therefore, with three and not four divisions: there cannot be an industry in which the factors

[1] A mathematical formulation of these relationships is given in J. E. Meade, 'External Economies and Diseconomies in a Competitive Situation', *Economic Journal*, March 1952.

TABLE IV

Marginal Values and Costs: a Classification of Industries

(1)	Competition			Monopoly or monopsony					
(2)	Divisibility of factors						Indivisibility of factors		
(3)	No external economies or dis-economies	Unpaid factors	Creation of atmosphere	No external economies or dis-economies	Unpaid factors	Creation of atmosphere	No external economies or dis-economies	Unpaid factors	Creation of atmosphere
	(*a*)	(*b*)	(*c*)	(*d*)	(*e*)	(*f*)	(*g*)	(*h*)	(*i*)
(4)	Full standard competitive position.	Production of apples provides food for bees.	Production of timber provides rainfall for wheat growing.	Monopoly protected by a patent right.	(*d*) together with (*b*).	(*d*) together with (*c*).	A large indivisible productive system such as a railway system between two places.	(*g*) together with (*b*).	(*g*) together with (*c*).

are indivisible and there is also a fully competitive situation. But there may, of course, be a situation in which there is full divisibility of factors of production but for some other reason (for example, the single legal ownership of a raw material or of a patent right) an element of monopoly.

(iii) Finally, row 3 of the table shows that any of the above types of industry may be one in which there are (*a*) no external economies or diseconomies, or (*b*) external economies or diseconomies due to unpaid factors, or (*c*) external economies or diseconomies which create an atmosphere.

This gives in all nine possible cases, and the table gives in the last row an example of each kind. As we have already seen, wherever there are indivisibilities of factors there are liable to be increasing or decreasing returns to scale (pp. 32–34) and also wherever there are external economies or diseconomies of the atmosphere-creating type there will be increasing or decreasing returns to scale for society as a whole. Thus in all these cases (columns *c*, *f*, *g*, *h*, and *i* of Table IV) the problem will arise that to pay rewards to all factors of production equal to the value of their marginal social net products may absorb more or less than the total product of the industries concerned. It will absorb more than the total product, and thus involve the problem of raising revenue from general taxation in order to subsidize the industry's losses, if an indivisible factor of production is not being used up to its optimum capacity or if there are external economies of the atmosphere-creating type. The opposite will be so in the case of an over-employed indivisible factor or of external diseconomies of the atmosphere-creating type.

4. *The Raising of Revenue*

In the first part of this chapter we enumerated the many forms of action which national governments may take in order to remove divergences between marginal social values and costs. But we were left with one important unresolved problem—namely, the raising of revenue. Revenue must be raised in order to finance communal forms of consumption like police, defence, etc.; it must be raised from the rich in order to give aid and relief to the poor if it is desired to increase equality of income in the interests of equity; it may also be desirable for the State to raise revenue in excess of its expenditure so that public savings through a budget surplus may supplement private savings and bring the community's total savings more nearly to the optimum level; and, as we have seen in the second part of this chapter, the removal of divergences between marginal social values and costs due to indivisibilities of factors of production or to external economies may involve fiscal arrangements requiring the raising of a net revenue from general taxation. As we have seen, this last point is not certain. If we had to deal solely with external diseconomies of an atmosphere-creating type or with indivisible factors which were overworked rather than underworked, the fiscal arrangements necessary to remove marginal divergences would actually make a net contribution to general tax revenues. But the sums that are required in modern societies to finance communal needs, for purposes of redistributing income, and for the supplementation of private savings are so large that we can safely conclude that, when all action has been taken to remove marginal divergences between costs and values, there will remain a vast problem of raising revenue to finance State expenditure. We have not up to now considered any way in which such large revenues could be raised without themselves introducing divergences between marginal social costs and values. We must now turn to a consideration of this problem.

It is clear that the normal methods of raising revenue will themselves introduce a divergence between marginal values and costs. Thus in the case of indirect taxation it is obvious that a 10 per cent *ad valorem* rate of duty imposed upon the purchase or sale of a particular commodity will give rise to a 10 per cent rate of divergence between the gross price paid by the buyer and the net price received by the seller. In the absence of external economies or diseconomies and if there were perfect competition in this market, this would cause a 10 per cent rate of divergence between marginal social values and costs in respect of this transaction.

In the case of a direct tax on income the result is a little more complicated because of the possibility that the tax may itself be a progressive one. This is illustrated in Table V. Let us consider first a proportionate income tax of 10 per cent of income, as illustrated in section i of Table V. When a man's income goes up from \$1,000 to \$1,100 (column *a*, rows 1 and 2) since the rate of tax is constant at 10 per cent (column *b*), the amount which he pays in tax rises from \$100 to \$110 (column *c*), so that his net tax-free income rises from \$900 to \$990 (column *d*). In other words, when his gross income rises by \$100 (column *e*) his net income rises only by \$90 (column *f*). In other words, on an additional earning of \$100 he pays \$10 in tax which represents a marginal rate of tax of 10 per cent on his additional earnings (column *g*). But in order to fit in with our definition of a rate of divergence we must reckon any divergence between marginal values and costs not as a percentage of values but as a percentage of costs. Now it is the marginal gross income which in equilibrium will represent the value of this man's services to those who hire him and it is his marginal net income which in equilibrium will measure the marginal cost of the effort to him. If we reckon the marginal tax payment of \$10 as a percentage of the marginal net income of \$90 instead of as a percentage of the marginal gross income of \$100, we obtain a marginal rate of divergence of $11\frac{1}{9}$ per cent (column *h*).

All this is different in the case of a progressive income tax. Suppose, as we do in section ii of Table V, that when a man's gross income goes up from $1,000 to $1,100 (column *a*, rows 3 and 4) the rate of tax is raised progressively from 10 per cent on the lower income to 15 per cent on the higher income (column *b*) so that the amount of tax paid rises from $100

TABLE V

Proportionate and Progressive Income Taxes

	Gross income	Rate of tax	Amount of tax	Net income	Marginal gross income	Marginal net income	Marginal rate of tax	Rate of divergence
	a	*b*	*c* $(a \times b)$	*d* $(a - c)$	*e*	*f*	*g* $\left(\frac{e-f}{e}\right)$	*h* $\left(\frac{e-f}{f}\right)$
				(i) *Proportionate Income Tax*				
	$	%	$	$	$	$	%	%
(1)	1,000	10	100	900	—	—	—	—
(2)	1,100	10	110	990	100	90	10	$11\frac{1}{9}$
				(ii) *Progressive Income Tax*				
	$	%	$	$	$	$	%	%
(3)	1,000	10	100	900	—	—	—	—
(4)	1,100	15	165	935	100	35	65	$185\frac{5}{7}$

to $165 (column *c*) leaving a net income which rises from $900 to $935 (column *d*). Now when the gross income goes up by $100, the net tax-free income rises only by $35 (columns *e* and *f*). This represents a marginal tax payment of $65 on the additional earnings of $100 or a marginal tax rate of 65 per cent (column *g*). This gives a rate of divergence between marginal values and costs, as we have defined it, of no less than $185\frac{5}{7}$ per cent (column *h*), although the average rate of income tax applicable to this man's income is only 15 per cent (column *b*).

Thus a system of taxation which, in the interests of economic equity, is introduced on a highly progressive scale will necessarily introduce very high rates of divergence between marginal values and costs.

An exactly similar phenomenon may appear on the expenditure side if a system of what may be called 'progressive income subsidies' is introduced in order to raise the incomes of the poorest citizens. Suppose that family allowances, unemployment benefit, health benefit, and the like are made payable on some principle of a means test so that the payments are tapered off as a man's income increases, in order that the payments may be made exclusively to those who most need them. Such a situation is illustrated in Table VI. Suppose that when a man's income rises from

TABLE VI

Progressive Income Subsidies

Gross income	Rate of subsidy	Amount of subsidy	Net income	Marginal gross income	Marginal net income	Marginal rate of tax	Rate of divergence
a	b	c $(a \times b)$	d $(a + c)$	e	f	g $\left(\frac{e-f}{e}\right)$	h $\left(\frac{e-f}{f}\right)$
$	%	$	$	$	$	%	%
100	10	10	110	—	—	—	—
110	5	$5\frac{1}{2}$	$115\frac{1}{2}$	10	$5\frac{1}{2}$	45	$81\frac{9}{11}$

$100 to $110 (column *a*) a rate of subsidy to his income is reduced from 10 per cent to 5 per cent (column *b*), so that the total subsidy paid to him falls from $10 to $$5\frac{1}{2}$ (column *c*) and his income after receipt of subsidy rises from $110 to $$115\frac{1}{2}$ (column *d*). This means that when his gross earnings rise from $100 to $110 (column *a*) or by $10 (column *e*), his net income rises only from $110 to $$115\frac{1}{2}$ (column *b*) or by $$5\frac{1}{2}$ (column *f*). Of his additional earnings of $10 he keeps only $$5\frac{1}{2}$ which represents, as it were, a marginal rate of 'tax' of 45 per cent (column *g*) which is the equivalent of a rate of divergence between marginal values and costs of $81\frac{9}{11}$ per cent (column *h*).

The problem of progressive income subsidies is not so acute as that of progressive income taxes. A subsidy to income which is fixed in amount and which does not vary at all with the recipients' income will be highly progressive in the sense that it will increase the small income by a much larger percentage than it increases the large income; and it will, of course, cause no divergence between the marginal gross income and the marginal net income. The income earner can keep all that he adds to his income by working harder. A tax on income which is fixed in amount and which does not vary with the recipient's earned income would in the same way cause no divergence between marginal gross and net incomes; but, unlike a fixed income subsidy, it would be highly regressive instead of progressive. It would represent a much larger percentage of tax on the small income than on the high income. Our problem is, therefore, especially one of progressive income taxation rather than of progressive expenditure to redistribute income.

The question, therefore, arises whether there are any ways in which revenue can be raised equitably, but without causing such high rates of divergence between marginal values and costs.

The first possibility is that the State should itself receive a revenue from sources other than taxation. This would be the case if the State itself owned a considerable amount of property and thus itself directly received rents from land or interest from capital which was in its own ownership. In fact, in modern societies the opposite is usually the case. There are normally large national debts which mean that the State, far from receiving a net income from property, itself has to pay out a considerable amount in interest on debt which it owes to private citizens. But if by a single once-for-all capital levy this role could be reversed, the State itself might become a net creditor instead of a net debtor and use its income from rents, profits, interest, etc., on State-owned property to finance part of its expenditure. If the State used its property (in nationalized industries or by hiring it out to private entrepreneurs) in an appropriate manner, this would be a method of raising revenue without there necessarily being a divergence between marginal values and costs. We can do no more than indicate this possibility, any full discussion of which would be an important topic in a Theory of Domestic Economic Policy.

There is, however, theoretically one possible way of raising tax revenue in a progressive manner without introducing any divergence between marginal values and costs. This method may be called that of progressive poll taxes.[1] What we need is a form of taxation which does not affect the relationships at the margin between gross income before tax and net income after tax. As we have already observed, the poll tax or lump-sum tax is of this character. Suppose that a man is earning $1,000 and that it is desired to take $100 from him in taxation. A proportionate tax of 10 per cent on his income will raise the necessary sum;[2] but in this case he will be told that for every additional $1 which he earns he can keep only $0·9. His net reward for an additional unit of work will be reduced by 10 per cent below the value of his services to his employer. But if a lump-sum tax of $100 were imposed upon him regardless of the amount which he worked, then if he decided to earn an additional $1, he would keep the whole $1 for himself.

A poll tax, i.e. a tax fixed in absolute amount which everyone must pay, does therefore pass the requirement that it raises revenue without

[1] See A. P. Lerner, *The Economics of Control*, Chapter 19, p. 237.

[2] Disregarding for the moment any adjustment of the total amount which he earns, an adjustment which he may make as a result of the tax.

introducing a divergence between marginal values and costs. But such a tax is, of course, open to obvious objections on grounds of equity. To raise the same lump sum of $100 from every citizen, rich and poor, is clearly to distribute the burden of taxation in an unacceptable way. Equity may demand not merely that the richer citizen shall pay more than the poorer, but that he should pay a larger proportion of his income than the poorer. But, as we have seen, if this principle of progression in taxation is introduced into a normal tax system, the effect of taxation in causing a divergence between marginal values and costs will be still more accentuated.

Theoretically, however, even this difficulty could be overcome if it were possible to assess people for taxation not on their actual income but on their earning capacity. Suppose that it were possible impartially to assess Mr. A as a man whose income would be $1,000 in the absence of taxation, and Mr. B as a man who, in view of his greater capacity or training, would earn $1,500 in the absence of taxation. Then a fixed lump-sum tax of $100 could be imposed on A and one of $300 on B. The tax system would be progressive; but since neither A nor B could vary the absolute amount of tax payable by them by actually earning more or less, the tax would cause no divergence at the margin between the gross and the net income earned through working harder and earning a little more.

In the same way, it would be theoretically possible to assess the poorer citizens according to their capacity to earn instead of according to their actual earnings for the purpose of paying lump-sum benefits or poll subsidies to supplement their low earnings. Once again, they would be able to keep all their marginal earnings, since their income subsidies would not vary with their actual earnings.

Such a system of progressive poll taxes and poll subsidies would be the complete theoretical answer to our problem of raising revenue in any manner considered equitable for the finance of any level of governmental expenditure without introducing thereby any rates of divergence between marginal values and costs. The system is obviously totally impracticable. It is introduced here merely in order to elucidate the nature of the problem requiring solution. But in the absence of such a system of taxes, the raising of revenue by the State is bound to introduce divergences between marginal values and costs somewhere in the economic system, unless the State owns sufficient income-bearing property to be able to finance its budget without the imposition of taxes for solely revenue purposes.

CHAPTER IV

THE MARGINAL CONDITIONS FOR UTOPIAN EFFICIENCY

WE can now turn to a consideration of the conditions which must be fulfilled in order to ensure that any given amount of the basic economic resources—land, labour, and capital—are used in the most efficient manner. We shall say that the maximum efficiency has been attained when it is impossible to alter the use of those resources in such a way as to make one citizen better off without making any other citizen worse off. In this chapter we shall be concerned solely with the marginal as opposed to the structural conditions for such an efficient use of resources (see pp. 6–7 above). That is to say, we shall be concerned solely with the possibility of making one citizen better off without making any other citizen worse off by means of small marginal adjustments of the use of resources; we shall postpone until Chapter VIII any discussion of the possibility of increasing economic efficiency by large-scale structural changes in the whole pattern of the economy.

The marginal conditions which must be simultaneously satisfied in order to achieve complete—or, as we have called it, utopian—efficiency can be discussed under four heads, which we shall call (i) the condition of optimum trade, (ii) the condition of maximum production, (iii) the condition of optimum production, and (iv) the condition of optimum effort.

It will be one purpose of this chapter to show that all these conditions will be simultaneously fulfilled if, by measures of the type discussed in the last chapter, all divergences between marginal social values and costs could be removed, and if at the same time all consumers were free to choose what they would buy with their incomes, if all owners of factors of production were free to decide what use they would make of their factors, and if all traders and entrepreneurs could freely aim at maximizing their profits in deciding what to trade and what to produce. We shall call this the solution by means of a 'modified laissez-faire policy', since it involves a laissez-faire policy modified only by those measures required to remove divergences between marginal social values and costs. The reader is reminded that such a solution would involve totally impracticable fiscal arrangements based upon a system of progressive poll taxes and poll subsidies and that in consequence it is not put forward as a feasible policy but merely as a standard of reference in the light of which other policies can be judged.

But it will also be a purpose of this chapter to point out that the complete removal of all divergences between marginal social values and costs is not a necessary condition for each of the four conditions considered separately. In order to fulfil all the four conditions simultaneously—that is to say, in order to reach a utopian solution—the complete removal of all divergences is necessary. But in order to fulfil some of the individual conditions separately a much less strict policy is necessary. In discussing each of the four conditions separately we shall indicate what divergences between marginal social values and costs are compatible with the fulfilment of that particular condition.

In our exposition in this chapter and, indeed, throughout Part I, we shall not only assume that there are no artificial obstacles put in the way of the movement of factors of production from one occupation to another or in the way of the free choice by consumers between different products. We shall also assume that there are no real costs of movement of factors when they turn from one industry to another and no real costs of transporting products from one market to another. Such costs of movement for factors and of transport for products make up an essential feature of the theory of international trade which is concerned with movements of products and factors between markets which are widely separated in space. We shall have to consider their influence in some detail in the subsequent Parts of this volume. But in this Part we shall provide a general outline of the theory of economic welfare which abstracts from such costs.

We can now turn to an examination of each of the four marginal conditions for utopian efficiency.

1. *The Condition of Optimum Trade*

It may be possible to make one consumer better off without making any other consumer worse off by a further exchange of commodities between the consumers. For example, it may be possible by giving citizen A one more blanket and one less apple to consume and, simultaneously, giving citizen B one less blanket and one more apple to consume to leave citizen A just as well off as before but to make citizen B better off. If this is so, then an exchange of one apple given by A to B for one blanket given by B to A will increase economic efficiency. If no further possibility of profitable trade of this kind exists in the community, we shall say that the condition of optimum trade is fulfilled.

As can be seen from Table VII, trade will not be optimized so long as it is possible to find any two commodities the ratio between whose marginal values is different to any two consumers. Thus in the table we suppose that the marginal value of an apple and of a blanket is $1 to A, whereas in the case of B the marginal value of an apple is $4 and of a blanket is $2. In this case for A to have one more blanket will add to his welfare just as much as he will lose by having one less apple. But B will gain more ($4 in value) by having one more apple than he will lose ($2 in value) by having one less blanket. Trade is not optimized because the ratio of the marginal value of an apple to that of a blanket is different for A and for B.

Now, as we have already seen, each consumer in a free market will buy each commodity until its marginal value to him is equal to the marginal payment which he has to make to acquire one more unit. The optimization of trade is, therefore, one of the easiest conditions to fulfil. If consumers have no monopsonistic powers, all that is necessary is that the prices at which commodities can be bought should be in the same ratio to each other for all consumers. This is obviously so if the

TABLE VII

The Optimization of Trade

	Marginal value to		Change in amounts consumed by		Change in welfare of	
	A	B	A	B	A	B
Apple .	$1	$4	−1	+1	−$1	+$4
Blanket .	$1	$2	+1	−1	+$1	−$2

price charged for any commodity were the same for all purchasers. It would even be true if the prices charged to B were all higher than those charged to A, provided that the price to B of all commodities were raised by the same proportion. For example, the condition of optimum trade would not be invalidated even if there were a tax on all commodities purchased by B without any tax on commodities purchased by A, provided that all B's purchases were charged at the same *ad valorem* rate.

The type of divergence which would not be compatible with the optimization of trade would be exemplified by a tax on apples consumed by B which was not offset either by a similar tax on apples consumed by A or by a similar tax on blankets consumed by B. A similar situation would arise if B had a large degree of monopsonistic power in the purchase of apples (so that the marginal payment which B had to make to acquire an additional apple were much higher than its price) without this being offset by a similar monopsonistic power either on the part of A in the purchase of apples or on the part of B in the purchase of blankets. Or a similar situation would arise if apples and/or blankets were rationed to consumers and A's and B's tastes were such that B had a stronger taste for apples relatively to blankets than had A.

So far we have argued as if neither A nor B were themselves producers of apples or blankets but as if each had money incomes which they could spend on either of these two commodities. But suppose A were a producer of apples and exerted a monopolistic power in the market for apples. The price of an apple charged by A for his sales might be, say, \$2 so that the marginal payment to be made by B for an apple was \$2. But the marginal revenue which A could obtain from the sale of another apple might be only \$1, because he would spoil the existing market for his apples by putting more on the market. Suppose that the price and marginal payment which A and B had to make for a blanket was \$1 to both of them. Then A would consume both apples and blankets until the marginal value of each to him was \$1. He will prefer to consume his own apples until their marginal value to him is only \$1, because by selling one more apple instead of consuming it himself he obtains a marginal revenue of only \$1. But B, to whom the price of a blanket is \$1 and of an apple is \$2, will consume apples only up to the point at which the marginal value of an apple is twice that of a blanket. Thus where a monopolistic producer of a product is also a consumer of that product, trade will not be optimized; the monopolistic producer will not only restrict production (with which we are not at present concerned) but he will also expand his own consumption of his product instead of selling it.

Apart from divergences of the types discussed in the preceding paragraphs trade will be optimized; and this is compatible with all sorts of other divergences between marginal values and costs. To illustrate in terms of divergences due to taxation, it is compatible with a general income tax, a tax on the production or the consumption of all commodities, a tax on the production or the consumption of one commodity but not of another commodity, a tax on one consumer's income or total expenditure but not on that of another consumer, and even with a tax on a particular product levied only when it is produced by one particular firm or producer. What is ruled out is a tax confined to one particular product which is levied when this product is consumed by some consumers but not when it is consumed by other consumers.

2. *The Maximization of Production*

A second obvious condition for economic efficiency is that resources should be so used that it is impossible to produce more of one commodity without producing less of another. When this condition is fulfilled we shall say that production is maximized. The attainment of this condition within any given unit of production is a matter of efficient technology and business administration which it is not our purpose to discuss. Economic issues arise as soon as we consider whether production could be increased by re-arranging the employment of factors or the production programmes as between different independent firms.

As Table VIII suggests, there are three possible ways in which such re-arrangements between different firms might lead to an increase in the production of one product without any reduction in the production of another product.

The first possibility is shown in section i of Table VIII. Suppose that the marginal product of labour is 2 apples in firm A and 1 apple in firm B. Then output will clearly be increased by a movement of a unit of labour from firm B to firm A. The first sub-condition for the maximization of production is, therefore, that the marginal product of any one factor in terms of any one product should be the same in all firms.

The second possibility is shown in section ii of the table. We suppose that both firms A and B employ some labour and some land, but that firm A produces apples and firm B blankets. But we suppose that the marginal product of labour is twice as high as that of land in firm A where apples are produced, while the marginal product of land is the same as that of labour in firm B where blankets are produced. At the margin labour is twice as productive as land in firm A, but only equally as productive as land in firm B (columns *a* and *b* of section ii). If in these conditions some labour moves from firm B to firm A where labour is relatively more productive and is replaced in firm B by some land from firm A where land has a relatively low productivity (columns *c* and *d* of section ii), then the output of firm A will be increased while that of firm B is unchanged. In firm A 1 less apple will be produced because of the loss of a unit of land whose marginal product is 1 apple, but 2 more apples will be produced because of the gain of a unit of labour whose marginal product is 2 apples—a net gain of 1 apple (column *e*). But in firm B output will remain unchanged; the loss of a unit of labour will be exactly balanced by the gain of a unit of land, since in firm B the two factors have the same marginal product (column *f*). Thus the second sub-condition for the maximization of production is that the ratio between the marginal product of one factor and the marginal product of another factor should be the same in all firms in which the two factors are employed side by side, regardless of the nature of the products produced.

The third possibility is shown in section iii of Table VIII. Suppose now that firm A and firm B both produce some apples and some blankets. But suppose that in firm A the marginal cost of an apple is only half that of a blanket in terms of any one factor (say, land), whereas in B the marginal cost of an apple is the same as that of a blanket in terms of any one factor (say labour) (columns *a* and *b* of section iii). Suppose then that in firm A there is a shift of land to the production of apples whose land-cost of production is relatively low at the margin and that in firm B there is a shift of labour to the production of blankets (columns *c* and *d*). This is, of course, only another way of saying that

TABLE VIII

The Maximization of Production

In firm		Change of employment in firm		Change of output in firm	
A	B	A	B	A	B
(*a*)	(*b*)	(*c*)	(*d*)	(*e*)	(*f*)
(i) The movement of a factor from one firm to another producing the same product.					
the marginal product of labour is					
2 apples	1 apple	+1 labour	−1 labour	+2 apples	−1 apple
(ii) An exchange of factors between two firms not necessarily producing the same product.					
the marginal product of labour is					
2 apples	1 blanket	+1 labour	−1 labour	+2 apples	−1 blanket
and of land is					
1 apple	1 blanket	−1 land	+1 land	−1 apple	+1 blanket
(iii) A change of production programmes in two firms not necessarily employing the same factors.					
the marginal cost* of an apple is		on the production of apples			
½ land	1 labour	+1 land	−1 labour	+2 apples	−1 apple
and of a blanket is		on the production of blankets			
1 land	1 labour	−1 land	+1 labour	−1 blanket	+1 blanket

* This is, of course, only another way of expressing the facts that in firm A the marginal product of land is 2 apples and 1 blanket and that in firm B the marginal product of labour is 1 apple and 1 blanket.

land shifts in A and that labour shifts in B to the production of the commodity in terms of which its marginal product is relatively high. In this case (columns *e* and *f*) the reduction in A's output of blankets will be exactly offset by the increase in B's output, while the increase in A's output of apples will be greater than the reduction in B's output. The third sub-condition for the maximization of production is, therefore, that the ratio between the marginal cost of producing one product and the marginal cost of producing another product should be the same in all firms which produce both products regardless of the nature of the factors employed.[1]

Now it is clear that with what we have called a modified laissez-faire policy all three types of adjustment called for in Table VIII will be made. In the situation depicted in section i of the table the marginal product of labour will be twice as high in firm A as in firm B and labour will therefore move to obtain the higher reward obtainable in firm A. In the situation depicted in section ii the ratio between the marginal product and so the reward of labour and that of land will be twice as high in firm A as in firm B. This will be incompatible with equilibrium since it must mean either that the reward of labour is higher in A than in B or that the reward of land is lower in A than in B or that both are true. In the situation depicted in section iii the ratio between the marginal cost and so the price of an apple and that of a blanket will be twice as high in firm B as in firm A. This also will be incompatible with equilibrium since it must mean either that the price of an apple supplied by A is lower than that of an apple supplied by B or else that the price of a blanket supplied by A is higher than that of a blanket supplied by B or that both are true. Consumers will shift their purchases accordingly.

But while the free and costless movement of factors and of products combined with the absence of divergences between marginal social values and costs will be sufficient to lead to the maximization of production, it is not necessary that such stringent conditions should be fulfilled. Many types of divergence are compatible with the maximization of production, though some are not. This matter is a little complicated,

[1] In passing it may be of interest to observe an important distinction between the types of adjustment called for in sections i, ii, and iii of Table VIII, a distinction which will be of major importance when we come to consider problems of international trade. The adjustment called for in section i involves both a movement of the factors of production from firm B to firm A (which will require a free movement of factors from locality B to locality A) and also a change in the locality of output since A's output goes up and B's output goes down (which will require the freedom of movement of the products from each locality to the market to be served). The adjustment called for in section ii involves the movement of labour from A to B and of land from B to A (i.e. a free movement of factors), but the commodities are still produced in the same firms so that no new problem of transporting the products arises. The adjustment called for in section iii involves no movement of factors between A and B but does involve a new location for the output of the two products. Thus adjustment i involves low costs for the movement of factors and for the transport of products; adjustment ii involves low costs for the movement of factors but not for the transport of products; and adjustment iii involves low costs for the transport of products but not for the movement of factors.

and it may be easiest to understand the principle involved by asking what types of direct taxation of incomes and of indirect taxation of products would not disturb a situation of maximum production which would otherwise exist.

First, it would be quite legitimate to impose a rate of tax on the incomes earned by one factor, say labour, even though it were not imposed on the incomes earned by other factors, provided that the tax on wages were levied in respect of all wages earned in all lines of production. In section i of Table VIII this would still leave an incentive for labour to move to the occupation in which its gross reward before tax deduction were highest, because its net reward after tax would also be highest in that same occupation. In section ii the ratio between the net rewards of labour and of land would still be higher in firm A than in firm B, and some adjustment would therefore still take place. In section iii the ratio between the costs to the entrepreneurs of the two products would still differ in the two firms, and adjustment would therefore still take place.

Second, it would be perfectly legitimate to impose a rate of tax on any one product without imposing it on any other product, provided that the tax were imposed at the same rate on the product regardless of the firm in which or the factor by which it was produced. In section i of Table VIII the fact that apples were taxed would not remove the incentive for labour to choose as between two firms producing apples that one in which its marginal product and so its reward was the higher. In section ii the fact that apples were taxed and blankets were not would not alter the fact that the ratio between the marginal product and so the reward of labour and of land would be higher in firm A than in firm B, which is clearly incompatible with equilibrium. In section iii the fact that apples were taxed and blankets were not would not remove the fact that the ratio between the marginal cost of apples and blankets differed in the two firms, which also is incompatible with a final equilibrium.

Third, any combination of taxes of the kind mentioned in the two preceding paragraphs would be compatible with the maximization of production. One could have a 10 per cent tax on wages, a 20 per cent tax on rents, a 30 per cent tax on the production or consumption of apples, and a 40 per cent tax on that of blankets, all combined together.[1] The incentives to maximize production would not thereby be removed. For it is clear from the analysis of the preceding paragraphs that the

[1] If the tax on labour is 10 per cent, then the net post-tax wage of labour will equal its pre-tax wage $\times$ 0·9. If the tax on apples is 30 per cent, then the price of apples to consumers inclusive of tax will equal the post-tax price received by the producers $\times$ 1·3. Thus the ratio of marginal value to consumers to marginal cost to labour in the case of labour used to produce apples will be $\frac{1 \cdot 3}{0 \cdot 9}$. Let us call this R_{ma} (i.e. the ratio of marginal value to cost in the case of *m*anpower used to produce *a*pples). Thus, with the numerical examples given in the text, the ratio of marginal value to cost will be

introduction of these duties one after the other will do nothing to remove the incentives to maximize production. All that must be avoided is the imposition of an arbitrarily chosen rate of tax which is levied only on some factors and not on others and only when those factors produce some commodities but not when they produce others. What must be avoided is anything which militates with exceptional severity against the use of a particular factor to produce a particular product; it is that sort of arrangement which will cause the production of that product to be inefficiently organized.

It would appear, therefore, at first sight as if fiscal arrangements would be unlikely to interfere with the maximization of production, since any rate of tax could be levied on the income of any factor of production or on the final consumption of any product. But a complication arises in the case of products which are also used as factors in other industries. Thus suppose that labour is employed to produce coal and that labour and coal are used to produce blankets, it being possible in the production of blankets to choose between methods which employ more labour and less coal or methods which employ less labour and more coal. Suppose now that a 10 per cent tax is levied on the production of coal. Then labour which is used to produce blankets directly will not be taxed but labour which is used to produce coal to produce blankets indirectly will be taxed 10 per cent and employers will therefore have an uneconomic incentive to produce blankets by labour used directly rather than by labour used indirectly through coal. We shall end in a position in which if a unit of labour were moved from the blanket

---

in the case of *m*anpower used to produce *a*pples, $R_{ma} = \frac{1\cdot3}{0\cdot9} = 1\cdot4$

„ „ „ „ *m*anpower „ „ „ *b*lankets, $R_{mb} = \frac{1\cdot4}{0\cdot9} = 1\cdot71$

„ „ „ „ *l*and „ „ „ *a*pples, $R_{la} = \frac{1\cdot3}{0\cdot8} = 1\cdot645$

„ „ „ „ *l*and „ „ „ *b*lankets, $R_{lb} = \frac{1\cdot4}{0\cdot8} = 1\cdot75$

Thus the rate of divergence between marginal values and costs can be different in the case of every factor employed to produce every product. But there must be certain relationships between these divergences. In our case the necessary condition is that

$$\frac{R_{ma}}{R_{la}} = \frac{R_{mb}}{R_{lb}}$$

In words, in order that the free movement of factors, free choice of consumers, and the free enterprise of entrepreneurs should lead to the maximization of production, it is necessary to ensure that there are no divergences which cause the proportion between the ratio of marginal value to cost in the production of apples by land and the ratio of marginal value to cost in the production of apples by labour to differ from the proportion between the ratio of marginal value to cost in the production of blankets by land and the ratio of the marginal value to cost in the production of blankets by labour.

industry in order to produce coal to provide to the blanket industry, the amount of blanket production gained through the increased coal supply would be 10 per cent greater than the blanket production lost by the contraction of labour directly employed in the blanket industry. But the incentive to make the change would not exist because the coal production is subject to a 10 per cent tax. The taxation of intermediate products is incompatible with the maximization of production.

Apart from fiscal arrangements of this kind, there may be divergences due to other causes which will impede the maximization of production.

First, there may be restrictions on the movement of factors of production. Thus a trade union organization which was more fully developed in one region than another and which therefore restricted the entry of labour into a firm in one locality without restricting entry into another firm in another locality might lead to a situation of the kind depicted in section i of Table VIII. Labour might not move from firm B to firm A even though its marginal product was higher in firm A than in firm B, simply because entry into firm A was made more difficult than entry into firm B.

Second, there might be different degrees of monopsony exercised by employers in different industries over different factors of production. Thus the entrepreneurs in the apple industry (but not in the blanket industry) might exercise a considerable monopsonistic power over the hire of labour (but not of land). In this case employers would refrain from employing labour up to its most economic level in the apple industry and would employ land instead in order to avoid driving up the wage of labour against them. One might end up in the situation depicted in section ii of Table VIII, where the ratio between the marginal product of labour and land remained higher in the apple industry (where employers had a monopsonistic reason for avoiding the employment of labour) than in the blanket industry (where employers had no such reason for avoiding labour as a factor of production).

Third, an external economy might be associated with the employment of labour (but not of land) in the blanket industry (but not in the apple industry). For example, a large labour force in the blanket industry might facilitate the diffusion of skills and know-how among the workers attached to the industry. In this case there would be a social advantage, but no private motive, to transfer the use of labour from the production of apples to that of blankets and to transfer the use of land from the production of blankets to that of apples. One might remain in the sort of situation depicted in section iii of Table VIII because while the marginal *social* net cost of producing another blanket might (as shown in column *b* of the table) be 1 unit of labour the marginal *private* net cost might be 2 units of labour, so that the transfer of labour would not be profitable to the private employer.

In any one of these three situations production would fail to be maximized.

3. *The Optimization of Production*

If trade is optimized and production is maximized, it will be impossible to produce more of one thing without producing less of another, and with any given output it will be impossible to redistribute the supplies among different consumers so as to make one consumer better off without making someone else worse off. But we may still be far away from maximum economic efficiency, because the community might be better off if more of one product and less of another product were produced. This would be the case in a community in which the citizens were overfed but underclad. Suppose that by shifting a small amount of resources from the apple industry to the blanket industry it were possible to produce 2 less apples but 1 more blanket; and suppose that there is one consumer who would feel better off if he sacrificed 2 apples but gained 1 blanket. Then it would be possible by that movement of resources to make that citizen better off without making any one else worse off. When there is no further possibility of altering the outputs of any two commodities so as to make one consumer better off without making any other worse off, then we shall say that production is optimized.

The necessary and sufficient condition for the optimization of production, as can be seen from Table IX, is that it should be impossible to find any one factor, any two products, and any one consumer such that the ratio between the marginal social net cost of the two products in terms of that factor should differ from the ratio between the marginal values of the two products to that consumer. In Table IX we assume that in terms of labour the marginal cost of a blanket is twice that of an apple (column *a*), while in the case of some particular consumer the marginal value of a blanket is four times that of an apple (column *b*).

TABLE IX

The Optimization of Production

	Marginal social net cost (*a*)	Marginal value (*b*)	Change in employment (*c*)	Change in output (*d*)	Change in welfare (*e*)
Apples	1 labour	\$1	−2 labour	−2 apples	− \$2
Blankets	2 labour	\$4	+2 labour	+1 blanket	+ \$4

It follows from the cost conditions that if 2 units of labour are transferred from producing apples to producing blankets (column *c*) there will be 2 less apples and 1 more blanket produced (column *d*). But since the marginal value of an apple is only \$1 and of a blanket is \$4 (column *b*), it follows that this will mean that the consumer will lose apples worth only \$2 to him in order to gain blankets worth \$4 (column *e*).

In a modified laissez-faire situation this state of affairs could not continue. The fact that the ratio of marginal value to marginal labour cost is twice as high in the blanket industry as in the apple industry must mean that marginal values exceed costs in the blanket industry and/or fall below costs in the apple industry. Thus competitive forces will cause the apple industry to contract and/or the blanket industry to expand.[1]

But while a modified laissez-faire policy would be sufficient to optimize production, it is not necessary that such stringent conditions should be fulfilled. Once again it may be easiest to understand the issues involved by asking what taxes (other than those required to provide a

[1] It is not, of course, necessary in the above argument to assume that all work, on the apple-farm and the blanket factory, is equally attractive. The marginal cost to a worker of an hour's work on a farm might be only half the marginal cost to him of an hour's work in a factory. If this is so, the optimization of production requires the worker to shift this hour's work from the farm to the factory only if the value of his marginal social net product is more than twice as high in the latter as in the former. For the worker to be as well off he must only work an additional half hour in the factory when he works 1 hour less on the farm, so that the consumer can be better off only if the value of the marginal product of work in the factory is more than twice as high as on the farm. Strictly speaking, this analysis is based upon the assumption that workers can spread out their work over different jobs—1 hour a week at apple-farming, 5 hours at blanket-making, 7 hours at road-sweeping, and so on; just as consumers can spread out their expenditure on different commodities—\$1 a week on jam, \$5 a week on books, \$10 a week on travel, and so on. In this case, in the modified laissez-faire situation, each worker will be faced by a wage rate for each type of work which measures the value of the marginal social net product of that type of work and will then spread his working hours over the different jobs until the marginal cost of each job to him is equal to the particular wage offered. In this way production would be optimized. But in fact the worker for institutional reasons can normally only choose between working full-time on a farm or full-time in a factory. To him the change is a structural change. But it may still remain a purely marginal change to the farms or factories concerned to take on 1 more or 1 less worker. In the modified laissez-faire situation, therefore, the wage offered for a worker in each industry will still measure the marginal value to consumers of the marginal product of labour in each job. Each worker will then, subject to his particular aptitudes, be offered a wage in each job equal to the value of his marginal product in each job. He can then choose which job to take. He can make the—to him—structural change of moving from a farm to a factory if the marginal product of his work is greater in the latter than in the former by an amount which exceeds the total cost to him of the structural change in his way of life. Subject to this limitation, production will still be optimized in the modified laissez-faire situation in the sense that he will still have an incentive to move wholly from one job to another if it is possible thereby to make himself better off without making consumers worse off. In the rest of this volume we shall therefore neglect this complication.

modified laissez-faire policy) would be compatible and what incompatible with the optimization of production. In the first place, any rate of tax on the income earned by any factor, even if it were not accompanied by a similar tax on the incomes earned by other factors, would be compatible with the optimization of production. Thus, in the example given in Table IX, a 10 per cent tax on the income earned by labour would not destroy the incentive to shift labour from the apple industry to the blanket industry even if no tax were levied on the income earned from rents on land, provided the tax on wages were levied at the same rate in both industries. Nor would a tax on the production or consumption of apples and blankets impede the optimization of trade provided that it were levied at the same rate on the production or consumption of all products. But a tax levied on the production or consumption of blankets but not on the production or consumption of apples would impede the optimization of production. For example, a 100 per cent tax levied on blankets only would mean that while the forces of competition would make marginal values equal to marginal costs in apple production, they would leave marginal values twice as high as marginal costs in blanket production and we would have a continuation of the situation depicted in Table IX.[1]

Thus any form of direct taxation of the incomes of ultimate factors of production would be permissible; but in the case of indirect taxation there must be a single rate of tax applicable to all products for final consumption. But, as in the case of the maximization of production, it is only final products ready for final consumption which must be subject to the tax; products must be exempt from the tax when they are used as factors of production in other industries.

We can illustrate this point by a slight elaboration of the example already given in the case of the maximization of production. Suppose that labour can be used to produce coal; that labour and coal can be used to produce blankets; and that coal can be used directly in domestic grates to give final warmth to final consumers as well as in the form of a factor of production in the blanket industry. Suppose now that both products, coal and blankets, are subject to a uniform rate of tax of 10 per cent. Then when labour is used directly to produce coal for

[1] If the $\frac{\text{marginal cost of apples}}{\text{marginal cost of blankets}}$ is to be equal to the $\frac{\text{marginal value of apples}}{\text{marginal value of blankets}}$ (which, as we have seen, is the necessary and sufficient condition for the optimization of production), then the $\frac{\text{marginal value}}{\text{marginal cost}}$ of apples must be equal to $\frac{\text{marginal value}}{\text{marginal cost}}$ of blankets in terms of any one factor. In other words, in the terminology used in the footnote on p. 59, we need $R_{ma} = R_{mb}$ and $R_{la} = R_{lb}$ instead of $\frac{R_{ma}}{R_{la}} = \frac{R_{mb}}{R_{lb}}$ which was all that was needed to ensure the maximization of production.

consumers it will be subject to a 10 per cent tax, but when it is used indirectly to produce coal to produce blankets it will be subject to (approximately) a 20 per cent tax—10 per cent on the coal and 10 per cent on the blankets produced from the coal. There will thus be a larger divergence between marginal values and costs in the case of blankets produced indirectly from labour employed in the coal mines than in the case of coal provided direct to consumers from the coal mines. The optimization of production requires that more coal should be used to produce blankets and that less should be sold for consumption in the domestic hearth. But this shift of resources from providing coal for final use to producing blankets will be impeded by the fact that coal is, as it were, taxed twice when it is used in the indirect fashion. The taxation of intermediate products is thus incompatible with the optimization of production. Coal, like blankets, must be taxed only when it is sold for final consumption.

What must be avoided if production is to be optimized is anything which causes there to be a larger divergence between marginal values and costs in the provision of one product for final consumption than in the provision of another. Such divergences may be caused by elements of monopoly or monopsony, by external economies or diseconomies, or by institutional regulations as much as by taxation. For example, if the blanket industry is more monopolistic than the apple industry, or if the apple industry suffers from an external diseconomy or the blanket industry enjoys an external economy which the other does not, or if there is some institutional barrier to the expansion of the blanket industry which is not so strong in the case of the apple industry, production will not be optimized and consumers could be made better off by having more blankets and less apples.

Theoretically it would be possible to imagine a situation in which there was the same degree of monopoly or of external economies in all industries, so that in the case of apples, blankets, coal, and everything else there was the same rate of divergence between marginal values and costs. In this case production would continue to be optimized; it would only be to the extent that the rates of monopolistic or external-economy divergences differed in the different industries that production was not optimized. But even this possibility would disappear if we consider a product which could be used both as a final consumption good and also as a factor of production. If, for example, coal could be used directly to give warmth to consumers or indirectly to produce blankets for consumers, it would be necessary that the degree of monopoly or of external economy in the provision of coal to final consumers should be the same as in the case of the provision of blankets to final consumers, while at the same time there should be no degree of monopoly or of external economy in the provision of coal to the blanket industry.

Otherwise production would not be optimized, since coal provided direct to final consumers would only have to encounter one divergence while coal used in the blanket industry to provide blankets to consumers would have to overcome two divergences. The possibility of avoiding this is, of course, very remote.

The optimization of production is, as we have seen, compatible with a tax on the income earned by any one ultimate factor of production even if it is not levied on other factors of production but provided that it is levied on the factor's income regardless of the way in which that factor is employed. In the same way the optimization of production would be compatible with a divergence between marginal values and costs in the case of the employment of any one factor, whether the divergence were due to a monopolistic element, an external economy or diseconomy, or an institutional regulation, provided that this cause of divergence operated with the same force in all uses of the factor. Such a possibility is not, perhaps, quite so remote. An example would be a monopolistic trade union which, while it could not discriminate in the price charged for the labour to different employers of the labour, could nevertheless raise the wage of the particular kind of labour above its marginal cost. This would cause a divergence between marginal values and costs for this labour, but the rate of divergence would be the same in all uses of the labour.

4. *The Optimization of Effort*

Even though trade is optimized and production is both maximized and optimized, it may still be possible to make one citizen better off without making anyone else worse off by a variation in the amount of work done or effort expended by an individual citizen. If someone does an additional hour's work a week, the disagreeableness to him of the additional work or of the loss of leisure may be more than compensated by his satisfaction in having the additional product of his labour to consume directly or to exchange with other people in order to add to his consumption of other things. When such an adjustment is no longer possible, we shall say that effort has been optimized.

The necessary and sufficient condition for the optimization of effort is easy to understand; it is that it should be impossible to find any two citizens A who is doing a particular type of work and B who is consuming the product of A's work, such that the marginal cost of a unit of effort to A differs from the marginal value to B of the marginal social net product of that effort. We have defined the marginal cost of the effort as the amount of additional money which A would in current market conditions have to receive in order just to be recompensed for the additional unit of effort; and we have defined the marginal value of the marginal social net product as the amount of money which in current market conditions B would be just willing to give up in order to acquire the additional product. Clearly, if the marginal value of the product exceeds the marginal cost of the effort in this sense, both A and B would be better off if A worked harder and were paid by B for the product something between its marginal cost to A and its marginal value to B. Conversely, if the marginal value of the product were lower than the marginal cost of the effort, both A and B would be better off if A worked less hard and B, no longer receiving the product, cut down his payment to A by something in between the marginal value to B and the marginal cost to A.

In a modified laissez-faire situation this condition will be satisfied. The marginal value of any product will be the same to every consumer of that product and will be measured by the price of the product. The marginal cost of the effort will be the same to every worker who will be free to provide more or less effort, and will be measured by the uniform wage rate offered per unit of effort. And the competitive process will bring it about that the wage rate is equated to the value of the marginal product, i.e. that the marginal value of the product is equal to the marginal cost of the effort.

But practically any divergence between marginal value and cost introduced into the economy at any point will upset the optimization of effort. An indirect tax on a particular commodity or a direct tax on any form of earnings from effort will cause a divergence between the value of the marginal product and the cost of the effort. Similarly, a monopolistic element, an external economy or diseconomy, or an institutional regulation at any such point will disturb the optimization of effort. In particular, as we have already noted (p. 23), it may for institutional reasons be inevitable that a uniform working week should be observed by all workers in a particular trade. Where this is so, it is not possible for each worker individually to adjust the amount of his effort until the value of its product on the market is equal to its marginal cost to him.

The only type of divergence between marginal value and cost which would be compatible with the optimization of effort would be one which affected only the earnings of some factor of production the supply of which did not depend at all upon human 'effort' of any kind. If land were a factor of production which did not depend in quantity or quality upon human work, risk-bearing, or investment, then a tax on the rent of land would cause a divergence between the value of the marginal product of land and the net rent offered to the owners of land for each unit of land. But it would in no way affect the supply of land; it would merely reduce the incomes of the owners of land. Effort would still be optimized.

We have now discussed the four marginal conditions for economic efficiency, namely: the optimization of trade, the maximization of production, the optimization of production, and the optimization of effort. Our discussion will have made it clear that the difficulties of ensuring that each condition is fulfilled increase in this order. We can illustrate this by summarizing the types of taxation which it is legitimate to introduce into a modified laissez-faire situation in order to raise revenue; but the same principle can, of course, be applied to divergences between marginal values and costs due to factors other than taxation. Thus the optimization of trade is compatible with any form of taxation whatsoever, except that if a particular product is taxed then the tax must be levied on the total consumption or on the total production of that product. The tax must not fall solely on trade in that product and thus cause a divergence between marginal value and cost when a product is bought from someone else for consumption which is absent if the product is consumed by the person who produces it. The maximization of production requires the additional tax conditions that if a tax is levied on the consumption of a particular product when it is produced by one factor it should also be taxed when it is produced by another factor, that if a tax is levied on one factor when it produces one product it should also be taxed when it produces other products, and that products should be exempt from tax when they are used as factors in other industries. The optimization of production requires the further tax condition that if one product is taxed for final consumption all other products for final consumption should be equally taxed. It will be observed, however, that all these three conditions are compatible with the raising of revenue by means of a progressive rate of income tax. But the optimization of effort requires that there should be no marginal rate of tax on any product or on any factor whose supply can be affected by human endeavour; there must be no divergence between the marginal values of marginal products and the marginal cost of the effort. Only the impracticable progressive poll taxes discussed in Chapter III (p. 50) would be legitimate. We shall return to this problem in Chapter VII.

CHAPTER V

THE MARGINAL CONDITION FOR UTOPIAN EQUITY

THE four marginal conditions which we discussed in the last chapter —the conditions of optimum trade, of maximum production, of optimum production, and of optimum effort—all have one important feature in common. So long as any one of them is not fulfilled it is possible, as we have seen, to make one citizen better off without making any other citizen worse off. Any economic policy which in fact results in making one citizen or group of citizens appreciably better off without making any other citizen or group of citizens appreciably worse off may be regarded as unequivocally desirable.

But the marginal condition for economic equity which we are about to discuss is of an essentially different nature. It involves, or may involve, the raising of economic welfare by increasing the welfare of one citizen or group of citizens at the expense of a smaller decrease in the economic welfare of another citizen or group of citizens. This raises a quite different issue. It is one thing to ask someone whether he prefers situation A or situation B, and to say that it is a good thing to allow him to move to the preferred situation, if that does not involve altering the situation of anyone else. It is quite a different matter to decide whether the total situation has improved or deteriorated when one citizen has moved from a less preferred to a more preferred situation at the expense of a reverse movement for some other citizen. In order to say whether the total situation is better or worse, we must have some absolute measure of how much the situation of the first citizen has improved and how much that of the second has deteriorated in order to see whether the improvement of the former is greater than the deterioration of the latter or vice versa. We shall have more to say about this later in this chapter. For the time being we shall simply assume that it makes sense to ask whether a given improvement in one person's welfare is more or less than counterbalanced by a given deterioration in the welfare of another.

Most people would agree that to give a crust to a starving beggar would give more satisfaction than to give it to a rich and replete alderman returning from a City dinner. This principle is raised, although often in a less obvious form, whenever we consider whether a redistribution of consumption from one citizen or group of citizens to another citizen or group of citizens would or would not increase total economic welfare. If the distribution of income is such that it is impossible by shifting income from one citizen to another to increase the satisfaction of the latter more than the satisfaction of the former is reduced, we shall say that the condition of optimum distribution is achieved.

There is no very obvious way in which institutional arrangements can be devised so as to provide private incentives which will automatically lead to the condition of optimum distribution. Freedom of movement of factors of production from lower-paid to higher-paid occupations—all, in fact, that is meant by freedom of opportunity—will, on the whole, exert an equalizing tendency in rewards. But even if such movements were complete, there would remain differences in factor endowment, differences in family responsibilities, and differences in tastes for which allowance must be made before the condition of optimum distribution is attained. One man may have less innate ability than another or may own less income-earning property than another; and he may thereby receive a smaller income than the other, even though the rates of reward for equal units of any factor are the same in every use. Or one income-earner may be responsible for maintaining a larger number of dependants than another. Or one income-earner may have different physical or psychological requirements than another; on grounds of physical health he may need a diet consisting of the more expensive foodstuffs. To such men, presumably, the addition of an extra dollar per annum may mean more than it does to the others.

If an attempt is to be made by the State to make allowance for any or all of these possibilities, it will involve the raising of revenue by the taxation of those to whom the last units of income are of less importance and the use of the revenue to increase the income of those to whom additional units of income are of special importance. The attainment of the condition of optimum distribution may thus require the taxation of high incomes and the subsidization of low incomes.

In this volume we cannot neglect the basic issues raised by this condition of optimum distribution. It must inevitably be an essential part of our present problem to consider (see Chapters XVII, XVIII, and XXVII) the effect of different international economic policies upon the distribution of income as between the trading countries and as between the different citizens within the trading countries. A fairly full treatment of this subject is inescapable.

We cannot make any progress on this part of our present inquiry unless we are prepared to make comparisons between the satisfactions of different citizens. Suppose that in any given situation at given market prices—or, more accurately, at given marginal payments for different goods to different consumers—it were possible to give \$1 more per annum to citizen A. Then one must be able to say how many dollars one would have to be in a position to give to citizen B in order to be indifferent between giving \$1 more to citizen A or this number of dollars more to citizen B. Suppose that one would feel that one would do exactly as much good by giving $1 extra to citizen A or by giving $2 more to citizen B. Then one can say that one judges the marginal utility of income to citizen A to be twice as great as the marginal utility of income to citizen B. If one is given a series of indices of this kind showing how much additional income one must give to B, to C, to D, and so on, in order to do as much good as can be done by giving $1 more to A, one can then proceed to judge whether a given redistribution of income will increase total economic welfare or not. The marginal condition for utopian distribution would demand that one should always transfer $1 of income from B to A so long as one could find any two citizens A and B such that the marginal utility of income to A was greater than the marginal utility of income to B. But, quite apart from such a utopian criterion, such a system of indices would enable one to say of any policy which made marginal changes in outputs and incomes whether, from the point of view of economic equity as well as of economic efficiency, the change added to economic welfare or not (see Chapter VII).

Now it is not suggested that such marginal utility indices are objective facts which can be objectively measured. They are bound to be political or moral assessments which the economist as such must accept as given by the policy-makers. In what follows, therefore, we shall assume that the policy-makers are prepared to allot certain 'distributional weights' to the incomes of the various citizens or groups of citizens, A, B, C, D, etc., in the sense that they are prepared to say whether to add $1 to the income of B is one-half, twice, or three times as important an objective of policy as adding $1 to the income of A. The economist's job can only be on the basis of any given schedule of distributional weights to say whether an economic policy would then lead to greater economic welfare or not. But although these distributional weights cannot be objectively tested, they are not altogether unnatural. Indeed, they are part of the normal stock in trade of politics. The vast majority of people would agree that an additional $1 to a pauper (group A) will cause more satisfaction than an extra $1 given to a millionaire (group B). But the adherents of one party will assess policies on the assumption that they are willing to see a gain to group A of $1 provided it does not mean a loss to group B of more than $10, while those of another party will be willing to see a gain to group A of $1 only provided that it does not mean a loss to group B of more than $2. The economist, as such, can merely advise each party about the implications for policy of its own weightings.

But since these distributional weights are bound to be less objective in character than the problems of economic efficiency which we were discussing in the previous chapter, it may be suggested that we should be well advised to reject all problems of equity from economic analysis and to confine our attention to problems of efficiency. Unfortunately, this solution is impossible because, as we shall try to show in the remainder of this chapter, it is impossible to divorce considerations of efficiency and of equity in economic analysis.

An attempt has been made in the past to divorce decisions about policies for economic efficiency totally from decisions about policies for economic equity in the following way. Suppose that some economic policy is under consideration—for example, the reduction of a duty on the production of apples and its replacement by a duty on blankets as a means of raising revenue. We want to consider the effect of this policy solely from the point of view of economic efficiency, although it is also likely to have some effect upon the distribution of income and thus upon economic equity as well. When we make the change in policy some people (e.g. the apple producers who are no longer taxed) will gain and some people (e.g. the blanket producers who are now subject to tax) will lose. It is not, therefore, a case in which everyone has been made better off since some gain and some lose; and we cannot, therefore, say directly that economic efficiency has been increased. But we can then ask the supplementary question: could the gainers from the change in policy make a transfer of income to the losers which would compensate the losers for their losses and yet leave the gainers better off than under the old policy? If such compensation is possible, then to make the change of policy has been said to mark an increase in economic efficiency; for—although it does not make everyone better off—it leads to a situation in which a mere transfer of income from gainers to losers would make everyone better off. The change of policy, therefore, marks an increase in economic efficiency; and we can judge later on purely equitable grounds whether the compensation should be paid, i.e. whether we want everyone to share the gains or whether we consider it an actual improvement in economic welfare from the point of view of equity that the gainers should in fact be permitted to gain at the expense of the losers.

If it were possible to argue in this manner, there would be a great simplification in the theory of economic welfare. We could consider all the efficiency aspects of any change of policy quite separately on the more or less objective grounds discussed in the last chapter. We could then turn to a quite separate discussion of the question whether steps should then be taken to rectify any of the effects which the policy may have had upon the distribution of income, a discussion which would have to be based upon the much less objective criteria of our policy-maker's distributional weights.

But unfortunately there are overwhelming reasons for believing that this hard-and-fast distinction between the efficiency and equity aspects of policy cannot be made. We will examine three such reasons.

The first objection to the use of this 'compensation principle' as the means of separating the efficiency from the equity aspects of an economic policy is that, in many cases, it may fail to provide an answer to the question whether on grounds of efficiency alone a change is desirable or not. Consider a change of policy which will move the economy from what we will call 'situation i' to 'situation ii'. We suppose that in situation ii some people will be better off and others worse off than in situation i; we will call these the 'gainers' and 'losers' respectively. The compensation principle states that situation ii is a more efficient one than situation i if in situation ii the gainers could compensate the losers and leave everyone better off than in situation i, even though in fact no compensation scheme is introduced.

Suppose then that the change from situation i to situation ii is contemplated without the gainers compensating the losers. The potential losers know that they will be worse off if the change is made. They would, therefore, be willing to pay those who stand to gain from the change a 'bribe' to persuade them to agree that the change should not take place. Now the loss to the potential losers through the bribe which they must pay to the potential gainers to make up for the gain which the latter would have forgone may be less than the actual loss incurred by the losers through the change itself; and it is not impossible that at the same time the actual gainers from the change would be able to compensate the losers. If this were so, then the compensation principle would state that situation ii was more efficient than situation i because if the change were made the gainers could compensate the losers; but it would also at the same time have to state that situation i was more efficient than situation ii because if the change were not made (i.e. if there were, as it were, a change back from situation ii to situation i) the potential losers could bribe the potential gainers to give up the change (i.e. those who gained from the change back from situation ii to situation i could compensate those who lost by this reverse change). Thus if the gainers can compensate the losers for the change, the new situation must be judged more efficient than the old; but if at the same time the potential losers can bribe the potential gainers to give up the change, the old situation must simultaneously be judged more efficient than the new—which is absurd.

At first sight it may appear improbable that a state of affairs could exist in which it would be possible for the gainers from a change to compensate the losers and yet at the same time for those potential losers to be able to bribe the potential gainers against a change. But this state of affairs is a perfectly possible one, as the example given in Table X may help to demonstrate.

In this example we raise the problem of economic efficiency by supposing that in the community only apples and blankets are produced and by considering the condition of optimum production (see pp. 61–5

TABLE X

The Principles of Compensation and Bribery

				Production programme gives priority to							
				blankets				apples			
				Consumption and price of		Income	Order of preference	Consumption and price of		Income	Order of preference
				apples (*a*)	blankets (*b*)	(*c*)	(*d*)	apples (*e*)	blankets (*f*)	(*g*)	(*h*)
Total consumption = total output			(1)	500	600	—	—	600	500	—	—
Distribution of income favours				*Situation* i				*Situation* ii *with compensation*			
	workers	Price	(2)	$1·75	$0·375	—	—	$1	$1	—	—
		Workers	(3)	400	400	$850	2nd	460	340	$800	1st
		Landlords	(4)	100	200	$250	4th	140	160	$300	3rd
				Situation i *with bribe*				*Situation* ii			
	landlords	Price	(5)	$1	$1	—	—	$0·375	$1·75	—	—
		Workers	(6)	160	140	$300	3rd	200	100	$250	4th
		Landlords	(7)	340	460	$800	1st	400	400	$850	2nd

above). Would the community gain if more apples and less blankets were produced? We introduce the problem of economic equity by assuming that there are only two groups of citizens, namely, workers and landlords. Blanket production, we assume, is technically of such a character that it requires a lot of labour and little land to produce a blanket. Apple-farming, however, is technically of the opposite kind; and a lot of land and little labour is needed to produce an apple. Income will be redistributed and problems of equity will arise as soon as anything is done which raises the rent of land and lowers wage rates, or vice versa.

Let us suppose that both apple-farming and blanket production are socialized. The authorities are producing 500 apples and 600 blankets (left-hand side of Table X) but could produce 600 apples and 500 blankets (right-hand side of the table) if they took steps to expand apple-farming at the expense of blanket-manufacturing. Such action would mean, however, that the apple-farming authority would have to take on a lot more land and only a little more labour, while the blanket-making authority would be releasing little land and much labour. The expansion of apple-farming and contraction of blanket-making would thus cause a scarcity of land and a surplus of labour in the market, and the rent of land would be driven up and the wage of labour would be reduced. The incomes of landlords would rise and of the workers would fall. This is shown in the table by the fact that in situation i the workers have an income of $850 and the landlords an income of $250, whereas the position is reversed in situation ii.

Finally, we assume that landlords happen to have a specially heavy demand for blankets while workers happen to have a specially heavy demand for apples.[1] As a result of this the price of apples will be very much higher in situation i than in situation ii for two reasons—both because the supply of apples is lower in situation i than situation ii and also because income is distributed more favourably in situation i than in situation ii to workers who have a specially high demand for apples. If the cost of an apple is approximately the same as that of a blanket, situation i will be one where the State is making a loss on its blankets which it can sell for only $0·375 and a profit on its apples which it can sell for $1·75. The opposite will be the case in situation ii when it has greatly reduced the supply of blankets on the market and has greatly increased the supply of apples.

We are now asked to judge on purely efficiency grounds between the production programme of 500 apples and 600 blankets in situation i and the production programme of 600 apples and 500 blankets of situation ii. Can this be done? Suppose that the change from situation i to

[1] It will be observed that in each of the four situations shown in Table X the ratio of apples bought to blankets bought is higher in the case of workers than in the case of landlords.

situation ii is made; and suppose (top right-hand quarter of the table) that the landlords who have gained from the change compensate the workers who have lost by transferring \$550 of their income so that the workers now have \$800 and the landlords \$300 to spend. The result of this transfer of income from the blanket-consuming landlords to the apple-eating workers will be to bring down the demand price for blankets from the high level of \$1·75 to \$1 and to raise the price offered for apples from the very low level of \$0·375 to \$1, where the demand prices are more nearly in line with the costs of producing the two products.

Now it is certain that both workers and landlords will be better off in situation ii with compensation (top right-hand quarter) than in situation i (top left-hand quarter). The landlords, for example, in situation i are using their \$250 of income to purchase 100 apples at \$1·75 an apple and 200 blankets at \$0·375 a blanket. In situation ii with compensation they have \$300 to spend and the price of an apple is \$1 and of a blanket is \$1. They could, therefore, purchase 100 apples at \$1 and 200 blankets at \$1, i.e. they could purchase exactly what they purchased in situation i. But because between situation i and situation ii with compensation the price of an apple has fallen (from \$1·75 to \$1) and of a blanket has risen (from \$0·375 to \$1) they choose to buy more apples (140 instead of 100) and less blankets (160 instead of 200). They must therefore prefer 140 apples plus 160 blankets to 100 apples plus 200 blankets since in situation ii with compensation they freely choose the former instead of the latter combination. They are, therefore, better off in situation ii with compensation than in situation i.

Similarly, it can be shown that the workers are better off in situation ii with compensation than in situation i. In situation i they use their \$850 to purchase 400 apples at \$1·75 each and 400 blankets at \$0·375 each. In situation ii with compensation with their income of \$800 they could purchase 400 apples at \$1 and 400 blankets at \$1, i.e. the combination of goods which they purchased in situation i. But because the price of apples has fallen and of blankets has risen, they too freely choose to purchase more apples (460 instead of 400) and less blankets (340 instead of 400). They also must therefore be in a preferred position.

We are required, therefore, by the compensation principle to say that situation ii is better than situation i since in situation ii with compensation everyone would be better off than in situation i. But let us now suppose that we start in situation ii and make the change of production programme to situation i. We can now prove by an exactly similar argument that situation i is better than situation ii. If from situation i (top left-hand quarter of the table) \$550 of income is transferred from workers to landlords, we have situation i with bribe (bottom left-hand quarter of the table). Since income has been transferred from apple-eaters to blanket-buyers the price of apples will have fallen from \$1·75 to, say, \$1 and of blankets will have risen from \$0·375 to, say, \$1. Prices will now more nearly reflect costs of production. If we compare situation i with bribe (bottom left-hand corner of the table) with situation ii (bottom right-hand corner), we see that everyone has gained by the change back to situation i with bribe. Workers with an income of \$300 could have bought 200 apples at \$1 and 100 blankets at \$1 (i.e. they could have bought what they had in situation ii); but they prefer to purchase 160 apples and 140 blankets because apples are more expensive and blankets less expensive than in situation ii. Similarly, landlords in situation i with bribe could have bought what they bought in situation ii but, in fact, buy another combination of products, and are better off in situation i with bribe than in situation ii. The workers could, therefore, have bribed the landlords not to make the change from situation i to situation ii; and on the same compensation principle situation i must therefore be judged superior to situation ii.

How is it that situation i with bribe can be preferred by everyone to situation ii, while at the same time situation ii with compensation can be preferred by everyone to situation i? In our example the essential feature is that workers have a taste for apples and landlords a taste for blankets. One cannot, therefore, consider the efficiency principle of optimum production without taking into account what is in fact going to be done about the distribution of income on equity grounds. If on equity grounds it is considered proper that the incomes of workers should be maintained at a high level relatively to those of landlords (top half of Table X), then it is efficient to produce many apples and few blankets since workers want apples rather than blankets (situation ii with compensation is better than situation i). If, however, on equity grounds it is considered proper that the landlords should be kept rich and the workers poor (bottom half of Table X), then it is efficient that many blankets and few apples should be produced, since landlords want blankets rather than apples (situation i with bribe is better than situation ii). Efficiency demands that the production programme should match the distribution of income which is judged proper on grounds of equity. The two sets of considerations cannot be separated.

We can, therefore, conclude that in a state of affairs like that depicted in Table X where the principle of compensation demands that the change should be made while the same principle of bribery demands that it should not be made, the one thing which we know for certain is that we do not want either of the situations between which we are asked to choose (situation i and situation ii). We do not want situation i because situation ii with compensation is better for everyone. We do not want situation ii because situation i with bribe is better for everyone. What we should choose between is situation i with bribe (i.e. adopting a policy for the redistribution of income in situation i) and situation ii with compensation (i.e. changing to situation ii and offsetting the effects of the change on distribution). If we like the distribution of situation i, we should move to situation ii with compensation, and if we like the distribution of situation ii, we should go for situation i with bribe. We cannot reach our efficiency decisions regardless of the considerations of economic equity.

It may be of interest to observe that if situation ii were a situation of utopian economic efficiency (i.e. a situation in which all the conditions discussed in the preceding chapter were simultaneously satisfied so that it was impossible to choose another situation in which anyone was better off without someone being worse off) then the situation i with bribe of Table X could not exist. Simply because situation ii was a situation of utopian efficiency, situation i with bribe could not be preferred by everyone simultaneously. The possibility of bribing against the change could not arise. Similarly, situation ii with compensation could not be preferred by everyone over situation i, if situation i were a situation of utopian economic efficiency. If therefore either situation i or situation ii were a fully efficient situation, the logical inconsistency of the compensation principle would disappear. If situation i were efficient and situation ii inefficient, it might be possible to bribe against the change but would be impossible to compensate for a change. If situation i were inefficient and situation ii were fully efficient, it might be possible to compensate for the change but would be impossible to bribe against it. If both situations were fully efficient, it would be impossible to compensate for the change or to bribe against it. If, therefore, we are confining ourselves to utopian situations, i.e. are only considering changes which bring us to a situation of utopian efficiency, the possibility of bribing against the change will not occur. The formal consistency of the compensation principle would be restored.[1]

If we were only concerned with utopian success in so far as our policies for economic efficiency were concerned, the compensation principle would not break down on the grounds of logical inconsistency which we have just discussed. But there might remain another reason for being unable to distinguish sharply the efficiency and equity aspects of the change of policy. Suppose that the state of affairs is as depicted in situation i and situation ii of Table X. When we apply the compensation principle we ask whether there is a situation like situation ii with compensation which is preferable to all concerned over situation i. In Table X we find that such a situation can be attained simply by starting from situation ii and transferring $550 of income from landlords to

[1] But it would still be open to the overwhelming objection discussed below (pp. 78–9) to the effect that to say that situation ii with compensation is better than situation i does not enable one to judge the relative merits of situation ii without compensation and situation i.

workers. But this is based upon the assumption that the transfer of income can be brought about by means—such as the progressive poll taxes and poll subsidies or the State ownership of sufficient income-bearing property discussed in Chapter III (pp. 49–50)—which do not themselves impede economic efficiency by introducing disincentives to the earning of income and thus disturbing, for example, the condition of optimum effort. The shift from situation ii to situation ii with compensation as depicted in Table X may be altogether too flattering to situation ii with compensation, because the raising of revenue from the landlords to transfer income to the workers might introduce disincentives of a kind that would reduce the supplies in situation ii with compensation below the 600 apples and 500 blankets there supposed to continue to be forthcoming. Presumably, we must modify the compensation principle to say that situation ii is to be preferred to situation i if in situation ii you could introduce a practical system of fiscal redistribution of income such that, even after taking into account any new inefficiencies introduced by these fiscal arrangements, everyone could be better off in situation ii with compensation than in situation i. It is thus impossible to consider equity policies designed merely to redistribute income without taking into account their effects upon efficiency.

But this last point merely serves to demonstrate the essential irrelevance of the compensation principle. If one is moving from situation i to situation ii and is not in fact going to compensate the losers, then it is of purely theoretical interest whether one could or could not introduce a completely efficient mechanism for the redistribution of income. If one is not going to redistribute in any case, it would seem irrelevant whether situation ii with compensation should be based upon a perfectly efficient scheme for redistribution or not. The question becomes relevant only if one is choosing not between situation i and situation ii, but between situation i and situation ii with compensation. In that case, while situation ii with a perfectly efficient method of compensation might make everyone better off than in situation i, situation ii with the best practicable but nevertheless not perfectly efficient method of compensation might necessarily leave everyone worse off than in situation i. In this case situation ii with compensation must in fact be given up in favour of situation i.

Indeed, the ultimate and essential argument against the compensation principle is the very simple one that, if one is not going to compensate, situation ii with compensation is utterly irrelevant and one must choose between situation ii and situation i; and if one is going to compensate, then situation ii is utterly irrelevant and one must choose between situation ii with compensation and situation i. Suppose we start with situation i of Table X. We may all agree that situation ii with compensation would be better. But if I am asked to agree with an economic policy which will move us to situation ii without a compensation scheme, I may quite logically and correctly oppose this change as vigorously as I can. If workers are in much greater need of income than landlords, I may rightly consider that the evil redistribution of income away from workers to landlords involved by any change to situation ii greatly outweighs any efficiency advantages which the change may have. This opposition might be perfectly correct and legitimate even if situation i were a very inefficient one and situation ii were a position of utopian economic efficiency so that no bribe against the change was possible. I might simply hold that the distributional evils of the move from situation i to situation ii outweighed the admitted efficiency gains. I might therefore properly oppose it unless it is combined with a compensation scheme, in which case I would support it.

We, therefore, need some apparatus for judging simultaneously the efficiency and the equity aspects of economic changes which are brought about by economic policy. Moreover, because of the difficulties of redistributing income without introducing inefficiencies—if for no other reason—we need an apparatus which will help us to choose between two policies even though neither one gives us utopian economic efficiency. We must therefore look for a method of analysis which enables us to combine the efficiency and the equity aspects of policy and which at the same time is applicable to second-best as well as to utopian policies. We shall turn our attention to this question in Chapter VII.[1] But before we do so we must consider two further marginal conditions for economic welfare which have not been covered in this or the preceding chapter.

[1] Even then we shall be considering a technique which is capable of dealing only with the *marginal* conditions for utopian and second-best efficiency and distribution. We shall leave the *structural* problems until Chapter VIII.

CHAPTER VI

OPTIMUM POPULATION AND OPTIMUM SAVING[1]

THE four marginal conditions for economic efficiency discussed in Chapter IV and the marginal condition for economic distribution discussed in the last chapter do not in fact exhaust the marginal conditions for economic welfare. Our argument in the two preceding chapters has in fact been based upon the assumption that there was a fixed supply of the ultimate factors of production in the community under examination, so that our problem consisted in determining how these resources could be most effectively used and how their product could be best distributed. But, in fact, the supply of the ultimate factors of production is not fixed. First, the total working population may rise or fall, and it may be possible for the authorities to adopt various policies which, within limits, will affect these demographic trends. Second, the total stock of capital in the community can be increased if the citizens as a whole spend on goods and services for consumption less than the total income which they produce, so that the difference can be saved and invested in addition to the community's capital equipment; and once again the authorities can adopt various policies to increase or to decrease the rate at which income is saved in the community.

Economic welfare can thus be affected by governmental policies which affect the rate of population growth and the rate of capital accumulation. In this chapter we shall say something about these two problems. There are a number of reasons for discussing them separately from the conditions discussed in the two preceding chapters and devoting a special chapter to them.

In the first place, it is convenient to treat them both together, since —as the following discussion will show—the optimum population depends very closely upon the size of the community's capital stock, and the optimum rate for the community's saving (and so the size of the community's capital stock) depends closely upon the size of the population. The two conditions are so dependent on each other that they must be treated together.

Secondly, a consideration of increasing population and of capital accumulation necessarily involves a consideration not merely of the optimum arrangements in a static economic but of the optimum rate of expansion (or possibly of contraction) of an economic system. This involves problems of a rather different nature from those raised in the two preceding chapters.

[1] The relationships between the conditions of optimum population and optimum saving are worked out more fully in Section I of the mathematical supplement to this volume.

Thirdly, it is peculiarly difficult in considering the optimum population or the optimum rate of capital accumulation to separate the efficiency aspects from the distributional aspects of the question. In Chapter IV we discussed in what conditions certain changes could be made (e.g. changes in production or trade) which would enable one citizen to be better off without making any one else worse off. In Chapter V we discussed the question in what conditions economic welfare could be increased by redistributing income between citizens. It is true that in that chapter we saw reasons for believing that in reaching policy decisions it was impossible to consider the efficiency aspects and the distributional aspects of any policy in isolation from each other; but conceptually the question whether a change in trade or production could increase the welfare of some citizens without decreasing that of any others is quite distinct from the question whether any given redistribution of income will in fact raise the welfare of the gainers by more than it reduces the welfare of the losers.

In discussing the optimum population and the optimum rate of savings the difficulties involved in maintaining this distinction between efficiency and distributional aspects take a rather special form. There are clear efficiency aspects of both these problems. Thus because of the existence of economies of large-scale production a growth of population may enable production to be carried on in a much more 'efficient' manner. Or a man who refrains from consuming goods at a time when they are relatively unimportant to him (e.g. when he is at the height of his earning powers) and who saves the income instead may be able to consume these goods at a time when they mean much more to him (e.g. during his old age when he is retired and not earning). His personal savings and subsequent dissavings may increase the total welfare which he obtains without hurting anyone else; a change in the rate of savings may make the time pattern of individual consumption more efficient.[1]

But while there are very real efficiency aspects to the questions of the optimum population and the optimum rate of capital accumulation, these aspects cannot ever be separated from the distributional question, for the simple reason that a change in the size of the population or a change in the rate of savings is bound to affect the interests of two separate and distinct groups of persons.

Suppose that the community's saving is increased. That means that

[1] Thus in so far as a man saves for his own future benefit, it might appear that the problem of comparing the satisfactions of different persons does not arise. But even in this case it is possible to doubt whether Mr. Smith of next year can really be treated as being the same person as Mr. Smith of this year. In 1950 Mr. Smith may prefer consumption in 1950 to consumption in 1951, but in 1951 he may prefer consumption in 1951 to consumption in 1950. Is he the 'same person' so far as decisions about saving for the future are concerned? Perhaps the State should take an interest in the distribution of income between Mr. Smith of 1950 and Mr. Smith of 1951.

consumers in future years can be better off at the cost of current standards of consumption; but because men are mortal consumers in future years will not be the same collection of persons as consumers in this year. An increase in savings will necessarily involve some conflict of interest between the born of this generation and the unborn of the next generation.

Consider next the size of the optimum population. Would the economic welfare of any given generation be greater if the total population in that generation were greater? The answer to this question obviously involves a consideration of the welfare of the existing members of the generation in question: would their welfare be increased or decreased by the addition of new members to the community? It equally obviously involves a consideration of the welfare of the newcomers: would they be better off than if they had never been born? Just as a change in the rate of savings necessarily involves some conflict of interests between the born of one generation and the unborn of the next, so a change in the size of the population may at least involve a conflict of interests between the born and the unborn of the same generation.

1. *The Condition of Optimum Population*

Let us turn then to a consideration of the meaning of an optimum population and of the conditions necessary for its achievement. If steps had been taken in the past to make the population in any community greater than it actually is, this might well affect the standard of living of the actually existing members of the community; and it would, of course, have brought into being a new group of citizens who do not actually exist and who, if the standard of living is above some basic minimum, would have enjoyed a certain amount of economic welfare or satisfaction. If the increase in numbers had the effect of raising the standard of living of the actually existing population, then the increase in population might be considered to be unequivocally desirable. It would increase the satisfaction of the existing number of citizens and add to that an additional number of citizens to enjoy life.

But suppose that the increase in numbers reduces the standard of living in the community. In this case it reduces the satisfaction of the existing number of citizens but adds an additional number of citizens to enjoy life. If a relatively small addition to the number of citizens would cause a very great reduction in the average standard of living, the total welfare of the community would be reduced. This, everyone would probably agree, is unequivocally undesirable. But suppose that a relatively large addition to the number of citizens would cause only a small reduction in the average standard of living. Total welfare, in the sense of the sum of the welfares of all individual citizens, might well be increased, although the average standard of living per head were reduced.

What do we want to do? To maximize total welfare or welfare per head? The author would accept the maximization of total welfare as the ultimate criterion.[1] Such a statement has a very academic ring. Yet it is a real issue which concerns very real things. Governments do in fact decide between different population policies. No doubt they do so on many grounds other than economic grounds—on grounds which are moral, religious, cultural, or military. But in so far as they do so at all on economic grounds, it is a matter of very real importance to decide whether they should prefer a small population with a high standard of living to a much larger population with a rather lower standard of living. For the purpose of this volume we shall say that if it is impossible by increasing the population to subtract from the satisfaction of the already existing citizens less than the satisfaction of those who are newly brought into existence (or by decreasing the population to add to the satisfaction of the remaining citizens more than the satisfaction of those who are now not brought into existence), then the condition of optimum population is achieved.

In order to start to analyse the implications of this criterion, there are three basic assumptions which we need to make. In the first place, we shall assume that technical knowledge is given, i.e. that a change in the size of the population is not accompanied by new inventions of technical processes which alter the productivity of a given collection of factors of production. Second, we shall assume that the community is endowed with a given supply of land and other natural resources, the amount of which remains constant in spite of changes in the size of the population. Thirdly, we assume that at any one given time there is a given stock of capital equipment to be used, but that there is also at any given time a given rate of savings and so of capital accumulation. That is to say, at any given time the whole body of citizens refrain from spending on the present consumption of goods and services a given fixed amount of their real income, this quantity of real savings being kept the same at any given time whatever the size of the total population at that particular time.[2]

We wish to consider the changes in the economic position in any community as the total population in that community becomes smaller or bigger, other things remaining equal. What we are essentially doing is to ask the question whether the community at any given time would be better off if its total population at that time were somewhat larger (or

[1] Previously, however, he accepted the criterion of the maximum welfare per head. (See J. E. Meade, *An Introduction to Economic Analysis and Policy*, 2nd ed. (London, Oxford University Press, 1937), Part IV, Chapter II).

[2] What the size of this amount of real savings should be is, of course, the subject-matter of the latter section of this chapter on the optimum supply of capital. For the moment we assume that the rate of real savings is fixed at some given level—a level which may or may not be the optimum rate of savings.

smaller) than in fact it is. For this purpose we shall assume that the ratio of the non-working population to working population—e.g. the ratio of dependent children and retired persons to people of working age—is constant, so that if the total population increases by 10 per cent the working population also increases by 10 per cent. On this assumption our subsequent arguments can run in terms of the optimum population without distinguishing between workers and non-workers; each worker has more than one mouth, but always the same number of mouths, to feed.[1]

Now a community with a very small population will have a very small scale of output for all its industries. If economies of large-scale production are important, then the growth in the scale of operations of the economy which would be caused by a growth in the size of the population might enable a greater amount to be produced per head of the working population. But after a certain size of population had been reached the economies to be derived from a further increase in the scale of operations would become less important, simply because the scale

[1] This assumption is legitimate so long as one is concerned with the comparison between two long-run static equilibria which differ solely in the size of their total populations. The fertility rate is assumed in each case to be at a level which maintains the population at a constant size. With the same given mortality rate in each case, the fertility rate will be the same regardless of the absolute size of the population. In these conditions the age distribution of the population, and so the ratio of non-working to working members of the community, will be the same regardless of the absolute size of the population. Accordingly, in the text (pp. 83–93) we shall be considering the optimum size for a static population of this kind. But subsequently in this chapter (pp. 93–101) we shall by implication at least be dealing with questions which involve not merely the optimum size for a static population in a stationary economy but also the optimum rate of growth (or decline) for a population in a growing economy. We shall be proceeding as follows. We shall be inquiring what is the optimum rate of savings; and in answering this question we shall assume that at every point of time the population is at the optimum level in the sense that its size is always adjusted in the best possible way to the changing stock of capital. This would involve a change in the population at a certain rate to keep in step with the changes in the stock of capital which may themselves—as we shall see—alter the optimum size of the population. But such a rate of change in the population might involve very considerable changes in the ratio of non-working to the working population. For this reason the optimum rate of population growth may differ from the rate of growth which would be necessary in order to keep the population always at its 'static' optimum in relation to the stock of capital existing at any time. This is a complication which in this volume we shall frankly ignore. We are providing only a sketch of a theory of the determination of the size of the optimum population in an otherwise static situation and of the optimum rate of savings in a world in which the population could always be kept at every instant at its static optimum. We require really a combined theory which explains what the simultaneous optimum rate of savings and optimum rate of growth of population are. The completion of the theory in this way would be an important task in any complete Theory of Domestic Economic Policy. But for the purposes of this volume we are concerned primarily with the international implications of these problems. These we shall discuss in Chapter XXVIII. For this purpose we must be satisfied with the sketch of an incomplete theory in this chapter. It would take us too far afield to try to complete it at this point.

was already more nearly that at which all economies could be enjoyed; on the other hand, it would become more and more important that each worker was equipped with less and less of the other co-operating factors of production, land and capital, which have been assumed to remain constant as the population grew. At some point the economies of large scale would be counterbalanced by the disadvantages of working with less land and capital per head, and output per head of the population would fall with any further growth of numbers.[1]

It is an interesting arithmetical truism that so long as a further growth of population would cause a rise in output per head the marginal product of labour will be above the average product of labour. The marginal product of labour measures the addition to the total product which would be brought about by employing one more worker. If this marginal product is higher than the previous output per head, the employment of the additional worker will raise the average output per head; if this marginal product is lower than the existing output per head, then the employment of the additional worker will lower the average output per head. In other words, so long as output per head would be raised by an increase in the size of the population, the marginal product of labour will be higher than the average product per head; when product per head has reached its maximum, the marginal product must be the same as the average product; and as soon as product per head would be reduced by a further increase of population, the marginal product will be lower than the average product.[2]

If the objective of policy is to raise welfare per head to the highest possible level, then the aim must be to raise real consumption per head to the highest possible level.[3] Now if no part of income were saved, real consumption per head would be at its highest point when real output per head (and so real income per head) was at its highest point. And the criterion for the attainment of this objective would be a simple one. If the marginal product is above the average product of labour, then a larger population is to be desired; if below, then a smaller population is wanted.

[1] In this discussion of the optimum population we are tacitly assuming (*a*) that all workers are alike in abilities, etc., and (*b*) that all output can be considered as if it were comprised of one single type of product. These two assumptions would need much more attention in any full treatment of this subject, but their discussion would take us too far away from our present purpose which is merely to prepare the ground for certain international applications.

[2] This arithmetical relationship is illustrated by the figures in columns (*c*) and (*d*) of Table XXXVII which is discussed in Appendix 1 (p. 574).

[3] This conclusion is certain only if income is not maldistributed. An increase in real consumption per head might be accompanied by a reduction in real welfare per head if it were associated with a redistribution of income which took income away from those to whom consumption had a high marginal utility and concentrated it on those to whom consumption had a low marginal utility.

This criterion needs a simple modification if we allow for our assumption that some fixed amount of real income is being saved. Consumption per head (as opposed to output per head) can be raised by an increase in the population so long as the marginal product of labour is higher than the existing level of consumption per head (as opposed to output per head).[1] For so long as this is so, an additional worker can add to real output an amount greater than the present level of consumption per head; and thus if the whole of this additional product is devoted to the consumption of the new worker and of the existing members of the community, consumption per head can be raised all round without any decline in the total amount of output devoted to savings. The size of the population which will maximize consumption per head when some fixed total is being saved will be somewhat larger than that at which output per head is maximized. For suppose that the population were at the size which maximized output per head. Then a small increase in the population would leave output per head practically unchanged; but with a larger population total savings can be maintained even though savings per head are reduced. But with output per head more or less constant and savings per head reduced, consumption per head will rise. Thus with a fixed total for savings, the maximum point for consumption per head will come at a later stage of population growth than the maximum point for output per head. When the marginal product of labour is above consumption per head, consumption per head would be increased by a growth of population; when the marginal product of labour is below consumption per head, consumption per head would be increased by a reduction of population. We will call this the criterion for the 'per-caput optimum' of population.

This criterion might be difficult enough to apply in practice. In particular it would not be easy to measure the marginal product of labour. Output per head would be maximized where economies of large-scale production still existed, but were just offset by the disadvantages to be experienced from using a smaller amount of land and capital with each worker. But it must be remembered (cf. pp. 32–43 above) that where economies of large-scale production exist there will either be important monopolies or important external economies. In either case the wage rate offered to labour will not automatically measure the value of its marginal social net product. To judge whether labour's marginal product exceeds or falls below the average level of real consumption will necessitate some assessment of the marginal product which is independent of the level of wages actually paid, unless positive steps of the kind already discussed in Chapter III have been taken to make the wage rate paid correspond to the value of labour's marginal social net product.

[1] This relationship is illustrated by the relationship between columns (*d*) and (*f*) of Table XXXVII (p. 574).

But to the present author it would seem improper to take the maximization of welfare per head as the ultimate objective. A consideration of one of the more extreme implications of this objective should be sufficient to demonstrate its inapplicability. Suppose two communities A and B to exist. Suppose that neither has any appreciable economic dependence on the other so that the disappearance of A would not appreciably affect the standard of living in B nor the disappearance of B the standard of living in A. Suppose, further, that the standard of living in B is somewhat lower than in A, though both communities are prosperous and enjoy high standards. The strict application of the objective of maximizing welfare per head would lead to the conclusion that the world would be a better place if community B ceased to exist, since output per head for all citizens of A and B would certainly be increased if that section of the community with the somewhat lower standard were to cease to exist. It is true that when A and B exist together the richer citizens of A may be being taxed in order, in the interests of a utopian distributional policy, to supplement the lower incomes in B. In this case the citizens of A would enjoy an increase in their average real incomes if the citizens of B were all to cease to exist. But this distributional arrangement can be judged on its own merits. It can be removed without the removal of the citizens of B. Suppose the taxation of A to subsidize B is stopped. Is it really reasonable to conclude that a prosperous B should be blotted out in order to raise the arithmetical calculation of the average real consumption of the world citizen to the slightly higher figure enjoyed in A? Yet this is what the acceptance of the objective would involve.[1]

[1] One paradoxical result of the objective may be noticed in passing, although it does not in any way disprove the validity of the objective. Consider an economy A which at first, because of policies of extreme protectionism, has no commerce with the rest of the world B. Suppose then that barriers to trade are removed and that A and B can freely exchange their products. The result will be to *lower* the size of the per-caput optimum population in A, i.e. of the population at which consumption per head will be maximized. Before trade takes place A must produce everything for herself—her own boots as well as her own shirts. After trade takes place she can concentrate on the production of that in which she has the greatest comparative advantage and obtain her requirements of other products by imports obtained from exports of her own produce—say, shirts. Now if there are economies of large scale in these industries, in the absence of international trade A must have a sufficiently large population to be able to build up a boot industry as well as a shirt industry so that each are on technically efficient scales. But with trade she need only have sufficient population to build up a shirt industry on a technically efficient scale. Of course, international trade will raise income per head to be enjoyed for any given population; but by increasing the scale of the market for the products of any one industry it will *lower* the size of the population which is needed to raise real income per head to the highest possible level. The size of the domestic market becomes less important as a means of enabling economies of large-scale production to be enjoyed, so that in population growth the point is more quickly reached at which the disadvantages of lowering the land and capital equipment of each worker outweigh the advantages of a further enlargement of the domestic market.

We shall accordingly abandon the maximization of welfare per head as the objective of policy. Let us consider the implications of the alternative objective of the maximization of total welfare.

For this purpose we must introduce the idea of a 'subsistence' level of income into our discussion. Now there is a 'physical subsistence' level of real consumption which is necessary for physical life. Only if a man's income is above this can he obtain the necessities of life so as to keep body and soul together. But some policy-makers will desire to introduce another and higher 'welfare subsistence' level. A man may be above the basic 'physical subsistence' level and yet his existence may be considered so wretched as to count as a minus quantity from the point of view of economic welfare. He must attain something appreciably above the bare physical subsistence level before he can be said to be counted as a positive contribution to economic welfare.

Making use of these two ideas of a 'physical subsistence' and a 'welfare subsistence' income, let us consider the implications for population policy of an attempt to maximize total economic welfare. Suppose that we start from a position in which welfare per head is maximized. That is to say, the population is of such a size that the marginal product of labour is equal to real consumption per worker. Suppose further that this level of real consumption is above the welfare subsistence level as defined in the previous paragraph. This means that an additional worker would add to the total output of the community an amount which, if he and his family enjoyed all of it but not more than all of it, would give him and his family real income sufficient to put them above the welfare subsistence level. In other words, without anyone else being better or worse off he and his family could live a full and enjoyable life. The maximization of economic welfare would clearly demand that he should exist. No one else need be affected and he himself is in a position with his dependants to enjoy a full measure of economic welfare.

Suppose now that the population has so grown that the marginal product of labour has fallen until it is equal to the welfare subsistence level. Is this to be regarded as the true size of the optimum population? Up to this point it has been possible, while keeping the welfare of every other individual unchanged, to add to total economic welfare a net positive welfare of the new members of the population. After this point the marginal product of a new worker will be less than his welfare subsistence level; and if everyone else's welfare is unchanged, it will be necessary to subtract from total economic welfare the net 'illfare' of the new members of the population. In one sense, therefore, the point at which the marginal product of labour is equal to the welfare subsistence level might from the point of view of efficiency be considered the optimum size of the population. We shall call this point the 'efficiency optimum' for the population.

But it is not really legitimate to abstract in this manner from the distributional effects of an increase in the size of the population. Suppose that the population does grow a little. This will somewhat depress the marginal product of labour and it will somewhat raise the marginal product of land and capital (since more labour is used with a given amount of land and capital). It will tend, therefore, as between the pre-existing members of the community to redistribute income away from labour and in favour of the owners of property. Now it is true that if the new worker is paid a reward neither greater nor smaller than the value of his marginal product, it must be just possible to compensate the existing workers for their loss due to the fall of wage rates by taking from the property owners their gains due to the rise in rents and interest; and only if this is in fact done can it in fact be argued that an increase in the population will enable the newcomers to enjoy an income equal to their marginal product without anyone else being made worse off.

But if policy is to be used to redistribute income in this way between the existing citizens, why should the new worker be excluded from any redistribution of income? As soon as we allow for the possibility that income might be distributed favourably to the new worker, it becomes apparent that the size of the population at which total economic welfare will be maximized is greater than what we have called the 'efficiency optimum', i.e. the size at which the marginal product of labour will be equal to the welfare subsistence level of consumption.

This can be proved in the following way. Suppose we are at the efficiency optimum. Then an increase in the population by one worker will increase output by an amount which is just equal to his welfare subsistence. If he received this real income, he would make a zero net contribution to total economic welfare. At the same time every other citizen could be left exactly as well off as before.

In these circumstances the increase of population would cause no net change in total economic welfare. But it is to be observed that in this situation the average consumption of the existing citizens must be higher than the welfare subsistence level. For since the population has passed the per-caput optimum, the consumption per head will be falling with further increases in population; the marginal product of labour, in other words, is lower than the average level of consumption; and since the new worker receives the marginal product and this is equal to the welfare subsistence income, the average consumption enjoyed by the existing citizens must be greater than the welfare subsistence income. In short, the new worker receives only a wage which is equal to the marginal product of labour and is just sufficient for his welfare subsistence; but the existing citizens on the average receive not only this wage but also some net income in the form of rent of land and interest on capital.

On the average, therefore, the existing citizens must have a higher standard of living than the new worker would have if he received only the marginal product of his labour. Now if the marginal utility of income diminishes as people have larger incomes, it follows that the loss of welfare due to taking a small amount of consumption away from the existing citizens would be less than the gain of welfare due to giving it to the new worker. There would, therefore, be a net increase in economic welfare if the population grew somewhat beyond the point of what we have called the efficiency optimum, provided that as it so grew income was redistributed between the existing citizens and the new citizens in favour of the latter.[1]

Now, as we have seen in the preceding chapter, if all citizens have the same tastes and needs, economic welfare will be maximized only when there is an equal distribution of income. If citizen A has a larger income than citizen B, the marginal utility of income will be lower to A than to B, and the transfer of a unit of income from A to B will tend to an increase in total welfare. Let us suppose, then, that there is an equal distribution of income between all citizens.

We can now examine how large the population would have to be in order to maximize total welfare if income were always equally distributed between all citizens in the interests of maximizing economic welfare. We have already seen that population would have to grow beyond the 'efficiency optimum' at which the marginal product of labour was equal to the welfare subsistence level. The additional worker would be on the borderline of finding his life just worth while if he received an income equal to his marginal product, while everyone else could enjoy an unchanged income in such circumstances. If now income were transferred from the old members to the new member of the community until income were equally distributed, there would be a net increase in economic welfare because the loss to the (rich) old members would be less than the gain to the (poor) new member.

But by how much must the population grow beyond the 'efficiency optimum' in order to maximize total economic welfare? When a new member is introduced into the community, there will now be one more person enjoying the average consumption of the community. This in itself represents a gain of economic welfare equal to the total welfare of one representative citizen. But against this must be set the loss of welfare to the old members. If total savings are to be kept constant, they must between them transfer an amount of income for consumption by

[1] Such a redistribution of income might come about either through the fiscal weapons of a welfare state (in which case as the population grew the proceeds of progressive taxation on the rich would be used to supplement the incomes of the poor, including the poor new members of the society) or else through the instrument of widespread inheritance (in which case the new members of the population would have inherited their 'fair share' of the property of the society from which their incomes, like those of the existing citizens, would be supplemented).

the new member equal to the excess of their average consumption over the marginal product of the new member. Their combined loss is therefore equal to the marginal utility of an amount of income equal to the excess of the average consumption of one worker over the marginal product of a worker. A further increase of population will therefore tend to a further increase in total economic welfare if

> the total utility enjoyed by a representative citizen is greater than the marginal utility of a unit of product to the representative citizen multiplied by the excess of the average consumption over the marginal product of a worker.[1]

Now as the population grows beyond the per-caput optimum, consumption per head will fall. Total utility for each citizen will therefore fall and the marginal utility of income to each citizen will rise. When the total utility of income for the representative citizen has so fallen and the marginal utility of income has so risen that the condition given in the preceding paragraph is fulfilled, total welfare would no longer be increased by a further growth of population. We should have reached what may be called the 'total-welfare optimum'. Whenever in what follows we speak simply of the optimum population, it will be this definition of the optimum which we shall have in mind.

Before we turn from this discussion of the meaning of the optimum population it is perhaps worth while to note certain other special cases in the process of population growth.

Thus at some point after the efficiency optimum—it may be either before or after the total-welfare optimum is reached—the marginal product of labour will have fallen below the welfare subsistence level and will have reached the physical subsistence level. This point may be of interest in certain conditions. For example, suppose that the population were divided into two parts—those citizens who owned property and whose rate of reproduction was controlled so that their numbers were stable and a propertyless group of citizens whose fertility was unchecked. Then, in the absence of any arrangements for a welfare state in which part of the income of the former was transferred by fiscal means

[1] This formula is treated more formally in Section I of the mathematical supplement to this volume. Among other things, it is there shown that at the optimum point described by this formula the population may have to be so large that the marginal product of labour is actually negative. We know that the population will have to be larger than the 'efficiency optimum' at which the marginal product of labour is equal to the welfare subsistence level. If the marginal product of labour falls very rapidly and if much greater numbers are needed to raise total economic welfare by distributing income more thinly over a much larger number of persons to each of whom the marginal utility of income is high because consumption per head is not too high, then the population may have to be so large that the marginal product of labour is actually negative.

to the latter, the population of propertyless workers would grow until their marginal product and so their wage were at the physical subsistence level at which point its further growth would be checked by famine. But the income from property of the property owners—though not their income from work—would be increased by any growth in numbers of the propertyless workers, since the higher the number of workers the greater the marginal product of the existing stock of land and capital. We may call this point 'the physical subsistence point in the absence of redistribution of income'.

But if there are institutional arrangements for a more or less equal distribution of income between all citizens—either through the fiscal policy of a welfare state or through the more or less equal inheritance of property—then the population can grow far beyond this point. At this point the marginal product of labour is equal to the physical subsistence level; but since the population is greater than the per-caput optimum the level of average consumption will be higher than the marginal product of labour, and therefore higher than the physical subsistence level. In this case there will continue to be growth of population provided that income is more or less equally distributed and there is any section of the community the growth of which is unchecked in numbers.

Now at some point after the efficiency optimum (at which the marginal product of labour is equal to the welfare subsistence income) the growth of population will have caused such a fall in the output per head of the population that consumption per worker will have reached the welfare subsistence level. Before this point is reached, with an equal distribution of income, every citizen would be above the welfare subsistence level so that total economic welfare would be positive. After this point, even with an equal distribution of income, every citizen would be below the welfare subsistence level so that total economic welfare would be negative. We may call this point the 'welfare subsistence point with redistribution of income'.[1] But this is not, of course, the point at which further growth of population will necessarily stop. Even when consumption is below the welfare subsistence level, it may still be above the physical subsistence level. In conditions in which income from property is more or less equally divided between all citizens,

[1] It might at first sight seem proper to conclude that if the population were greater than this and consumption per head were below the welfare subsistence level, then from the economic point of view it would be better if the community did not exist at all, since every individual citizen is below the welfare subsistence level, i.e. below the break-even point at which positive welfare gives place to negative 'illfare'. But this would be a false deduction. The low standard of consumption might be due to a high level of savings which through the accumulation of capital will greatly raise standards in the future. The illfare of the present generation will in this case promote the welfare of future generations, and the welfare of future generations may greatly outweigh the illfare of the present. The conditions in which this will be the case are discussed in Section I of the mathematical supplement to this volume.

if there is any section of the population for which the growth of numbers is unchecked, the total population will continue to grow until average consumption per head is as low as the physical subsistence level. We may call this point 'the physical subsistence point with redistribution of income'.

At this point the marginal product of labour may be very low indeed. In fact it may actually be negative. Such cases may well exist in conditions of agricultural over-population and of what is often called disguised agricultural unemployment. If numbers have grown to a sufficient extent, the land may be so overcrowded that one additional worker would add nothing whatsoever to the farm's output. Indeed, there might be such overcrowding that the total output from the farm would be increased if the numbers on the farm were diminished. In such a case the marginal product of labour is negative; the last additional worker causes an actual decrease in total output. But in an institutional arrangement in which all on a farm share and share alike in the total product, numbers may increase until the average product has been reduced to the physical subsistence level, and at this point the marginal product of labour may well be a negative quantity.[1]

2. *The Condition of Optimum Saving*

So long as the marginal product of capital is positive, an act of saving means that the community by sacrificing the consumption of a given finite amount of goods and services can add to its real annual income a certain additional output of goods and services which will continue for ever. By giving up the consumption of $100 worth of goods and services from consumption this year, a machine costing $100 can be produced. With a rate of interest of 5 per cent this would mean that the new machine will add to the output of the plant in which it is employed an amount of goods which are of sufficient value both to replace the machine as it wears out (i.e. to cover its depreciation) and to earn $5 a year on the original investment. The sacrifice of $100 worth of consumption goods once and for all will add to the annual output of the community for every subsequent year *ad infinitum* an output of goods worth $5.

From this it is clear at once that if the welfare of all generations is to be maximized the community must go on saving and accumulating more and more real capital so long as the value of the marginal product of capital is greater than zero. For as long as this is true a single finite sacrifice in one year will lead to an infinite series of gains in future years.

[1] Readers who are helped by numerical examples are advised at this point to read Appendix 1 (p. 574), which contains a numerical example of the various points of population growth to which reference has been made in the preceding paragraphs.

Saving should cease only when so much capital has been accumulated that the value of the marginal product of capital has fallen to zero.

This point might ultimately arrive for either of two distinct reasons.

First, as capital became more and more plentiful there would be fewer and fewer productive opportunities for its use. Even though the supply of labour to co-operate with the capital might be increased by a growth in the population, the supply of land on which the labour and capital can work will be fixed. At some stage so much capital may have been accumulated that there is literally no point in accumulating any more. The physical marginal product of capital will have fallen to zero. Consumers in the community may still have many needs for further products unsatisfied. They would dearly like to enjoy a further output of goods and services; but, alas, a further accumulation of capital can no longer help them to do so. This we may call the position of 'capital glut'.

Second, it may be that the opportunities for further profitable investment of capital fall off very slowly as more and more capital is accumulated. Capital accumulation continues indefinitely to enlarge the total output of goods and services in the community. It is possible that the stage at which all consumers' needs had been satisfied might be reached sooner than the stage at which the marginal physical product of capital had fallen to zero. The value of the marginal product would now be zero, because the value of any further products was zero. In this case the whole problem of economic welfare would be solved. No one would be made better off by having his real standard of living raised. People would not necessarily be blissfully happy; that depends upon many factors other than the economic. But economic advance would have no further contribution to make to human welfare. We may call this position one of 'product glut'.[1]

Now if there is a given population in the final state of glut, this state may ultimately be reached either because of capital glut or because of product glut. But if in the ultimate state of glut the population is adjusted until it is at the optimum level, then the final state of glut must be due to capital glut and not to product glut. This can readily be seen from a consideration of the formula for the optimum population given on p. 91. If there were a position of product glut, then the marginal utility of real income would be zero, since an addition to the amount of goods available for consumption would add nothing to welfare. But the formula on p. 91 indicates than in this case the population is bound to be below the optimum; for in this case the total utility enjoyed by a representative citizen is bound to be greater than the marginal utility of

[1] Mr. F. P. Ramsay in his well-known article in the *Economic Journal* for December 1928, on which much of what follows is based, uses the term 'Bliss' to describe the final state at which capital accumulation must aim. But for the reasons given in the text I feel that the term 'Bliss' is rather a misnomer.

income times the excess of the average consumption over the marginal product of a worker. The common sense of this is obvious. The addition of one worker to the community would add to the welfare of the community one more person at the average level of consumption; and—however low his marginal product might be—it would cost the existing population nothing to bring the newcomer's consumption up to this average level, since the marginal utility of income to them is zero.

If, therefore, population is adjusted to the optimum level, the ultimate state of glut must be one in which capital is so plentiful relatively to land and labour that its physical marginal product has fallen to zero; that the working population has grown in numbers until even with this glut of capital equipment the marginal product of labour has declined relatively to the average output per head sufficiently to satisfy the formula for an optimum population; and that the indefinite expansion of population and capital supply in fulfilment of these conditions is held in check only by the limited amount of land and other natural resources, which in the end is bound to cause the marginal products of labour and capital to decline as more and more population and man-made equipment is crowded on to the given amount of land.

To return to our main theme, it is clear that savings should continue and real capital should be accumulated until a position of capital glut is finally reached, and at this point further accumulation becomes pointless. But this does not answer the question how much should be saved in any one year. Positive savings should continue until the state of glut is reached. But should we aim at reaching the state of glut 10 years hence, 40 years hence, or 200 years hence? It is this which will determine whether 20 per cent, 5 per cent, or 1 per cent of the current national income should be saved. What determines the optimum rate of saving?

The basic consideration is how soon one should try to reach the ultimate goal. This final position of glut will require a certain total amount of capital accumulation. If more is saved this year, then the position of glut can be reached so much the sooner. There are 365 days in the year. Suppose that at present 2 units of real goods are being saved per day or 730 units per annum. Suppose that the rate of saving this year were raised by 2 units to 732 units of goods per annum. Then by December 31st of this year (say, 1950) the community would have accumulated an amount of capital which at the old and lower rate of saving it could have reached only by January 1st of next year (i.e. 1951). The result would be that by the end of the year the community would be one day ahead of its previous schedule of capital accumulation for the final attainment of the state of glut. Now suppose—and this is the basic assumption whose validity we shall have to examine at some length in what follows—that the date at which it is used makes no difference to the welfare to be derived from the use of a given stock of capital. Then the effect of the increased rate of saving this year on the whole of the community's welfare over all future time can be resolved into the four following components:

(1) The community can now reach the stock of capital which is necessary to introduce and to perpetuate the state of glut one day sooner than before. For example, it will start its enjoyment of the final state of glut on December 31st, A.D. 3000, instead of on January 1st, A.D. 3001. This represents a gain of one day's welfare in the state of glut.

(2) Between now and this far-distant date it will enjoy each stage on its journey to the state of glut one day earlier than before. Thus it will enjoy on November 1st, 1982, the capital stock which it would otherwise have enjoyed on November 2nd, 1982. But, on our basic assumption that the date on which it enjoys any given stock of capital is immaterial, this will represent no net gain or loss to it.

(3) But the community will now enjoy on January 1st, 1951, the stage of welfare which it would otherwise have enjoyed on January 2nd, 1951. In the whole infinite span of days which lie before it after December 31st, 1950, it will, as it were, have skipped the welfare which it would otherwise have enjoyed on January 1st, 1951. The net gain to the community from the three components so far discussed is therefore the excess of one day's welfare in the state of glut over one day's welfare at the stage of capital accumulation which it would have reached by the end of 1950. This we may call the excess of a day's utility in the state of glut over a day's utility in the present state of scarcity of capital.

(4) But this net gain has been brought about only by saving this year, i.e. in 1950, an additional 2 units of real goods, i.e. an additional day's savings. The current marginal utility of 2 units of real consumption is a measure of this sacrifice in 1950.

Thus total welfare over time will be maximized only if the current rate of savings is increased so long as the marginal utility of an additional day's savings concentrated in this year is less than the excess of a day's total utility in the state of glut over a day's total utility in present conditions. In other words, the condition for the optimum rate of savings is that the present rate of savings should be increased if

> the present rate of savings (e.g. amount saved per day) multiplied by the present marginal utility of income is less than the excess of the rate of total utility (e.g. total welfare per day) which will be enjoyed by the community in the state of glut over the rate of total utility which it enjoys in present conditions.[1]

[1] Suppose we start from a position in which savings are too low according to this formula, because the rate of savings multiplied by the marginal utility of income is less than the excess of the rate of total utility in the state of glut over the rate of total utility in current conditions. It can be shown that as the

The whole of the foregoing argument has been based upon the fundamental assumption that the actual date in the future at which a given stock of capital is enjoyed is immaterial to the calculation of economic welfare. Thus, to repeat the example already given in paragraph 2 on p. 96 above, we assume that no difference is made to the sum total of economic welfare by the mere fact that a certain stock of capital is enjoyed on November 1st, 1982, instead of on November 2nd, 1982.

For this assumption to be true at least three conditions must be fulfilled.

(1) First, the policy-makers, i.e. those people whose task it is to determine what the objective of policy should be, must not discount future welfare. That is to say, they must not prefer a given enjoyment of income by future citizens on November 1st, 1982, over that same amount of enjoyment by citizens on November 2nd, 1982, on the sole ground that the former date is earlier than the latter. The interest of each generation in the community—the present generation and each generation in the near or distant future—must count equally in the calculations of the policy-makers. If this objective is not adopted, if—that is to say—the interest of each generation is preferred to that of the next, then the amount which the community ought to save will be less than that which is indicated by the formula on p. 96. The welfare of the citizens of one generation can always be improved at the expense of the welfare of the citizens of the next if less is saved by the former and more is, therefore, available for their consumption. This will raise standards of living for the former at the expense of a smaller stock of capital and thus a smaller output of goods and services for the latter.

(2) Second, the formula on p. 96 will give a correct indication of the optimum rate of savings only if technical knowledge is not improving over time. Suppose, however, that a steady stream of inventions and of improvements in productive techniques is taking place over time, and that these improvements are to some extent at least independent of the amount of capital that has been accumulated. In other words, output per head would go on rising as time passed even though no further capital were accumulated. It is now no longer true that to have a given stock of capital on November 1st, 1982, will provide as much enjoyment

rate of savings is increased the condition of optimum savings will be approached. As savings increase, there will be (i) a rise in the rate of savings to be reckoned as a cost at the current marginal utility of income, and (ii) a rise in the current marginal utility of income itself (because a smaller amount of goods is being consumed so that an additional unit of income is currently worth more to consumers), but (iii) some fall in the rate of total utility in current conditions (because less is consumed now). Items i and iii will cancel out. For if one more unit of real goods is saved and not spent, the fall in total utility at current standards (item iii) is the marginal utility of a unit of real goods, which is the same as the marginal utility of the one more unit of real goods saved (item i). Item ii will remain to bring the condition of optimum saving nearer to fulfilment.

to the community on November 1st as would be provided on November 2nd by the same stock of capital on November 2nd (cf. paragraph 2 on p. 96). Since the technique of production is continually increasing, the output and so total enjoyment on November 2nd derived from a given stock of capital will be greater than that which could be derived from the same stock of capital on November 1st. It is still true that an extra day's saving in 1950 will enable the community to bring forward by one day each stage of capital accumulation on the way to the ultimate state of glut. But it is no longer true, as was argued in paragraph 2 of p. 96, that the bringing forward by one day of each intermediate stage on the journey to glut will not in itself affect the total of economic welfare enjoyed over the whole process. A given stage in the process of capital accumulation will now, simply because of the growth of technical knowledge over time, produce a smaller output on one day than it would have done on the next day. The bringing forward of each stage on the journey to the state of glut will itself involve some sacrifice of welfare which is neglected in the formula on p. 96 and the optimum rate of savings will be less than is indicated in that formula. Since the mere passage of time is going to improve the lot of future generations, there is less call on the present generation to make sacrifices on their behalf.

(3) Third, for rather similar reasons the formula given on p. 96 for the optimum rate of savings will not hold good if there is in fact a steady growth of population over time, a growth which is to some extent independent of the actual size of the capital stock at any point of time. Suppose that, as before, by putting in an extra day's savings in 1950 every subsequent stage in the accumulation of the ultimate stock of capital is brought forward one day in time. Then in every one of the intermediate stages on the journey to the state of glut each given capital stock will be employed with the smaller population of the preceding day. On each intermediate day, therefore, the marginal product of capital will be smaller than it would have been if the process of capital accumulation had not been brought forward by one day, for the simple reason that the ratio of capital to labour will now be lower than before. This is clearly a material factor which can no longer be neglected in the final calculation of the optimum rate of savings.[1]

Now if the population were constant over time, this complication would not arise. The bringing forward by one day in time of any stage in the process of capital accumulation would now make no significant difference except in the actual date at which that stage was reached. The given stock of capital would be employed with the same population

[1] It is not very evident exactly how the introduction of this factor would affect the final calculation. This is one of the many possible lines of further inquiry on the subject of the optimum rates of growth of population and of capital which we cannot pursue in this volume.

whether it was reached on November 2nd, 1982, or November 1st, 1982. The welfare obtained would be the same whatever the date on which the capital stock was available for use.

But it is not necessary to make quite so severe an assumption as this about the future population in order to justify use of the formula for the optimum rate of savings given on p. 96. This formula will be correct provided that one given size of population is associated with every given size of capital stock. If bringing forward in time by one day the attainment of a given stock of capital also involved bringing forward by one day the attainment of the associated size of the population, the formula on p. 96 would clearly need no modification. Once again the achievement of a given stock of capital on November 1st instead of on November 2nd would mean that the welfare now enjoyed on November 1st is the same as that which would otherwise have been enjoyed on November 2nd.

This means that the formula for the optimum rate of savings given on p. 96 will be correct if one can assume that the size of the population is always kept strictly at the optimum indicated by the formula given on p. 91. The optimum size of the population as defined in that formula will depend upon the actual size of the stock of capital. There may be some presumption that an increase in the size of the capital stock with which labour can co-operate in production will increase the optimum size for the population.[1] In any case there is no reason at all to suppose that the optimum size for the population is independent of the size of the co-operating stock of capital. But if the population could be always at once adjusted to the size of the capital stock so as to keep the population always at the optimum size, then with each stock of capital, regardless of the date at which it was accumulated, there would always be associated one—namely the optimum—size of population. The formula on p. 96 for the optimum rate of savings would require no modification on grounds of population changes.[2]

[1] According to the formula given on p. 91 the population should be increased so long as the total utility enjoyed by a representative citizen is greater than the marginal utility of income multiplied by the excess of the average consumption over the marginal product of a worker. An increase in the capital supply (i) will increase the total utility of a representative citizen since it will raise total output, will raise the average product of labour and so, with a constant amount being saved, will raise the average consumption of a worker; (ii) it will also raise the marginal product of labour though the effect on the excess of consumption over marginal product will be uncertain; and (iii) it will reduce the marginal utility of income, since each citizen will enjoy a share in the larger total output. Both items i and iii above work in the direction of an increase in the optimum size of the population, while the direction of the influence of item ii is uncertain.

[2] In actual fact, since population changes take time and since during the process of change there will be variations in the ratio of working to non-working members of the population, with even the most extreme forms of population control it might be impossible to keep the population at the optimum size

Now there are many reasons why private citizens if left to their own devices may not save the amount which should be saved according to the formula on p. 96.

(1) Private citizens may discount their own satisfactions over time in the sense that in 1950 Mr. Smith may prefer enjoyment in 1950 to enjoyment in 1951, although Mr. Smith in 1951 is equally certain to prefer enjoyment in 1951 to enjoyment in 1950. The policy-makers may be able to take a more rational line and to give equal weight to enjoyment regardless of the actual date of the enjoyment.

(2) Private citizens are mortal and they may prefer their own enjoyment to that of their heirs—to say nothing of their heirs' heirs. The policy-makers may be able to take the more rational line and to give equal weight to enjoyment of one generation as to that of another.

(3) Private citizens may not be offered for enjoyment the whole marginal product which is to be ascribed to any act of saving on their part. Because of progressive income taxation, because of external economies, or because of elements of monopoly, they may enjoy less than the value of the marginal social net product of any capital which they accumulate. They, unlike the policy-makers, cannot be expected to take into account the full effects of their action in saving.

(4) Private citizens may not be able to foretell well the effect which future changes in technical knowledge and invention and in population growth will have upon the productivity of their capital and upon their future standards of living; and yet, as we have seen above, these considerations are very important from the point of view of determining the best level for savings. Policy-makers may be able to make better allowance for these factors.

Now a full theory of economic growth would at this point consider the discrepancies which are thus likely to arise between the actual rate and the optimum rate of capital accumulation and between the actual and the optimum rates of population growth; and it would examine the various ways in which the authorities could influence the rates of saving and of population growth so as to bring them more nearly into line with the optimum rates. As far as the promotion of savings is concerned, much might perhaps be achieved if progressive income taxes could be turned into progressive consumption taxes, so that taxpayers were exempt from paying tax on any part of their incomes which they saved but were taxed on any consumption expenditure which they financed not out of their incomes but by dissaving part of their accumulated

---

according to the formula on p. 91, when capital is in the process of accumulation. A complete theory would at this stage take into account the rates at which population can be increased or decreased and the implication of various rates of growth upon the ratio of working to non-working population over time; and on this basis it would then work out the simultaneous formulae for an optimum rate of savings and an optimum rate of population growth.

capital wealth. Moreover, the State itself by raising a tax revenue in excess of its current expenditure can supplement private savings by the public savings which this budgetary surplus represents. (But see Chapter III, pp. 45–50, for some of the further implications of this proposal.) All this would constitute a major topic for any Theory of Domestic Economic Policy. We cannot embark upon that task in this volume. But enough has presumably been said to establish the fact that the rates of savings and of population growth will not necessarily be automatically adjusted through private incentives to the optimum levels. If, therefore, policies which are introduced for other purposes have the incidental effect of influencing the rate of savings or of population growth, this effect of such policies must be weighed in the balance before a final verdict is passed upon them. Accordingly, at a later stage (Chapter XXVIII) we shall consider some of the effects upon the world supplies of capital and labour of some of the international policies whose usefulness for other purposes will have been considered in other chapters in this volume.

CHAPTER VII

THE MARGINAL CONDITIONS FOR THE SECOND-BEST

We suppose now that we start from a position in which the marginal conditions for utopian efficiency and equity are not all simultaneously fulfilled. Suppose first of all that there are a large number of divergences between marginal values and costs in the economy due to taxes, elements of monopoly, and external economies. There is one particular divergence which it would be possible to reduce by some act of policy—for example, by a change of taxation or by some anti-monopoly policy. The questions which we now wish to raise are as follows. Will the reduction of one particular divergence between marginal values and costs in one part of the economy invariably lead to an increase in economic welfare, even though many other divergences between marginal values and costs continue unchanged in other parts of the economy? And if not, in what conditions will the reduction of one particular divergence raise and in what conditions will it lower economic welfare?

Our contention in this chapter is that if there are a number of existing divergences between marginal values and costs, then the reduction of one of these divergences—the others all remaining unchanged—will not necessarily lead to an increase in economic welfare, but may very well reduce it. The reason for this view is perhaps best understood by means of an illustration. Suppose that there are two industries producing the same, or at least highly substitutable, products. The provision of transport services by the railways and by road haulage is a case in point. Let us suppose that in both industries the marginal value exceeds the marginal cost of the service—because of taxation on the two systems or because of elements of private monopoly in either or both of the transport systems. But suppose that the rate of divergence between marginal value and cost is considerably higher in the one system (say, the railways) than in the other (say, road transport). In such circumstances the reduction of the divergence in road haulage —e.g. by an anti-monopoly policy applied to the road haulage industry —might do harm. Such a policy might well help to improve production as between transport services on the one hand and other products on the other hand, if the rate of divergence between marginal values and costs were lower throughout the rest of industry; for it would encourage people to make a greater use of road transport services—which had a high value in relation to their cost—at the expense of other products—which had a lower value in relation to their cost.

But it would undoubtedly considerably worsen the productive use of resources within the transport industry as a whole. The cheapening of road transport without the cheapening of rail transport would induce those users of transport for which the two forms of transport were good substitutes to use the roads instead of the railways. But, *ex hypothesi*, for a given value of transport service the marginal cost on the roads is considerably higher than on the railways, since we are assuming that the rate of divergence is low on the roads and high on the railways. To reduce the lower of the two divergences will, therefore, induce a shift of resources out of the more economical into the more costly method of providing the service. If, in the example which we have taken, there were little competition in demand between transport services as a whole and other products on which initially the rate of divergence was low, the reduction of the divergence in the case of road transport would do little good; but if at the same time there were very high competition in demand between road transport and rail transport, the reduction of the divergence on road transport would do a great deal of harm within the transport industry as a whole by diverting traffic from the socially more economical railways on to the socially more expensive roads.

But in the above example there would be a very high probability that welfare would be increased by a lowering of the rate of divergence between marginal value and costs in the railway industry, where the rate of divergence is higher than it is in the road transport industry and than it is in the general run of the rest of industry. For the lowering[1] of the rate of divergence in the railway industry by attracting traffic from the roads where values were lower relatively to costs would improve the efficiency of the transport industries as a whole; and in so far as it attracted demand away from other industries it would also help towards the optimization of production, since *ex hypothesi*, the ratio of marginal value to marginal cost is higher in rail transport than in other industries.[2] We may, therefore, conclude that if there are a number of divergences between marginal values and costs throughout the economy it is not

[1] But not its elimination. The argument in the text is valid for a lowering of the rate of divergence in the railway industry only so long as it remains higher than it is in other industries.

[2] The only possible adverse factor would be that within these other industries there are some products which are jointly supplied or jointly demanded with rail transport and whose production and consumption is therefore expanded when travel by rail is expanded. These may in turn be close substitutes in production or consumption for a third group of products. For example, railway passengers may be provided with many cups of tea, the consumption of which reduces their demand for lemonade when they reach the end of their journeys. Now if the rate of divergence were specially high in the case of lemonade and low in the case of tea, the indirect effects of shifting demand within these other industries from lemonade in the case of which values were high relatively to costs on to tea in the case of which values were low relatively to costs, might conceivably outweigh the good done by the expansion of the railway industry. But such repercussions are not very probable.

always desirable to reduce any one particular divergence, but that the higher—relatively to the divergences in the rest of the economy—is the rate of divergence which it is the object of policy to reduce, the more likely is the policy to improve economic welfare.

So far we have ignored the possible effects of a reduction of a particular divergence upon the distribution of incomes. Indeed, in the preceding example about the competition between road and rail transport we were tacitly assuming that the marginal conditions for utopian equity were fulfilled or, in other words, that income were so distributed that the policy-makers allotted the same distributional weights to all citizens. For it is only in these circumstances that a gain in economic welfare can be measured by the difference between the marginal value to the consumers and the marginal costs to the producers of the things which are produced in greater amount. If different distributional weights were given to the buyers and to the sellers of any product, then we could not calculate the contribution to welfare of an increased supply of this product merely by comparing its money value to the consumers with its money cost to the producers.

Let us consider this distributional problem by supposing for the moment that there is some one divergence between the marginal values and costs in the economy—say, in railway transport; that no other divergence exists between marginal values and costs in any other part of the economy; but that different distributional weights have been allotted to different citizens, a much higher distributional weight being given to the producers of railway services than to the rest of the community. In these circumstances the reduction of the divergence in the provision of railway transport—for example, by some price control which prevented the monopolized producers of railway transport from raising the price charged for it so far above its marginal cost—would not necessarily lead to an increase in economic welfare. On all the efficiency[1] grounds which we have so far examined in this chapter it would do so. It would lead to an increase in the number of units of railway transport which were bought in circumstances in which railway transport provided a high value for each unit of cost and in which marginal value equalled marginal cost in every other occupation.

But the change might redistribute income between the various classes

[1] The attentive reader will realize that the distinction between efficiency and equity considerations in dealing with the second-best problems of this chapter is not quite the same as the distinction between efficiency and equity as it has been used in the two preceding chapters in connexion with the marginal conditions for utopian efficiency and equity. In terms of the utopian conditions, a policy leads to greater efficiency when it enables one citizen to be better off without making any other citizen worse off: in terms of our present analysis of the second-best, a policy leads to greater efficiency when it would increase total economic welfare if the same distributional weights were given to all citizens.

in the community. Suppose that the elasticity of demand for railway transport by the rest of the community were less than unity so that a reduction in the price charged for such transport caused only a relatively small increase in the amount bought. Then the rest of the community would spend a smaller total amount on rail transport after the reduction of the divergence: the reduction in the price charged per unit would outweigh the increase in the amount bought. The reduction of the divergence would, therefore, have a twofold effect. It would increase the amount of rail transport produced at the expense of some contraction in the production of other things; but it would reduce the real income of the producers of rail transport to the benefit of an increase in the real income of other classes in the community. The efficiency aspects of the change would be all to the good. Since the price charged for rail transport, like that charged for all other products, would now more nearly measure its marginal social cost, any class of citizens would with a given distribution of income make a more efficient use of their purchasing power. Production would be more nearly maximized and optimized, and trade and effort would be more nearly optimized. But simultaneously there would have been a distribution of income away from the railway producers to whom, *ex hypothesi*, it meant most to other classes to whom it meant a great deal less. In spite of the greater efficiency of the economic system, total welfare might well have been reduced because of these adverse effects upon economic equity.

We can then theoretically proceed in the following manner. Suppose that there is any small marginal change in policy, such as a small reduction in a particular rate of tax or a small reduction in the degree of monopoly in some particular market. This will cause a change in relative prices which in turn will cause small shifts in the amounts of goods and services bought and sold in a large number of markets—theoretically in every market in the economy.

Let us start by considering any one such change. When more of a particular product is sold by A to B, real goods will pass from A to B and money will pass from B to A. But welfare arises from the enjoyment of real goods; money is desirable only in so far as it enables more real goods to be purchased. The passing of the real goods from A to B will in itself raise B's welfare (since B now has more of the real product to enjoy) and lower A's welfare (since A now has less of it to enjoy). Against this, of course, A will now be able to obtain more goods from someone else, say C, by using the extra money received from B for the purchase of additional supplies from C. But we can once more confine our attention to the real, as opposed to the money, aspect of this transaction, in which the passing of the goods from C to A will in itself increase the welfare of A and reduce the welfare of C. Similarly, B who is spending more on A's product will have less to spend on, say, D's product; and the direct effect of this on welfare can be measured by the loss of B's welfare through having less of D's real product to enjoy and the increase of D's welfare through having so much more of this product. Now in turn C may purchase more of something from someone else since C is earning more money from A, and D may purchase less of something else from someone else since D is earning less money from B. But the contributions of each of these transactions to welfare can be measured in the same way by considering in each case the changes in the flows of the real goods and services concerned.

We can proceed, therefore, to consider the final effect upon economic welfare of any small change in policy by confining our attention to all the changes in the flows of real goods and services to which, directly or indirectly, it gives rise and by considering in turn in each case how much the welfare of the man who parts with the good or service is reduced merely by parting with that amount of that good or service and how much the welfare of the man who receives the good or service is increased merely by receiving that amount of that good or service. The sum of all the increments and decrements of welfare so calculated gives the total change in economic welfare which is caused by the change in economic policy under consideration.

Let us suppose then that there is a small change of policy; and let us start by considering in isolation the effect upon economic welfare of the change in the amount of any one particular good or service which is traded in one particular market as the result of the change in policy. For example, let us consider the sale of his labour by a worker to an employer. Let us suppose that as a direct or indirect result of the change of policy a particular worker provides a little more work to a particular employer. Now if there were no divergence between the marginal value to the employer and the marginal cost to the worker of this extra work, and if the same distributional weights were allotted to employer and worker, this small marginal change in the amount of work done would have no effect upon total economic welfare. The marginal cost of the extra effort to the worker would be equal to the marginal value of the extra labour to the employer, and the welfare lost through the cost of the work would be equal to the welfare gained through the use of the extra work done. But if the marginal value of the work exceeded its marginal cost and/or a higher distributional weight were given to the employer than to the worker, then the provision of this extra amount of work considered in isolation would increase economic welfare, because the welfare lost through the additional work done would be less than the welfare gained by the employer through the use of the additional work.

Of course this one transaction cannot be considered in isolation. The worker who was losing through providing more work to the employer would be gaining through the additional goods and services which he bought with the additional wages he earned. Similarly, the receipt of the worker's additional work would not be a net additional gain to the employer, since he would be giving up part at least of the product of the worker by sale in the market in order to acquire the funds to pay the additional wages. But both the purchase of new goods for consumption by the worker and the sale of new products by the employer are different transactions in different markets. Each of these must be subject to a separate evaluation to see how much it increases or decreases economic welfare. Thus in the case of the goods bought by the worker one must evaluate their marginal cost to the supplier and their marginal value to the worker, and one must weight their marginal cost to the supplier by the supplier's distributional weight and their marginal value to the worker by the worker's distributional weight. When one has done this for all markets throughout the economy and has added all the marginal gains or losses so obtained, there is an increase in economic welfare if the final sum is positive and a decrease in economic welfare if the final sum is negative.[1]

A numerical example may help to make this procedure clear. Such an example is given in Table XI. We there suppose that there are two groups of citizens: citizens A are producers and sellers of commodities W and X and buyers and consumers of commodities Y and Z; and citizens B are producers and sellers of commodities Y and Z and are buyers and consumers of commodities W and X (rows 1 and 2 of Table XI). Let us choose our units of these commodities so that the marginal cost of each product to the seller is \$1 (row 3). That is to say, we assume that in present market conditions citizens A would have to receive an additional \$1 to be willing to give up one more unit of either W or X, and citizens B would likewise have to receive an additional \$1 to be willing to give up one more unit of either Y or Z. We suppose, also, that the rates of divergence in the sale of these commodities is 100 per cent, 50 per cent, 25 per cent, and zero in the case of commodities W, X, Y, and Z respectively, so that their respective marginal values to the buyers are \$2, \$1·5, \$1·25, and \$1 (rows 4 and 5).

In these conditions we suppose that there is some change of policy which affects at the margin the amounts of the various products which will be supplied and demanded. Thus we suppose that the change is such that 15 more units of W and 5 more units of Y are put on the market, while 5 less of X and 15 less of Z are traded (row 6).

Now there are a great number of different types of policy changes which might have this result, and the argument which follows would be valid whatever was the policy change which caused the changes. But

[1] For a formal proof of the validity of this procedure see Section II of the mathematical supplement to this volume.

TABLE XI

The Effect of a Marginal Change of Policy upon Economic Welfare

Commodity	1	W	X	Y	Z	
Commodity is sold	2	by A to B		by B to A		
Marginal cost to seller	3	$1				
Rate of divergence	4	100%	50%	25%	Nil	
Marginal value to buyer	5	$2	$1·5	$1·25	$1	
Increase (+) or decrease (−) in amount sold	6	+15	−5	+5	−15	
		(i) *Distributional weights for* A *and* B = 1.				
Loss (−) or gain (+) to sellers	7	− $15	+ $5	− $5	+ $15	
Gain (+) or loss (−) to buyers	8	+ $30	− $7·5	+ $6·25	− $15	
Net gain (+) or loss (−)	9	+ $15	− $2·5	+ $1·25	Nil	Total + $13·75
		(ii) *Distributional weight for* A = 1 *and for* B = $\frac{1}{2}$.				
Loss (−) or gain (+) to sellers	10	− $15	+ $5	− $2·5	+ $7·5	
Gain (+) or loss (−) to buyers	11	+ $15	− $3·75	+ $6·25	− $15	
Net gain (+) or loss (−)	12	Nil	+ $1·25	+ $3.75	− $7·5	Total − $2·5

in order to make the example clearer we will confine our attention to one possible cause of these changes. Let us suppose that the divergences between marginal values and costs are in all cases due to different degrees of monopolistic power on the part of the sellers of these commodities. Citizens A have been able to form a fairly tight monopoly in the case of product W and to raise the price charged to B 100 per cent above the marginal cost; in product X they have a less powerful monopoly and can raise the price only by 50 per cent above marginal cost. Citizens B have some small monopoly power over product Y and can raise the price 25 per cent above marginal cost. But in product Z they have no monopoly power and sell to citizens A at a price equal to the marginal cost.

In these conditions we suppose that the authorities adopt a new policy for the control of monopoly. Steps are taken to reduce somewhat the monopolistic powers of citizens A over product W. For example, the price which they can charge for W is somewhat reduced by means of a price-control regulation. Let us further suppose that the reason why citizens B did not raise the price charged for Z above its marginal cost was because of a strict anti-monopolistic price regulation which was applied to this market. Otherwise they could have raised the price somewhat against citizens A. Let us suppose that the government at the same time at which it makes more severe its price-control regulation in the case of sales of W relaxes its price-control regulation in the case of sales of Z. The price charged for W is slightly reduced and that charged for Z is slightly raised.

As a result of these changes, citizens B buy 15 more units of W which is now cheaper to them. But since W has fallen in price relatively to X, they buy somewhat less X (5 units less) when they buy more W from citizens A. On the other hand, citizens A buy 15 less units of Z which is now more expensive to them; but since the price of Z has gone up relatively to that of Y, they buy a little more Y (namely 5 units more) from citizens B. The slight fall in the price charged by A for W and the slight rise in the price charged by B for Z—these price changes being themselves the result of changes in monopoly policies—thus account for the changes in the quantities traded as recorded in row 6 of the table.[1]

We assume that these transactions in W, X, Y, and Z represent all the transactions that take place in the whole economy. We can then consider these changes both from their efficiency and from their equity aspects.

As far as efficiency is concerned, the change of policy would appear to be a desirable one. The authorities have taken action to reduce the rate of divergence on product W, where the rate of divergence was very high, namely 100 per cent; and they have taken steps to raise the rate

[1] It is to be observed that although A is buying less of Y and Z combined from B, while B is buying more of W and X combined from A, it can still be true that the total value of A's purchases from B is equal to the total value of B's purchases from A. The rise in the price of Z means that A is paying to B somewhat more for all the units of Z which A continues to purchase; and the fall in the price of W means that B is paying less to A for all the units of W which B was previously buying.

of divergence on Z, where the rate of divergence was very low, namely zero. The rates of divergence on the various products will therefore be more nearly equalized, and there is likely for this reason to be a closer approximation in the economy to the fulfilment of the marginal conditions for the optimization of trade and for the maximization and the optimization of production, as explained in Chapter IV. It can be seen from Table XI that the change in monopoly policy shifts B's purchases and A's sales away from commodity X, of which 5 less units are traded on to commodity W, of which 15 more units are traded. And similarly the change in policy shifts A's purchases and B's sales away from commodity Z to commodity Y. But both these shifts are away from a commodity with a smaller on to a commodity with a higher rate of divergence: W has a rate of divergence of 100 per cent as compared with only 50 per cent in the case of X, and Y has a rate of divergence of 25 per cent as compared with a zero rate of divergence in the case of Z. From the efficiency point of view the change would appear to be in the right direction.

But the change in policy also has effects upon the distribution of income between A and B. It causes a movement of the terms of trade against citizens A and in favour of citizens B, who thus obtain a redistribution of income in their favour. Citizens A reduce their supply of X to citizens B by only 5 units costing $1 each, but they have to increase their supply of W to citizens B by no less than 15 units costing $1 each. In return they acquire from B 5 more units of Y costing $1 each, but they face a reduction of no less than 15 units costing $1 each in the amount of Z which they obtain from B. This redistribution of income in favour of B is the natural outcome of the change of monopoly policies which enables A to exercise less monopolistic power over sales to B and enables B to exercise more monopolistic power over sales to A. For this reason the change will have a less favourable effect, or even a positively unfavourable effect, upon economic welfare if citizens A are given a higher distributional weight than citizens B.

The remaining rows of Table XI are devised to calculate these efficiency and equity effects upon economic welfare. In rows 7, 8, and 9 of the table we disregard the equity effect by assuming that the same distributional weights are allotted to both sets of citizens, so that $1 can be taken as a measure of economic welfare at the margin to buyers and sellers in all four markets. Row 7 shows the quantity changes of row 6 multiplied by the marginal cost of row 3. Thus citizens A give up to citizens B 15 more units of commodity W (row 6). But a unit of W has a marginal cost to citizens A of $1 (row 3), which means that by giving up 15 more units of W citizens A lose something which they value at $15 (row 7). And similarly for the other figures in row 7. Row 8 shows the quantity changes of row 6 multiplied by the marginal values of row 5. Thus citizens B receive from citizens A 15 more units of commodity W (row 6). But a unit of W has a marginal value to citizens B of \$2 (row 5), which means that by receiving 15 more units of W citizens B obtain something which they value at \$30 (row 8). And similarly for the other figures in row 8. Row 9 merely gives the sum of the figures in rows 7 and 8. Thus when 15 units of W pass from citizens A to B the former lose something worth \$15 to them and the latter gain something worth \$30 to them, a net gain to the community of \$15 (row 9), if the same distributional weight is given to the money income of both sets of citizens. The total of all the figures in row 9 is a gain of \$13·75 (right-hand side of row 9), which illustrates the fact that the policy change is an efficient one; by shifting the trade for both sets of citizens from a commodity with a lower to a commodity with a higher rate of divergence, the economic system more effectively satisfies the wants of the citizens.

But the change is one which has caused a considerable redistribution of income. Indeed, while citizens B have gained, citizens A have lost. The gains and losses of citizens A as sellers or givers-up of commodities are — \$15 + \$5 (row 7, columns W and X) and as buyers or receivers of commodities are + \$6·25 — \$15 (row 8, columns Y and Z), a net loss of \$18·75. On the other hand, the gains and losses of citizens B as sellers or givers-up of commodities are — \$5 + \$15 (row 7, columns Y and Z) and as buyers or receivers of commodities are + \$30 — \$7·5 (row 8, columns W and X), a net gain of \$32·5. Thus while citizens B gain \$32·5, citizens A lose \$18·75, which gives a net gain of \$13·75 if one gives the same distributional weights to the incomes of both sets of citizens.

But suppose that for some reason or another—perhaps because citizens A are poorer than citizens B—the policy-makers allot only half as high a distributional weight to citizens B as to citizens A. Then with distributional weights of 1 for A and ½ for B, the losses of A continue to be evaluated at \$18·75 but the gains of B are now evaluated at \$16·25 instead of \$32·5. This gives a net loss to the community of \$2·5 [1] instead of a gain of \$13·75. Thus while the change of policy is one which is efficient in the sense that it would increase total economic welfare if one gave the same distributional weight to every citizen, it

[1] This net loss is shown at the right-hand side of row 12. Rows 10, 11, and 12 merely give the detailed working when B receives a distributional weight of only ½. The figures for A remain unchanged; (the figures in row 10, columns W and X, are the same as those in row 7, columns W and X, and those in row 11 columns Y and Z, are the same as those in row 8, columns Y and Z). But the figures for B have been halved—(the figures in row 11, columns W and X, are half those in row 8, columns W and X, and those in row 10, columns Y and Z, are half those in row 7, columns Y and Z). With these changes in weight the rest of the calculation for rows 10, 11, and 12 is the same as in the case of rows 7, 8, and 9.

nevertheless reduces economic welfare if citizens B are given only half as great a distributional weight as citizens A.

In the rest of this chapter we will give one more illustration of this principle in order to show how this analysis of a second-best policy may be applied to a quite different type of market. We assume that the government does not itself own sufficient income-bearing property and that it must therefore raise a certain tax revenue in order to finance its inevitable expenditures. We assume further that it is not possible administratively to apply the type of progressive lump-sum taxation which—as we saw in Chapter III (pp. 49–50)—would theoretically enable the government to raise any amount of revenue which it desired with any degree of progressive incidence upon the rich which was thought equitable but without introducing any divergence in any part of the economy between marginal values and costs. We assume, therefore, that the revenue is being raised by a progressive income tax which, as explained on p. 47, introduces throughout the system a large rate of divergence between the value of the marginal product of effort and the marginal cost of that effort. This is then necessarily a second-best position, since the marginal condition for the optimization of effort (see pp. 65–7) will clearly not be satisfied.

The question which we shall now discuss is whether, given this situation, it would be desirable to turn to some extent from the direct taxation of income to the indirect taxation of particular goods and services as a means of raising revenue.[1] At first sight it would seem most probable that such a change would only make matters worse. An income tax is comparable to a tax levied at the same *ad valorem* rate on the consumption of all goods and services; the income receiver is taxed at the same rate, whatever he spends his money on.[2] To reduce the income tax and to raise the revenue in its place by means of an indirect tax on one particular product would, therefore, be equivalent to a system of indirect taxes on all goods and services which started at the same *ad valorem* rate on all purchases but which were then lowered on all goods and services except the one on which a higher rate was charged.

It would appear at first sight that this change would be bound to be for the worse. It would do nothing to reduce the average rate of divergence between the value of marginal products and the rewards paid to factors of production; it would merely raise this rate of divergence in

[1] Certain aspects of this problem are discussed in a more rigorous form in Sections III and IV of the mathematical supplement to this volume.

[2] We omit from the present discussion the fact that while the income tax falls equally on income saved as on income spent, a general tax on goods and services consumed would leave savings untaxed. A more accurate comparison would be between a system of indirect taxes on goods and services consumed and a general expenditure tax rather than between a system of indirect taxes and a general income tax.

the case of the product subject to the higher rate of tax and reduce it slightly in the case of the other products on which taxation was lowered. The marginal condition for the optimization of effort would appear to be as far from being satisfied as before; and in addition to this the marginal condition for the optimization of production which was previously satisfied would now fail to be satisfied. Now the rate of divergence between marginal value and cost would be higher in the case of the product on which the special indirect tax was levied than in the case of all other products; consumers would be induced to shift their demands uneconomically away from the former commodity; production would no longer be optimized and it would now become possible, as it had not been possible before, by producing a little more of the heavily taxed commodity to make one consumer better off without making anyone worse off.

All this is true; but it still does not follow that the uniform income tax is necessarily preferable to the system of indirect taxes of varying incidence on different products. The uniform income tax can be regarded as a tax at a uniform rate on the consumption of every good except one—namely leisure—on which no tax at all is levied. If a man refrains from working for an extra hour a week, he will earn a smaller income but will obtain more leisure. He can be regarded as having purchased the leisure with the income which he would have earned if he had worked. But when he chooses the extra leisure he does not earn income, and therefore he pays no tax. In other words, if he spends his income on the purchase of apples, blankets, coal, or any other product, he will pay the uniform rate of income tax on such transactions; but if he spends any part of his income on extra leisure, he pays no tax on the leisure so acquired.

In this sense the income tax is already a tax which differentiates in its incidence on the purchase of different goods. It taxes everything except leisure at one rate and leisure at a zero rate. If one must have a tax system which differentiates by taxing leisure at a zero rate, may there not be a superior system of differentiation? To this problem we can apply the technique developed in this chapter. If we can make a small marginal change in the tax system which shifts demand and/or supply away from leisure which is the thing taxed at a very low rate (i.e. with a low rate of divergence) on to the other products which are taxed at a high rate (i.e. with a high rate of divergence), we shall have improved the efficiency of the economy; and we shall thereby have increased economic welfare provided that the improvement in economic efficiency is not offset by a redistribution of income which has an adverse equity effect.

Suppose, then, that we levy a special indirect tax on one commodity, say on apples, and that we use the additional revenue to reduce a uniform rate of tax on all other products, which we will call blankets. In what circumstances, if any, is this likely to cause such a shift in demand and supply that people 'consume' less leisure (on which there is a zero rate of divergence) and more of the other products (on which there is a rate of divergence due to the income tax)?

Let us first deal with the case in which apples and blankets are very good substitutes for each other in demand. If the price of apples were to go up at all markedly as a result of the special tax imposed on apples and if the price of blankets were to go down at all markedly as a result of the reduction in the general rate of tax on blankets, there would be a very large shift of demand away from apples on to blankets. In view of the great decrease in the demand for apples the producers of apples would in fact have to accept a lower price; and in view of the great increase in the demand for blankets the producers of blankets would be able to charge a somewhat higher price. In other words, in these circumstances in which apples and blankets were very good substitutes for each other in consumers' demands, the prices charged for the two products to consumers would not be very much changed; the producers of apples would have to pay the greater part of the tax on apples themselves rather than raise the price of apples to the consumers of apples; and the producers of blankets would not have to pass on much of the reduction in the tax on blankets to the consumers of blankets but could add it to their own income.

Now suppose that in these circumstances apples are produced very largely by some factor of production which we will call land and which, while it is very important in the production of apples, cannot readily be used to produce other products, namely blankets. And suppose further that land is a factor which is more or less rigidly fixed in total supply and which cannot (or does not desire) to purchase 'leisure' or 'idleness' with any of its potential earnings. Then the supply of apples will be very inelastic. When apples are more heavily taxed, the tax will fall mainly on the rent of land used for apple production, but as a result of this land will not disappear in idleness or go off to blanket production. As the tax on apples is raised, the largest rate of divergence will be in respect of apples; but it will cause only a small reduction in the amount of apples put upon the market, so that the net loss of economic welfare in respect of apple production will not be great.

Suppose, on the other hand, that blankets are produced mainly by a factor of production—labour—which, it is true, is not very much used in apple production but which can be easily used in the production of 'leisure'. When the tax on blankets is lowered, in the circumstances which we are at present examining the incomes of blanket producers—namely, mainly the wages of labour—will be raised. More labour cannot be induced on any large scale to come into blanket production from apple production, since labour is not much used in apple production. But the rise in the reward offered for labour in terms of goods in general—namely blankets—might quite well induce some labour to move from leisure into blanket production. And this move would increase economic welfare, since it would represent a reduction in 'transactions' (namely, the purchase of leisure with potential wage earnings) in the case of which there was a zero divergence between marginal values and costs and an increase in transactions (namely the sale of labour to produce blankets) in the case of which there was a rate of divergence due to the uniform rate of tax on blankets. In the conditions so far assumed it is quite possible that the loss due to any small reduction in the output of apples—the high rate of divergence there having to be applied to only a very small reduction in output—would be less than the gain due to the expansion of the production of blankets (on which there was a considerable divergence due to the uniform rate of tax on blankets) at the expense of the 'production' of leisure (on which there was a zero rate of divergence).

These would seem, then, to be circumstances in which some shift from a general income tax on to a special indirect tax on apples would be desirable. Yet this is not in fact the case. The raising of the tax on apples and the lowering of the tax on blankets in our example leads to greater economic efficiency solely because the demand for apples is indirectly a demand for land and the demand for blankets indirectly a demand for labour; it is, therefore, in part equivalent to a raising of the rate of tax on the rent of land and a lowering of the rate of tax on the wages of labour; and this leads to greater efficiency because the raising of the tax on the rent of land does not reduce the amount of land supplied, whereas the lowering of the rate of tax on the wages of labour does increase the amount of effort supplied, so that there is an increase in welfare through the increased supply of effort—a transaction on which there is a large divergence between marginal values and costs.

But this result could have been brought about more directly simply by raising the rate of income tax on the rent of land and lowering it on the wages of labour. Indeed, this method would have been more advantageous than the method of taxing apples more heavily and blankets less heavily. For if any land is used in the production of blankets and any labour is used in the production of apples, the higher taxation of apples and lower taxation of blankets (while its main effect may be to lower the net reward of land and to raise the net reward of labour) will to some extent cause a shift of labour and land out of the production of the more heavily taxed apples into the production of the less heavily taxed blankets, i.e. from the industry with the larger into the industry with the smaller rate of divergence between marginal values and costs. This interference with the optimization of production would be completely avoided if the higher taxation were levied not on apples but on the rent of land, regardless whether the land were used to produce apples or blankets, and if the lower rate of tax were levied not on blankets but on the wages of labour, regardless whether the labour were used to produce blankets or apples. But this would not be a system of indirect taxation on products; it would be a system of direct taxation on incomes, the rate being higher on income from the rent of land than on income from the wages of labour. Whether or not this would be desirable on grounds of equity would depend upon the distributional weights allotted to landlords and workers. If landlords were given a lower distributional weight than workers, simply because landlords were richer than workers, then the system of income taxation which taxed rents more heavily than wages would be a straightforward progressive income tax. If, however, landlords were given a higher distributional weight than workers, then there would be a straightforward conflict between the requirements of economic efficiency (which would call for a specially high rate of tax on the rent of land) and of economic equity (which would demand a specially low rate of tax on rents).

So far we have dealt with the case in which apples and blankets were very good substitutes for each other in the demand of consumers; and we have seen that conditions on the supply side may in this case be such as to suggest that a higher rate of tax should be levied on apples than on blankets, but that on further examination this is really only a case for a higher rate of income tax on the earnings of one factor than on the earnings of another.

Let us now turn to the case in which apples and blankets are very good substitutes for each other on the side of supply. That is to say, let us assume that both products are made with much the same combinations of factors of production. In this case, when the price which producers receive for apples falls relatively to the price received for the production of blankets, a large amount of resources will be shifted from the apple industry to the blanket industry. If in these conditions the rate of tax on blankets is lowered and on apples is raised, the output of apples will be considerably reduced and the output of blankets considerably increased. The scarcity of apples will cause the price which consumers offer for them to rise, and the increased supplies of blankets will lead to a reduction in the price offered for them by consumers. In other words, the higher tax on apples will now not much lower the price received by the producers, but will rather raise the price paid by consumers of apples; and similarly the lower tax on blankets will lead to a reduction in the price charged to consumers for them rather than to an increase in the net price received by the producers.

In these conditions there is a real possibility that the indirect taxation of apples as opposed to the direct taxation of income might increase economic efficiency. Suppose that apples and blankets are poor substitutes for each other in consumption. Suppose further that apples and leisure are also poor substitutes in consumption (you really enjoy eating apples when you are on holiday and they seem to lose their flavour in the office); but suppose that blankets and leisure are good substitutes for each other (you can enjoy warmth in winter either by taking a holiday to a warmer climate or by wrapping yourself up in blankets in the office). A change in the tax system which raised the price of apples and lowered the price of blankets would now make your apple-eating holidays more expensive and would simultaneously make it cheaper to keep warm by blankets rather than by holidays. Such a change would decrease the demand for leisure by raising the price of those things (apples) which are jointly demanded with leisure and lowering the price of those things (blankets) which are good substitutes for leisure. And since the 'purchase' of leisure is a transaction in which there is a zero divergence between marginal values and costs whereas there is a considerable divergence due to taxation in the case of all those other things (blankets) which would be purchased in additional quantity out of the increased incomes earned by working harder, this part of the change would represent a net increase in economic efficiency. Against this would have to be set some loss in economic efficiency due to the shift of demand away from apples on to blankets, since the rate of tax and therefore the rate of divergence would be higher in the case of apples than of blankets. But this would represent a loss only in so far as the rate of tax on apples exceeded that on blankets. For a small differentiation in the rate of tax between apples and blankets the gain would, therefore, necessarily exceed the loss, since the gain on the shift from leisure to blankets would be measured by the whole rate of tax on blankets while the loss on the shift from apples to blankets would be measured only by the very slight excess of the rate of tax on apples over that on blankets. The possible loss in welfare on apples would become serious only if the policy of differentiation in the rates of tax were carried too far.

In order that this improvement in economic efficiency should not be offset by any deterioration from the point of view of economic equity, it would be necessary in our example that those with a small distributional weight (e.g. the rich) should spend a specially large proportion of their income on apples and those with a high distributional weight (e.g. the poor) should spend a specially large proportion of their income on blankets. In order that such a system of indirect taxation should make a real contribution to economic welfare as an alternative to a progressive income tax for the raising of revenue, it is necessary to choose for specially heavy taxation those goods (e.g. luxury cruises) which are consumed by the rich and which are jointly demanded with leisure and for specially low taxation those goods (e.g. evening performances in the cinema) which are consumed by the poor out of normal working hours and which provide some alternative to relaxations, such as mid-week horse-racing, the enjoyment of which requires an absence from work.

CHAPTER VIII

THE STRUCTURAL CONDITIONS FOR ECONOMIC WELFARE

THE problems which we have so far been discussing, in Chapters II to VII, have all related to small marginal adjustments. For example, we have been considering a factor's *marginal* product, i.e. how great is the additional product which would be produced if a small additional amount of the factor were employed in an existing firm or industry which already employed a certain amount of that factor. On the basis of this marginal analysis—relating to small marginal adjustments in amounts of production or of trade or in the transfer of purchasing power from rich to poor or from present to future generations—we constructed in Chapters IV, V, and VI seven conditions of economic welfare, all of which must be simultaneously fulfilled if it is to be impossible to increase economic welfare by any further marginal adjustment.

These seven conditions are necessary conditions for the maximization of economic welfare. If they are not all fulfilled, it will always be possible by making some small marginal adjustment to increase economic welfare somewhat. But they are not, unfortunately for the simplicity of our analysis, sufficient conditions for the maximization of economic welfare. Even though all the seven conditions are fulfilled so that it is no longer possible to increase welfare by making any small marginal adjustment, yet it may still be possible to improve economic welfare by making a large structural change in the economy.

Consider a mountaineer who wishes to reach the highest point in a mountain range. He can always get higher so long as he moves uphill. Whenever he is on a slope, the marginal conditions for maximizing his height are not fulfilled; by moving a little way in the uphill direction he can always reach a higher point. When he is no longer on a slope he may either be on a peak, or at the bottom of a hollow, or at a point on the side of the mountain at which the slope has temporarily flattened out. Which of these positions he is in he can test by walking a little way in each direction from where he stands. If he is on a peak, then he will soon begin to go downhill in whatever direction he moves; if he is at the bottom of a hollow, then he will soon begin to go uphill in whatever direction he moves; if he is at a point of temporary flattening of the slope, then when he walks in the right direction he will soon start to go up again. The important point for our analogy is that he can find the answer to these questions by making small 'marginal' excursions in all directions in turn. If, then, whenever he finds an upward slope he moves up it, he must eventually reach a peak. But he may not be on the highest peak of the mountain range; he might be able to get still higher if he came down again and went up the next mountain. The structural changes in the economy which we propose to discuss in this chapter concern the rules, not for climbing a mountain, but for choosing the right mountain to climb. This choice cannot be made simply by making small marginal excursions in every direction from the particular point from which one happens to start.

What, then, are the conditions in which society should start up the production of some new commodity which it is now not producing at all or close down entirely the production of some existing commodity which it is at present producing on a considerable scale? In fact, in what follows we shall deal only with the former of these two questions—the introduction of an entirely new product; because the latter problem—the exclusion of an existing product—can be analysed very simply as the former problem in reverse. If we want to know whether the production of commodity X should be dropped, we can ask whether X ought to be introduced if we did not already produce it. If it ought to be introduced into the economy which does not produce it, then it ought not to be dropped from the economy which does produce it and which in other respects is quite similar.

One preliminary observation. In this chapter we shall be primarily concerned with the measurement of the highest mountain peak. That is to say, we assume that whatever mountain is selected the mountaineer is able and willing to move uphill until he is at the top. In other words, we shall assume that, whether we introduce the new product or not, all the marginal conditions for economic welfare of Chapters IV, V, and VI will be fulfilled, so that we always get the most out of any structure.

In fact, as we have seen in Chapter VII, it is not always easy to satisfy all these utopian conditions simultaneously; and it might be more difficult to satisfy them simultaneously in one economic structure than in another. It might be more difficult to get to the top of one mountain than to the top of another, so that maximum height would not always be achieved by choosing the highest mountain to climb. But for the purpose of simplification we shall at first avoid this difficulty by assuming that in any economic structure which we wish to consider all the marginal conditions for economic welfare are simultaneously completely fulfilled; we can reach the top of any mountain which we choose to climb. We shall maintain these assumptions until the closing paragraphs of the chapter, where we will briefly indicate the sort of difference which would have to be made in the analysis if the marginal conditions for economic welfare were not universally satisfied.

Part of our initial set of assumptions is, therefore, that the marginal conditions for utopian equity are fulfilled; that is to say, we are assuming that income is in all circumstances so distributed that the policy-makers allot the same distributional weights to all citizens. In evaluating any structural change we can set off any $1 gain (or loss) to one individual against a $1 loss (or gain) to any other individual. This will be an important feature of the following analysis.[1]

Let us start, then, with an economy which is producing Y, Z, etc., and consider whether it should also produce X. Table XII has been devised to illustrate this problem. Let us explain the construction of the table by reference to case i of it. We suppose that if 1 unit of product X is produced (column *a*), then the price which will be offered for it by consumers will be $60 (column *b*) and the price of the factors of production required for its production will be $50 (column *e*). On our assumption that the marginal conditions for economic efficiency are all fulfilled, the price paid by the consumers will measure the marginal social net value of the first unit of the product, and the price paid to the factors of production will measure the marginal social net cost of the first unit of the product; and on the assumption that the marginal conditions for economic equity are also fulfilled, we can set the marginal cost to the producers against the marginal value to the consumers. In these circumstances, in the case illustrated in case i of Table XII it will certainly pay society to produce this first unit of X (column *g*). The fact that consumers will pay $60 for it means that it is worth to them as much as an output of other commodities which is priced $60; and the fact that the factors of production needed for its production cost only $50, means that these factors of production, if used in alternative lines of production, could produce commodities worth only $50 to consumers. There is a net gain to society of $10.

When a second unit of the product is produced, the price offered by consumers is assumed to fall to $55 (column *b*); and the cost of the additional factors of production is assumed to be $47·5 (column *e*).

[1] In order to employ the analysis which follows there is, strictly speaking, one further assumption which we must make. When a new industry is set up there may have to be a change in the price relationships ruling between the various goods and services which are traded, in order to preserve equilibrium and to continue to satisfy all the marginal conditions for economic welfare. Now these changed price relationships would be compatible with a rise in the general level of money prices (some money prices having gone up more than others) or with a fall in the general level of prices (some money prices having fallen less than others) or with any intermediate position. The technique which we shall use for measuring the effect upon economic welfare will involve using a unit of money (e.g. $1) as a measuring rod of marginal increments or decrements of economic welfare, in order to reach our final conclusion by adding together all these marginal changes into one large structural change. But this implies not only that $1 has the same marginal utility to all citizens (i.e. that the same distributional weights are allotted to all citizens), but also that the marginal utility of money remains the same to each citizen throughout the process of structural change. In other words, we must assume a monetary policy which so controls the general level of money prices that throughout the change the importance to any one citizen of having $1 added to his income remains unchanged.

TABLE XII

Total Social Value and Total Social Cost

Number of units produced	Price offered by consumers	Total amount spent by consumers	Total value to society	Price of additional factors required to produce last unit	Total cost to society	Net social gain (+) or loss (−)	Private profit (+) or loss (−) if factor prices constant
(*a*)	(*b*)	(*c*) (*a*) × (*b*)	(*d*) Sum of (*b*) column	(*e*)	(*f*) Sum of (*e*) column	(*g*) (*d*) − (*f*)	(*h*) (*c*) − (*f*)
Case (i). *First Unit Profitable. Production Socially Advantageous.*							
	$	$	$	$	$	$	$
1	60	60	60	50	50	+10	+ 10
2	55	110	115	47·5	97·5	+17·5	+ 12·5
3	50	150	165	45	142·5	+22·5	+ 7·5
4	45	180	210	42·5	185	+25	− 5
5	**40**	200	250	**40**	225	+**25**	− 25
6	35	210	285	37·5	262·5	+22·5	− 52·5
7	30	210	315	35	297·5	+17·5	− 87·5
8	25	200	340	32·5	330	+10	−130
9	20	180	360	30	360	0	−180
10	15	150	375	27·5	387·5	−12·5	−237·5
Case (ii). *First Unit Unprofitable. Later Units Profitable. Production Socially Advantageous.*							
	$	$	$	$	$	$	$
1	60	60	60	70	70	−10	− 10
2	55	110	115	50	120	− 5	− 10
3	50	150	165	30	150	+15	0
4	45	180	210	20	170	+40	+ 10
5	40	200	250	20	190	+60	+ 10
6	35	210	285	25	215	+70	− 5
7	**30**	210	315	**30**	245	+**70**	− 35
8	25	200	340	35	280	+60	− 80
9	20	180	360	40	320	+40	−140
10	15	150	375	45	365	+10	−215
Case (iii). *No Units Profitable. Production Socially Advantageous.*							
	$	$	$	$	$	$	$
1	60	60	60	68	68	− 8	− 8
2	55	110	115	52	120	− 5	− 10
3	50	150	165	46	166	− 1	− 16
4	45	180	210	41	207	+ 3	− 27
5	40	200	250	37	244	+ 6	− 44
6	35	210	285	33	277	+ 8	− 67
7	**30**	210	315	**30**	307	+ **8**	− 97
8	25	200	340	28	335	+ 5	−135
9	20	180	360	26	361	− 1	−181
10	15	150	375	25	386	−11	−236
Case (iv). *No Units Profitable. Production Socially Disadvantageous.*							
	$	$	$	$	$	$	$
1	60	60	60	69	69	− 9	− 9
2	55	110	115	61	130	−15	− 20
3	50	150	165	52	182	−16	− 32
4	45	180	210	45	227	−16	− 47
5	40	200	250	39	266	−15	− 66
6	35	210	285	34	300	−14	− 90
7	**30**	210	315	**30**	330	−**14**	−120
8	25	200	340	27	357	−16	−157
9	20	180	360	25	382	−21	−202
10	15	150	375	24	406	−30	−256

From this we can deduce the total value to society of the two units and the total cost to society of the two units. So far as the total value to society is concerned, we proceed as follows. If the price which consumers would pay to have one unit rather than none was \$60, the value to them of the first unit was \$60; and if the price which they would pay to have two units rather than one was \$55, the second unit must add a value of \$55 for them. Thus, the total value to consumers of two units rather than none is \$60 + \$55 or the \$115 of column *d*, although they spend only \$110 (column *c*) on two units. As for the total cost to society, we proceed as follows. The cost of the factors required to produce one unit instead of none is \$50 (column *e*) and \$50 therefore represents the value of the other products whose production is given up in order to produce this first unit of commodity X. The cost of the factors required to produce two units rather than one unit is \$47·5 (column *e*), so that this sum measures the value of the other products whose production must be given up in order to produce two units instead of one unit of commodity X. Thus \$50 + \$47·5, or the \$97·5 of column *f*, represents the total sacrifice in terms of the value of other products which must be given up in order to produce two units instead of none of commodity X. The net gain or loss to society from any output of commodity X is thus the difference between the figures in columns *d* and *f*, and these figures are shown in column *g*.

We can, therefore, from Table XII, give a rule for deciding whether a new line of production should be introduced or not. It is necessary to consider what would be the schedule of prices offered by consumers for the various levels of output (as in column *b*) and from this to construct a series showing the total value to consumers of different levels of output (as in column *d*). It is necessary also to consider what would be the price of the additional factors required to produce successively larger outputs of the commodity (as in column *e*) and from this to construct a series showing the total cost to society of different levels of output (as in column *f*). If at any output the total value to society is greater than the total cost to society (column *d* greater than column *f*, i.e. column *g* positive), then the production of commodity X should be undertaken. And, of course, if the output is undertaken at all, it should be carried on on the scale necessary to satisfy the marginal conditions in its production. This will be attained, if the output is increased so long as the marginal social net value of the product is greater than its marginal social net cost, i.e. so long as the price of a unit of the product (column *b*) is greater than the price which has to be paid to the additional factors required to produce it (column *e*). This marginal rule will involve that, if commodity X is produced at all, then in case i 5 units should be produced (at which level the figures in columns *b* and *e* are both \$40), and in cases ii, iii, and iv 7 units should be produced (at which level the figures in columns *b* and *e* are both \$30). An inspection of the figures in column *g* will show that these are the levels of output at which the net social gain is a maximum or the net social loss a minimum.[1]

In reality this process of estimation of the schedules of prices and costs in columns *b* and *e* is a most difficult one. Apart from other difficulties there are certain complications which arise from the nature of the schedules themselves. Thus the schedule of demand prices drawn up in column *b* is not simply a list of the various prices which consumers would offer for the various outputs on the assumption that either the prices or the outputs of all other complementary or competitive products remained constant. Each price in column *b* shows the price which consumers would pay for an additional unit of product X on the assumption that the outputs and prices of products Y, Z, etc., had all adjusted themselves to whatever particular levels they would have had if all the marginal conditions of economic welfare were satisfied when the output of X was at the level indicated in column *a*. And similarly with the schedule of the price of additional factors in column *e*. This schedule must not be drawn up on the assumption that the factor prices are constant, but on the assumption that they are what they would actually be if the output of all other products, and so the alternative demands for the factors, were what they would actually be if all the conditions of economic welfare were satisfied when the amount of commodity X shown in column *a* were being produced. To take one possible example, suppose that the output of X is increased from 3 units to 8 units, that this reduces the demand for commodity Y which is a close substitute for X, that this causes a fall in the price of Y, that this causes a reduction in the demand for a factor of production which is also used in the production of X, and that this causes a fall in the price of that factor. Then the fall in the price from \$50 a unit for 3 units to \$25 a unit for 8 units which is shown in column *a* must be the fall which would take place after allowing for the accompanying fall in the price of the substitute commodity Y; and the fall in the cost of the factors required to produce one more unit of output from \$45 when 3 units are produced to \$32·5 when 8 units are produced (column *e*) must allow for the fall in the price of the factor which is now less needed in the production of Y. The price schedules in columns *b* and *e* thus depend not only upon the usefulness to consumers of commodity X and the technical costs of expanding the production of X, but also upon the interrelation of conditions of supply and demand in industries

[1] With the exception of the output of one unit in case iv, where a loss of only \$9 would be incurred. But in this case, where the output always involves a loss, the absolute minimum can always be reached by producing zero. The minimum social loss of \$14 incurred at an output of 7 units is the minimum achievable apart from producing zero or practically zero.

Y, Z, etc. The schedules in columns *b* and *e* are therefore peculiarly difficult to assess; but unless an attempt is made to assess them so that they measure the price which would actually be offered by consumers and the price which would actually be demanded by the factors of production technically required to produce another unit of output, in the actual conditions of supply and demand which would in fact rule at each output of X, they cannot serve their purpose of determining whether some output of X is socially desirable or not.

From the above analysis it can be seen that the question whether a new product should be introduced into the economy or not presents difficulties only if there are economies of large-scale production in the industry concerned. If the figures in column *e* of Table XII remained constant or rose (constant or decreasing returns to scale) while the figures in column *b* always fell (diminishing marginal importance of successive units of consumption), at no point could any figure in column *e* be below the corresponding figure in column *b*, unless the figures in column *e* started below the figures in column *b*. In other words, total value can exceed total cost only if at some points marginal values exceed marginal costs. But if marginal values always fall and marginal costs always rise, the former will exceed the latter only if they start by doing so. In other words, if it is socially desirable to produce at all in the absence of economies of large scale, then the first units will be profitable; and it will, therefore, pay private enterprise to embark on the production. The question of State action to introduce the industry can arise only if there are economies of large-scale production.

From our present point of view the two familiar types of large-scale economy are both relevant, and can both be illustrated by a suitable interpretation of Table XII.

First, the question may arise of introducing a new firm (e.g. in railway transport or in electrical generation) such that, because of indivisibilities of capital equipment, this single firm or productive unit could produce all that the local market requires of the new product. In this case economies of large scale will exist up to a certain level of output for the newly introduced product, because up to a point an expansion of output will enable the same indivisible productive equipment to be more fully used.

If Table XII is used to illustrate this type of problem, then the outputs measured in column *a* of the table are the outputs of the single new firm; and the cost conditions shown in column *e* are those which are caused by the fact that, up to a point, as the fixed equipment of the single plant is more and more fully utilized, so production becomes more efficient and economic.

Second, the question may arise of introducing a new industry made up of a large number of small competing firms but of a kind in which each firm carries with it important atmosphere-creating external economies.[1] In this case the outputs of column *a* are the outputs of the whole industry and the cost conditions of column *e* are calculated after allowing for the fact that, up to a point, the expansion of output of any one firm enables other firms in this same industry or in other industries to produce efficiently, so that the net additional factors required by society to produce the additional output is less than those required by the firm to increase the additional output.

One simple special case will illustrate the principle well. Suppose that the economies of large scale while they are 'external' to the individual firms in the industry are 'internal' to the industry itself. This would be the case where the expansion of the output of any one firm in the industry lowered the costs of other firms in the same industry but had no effect upon the costs of firms outside this particular industry. In this case we could make the following interpretation of Table XII. We could assume that each firm produces a given optimum output, which we would call one unit of output. We could then use the figures in column *a* to represent the number of firms in the industry as well as the output of the industry. Column *e* would then show how the cost conditions of the industry behaved simply because the number of firms in the industry increased. Column *f* would then show the total expenses or costs

[1] If there are external economies of production in the industry due to the existence of unpaid factors (see pp. 39–41), then it may fail to be set up because it does not receive payment for the whole of its output. Thus, apple-farming might be altogether unprofitable if the farmers had to rely upon the sale of their apples alone and might become profitable if they were also able to sell the nectar which the apple blossom incidentally supplied to bee-keepers. State action to subsidize apple-farming (subsequently to be paid out of the proceeds of a tax on bee-keeping) might be necessary to get the desirable industry of apple-farming started at all. But we need not consider this case in this chapter which is devoted to *structural* problems, because if as a result of a 'modified laissez-faire' policy the *marginal* conditions of economic welfare are all observed, no further State action need be taken in this case in order to alter the structure of industry. Suppose that apples are produced under constant returns to scale and suppose also that it does not pay to produce the first unit of output of apples even though the bee-keepers pay the proper price for the bee food which is simultaneously provided, i.e. even though all the marginal conditions of economic welfare are fulfilled. In terms of Table XII the figure in column *b* for the first unit of output is lower than the corresponding figure in column *e*. Now since the figures in column *b* are bound to fall as more output is produced (the price of apples and of bee food both decline as more is put on the market) and the figures in column *e* either rise or stay stationary (there are no economies of large scale in the production of apples), the figures in column *f* will for every level of output remain higher than the figures in column *d*. Total value to society will never exceed total cost to society, if the market value of the first unit of output is lower than the cost of producing the first unit of output. In this case, if the *marginal* conditions are fulfilled for the first unit of output (i.e. are fulfilled when no output is being produced) the State need take no *structural* action to ensure that a socially desirable industry is in fact set up. Its social desirability can be judged by the criterion whether it pays to produce the first unit of output.

of the industry at different sizes of the industry;[1] and if we divided the figures of column *f* by the corresponding figures of column *a* we should obtain the cost per unit of production when there were different numbers of firms in the industry, thus:

No. of firms	Cost per unit of output
	$
1	50·0
2	48·75
3	47·5
4	46·25
etc.	etc.

In other words, when the number of firms rose from 2 to 4 the cost per unit of production in each firm would fall from $48·75 to $46·25 simply because of the increased size of the industry.

But whichever type of problem we wish to consider—the setting up of a single large-scale plant or of a many-firm industry—the basic arithmetical procedure is the same and is illustrated in Table XII.

So far we have made no reference to column *h* of Table XII. Suppose that commodity X in any case makes up only a very small proportion of the output of the economy and that it employs only those factors of production which are in general use throughout industry. In this case we should not be far wrong in assuming that variations in the output of commodity X would not appreciably affect the price which would have to be paid for the factors of production used in the production of X; more factors could be attracted away from the margin of the large number of other occupations in which they were employed without making any significant difference in those other industries. In this case the figures in column *f* (besides measuring the total cost to society of the production of X, which they will do whether or not the prices of the factors used in X remain constant) will also measure the total cost of production in X to the actual private producers in X. Thus in case i the production of one unit will cost the private producers factors worth $50, and the additional production of a second unit will cost them an additional amount of factors worth $47·5 (column *e*). But since the employment of the second block of factors will not have raised the prices payable to the factors already employed for the production of the first unit of output, the total cost to the private producers of producing two units will be $50 + $47·5 or $97·5 (column *f*).

In these special circumstances the figures in column *f* represent the private costs of production; the difference between the figures in

[1] Except in so far as a change in the size of the industry caused a change in the price payable for particular factors of production employed in the industry (see next paragraph but one).

column *c* which show the total receipts from the sale of the product and the figures in column *f* which show the total cost of producing the product would therefore show the net profit or loss which would be made by the private producers and which must be counteracted by a tax or subsidy (paid on the principles discussed on p. 30 above) if the actual reward of each factor is to be equated to the value of its marginal social net product (see pp. 32–43 above). This difference between total receipts and total costs is shown in column *h*.

But if the prices of the factors employed in X are affected by the scale of operations in X, then the total cost to private producers of producing various outputs of X may differ from the figures given in column *f*. The example which we gave on p. 124 above provides a case where the figures given in column *f* would exaggerate the private costs of production. Suppose that, when a second unit of X is produced, this reduces the demand for a close substitute Y which leads to the reduction in the demand for and so in the price of a factor also employed in the production of X. It is just possible (though perhaps improbable) that the reduction in the demand for this factor in Y is more important than the increase in the demand for it in X. In this case the price of the factor will fall. The total private cost of production of two units will be reduced below the $97·5 shown in case i of the table by the saving on the $50 paid (column *e*) as a reward to the factors needed to produce one unit as a result of the fall in the reward now payable to one of these factors.

A more probable case is where the expanded production of X requires the use of some factor which is specially important in the production of X and which is little used in other lines of production. The increased output of X may drive up the price of this factor against the producers in X so that the production of two units costs not merely the $97·5 of column *f* of case i, but also the rise in the rewards of $50 payable for the factors needed to produce one unit as a result of the rise in the price payable to this factor which is specially important in the production of X. In this case the figures in column *h* will underestimate the private loss which requires to be met by subsidy.

An examination of the four cases in Table XII will reveal the following general conclusions:[1]

(i) If the first units of production of X are profitable (case i), then the commodity should be produced; but in this case private enterprise will, of course, have an incentive to embark on its production.

(ii) If the first units of production are unprofitable, then it may (cases ii and iii) or may not (case iv) be socially desirable to produce the product.

[1] Provided always that the factor costs are constant so that column *f* measures the total private costs of production.

(iii) If there are any units for which production is profitable (cases i and ii), then these outputs will always represent outputs for which total social value exceeds total social costs and the commodity should be produced.

(iv) If there are no units for which total receipts exceed total costs, yet it may be socially desirable to produce (case iii) because the total value to consumers of the product (column *d*) exceeds the total amount spent by consumers on the product (column *c*).[1]

(v) As we have seen, the whole problem arises only because of increasing returns to scale. If the figures in column *e* remained constant or rose (constant or decreasing returns to scale) while the figures in column *b* always fell (diminishing marginal importance of successive units of consumption), then the figures in column *d* could exceed those in column *f* only if for the first unit of output the figure in column *f* exceeded that in column *e*. It would be socially desirable to produce X only if it were profitable to private producers to start the production of X.

(vi) Nor could the need for State subsidization of a new single firm arise if the price offered for the product by consumers did not fall when the output was increased. Suppose there were a question of setting up a new firm in a particular region or country to produce for a world market which was so large in relation to the productive resources of the particular region that the setting up of the firm in that region could not appreciably affect the world price. In such conditions the outputs measured in column *a* of Table XII would represent changes in the output of the one firm in question and the price in column *b* would remain constant. In this case there would be no appreciable difference between the total value to society (column *d*) and the total amount spent by consumers on the product of this particular firm (column *c*). Therefore if total value to society exceeded total cost to society (figure in column *g* positive), then the total receipts of producers would also exceed their total costs (figure in column *h* positive). If the new firm were socially desirable it would also be privately profitable.

(vii) But even in these circumstances in which the world price offered for a product is constant there might be a case for State action to set up an industry consisting of a number of firms in a new region to produce the product. This would be the case if there were appreciable external economies in the sense that within certain limits the greater the number of firms in the region the lower the costs incurred by each firm. With such external economies of conglomeration, as we may call them, it may not pay any one firm to set up in the first instance, since it would not enjoy any such economies. But it might pay a large number of firms to be set up simultaneously. In terms of Table XII, changes in

[1] This excess is often known as 'consumers' surplus'.

output (column *a*) would now represent changes in the number of individual firms which were producing; and with the price offered for the product (column *b*) constant, there might be a case where total costs (column *f*) were less than total receipts (column *c*), which in this particular case coincided with total value to society (column *d*), when there was a large output produced by a large number of firms but did not do so when there was a small output produced by only a small number of firms.

So much for the problem of deciding whether the production of X should be started in an economy which is already producing Y, Z, etc. But this is only the most simple and straightforward type of structural decision. Let us consider a second group of structural decisions. Suppose that in our economy, as before, commodities Y, Z, etc., are being produced, but that we want to know whether to introduce the production of either or both or neither of the commodities W and X. In the previous case we had only one comparison to make: was an economy producing X, Y, Z, etc., better or worse than one producing Y, Z, etc.? In our present case three calculations have to be made. We have to calculate the size of the net social gain or loss from introducing (i) W alone, (ii) X alone, and (iii) W and X together into the existing economy. We cannot take it for granted either that it is worth while introducing W and X together into the economy from the fact that it is worth while introducing each one separately or that it is not worth while introducing W and X together into the economy from the fact that it is not worth while introducing either of them separately. This arises from the nature of the special relationships which may exist between the two products W and X.

(1) Suppose that W and X are close substitutes for each other, for example leather shoes and rubber shoes. Clearly it might be worth while introducing a new industry to produce leather shoes or a new industry to produce rubber shoes into an economy which was producing no shoes at all. But, because of the economies of large-scale production which would be sacrificed, it might not be worth while introducing the production of rubber shoes into an economy which was already producing leather shoes or the production of leather shoes into an economy which was already producing rubber shoes. Indeed, the expense of producing small quantities of rubber shoes and of leather shoes might be so great as to make it better to produce no shoes at all rather than to try to produce both.

(2) Suppose, on the other hand, that our two commodities W and X, far from being close substitutes for each other in consumption like leather and rubber shoes, were important complements for each other in consumption like tennis rackets and tennis balls. It is not much use having the balls without the rackets or the rackets without the balls.

It might not, in this case, be worth while introducing the production of rackets into an economy which did not produce balls or that of balls into an economy which did not produce rackets. But it might still be worth while introducing the production of both simultaneously.

(3) Suppose next that the commodities W and X have no specially close relationship in consumption; they are neither close substitutes for each other nor are they complements in consumption. But suppose that they both rely very largely indeed upon the same factor of production for their manufacture and that this factor of production is not much used in other lines of production. Once again, as in (1) above, it may be worth while to introduce the production of either W or X but not of both together. The production of W or of X alone would enable good use to be made of the particular factor of production which would otherwise be idle or used only in relatively unproductive employments in other lines of production. But the introduction of both W and X might so raise the demand for this special factor of production and so raise its cost that both W and X would be produced only on a small scale with the result that the economies of large-scale production were realized in neither commodity.

(4) It is possible that the production of W requires the use mainly of one factor of production (say, summer work) while that of X requires the use mainly of another factor of production (say, winter work) which is complementary with the former. In this case it is possible that, as in (2) above, the introduction of W alone or of X alone would not be socially worth while, but the introduction of both together would give a net social gain. The introduction of W would attract labour for summer work and thus increase the supply, and lower the price, of labour for seasonal winter work. To introduce W alone might work out as socially unprofitable; but it would reduce the social cost of introducing X, so that the simultaneous introduction of both might be worth while.

In order, therefore, to obtain a clear guide as to whether the production of W or of X or of both together should or should not be introduced into an economy which starts with neither, it is necessary to calculate the net social gain from W alone, from X alone, and from W and X together, and to choose that combination (if any) which gives the highest positive net social gain.[1] Now the calculation of the net social gain to be obtained from the introduction of W alone or of X alone involves no more than the analysis discussed in connexion with Table XII. The introduction of W alone is to be preferred if it shows a higher positive value in column *g* of the table than is shown in the case of the introduction of X alone.

[1] If there are three products V, W, and X involved, then the net social advantage from V, W, X, VW, VX, WX, and VWX must be separately calculated; and so on, with still larger numbers.

The calculation of the net social gain or loss from the introduction of W and X together requires only a simple extension of this same method. By the means outlined above one can calculate the net social gain or loss obtained by introducing the production of X into an economy which is producing Y, Z, etc.; and one can then calculate the net social gain or loss obtained by introducing the production of W into the economy which is already producing X, Y, Z, etc. The sum of these two net gains or losses is the net gain or loss obtained from the introduction of W and X together into an economy which is producing Y, Z, etc.

If commodities W and X are very complementary with each other in consumption, it will be rather worthless having much X without any W. The introduction of X into the economy without W may well result in a net social loss and the output of X which in these circumstances satisfies the marginal principles may be very low. But when W is now introduced into the economy which already produces X the net social gain may be positive since W is very useful when X can be also obtained and the output of W and of X which satisfy the marginal conditions may be great. The net social gain or loss will be obtained by balancing the loss from the introduction of X into an economy which does not produce W against the gain from introducing W into the economy which already produces X.

On the other hand, if W and X are very close substitutes for each other, the introduction of X into an economy which does not produce W may bring a positive net social gain. The absence of W makes it very desirable to have X. But the subsequent introduction of W into the economy which already produces X may bring a net social loss. The fact that X is available makes it very unimportant to be able to obtain W, for which X is a close substitute; and the production of both would mean a waste since neither could then take full advantage of the economies of large-scale production. In this case the net social gain or loss for introducing W and X together will be obtained by balancing the gain from introducing X into an economy without W against the loss from introducing W into an economy which already produces X.[1]

It is difficult enough in the real world to apply the marginal analysis discussed in Chapter VII in order to decide whether any particular small adjustment of policies would do good or harm. But an attempt can perhaps in some cases be made to estimate the main changes in transactions which a marginal change of policy would bring about and to assess the order of magnitude of the divergences in the transactions, given always that certain distributional weights have been allotted to the main classes concerned.

[1] The above analysis rests upon the quite plausible assumption that no difference is made by the order in which W and X are introduced.

But the difficulties of assessing whether a structural change of policy is desirable are of a quite different order of magnitude. Even in the simplest case where, first, it is a question of introducing only one new industry and, second, it can be assumed that throughout the rest of the economy all the marginal conditions for economic welfare are satisfied, the problems are formidable. To draw up the schedules of marginal values and of marginal costs (columns *b* and *e* of Table XII) involves estimating such quantities as: what prices consumers would be willing to offer for a particular product if its supply were totally different from what it now is and if there had been appropriate adjustments in the supplies of other competing and complementary products; or what the marginal cost of a product would be if its scale of production were totally different from what it now is and if there had been appropriate changes in the other demands for factors of production which were highly competitive with or complementary to those used to produce the product in question.

The difficulties are multiplied when it is a question of introducing more than one new industry at the same time. As we have just seen, the problem then arises not only of constructing the schedules of marginal values and costs for one new industry introduced into present *actual* conditions but then of constructing such schedules for another new industry introduced into the new *hypothetical* conditions which would exist if the first new industry had been set up.

But still greater theoretical complications are introduced as soon as we allow for the fact that the marginal conditions of economic welfare will not be universally satisfied. We would no longer be able to rest content with calculations, such as those shown in Table XII, of the schedules of marginal values and marginal costs in the new industry. We should at each stage have to make concurrent calculations for the changes being made in every other industry.

Thus let us suppose that 1 unit of a new commodity X is produced. We could, as before, calculate whether a net loss or gain was made in industry X by setting up the industry to produce 1 unit of X, by considering the marginal values and costs of columns *b* and *e* of Table XII, the only difference being that we should have to weight the figure in column *b* by the distributional weight of the consumers concerned and the figures in column *e* by the distributional weight of the owners of the factors of production concerned.

But this would not now be the end of the calculation. The production of 1 unit of X would affect the output of other products. For example, it might lead to a reduction in the output of a product which was a very close substitute for X in consumers' demand or which was previously produced by those factors which are specifically needed in the new X-industry. Or it might lead to the expansion of an industry which produced a product complementary in demand with X or which employed factors of production which were complementary in supply with those used in X (see pp. 130–1). Previously we could neglect the effect on welfare of this marginal change in other industries simply because we were assuming that marginal values equalled marginal costs in all other industries and that every dollar of marginal value and cost had the same distributional weight.

But we could no longer make this assumption. There might be an excess of marginal value over marginal cost or the distributional weight assigned to the consumers might be higher than the distributional weight assigned to the producers in some other industry which underwent some indirect marginal contraction or expansion as a result of the production of X. In the case of a contracting industry when the first unit of X is produced we have to add to any net social loss made in industry X the net social loss due to the marginal contraction in an industry in which there was an excess of marginal value over marginal cost or an excess of the consumers' over the producers' distributional weight. And vice versa in the case of an industry which expands when X is produced.

And similarly when we consider the effect of adding a second unit of output of X to the first, or a third to the second. We must not only calculate the additional social gain or loss in industry X by the means employed in Table XII, always modified by applying the appropriate distributional weights on the value side and on the cost side. We must also take into account all the further marginal repercussions on other transactions in which there is either a significant rate of divergence between marginal values and costs or a significant difference between the distributional weights assigned to the buyers and sellers. At each stage the consequential social gains or losses in all these other industries must be added into the sum of total social gain or loss.

Clearly it would be an utter impossibility to attempt any precise calculation of this kind. A decision about a structural change of policy is bound to remain a much more hit-or-miss affair than a decision about a marginal change—which itself will always be a matter of great uncertainty. All that one can hope to do is to bear in mind the main features which this analysis has brought out. First, is the new industry one in which there is likely to be a large total excess of value to consumers (column *d* of Table XII) over amount spent by consumers (column *c*)? This is likely to be so in the case of a commodity for which consumers would pay a very much higher price for the first units than for later units. Second, is the new industry one in which costs are likely to fall a lot when it has been instituted on a scale which will be of a reasonable size in view of the probable demand for the commodity? This is likely to be the case where there are important external economies of the 'atmosphere-creating' kind or an important indivisibility of some necessary factor of production. Third, are the consequential changes in the rest of the economy likely to be such as to cause an expansion of other industries in which there are abnormally large divergences between marginal values and costs, and so to confer an important indirect social benefit? And, fourth, are the consequential changes in the rest of the economy likely to improve the distribution of income by lowering the price of products bought by the poor or raising the rewards offered to factors owned by the poor? An affirmative answer to each of these questions increases the chance that the structural change will lead to an increase of economic welfare; and it is only by considering the answer to questions of this kind that the policy-maker can hope that his hunches will be at all well founded.

PART II. THE CONTROL OF TRADE

PART II. THE CONTROL OF TRADE

CHAPTER IX

THE CASE FOR FREE TRADE

In this Part we intend to apply the analysis of Part I to the question whether free trade will lead to the maximization of economic welfare or whether some forms of control over international trade should be introduced for this purpose. Throughout this Part II we shall assume that the factors of production, labour, and capital are unable to move from country to country; and we shall be considering the problem of maximizing economic welfare, always subject to this condition that the factors cannot move internationally. In Part III we shall turn to the possibility of international factor movements and shall ask whether trade in goods and services alone is sufficient to attain a complete maximization of economic welfare or whether a still higher level of economic welfare could be achieved if there were some international movement of factors of production. At that point we shall have to ask whether a completely free international movement of factors of production is desirable for the maximization of economic welfare or whether some controls over the international movement of labour and capital are required. Moreover, in this Part and in Part III we shall argue as if the world were made up of only two countries, A and B, and we shall relegate the special problems which arise in a many-country world to Part IV.

Our programme in this Part is as follows. In this chapter we shall state the general case for free trade, which, as we shall see, rests upon the contention that in a world of *utopian* domestic economic policies it sets internationally the proper *marginal* conditions for economic *efficiency*. In Chapters X and XI we shall then describe the various forms of trade control which might be introduced into a free-trade world and will consider some of the effects which these different forms of trade control might have.

In the remaining chapters of this Part we shall then turn to the basic arguments which can be brought against a free-trade policy. The first of these, which we shall examine in Chapters XII–XV, is that the freeing of trade is not necessarily the best policy if the marginal conditions for utopian economic efficiency are not otherwise satisfied throughout the various economies of the world. The second basic argument against a free-trade policy, which we shall examine in Chapter

XVI, is that some intervention with international trade may be desirable to obtain an improvement in the world's economic structure. The third basic argument against free trade, which we shall examine in Chapters XVII and XVIII, is that some intervention in international trade may be desirable in the interests of economic equity.

We start then with a world of two countries A and B in order to consider the case for a policy of free trade between them. We make two basic assumptions about this two-country world for the purpose of this chapter. The first (which we shall not modify until Part III) is that the factors of production—land, labour, and capital—cannot move between A and B. The second (which we shall modify in Chapters XII–XV) is that within each country A and B there is a domestic policy of what we have called (p. 51) 'modified laissez-faire'. In other words, consumers are free to choose what they will purchase; owners of factors of production are free to decide what they will use their factors to produce; and there is such a system of governmental fiscal and other policies that there are no divergences between marginal social values and costs in any market. Each factor is offered in each industry within each country a net reward equal to the value of its marginal social net product. Each consumer is charged for each product with each country a net payment which is equal to the marginal social net cost of its production.

Now world economic efficiency demands that conditions should be such that it is impossible to make any one citizen of the world better off without making any other citizen of the world worse off. If we assume—as we are doing for the purposes of this Part—that it is possible to move products but impossible to move factors between countries, and if we further assume—as described above—that there is a policy of modified laissez-faire within each country, then it is easy to show that the marginal conditions for world economic efficiency require the free movement of products between countries in world markets which are so arranged that there are no divergences between marginal social values and costs in any international trade transactions.

This last qualification is important. It is possible that complete free trade would still leave some divergences between marginal social values and costs in international markets. For example, it is possible that the traders importing, say, blankets into A might for one reason or another be monopolized. In this case the marginal payment which they would have to make to import another blanket into A would not be merely the price charged for a blanket in B but this price plus any rise in price of all the other blankets already being imported by them, which might result from an expansion of their purchases (see Table I, p. 16). In this case they would exercise their monopsonistic powers and would charge to the consumers of imported blankets in A a price which was related not to the price (and so to the marginal social cost) of a blanket in B but to the higher marginal payment which they would have to make to acquire one more imported blanket. There would be a divergence between marginal social values and costs in the international market for blankets even though there were a policy of free trade and even though there were no divergences within the domestic economy of either A or B.

Another possible example would be if there were an external economy or diseconomy which was associated with the international trade in a particular economy. It seems doubtful whether this case is likely to be of any importance in fact. Most external economies or diseconomies are associated with the production or the consumption of products; and all these we have assumed to be offset by the domestic policies for modified laissez-faire in the two countries A and B. But if one can imagine some indirect social benefit which accrues not from the production of blankets in B nor from the consumption of blankets in A, but from the movements of blankets from B to A, then in a free-trade world there would be a divergence between marginal social values and costs in the trade of importing blankets from B to A.

We assume, therefore, for the purpose of this chapter that in addition to the policies for modified laissez-faire in A and B there is a policy of 'modified free trade' between A and B; that is to say, we assume that by appropriate fiscal or other policies any divergences between marginal social values and costs in trade between A and B are removed. What we intend to demonstrate in this chapter is that in these conditions a policy of free trade, i.e. a policy of leaving traders free to import and export without any duties, subsidies, or governmental intervention other than those required for our 'modified free trade' position, will lead to the fulfilment of the marginal conditions for utopian world efficiency.

This conclusion really follows immediately from the analysis of Chapter IV. We there showed that for any closed domestic economy—i.e. for any economy which had no economic relations with any other economy—a governmental policy which allowed consumers freely to choose what they would purchase, and owners of factors of production freely to choose what they would produce, and which at the same time took steps by fiscal or other measures to remove all divergences in all markets between marginal social values and costs, would necessarily lead to the fulfilment of all the marginal conditions necessary for economic efficiency. Trade would be optimized; production maximized and optimized; and effort optimized. We are now dealing with a closed world economy in each part of which (countries A and B) there is *ex hypothesi* a suitable policy for modified laissez-faire. But our modified free-trade policy for transactions between A and B is just such as will ensure that throughout the whole world economy there is a policy of modified laissez-faire. Consumers are free everywhere to decide what they will buy; owners of factors of production are free to produce what they will; and there are no divergences between marginal social net values and costs in any transaction. In the closed-world economy the stage is set for a complete fulfilment of all the marginal conditions for economic welfare.

As a formal proof of the case for free trade there is really nothing to be added to this simple extension of the argument of Chapter IV. Nevertheless, it is probably worth while briefly to describe the particular way in which the arguments of Chapter IV apply to the problem of international trade. This description will help to clarify a number of subsequent arguments in this volume.

We will start then with a discussion of the effect of a policy of modified free trade upon the *marginal condition for the optimization of trade.* Let us suppose that in each of our countries both apples and blankets are produced and consumed. At first the two economies are completely isolated and no trade takes place between them. For one reason or another the market price of apples relatively to that of blankets is lower in A than in B. For our present purpose it does not matter what is the cause of this price disparity. It may be due to the fact that the tastes of consumers are different in the two countries; people in A have an exceptionally low demand for apples and an exceptionally high demand for blankets, the low demand for apples in A thus tending to depress the price of apples in A. Or it may be due to the fact that the producers in A are for one reason or another better qualified to produce apples than blankets, so that the supply of apples in A is high relatively to the supply of blankets, the high supply of apples in A thus tending to depress their price in A.

But whatever the cause, we assume that the ratio of the price of apples to that of blankets is only one-quarter as much in A as it is in B. This means that in A consumers for a given price can buy, let us say, 1 blanket or 2 apples, whereas in B consumers for a given price can buy 2 blankets or 1 apple. Since we are assuming that in both countries consumers are free to decide what they will buy and that in both countries the individual consumer cannot appreciably affect the price of blankets or of apples by altering the scale of his own individual purchases, this will mean that blankets and apples are being consumed in A in such amounts that to each individual 1 more blanket has just the same importance as 2 more apples. But in B to each consumer 2 more blankets will have just the same importance as 1 more apple.

Here is a clear case in which the condition of optimum trade is not achieved. If 1 apple were exported from A to B and 2 blankets from B to A, then the welfare of every citizen in B could be left unchanged; all that would be necessary would be for one consumer in B to consume 1 more apple and 2 less blankets, and *ex hypothesi*, 1 more apple just makes up in his consumption for 2 less blankets. But in A welfare could be increased. One consumer could be asked to give up 1 apple in return for 2 blankets; but *ex hypothesi* he would be willing to give up 2 apples for 1 blanket, i.e. no less than 4 apples for 2 more blankets. His welfare would thus be increased.

This situation is illustrated in case i of Table XIII. We assume that before trade takes place the price of an apple is $3 and of a blanket is $1·5 in B, but that the price of an apple is $1·5 and of a blanket is $3 in A (case i, columns *a* and *d* of Table XIII). The export of 1 apple from A to B and of 2 blankets from B to A (columns *b* and *e*) means to A's consumers a net gain (since they lose something worth $1·5 and give something worth $6 to them) without any change of welfare to consumers in B (since what they lose and what they gain are both worth $3 to them)—(columns *c* and *f*).

Now free trade will in fact lead to the export of apples from A to B and of blankets from B to A so long as the ratio of the price of apples to the price of blankets is lower in A than in B. The trader will purchase apples in A, sell them in B, with the proceeds purchase blankets in B, and sell them in A for the value of a larger number of apples than those originally exported to B.

We are assuming that the individual trader cannot by his own action appreciably affect the price of apples or of blankets in either country. The traders as a whole will, therefore, continue to expand the volume of trade so long as the ratio of the price of apples to that of blankets is lower in A than B. But as apples become scarcer in A owing to their export and blankets become more plentiful in A owing to their import, the price offered by consumers for apples in A will tend to rise and that offered by consumers for blankets in A to fall. The opposite will be happening in B, where the import of apples and the export of blankets is making the former more plentiful relatively to the latter.

At some point the ratio of the price of apples to that of blankets will have so risen in A and fallen in B that it is the same in the two countries, and at this point traders will have no further incentive to expand the trade. But it is precisely at this point also that the condition of optimum trade will be fulfilled. If, for example, in both countries the ratio of the price of apples to that of blankets is one to one, so that 1 apple exchanges for 1 blanket, this will mean that in both countries each consumer finds 1 apple equally as important as 1 more blanket. There is no further gain possible from trade.

This free-trade position is illustrated in case ii of Table XIII. The price of apples has risen in A from $1·5 to $2 and has fallen in B from

TABLE XIII

The Optimization of World Trade

	Country A				Country B			
	Marginal value	Change in quantity consumed	Change in value		Marginal value	Change in quantity consumed	Change in value	
	(*a*)	(*b*)	(*c*) = *a* × *b*		(*d*)	(*e*)	(*f*) = *d* × *e*	
	Case (i). *Before Trade*							
Apples	\$1·5	−1	−\$1·5	+ \$4·5	\$3·0	+1	+\$3·0	= \$0
Blankets	\$3·0	+2	+\$6·0		\$1·5	−2	−\$3·0	
	Case (ii). *After Trade. No Transport Cost*							
Apples	\$2·0	−1	−\$2·0	= \$0	\$2·0	+1	+\$2·0	= \$0
Blankets	\$2·0	+1	+\$2·0		\$2·0	−1	−\$2·0	
	Case (iii). *After Trade. With Transport Costs*							
Apples	\$1·8	−1	−\$1·8	= \$0	\$2·7	+1	+\$2·7	= \$0
Blankets	\$2·7	+1½	+\$4·05		\$1·8	−1½	−\$2·7	
Transport	\$0·9	−2½	−\$2·25		—	—	—	

\$3 to \$2 because the export of apples from A to B has made them scarcer to A's consumers and more plentiful to B's. Since the price of apples is now the same in both markets, there is no further tendency to expand the trade in them. At the same time the price of blankets has fallen in A from \$3 to \$2 and has risen in B from \$1·5 to \$2 because their export from B to A has made them scarcer in B and more plentiful in A. The price of blankets is now the same in both markets, so that there is no tendency to develop further the trade in blankets.

Now with the ratio of the price of blankets to the price of apples the same in both countries, it is impossible for consumers in the one country to gain without those in the other losing from a further marginal development of trade. Suppose that 1 further blanket is exported from B to A. Consumers in B will lose something worth \$2 to them. In order to be just compensated for this loss they must receive in return 1 more apple from A which also has a marginal value of \$2 to them (column *f* of Table XIII). But in this case consumers in A will receive a blanket worth \$2 to them and lose an apple also worth \$2 to them (column *c*). It is no longer possible to make A's consumers better off without making B's worse off.

The preceding paragraphs have been written on the assumption that there are no costs of transporting apples from A to B nor of blankets from B to A. The analysis can, however, very easily be modified to allow for such costs. We have now to introduce another industry, the transport industry, into the analysis. Suppose for simplicity of exposition that transport, e.g. shipping services, is all produced in A. Suppose that it costs 1 unit of transport to carry a blanket from B to A or an apple from A to B; and let us suppose further that the marginal value in A of a unit of transport (or of the things which could have been produced instead of the unit of transport) is \$0·9 (see last row of Table XIII).

If we now look at Table XIII we can see that in these circumstances trade ought not to be developed as far as it is in case ii of that table. If 1 *less* blanket were taken from B to A in the conditions depicted in case ii, then 1 less apple need be taken from A to B to pay for the blanket. This would leave consumers in B as well off as before; they would have 1 more blanket worth \$2 to them and 1 less apple which is also worth \$2 to them. But consumers in A would be better off than before. They would have 1 less blanket worth \$2 to them; but against this they would have not only 1 more apple worth \$2 to them, but also the additional transport services which were no longer required to bring the blanket from B and to take the apple from A to pay for it. In our example this requires 2 units of transport (1 unit to carry the blanket and 1 to carry the apple) each with a marginal value of \$0·9, so that consumers in A would, in fact, be \$1·8 better off than before.

In fact trade would not develop as far as in case ii, because on the last units of trade in case ii private traders would be making a loss. The trader who was purchasing an apple for \$2 in A and selling it for \$2 in B would be making a loss of the \$0·9 cost of transporting it; and similarly, the trader who was buying a blanket for \$2 in B and selling it for \$2 in A would be making a loss of the \$0·9 cost of transporting it from B to A.

But if because of the transport costs trade were less developed than in case ii, we might end up in a situation like that shown in case iii. There is some flow of apples into B and of blankets out of B, so that the price of apples in B is lower and of blankets in B is higher than in case i; but the change is not as great as in case ii; and we thus suppose that the price of apples in B has fallen from \$3 (case i) to \$2·7 (case iii) instead of to \$2 (case ii). Similarly, we suppose that the price of blankets in B has risen from \$1·5 to \$1·8 instead of to \$2. The ratio of the price of blankets to the price of apples in B which had risen from $\frac{1}{2}$ to 1 in the absence of transport costs has now risen from $\frac{1}{2}$ to $\frac{2}{3}$. In A also the trade has been less developed, so that the price changes have been less great. The price of apples has risen from \$1·5 to only \$1·8 instead of to

$2 in the previous free-trade position; and the price of blankets has fallen from $3 to $2·7 instead of to $2.

In case iii it is now no longer possible to improve the position of the consumers in either country by a small marginal change in the amount of trade without making the consumers in the other country worse off. Thus if 1 more apple were exported from A to B, the consumers in B would gain something worth $2·7 to them. To compensate for this they could give up 1½ more blankets to A, since at a price or marginal value of a blanket in B of $1·8 the loss of 1½ blankets would also be worth $2·7 to them. But consumers in A would, therefore, have 1 less apple and 1½ more blankets to consume. If this were the only change they would be better off, since 1 apple has a marginal value of only $1·8, whereas 1½ more blankets at a marginal value of $2·7 a blanket has a value of $4·05 to them. There would therefore be a net gain of $4·05 less $1·8, or $2·25. But in addition they would lose the cost of the transport necessary to bring the 1½ blankets from B and to take the apple to B to pay for it. In our example this requires 2½ units of transport each having a marginal value of $0·9, so that the transport would involve a loss to consumers of $2·25, which is exactly equal to the net gain from an exchange of 1 apple for 1½ blankets.

And not only is this the point at which trade is optimized; it is also clearly the point at which, with our modified free-trade policy, it would pay traders to stop developing the trade. The trader in case iii who spent $1·8 to purchase an apple in A, took it to B and sold it there for $2·7 would make a gross profit of $0·9. But this would only just serve to pay for the cost of transport of the apple. And similarly the trader who bought a blanket in B for $1·8 and sold it in A for $2·7 would only just cover the $0·9 cost of transport involved. In these conditions it would be profitable for private traders to develop the trade until the marginal condition of optimum trade was reached, but no further. The existence of transport costs makes no difference to this conclusion.

We turn now to a consideration of the way in which a free-trade policy would lead to the fulfilment of the *marginal condition for the maximization of world production* in our world in which there is a modified laissez-faire policy inside both A and B. Throughout this discussion, it will be remembered, we are considering the maximization of production subject always to the assumption that it is impossible for any factor of production to move between the countries.

Let us assume, as in our previous example, that before trade takes place between A and B the ratio between the price of an apple and that of a blanket is four times as high in B as in A. This, as we have already explained, might be due either to the fact that in B there was a relatively high demand for apples or else that in B the cost conditions were such as to favour the production of blankets. But, whatever may be the cause of the initial price discrepancy, the fact that we are assuming no divergences between marginal values and costs domestically, will mean that before trade is opened up the ratio between marginal cost of production of an apple and that of a blanket will also be four times as high in B as in A. This will mean that if B expanded her blanket industry in which her costs are low and contracted her apple industry in which her costs are high, and if A changed her output in the opposite direction, it would be possible for the two countries in combination to produce more of both commodities than they did before.

TABLE XIV

The Maximization of World Production

	Country A			Country B		
	Marginal cost	Change in quantity produced	Change in total cost	Marginal cost	Change in quantity produced	Change in total cost
	(*a*)	(*b*)	(*c*) = *a* × *b*	(*d*)	(*e*)	(*f*) = *d* × *e*
	Case (i). *Before Trade*					
Apples	$1·5	+1	+$1·5 } = −$4·5	$3·0	−1	−$3·0 } = $0
Blankets	$3·0	−2	−$6·0	$1·5	+2	+$3·0
	Case (ii). *After Trade. No Transport Costs*					
Apples	$2·0	+1	+$2·0 } = $0	$2·0	−1	−$2·0 } = $0
Blankets	$2·0	−1	−$2·0	$2·0	+1	+$2·0
	Case (iii). *After Trade. With Transport Costs*					
Apples	$1·8	+1	+$1·8 } = $0	$2·7	−1	−$2·7 } = $0
Blankets	$2·7	$-1\frac{1}{2}$	−$4·05	$1·8	$+1\frac{1}{2}$	+$2·7
Transport	$0·9	$+2\frac{1}{2}$	+$2·25	—	—	—

This possibility is illustrated in case i of Table XIV. We suppose that before trade takes place the marginal cost of an apple ($1·5) is half that of a blanket ($3) in A, whereas the marginal cost of an apple ($3) is twice that of a blanket ($1·5) in B (columns *a* and *d* of Table XIV). If now in B 1 less apple was produced, this would release the resources necessary to produce 2 more blankets, since the marginal cost of an apple is twice that of a blanket in B. But if in A 1 more apple and 2 less blankets were produced in order to compensate for the changes in production in B, there would be a net saving of factors of production in A. The production of 2 less blankets in A would have released $6 worth of factors, whereas the production of 1 more apple would have called for the use of only $1·5 worth of these factors. The remaining

$4·5 worth of factors would have been freed to increase the total world output of either or both commodities.

And in these circumstances a modified free-trade policy would bring about just those shifts of production in A and B which were necessary for the maximization of production. In the position shown in case i of Table XIV, producers of apples in A would now be able to obtain a price of $3 an apple in B when their marginal cost in A was only $1·5, whereas the producers of blankets in A, whose marginal cost is $3, would find their market in A invaded by B's blankets which cost only $1·5. A's productive resources would thus, under the influence of the profit motive, be shifted from blanket production to apple production. Similarly, in B producers of blankets can obtain a $3 price for blankets in A while their costs are only $1·5, but producers of apples whose costs are $3 would be confronted with increased imports from A at a cost of $1·5. B's blanket industry would expand and her apple industry would contract.

This change in production would continue until either of two things happened. First, one or both countries might give up entirely the production of one commodity. Thus resources might be shifted from A's blanket industry into her apple industry on such a scale that A produced no more blankets; and/or resources might be shifted out of B's apple industry until no more apples were produced in B. Or, second, the marginal costs of apples in A and of blankets in B might so rise as the result of the expansion of these industries, and the marginal costs of blankets in A and of apples in B might so fall as a result of the contraction of these industries, that the ratio of the marginal cost of apples to the marginal cost of blankets became the same in both countries while each country continued to produce something of both commodities. Which of these two things is likely to happen we shall discuss at a later stage (see Chapter XIX). For our present purpose it is sufficient to point out that whichever happens the policy of modified free trade will have led to the maximization of world production.

Thus if A gives up the production of blankets or B gives up the production of apples, there clearly cannot be any further increase in the production of both commodities by a further shift of resources from blanket production to apple production in A combined with a further shift from apple production to blanket production in B, for the simple reason that one or other or both of these shifts is now impossible.

The case in which the shifts of production lead to an equalization of marginal production costs in both countries is illustrated in case ii of Table XIV. We assume that as a result of the expansion of A's apple industry the marginal cost of apples rises from $1·5 to $2, as a result of the contraction of A's blanket industry the marginal cost falls from $3 to $2, as a result of the expansion of B's blanket industry the marginal cost rises from \$1·5 to \$2, and as a result of the contraction of B's apple industry the marginal cost falls from \$3 to \$2. Now it is clear that production is maximized. If 1 more blanket is produced in B this would take up resources costing \$2, which would mean that 1 less apple would be produced since the marginal cost of an apple in B is also \$2. But if an exact compensation is made in A's production, A will have to produce 1 less blanket and 1 more apple, both of which changes will involve her in the same costs, namely \$2. There will thus be no net change in world output. Moreover, it is clear that at this point at which the marginal conditions for the maximization of world production are satisfied, private producers will have no further incentive to change their production programmes, since the marginal cost of each product is now the same in A as in B.

So far we have considered the problem on the tacit assumption that there are no costs of transport. But suppose that, as in the example given for the optimization of trade, it takes a unit of transport to take 1 apple from A to B or 1 blanket from B to A, that transport services are produced only by A, and that a unit of transport has a marginal cost in A of \$0·9. It is clear that in these circumstances case ii of Table XIV represents too large a shift of resources from blanket production to apple production in A and vice versa in B. Suppose that, starting in the position shown in case ii of the table, 1 less blanket and 1 more apple were produced in B. There would be no net change in the demands on B's productive resources, since each of these changes involves the same cost. B's consumers could then consume as much as before if 1 less apple were imported from A and 1 less blanket were exported to A. The consequential change in supplies in A could be offset if in A 1 less apple and 1 more blanket were produced; and since the marginal cost of each of these changes is the same in A, there would be no net change in the demands made on A's productive resources engaged in the apple and blanket industries in A. But there would now be a saving of resources used in A to provide transport services; 2 units of transport services (1 to carry the apple from A to B and 1 to carry a blanket from B to A) would be saved which, at \$0·9 a unit, would represent an increase of \$1·8 to A's consumers. Moreover, in these circumstances there would also be an incentive to producers to make these productive shifts. A's producers of apples would in fact produce less apples for B's markets, since the marginal cost in A is \$2 and the price obtained by sale in B is also \$2, so that the \$0·9 cost of transport on each apple produced in A for B would represent a net loss. And similarly B's producers of blankets would be making a net loss on blankets sent from B to A.

With transport costs at \$0·9 a unit, we might end up in a position like that shown in case iii of Table XIV. As compared with the pre-trade position shown in case i, resources have been shifted in A from the production of blankets to that of apples, and vice versa in B. But these shifts have not gone to the extent indicated in case ii. As a result, the marginal cost of producing apples in A has risen from \$1·5 (case i) to \$1·8 (case iii) instead of to \$2 (case ii), the marginal cost of producing blankets in A has fallen from \$3 to \$2·7 instead of to \$2, the marginal cost of producing blankets in B has risen from \$1·5 to \$1·8 instead of to \$2, and the marginal cost of producing apples in B has fallen from \$3 to \$2·7 instead of to \$2. There is now no private incentive to change the scale of trading operations. An apple costs \$1·8 in A and can be sold for \$2·7 in B, but this difference of \$0·9 only just covers the cost of transport; and similarly a blanket costs \$1·8 in B and sells for \$2·7 in A, but this difference in price of \$0·9 again only just covers the cost of transport of 1 blanket from B to A. But this position is one in which production is maximized. If, for example, 1 less apple were produced in B, this would save \$2·7 worth of factors in B which, at a marginal cost of blankets of \$1·8 in B, would enable 1½ more blankets to be produced in B. If A offset these changes and produced 1 more apple and 1½ less blankets, she would save \$2·25 in costs, since the 1 more apple would cost her only \$1·8 and the 1½ less blankets, at a marginal cost for blankets of \$2·7 in A, would save her \$4·05 of costs. But apples-in-A are not the same thing as apples-in-B, and blankets-in-B are not the same things as blankets-in-A. If all consumers in all countries are to have the same amount of everything as before, 1 more apple must now be carried from A to B and 1½ more blankets from B to A. But this would absorb just the \$2·25 worth of resources in A which were released by the shift from blanket production to apple production in A.

A comparison of Tables XIII and XIV will serve to show the close analogy between the effect of a modified free-trade policy upon the optimization of world trade and the maximization of world production.[1] Transport costs aside, trade will be optimized when (in the absence of monopsony among buyers) the *prices charged to consumers* for apples and for blankets are in the same ratio to each other in A and in B; but production will be maximized when (in the absence of monopoly among sellers) the *prices offered to producers* for apples and for blankets are in the same ratio to each other in A and in B. It may be helpful at this point, in order to underline this distinction, to give illustrations of types of fiscal policy (other than those required for a modified laissez-faire policy within each country or for a modified free-trade policy between them) which would interfere with the optimization of trade and the maximization of production.

[1] All the figures in Table XIV are the same as those in Table XIII except that the signs are reversed. In Table XIV we are dealing with changes in quantities produced and in costs, whereas in Table XIII we are dealing with changes in quantities consumed and in values.

(1) A tax or a subsidy on the trade between A and B will interfere with both the optimization of trade and the maximization of production. Thus a duty levied on the import of blankets into A from B will cause the price of blankets charged to consumers and offered to producers to be higher in A than in B, while the price of apples will be the same in both countries.

(2) A tax or subsidy on the consumption of a particular product in A will interfere with the optimization of trade but not with the maximization of production. Thus a tax levied in A on the consumption of blankets will cause the price charged to consumers of blankets to be higher in A than B; but it will not cause the price offered to producers of blankets to be higher in A than in B, since the tax is levied on blankets produced in A for A's consumers as well as on those imported from B for A's consumers. With the price of apples the same in both countries to producers and consumers, this will interfere with the optimization of trade but not with the maximization of production.

(3) A tax or subsidy on the production of a particular product in A will interfere with the maximization of production but not with the optimization of trade. Thus a tax levied in A on the production of blankets in A will not cause the price charged to consumers of blankets to be higher in A than in B, since blankets can still be freely imported into A from B. But it will cause the price offered to producers of blankets in A to be reduced below that offered to producers of blankets in B. With the price of apples the same in both countries to producers and consumers this will interfere with the maximization of production but not with the optimization of trade.

These effects of a free-trade policy upon the optimization of trade and the maximization of production form the core of the case for free trade. It is easy to show that if a modified laissez-faire policy is adopted within each country and if, in addition, as a result of a modified free trade policy world trade is optimized and world production is maximized, then it will also automatically follow that the marginal conditions are fully satisfied for the *optimization of production and of effort*.

As far as the optimization of production is concerned, the adoption of domestic policies for modified laissez-faire will ensure that it is impossible within any one country to make one consumer better off without making others worse off by producing more of one product within that country for consumption within that country at the expense of producing less of another product within that country for consumption within that country.

In this sense we may say that production would be optimized nationally. It would be impossible to make any one consumer in A better off by making him give up the consumption of 1 blanket and by using the factors of production in A which were released by the contraction of A's blanket industry to produce for this consumer an additional amount of apples which he would prefer to 1 blanket. But would production necessarily be optimized internationally as well? Might it not be possible to make a consumer *in B* better off by making him give up the consumption of a blanket and by using the factors of production which might thereby be released from the blanket industry *in A* to produce for the consumer *in B* an additional amount of apples?

The answer is that this will not be possible if not only is production optimized nationally in A but trade is also optimized internationally between A and B. This proposition is illustrated in Table XV. Throughout that table we assume that the production of an apple and of a blanket in A has the same marginal cost of $1 (column *a*). If, then, A gives up the production of 1 blanket, she can produce 1 more apple at the same total cost (columns *d* and *e*). We wish to see in what conditions, if the change in world supplies of 1 more apple and 1 less blanket all fell on consumers in B, the total value of consumption in B might be increased (column *f*).

In case i we assume both that production is optimized nationally in A and that trade is optimized internationally between A and B. The optimization of production in A requires that the ratio between the marginal social values of the two commodities in A should be the same as the ratio between their marginal social costs. This is so in case i, where the marginal value of each commodity is $2 and the marginal cost of each commodity is $1 (columns *a* and *b*).[1] The optimization of trade between A and B requires that the ratio between the marginal values of the two commodities should be the same in B as in A. This is so in case i where the marginal value of each commodity is $3 in B and $2 in A (columns *b* and *c*).[2] If, now, 1 less blanket and 1 more apple is produced in A and B's consumption is changed by these amounts, the total value to B's consumers is unchanged. They gain an apple worth $3 and lose a blanket worth $3 (column *f*). Since production is optimized in A and trade is optimized between A and B, it is impossible to make consumers better off in B by changing the composition of A's production. Production is optimized internationally.

But if trade between A and B is not optimized (case ii), then it is possible to make B's consumers better off by altering the composition of A's production. In case ii the figures in column *c* differ from those in

[1] The absolute difference between the marginal value and marginal cost might be due, for example, to a 100 per cent consumption tax which falls in A at the same rate on all commodities. This, as we have seen, does not interfere with the optimization of production.

[2] The absolute difference between the marginal values in the two countries might, for example, be due to the fact that there was a higher general level of tax on the consumption of all commodities in B than in A.

TABLE XV

The Optimization of World Production

	Marginal costs in A	Marginal values in A	Marginal values in B	Change in production in A and in consumption in B	Change in cost in A	Change in value in B
	(*a*)	(*b*)	(*c*)	(*d*)	(*e*) = *d* × *a*	(*f*) = *d* × *c*
	Case (i). *Production in A optimized. Trade between A and B optimized*					
Apples	\$1	\$2	\$3	+1	+\$1 } = \$0	+\$3 } = \$0
Blankets	\$1	\$2	\$3	−1	−\$1	−\$3
	Case (ii). *Production in A optimized. Trade between A and B not optimized*					
Apples	\$1	\$2	\$6	+1	+\$1 } = \$0	+\$6 } + \$3
Blankets	\$1	\$2	\$3	−1	−\$1	−\$3
	Case (iii). *Production in A not optimized. Trade between A and B optimized*					
Apples	\$1	\$4	\$6	+1	+\$1 } = \$0	+\$6 } + \$3
Blankets	\$1	\$2	\$3	−1	−\$1	−\$3

case i. Because, for example, the consumption of apples is taxed in B at a higher rate than that of blankets while they are taxed at the same rate in A, the ratio between the marginal values of the two commodities is higher in B than in A. Trade between A and B is not optimized. It is now possible to make B's consumers better off by giving them 1 more apple and 1 less blanket to consume (column *f*), although this makes no greater claim on A's resources (column *e*). Production is not optimized internationally.

And similarly, if production is not optimized in A (case iii). Because, for example, of a higher tax on the production of apples than on that of blankets in A, the ratio between the marginal value of the two commodities (column *b*) differs from the ratio between their marginal costs (column *a*); production is not optimized in A. But the ratio between the marginal values of the two commodities is the same in A and in B (columns *b* and *c*); trade is still optimized between A and B. But because of the failure to optimize production in A it is now possible by giving B's consumers 1 more apple and 1 less blanket to consume to make them better off (column *f*) even though there is no additional strain on A's resources (column *e*).[1]

[1] The above argument has proceeded on the assumption that there are no marginal transport costs. But the argument could easily be generalized to allow for such transport costs. As in the problems of the optimization of world trade and the maximization of world production illustrated in Tables XIII and XIV, this would be found to make no difference to the general conclusion.

Thus we may conclude that if production is optimized within each country and trade is optimized between them, then production will be optimized internationally as well as nationally. It is also true that if effort is optimized nationally and production is maximized internationally, then effort will be optimized internationally as well as nationally. This can be shown in the following way.

The adoption domestically of modified laissez-faire policies will lead to the optimization of effort nationally in the sense that it will not be possible for anyone in A by exerting more effort in A to improve his own position without making anyone worse off. But will effort also be optimized internationally? May it not be possible for someone *in A* by exerting and applying more effort *in B* to improve his own position without making anyone else worse off? This will clearly be impossible if the marginal product of effort in B is the same as in A. If the individual in A has the correct balance between extra effort and the return to effort in A, and if the return to effort in B is the same as in A, he could not improve his position by applying in B a different amount of effort from that which he is applying in A. But if the return to effort in B differs from the return to effort in A, he might be able to do so.

Whether or not, therefore, our modified free-trade policy will have led to the international optimization of effort is seen to depend upon whether it will have led to the equalization of the marginal product of any one factor throughout the world. We shall postpone any discussion of this problem until Part III (Chapters XX–XXIII). At this point we need only say: that if free trade leads to the equalization of marginal products in the different countries, then it will have led to the full maximization of production internationally and so, as we have just shown, also to the international optimization of effort; that if free trade alone is insufficient to equalize marginal products throughout the trading countries, then the full maximization of world production requires the movement of factors from the country of low to the country of high marginal productivity; and that if production is thus maximized by the movement of factors, it will then once more follow, by the argument developed in the preceding paragraph, that effort will also be optimized internationally.

We may conclude, therefore, that the essential argument for free trade is that it will help to optimize world trade and to maximize world production and thus to maximize world economic efficiency. More precisely the case is that free trade in otherwise *utopian* marginal conditions will provide the remaining *marginal* conditions required for world economic *efficiency*. But we have not claimed to show (i) that it is desirable in a *second-best* world in which other marginal conditions necessary for economic efficiency are not fulfilled; or (ii) that it will necessarily give rise to any *structural* changes that may be desirable in the interests of economic welfare; or (iii) that it will ensure the marginal conditions necessary for economic *equity*. To these three aspects of the question we shall revert in Chapters XII–XVIII.

CHAPTER X

FORMS OF TRADE CONTROL: (1) TAXES AND SUBSIDIES

THUS the general case for free trade rests upon the contention that it will help to increase world economic efficiency. We shall turn to a critical examination of this case in Chapters XII–XVIII. But before we analyse the arguments for the imposition of trade controls we must catalogue the various forms which trade controls may take; and we must consider the differences in the effects which different trade controls may have upon the economy. This task we shall undertake in this and the following chapter. Only when we have done this shall we be in a position to consider whether there is any particular form of trade control which can be used to achieve any particular result in raising economic efficiency or in improving economic equity.

In this chapter we shall consider trade controls which are imposed for the purpose of influencing prices by means of taxes and subsidies; in the following chapter we shall consider those which operate through a control of the quantities of the products which may be produced, consumed, or traded, whether these be administered by the State licensing of private trade or by direct State trading.

Now taxes or subsidies may be imposed upon the import, export, total consumption, or total production of a commodity. We have, therefore, really eight forms of trade control to enumerate in this chapter:

1. An import tax.
2. An export tax.
3. An import subsidy.
4. An export subsidy.
5. A consumption tax.
6. A production tax.
7. A consumption subsidy.
8. A production subsidy.

We shall consider these 'pure' forms of tax and subsidy in this order, examining the problems of an import tax at length and then indicating briefly the application of the same principles of analysis in the other cases. We shall then have to say something of those 'complex' forms in which various taxes and subsidies of different kinds are combined into a single scheme of control.

We start then with the familiar import duty. If a duty is imposed upon the import of a particular commodity into country A, the obvious and universal effect in a competitive economy—provided always that some amount of the commodity is in fact imported after the imposition of the duty—is that the market price of the commodity to its purchasers in A will be above its market price to purchasers in B by the amount of the duty as well as by the amount of any cost of transport from B to A. We shall call the import duty levied on a unit of the commodity expressed as a ratio of the price of the import exclusive of the import duty the *ad valorem* incidence of the import duty. Thus if a particular imported commodity in A costs the consumer in A \$120, and if the import duty is \$20, the *ad valorem* incidence of the duty is said to be 20 per cent $\left(\text{i.e. } \frac{\$20}{\$120-\$20}\right)$.

In passing it may be worth noting that in order to obtain a correct estimate of the *ad valorem* incidence of a duty on any particular commodity it is very important to define correctly the commodity which is, in economic fact as opposed to legal fiction, the subject of the duty. Suppose that it costs \$10 to produce a shirt in B and to transport it to A, and suppose that, of this total cost of \$10, \$4 represents the cost of producing the necessary raw cotton for the shirt. Suppose, further, that raw cotton can be imported into A free of import duty, but that there is a \$2 import duty on a shirt when it is imported into A, so that the market price of a shirt in A is \$12. It might appear that the *ad valorem* incidence of the import duty on shirts is 20 per cent $\left(\text{i.e. } \frac{\$2}{\$12-\$2}\right)$. But in fact it is not the production of shirts including the production of the necessary raw cotton which is being protected in A. Raw cotton can be freely imported into A to be made up into shirts in A. The whole of the \$2 import duty in A protects the making up of the raw cotton into shirts. The market price in A of the making up of the foreign shirt, i.e. of the shirt less the value of its raw cotton content, is only \$8; and thus the *ad valorem* incidence of the duty on the manufacturing of shirts from raw cotton, which is what is in fact being protected, is $33\frac{1}{3}$ per cent $\left(\text{i.e. } \frac{\$2}{\$8-\$2}\right)$. In what follows when we speak of the *ad valorem* incidence of an import duty we shall have in mind, unless we state the contrary, its *ad valorem* incidence measured in respect to that commodity or part of a commodity which it is in fact designed to protect.

Import duties may in fact be imposed on an *ad valorem* or on a specific basis or on a combined basis. Thus the duty of \$2 on the imports of shirts into A might be legally fixed as a duty of 20 per cent on the value of imported shirts (the *ad valorem* basis), or as a duty of \$2 on each shirt imported (the specific basis), or as a combined duty of, say, 15 per cent of the value of the imports plus a duty of $0·5 on each shirt (the combined basis). Whether the *ad valorem* or the specific basis is chosen may be of importance from certain points of view. Thus the *ad valorem* basis means that the actual duty levied on cheaper qualities of a commodity will be lower than the duty levied on the more expensive qualities, whereas the specific duty levies the same absolute duty on all qualities and in this sense discriminates by imposing a higher *ad valorem* incidence and so a larger protective effect on the cheaper grades. Another important difference is that in a period of generally declining commodity prices the *ad valorem* incidence and so the protective effect of a set of specific duties will rise, and during a period of generally rising commodity prices it will fall, whereas the protective effect of a set of *ad valorem* duties will not be affected by general changes in the level of commodity prices. Differences of this kind, while they are of importance for certain purposes, are not relevant to the central analysis of this volume, and we shall not consider them. In what follows we shall take for granted that import duties have a given *ad valorem* incidence and so a given protective effect, and shall examine the consequences of given import duties on this basis.

In analysing the economic effects of an import duty it is essential to take into account the effects of the use by the taxing authority of the revenue collected by means of the duty. The neglect of this side of the question is a frequent source of muddle and error. Broadly speaking, there are three things which the taxing government can do with the revenue: (i) it can use the additional revenue to add to its budget surplus; (ii) it can use the additional revenue to increase its own consumption of goods and services—for defence, justice, education, and the other forms of communal consumption of goods and services; and (iii) it can use the additional revenue to decrease the revenue which it raises in other forms of taxation on its citizens—income tax, death duties, indirect taxes on consumption, and so on.

Before we consider the different effects of these different ways of using the revenue from the import duties, we must make clear certain general assumptions which we shall make throughout this volume about governmental policy. Following the analysis of Volume I, we assume variable exchange rates to keep the balance of payments between A and B in equilibrium. Abstracting from changes in autonomous capital movements, we shall therefore assume that the total value of A's exports *after* adding any export duty or subtracting any export subsidy (and so the amount received from foreigners) always varies by exactly the same amount as the total value of A's imports *before* adding any import duty or subtracting any import subsidy (and so the amount paid to foreigners for A's imports). In the context of our present problem of the effect of a new import duty this means that, if out of any given income buyers in A spend the same amount at market prices on goods and services as a whole, the additional amount which they now pay in import duties as revenue to the State must cause an exactly equal reduction in the amount (at factor cost) spent on A's own products.[1] To this extent the levying of the new import duties is deflationary. Since, following the analysis of Volume I, we shall assume throughout this second volume that the authorities adopt a domestic financial policy for internal balance, we shall assume that by means either of fiscal or of monetary policy the authorities take steps to stimulate once more the total domestic expenditure in A to the extent necessary to offset these primary deflationary tendencies of the raising of additional import duties.

Bearing these general assumptions in mind, we can now consider the effects of the government using the additional revenue from the import duties in any of the three ways enumerated above.

Suppose, first of all, that it adds the new revenue to its budgetary surplus. The net deflationary effects of the raising of the new revenue will not be directly offset by the government's use of the revenue. It will on our assumptions, therefore, adopt either a fiscal or a monetary policy to stimulate total domestic expenditure in A. If it adopts a fiscal policy for this purpose, this will involve the stimulation of demand either by an increased governmental demand for goods and services or by a reduction in other taxes to stimulate private buying. In effect, the new revenue would not have been used to add to the budgetary surplus, but would have been used either to increase the governmental demand for goods and services—the second possibility enumerated above—or to reduce other taxes—the third possibility in our list. If, however, the authorities adopt a monetary policy for the offsetting of the deflationary effects of the collection of the additional import duties, then the increased revenue may be added to the budget surplus. In this case supplies of money must be increased and the rate of interest reduced until additional private investment has been stimulated or private savings discouraged (and so consumption encouraged) by an amount equal to the direct deflationary effect of the raising of the new import duties.

Because of our assumption that the exchange rate will be varied so as to keep the balance of payments in equilibrium, this statement is true

[1] It might be that the rise in the market price of imported products would induce buyers in A to spend a greater total amount on all products, i.e. to finance part of the payment of import duties out of money that would otherwise have been saved. Or they might conceivably be induced to spend a smaller total amount on all products, if their demand for imports were very elastic and the next preferred use of the funds were to save them. In the former case something rather less, and in the latter case something rather more, than the whole revenue from the new import duties would represent a decline in the demand of private buyers for A's own products.

however much or little of the investment expenditure which is stimulated by the reduced interest rates is devoted to the purchase of imported goods and services. Such a demand for imported goods would tend to cause a deficit in the balance of payments, whereupon the exchange rate would depreciate until the expenditure on imports had been reduced or that on exports increased to an extent sufficient to remove this deficit. At this point there would in fact have been a net increase in the demand for A's products equal to the total amount of the additional domestic expenditure which was stimulated by the expansionary monetary policy. This conclusion would need some modification if the change in monetary policy led to a change in the autonomous flow of capital between A and B. Suppose that the lower interest rates in A caused an outflow of capital funds from A to B. This would cause a strain on A's balance of payments; A's currency would depreciate until the value of A's imports had been reduced and the value of A's exports increased by an amount sufficient to cover the flow of capital funds from A to B. This improvement in A's balance of trade would itself be an inflationary factor so that the fall in the rate of interest and the consequential stimulus to domestic expenditure in A would need alone to be somewhat less than the initial deflationary gap caused by the raising of the new import duties.

Little need be added to the above argument to cover the case where the government uses the revenue from the additional import duties to cover new governmental expenditure on goods and services. Because of our assumption that the exchange rate varies so as to maintain external balance, this will indirectly cause an exactly equivalent increase in the demand for A's products, a conclusion which will not in this case be complicated by possible capital movements due to changes in the level of interest rates in A. If the direct deflationary pressure due to the levying of the new import duties is exactly equal to the amount of new revenue raised, that is the end of the story. If the deflationary pressure is slightly less than this, then the expenditure of the whole of the new revenue by the government on goods and services may need to be combined with a somewhat more restrictive monetary policy in order to deal with the small net inflation resulting from the total fiscal change; and vice versa if the deflationary pressure due to the raising of the new revenue from import duties were greater than the total revenue so raised.

The third possibility is that the revenue from the new import duties should be used to reduce the revenue from other duties such as the income tax. If the persons who enjoyed the reduction in the income tax spent the whole of their additional tax-free incomes on goods and services, so far as the total inflationary or deflationary situation is concerned the case would be exactly the same as when the government used the whole of the revenue to increase its own demand for goods and services. The only difference would be that the increased demand for goods and services which offset the deflationary effect of the increased import duties would be a private demand instead of a public demand. But private taxpayers may save some part of the reduction in their income-tax payments. If they save a larger part out of their reduced income-tax payments than the possible reduction in the savings of those who are paying the higher price for the newly taxed imports—which seems a probable case—then in this case the reduction of the income tax by an amount equal to the increased revenue from import duties will have to be combined with some expansionary monetary policy to stimulate investment or to reduce savings if all deflationary effects are to be avoided.

In this volume we shall be primarily interested in the use of import duties as protective devices, that is to say, as instruments designed to reduce the demand for certain foreign products in favour of certain home-produced products. In order to isolate, as far as possible, these aspects of import duties we shall neglect the first two possible uses of the revenue from import duties enumerated above (p. 158) and shall restrict ourselves to the third possibility, namely, the use of the revenue to reduce other forms of taxation and, in particular, a general income tax. If the revenue is used to add to the budget surplus and this is combined with an appropriately expansionist monetary policy, then the use of the revenue will ultimately cause an increased demand for new capital goods. This will represent a shift of demand away from those particular products which the consumers would have bought if they had not had to pay the new import duty on to those capital goods and services which will be bought as a result of the increased expenditure on capital development stimulated by the expansionist monetary policy. If the revenue from the import duties is used to finance increased governmental demand for goods and services, there is an even more obvious shift of demand away from the goods and services which the consumers would have bought if they had not had to pay the new import duties on to the goods and services needed for the enlarged public-expenditure programme.

On the other hand, if the increased revenue is used to finance a reduction in the general level of income tax, consumers as a whole will be given by the reduced income tax an increase in spendable incomes which is exactly equal to the total amount of money which they have to pay in increased import duties. There will be a shift in demand, but a shift which is solely due to the change in the price relationships between imported and home-produced products. They could go on buying exactly the same amount of each product as before, the increased duty payable on imported goods being exactly offset by increased tax-free incomes.[1] They will in fact buy less imports and more of other things because the price of imports has risen relatively to that of other things. We shall thus have succeeded in isolating the price effects of the import duty in shifting demand.

For this reason, throughout the rest of this volume, unless it is otherwise expressly stated, we shall assume that the revenue from any trade taxes is used to reduce the general level of income tax. And, similarly, we shall assume that the funds required for the payment of any trade subsidy are raised, not by reducing a budget surplus or some existing programme of public expenditure, but by raising a general income tax.

So much for the general nature of import duties. Exactly similar points can be made about export duties. They may be imposed upon a specific or an *ad valorem* basis. As in the case of an import duty, a specific export duty will rise or fall in *ad valorem* incidence according as the general level of prices moves in a downward or upward direction; and a specific duty will fall with greater incidence upon the cheaper qualities.

Moreover, the *ad valorem* incidence of an export duty must be carefully considered in relation to the thing or activity the export of which is actually taxed. Thus, suppose that a country taxes the export of shirts costing \$10 at a rate of \$2 a shirt. The *ad valorem* incidence of this export duty would naturally be reckoned as 20 per cent $\left(\text{i.e. } \frac{\$2}{\$10}\right)$.[2] But suppose that the country also exports raw cotton, that the raw cotton content of the shirt is \$4, and that raw cotton can be exported free of export duty. Then the whole of the \$2 tax on the export of the shirt is a tax on the export of the home manufacturing process embodied in the shirt, and no part is a tax on the raw cotton embodied in the

[1] It is to be observed that this statement need not be modified by allowing for changes in the terms of trade which may cause foreigners to bear some part of the burden of the tax, thus making home consumers better off. For if home consumers did buy exactly the same amount of imported products and of home products as before, then there would be no reduction in the demand for foreign products and so no change in the terms of trade against the foreigner. The change in the terms of trade is in our case always a consequence of the purely protective effect of the import duty in shifting demand away from foreign products. The statements in the text do, however, need to be modified in such a way as to allow for the possible effects upon the relative demand for imports and for home produce which may result from the redistribution of real income at home which results from the fact that those who gain from the reduction in the income tax may not be the same persons as those who lose from the higher price of imports.

[2] The shirt costs \$10 at home and sells for \$12 in the foreign market, including the tax. The *ad valorem* incidence is 20 per cent, which can be reckoned as \$2 on the cost of \$10 or as \$2 on the price ex tax in the foreign market $\left(\text{i.e. } \frac{\$2}{\$12-\$2}\right)$.

shirt. The tax is, therefore, economically best represented not as a tax of 20 per cent $\left(\text{i.e. } \frac{\$2}{\$10}\right)$ on the export of shirts but as a tax of $33\frac{1}{3}$ per cent $\left(\text{i.e. } \frac{\$2}{\$10-\$4}\right)$ on the export of the manufacturing processes embodied in the shirt.

The revenue from export duties can be used in either of the three ways which we discussed in the case of import duties: to add to the budget surplus; to finance an enlarged programme of governmental expenditure on goods and services; or to finance a reduction in other taxes and, in particular, in a general income tax. For the reasons discussed at length in the case of import duties we shall assume that the revenue from any export duties is used to reduce the general level of income tax. By this means we shall be able to abstract from those extraneous shifts in demand as between home-produced and foreign products which would be likely to result from the stimulation of capital expenditure by the expansionist monetary policy which, to preserve internal balance, would have to accompany an increase in the budget surplus or from the increased governmental demand for the particular goods and services needed for its new programme of public expenditure.

The raising of export duties is likely in itself to exert a deflationary pressure. Because of the policy of exchange-rate adjustments for the preservation of external balance, we assume that the total expenditure by foreigners on the country's exports varies in the same way as the total amount of the home country's purchasing power which is devoted to the purchase of imports. But of the foreigners' expenditure on the home country's export an amount equal to the export duties is siphoned direct into the government's budget without its having represented a demand for the home country's labour or other factors of production. This deflationary influence is, however, counterbalanced in part at least by the inflationary effects of the reduction in income tax which accompanies the improved budgetary position. We assume that to the extent to which there remains any slight net deflationary influence (or appears any slight net inflationary influence) this is offset by a suitably expansionary (or restrictive) banking policy for the maintenance of internal balance.

So much then for trade taxes, whether they be levied on imports or on exports. A complete catalogue of different forms of trade control would, of course, have to include a discussion of trade subsidies, paid either on imports or on exports. In fact subsidies are merely negative taxes; and the consideration of import and export subsidies would require only a reproduction of the preceding arguments reading everywhere 'subsidies' for 'taxes', 'increase' for 'decrease', 'expenditure' for 'revenue', and so on. The reader will be left to carry out this exercise for himself in the case of import subsidies which are in fact of little importance. But export subsidies are in fact a very important form of trade control; and in their case it may therefore be worth while briefly to recapitulate the main arguments.

An export subsidy of $2 will cause a shirt which costs $10 to produce in the home country and which sells at $10 in the home country to be offered for sale at $8 in the foreign country.[1] This may naturally be reckoned as a subsidy with an *ad valorem* incidence of 20 per cent. It may be levied on an *ad valorem* basis, in which case this incidence remains always the same, or on a specific basis, in which case the incidence is higher in times of low prices than in times of high prices and higher in respect to low qualities than in respect to the more expensive qualities. And once again it is important to realize what it is, the export of which is in fact subsidized. If the shirt contains $4 of home-produced raw cotton the export of which was not subsidized, then a subsidy of $2 on a shirt which cost $10 inclusive of raw-cotton content, but only $6 exclusive of raw-cotton content, would be best regarded as a subsidy of 33⅓ per cent on the export of the manufacturing processes embodied in the shirt.

In considering export subsidies we shall assume that the funds required for their finance are raised, not by cutting down either a budget surplus or existing governmental programmes for expenditure on goods and services, but by levying an additional income tax. The payment of the export subsidy is likely to be inflationary, since the home exporters now receive the subsidy in addition to the amount which foreign importers spend on the home country's exports. On the other hand, the raising of the funds by means of a higher income tax will exert a deflationary influence. We assume that any remaining net inflationary or deflationary influence is offset by an appropriate monetary policy, so that internal balance is preserved.

One very important distinction to make in considering the effects of import and export duties and subsidies depends upon whether the duty or subsidy is levied or paid on all imports or exports at the same *ad valorem* rate, or whether it is levied or paid only in respect to the trade in a particular commodity or group of commodities. Thus, if in country A an *ad valorem* import duty of 10 per cent is levied on all imports of every kind, then, so far as concerns the direct effect of this on prices charged to consumers for imports, it is equivalent to a depreciation of A's money in terms of B's money by 10 per cent. In the one case consumers in A pay 10 per cent more in their own money to obtain the foreign exchange to purchase imports from B; and in the other case

[1] Except, of course, to the extent that this price is raised by transport costs or by an import duty in the foreign country.

they pay the same amount of their own money in order to obtain the foreign currency, but must pay also a 10 per cent duty when the foreign goods are imported. The difference between a 10 per cent *ad valorem* duty on all imports and a 10 per cent depreciation of the currency, so far as trade is concerned, is, of course, that the former does not directly affect the terms on which consumers in country B can purchase A's exports whereas the latter does. When A's currency is depreciated by 10 per cent in terms of B's, then consumers in B can obtain 10 per cent more of A's money with a given amount of B's money. From the point of view of the direct effect upon their trading relationship with A it is to the consumers in B exactly as if the government in A had paid a 10 per cent subsidy on the price of all products exported from A to B.

It follows, therefore, that a 10 per cent duty on all imports into A from B combined with 10 per cent subsidy on all exports from A to B, is exactly equivalent in its direct effects on trade to a 10 per cent depreciation of A's currency. But we are assuming that exchange-rate variations are used to preserve external balance between A and B. A 10 per cent duty on all imports into A combined with a 10 per cent subsidy on all exports from A, on the assumption that the sum of the elasticities of demand for imports in A and B was greater than unity,[1] would cause an improvement in A's balance of trade. This improvement in A's balance of trade would lead to an appreciation of A's currency in order to restore external balance. But when A's currency had appreciated by 10 per cent, the appreciation of the exchange rate would have exactly offset the effects both of A's general tax on imports and of her general subsidy on exports. So far as any real effects on trade were concerned, it would be exactly as if nothing had happened at all. We can, therefore, reach the very important conclusion that, on the assumption that the price mechanism is used to keep the balance of payments in equilibrium, a general tax on imports combined with an equal general subsidy on exports makes no real difference at all; it will have only a purely monetary effect, such as a change in the exchange rate.

An exactly similar argument could, of course, be used to show that a 10 per cent general import subsidy combined with a 10 per cent general export tax would have exactly the same effect upon trade as a 10 per cent appreciation of the currency, and would, therefore, in effect be exactly offset by an actual 10 per cent depreciation of the currency. It would thus have no real effect upon trade.[2]

[1] See Volume I, Chapter VI, pp. 68–73.

[2] These conclusions rest upon the assumption that in real terms the effect of a 10 per cent exchange-rate adjustment on items in the balance of payments other than imports and exports is the same as the effect of a combination of a general 10 per cent trade tax and subsidy. But there are at least two reasons why this is not likely to be strictly true. First, some items in the balance of payments other than trade items may be fixed payments set in terms of the

This argument will also enable one to see the truth of another very important proposition about general taxes or subsidies on all imports or exports. Suppose that a 10 per cent tax levied on all exports is removed and is replaced by a 10 per cent tax levied on all imports. This change is exactly equivalent to the introduction, into a system containing only a 10 per cent export duty, of a 10 per cent duty on all imports combined with a 10 per cent subsidy on all exports, this latter subsidy in fact merely cancelling the effect of the existing 10 per cent duty on all exports. But, as we have just argued, a 10 per cent duty on all imports plus a 10 per cent subsidy on all exports must be accompanied by a 10 per cent depreciation of the home country's exchange rate in order to preserve external balance; but the change will have no other real effect at all. Thus, provided always of course that the same use is made of the revenue from the two duties, a 10 per cent general import duty will have exactly the same real effect as a 10 per cent general export duty; the only difference will be that with the export duty the exchange value of the country's currency must be depreciated by 10 per cent as compared with its position with the import duty. And similarly, of course, it could be shown that a general 10 per cent export subsidy would have exactly the same real effect as a general 10 per cent import subsidy, provided always that the unfavourable effect upon the balance of trade caused by the substitution of the import subsidy for the export subsidy was offset by a 10 per cent depreciation of the foreign-exchange value of the country's currency.[1]

But import and export duties and subsidies are not, of course, normally levied indiscriminately on all imports or on all exports. Commercial policy consists very largely in deciding which particular

money of the one country or the other. Clearly such payments would be differently affected by the two types of adjustment. Secondly, the theorems in the text would be true only if the 10 per cent tax and 10 per cent subsidy referred to all transactions and not only to transactions in respect of commodity trade. The conclusions of the text, therefore, need some modification, because the effect on items other than trade may mean that an appreciation of somewhat more or less than 10 per cent may be necessary in order to preserve external balance when a 10 per cent import tax is imposed together with a 10 per cent export subsidy. But if trade items make up the largest part of all transactions both on the payments and the receipts side of a balance-of-payments account, the statements in the text will approximate to the truth.

[1] The plausibility of these conclusions may be increased by remembering that trade between A and B consists essentially in the exchange of A's products for B's products. A trader purchases A's products, sells them in B, with the proceeds he buys B's products, and sells them in A. If he is taxed on his trade turnover, it makes no difference to him whether he is taxed 10 per cent on the value of the A-products which he sells in B (an export duty in A) or on the value of the B-products which he sells in A (an import duty in A). Either arrangement will have the same real effect upon his trade; and it will have the same real effect upon the total trade of all traders, provided that both taxes are paid to the same taxing authority and that the revenue from both is used in exactly the same way.

imports or exports should be subject to what particular rates of duty or subsidy; and in the following chapters of this volume we shall have to make frequent reference to this sort of choice.[1]

Up to this point in this chapter we have been considering taxes and subsidies on those parts of the production or consumption of a commodity which enter into international trade. But taxes and subsidies may be introduced in respect to the total production or consumption of a commodity. Such taxes or subsidies may be introduced on an *ad valorem* or on a specific basis; but we shall not discuss the differences brought about by this distinction, since the same principles are at work as those which we have already considered in the case of imports and exports. Moreover, the revenue from taxes on the total production or consumption of a commodity may be employed in any of the three ways which we discussed in the case of the revenue from import or export duties, namely, to add to a budget surplus, to finance an enlarged governmental programme of expenditure on goods and services, or to reduce a general income tax; or the funds needed to finance subsidies on the total production or consumption of a commodity may be raised from any one of the three corresponding sources. For the reasons given in connexion with taxes and subsidies on imports and exports we shall assume throughout that the revenue from taxes on total production or consumption is used to reduce a general income tax and that the expenditure on subsidies on total production or consumption is financed by an increase in a general income tax.

The effect upon international trade of a general tax or subsidy in respect to the total home production or consumption of a particular commodity is likely to be as follows.

A tax on the total consumption of a commodity in any country is likely to cause a decrease in the import or an increase in the export of that commodity. Its effect will be to raise the price to the home consumer of the commodity above the price received by the home or foreign producer. This will cause some reduction in the total home demand for the product. If the product is imported, some of the reduction in the home demand will take the form of a reduced purchase of imported supplies; if the product is exported, some of the surplus supply which is no longer necessary to satisfy the reduced home demand will be available for export.

A tax on the total home production of a commodity will decrease exports or increase imports. It will discourage home production so that, in the case of an exported product, less will be available for export or, in the case of an imported product, larger imports will be needed to satisfy the home demand.

[1] We have already pointed to some of these considerations in Chapter XXIII of Volume I.

A subsidy on the total consumption of a commodity will encourage the home consumption of it, so that either larger imports will be purchased or less of the commodity will be available for export.

Finally, a subsidy on the total production of a commodity will encourage home production so that more of the commodity is available for export or less imports are needed to satisfy the home demand.

Thus we can summarize the effect of various forms of tax and subsidy on the international trade in the commodity concerned in the way outlined in the first three columns of Table XVI. Thus imports can be discouraged by an import tax, or by a subsidy to total home production of the commodity, or by a tax on the total home consumption of the commodity. For each of the four purposes shown at the head of each of the first four columns of the table any one of three basic instruments of tax and subsidy policy may be used to bring about the desired result.

But the method adopted will have fundamentally different results. Consider, for example, the measures which might be taken to reduce imports. An import duty of, say, 20 per cent *ad valorem* will cause the price of the imported product both to the consumer and the producer to rise by 20 per cent above the price in the supplying market. It will thus disturb the maximization of world production since the ratio of the price offered to producers of this commodity to the price offered to producers of other commodities will be raised in the taxing country relatively to the other country. It will also disturb the optimization of world trade, since the ratio of the price payable by consumers of this commodity to the price payable by consumers of other commodities will also be raised in the taxing country relatively to the other country. It will not, however, disturb the national optimization of production or the national optimization of trade, since the price paid by consumers will remain equal to the price received by producers of the commodity in the taxing country.

But a production subsidy of 20 per cent will have a quite different effect. It will disturb the maximization of world production in the same way as a 20 per cent import tax, because the ratio of the net price (including subsidy) offered to producers of this commodity to the price offered to producers of other commodities will be raised by 20 per cent in the subsidizing country relatively to the other country. But it will not disturb the optimization of world trade, since it will not introduce any new factor tending to cause the ratio of the price charged to consumers for this commodity to the price charged for other commodities to differ as between the two countries. It will, however, disturb the national optimization of production and effort because it will cause the price (including subsidy) received by the domestic producer to rise relatively to the price charged to the domestic consumer.

Finally, a tax on total consumption will not disturb the maximization

TABLE XVI

The Effect of Different Forms of Tax and Subsidy

Purpose and method of tax or subsidy				Does the chosen method disturb the		
Reduction of imports by	Expansion of imports by	Reduction of exports by	Expansion of exports by	maximization of world production?	optimization of world trade?	national optimization of production and effort?
(1) Import tax	(1) Import subsidy	(1) Export tax	(1) Export subsidy	Yes	Yes	No
(2) Production subsidy	(2) Production tax	(2) Production tax	(2) Production subsidy	Yes	No	Yes
(3) Consumption tax	(3) Consumption subsidy	(3) Consumption subsidy	(3) Consumption tax	No	Yes	Yes

of world production since, unlike an import tax, it will keep down the price offered to the home producer as well as the price offered to the foreign supplier, so that the ratio of the price offered to the producer of this commodity to the price offered to the producers of other commodities will not be raised or lowered in the taxing country relatively to the other country. It will, however, like an import duty, disturb the optimization of world trade since it will tend in the same way to raise the ratio of the price charged to consumers for this product to the price charged for other products in the taxing country relatively to the other country. Moreover, like a production subsidy, it will disturb the national optimization of production and effort; but it will do so in the reverse direction, since it will tend to reduce the price offered to the producer relatively to the price charged to the consumers of the product.

A similar analysis could be applied to the three methods of tax or subsidy which were appropriate for the expansion of imports, the reduction of exports, or the expansion of exports. The reader must work the results out for himself, but the conclusions are summarized in the last three columns of Table XVI. It is in fact plausible that a tax or subsidy on trade (i.e. on imports and exports) should be found to disturb the maximization of world production and the optimization of world trade, but not the national optimization of production or of effort; that a tax or subsidy on total production should be found to disturb the maximization of world production and the national optimization of production and of effort, but not the optimization of world trade; and that a tax or subsidy on total consumption should be found to disturb the optimization of world trade and the national optimization of production and effort, but not the maximization of world production.

So far we have considered what we may call simple cases of a tax or a subsidy on one line of trade, production, or consumption. But in fact there may be more complex forms in which a combination of different taxes and subsidies is used to affect imports or exports. Such arrangements often take the form in which a tax is combined with a subsidy in such a way that the revenue from the tax is used to finance the subsidy.[1] Such arrangements we shall call 'levy-subsidy' arrangements. They may take many different forms, as can be seen from an examination of Table XVI. For our purpose it will suffice to give one simple illustration.

Suppose that it is desired to give 30 per cent protection to the home producers of wheat against wheat imported from abroad. Suppose that \$200 m. worth of wheat is being imported into the country and \$100 m.

[1] Such arrangements do not offend against our assumption that the revenue from commodity taxes is always used to reduce the income tax and the expenditure on commodity subsidies is always financed from a rise in the income tax. If the revenue from a tax is exactly equal to the expenditure on a simultaneous subsidy, on our assumption there will be a zero net effect upon the income tax, and the tax revenue will in effect be used to finance the subsidy.

worth is being produced at home. A simple import duty of 30 per cent on the import of wheat into A would raise $60 m.—abstracting for the moment from any alteration consequent upon the duties in the quantity or the ex-tax price of imported wheat. On our assumptions this revenue of $60 m. would be used by the government in A to finance a reduction in the income tax in A. But there is a second possibility. A duty of 10 per cent could be levied on the $200 m. worth of wheat imports, and the resulting revenue of $20 m. could be paid in subsidy to the home producers of wheat. This enables a rate of subsidy of 20 per cent ($20 m. on $100 m.) to be paid on home production. Once again 30 per cent protection would be given—10 per cent by import duty and 20 per cent by production subsidy.

There are in fact a number of different administrative arrangements by means of which this levy-subsidy might be operated. Thus a 10 per cent tax on all consumption, the proceeds from which were used to subsidize home production, would in fact achieve exactly the same effect economically. Total consumption of home produce plus imports is $300 m. (i.e. $100 m. + $200 m.); a 10 per cent duty on this would raise $30 m.; this would enable a subsidy to be paid on the home produce of $100 m. at a rate of 30 per cent; and of this subsidy of $30 m., $10 m. would merely offset the 10 per cent duty raised on the consumption of home-produced wheat. The effect would be exactly the same as the 10 per cent duty on imports only, the revenue from which was used to pay only a 20 per cent rate of subsidy on home production.

Another arrangement which would have exactly the same effect would be a tax of 30 per cent on imports (raising $60 m. in revenue) the proceeds of which were used to pay a subsidy at the rate of 20 per cent on the total consumption of $300 m. of imported and home-produced wheat. Once again the home-produced wheat would obtain a subsidy of 20 per cent when it was sold for consumption, and the imported wheat would bear a net tax of 10 per cent, the 30 per cent import duty being partially offset by the 20 per cent consumption subsidy. This again would be equivalent to a tax of 10 per cent on imports the revenue from which was used to pay a subsidy of 20 per cent on home production.

A levy-subsidy arrangement may thus have many forms which may tend to disguise its true economic meaning;[1] but it can always be reduced to a simple formula in which one thing is subject to a net tax and something else enjoys a net subsidy financed by the revenue from the tax.

[1] This will be particularly the case if, for example, a subsidy on total wheat consumption is paid by one department (say, a Ministry of Food) and is called a subsidy paid on all consumption for the promotion of nutrition, while a charge on imported wheat is levied by another department (say, a Ministry of Finance) on some other ground. The net effect of the two, however, is the economically significant factor.

In the example which we have given, the protective effect of the 30 per cent import duty is the same as that of the 10 per cent import duty combined with a 20 per cent production subsidy. The home producer in both cases gets a 30 per cent preference in price over the foreign supplier. The effect on the maximization of world production is the same in the two cases. But in their effects on the optimization of world trade and on the national optimization of production and effort they differ. The import duty causes a larger difference than the levy-subsidy between the price to consumers of the product in A and B, and thus causes a larger disturbance to the optimization of world trade; the levy-subsidy causes a larger divergence domestically between the price charged to consumers and the price received by producers and thus causes a larger disturbance to the national optimization of production and effort. But all such effects can be regarded as the combined effect of one of the 'simple' taxes with one of the 'simple' subsidies of Table XVI. We shall treat all levy-subsidy arrangements in this way.[1]

[1] One particular method of arranging for combinations of taxes and subsidies on imports and exports (but not on production and consumption) is by means of multiple-exchange-rate systems under a regime of exchange control. Such methods have been described in Chapter XX of Volume I.

CHAPTER XI

FORMS OF TRADE CONTROL: (2) QUANTITATIVE RESTRICTIONS AND STATE TRADING

THE second main class of instruments of trade control is the quantitative restriction by administrative action of the amount of private production, consumption, or trade of a particular commodity or group of commodities which is allowed to take place. Such quantitative restrictions may apply to production, consumption, exports, or imports. Thus the producers of a commodity may be permitted under a licensing scheme only to produce certain quotas of output; consumers under a rationing scheme may be permitted to consume only a certain quantity or value of the commodity; exporters may be licensed to sell abroad only a restricted quota of the product; and importers may be licensed to import from abroad only a limited quantity or value of the commodity.

In some essential respects quantitative restrictions have the same effects as taxes. Thus a tax on the production of a particular commodity will discourage the producers of that commodity and thus cause a reduction in its supply. This reduction in its supply will cause consumers to offer a higher price for the commodity which is now scarcer on the market, and the reduction in output may have driven out the high-cost units of production so that the producers can continue to supply the remaining output at a somewhat lower price to themselves. The tax will, therefore, lead to a reduction of production until the price offered by consumers has so risen and the price needed by producers to cover their costs has so fallen that the margin between the higher price paid by consumers and the lower price received by producers is sufficient to cover the tax.

Exactly the same degree of reduction of production could have been achieved by the alternative method of a quantitative restriction on the amount of the product which producers are permitted to produce. This would normally tend to cause the same rise in the price offered by consumers for the commodity, because the supplies of the commodity are equally diminished under the two systems and the scarcity is therefore the same in the two cases. The reduction in production brought about by quantitative restriction may also as a general case be assumed to have the same effect upon producers' costs as an equal reduction brought about by a tax. Thus a quantitative-restriction scheme is likely to have the same effect as a tax (i) in reducing the amount of the thing restricted or taxed, and (ii) in causing a divergence between the demand price offered for, and the supply price of, the thing restricted or taxed.

In these respects quantitative-restriction schemes can be devised which have comparable effects to those of taxes. But it is not, of course, easy to imagine quantitative restriction schemes which have the same effects as subsidies. It is one thing to restrict by licensing the amount of a thing which an individual may produce, consume, import, or export; it is a totally different administrative matter in a free community to compel an individual to produce, consume, import, or export a quantity greater than he finds it profitable to do. The reader may turn to the first four columns of Table XVI (p. 169), cross out all methods of control which depend upon subsidy, and replace the word 'tax' by the word 'restriction'. He will then obtain the following account of the effects upon international trade which may be achieved by various forms of restriction scheme:

Reduction of Imports	*Expansion of Imports*	*Reduction of Exports*	*Expansion of Exports*
Import restriction. Consumption restriction.	Production restriction. —	Export restriction. Production restriction.	Consumption restriction. —

In the case of a tax the divergence between the raised demand price and the lowered supply price will accrue to the government of the taxing country and on our assumption will be used to reduce the general level of income taxation. But with a quantitative restriction scheme the divergence between the demand price and the supply price will not automatically accrue to the government. Some of the most significant differences between the tax method and the quantitative-restriction method can be best examined by considering what happens to this price margin in the case of quantitative restrictions. This analysis we have already undertaken at some length in the case of quantitative import restrictions in Chapter XXI of Volume I, where we reached the conclusion that (apart from the bribery of the officials administering the scheme) the margin between the demand and supply prices might accrue (i) to the licensed middlemen trading between the producers and the consumers, (ii) to the foreign producers of the commodity, (iii) to the domestic consumer of the commodity, and (iv), in the form of a licence fee, to the government administering the scheme. Exactly the same four possibilities clearly exist in the case of quantitative restrictions over domestic production, domestic consumption, or export. We shall not repeat at this point the detailed analysis already given of the conditions which are likely to lead to each of these four possibilities. The reader must turn to Chapter XXI of Volume I. Here we shall assume as the normal case that with the licensing system goes some fee or charge for the licence which means that, as in the case of a tax, the administering government receives as part of its revenue the consequential divergence between the price charged to the purchaser and the price offered to the supplier. And, as in the case of the taxes discussed in the last chapter, we shall assume that this additional revenue is used as a means of reducing the general level of income tax from its previous level.

There is one more essential difference between a quantitative restriction and a tax. An *ad valorem* tax is a governmental intervention which fixes the *ad valorem* rate of divergence between the price which the purchaser pays and the price which the seller receives and then leaves the market to determine how much shall be bought and sold. A quantitative restriction on the other hand fixes the amount which may be bought and sold and then leaves the market to determine the *ad valorem* rate of divergence between the price which the purchasers would be willing to pay for that amount of the commodity and the price at which the suppliers would be willing to supply that same amount. If the *ad valorem* rate of tax and the quantity licensed for purchase or sale are appropriately chosen, the two forms of intervention can achieve, broadly speaking, the same result in any given market situation. But the effect of any subsequent change in the market situation will be very different in the two cases. Suppose, for example, that the demand for the product is subsequently increased for one reason or another so that consumers offer a higher price for the same amount of the product. With a fixed *ad valorem* rate of tax the amount bought and sold will increase until the demand price has so fallen again and/or the supply price has so risen that the *ad valorem* divergence has fallen back to its previous level. But with a fixed quantitative restriction the amount bought and sold will remain the same, but the *ad valorem* divergence between the price offered by buyers and the price acceptable to suppliers will increase so as to give a new market equilibrium with the same volume of transactions. This distinction will be seen to be of great importance when we come to discuss the second-best arguments for trade controls in Chapters XII–XV.[1]

[1] Such is the general analysis of the effects of a quantitative restriction. But in Chapter XXI of Volume I a number of elaborations and modifications of this analysis have already been developed. In particular, attention is there paid to the case in which the direct control limits not the *amount* but the *value* of a commodity which may be bought. There is also some discussion of the effect which various ways of administering the restriction may have upon the extent to which the trade is monopolized or monopsonized and of the effect which various ways of distributing the licences may have upon the real costs of supplying the commodities. These points are, of course, equally relevant for the analysis undertaken in this volume; but it would be tedious to repeat them all here.

Another instrument through which a government can control the volume of trade is through the institution of State-trading monopolies. Thus the State could theoretically at least reduce (or increase) the volume of imports (i) by setting up a State import monopoly which then proceeded to import less (or more) than would otherwise have been imported, (ii) by socializing the whole domestic production of the commodity and then proceeding to produce more (or less) than would otherwise have been produced, and (iii) by instituting a State monopoly for the consumption of the product and then proceeding to consume less (or more) than would otherwise have been the case. In practice, it is always conceivable that the State should monopolize the import or export trade in a product or that it should monopolize the home production of that product. But the State monopolization of the final consumption of a product would be meaningless in those many cases where the good or service concerned is one which must ultimately be enjoyed by the individual citizen, except in the sense that the State might set up a monopoly which would have the sole right to purchase the commodity from the home and foreign producers and which would then distribute the commodity in some more or less arbitrary manner to the individual consumers.

In an economic system in which other activities are carried on in a more or less free competitive regime the consequences of the State monopolization of production, consumption, or trade in any commodity are essentially similar to the consequences of State intervention through taxes or subsidies and through quantitative restrictions which we have examined in the last two chapters. Consider the problem of restricting imports by some State action directly influencing imports. This could be done by an import duty, by a scheme of import licences restricting the volume of privately imported supplies, or by the institution of a State monopoly for the import trade which then bought imports from the foreigner and resold them in the domestic market only on a restricted scale. If the rest of the economy remained free and competitive, each of these three schemes would have essentially the same effects. The restriction of the amount demanded from the competitive foreign suppliers would reduce the price at which they would be willing to supply; the restriction of the supplies available to the competitive home consumers would raise the price which they would offer; and there would thus arise a divergence between the new demand and supply prices for the imported product. In the case of the import duty this price margin would cover the tariff; in the case of the quantitative import restriction it could and, in accordance with the assumption made above (p. 175), it would be made to accrue to the State budget through the charge of an appropriate import licence fee; and in the case of the State-trading monopoly it would represent a profit on the trade turnover which would be available for the State budget.

Similarly, any State monopoly over production, consumption, or export which was used to restrict the turnover would cause a margin to develop between the State monopoly's buying prices or costs and its selling prices or revenue. This profit would accrue to the State budget; and for the reasons given in Chapter X we shall assume that it is used to reduce the general level of income tax below what it would otherwise be. Conversely, a State monopoly which was used to raise the level of production, consumption, or trade above the competitive level would raise the State monopoly's buying prices or costs above its selling prices or revenue. This would involve a loss which, like a subsidy on the turnover, would have to be financed out of the State budget. Here again, for the reasons given in Chapter X, we shall assume that the funds necessary to meet this loss are found by raising the general level of income tax.

In two respects, therefore, a State-trading monopoly is likely to be more like a tax or subsidy system than is a quantitative restriction of private trade. In the first place, a State-trading monopoly like a system of taxes or subsidies can be used to restrict or to expand the volume of trade, whereas a quantitative licensing of private trade can be used only to restrict. In the second place, with a State-trading monopoly or a system of taxes any divergence between the price paid by the ultimate consumers and the price paid to the original supplier will accrue as a revenue to the State in the form of a trading profit or of a tax revenue, whereas in the case of a quantitative restriction the special profit, as we have seen on p. 174, may accrue to other specially interested parties.

The third main difference between a quantitative restriction and a tax we have seen (p. 175) to consist in the fact that subsequent changes in supply and demand will cause the amount to remain unchanged and the divergence between the demand and supply price to vary in the case of a quantitative restriction, whereas it will cause the quantity to vary and the price divergence to remain unchanged in the case of a tax. Whether a State-trading monopoly will in this respect be more like a tax or more like a quantitative restriction cannot be determined *a priori*. It will depend upon the policy adopted by those in charge of the State monopoly. If their policy is to fix a quantity and to keep it fixed regardless of subsequent variation in demand and supply conditions, it will be more like a quantitative restriction. If, on the other hand, their policy is to make a more or less fixed monopolistic rate of profit on turnover, it will be more like a tax.[1]

[1] The discussion of this and the preceding paragraph is to suggest that State trading and excise or customs duties are like each other and are both to be contrasted with the quantitative licensing of private trade. In certain purely

But there is one respect in which State trading may give rise to problems which are essentially different from those which arise when all trade is in private hands and is subject only to taxation, subsidization, and quantitative limitation. These problems arise when the institution of a State import (or export) monopoly in country A is matched by the institution of a State export (or import) monopoly in country B. This is a not improbable or unusual case. Suppose that country A sets up a State-trading organization which has the monopoly over the import of blankets from B into A and that this import monopoly then begins to use its monopolistic power to exploit the private competitive exporters of blankets in B. It is a quite natural outcome that a State monopoly over the export of blankets from B should be set up in B to bargain with the State import monopoly in A.

In such circumstances of so-called bilateral monopoly the State import monopoly in A and the State export monopoly in B must come to agreement upon some 'barter' deal between the blankets (which B is exporting) and the dollars (with which A is paying and which represent purchasing power over the general output of A-products). The deal may be, for example, that B should provide 175 blankets this year in return for \$350 in payment from A, i.e. 175 blankets at a 'barter' price of \$2 a blanket making a total payment of \$350. Now we assume (i) that the export monopoly purchases the blankets in B from a competitive industry in B which is also able to sell the blankets in a free market in B to B's consumers and that the State export monopoly in B pays a price (which may or may not correspond to the barter price of \$2 which is charged to A's import monopoly) which is just sufficient to obtain the necessary supplies of 175 blankets from this free production-consumption market in B; (ii) that any profit (or loss) which the State export monopoly in B may make by acquiring the 175 blankets at a market price in B which is lower (or higher) than the barter price at which it sells them to A's import monopoly is used to lower (or is covered by raising) a general income tax in B; (iii) that similarly the State import monopoly in A sells the 175 imported blankets in a free market within A in which blankets are freely produced and consumed in A at a price which may or may not correspond to the barter price of \$2 which is paid to B's export monopoly; and (iv) that any profit (or loss) made by A's import monopoly as a result of a divergence of the barter price from the free market price in A is used to lower (or is covered by raising) the general level of income tax in A.

Now we can best analyse the economic significance of the different

---

economic effects this is undoubtedly true. But from certain other political and administrative aspects, which are not the main subject of this study, it may of course be more relevant to make the contrast between the taxation and quantitative licensing o fprivate trade on the one hand and State trading on the other.

barter deals which may be reached between the two trading monopolies in A and B by considering the relationship between the three relevant price relationships—first, the barter price at which the two trading monopolies exchange blankets for dollars; second, the market price of blankets in B; and, third, the market price of blankets in A. There are certain propositions which we can lay down about the relationships between these three prices.[1]

(1) If the market price of blankets in the importing country A is higher than the market price in the exporting country B, there is 'undertrading' in the product, in the sense that the two trading monopolies by fixing another barter deal in which rather more blankets were exchanged for rather more dollars could make the citizens in both countries better off than before. Thus, suppose that the free-market price of a blanket in A is \$3 and in B is \$2. This means that consumers in A would be better off by having 1 more blanket to enjoy if they had to sacrifice anything less than \$3 worth of A-products in return for the extra blanket, and that consumers in B would be better off by giving up 1 more blanket if they could receive anything more than \$2 worth of A-products in return. If, therefore, the two trading monopolies would strike another barter deal in which 1 blanket was added to the total exports of blankets from B and something between \$2 and \$3—say, \$2½—to the total amount which the import monopoly in A was to pay for these blankets, the welfare of the citizens in both countries would be raised. Such an expansion of trade would help to optimize world trade.

(2) Conversely, if the market price of blankets in A was less than the market price of blankets in B, the two monopolies are 'overtrading'. Suppose the free-market price is \$2 in A and \$3 in B. This means that if the consumers in A imported 1 less blanket and so had 1 less blanket to enjoy, they would still be better off if they reduced their exports of A-products by anything more than \$2 worth so that they had more than \$2 worth of additional A-products to consume instead of the extra blanket. Simultaneously, if, by refraining from exporting 1 blanket, the consumers in B had an extra blanket to consume they would be better off provided that they gave up the import of anything less than \$3 worth of A-products. Thus, if the two State-trading organizations fixed a new barter deal in which 1 blanket was subtracted from the total number to be exported from B to A and \$2½—or any other sum between \$2 and \$3—was subtracted from the total amount to be paid from A to B in return, the citizens of both countries would be better off. Such a contraction of trade would help to optimize world trade.

[1] In what follows we shall assume that there are no transport costs. This enables the arguments to be put clearly and succinctly. But the points would be essentially the same even if allowance were made for some costs of transport.

(3) Suppose that after the barter deal it so turns out that the market price in A is the same as the market price in B and that both coincide with the barter price between the two trading monopolies. Then this would mean that the two trading organizations happened to have hit upon the deal which corresponds exactly with the flow of trade which would take place in free-trade conditions. In conditions of free trade the trade would adjust itself, in the absence of transport costs, until the market price of blankets was the same in the two countries and this price would correspond also to the price at which the traders in A actually purchased blankets from the traders in B. Certain quantities of blankets would then flow from B to A and of dollars from A to B. It is only if the two State-trading monopolies happened to fix on these same quantities in their deal that the quantities of blankets and of A-products in both A and B would be such as to give rise to market prices in A and B which were both equal to the price actually paid by A-traders to B-traders for the blankets. A barter deal between the two State-trading organizations which happened to leave all three prices at the same level can be seen to correspond to the free-trade position by asking what would happen if the monopoly privileges of the State-trading organizations were then removed. Since the market prices of blankets in A and B are the same and since these are also equal to the prices at which blankets are internationally traded, there would be no reason to expect any change either in the quantities traded or in the prices.

(4) Suppose next that the barter deal between the two State-trading organizations was such that the barter price was the same as the market price in, say, country B but differed from the market price in A. Suppose the market price in A was higher than the barter price and the market price in B. Then this would correspond to the flows of trade which would result if a free-trade policy were adopted in B but a duty on imports were imposed in A. Since the barter price is the same as the market price in B, the removal of the State export monopoly in B would not be likely to cause any change in the flow of export trade from B since B's traders can obtain the same price in the international market as they can obtain at home. The position corresponds to a free-trade position for B. But in A the price in the home market exceeds the barter price at which blankets are obtained from B. The removal of the State import monopoly in A would, therefore, leave private importers in A with an incentive to increase imports from B. This incentive would, however, be removed by the imposition of an import duty in A equivalent to the difference between the price in B and the price in A. This import duty would merely take the place of the profit margin which the State import monopoly in A makes by selling the blankets in A at a market price in excess of the barter price at which it had acquired them.

(5) Suppose now that the barter deal is one which causes the barter price greatly to exceed or fall below the two market prices in the two countries. Suppose that the market prices in the two countries are the same but that the barter price greatly exceeds them. Then the State import monopoly in A will be making a loss, since it is paying a high barter price for the imports which it sells at a low market price in A. On the other hand, the State export monopoly in B will be making a profit, since it is paying a low market price in B to acquire blankets for export for which it is obtaining a high barter price. If the State import monopoly were removed in A, competitive traders would have an incentive to import less since a loss is made on imports at present; and this incentive would be removed if the authorities in A paid a subsidy on the import of blankets into A at a rate equivalent to the present loss made by the State import monopoly. Similarly, if the State export monopoly were removed in B, competitive traders would have an incentive to export more since a profit is at present being made; but this incentive would be removed if the authorities in B imposed an export duty on blankets at a rate corresponding to the profit at present made by the State export monopoly in B. Moreover, since the market price of blankets in A and B is the same, the total loss made by the State import monopoly in A (due to the difference between the barter price and the market price in A) would be exactly equal to the profit made by the State export monopoly in B (due to the difference between the barter price and the market price in B). In other words, the position in which the two market prices are the same but the barter price is higher is one which could be sustained without any import or export monopoly if the government in A subsidized the import trade and the government in B taxed the export trade by the same amount.

But this is a position which could be sustained by a totally different mechanism. Suppose that the government in A raised by a general income tax this amount of money and instead of using it to subsidize the import trade or to finance a State-trading loss on its import trade paid the money over to the government of B; suppose, further, that the government of B used this money, instead of any funds obtained from the taxation of its export trade or from a State-trading profit on its export trade, to finance a general reduction in the income tax in B, and suppose that free trade was then permitted between A and B. Then the result would be exactly the same as that which occurred as a result of the State-trading deal in which the barter price was high (and thus favourable to B) but the market prices in A and B were equal to each other at a lower level.

That this is so can be seen from the following argument. Under the two systems the consumers in A would be in exactly the same position. In the one case they would be taxed to subsidize imports or to make up for a State-trading loss; and in the other they would be taxed to the same amount to raise the funds to make a direct transfer to the government in B. In both cases they would, therefore, have the same income to spend. Moreover, in both cases imported goods would cost them the same price; in the one case the high barter price paid by A's import monopoly would tend to raise the price of blankets in A above the market price at which they could be obtained in B but the whole of this would be offset by the loss on imports sold in A, and in the other case free trade would directly allow the import of blankets in A at the market price charged for them in B. Similarly, the consumers in B would under both systems be in the same position. Their incomes would be increased by the reduction in the income tax made possible in the one case by the profits made on the export of blankets to A at the high barter price and in the other case by the direct transfer of money from A's government. Moreover, the price they received for their exported blankets would in both cases be the same as the market price in A; in the one case part of the high barter price paid by A's import monopoly would fail to reach the producers in B because of the export tax or the profit of the export monopoly in B, and in the other case free trade would permit the direct sale of the blankets at the market price in A.

So far, therefore, as the citizens of A and B are concerned there is no difference in the two situations. The only difference is in the pure mechanics of the transfer of purchasing from A's citizens to B's. In the State-trading case real income is transferred from A to B through the barter price for blankets (i.e. the amount of dollars given by A's authorities to B's authorities for a given number of blankets) being unnaturally high in the sense that it is higher than the price of blankets either in A's or B's market; in the tariff-subsidy case real income is transferred from A to B by the raising of a tax on blanket exports by B's government the source of which is not in fact a higher price charged to A's consumers of blankets or a lower price enjoyed by B's producers of blankets but simply the equal subsidy paid on these same blankets by A's government; and in the free-trade case the transfer is made by the straightforward transfer of funds from A's government to B's government.

We reach the following important conclusion. If as a result of a barter deal between State-trading monopolies in A and B a position is reached in which the market prices in A and B are the same but the barter price is higher than these market prices, this is equivalent to either (*a*) a position in which a tax is levied on B's exports by B's government and an equal subsidy paid on A's imports by A's government, or (*b*) a position in which free trade is allowed but an exactly equal sum is transferred directly from A's consumers to B's consumers by a rise of income tax in A and a reduction in B. And conversely, of course, a case in which the barter price was low relatively to the two equal market prices would be one which corresponded to a direct transfer of purchasing power from B's citizens to A's.[1]

We have argued above that if the market prices differ in A and in B, the two State-trading monopolies could strike another bargain which would leave the citizens in both countries better off than before. Let us suppose that barter deals of this kind are always avoided. This would mean that we could confine our attention to deals in which the market price in A was left equal to the market price in B. But the barter price might differ from these free market prices. As we have seen if the barter price of blankets (B's export) is greatly above the market prices in A and B, this represents a deal which is more favourable to B than the free-trade position would produce; and vice versa.

Therefore even if all deals are avoided which would still permit both countries to be better off than before, there remains the question what determines whether the final bargain will be favourable to A or to B. What factors are likely to give A the bargaining strength, and B the bargaining weakness, which will enable A to extract better terms from B? The pressure which A can exert on B is to refuse to trade at all with B unless B gives improved terms, and the resistance which B can put up against A is similarly to refuse to trade at all except on the old terms. Bargaining strength or weakness can be measured, therefore, by the ability and willingness to face a period of no trade. The longer the period of no trade which A thinks that it would be worth while risking in order to obtain a given improvement in the terms of the barter deal and the shorter the period of no trade which B thinks that it would be worth while risking in order to resist a given deterioration in her own position, the more likely is A to be able to obtain some improvement in the terms of the exchange by threatening otherwise to break off trading relations.

It is not, of course, necessary that the trade should actually be broken off for any period in order that these elements of bargaining strength and weakness should in fact be operating. Indeed, if A knows B's position and B knows A's position accurately, trade will never be broken off in actual fact. Both sides can always gain from trade, and a period of no trade means a net loss to both taken together. But even though trade is never broken off, the knowledge of each other's relative willingness to do without trade in order to exact better terms from the other will remain as a main determining factor of the actual bargain struck.

Now the more favourable the initial terms are to A (and the less

[1] In Appendix 2 (pp. 578–85) some numerical examples are given of the various types of barter deal which are possible, and these deals are also represented geometrically.

favourable, therefore, to B) the smaller will be A's bargaining power to obtain a still further improvement and the greater will be B's bargaining strength to resist this further change. A's bargaining power to exact a still further improvement will be low for two reasons. First, the more favourable are the initial terms to A (i.e. the more A is already gaining from the trade), the more will A stand to lose from any given period without any trade at all. The more favourable are the terms to A, the greater the cost to A of carrying out any threat to cut off trading relations. Secondly, the more favourable are the existing terms to A (i.e. the more A-products and B-products which A's consumers are already enjoying) the less does A gain by achieving any further small improvement in the terms (i.e. the less important is it to A's consumers to achieve a small further amount of these products to consume). For the higher is the standard of living in A, the less important it is to raise that standard by a further absolute amount.

The combination of these two factors means that the more favourable the terms of trade become to A, the less is A's bargaining strength in exacting yet a further improvement. For exactly converse reasons, the less favourable the terms of trade become to B, the greater will be B's bargaining power to resist A's pressure; for, first, B will face a smaller total loss from breaking off the trade and, second, B will find any further small deterioration in the terms of her trade more important to resist. If the initial terms were very favourable to B, therefore, it would be probable that A could exact better terms from B; but if the initial terms were very favourable to A, B could probably exact better terms from A. The ultimate bargain would settle down at some intermediate position, where neither country's bargaining strength is excessively large relatively to the other's.

What then determines whether A's and B's relative bargaining powers will balance each other at a point which is rather more favourable to A or rather more favourable to B? We have to consider the factors which would make it easy or difficult for A or for B to face a period of no trade. The following are the conditions which are likely to make the terms of trade settle at a position relatively favourable to A.

(1) If the A-products and B-products are good substitutes for one another in A's consumption, then A can more readily face a period of no trade with B. When A breaks off trade with B, she will no longer export A-products or import B-products; she will, therefore, have more of the former and less of the latter. If the former can fairly readily replace the latter in A's consumption, then A will be ready to face the severance of trade relations. But if at the same time the A-products and B-products are poor substitutes for one another in B's consumption, then when trade stops B cannot readily use the B-products which she

was formerly exporting to A to replace in her consumption the A-products which she was formerly importing from A, and B will be the less willing to face a stoppage of trade.[1]

(2) If in A it is relatively easy to turn from the production of A-products to the production of B-products, a period of trade stoppage will be the less costly because A can use the factors previously employed in exporting A-products to B to make (albeit at some extra cost) the B-products previously imported from B. But if at the same time B's endowment with resources makes it difficult for her to turn from the production of B-products to those of A-products, B cannot reduce the cost of a trade stoppage by this means.

(3) If A exports essentials to B and imports luxuries from B, A will be able to face a period of trade stoppage more readily than can B.

(4) If B-products can be stored so that A's trading monopoly can build up a strategic reserve of imports, then A's monopoly can put itself into a position to be able to face a considerable trade stoppage with smaller loss. If A-products cannot be stored, B's monopoly cannot put itself in this position.

(5) Finally, if the importance to A's consumers of having yet more A-products and B-products does not diminish very rapidly as they have more of them, then the importance to A's trading organization of obtaining more and more favourable terms will not rapidly diminish as the terms improve. On the other hand, if the importance to B's consumers of avoiding a given additional loss of A-products and of B-products does not rise at all rapidly as they have less of them, then the importance to B's trading organization of resisting any further worsening of its terms of trade will not increase rapidly as A's terms of trade improve. This will help to tip the balance in A's favour.

[1] If A-products and B-products are good substitutes in A's consumption they are likely to be good substitutes in B's consumption also. But this is not necessarily so. Suppose A to be a country of Snobs which exports Cups and B a country of Democrats exporting Saucers. The Snobs in A would die sooner than be seen drinking tea out of one of their own Cups without a Saucer for it to stand in; the Democrats in B will quite willingly drink tea out of one of their own Saucers if they can't get any Cups from A. The two products are good substitutes in B's consumption, but bad substitutes in A's consumption, and B will be able to exert a bargaining pressure on A.

CHAPTER XII

THE SECOND-BEST ARGUMENT FOR TRADE CONTROL: (1) THE RAISING OF REVENUE

THE case for free trade which was argued in Chapter IX depended upon the assumption that in each of the trading countries there was a successful policy of modified laissez-faire. As the reader will remember this includes the assumption that revenue is raised for the necessary purposes of State expenditure by means which do not involve any divergence between marginal values and costs throughout the economy. But as we have seen, this is a hopelessly unrealistic assumption, unless the State itself owns sufficient income-bearing property to cover its net expenditure. All forms of practicable taxation, whether direct or indirect, are likely to cause a divergence between marginal values and costs in the transactions subject to the tax. An income tax causes the value of the marginal social net product of the income earner to exceed his net reward; an indirect tax causes the marginal value of the product to exceed its marginal cost.

Suppose first that it is decided that a general income tax, whether progressive or not, is the type of taxation which will raise revenue with the least interference with economic welfare in each of the trading countries. It is considered, that is to say, that any adverse effects of the general income tax upon the optimization of effort are less serious than the adverse effects of alternative forms of indirect taxation upon the optimization of production or of distribution. Then there will be little or no argument to be produced in favour of abandoning a free-trade policy because of the existence of the divergences between rewards and marginal products which will be introduced into the trading countries by the general income taxes. Such general income taxes do nothing to cause the price charged to consumers for a particular product to differ in country A and in country B. They do nothing, therefore, to disturb the optimization of world trade. Moreover, such general income taxes—assuming always that factors of production cannot in any case move from one country to another but only from one industry to another within any country—will do nothing to interfere with the maximization of world production. The income tax falls at a given rate on a factor's earnings regardless of the industry in which the factor is employed. With free trade between A and B the market price of apples will be the same in A as in B, and similarly with the market price of blankets. With a uniform income tax in A the net tax-free earnings from the production and sale of an apple will be lower in A than in B; but the net tax-free earnings from the production and sale of a blanket will be lower in A than in B by the same proportion. The ratio of the marginal cost of producing an apple to the marginal cost of producing a blanket will be the same in A as in B, and in consequence world production will continue to be maximized (see p. 147).

In passing, it is interesting to observe that exactly the same argument could be applied to the raising of revenue in either country either by a general uniform rate of tax on all lines of domestic production (whether the goods were consumed at home or abroad) or by a general uniform rate of tax on all lines of domestic consumption (whether the goods were produced at home or abroad). Indeed, in a 'closed' economy which has no contacts with other countries and therefore no imports or exports, a 10 per cent tax on all final products bought must be the same thing as a 10 per cent tax on all final products sold, which is the same as a 10 per cent tax on all income earned from the production and sale of the real national output.[1]

But with an 'open' economy which exports some products to the rest of the world and imports others from the rest of the world the proposition is not quite so obvious. Let us start with the case of a 10 per cent tax on all incomes earned in a country. This is clearly the equivalent of a tax of 10 per cent on all the goods and services produced and sold by the income-earning factors of production. Now in so far as the goods are produced at home for consumption at home it clearly makes no difference whether the 10 per cent tax is called a tax on their production or a tax on their consumption. As far as international trade is concerned, our production tax of 10 per cent (which, as we have seen, would be the equivalent of a 10 per cent income tax) would involve the levying of a tax of 10 per cent on all goods produced at home and exported for consumption abroad and the levying of no rate of duty on goods produced abroad and imported for consumption at home.

Suppose now that we changed this uniform 10 per cent production tax (which, as we have seen, is equivalent to a 10 per cent income tax) into a uniform 10 per cent consumption tax. In so far as goods are produced at home for consumption at home no change is needed. We merely call the tax a tax on the consumption instead of a tax on the production of these products. But in so far as foreign trade is concerned we would have to remove the 10 per cent duty on all exports of home products and to impose a 10 per cent duty on all imports for home consumption. We have, however, already shown in Chapter X (p. 166) that to replace a 10 per cent uniform export duty by a 10 per

[1] This proposition is true only if the tax on purchases or sales is confined to purchases or sales of finished products. If it falls also on sales of intermediate products (e.g. on coal used in manufacturing blankets as well as on coal and blankets sold for final consumption), then lines of production which include many intermediate stages will be more heavily taxed than those which do not. (See p. 63.)

cent uniform import duty makes no real difference. It will, of course, have a monetary effect. With the export duty the money prices of the taxing country's imports will be the same in both countries but the money prices of its exports will be lower in the taxing country than in the rest of the world; with the import duty the money price of the taxing country's exports will be the same in both countries but the money price of its imports will be higher in the taxing country than in the rest of the world. The shift from a general export duty to a general import duty would, therefore, have to be accompanied by an inflation of all money prices and costs in the taxing country, a deflation of all money prices and costs in the rest of the world, or an appreciation of the taxing country's currency. When this had happened there would be no real change at all in any price relationship or levels of production, consumption, or trade.

Now it is easy to see that neither the general uniform 10 per cent production tax nor the general uniform 10 per cent consumption tax would interfere with the optimization of world trade nor—subject to the assumption that factors of production could not in any case move from one country to another—with the maximization of world production. The imposition of a uniform 10 per cent tax on all production would not cause the price charged to consumers for apples or for blankets to be different in the taxing country, A, from the rest of the world, B; and in a free market trade would continue to be optimized. The imposition of a uniform 10 per cent tax on all production in A would, of course, cause the price offered to producers for apples and for blankets to be 10 per cent lower in A than in B; but it would cause the A-price to be lower than the B-price by the same percentage in the case of each product, so that there would be no interference with the maximization of production. (See p. 147.) Conversely, the imposition of a 10 per cent uniform tax on all consumption would not cause the price offered to producers for apples or for blankets to be different in A than in B; and in a free market production would continue to be maximized. The imposition of a uniform consumption tax would, of course, cause the price charged to consumers for apples and for blankets to be higher in A than in B; but it would cause the A-price to exceed the B-price by the same percentage in the case of each commodity, so that trade would continue to be optimized. (See p. 144.)

The case is, however, very different if a tax is imposed upon the production or consumption not of all final products but upon the production or the consumption of one particular product. In general, one may say that the imposition of a tax upon the production of a particular commodity in a particular country will interfere with the maximization of world production but not with the optimization of world trade, whereas the imposition of the tax upon the consumption of the commodity will interfere with the optimization of world trade but not with the maximization of world production.

Let us consider first an export product (e.g. apples in A). If a production tax is imposed, then A's apples will be taxed whether they are consumed in A or exported to B. The price charged to consumers of apples will be the same in A as in B; and with all other prices the same in both countries trade will be optimized. But the price offered to producers of apples will be lower in A than in B; and with all other prices the same in both countries production will fail to be maximized. If a consumption tax is imposed on apples in A, then the price charged to consumers for apples will be higher in A than in B by the amount of the tax, and trade will not be optimized. But in these circumstances the price offered to producers will be the same in both A and B, since A's and B's producers will obtain the same price for apples sold in B and no tax will be deducted; and in consequence production will be maximized.

We can deal with an import product (e.g. blankets in A) in exactly the same way. A production tax in A will fall on A's blankets consumed in A but not on B's blankets imported into A. The price charged to consumers for blankets will be the same in A as in B; and trade will be optimized. But the price received by A's producers will be below that received by B's producers by the amount of the duty; and production will not be maximized. A consumption tax in A will fall on A's blankets consumed in A and also on B's blankets imported into A. The price charged to consumers of blankets will now be higher in A than in B, and trade will not be optimized. But the price received by producers of blankets will in this case be the same in A as in B, since both will receive the market price in A less the tax; and in consequence production will continue to be maximized.

We can summarize the argument up to this point in the following way. A general 'purchase' or 'sales' tax levied at the same rate on all final products but on no intermediate products will not interfere at all with the optimization of trade or the maximization of production whether it is imposed as a production tax (exempting all imports but taxing all exports) or as a consumption tax (exempting all exports but taxing all imports). What it must not do is to tax both imports and exports or to exempt both imports and exports. On the other hand, a 'purchase' or 'sales' tax levied on only one particular product will disturb the optimization of trade but not the maximization of production if it is levied as a consumption tax (i.e. exempting exports but not imports); and it will disturb the maximization of production but not the optimization of trade if it is levied as a production tax (i.e. exempting imports but not exports).

The other possibility is that the revenue should be raised not by a tax upon the production or the consumption of the product in question, but upon the trade in the product. This would, of course, interfere with both the optimization of world trade and the maximization of world production. A tax on the export of apples from A to B will cause the price charged to consumers and the price offered to producers to be higher in B than in A by the amount of the tax; trade will not be optimized nor production maximized. Similarly, a tax on the import of apples into A from B will raise the price charged to consumers and that offered to producers in A above its level in B; and once again trade will not be optimized nor production maximized.

Consider the blanket industry in A, blankets being a product which is also imported from B. Suppose that a revenue is to be raised of a certain amount by the taxation of blankets in A. If we start with a tax levied solely on those blankets which are produced in A for consumption in A, we have a production tax. If now we include imported blankets as well in our tax and levy it upon A's blankets and upon imports of B's blankets, we have a consumption tax. If we went further and continued to levy the tax upon B's blankets consumed in A but exempted A's blankets from the tax, we should have a pure trade tax. There are in fact two distinct objects of tax, A's blankets produced and consumed in A and that part of B's blankets which is sent to A for consumption in A. If we start by raising our given revenue solely by taxing A's blankets, we have a pure production tax. But now, in order to raise the same total revenue, we may slightly reduce the rate of tax on A's blankets and replace the revenue so lost by a small tax on imports of blankets from B. If we go on with this process long enough we shall reach the point when the rate of duty on A's blankets has been so lowered and that on imports of B's blankets has been so raised, that they are at the same level and we have the pure consumption tax. If we still go on lowering the duty on A's blankets and replacing the lost revenue by raising the duty on B's blankets imported into A, we shall now raise the rate of tax on imports somewhat above that on home products. The end of this process is the pure trade tax when the rate of duty on home products has been reduced to zero and the whole revenue is being raised on the imported supplies.

Where in this process of shifting incidence of the tax from home products on to imports do we wish to stop from the point of view of economic welfare? In attempting to deal with this question in the remaining pages of this chapter we shall assume that we are concerned only with the effects of the tax arrangement upon world economic efficiency. We shall assume that the distributional weights are the same for all citizens of the world, i.e. that a $1 increase of income should be equally regarded whether it accrued to the citizens of B or to the citizens of A and whether it accrued to landlords or wage-earners. It may seem an unreal assumption that, though we are dealing with a tax imposed by the national government of A to raise a revenue for its own expenditure, yet the policy-makers in fact give equal weight to the welfare of all citizens in all countries. We do so, however, solely in order to illustrate certain principles of economic efficiency. In Chapter XVII we shall turn to the use of commercial policy for the purpose of affecting the distribution of income between the citizens of A and of B by altering the terms of trade between them, and the analysis of that chapter can easily be used to modify our present conclusions. We shall start off our analysis with another very important assumption, namely that, apart from the divergences between marginal values and costs due to the particular tax under consideration, there are no other divergences in the rest of the world economy. We must assume that policies of modified laissez-faire are adopted in A and in B, including the raising of revenue in B and of the remainder of the governmental revenue in A by means (such as progressive poll-taxes) which do not introduce a divergence between marginal values and costs. This again is an unnatural assumption which we make merely in order to isolate certain central considerations which depend solely upon the nature of the market for the taxed product.

The problem with which we are concerned is clearly a problem of the second-best. The utopian solution would no doubt be to give up altogether the use of this particular tax which introduces a divergence in this market between marginal values and costs and to turn to the raising of the whole of the revenue in a way which does not have this effect. But given that a certain amount of revenue is to be raised in this way we have a second-best problem to solve. Given that a tax is being levied on, and causes a divergence between marginal values and costs in, the production of blankets in A for consumption in A, would it improve matters to tax imports as well even though that were to introduce a new divergence between values and costs in the market for imported supplies? [1]

There are two general observations to be made on this question.

In the first place, whether or not a movement of taxation away from the basis of a tax on production towards the basis of a tax on consumption will do good or harm, will depend upon whether, in the case of this particular product, it is more important to preserve the maximization of production or the optimization of trade. If the product is one in the case of which there is very little possibility of productive resources being moved into or out of that line of production (because, for example, blankets are produced with one distinct specialized factor of

[1] The rest of this chapter is merely a particular application of the general technique developed in Chapter VII. The reader must be familiar with that technique if he wishes to understand what follows.

production and apples with another), and if, at the same time, the product is one which in consumption can fairly readily be substituted for others, then a shift away from a production tax to a consumption tax is liable to do harm. The production tax will not much harm the use of productive resources which will be employed to produce what they do produce in any case; but the consumption tax might do much harm in interfering with and diminishing the desirable trade whereby the citizens of A give up the consumption of some of their apples in order to increase their consumption of B's blankets. And conversely, if there was little or no substitutability between apples and blankets in consumption but if economic resources could be fairly readily shifted from producing one to producing the other, a tax on the consumption of blankets in A might cause little harm (since much the same amount of blankets and apples would be consumed in any case) while a production tax in A might do serious damage to total world production by diverting A's resources too much out of blanket production and into apple production.

But there is a second general consideration to bear in mind. Suppose that we have a 10 per cent production tax on A's home output of blankets. When we turn this into a consumption tax by taxing imported blankets as well, we are not considering the addition of a 10 per cent tax on imported blankets to the 10 per cent tax on home-produced blankets. Our concern is only to raise the same revenue as before and if we broaden the basis of taxation we can lower the rate. Broadly speaking, if imports are of the same magnitude as home production we shall be comparing a 10 per cent duty on home production on the one hand with a 5 per cent duty on home production plus a 5 per cent duty on imports on the other hand. To add a 10 per cent divergence in the case of imports to a 10 per cent divergence in the case of home production may do good in so far as it diverts transactions away from the import market (in the case of which there was at first no excess of marginal value over marginal cost) on to the market for the domestic products (where throughout marginal value has exceeded marginal cost by 10 per cent). But it will also do harm in so far as the diversion of transactions in the import market which do begin to have a divergence between marginal values and costs is on to completely different products (say, apples) where there is no divergence between values and costs at all. However, to add a 5 per cent divergence on imports and simultaneously to reduce the divergence on home supplies from 10 per cent to 5 per cent is much more likely to increase welfare. The diversion out of imported products will be smaller in amount and subject to a lower rate of divergence; and the diversion on to home products will be greater in so far as the duty on home products is being reduced. There is always some presumption in favour of the largest base for a tax because this gives a lower rate of tax spread equally over a large range of transactions. In the case of the imported product, blankets consumption is greater than either domestic production or imports alone so that we start with a presumption in favour of a general consumption tax.

Suppose then that we have a 5 per cent rate of tax on the consumption of imported blankets. Suppose then that we reduce very slightly (say, from 5 per cent to 4·9 per cent) the rate of duty on imports and increase by a similar slight extent, i.e. to the extent necessary to preserve the yield of the revenue, the rate of duty on home production. Will world economic welfare be increased or reduced?

There is likely to be (i) some increase in A's imports of blankets because the reduction in the tax on such imports will increase the incentive to purchase them in A and to export them in B, and (ii) some decrease in A's home production of blankets because the rise in the tax on them will reduce the incentive to purchase them and to produce them. Now if the elasticity of supply of the production of blankets in A is low and the elasticity of supply of the export of blankets from B is high, then the increase in imports—(i) above—is likely to be larger than the decrease in home production—(ii) above. The supply of exports from B will be much encouraged by the better price obtained because of the reduced import tax in A, while the home production of blankets in A will not be much discouraged by the reduced price obtainable because of the raised tax on their production. The extent to which in such circumstances the increase in imports will exceed the reduction in home supplies will depend upon the elasticity of demand for blankets in A. In the circumstances which we are assuming, the price charged to consumers of blankets in A will fall. The reduction in the duty on imports will cause a fall in the price of imported blankets which will not quickly be offset by any rise in the cost of imported blankets as more are imported, because the supply of exports of blankets from B is assumed to be very elastic. The rise in the duty on home production would tend to cause a rise in the price of home-produced blankets but this is very quickly offset by a reduction in the cost of home-produced blankets as their output is reduced, because the elasticity of supply of their production is assumed to be small. Now if the elasticity of the demand for blankets in A were zero, there would be no increase in their total consumption even though the price charged to consumers of blankets in A fell. In this case the increase in imports would necessarily be exactly equal to the reduction in home production. But if the elasticity of demand for blankets in A is high, then when their price falls there will be a large net increase in their consumption; and in this case the increase in imports must be much bigger than the decrease in home production.

We reach the conclusion that a shift of taxation away from imports on to home production will cause an increase in imports which is much larger than the decrease in home production if (i) the elasticity of supply of the exports from B is high, (ii) the elasticity of supply of the production in A is small, and (iii) the elasticity of demand for consumption in A is large. These are the conditions in which such a change in taxation will add to economic welfare. At the outset the divergence between marginal values and costs is 5 per cent in the case of both imports and home production. A large increase in imports and a small decrease in home production will, therefore, add to welfare, since the increase in welfare on imports will be greater than the loss in welfare on home production and there will be no change in welfare in other markets where there is no divergence between marginal values and costs. But as the process of reducing the tax on imports and raising that on home production continues, the gain will become less and less and will ultimately give place to a loss. With a high elasticity of exports from B, a low elasticity of supply in A, and a high elasticity of demand in A, it may still be true that, say, the increase in imports is twice as big as the decrease in home production. But suppose that the rate of tax on imports has already been so much reduced and that on home production so much increased that the divergence in the case of home production is now more than twice as great as in the case of imports. In this case though the reduction in home production is only half the increase in imports, the divergence on home production will be so great relatively to that on imports, that the loss of welfare on home production would outweigh the gain on imports. All one can say is that to maximize welfare the rate of tax should be higher on home production than on imports (i.e. there should be some move from a consumption to a production tax), if the elasticity of supply of home production is smaller than the elasticity of supply of the foreign country's exports. The best ratio between the rate of tax on home production and the rate of tax on imports will be the higher, (i) the higher is the elasticity of supply of exports by the foreign country, (ii) the lower is the elasticity of the home supply, and (iii) the higher is the elasticity of the home demand.[1]

Of course, if the elasticity of the supply of exports by the foreign country were smaller than the elasticity of supply of the home output, then the duty on imports should be higher than the duty on home production. Starting once more with the same rate of duty on home production and on imports, we now somewhat reduce the rate of duty on the former and raise it on the latter. This causes a considerable increase in home production (where the supply is elastic) and no very great fall in the foreign country's supply of exports (where the supply is inelastic). Imports fall less than home production rises; and since there is initially the same rate of tax and so the same rate of divergence

[1] The precise formula is given in Section V of the mathematical supplement to this volume.

between marginal values and costs in both markets, this represents a net gain in welfare. The price charged to consumers for home produce will fall as a result of the tax and this fall will not be much offset by higher costs of production as home output rises because the supply is elastic; on the other hand, any rise in the price charged to consumers for imports as a result of the higher tax on imports will be quickly offset by a reduced cost of imports as the supply of imports falls, because their supply is inelastic. The price of the product will thus fall in A. The more elastic the demand in A, the greater will be the net increase in the amount consumed. In other words, the more elastic is the demand in A, the greater will be the amount by which the increase in home production exceeds the decrease in imports, and the greater therefore will be the gain in welfare to be achieved from the shift of the taxation.

If, therefore, we start with a consumption tax in the case of an imported product, we should shift towards a production tax if the elasticity of home supply is less than the elasticity of the foreign country's supply of exports; and we should shift in the opposite direction towards a trade tax if the elasticity of home supply is greater than the foreign elasticity of supply of exports. One cannot, of course, say which is the case unless one knows the particular circumstances of the particular product which is the subject of tax. Nevertheless, there is one general consideration which may give some presumption in favour of the view that home production should be taxed more heavily than imports. The elasticity of supply of home production depends solely upon the ease with which the factors of production can be shifted off to the production of alternative products when this particular product is subject to tax. On the other hand, the elasticity of supply of exports by the foreign country depends not only upon the ease with which the factors of production can be shifted away from the production of this product, but also upon the ease with which the product in question can be substituted for other products in the consumption of the citizens of that country.

This is illustrated in Table XVII. Thus suppose (column *a*) that the price offered for B's blankets falls by 10 per cent from \$1 to \$0·9; suppose (column *b*) that the elasticity of production of blankets in B is unity so that this causes a 10 per cent decrease in the output of blankets in B from 200 to 180; suppose, further (column *c*), that the elasticity of demand for blankets in B is also unity so that the amount consumed rises by 10 per cent from 100 to 110. Then (column *d*) the fall in price by 10 per cent from \$1 to \$0·9 has reduced the supply available for export by 30 per cent from 100 to 70. The elasticity of supply of exports from B is 3 although the elasticity of supply of production in B is only unity. Thus if the elasticity of supply of production

TABLE XVII

The Elasticity of Supply of Exports

Price offered by A for B's blankets (*a*)	Amount of blankets produced in B (*b*)	Amount of blankets consumed in B (*c*)	Amount of blankets exported by B (*d*) = (*b*) − (*c*)
\$1·0	200	100	100
\$0·9	180	110	70
	Elasticity of supply of output = 1	Elasticity of demand = 1	Elasticity of supply of exports = 3

were the same in both countries (which it might well be if the technical problems of production were similar), the elasticity of supply of exports from B would be appreciably larger than the elasticity of production in A, provided that a considerable part of B's production were consumed at home. There is, therefore, this degree of presumption in favour of the view that the tax on imports in A ought to be lower than the tax on home production in A.[1]

We can apply exactly the same sort of argument to the taxation of an export product, e.g. of apples produced by A partly for consumption in A and partly for export to B. Let us start with a uniform rate of tax on the total production, i.e. on the amount consumed in A as well as on the amount exported to B. We do this because this gives us the largest base for our tax and, therefore, the lowest initial rate of tax necessary to raise the given revenue for A's government. Suppose now that we slightly raise the tax on home consumption and reduce correspondingly the rate of tax on exports. If the home demand is less elastic than the foreign demand for A's exports of apples, then the decrease in transactions in A's consumption will be less than the increase in B's imports. Since both have initially the same rate of tax and so the same rate of divergence between marginal values and costs, this will represent a net gain in world economic welfare.

[1] This presumption is essentially due to the fact that we are assuming that A's government is trying to maximize world welfare while it can tax only A's production or consumption. If A's government (or a supranational government) could, in raising the fixed revenue, tax B's production of blankets for B's consumption as well as B's production of blankets for export, this presumption in favour of a heavier tax on A's than on B's blankets would disappear. It is due solely to the fact that our problem requires that part of B's output of blankets should be totally free of tax.

This gain will be the greater, the greater is the elasticity of supply of total production of apples in A. The increased rate of tax on home consumption will be more than fully absorbed by a rise in the price charged to the home consumer without much decrease in the amount consumed at home, since the home demand is inelastic. The reduced rate of tax on exports will mainly cause a rise in the price received by the producer, since the foreign demand is elastic and will require only a small fall in the price including tax to cause a large increase in the amount imported. As a result the price received by the producer in A will rise. The more elastic his supply, the greater will be the consequential increase in his output. In other words, the increase in exports will greatly exceed the reduction in home consumption, and there will be a large increase in welfare.

After a time, however, when the rate of tax on home consumption has been much raised and that on exports has been much lowered, there will be no more gain—indeed only a net loss—to be obtained from a further shifting of taxation. It might still be true that there would be a much larger increase in exports than decrease in home consumption as a result of a further shift of taxation from the former to the latter; but if the tax rate and so the rate of divergence on exports is now very low and on home consumption very high, there would be only a small gain per unit on increases in exports and a large loss per unit on decreases of home consumption. At this point the shift of tax would have to cease.

If, then, home demand were less elastic than the foreign demand for imports, we ought to shift away from a production tax towards a consumption tax. If, on the other hand, home demand were more elastic than the foreign demand for imports, we ought to shift away from a production tax in the opposite direction towards a trade tax on the exports of the product. In this case a reduction of the tax on home consumption balanced by a somewhat higher tax on exports would increase home consumption more than it reduced foreign imports; and starting with the same rate of divergence due to the same rate of tax in both markets this would raise economic welfare.

But, as Table XVIII shows, the elasticity of demand for imported apples in B will be greater than the elasticity of demand for apples in general in B if B produces some part of her own supply of apples. If the price at which A offers apples in B falls by 10 per cent from $1 to $0·9, and if this causes a 10 per cent increase in B's demand from 200 to 220 and a 10 per cent decrease in B's output from 100 to 90, it will cause a 30 per cent increase in B's imports from 100 to 130. If the elasticity of demand for apples were the same in A and in B and if B produced apples for herself, then the elasticity of B's demand for imports of apples would be greater than the elasticity of A's demand for apples in general. There would be a case for taxing A's exports less heavily than A's own consumption.[1]

TABLE XVIII

The Elasticity of Demand for Imports

Price charged for apples in B (*a*)	Amount of apples consumed in B (*b*)	Amount of apples produced in B (*c*)	Amount of apples imported into B (*d*) = (*b*) − (*c*)
\$1·00	200	100	100
\$0·90	220	90	130
	Elasticity of total demand in B = 1	Elasticity of supply in B = 1	Elasticity of demand for imports in B = 3

In the above analysis we have made a very large number of severe assumptions in order to isolate certain factors which will help to determine whether, in the interests of world economic welfare, a national government should prefer production, consumption, or trade taxes as a means of raising revenue. We have found some reasons for a general preference for moving somewhat away from trade taxes towards a production tax in the case of an imported product and towards a consumption tax in the case of an exported product. But it must be recognized that there are many reasons why this conclusion may need to be modified in particular cases.

First, there may be special reasons for believing that the elasticity of the foreign supply of an import or of the foreign demand for an export is very specially low. In this case there would be an argument for shifting rather towards trade taxes.

Second, it may be legitimate in our problem to believe that welfare would be increased by a distribution of income in favour of the citizens of the taxing country at the expense of the citizens of the other countries. The distributional weights for the taxing country may be higher than for the others. In this case, as we shall see in Chapter XVII, there would be a case for shifting towards trade taxes—though, of course, if the distributional weights to be given to the foreigner were higher than those allotted to the citizens of the taxing country, then there would be

[1] For the precise analysis in the case of the taxation of an export product see Section VI of the mathematical supplement to this volume.

a still stronger argument for shifting away from trade taxes to a production tax in the case of an imported product and to a consumption tax in the case of an exported product.

Third, the analysis would be quite different if the taxing government could levy its taxes on production and consumption in the foreign as well as in the home country. In this case all presumption against the taxation of the foreign production or consumption would disappear.

Fourth, the analysis might need to be altered if we modified the assumption that there were no divergences between marginal values and costs in any other part of the economy. Suppose, for example, that blankets which are being taxed in A are jointly demanded with leisure. Suppose also that we have the normal case in which the elasticity of supply of exported blankets by B is greater than the elasticity of supply of home-produced blankets in A. Then a tax on imports rather than on the home production of blankets will keep up the price of blankets to consumers in A and will make them reduce their consumption of blankets. This, if blankets are jointly demanded in A with leisure, would make the citizens of A desire less leisure, supply more effort, earn more income, and so consume more of other things. Now if there is a divergence between marginal values and costs in the earning of income from effort—due, for example, to the existence of a marginal income tax for the raising of some part of the revenue—this increased supply of effort weighted by its marginal divergence would make a positive contribution to welfare. In other words, if the whole point of taxing the particular product were to raise its price in order—on the lines discussed in Chapter VII, pp. 112–18—to make leisure less attractive, these indirect secondary effects would have to be taken into account.

It is not possible, therefore, in this chapter, to reach any hard-and-fast rules about the best type of indirect taxation on production, consumption, and international trade for the purpose of raising revenue. This is always a problem in the second-best. It can only be solved in each particular case by applying the general method discussed above in Chapter VII. In this chapter we have merely tried to give certain illustrations of this method and in particular of its application to the markets most directly affected.

CHAPTER XIII

THE SECOND-BEST ARGUMENT FOR TRADE CONTROL: (2) THE PARTIAL FREEING OF TRADE

LET us now leave on one side the problems raised by the existence of divergences between marginal values and costs due to the necessity for taxation for the purpose of raising revenue. We will assume, that is to say, that sufficient is received from State-owned income-bearing property or can be raised by other means—such as progressive lump-sum taxes—which do not cause any divergence between marginal values and costs. It is no longer required that taxes on international trade should raise any given revenue.

The problem which we intend to discuss in this chapter is whether it is always desirable on grounds of economic efficiency to eliminate a particular divergence between marginal values and costs in international trade by removing a tax or subsidy or other control of the international trade in the commodity concerned, when there are other divergences between marginal values and costs in the case of other commodities entering into international trade.

We wish to confine ourselves in this chapter to problems of economic efficiency. We shall, therefore, continue to assume that the same distributional weights are allotted by the policy-makers to all citizens in all the trading countries. That is to say, we should consider it an improvement if, at current prices, we could give an additional $1 of income to any one individual provided that that involved taking less than $1 of income away from any other individual.

We wish to confine ourselves in this chapter also to marginal changes. We shall, therefore, continue to assume that the structure of industry remains unchanged in each trading country and that we are concerned solely with such changes in trade taxes or other controls as will cause only marginal changes in the amounts produced, consumed, and traded of the products concerned.

But we are concerned in this chapter with another problem of second-best, as opposed to utopian, policy. We wish to consider in what conditions a reduction in one particular rate of import tax or other trade control will increase economic welfare not on the assumption that no other trade taxes exist, but on the assumption that for one reason or another a given structure of trade controls on the rest of international trade exists and will continue to exist.[1] But, in order to isolate certain

[1] In this chapter we shall argue as if these existing divergences between marginal values and costs in international trade were all due to trade controls—import and export duties, subsidies, quotas, State-trading controls, etc. There

basic considerations, we shall assume in this chapter that these unalterable divergences between marginal values and costs exist only in international trade and not in domestic production, consumption, or trade. In other words, we assume that within each of the trading countries a policy of modified laissez-faire is successfully adopted so that there are no domestic divergences between marginal values and costs.

We are left then with the following type of problem. Suppose that there is a duty in A on the import of blankets from B, and that the government in A reduces this duty. Suppose at the same time that there are duties or subsidies in A or in B on the movement of other goods from B into A or on some or all of A's exports to B. In these conditions does the reduction of the particular barrier on the sale of blankets by B to A necessarily lead to an increase in economic efficiency?

In accordance with the analysis of Chapter VII, in order to answer this question, we need to know what will be the effect of the reduction in A's duty levied on imports of blankets from B upon the amount of blankets which will be exported from B to A and, indirectly, upon the amounts of all the other products which will be exported from B to A and from A to B. We need to value the change in the volume of trade in each particular product by the supply prices of each product in the exporting country, since with modified laissez-faire policies within each country these supply prices will be equal to the marginal social net costs of production. We must then weight each of these changes in trade by the *ad valorem* rate of incidence of the trade barrier to which that particular line of trade is subject, since the trade barrier is the only cause of an excess of marginal value over marginal social cost. If the sum of all such changes so valued and weighted is greater than zero, then there is an increase in economic efficiency as a result of the partial move to free trade which the reduction of A's duty on imports of blankets represents. If, however, this sum is less than zero, the partial move towards free trade will have reduced and not increased world economic efficiency.

In making these calculations it is interesting to note the following points.

First, we can leave out of our calculation all changes in domestic trade within each country because we are assuming that there are modified laissez-faire policies within each country, which have the result that there is no divergence between marginal values and costs in any line of domestic transaction.

might, however, be divergences between marginal values and costs in international markets due to elements of monopoly or monopsony or, less probably, to external economies or diseconomies. The analysis is, of course, exactly similar in these cases, and the reader is left to apply the conclusions of this chapter to these other kinds of divergence for himself.

Second, we can leave out of our calculations all changes in international trade in commodities in which there is free trade, because in these cases too there are no existing divergences between marginal values and costs so that marginal changes in these transactions also have no effect upon economic welfare.

Third, we can leave out of our calculations all those products in international trade which are controlled not by taxes and subsidies but by quota arrangements which fix a rigid quantitative limit to the volume of trade. The reason for this is obvious. There will normally be no change in the volume of such trade, so that it can make no marginal contribution to an increase or decrease in economic welfare.[1]

Fourth, if subsidies to certain lines of international trade exist, then in those cases marginal costs will exceed marginal values and we shall be dealing with negative rates of divergence. An increase in the volume of such trade reduces economic efficiency since the marginal value of the increase in trade is less than its marginal cost. In such a case, therefore, any reduction of trade which would result as an indirect effect of the reduction of A's duty on the import of blankets from B will raise economic efficiency.

Our essential task is, therefore, to inquire what will be the effects upon the various flows of trade between A and B of a reduction in A's duty on the import of blankets from B. A complete answer to this question would involve a complete analysis of every change in both economies, since the supply and demand of each product entering into trade depends to a smaller or greater degree upon what has happened to the income of every factor of production in every country and to the price of every other product being produced or consumed in either country. Such a total analysis is completely impracticable except in a very elaborate mathematical form, and even this would provide results only of such generality that very few useful conclusions could be drawn from it. We must be content with a less rigorous analysis which will neglect a number of possible indirect repercussions but which may enable us to understand some of the most important tendencies at work.

Accordingly, in considering the effect of the reduction of A's duty on

[1] The one case in which imports which are restricted by a quantitative quota might be changed is where the repercussions of the reduction in A's duty on imports of blankets are such as to reduce the demand for or supply of this other product below the permitted quota. In such a case there would be a reduction in the volume of trade in this commodity. But we could still neglect the change in our calculations. The volume would not fall below the permitted quantity until the quota arrangement had lost all its protective effect, i.e. until all divergence between supply and demand price had disappeared as a result of the reduction in demand or the reduction in supply. Either the volume of trade is not changed or else there is no remaining divergence between marginal values and costs in the case of this commodity. In either case it makes no marginal contribution to increased or decreased economic welfare.

imports of blankets from B upon the flows of trade between A and B, we shall treat these effects under three separate headings, although in a full analysis these three types of effect could not be assumed to be independent of each other. We shall call these three types of effect the primary, secondary, and tertiary effects.

The direct effect of a reduction in the duty on imports of blankets from B into A will be to lower the price at which A's consumers can purchase B's blankets and/or to raise the price at which B's producers can sell blankets to A's consumers. By the *primary effect* of a reduction in A's duty on imports of B's blankets we mean the change in the amount of blankets which would be imported from B into A if there were no change of incomes in A or B and no change in the price of any product in A or B except the changes in the prices of blankets in A and B which were directly caused by the change in the duty on blankets.

But blankets may be a close substitute for or complement with some other particular product in A and/or in B. Because of this the change in the prices of blankets in A and B which are directly caused by the change in duty may cause shifts of supply and demand for these other products for which blankets are close substitutes or with which blankets are very complementary. This may, therefore, lead to shifts in the trade between A and B in these other products. By the *primary plus secondary effects* of the reduction in A's duty on imports of B's blankets we mean the changes which would take place in the amount of trade between A and B in blankets and in these other products which are close substitutes for or complements with blankets, if incomes remained constant in A and B and if the prices of all products remained constant in A and B except the prices of blankets and of these other products which were close substitutes for or complements with blankets in A or B.[1]

But when we have allowed for all the primary and secondary effects so defined, we may still not have reached a final equilibrium. We can illustrate this best in our present problem by saying that there might still remain a disequilibrium in the general balance of payments between A and B. The reduction in the import duty on blankets from B is likely to have caused A's consumers to purchase more imports from B and thus to have imposed some strain upon A's balance of payments with B. There is no reason to believe that the secondary changes, if any, as we have defined them will have removed this deficit on A's balance of payments. Its removal may, therefore, involve a fall in the general level of the incomes of the factors of production and of costs of products in A relatively to those in B, brought about either by the gold standard mechanism of general deflation in A and inflation in B or by

[1] Some important examples of primary and secondary effects are analysed in Sections VII–X of the mathematical supplement to this volume.

a depreciation of A's currency in terms of B's currency.[1] Such a development will encourage exports from A to B and discourage imports from B into A. These changes in trade flows due to the general adjustments required to restore equilibrium to the balance of payments between A and B we shall call the *tertiary effects* of the change in duty.

We do not need a very lengthy discussion of the primary effect of the reduction in A's duty on imported blankets. The effect will be partly to reduce the price of the imported blankets in A and partly to raise the price of the exported blankets in B. The reduction in the price charged to consumers in A for imported blankets will encourage them to purchase more of them,[2] and the better price which B's exporters can obtain for blankets sold to B will encourage them to export more of them. There will therefore be an increase in the volume of sales of blankets from A to B; and since there is a positive excess of marginal value over marginal cost in this trade due to the existing duty the primary effect of the reduction in the duty will always be to improve economic efficiency.

How great the increase in economic efficiency due to this factor will be depends upon two factors, the initial height of the duty and the size of the increase in the volume of trade caused by the reduction in the duty. With any given increase in the volume of trade the gain will be the greater, the greater is the initial level of the duty, since a high rate of duty will mean that there is a large excess of marginal value over marginal cost on the increment of trade. With any given duty the gain will be the greater, the greater is the increase in the volume of trade on which this excess of marginal value over marginal cost is enjoyed.

Now the increase in the volume of trade will be greater, the greater is the increase in the volume which A's consumers will want to import when the price they must pay for imported blankets falls by any small amount and the greater is the increase in the volume which B's exporters will want to sell abroad when the price they can obtain for exported blankets rises by any small amount. In other words, the primary increase in the trade in blankets will be large if the elasticity of demand for imports of blankets in A is large and if the elasticity of supply of exports of blankets in B is large.

Now the demand for imports of blankets in A will be the greater, the greater is the elasticity of demand in A for blankets in general—i.e. whether home-produced or imported. This is obvious. A fall in the price of imported blankets will cheapen the price of blankets in A, and the more this leads to an expansion in the consumption of blankets the more it will raise imports of blankets. But imported blankets may

[1] See Part IV of Volume I of this work.

[2] We rule out of consideration the remote possibility that the imported blankets may be so inferior a good in A's consumption that A's consumers purchase less of them when they become cheaper.

compete with home-produced blankets in A. The fall in the price of blankets in A due to the reduction in the duty on imported blankets will then reduce the price which home producers in A can obtain for their blankets. If as a result of this fall in price producers of blankets in A greatly cut down their supply, a large void will exist in the market for blankets in A to be filled by increased imports. In other words, the elasticity of demand for imported blankets in A will be the greater, the greater is the elasticity of supply of home-produced blankets in A. And, finally, the elasticity of demand for imported blankets in A will also be the greater, the smaller is the proportion of the total consumption of blankets in A which is supplied by imports. If imported blankets in A make up only a very small part of the total consumption of blankets in A, then only a very small proportionate increase in the total demand for blankets in A and only a very small proportionate decrease in the home supply of blankets in A is required to lead to an enormous proportionate increase in the amount of imported blankets which are required to fill the gap in A's market.[1]

Similarly, it can be shown that the elasticity of supply of exports of blankets from B will be the greater, (i) the greater is the elasticity of supply of the production of blankets in B whether for home consumption or for export, (ii) the greater is the elasticity of demand for blankets for home consumption in B, and (iii) the smaller is the proportion of the output of blankets in B which is exported. The reduction in A's duty on imports of blankets will raise the price offered for blankets in B. If this rise in price causes a large increase in B's production and a large decrease in B's consumption of blankets, this will release a large quantity for export. And if existing exports are small relatively to the total production of blankets in B, this increase in the supplies available for export will represent an enormous proportionate increase in the volume of exports.[2]

We may, therefore conclude that the primary effect of a reduction in A's duty on imported blankets will be to increase economic efficiency, and that the increase in economic efficiency will be the greater, (i) the higher is the initial rate of duty, (ii) the greater is the elasticity of demand for blankets in A, (iii) the greater is the elasticity of supply of blankets in A, (iv) the smaller is the proportion of A's consumption of blankets which comes from imports, (v) the greater is the elasticity of supply of blankets in B, (vi) the greater is the elasticity of demand for blankets in B, and (vii) the smaller is the proportion of B's output of blankets which is sold for export.[3]

[1] See Table XVIII (p. 198). [2] See Table XVII (p. 196).

[3] The above propositions can readily be proved algebraically. Let x be the volume of trade in blankets; $D_a(p_a)$ the volume of blankets consumed in A where p_a is the price of blankets in A and D_a is the demand function in A; $S_a(p_a)$ the supply of blankets produced in A; $D_b(p_b)$ the amount of blankets

We can turn next to the *secondary effects* of the reduction of B's duty on imported blankets upon the flows of trade. The reduction in the duty will, as we have seen, have the effect of lowering the price of blankets in A and increasing the amount of blankets flowing into the market in A and the opposite effect of raising the price of blankets in B and increasing the amount of blankets flowing out of the market in B. We will first consider the possible secondary effects of this which may take place in A's market, and we will then turn to the corresponding effects which may take place in B's market.

The extra blankets imported into A may be close substitutes for or close complements either with other goods which A imports or with goods which A exports. This gives us four possible types of secondary effect upon A's trade, namely: (1) where the extra blankets imported

---

consumed in B; $S_b(p_b)$ the amount of blankets produced in B; and t the *ad valorem* rate of import duty in A. We have the following three equations:

$$x = D_a(p_a) - S_a(p_a) = S_b(p_b) - D_b(p_b), \text{ and } p_a = p_b(1 + t)$$

since the volume of trade equals the excess of demand over supply in the importing country and the excess of supply over demand in the exporting country and since the price in A equals the price in B raised by the *ad valorem* rate of duty. Differentiating these equations we have:

$$dx = -(\varepsilon_a D_a + \eta_a S_a)\frac{dp_a}{p_a} = (\varepsilon_b D_b + \eta_b S_b)\frac{dp_b}{p_b}, \text{ and } \frac{dp_a}{p_a} = \frac{dp_b}{p_b} + \frac{dt}{1+t}$$

where ε_a and ε_b are the numerical values of the elasticities of demand for blankets in A and B and η_a and η_b are the corresponding elasticities of supply. If we eliminate $\frac{dp_a}{p_a}$ and $\frac{dp_b}{p_b}$ from the last three equations and remember that $D_a = S_a + x$ and $S_b = D_b + x$ we have:

$$dx = \frac{-dt}{1+t} \cdot \frac{\left\{\varepsilon_a + (\varepsilon_a + \eta_a)\frac{S_a}{x}\right\}\left\{(\varepsilon_b + \eta_b)\frac{D_b}{x} + \eta_b\right\}}{\varepsilon_a + (\varepsilon_a + \eta_a)\frac{S_a}{x} + (\varepsilon_b + \eta_b)\frac{D_b}{x} + \eta_b}$$

The gain in economic welfare is measured by the change in the volume of trade valued at the supply price and weighted by the *ad valorem* tax, i.e. by $dx \cdot p_b \cdot t$. The gain due to a given fall in duty $(-dt)$ is therefore measured by the expression:

$$p_b \frac{t}{1+t} \cdot \frac{\left\{\varepsilon_a + (\varepsilon_a + \eta_a)\frac{S_a}{x}\right\}\left\{(\varepsilon_b + \eta_b)\frac{D_b}{x} + \eta_b\right\}}{\varepsilon_a + (\varepsilon_a + \eta_a)\frac{S_a}{x} + (\varepsilon_b + \eta_b)\frac{D_b}{x} + \eta_b}$$

It is clear that an increase in t will increase this expression.

The right-hand fraction of the expression is of the form $\frac{(a + b)(c + d)}{a + b + c + d}$.

Let this equal e. Now $\frac{de}{da} = \left(\frac{c + d}{a + b + c + d}\right)^2$ and is therefore positive, and similarly $\frac{de}{db}$, $\frac{de}{dc}$, and $\frac{de}{dd}$ are positive.

It follows that the expression for the increase in economic welfare consequent upon a given decrease in duty $(-dt)$ will be greater, the greater are t, ε_a, η_a, $\frac{S_a}{x}$, ε_b, η_b, and $\frac{D_b}{x}$.

are substitutes for other goods imported by A, (2) where they are complementary with other goods imported by A, (3) where they are substitutes for goods exported by A, and (4) where they are complementary with goods exported from A.

(1) Where the extra blankets imported into A—which we will call the primary goods—are close substitutes for other imports in A, we shall have a case of what may be called *secondary import trade destruction in A.* Thus suppose that A imports two types of blanket from B—wool blankets and cotton blankets—and suppose that these two products are close substitutes for each other in A's consumption. Suppose then that there were a reduction in A's duty on imports of wool blankets without any reduction in her duty on imports of cotton blankets. Then the lower price and increased supplies of wool blankets in A would cause A's consumers to purchase less cotton blankets. Thus there would be a secondary destruction of the import trade in cotton blankets due to the primary increase in imports of wool blankets.

In the above example we have given a case in which there is direct competition in the demand of A's final consumers between the primary import (wool blankets) and the secondary import (cotton blankets). But there are at least two other forms of substitutability between the two imported products on A's market which may have exactly similar effects.

Suppose that A imports from B not only wool blankets but also raw wool which is used in A's industry to work up into home-produced blankets. Suppose then that in A an import duty on blankets is reduced without any accompanying reduction in duty on imports of raw wool. There will now be especially strong pressure on A's blanket industry to contract, since the price of the imported finished product will have been reduced without any corresponding reduction in the price of the imported raw material. As a result of this contraction in A's blanket industry, A's imports of raw wool will be reduced. In A's import demand finished blankets and raw wool are to a considerable extent substitutes for each other; according to the relative prices of imported raw wool and imported finished blankets, A's traders can choose between importing raw wool to be made up into blankets at home or importing the finished product itself.

There is yet another way in which substitutability may show itself between A's primary and secondary imports. Suppose that A imports from B both blankets and underwear and suppose that these are not close substitutes for each other in A's consumption. But suppose that blankets and underwear are close substitutes for each other in A's production in the sense that the factors of production which are used in A to produce blankets are extremely well suited to produce underwear—the same skill of labour and the same machines being required in both lines of production. Then a reduction in the price of blankets will cause a contraction in the blanket industry in A; this will release resources which will move into the production of underwear, which in turn will compete with imported supplies of underwear. As a final result the increased imports of blankets will have led to some reduction in the imports of underwear because of the competition of the two industries in A for the same factors of production.

Where there are secondary imports into A which in any one of these three ways are close substitutes for A's primary imports of blankets, the reduction in the import duty on blankets will cause a reduction in the imports of these secondary products. If there is any duty in A on the import of the secondary products, the reduction in the imports of the secondary product will in itself tend to reduce economic welfare, since there will be a smaller import of something whose marginal value in A exceeds its marginal cost in B. Now whether there is a net increase in economic welfare or not as a result of these combined primary and secondary changes will depend upon two things: first, upon the relationship between the rate of *ad valorem* import duty on the primary imports and the rate of duty on the secondary imports; and, secondly, upon the relationship which the reduction of the secondary imports bears to the increase of the primary imports.[1]

It is obvious that there is more likely to be a gain in economic welfare if the rate of duty is high on the primary imports which will come in in increased volume and is low on the secondary imports which will come in in reduced volume. We can be more confident about the good effects of a reduction of duty if it is high relatively to the rates of duty on the goods which may be the subject of secondary trade destruction.

It is equally obvious that the partial tariff reduction will do more

[1] By the primary imports we mean, of course, the imports of the product on which the duty is reduced, and by the secondary imports the imports of the product which is a close substitute for or complement with the primary import. But the increase in the primary imports is not, strictly speaking, the same as the primary increase in imports. Suppose that there is a reduction in a duty levied on the import of woollen blankets into A. We defined the primary increase in imports as the increase in the imports of woollen blankets which would then take place if money incomes and the price of everything other than woollen blankets remained unchanged. But suppose that this leads to a decreased import of some close substitute—cotton blankets. The decreased demand for cotton blankets may cause the supply price of cotton blankets to fall, and this may to some extent divert demand back again away from woollen blankets. This consequential reduction in the import of woollen blankets is part of the secondary change in imports. Thus the change in the amount of primary imports is equal to the primary increase in imports plus any parts of the secondary and tertiary changes in trade which may happen to take the form of changes in the amount of trade in the primary import. The reader should bear this distinction in mind in what follows where, solely for simplicity of exposition, we shall talk of changes in the amounts of primary and secondary commodities which are traded rather than of the primary and secondary changes in the volume of trade.

good if the volume of secondary trade destruction is low, relatively to the volume of primary trade creation.[1] The factors which will cause the ratio of secondary trade destruction to be low relatively to the primary trade creation are fairly clear. The first point is almost too obvious to need mention. The greater is the degree of substitutability in A's demand between the primary imports and the secondary imports in any of the three ways described above, the greater will be the shift of demand away from the secondary on to the primary goods and the greater, in consequence, the fall in the volume of the secondary imports relatively to the rise in the volume of the primary imports.

But this leads to a second consideration. A given shift of demand away from the secondary imports, however large, will have little effect upon the volume of those imports if the elasticity of supply of their export in B is sufficiently low. If when consumers in A shift from purchases of imported cotton blankets to imported wool blankets the exporters of cotton blankets in B—having no alternative uses for their factors of production—merely lower the price of cotton blankets and continue to export as many as before, there will be no decline in the volume of trade in cotton blankets. The reduction in the volume of the secondary imports will be large relatively to the increase in the volume of the primary imports only if the elasticity of supply of the exports of the secondary goods from B is large.

The primary increase in imports of blankets into A as a result of the reduced price of blankets in A is due to the substitutability between imported blankets on the one hand and home-produced goods and other imports on the other hand. The secondary reduction in imports will be the smaller relatively to the primary increase in imports, not only the smaller is the substitutability between the primary imports and other secondary imports (as we have already observed) but also the greater is the substitutability between the primary imports and other goods which are produced domestically in A. Thus if A also produces blankets or other goods which are close substitutes for blankets, the increase in the primary import of blankets can be large without relying upon an equivalent reduction in the import of other things.

Finally, the degree to which the volume of secondary imports will fall off will also depend upon the degree to which these secondary imports are good substitutes for other things produced in A. Thus when the demand for the secondary imports declines their price will be reduced unless the elasticity of supply of their export from B is infinitely high. As their price falls demand will shift back on to them away from

[1] On the assumption, of course, that the secondary product is subject to a trade duty and not to a trade subsidy. If trade in the secondary product were subsidized, reduction in it would increase economic welfare. In this case both the primary trade creation and the secondary trade destruction would raise economic welfare.

other goods produced in A if these secondary imports are good substitutes in A for other goods produced in A. We can, therefore, say that the reduction in the volume of secondary imports will be smaller relatively to the increase in the volume of primary imports, the greater is the substitutability between the secondary imports and the whole range of other products produced in A.

To summarize, where the blankets on which A's duty is reduced are close substitutes in A (in any of the three ways which we have described) for some other imports from B into A, there will be a secondary reduction in A's imports of these substitutes associated with the primary increase in A's imports of blankets. If there is a positive divergence between marginal values and costs (due, for example, to an import duty) in the case of the import of these substitutes, this secondary effect will tend to reduce economic welfare. The increase in economic welfare due to the primary increase in the import of blankets is, however, the more likely to outweigh this secondary loss, (i) the higher is the rate of duty on the primary trade relatively to the rate of duty on the secondary trade, (ii) the less the degree of substitutability between the primary import and the secondary import, (iii) the greater the degree of substitutability between the primary import and the general range of goods produced in A, (iv) the smaller the elasticity of supply of export from B of the secondary imports, and (v) the greater the degree of substitutability between the secondary imports and the general range of goods produced in A.

We have dwelt at very considerable length with this case of substitutability in A between the blankets on which A's import duty is reduced and other imports into A from B. We shall now deal much more shortly with the remaining three cases of substitutability or complementarity in A between the blankets imported from B and other of A's traded products, and with the corresponding four cases in B's market. The reader must for himself apply to these remaining seven cases the detailed analysis which corresponds to the points which we have discussed in detail in this first case.[1]

(2) We turn then to the case in which the blankets imported into A from B are complementary with some other good—let us say beds—which are also imported into A from B. The more blankets are available in A the more beds are required. A reduction in the duty on imported blankets in A is therefore likely to increase the demand in A for imported beds, so that we now have a case of ***secondary import trade creation in A.***

This complementarity is perhaps more likely to show itself in the import of two materials which are jointly used in A to produce some

[1] The mathematical reader may be helped in this task by consulting Sections VII–X of the mathematical supplement to this volume.

finished product. For example, A may import coal and iron ore to produce steel. A reduction in a duty on imported coal may reduce the cost of producing steel and thus, by increasing the demand for home-produced steel in A, raise the demand for imported iron ore. Or the complementarity between A's two imports may not be in A's consumption at all but in her production. Suppose that blankets in A can, for technical reasons, be produced only in the winter and that some other product—wireless sets—which are also imported into A can also be made in A in the summer by the same labour which produces blankets during the winter. Then a reduction in the duty on imported blankets will contract the blanket industry in A; this will reduce the labour available in the summer to produce wireless sets; and this will raise A's demand for imported wireless sets.

In any of these three cases a reduction in the import duty on blankets in A will lead to a secondary increase in the demand in A for some other import. If this import is also subject to an import duty so that there is a positive excess of marginal value over marginal cost in this case, then the increase in these secondary imports will also raise economic welfare so that the secondary change will in this case reinforce the primary change.

How much it will reinforce the primary change will depend upon two factors: the rate of tax on the secondary imports as compared with the rate of tax on the primary imports, and the increase in the volume of the primary imports as compared with the increase in the volume of the secondary imports. The greater are both these ratios, the greater the secondary reinforcement to the increase in economic welfare.

The secondary increase in imports will be the greater: (i) the greater the degree of complementarity between the primary and secondary imports, which is obvious; (ii) the more elastic is the supply of exports of the secondary product from B, so that their export is much increased when the demand for them in A is raised; (iii) the less good substitutes are the secondary imports for other products in A, so that when the increase in their importation raises their supply price this will not choke off A's demand for them; and (iv) the less good substitutes the primary import is in A with the other products of A, so that the reduction of duty on the primary import can lead to a fall in the price of the import in A and so to a large increase in demand for the complementary secondary import.

In this complementary case the increase in economic welfare due to the primary increase in imports when the duty on imports of blankets into A is reduced, will be reinforced by the increase in imports of the complementary secondary product, beds. It follows that the duty on blankets should not merely be reduced to zero, but should be still further lowered, or, in other words, the import of blankets should be subsidized. Suppose blankets are imported freely. The payment of a small subsidy on imported blankets will also increase the import of beds, upon which an appreciable rate of import duty is levied. The increased import of blankets will now do harm, since the subsidy lowers the marginal value in A below the marginal cost in B. But the increased import of beds will still do good since the marginal value in A exceeds the marginal cost in B by the amount of the duty. But the secondary good exceeds the primary damage when the rate of duty on beds is high relatively to the rate of subsidy on blankets. The raising of the subsidy on imports of blankets should obviously go further the greater is the increase in the volume of the secondary import (beds) in relation to any given increase in the volume of the primary import (blankets). The four considerations enumerated in the previous paragraph show, therefore, the conditions in which the rate of subsidy on the primary import should be raised to a high level relatively to the rate of duty on the secondary import.

(3) We pass now to the case of *secondary export trade creation in A*. This is the case in which the primary imports into A on which the duty is lowered are close substitutes in A for some products which are exported from A. Thus if the duty on imports of wines into country A is reduced, this may cause people in A to drink more wine at the expense of drinking less home-produced whisky, and this may release more whisky for export from A. Or the substitutability may be between a raw material and the finished product. Thus a reduction in a duty on the import of raw cotton into A may lead to an increase in the output of finished cotton textiles in A and so to an increase in the export of cotton textiles from A. Or the substitutability may be on the side of production. A reduction in the duty on the import of machine tools in A may lead to a contraction of the machine tool industry in A. This in turn may release factors of production—skilled engineering labour—which are most readily re-employed in the industry producing motor cars; and this may lead to an increase in the export of motor cars from A.

If there is a duty and so a divergence between marginal social values and costs on the export of the secondary products from A to B, then any reduction in the duty on the primary import into A will be bound to increase economic welfare. It will cause an increase in the primary import (on which there is a divergence between value and cost) as well as in the secondary export (in which there is also such a divergence). Indeed, if the rate of duty on the export of the secondary product from A to B cannot be reduced—and such is our present assumption—economic welfare demands that there should be some subsidy paid on the import of the primary product into A. If the primary import is subsidized, this means that there will be some direct loss incurred by a further stimulation of this import, since its marginal cost will now exceed its marginal value; but if the rate of subsidy on the primary import is not too high relatively to the rate of duty on the secondary export, some increase in the rate of subsidy and in the volume of the primary import will still raise economic welfare, because the direct loss due to the greater import of the primary product (on which marginal cost slightly exceeds marginal value) will be more than outweighed by the indirect gain from the stimulation of exports of the secondary product (on which marginal value greatly exceeds marginal cost).

The increase in the secondary exports will be large relatively to the increase in the primary imports (and thus the rate of subsidy on the primary imports should be high relatively to the rate of duty on the secondary exports) (i) if the degree of substitutability in A between the primary import and the secondary export is high; (ii) if the elasticity of demand for the secondary export in B is high, so that there can be a large increase in the secondary export without much fall in its price and so without much discouragement to its supply in A; (iii) if the secondary export is not a very good substitute in production in A with all other products in A, so that any given fall in the price offered for it in B does not much reduce its supply in A; and (iv) if the primary import in A is not a very good substitute with all the other products in A (apart from the secondary export) so that its price will fall considerably in A when the duty on it is reduced (or the subsidy on it is raised) with the consequence that there will be a large stimulation of the secondary export which is a close substitute for it.

(4) The last type of repercussion in A is that of *secondary export trade destruction in A*. This occurs when, in one of the three ways already mentioned, the primary imports in A are complementary in A's consumption or production with some export from A. In this case the increased import into A of the primary import will increase the home demand (or reduce the home supply) of the secondary commodity and the volume of its exports will in consequence be reduced. In this case some rate of duty should be maintained upon the primary import if the secondary export is also subject to a duty. A rise in the duty on the primary imports will reduce the primary imports and thus increase the secondary exports; and while there will be some direct loss of welfare on the decrease in the trade in the taxed primary imports, there will be a more than counterbalancing gain of economic welfare in the increased trade on the taxed secondary exports provided that the tax on the latter is high enough relatively to that on the former.

The tax on the primary imports should be high relatively to that on the secondary exports if the increased volume of secondary exports which will be associated with any decreased volume of primary imports is large. This will be so, if (i) there is a high degree of complementarity in A between the primary imports and the secondary exports; (ii) if the elasticity of demand in B for the secondary export is high; (iii) if the secondary export is not a very good substitute in A with all the rest of A's products, so that its supply to B is not much discouraged by any fall in its price in B; and (iv) if the primary import in A is not a very good substitute with all the other products of A so that its price will rise considerably in A when the duty on it is raised with the consequence that there will be a large stimulation of the secondary export which is a close substitute for it.

So far we have considered the repercussions of a reduction of a duty on imports into A only upon the demand or supply in A of exports or imports. But the reduction in the duty and the consequential increase in the flow of the primary commodity from B to A may also have similar repercussions in B, if the primary export from B is a particularly close substitute for or complement with other imports or exports of B. These possible repercussions may also take any one of four forms. Here we shall merely enumerate the four possibilities. The reader is left to apply to them the same detailed analysis which we have already applied to the similar repercussions in A.

(1) *Secondary export trade destruction in B.* The primary export from B may, in B's production or consumption, be a close substitute for some other secondary commodity which is also exported from B. In this case a reduction in the duty on the import of the primary product into A will reduce the consumption or increase the production of that primary product in B which will lead to a reduction in the export of the secondary substitute commodity from B.

(2) *Secondary export trade creation in B.* The primary export from B may be complementary in B's consumption or production with some other product which is exported from B. In this case an increase in the export of the primary product from B to A will release larger supplies of the secondary product also for export from B to A.

(3) *Secondary import trade creation in B.* The primary export from B to A might be a close substitute in B's consumption or production for some commodity imported into B. In this case an increased export of the primary commodity would lead to increased imports of the secondary product.

(4) *Secondary import trade destruction in B.* The primary export from B to A might be complementary in B's production or consumption with some commodity which is imported into B. In this case the increased export of the primary commodity would lead to a reduced import of the secondary complementary commodity.

These primary and secondary repercussions of a reduction in an import duty in A upon the volume of trade between A and B are summarized in columns *a* and *b* of Table XIX.[1] Thus the primary effect

[1] Columns *c* and *d* will be used at a later stage in this chapter to illustrate different points.

of a reduction in A's duty is to increase the flow of the product directly affected from B into A, and this represents a primary creation of import trade in A and of export trade in B (column *b*, rows 1 and 2). Rows 3–6 of the table deal with the four possible secondary repercussions on A's trade with B which may result from repercussion in A's markets (see pp. 206–14 above). To take row 3 as an example, if the primary imports into A are close substitutes with other imports into A (SI in column *a*), then there will be a secondary reduction of these other imports which have now to face fiercer competition from the primary imports into A on which the import duty has been reduced (ID in column *b*). And similarly for all the other rows of columns *a* and *b* in the table.

Now if one takes into account the possible secondary repercussions in B (rows 7–10 of Table XIX), as well as the possible secondary repercussions in A (rows 3–6 of the table), it becomes clear that quite large indirect gains or losses might be associated with any given reduction in duty on a primary import from B into A. Let us consider an example of great secondary gain. Suppose that A reduces a duty on the import of raw wool from B. Suppose that A also exports woollen textiles manufactured out of imported raw wool, and suppose that the raw wool in B is jointly produced with mutton, which is also exported from B to A. Then the reduction in A's import duty on raw wool will increase A's imports of raw wool from B. But this will cause both a secondary export trade creation in A (which will now have more woollen textiles to offer for export) and secondary export trade creation in B (which will now be producing more mutton for export as a result of its increased production of raw wool). It is quite possible that the value of the increased trade in mutton and in woollen textiles might be greater than the value of the increased trade in raw wool. In this case the maximization of economic welfare might require a rate of subsidy to be paid on the import of raw wool into A which was higher than the rate of duty levied either on the export of woollen textiles from A to B or of mutton from B to A.

Other combinations of repercussion in A and B might mean that very large secondary losses were associated with any primary increase of imports into A. Suppose that A reduces a duty on the import of butter from B. Suppose that in A's consumption imports of butter are closely substitutable for imports of margarine, and suppose that in B's production the preparation of butter for export competes very closely with the same factors of production which are needed to produce cheese for export. Then the reduction in the duty in A on imports of butter and the consequential primary increase in butter imports will be associated with a secondary import-trade destruction in A (since a smaller amount of margarine imports will now be wanted in A) as well

TABLE XIX

The Primary and Secondary Effects of a Partial Reduction in A's Import Duties on the Volume, Balance, and Terms of Trade

(a)		Import (I) or export (E) trade is created (C) or destroyed (D) (b)	Movement of balance of trade in favour of A or of B (c)	Movement of terms of trade in favour of A or of B (d)
Primary effect in A	(1)	IC	} B	B
,, ,, ,, B	(2)	EC		
Secondary effects: In A the primary import is a substitute (S) or complement (C) for A's other imports (I) or exports (E)				
(i) SI	(3)	ID	A	A
(ii) CI	(4)	IC	B	B
(iii) SE	(5)	EC	A*	B
(iv) CE	(6)	ED	B*	A
In B the primary export is a substitute (S) or complement (C) for B's other exports (E) or imports (I)				
(i) SE	(7)	ED	A†	B
(ii) CE	(8)	EC	B†	A
(iii) SI	(9)	IC	A	A
(iv) CI	(10)	ID	B	B

* These two letters would be reversed if the elasticity of demand in B for the relevant imports was less than unity.

† These two letters would be reversed if the elasticity of demand in A for the relevant imports was less than unity.

as a secondary export-trade destruction in B (since less cheese will now be produced for export by B). It is now possible that the rate of duty on butter imports into A should be kept at a higher level than that on either margarine or cheese imports, since any loss in the trade in butter may be offset by a still greater increase in the value of the trade in margarine and cheese combined.

It may be worth while noting before we leave these secondary repercussions that they may take rather more complicated forms than those which we have already discussed. For example, the relationship of substitutability or complementarity may be indirect through some third commodity. Thus coal and fertilizers may be close substitutes in one country's imports, not because coal can be used as a fertilizer or the fertilizer used as a fuel, but because there is some third commodity produced at home—such as cow-dung—which can be used as a fuel or as a fertilizer. Then increased imports of coal will mean that less home-produced cow-dung will be used as a fuel, more will be used as a fertilizer, and less imported fertilizer will be needed. Or, to take another example, imports of thick underwear may not be directly complementary with imports of iron ore. But increased imports of warm underwear may reduce the demand for coal for domestic heating; increased supplies of coal for industrial purposes may stimulate the steel industry and so the import of a complementary material, iron ore.

In the examples which we have so far discussed we have not allowed any of the secondary changes in trade themselves to have secondary repercussions. But it may not always be possible to neglect such changes. For example, a reduced duty on the import of wheat into A by causing an increase in the supply of wheat in A may lead to a secondary reduction in the demand for imported barley into A. But the reduced demand for exports of barley from B may itself have a marked secondary repercussion—the land and labour previously used for the production of barley exports in B being almost wholly shifted to the production of, say, cheese exports from B. There would then be an increase of cheese exports from B to A as a secondary secondary repercussion of the primary increase of wheat imports into A.

How far it is useful to carry an analysis of this kind will always depend upon the particular problem which is under discussion. When the effects of any particular duty reduction are under consideration, we must always consider the principal secondary changes which will take place in other lines of trade which are subject to a duty or subsidy or to any other form of divergence between marginal values and costs. Only the particular circumstances of each case can finally decide how far it is worth while carrying through each series of repercussions. Normally direct primary repercussions will be greater than indirect secondary repercussions, and secondary will be greater than secondary secondary repercussions. At each link in the chain of repercussions the amount of change which is passed on to another single specific commodity is likely to become smaller and smaller. The changes are soon likely to be diffused in the form of very small changes affecting a very large number of commodities.

This consideration leads to an examination of the *tertiary* repercussions of any primary change. When we have made allowance for all the primary and noticeable secondary changes, we shall have allowed for all the significant changes which are concentrated upon trade in the one or two commodities most markedly affected by the change. But we shall not necessarily have considered all the relevant changes. The attainment of full equilibrium may still require many very small further changes spread over the trade in a very large number of other commodities, and if these other commodities are all subject to taxes or subsidies, the aggregate effect of a very large number of changes, even though each change is very small in itself, may not be negligible *in toto*. In our present problem these further, or what we shall call tertiary, changes will show themselves most clearly in what we may call balance-of-payments adjustments.

The primary and secondary changes are those changes in the trade in the commodities most directly affected which would take place if money incomes in A and in B remain unchanged and if all prices other than those of the primary and secondary commodities remained unchanged. But there is no reason to believe that general equilibrium can be restored after the primary reduction of duty without some change in the general level of money incomes and prices in A relatively to the general level of money incomes and prices in B. Such a general adjustment of money incomes and prices will be necessary if the primary and secondary changes alone so affect the trade between A and B that a general balance-of-payments problem remains which requires a solution by means of a domestic deflation of money prices and incomes in the deficit country combined with a domestic inflation of money prices and incomes in the surplus country (the gold-standard mechanism), or by means of a depreciation of the domestic currency of the deficit country in terms of the domestic currency of the surplus country (the method of variable exchange rates).[1]

The primary change itself will certainly put A's balance of payments into deficit, assuming that previously A was in balance. When the duty on A's imports of, say, blankets from B is reduced, there will be an increase in the amount of blankets bought by A from B, and in consequence A will spend a greater amount of money than before on her imports of blankets from B.

This effect of the primary change upon A's balance of payments with B may be aggravated or may be in whole or in part offset by the secondary changes. Let us first give an example where it will be much aggravated by the secondary changes. Suppose A reduces a duty on imports

[1] Cf. Part IV of Volume I of this work.

of raw wool from B. If the raw wool in A is jointly demanded with imported spinning and weaving machinery to make woollen textiles, A's demand for imports will be further stimulated by the secondary repercussions in A. If the raw wool is jointly produced with exported mutton in B, more mutton will be offered for export by B to A; and if A's demand for imported mutton has an elasticity greater than unity, then A's expenditure on imports will increase still further because of this secondary repercussion upon the supply of mutton in B. In this case the reduction in A's duty on imported raw wool will have caused a threefold strain on A's balance of payments—because of the primary effect upon imports of raw wool and because of the secondary effects upon the imports of textile machinery and of mutton.

But the secondary effects may be to mitigate and even—though this is less likely—more than to offset the primary strain on A's balance of payments. Thus suppose, to repeat an example which we have already used, that A reduces a duty on imports of butter from B, that the butter imports into A are close substitutes in A's consumption for imports of margarine, and that the butter exports from B are close substitutes in B's production for exports of cheese. Then if, broadly speaking, more than one-half of A's increased expenditure on butter imports were met by an economy of A's expenditure on margarine imports, and if, at the same time, more than one-half of the value of the factors newly used in butter exports in B were drained away from the provision of cheese exports by B to A,[1] and thus represented a reduction in the value of A's cheese imports from B, then the secondary changes might more than outweigh the primary deterioration in A's balance of payments, so that there was a net surplus on A's balance of payments to be cared for by the remaining tertiary changes.

The possible effects of the primary and secondary changes in trade upon the balance of trade between A and B are summarized in column *c* of Table XIX. The primary effect (rows 1 and 2) will necessarily be favourable to B's balance of trade, since it represents an increase in A's demand for B's exports. Whether the secondary repercussions will be favourable to A's or to B's balance of trade will depend upon the character of the secondary repercussion itself. Thus (row 3) if the primary import into A competes closely with other imports into A, there will be a secondary decline in A's other imports and so some secondary improvement in A's balance of trade. But (row 4) if the primary imports into A had been complementary with some other imports, there would have been an additional secondary increase in A's demand for imports and so a secondary intensification of the improvement in B's balance of trade. If the primary imports into A were substitutes in A (row 5)

[1] Assuming that A's demand for imports of cheese were very elastic so that she did not pay a much higher price for the cheese which B continued to export to her.

with exports from A to B, then they would increase the supply of products available for export from A to B, and thus—provided that the elasticity of demand for imports of these products into B was greater than unity—would improve A's balance of trade. And the opposite would be the case if the primary imports into A were complementary in A with other products exported from A to B.

Similar repercussions on the balance of trade may arise from repercussions in B's markets. If the primary exports from B are substitutes in B for other exports from B (row 7), then the supply of these other exports from B to A will be reduced, which will improve A's balance of trade, provided that the elasticity of demand for imports of these products into A is greater than unity. The opposite would be the case if the primary exports from B were complementary in B with other exports from B to A and so increased the supply by B of these other exports to A (row 8). If the primary exports from B are substitutes in B with imports of B from A (row 9), then B's demand for these other imports will be raised, and this will aid A's balance of trade. And, finally (row 10), the opposite will be the case if the primary exports of B are complementary in B with imports into B, so that B's demand for these imports is reduced.

Now any element of substitutability between the primary product and tradeable products (whether imports or exports) in either country (whether A or B) will give rise to secondary repercussions which will help to offset the primary strain on A's balance of trade. In Table XIX this is shown by the fact that whenever an S (i.e. substitutability) appears in column *a*, an A (i.e. an improvement in A's balance of trade) appears in column *c*. But it is to be noted that there is no direct corelation between secondary trade creation or trade destruction on the one hand and a secondary alleviation to A's balance of trade on the other. In Table XIX, in rows 3–10, D and C in column *b* are associated an equal number of times each with A and B in column *c*. A frequent secondary connexion may be where most of A's imports are fairly good substitutes for each other (A importing products of the same type which can serve similar purposes in consumption and/or need similar factors for their production), and where most of B's exports are fairly good substitutes for each other (B exporting products of the same type which can serve similar purposes in consumption and/or which need similar resources for their production). In this case we should have secondary adjustments of the kinds shown in rows 3 and 7 of Table XIX. There would be secondary trade destruction and so a secondary loss of economic welfare to set against the primary gain. But at the same time and for similar reasons there would be a secondary improvement in A's balance of trade to set against the primary strain on A's balance of trade.

But this is by no means the only possible case. In the real world the actual secondary repercussions will depend upon the particular country which reduces the duty and the particular product on which the duty is reduced. As we have seen (p. 219), if all the secondary repercussions were favourable, it is possible that the secondary relief to A's balance of trade might outweigh the primary strain on A's balance of trade. But if all secondary repercussions were unfavourable, there might be a very heavy combined primary and secondary strain on A's balance of trade.[1]

But whatever is the outcome, it would be a mere coincidence if the secondary repercussions exactly offset the primary strain on A's balance of payments and left the payments between A and B in full equilibrium. There is likely to be some balance-of-payments problem in one direction or the other. In what follows we shall suppose that the primary and secondary changes leave A with some deficit on her balance of payments, and shall consider the effect upon economic welfare of the further or tertiary adjustments which are necessary to remove this deficit. We have chosen to consider the case of a deficit on A's balance of payments because this would seem to be on balance the more probable case. But the reader can readily apply for himself the following type of analysis to the case in which there is a surplus, and not a deficit, on A's balance of payments which needs to be corrected.

If the primary and secondary changes leave a deficit on A's balance of payments, we assume that this will be closed by means of the price mechanism—i.e. either by a domestic deflation of money prices and incomes in A and a domestic inflation of money prices and incomes in

[1] For our present purpose, since we are not concerned with the distribution of income between A and B, we are not interested in the effect of the primary and secondary trade changes upon the real terms of trade between A and B. But in Table XIX, column *d*, these effects are also summarized. It is clear that the primary effect of the increased demand for imports in A will be to raise the price which must be paid to producers of the primary export in B and so to turn the terms of trade against A. This primary movement of the terms of trade against A may be mitigated or intensified by the secondary repercussions. Anything which reduces A's demand for imports (and thus reduces the price which B's exporters can profitably charge), or which reduces A's supply of exports (and thus encourages B's importers to offer a better price for the reduced supplies), will tend to move the terms of trade back in A's favour. Thus (rows 3 and 6 of Table XIX) anything which causes a secondary destruction of trade in A will help A's terms of trade, whereas (rows 4 and 5) anything which causes a secondary creation of trade in A will worsen A's terms of trade—either by increasing A's demand for imports or by increasing the supply of exports which she puts on B's market. In B, on the other hand, anything which creates trade will help A's terms of trade either by increasing B's demand for imports from A (row 8) or else by increasing the supply of exports which B puts on A's markets (row 9). Conversely, anything which destroys trade in B (rows 7 and 10) will worsen the terms of trade for A. It can be seen from Table XIX that there is no correlation between the three effects—on volume, balance, and terms of trade in columns *b*, *c*, and *d*—of the various interrelationships of substitutability and complementarity between traded goods in column *a*.

B, or else by a depreciation of A's currency in terms of B's currency. As we have already argued (see Chapter XV of Volume I of this work), the ultimate real effects of both methods will in all relevant aspects be the same. The fall in A's prices and incomes relatively to B's prices and incomes will lead to a general contraction in the volume of A's imports from B and a general expansion in the volume of A's exports to B; and if these changes in the volumes of trade are sufficiently large relatively to the price changes which cause them, the result will be to remove the deficit on A's balance of trade.

Now these tertiary changes in the volume of trade—the general contraction of A's imports and expansion of her exports—will be spread over the whole range of A's imports and exports. It will affect the primary and the secondary commodities as well as all the other items in A's import and export list. Thus the reduction in A's incomes and prices may cause A's consumers to reduce their consumption slightly of the primary product, the initial increase in the import of which has been the cause of the whole disequilibrium. It may also cause them to reduce slightly their consumption of some other imports, the volume of which has already been powerfully affected by some secondary repercussion from the change in A's primary import. But the tertiary or balance-of-payments adjustments will be spread over all A's imports and exports and, unless the primary and secondary products make up an important section of A's total international trade, their effect on the balance of payments is likely to operate mainly through all the other items of A's imports and exports. We will call these the tertiary products and will examine the effect of changes in them upon economic welfare, although the careful reader will realize that the tertiary effects influence all commodities—primary, secondary, and tertiary—and not only these other imports and exports which we are calling the tertiary products.

As we have seen, the restoration of balance to A's international payments comes about through an expansion of A's tertiary exports and a contraction of her tertiary imports. Now if there are taxes levied on most of A's imports and exports, so that there is an excess of marginal value over marginal cost in the case of most of her trade, then there will be a loss of economic welfare due to the tertiary contraction of A's imports and a gain of economic welfare due to the tertiary expansion of her exports. In what circumstances will the tertiary gain exceed the tertiary loss, and vice versa?

Now if A is a heavily protectionist country and B has only a moderately protectionist policy, then the *ad valorem* incidence of the general level of duties on A's imports is likely to be much higher than the *ad valorem* incidence of the general level of duties on A's exports.[1] In this

[1] It is assumed that both countries carry out their protectionist policies by taxing imports and not exports.

case the loss of economic welfare due to a tertiary reduction in the volume of A's imports will be greater than the gain of economic welfare due to an equal tertiary expansion of A's exports. A high level of import duties in A relatively to the level in B will be a factor tending to cause a net tertiary loss of economic welfare.

But suppose that the general level of duties on the tertiary trade was the same in both countries. It would still be possible for there to be a net tertiary gain or loss to economic welfare. For example, there would still be a net tertiary loss if the tertiary adjustment to A's balance of payments was brought about mainly by a contraction in the volume of her imports and very little by an expansion in the volume of her exports. Now this would be the case if the elasticities of demand for imports in A and of the supply of exports in B were very high (so that a small rise in the price charged for B's products by B's exporters in terms of A's currency caused A to import very much less of them, and a small fall in the price offered for B's products by A's consumers in terms of B's currency caused B to export very much less of them), and if, at the same time, the elasticities of demand for imports in B and of the supply of exports in A were very small (so that a large fall in the price charged to B's consumers for A's products in terms of B's currency did not cause B to buy very much more of them and a large rise in the price offered to A's producers for A's products in terms of A's currency did not cause A to export very much more of them). In this case the adjustment of A's deficit would be mainly by tertiary trade destruction (contraction of her imports) rather than by tertiary trade creation (expansion of her exports). But unless there is reason in any particular case to believe either that A's tertiary imports will be subject to a markedly different rate of tax than B's tertiary imports, or else that the elasticity of demand and supply for A's tertiary imports is much bigger or smaller than that for B's tertiary imports, there is no reason to believe that the tertiary adjustments will cause any significant net addition to or subtraction from economic welfare.

It may be useful at this stage to summarize this chapter by enumerating briefly the conditions which will make it probable that a reduction in the rate of import duty on one particular import will lead to a rise rather than a fall in economic welfare.

(1) First, the reduction in duty is likely to cause an increase of imports of the commodity concerned. This will certainly increase economic welfare. This primary increase in economic welfare will be the greater, (*a*) the greater the consequential increase in the volume imported, i.e. the more elastic is the demand for the import in A and the supply of the export in B, and (*b*) the higher is the initial rate of duty on the commodity concerned. This last point means that if a particular duty is reduced in successive stages—e.g. from 60 per cent to 50 per cent,

from 50 per cent to 40 per cent, and so on—the earlier stages of reduction are more likely to cause a net increase in economic welfare than the later ones.

(2) Second, if we assume that all other elements of trade between A and B are subject to some degree of tax and that none are subject to subsidization, there may be further increases of economic welfare if the commodity primarily concerned has the appropriate close relationships of substitutability or complementarity in consumption or production in A or B with other goods which may enter into trade between A and B. The relationships which will cause a secondary expansion of trade and so a still further increase of economic welfare are (i) substitutability in A between the primary product and other goods which are exportable from A and in B between the primary product and other goods which are imported into B, and (ii) complementarity of the primary product in A with other imports into A and in B with other goods which are exported from B. The opposite relationships will lead to a secondary destruction of trade and so to a loss of economic welfare which might outweigh the gain of welfare through increased trade in the primary good. The secondary gains are, of course, more likely to outweigh any secondary losses if the rates of duty which are currently levied on any secondarily created trade are high relatively to those currently levied on any secondarily destroyed trade.

Since we want to avoid substitutability between the primary import into A and A's other imports and substitutability between the export from B and B's other exports, there will be a greater chance of gain from the primary reduction of an import duty in A if the duty is cut on a whole class of goods than if it is cut on only one particular good in a whole class of goods. For in the latter case the particular commodity in question is very likely to be a close substitute in A's consumption for some other imported products in the same class and also a close substitute in B's production for some other exported products in the same class of goods.

(3) Third, if we assume that the primary and secondary changes just described will leave A with some deficit on its balance of trade, there may be some further tertiary gain of economic welfare if the general level of duties on A's imports (which must be contracted on balance-of-payments grounds) is low and the general level of duties on A's exports (which will be generally expanded) is high. Also the tertiary gain is likely to outweigh the tertiary loss if the elasticities of supply and demand for A's imports are less than the elasticities of supply and demand for A's exports, so that the balance-of-payments adjustment comes about more by a tertiary expansion of A's export trade than by a tertiary contraction of her import trade.

It is very difficult to reach any really general conclusions on this subject. There would seem to be some presumption in favour of a reduction in a particular duty, since the primary effect is always beneficial and the secondary and tertiary effects may be unimportant and may work one way or the other. There is a still stronger presumption in making cuts in those particular duties which have a specially high *ad valorem* incidence, because in this case the certain primary expansion of trade will receive a very high welfare weight (being the subject of a high rate of divergence between marginal values and costs) relatively to the welfare weights to be applied to any possible secondary or tertiary trade destruction. Finally, the presumption in favour of the cut is increased if it applies to a whole class of similar goods rather than to a particular good in a general class.

CHAPTER XIV

THE SECOND-BEST ARGUMENT FOR TRADE CONTROL: (3) DOMESTIC DIVERGENCES

WE turn now from the case in which there is some initial and fixed divergence between marginal values and costs in international trade to the case in which there is some initial and fixed divergence between marginal values and costs within the domestic economy of one of our trading countries. We assume that there are no other domestic divergences within any of the trading countries and that there are initially no import or export duties and subsidies or any other cause of divergence between marginal values and costs in international trade. Our purpose is to inquire whether in these circumstances the damage to economic welfare caused by the domestic divergence between marginal values and costs might not be in part offset by a departure from free trade, i.e. by introducing a counterbalancing divergence through some commercial-policy control over a relevant part of the country's international trade. In examining this question we shall continue to abstract from the equity aspects of the problem and will consider only the efficiency aspects. That is to say, we shall assume that the policy-makers have allotted the same marginal distributional weights to the money income of every person throughout the world economy.

Let us suppose then that in country A in some industry producing goods which are highly competitive with some of A's imports there is a divergence between marginal values and marginal costs. This excess of marginal value over marginal cost might, as we have seen in Chapter II, be due to any one of a number of causes. There might be an element of monopoly in the production of the home product in which case home production will have been restricted until the marginal cost of production is equal, not to the price or marginal value of the product to the consumer, but to the marginal revenue to be obtained from adding the last unit of output to the sales of the product. Alternatively, there might be some external economy involved in the domestic production which meant that the marginal social cost was below the marginal private cost and so below the marginal value of the commodity to consumers. Or the divergence might be due to the existence of some rate of tax levied on the domestic production which raised the price charged to the consumer above the net price received by the producers. Our analysis will be relevant for any divergence between marginal values and costs, no matter what the cause of it may be.[1]

[1] In this chapter we shall confine our attention to certain positive domestic divergences. But there may, of course, be negative divergences in which marginal costs exceed marginal values, due, for example, to an external

Now if there is such a divergence in the production in A of goods which compete closely with A's imports (e.g. in the production of home-produced blankets in A competing with blankets imported from B), this will prevent production from being maximized but it will not prevent trade from being optimized. Suppose the divergence took the form of a 10 per cent excess of marginal value over marginal cost in A's blanket industry. Then the marginal social cost of producing blankets would be 10 per cent lower in A than in B. But, since we are assuming no other divergences to exist, the marginal social cost of all other traded products will be the same in A as in B. The two countries together could therefore have more blankets without having any less of any other product if A produced a few more blankets and a few less of some other traded product—say, apples—while B produced so many more apples and—because her marginal social cost was higher—reduced her output of blankets by less than A had increased hers. This could be brought about if A imported less blankets and made more at home for her own consumption with factors which previously produced apples for export, while B produced less blankets for export and more apples to replace the reduced exports of apples from A. A duty in A levied on the import of blankets would have this sort of effect and might thus, in the conditions which we are examining, have helped to maximize production.

On the other hand, the existence of the 10 per cent excess of marginal value over marginal cost in A's blanket industry would not in itself have done anything to interfere with the optimization of trade between A and B. As far as consumers are concerned the price charged for blankets, for apples, or for any other traded product would be the same in A as in B. It would not be possible for consumers in A to be made better off without consumers in B being made worse off simply by trading more or less between A and B out of fixed output of blankets, apples, etc., in A and B. But if a duty were imposed on the import of blankets from B into A in order to help to maximize production, then it would no longer be true that trade would be optimized. Suppose that a 10 per cent duty were imposed on the import of blankets into A, then production would be maximized. The price of blankets in A would be raised 10 per cent above their price in B; but since marginal social cost equalled the price of blankets in B but was 10 per cent below the price in A which was, in turn, 10 per cent above the price in B, the output of blankets in A and B would now be adjusted until the marginal social cost of a blanket was the same in A as in B. But the price charged to consumers for blankets in A would now be 10 per cent above the price charged for them in B, so that the marginal value of blankets would now be higher in A than in

diseconomy. The reader is left to apply the analysis of this chapter for himself to such cases. The analysis is, of course, essentially the same, requiring only a discussion of subsidies to trade instead of duties on trade or vice versa.

B. Consumers could now gain if, out of fixed outputs of blankets and apples in A and B, more apples were exported from A to B and more blankets exported in turn from B to A. Trade would no longer be optimized.

It follows that in the conditions under examination free trade will lead to the optimization of trade, but the 10 per cent divergence between marginal values and costs will mean that production is not maximized. A 10 per cent duty on the imports of blankets into A will offset this divergence and cause production to be maximized; but now trade will not be optimized because the marginal value of blankets will be 10 per cent higher in A than in B. Our problem is to find out whether more is gained through the consequential maximization of production or is lost through the consequential de-optimization of trade by imposing the duty, or whether some intermediate duty—higher than zero but less than 10 per cent—should be imposed in order to achieve the highest level of economic welfare when both the maximization of production and the optimization of trade are taken into account.[1]

Suppose then that a duty is imposed upon the import of blankets into A. This will have a twofold effect. (i) By protecting the home industry it will cause an increase in the volume of blankets produced in A for consumption in A; and (ii) by taxing imports of blankets it will cause a decrease in the amount of blankets imported into A from B. The increase in A's output under (i) will, however, be less than the reduction of imports under (ii). This is so because the imposition of the duty will raise the price in A, and it is only because the price is raised that there is any increase in output in A. But since the price in A is higher, the amount consumed in A will be reduced, so that the increase in home output under (i) will be less than the decrease in imports under (ii). Now it follows from this that, starting with a zero rate of import duty, the imposition of a small duty would increase economic welfare. This would cause some increase in domestic production on which there would be a gain equal to the 10 per cent divergence between marginal value and cost. It would, it is true, cause a still larger fall in the volume of imports; but on this there is initially no divergence and therefore no marginal loss.

But if the duty is now raised to a higher level there will once more be a gain equal to the whole 10 per cent divergence between marginal value and cost on the further increase of home production; but now there will be some loss equal to the rate of duty—which causes a divergence between marginal value and cost on the import trade—on the further reduction in import trade. Since the reduction in the volume of import trade is at each successive rise of import duty greater than the

[1] Much of the rest of the analysis in this chapter is outlined in mathematical form in Sections XI–XIV of the mathematical supplement to this volume.

accompanying increase of home output, the loss of welfare on the lost import trade will just counterbalance the gain on the new home production when the rate of duty on imports (which will operate on a relatively large decrease in the volume of imports) is lower than the rate of divergence on home production (which will operate on a relatively small increase in home production).

It will, therefore, do good to impose a duty on imports, but the rate of duty should be at a rate lower than the rate of divergence on home production, the wasteful effects of which it is designed to offset. But how much less? This clearly depends upon how much smaller the increase in home production is than the reduction in imports at each successive stage of raising of the duty. Now the increase in home production will be larger relatively to the decrease in imports, the greater is the elasticity of supply of the home product in A and the smaller is the elasticity of demand for the commodity in A. Thus a tax on imported blankets will raise their price in A. If this rise in price causes a large increase in the output of A's blankets and if, at the same time, it causes only a very small decrease in the total consumption of blankets in A, then there will be a large increase in the home production with only a very slightly greater fall in the volume of imports. There are in fact two possible limiting cases in which the increase in home production will be equal to the reduction in imports. The first is when the elasticity of demand for blankets in general in A is zero. In this case the rise in the price of blankets in A will not cause any reduction in the total amount bought in A, so that the increase in home production must be on a scale which exactly offsets the reduction in imports. The second limiting case is when the elasticity of supply of blankets in A is infinite. In this case the raising of the duty in imports cannot in fact lead to any increase in the price of blankets in A, because if it did so the domestic output of blankets in A would be indefinitely expanded until the price had been brought back to its former level. The whole of the duty would fall on the exporter of blankets from B and would cause a reduction in the price of blankets in B. But since the price of blankets would not have risen in A, consumers would have had no incentive to reduce their consumption of blankets. Once again the increase in home production must have completely replaced the reduction in imports.

In either of these two limiting cases, therefore—where the elasticity of demand for blankets in A is zero or where the elasticity of their production in A is infinite—the increase in home production would be as great as the reduction in imports; and the greatest contribution to economic welfare would therefore be attained if the import duty were raised to equality with the rate of divergence on the home production which it is designed to offset. But in the normal case where the elasticity of supply is less than infinite and the elasticity of demand is greater than zero, the loss of imports will exceed the gain of home production in volume, so that the duty which will maximize economic welfare will be less than the rate of divergence on home production. The best rate of duty will approach the rate of divergence on home production the more nearly, the smaller is the elasticity of A's demand for and the greater is the elasticity of A's supply of the product in question.

The nature of this argument for a protective duty should not be misunderstood. The argument is not that the imposition of a duty is the best policy to adopt, but merely that it is better to impose an import duty (provided it is at not too high a rate) than to do nothing at all about the problem. If one starts with the moderate duty on imports, the position can be improved if out of the revenue raised by the duty on imports a small subsidy is paid on home production. This would encourage the home production on which there is still a 10 per cent divergence between marginal value and cost at the expense of a smaller reduction of imports[1] on which in any case the divergence is less than 10 per cent because *ex hypothesi* the duty is less than 10 per cent. A still better situation could be achieved by still further reducing the rate of duty on imports and increasing the rate of subsidy on home production in such a way that there was some simultaneous increase in the amount produced at home (on which there is now a rate of divergence equal to 10 per cent less the rate of subsidy on home production) and in the amount imported (on which there is a divergence equal to the remaining rate of duty). Clearly this series of adjustments can be continued with a continuing favourable effect upon economic welfare until the rate of import duty has been eliminated and a rate of subsidy is being paid on home production equal to the initial 10 per cent divergence between marginal value and cost.

In other words, if there is a divergence between marginal value and costs in A's blanket industry, a moderate duty on the import of competing blankets from B will be better than nothing. But it will be better still to tackle the problem directly and to take action directly on A's blanket industry to remove or offset the initial divergence there, for example by means of a direct subsidy to the output of blankets in A. This argument, however, tacitly assumes that there are no problems involved in raising the revenue for the payment of the subsidy to A's blanket industry—that, for example, the State owns sufficient income-bearing property or else it is possible to raise the necessary funds by a system of progressive lump-sum taxes. But as we have seen in earlier chapters[2] the fact that taxes imposed for the purpose of raising revenue

[1] The reduction in imports would be smaller than the increase in home production since the subsidy on home production would tend to lower the price of the product in A and so to increase the total amount consumed in A.

[2] See Chapters VII and XII.

themselves cause divergences between values and costs is a complicating factor. Suppose then that a subsidy is being paid on the home production of blankets. It is probable that the rate of subsidy should be less than 10 per cent, i.e. less than sufficient to offset the whole of the initial divergence. The raising of the revenue for the payment of the subsidy will also do some damage elsewhere; and since to raise the subsidy from 9 per cent, say, to 10 per cent will cause an increase in home production on which there is now a divergence of only 1 per cent (i.e. the initial divergence of 10 per cent less the existing rate of subsidy of 9 per cent), the gain from raising the subsidy might be more than outweighed by the loss from raising the revenue. When, however, a search is made for suitable objects of taxation for the finance of the subsidy, it is most unlikely that the import of blankets would be found alone to constitute the best basis for the new taxation. If it were simply a case of finding a given revenue to pay a given total subsidy, it would be the merest of coincidences that the import of blankets should happen to be the most appropriate basis for a revenue duty when the home production of blankets happened to be the economic activity which needed to be subsidized. In this particular case, however, there would be an argument for taxing rather more heavily than the purely revenue considerations would demand those goods and services which either in production or consumption in A are closely competitive with A's home-produced blankets. If something is taxed in A which competes in A's consumption with home-produced blankets, then—in addition to raising a revenue—this will to some extent encourage the consumption of home-produced blankets; and since there is some divergence left between marginal value and cost in the production of these blankets, this incidental effect of the revenue duty will not be without value. Similarly, if some other product were taxed which used exactly the same factors of production as were used in A's blanket industry, then the discouragement of the production of this alternative product by the tax would reduce the demand for, and so lower the price of, these particular factors which would reduce the costs of producing blankets in A. The consequential increase in the supply of A's blankets would bring with it a net advantage since there is still some net divergence between marginal value and cost in the production of blankets in A.

To summarize, if revenue can be raised (e.g. by progressive lump-sum taxation) in such a way as to cause no divergences elsewhere, then the expansion of the blanket industry in A should be brought about by a subsidy which totally offsets the initial divergence between marginal value and cost in the industry. But if revenue cannot be raised in this harmless way, then a somewhat lower rate of subsidy should be paid, leaving some of the initial divergence uncompensated. Since some net divergence would still remain, it is still desirable to encourage the production of blankets in A. This means that in searching for suitable sources of revenue to meet the subsidy, there is a special case for taxing rather more heavily than would otherwise be done those goods and services which in consumption or production compete most closely with A's home-produced blankets. Since imported blankets compete in consumption very closely with home-produced blankets, there is an argument for some degree of protective duty as a means of promoting blanket production in A.[1]

But the force of this argument for some element of protective duty to expand the blanket industry in A depends upon the nature of the divergence between marginal value and cost in the production of blankets in A. In some cases it may be considerably weaker than the preceding analysis would suggest.

Suppose, for example, that the divergence between marginal value and cost in A's blanket industry was due to some external economy associated with the employment of a particular factor of production in that industry. Thus suppose that the employment of labour in any firm in A's blanket industry gives rise to the development of certain skills which are likely to become thereby more widely diffused and so to reduce costs in other firms in A's blanket industry and perhaps also in other similar industries. If this external economy relates only to the employment of labour, there will be no divergence between marginal value and cost in the employment of other factors—capital and land—in A's blanket industry but only in the employment of more labour. The thing which it is desirable to encourage in this case is not an expansion of the output of blankets in A but an expansion of the employment of labour in A's blanket industry.

Now if the ratio in which labour is employed with other factors such as capital and land were more or less rigidly fixed for technical reasons, then for all practical purposes the expansion of employment and the expansion of output in the industry would be the same thing. A 5 per cent increase in output would require a 5 per cent increase in the employment of labour, and a 5 per cent increase in the employment of labour would lead to a 5 per cent increase in output. But if it were technically possible to vary the proportions in which the factors of

[1] The above argument about the choice between an import duty on the one hand and a subsidy financed by general revenue on the other hand applies only to A's government. B's government cannot subsidize A's blanket production; but B's government can put a tax on the export of blankets from B to A which will have the same effect in stimulating the production of blankets in A as a duty imposed by A on the import of blankets would have. If, therefore, we are considering what B's government can do to increase world economic welfare, we should have to confine ourselves to the earlier discussion of the merits of a moderate rate of duty upon the movement of blankets from B to A. We could not aim at improving upon that policy by turning to a subsidy on the domestic production in A.

production were used in the blanket industry in A to produce blankets, then the two things are not at all the same. A 5 per cent increase in the employment of labour might mean either a 5 per cent increase in output (with the use of the other factors being increased also by 5 per cent) or else an unchanged output with a certain reduction in the employment of other factors for which the labour was being substituted. Or it might mean something of both, partly an increase in output and partly a replacement of other factors of production by labour.

Whether or not in any given situation it would be most economic to expand the employment of labour by expanding output or by using labour to replace other factors of production can be seen in the following way. Suppose there is a 10 per cent marginal external economy associated with the employment of labour in A's blanket industry, in the sense that the employment of an additional unit of labour in any firm in that industry will indirectly increase output in other firms in that industry or elsewhere by an amount which is worth 10 per cent of the labour's wage. Then the ideal way of getting rid of this divergence would be to pay a 10 per cent subsidy on the employment of labour in the blanket industry in A so that the individual employer received a return on the labour employed equal not only to the value of its marginal private net product in his firm, but also to the value of the external economy enjoyed by employers in other firms. The individual producers in A's blanket industry would then be left free to employ labour in the most economic manner in view of this new subsidized return on labour to them. The subsidy to the wage rate would lower the cost of producing blankets and this would to some extent encourage an increase in the production of blankets. It would also lower the cost of labour relatively to other factors of production such as land and capital, and thus lead to a displacement of those other factors by labour.

If the elasticity of demand for A's blankets were very low[1] but the substitutability of labour for other factors of production in A's blanket industry were very high, then there would be very little expansion of the total output of blankets but a considerable increase in the employment of labour in the blanket industry to replace other factors. If the elasticity of demand for A's blankets were high but the substitutability between labour and other factors in A's blanket industry were very small, then again there would be a considerable increase in employment but in this case with a more or less corresponding increase in output.

Now the protection of A's blanket industry from foreign competition

[1] This would be the case if the elasticity of demand for blankets by A's consumers were low and also the elasticity of supply of blankets for export by B were low. In this case a reduction in the price charged for home-produced blankets in A would expand the market for such blankets neither by inducing consumers to consume more blankets nor by inducing foreign producers to put less blankets on the market.

will increase the employment of labour in the industry only by expanding the demand for and so the output of blankets in A. As compared with a subsidy on the employment of labour in A's blanket industry, it will therefore be a most uneconomic method of adjustment if there is considerable substitutability between labour and the other factors of production in the industry. In such circumstances the argument for protection is very much weaker. The necessary adjustment would be much better carried out by a subsidy to the employment of labour in A's blanket industry—financed in part if there is a revenue-raising problem by a special tax on the employment of the other factors in the industry, since in this case these are the things which are particularly competitive with the thing (labour employed in the blanket industry) with which the divergence between marginal value and cost is directly associated. The argument for some element of protection is strong only when the divergence between marginal value and cost in the competing domestic industry is associated with the total output of that industry rather than with a particular way of producing it.

There is a second form of divergence between marginal value and cost in the blanket industry in A which will mean that the argument for protection is a good deal weaker than might appear from the argument as it has been so far developed. Suppose that the divergence between marginal value and cost is directly associated with the output of blankets in A so that it is the output which we wish to stimulate. But suppose that this divergence is due to the existence of an element of monopoly in the production of blankets in A. Let us take the extreme example and suppose that, for one reason or another, the whole of the output of blankets in A is produced by a single firm. In this case the monopolistic producer of blankets in A will be able to affect their price by restricting his output.[1] In fact he will restrict his output and raise his price until his marginal cost of production is equal not to the price offered by consumers for a blanket but to the marginal revenue obtainable by him from the sale of an additional blanket on the market. There will then be a divergence between marginal value and cost equal to the divergence between the price of a blanket and its marginal revenue, i.e. its marginal cost.

Now this divergence will be the greater, the smaller is the elasticity of demand for home-produced blankets in A. Thus suppose that the producer is considering restricting his output still further, raising his price still further, and thus increasing the margin between price and marginal cost still further. He is more likely to gain by such a further

[1] On the assumptions (i) that the output produced in A is not an insignificantly small part of the total supplies coming on to A's market from A's and B's industry, and (ii) that the elasticity of the supplies coming from B is not infinite.

restriction, the more the price of his output can be raised by restricting his sales, i.e. the less elastic the demand for his product.[1]

Now we cannot assume that the elasticity of demand for home-produced blankets in A will be independent of the duty levied on imported blankets. Indeed, there is some presumption for the view that the higher the rate of import duty the lower will be the elasticity of demand for the home-produced product.[2] The essential reason for this

[1] Suppose $x = D(p)$ represents the demand conditions for his output (x) in terms of the price charged (p). Then he adds to his receipts by selling one more unit $\frac{d(xp)}{dx} = p\left(1 + \frac{x}{p} \cdot \frac{dp}{dx}\right) = p\left(1 - \frac{1}{\varepsilon}\right)$, where ε is the numerical value of the elasticity of demand for x. He will go on producing until his marginal cost is equal to his marginal revenue or what he adds to his receipts by selling one more unit, i.e. until $c = p\frac{\varepsilon - 1}{\varepsilon}$, where c is his marginal cost. But the marginal value to consumers will equal the price p, and the rate of divergence between marginal value and marginal cost is $\frac{p - c}{c} = \frac{1}{\varepsilon - 1}$. Thus the smaller is the elasticity of demand ε, the greater is the rate of divergence between marginal value and cost.

[2] Let $a + i = D_a(p)$, $b = S_b\left(\frac{p}{1 + t}\right)$, and $b - i = D_b\left(\frac{p}{1 + t}\right)$ express the demand for blankets in general in A, the supply of blankets in general in B, and the demand for blankets for consumption in B respectively, where a = output of blankets in A, b = output of blankets in B, i = import of blankets into A from B, p = price of blankets in A, and t the *ad valorem* rate of duty on the import of blankets into A, so that $\frac{p}{1 + t}$ = the price of blankets in B. If we differentiate these three equations, keeping t constant and eliminate db and di between them, we obtain

$$\varepsilon = \varepsilon_a + \frac{b}{a}(\eta_b + \varepsilon_b) + \frac{i}{a}(\varepsilon_a - \varepsilon_b)$$

where $\varepsilon\left(\equiv -\frac{p}{a} \cdot \frac{da}{dp}\right)$ is the numerical value of the elasticity of demand for home-produced blankets in A, $\varepsilon_a\left(\equiv -\frac{p}{a + i} \cdot \frac{d(a + i)}{dp}\right)$ is the numerical value of the elasticity of demand for all blankets in A, $\varepsilon_b\left(\equiv -\frac{\frac{p}{1 + t}}{b - i} \cdot \frac{d(b - i)}{d\left(\frac{p}{1 + t}\right)}\right)$ is the numerical value of the elasticity of demand for blankets in B, and $\eta_b\left(\equiv \frac{\frac{p}{1 + t}}{b} \cdot \frac{db}{d\left(\frac{p}{1 + t}\right)}\right)$ is the elasticity of supply of all blankets in B. Let us suppose that the basic elasticities ε_a, ε_b, and η_b are constant and are unaffected by the level of blanket prices in A and B. We have no reason to believe that they will move in the one or the other direction. But as the import duty is raised, output in A (a) will be expanded, output in B (b) will be contracted, and imports into A (i) will be reduced. Thus $\frac{b}{a}$ and $\frac{i}{a}$ will both fall. It can now be is that as the rate of duty is increased the blanket industry in A will become larger and larger and the blanket industry in B will become smaller and smaller. Now the greater the proportion of the world supply of blankets which is produced in A the greater the influence which the producers in A will be able to exercise over the prices offered for blankets in A and in B. In other words, the higher the rate of duty, the lower the elasticity of demand for home-produced blankets in A.

If this is the case, a rise in the duty on imports of blankets into A will itself reduce the elasticity of demand for blankets in A. But, as we have seen, the divergence between price and marginal revenue and so between marginal value and marginal cost in A's blanket industry will itself be increased when the import duty on blankets is raised. The case for using an import duty to offset an element of monopoly in a competing domestic industry is to this extent weaker than the case for using an import duty to offset, for example, an external economy in a competing domestic industry. In the case of the monopolistic element the degree of monopoly and so the divergence between marginal value and cost will itself be increased by the raising of the duty, but in the case of the external economy there is no reason to believe that the raising of the duty will increase the divergence between marginal value and cost in the domestic industry. In the monopolistic case a duty will have a less advantageous effect in stimulating home production; for it will not merely stimulate home production by diverting demand on to home

---

seen from the above formula that ε, the elasticity of demand for home-produced blankets in A, will fall as t increases, if ε_a, ε_b, and η_b do not rise and if ε_b is not much greater than ε_a. As there is no reason to believe that ε_a, ε_b, and η_b are more likely to rise than to fall or that ε_b will differ materially from ε_a, there is a presumption that ε will fall as t rises. It may to some readers appear that this proof is not sufficiently rigorous, since it is not certain that a will increase, and if a decreased then $\frac{b}{a}$ might increase instead of decreasing. But this is in fact impossible. The increased duty will divert demand on to the home output and the demand price offered for any given home output will rise. If the elasticity of the demand for home output remained unchanged, the marginal revenue in the blanket industry would rise and output would be expanded. Output could only fall in the industry if the rise in the demand price offered for home output were more than compensated by a decline in the derived elasticity of demand ε and so a decline in the ratio of the marginal revenue to the price. But from the formula for ε (assuming ε_a, ε_b, and η_b constant and ε_a approximately equal to ε_b) it is clear that ε can decline only if $\frac{b}{a}$ falls. Thus that $\frac{b}{a}$ is bound to fall can now be proved by a *reductio ad absurdum*. Assume $\frac{b}{a}$ rises because a falls more than b. Then from the formula for ε it is clear that ε will rise. The ratio between marginal revenue and price will therefore rise, and since the price offered for the previous output will have risen the marginal revenue will have risen for two reasons. Output (a) will therefore have increased, so that $\frac{b}{a}$ will have fallen, which is absurd.

output from competing foreign supplies, but it will also discourage home output by reducing the elasticity of demand for home output and thus giving an increased incentive to reduce output.

This is merely a particular way of expressing the familiar argument that one advantage of free trade is that it will reduce monopolistic powers and thus reduce divergences between marginal values and costs and thus promote economic welfare. In the particular case under examination, therefore, the argument for protection is much weakened: it is true that it will divert demand on to the home output which needs to be stimulated, but it will also increase monopoly power in that industry and to this extent be less effective in stimulating the output.

So far we have considered the case in which there is an excess of marginal value over marginal cost in some industry in A which competes with imports. There may, of course, be a case in which—due, for example, to an external diseconomy—there is an excess of marginal cost over marginal value in such an industry. For the most part such a case is merely the reverse of the case which we have just considered at length. Domestic production needs to be discouraged instead of expanded; and this can be done by means of a subsidy on the competing imports instead of by means of a tax on imports. The subsidy on imports should be somewhat less than the excess of marginal costs over marginal values; but it should be higher relatively to that excess, the greater the restriction in the home production which will be brought about by any given expansion of competing imports. Thus the rate of subsidy should be the higher, the smaller the elasticity of demand and the higher the elasticity of supply of the product in A.

But this symmetry between an excess of marginal cost over value and an excess of marginal value over cost breaks down when one turns to a consideration of the alternative lines of policy which might be adopted. In the case in which the domestic output needs to be expanded, the ideal policy involves a subsidy to be paid on domestic production. But since the raising of revenue itself causes a divergence between marginal values and costs there may be some case for relying partially upon the second-best method of an import duty, since that is a duty which does have some beneficial repercussions and may therefore do less harm than the alternative possible forms of taxation. But where the domestic production requires to be discouraged, it is the 'ideal' policy of taxation of that output which has the advantage from the revenue point of view, whereas it is the indirect (and for that reason less desirable) form of policy, namely the subsidization of competing imports, which also suffers from the disadvantage of involving the raising of general revenue to finance the subsidy. There is, therefore, very little to be said in favour of a subsidization of imports as opposed to the direct tax of domestic production if the purpose is to contract domestic production, though there may be something to be said for some element of protective import duties if the purpose is to promote domestic production.

We have spent some time considering this case in which there is a divergence between marginal values and costs in production in an industry in A which competes with imports. But there are other kinds of domestic divergence which may provide some argument for a deviation from a full free-trade policy. We will complete this chapter by indicating very briefly the way in which the same type of analysis can be applied to some of these other types of domestic divergence.

The case which we have already examined is one in which there is a divergence between marginal value and cost in the *production* in A of some product which competes with imports. There might, however, be a case in which there was a divergence between marginal value and cost in the *consumption* in A of some product of which imported supplies competed with domestically produced supplies. Thus instead of its being socially desirable to promote the production of blankets in A, it might be socially desirable to promote the consumption of blankets in A. In this case the appropriate form of commercial policy would be, not the imposition of a duty on the import of blankets into A, but the payment of a subsidy on their import. A subsidy would promote imports and lower the price of blankets in A; this lower price in A would discourage A's home production but would expand A's consumption of blankets. In other words, imports would rise and home production would fall, but imports would rise more than home production fell.

Thus some import subsidy would help and normally the subsidy should be paid at a rate intermediate between zero and the rate of divergence on home consumption. The effect of a rise in the rate of import subsidy would be to increase home consumption but to increase imports by a greater amount. Now there would be a gain on the increase in home consumption equal to the rate of divergence on home consumption, but there would in addition be a loss on the increase in imports equal to the excess of marginal cost over the price of the imported product, i.e. equal to the rate of subsidy on imports. This additional loss would just offset the gain when the rate of subsidy on the relatively large increase in imports was less than the rate of divergence on the relatively small increase in total consumption. The rate of subsidy on imports should be higher relatively to the rate of divergence on consumption, the greater is the expansion of consumption relatively to the increase in imports which an import subsidy brings about. In other words, the rate of import subsidy should be the greater, the more elastic is the demand for the commodity in A and the less elastic is its supply in A; for these are the conditions which will make total consumption increase a lot with the least reliance upon the expansion of imports to provide the additional supplies for consumption.

Or the divergence might take the form of an excess of marginal value over cost in the production in A of some commodity (say, apples) which is exported from A. In this case the appropriate form of commercial policy would be the payment of a subsidy on the export of apples. The subsidy should, however, not be as high as the rate of divergence between marginal value and cost on home production which it is devised to offset. An increase in an export subsidy will raise the price received by producers of the product in A and will lower the price in B. It will thus cause an expansion of output in A and so raise the cost price in A. This will raise the unsubsidized price charged to consumers in A and will thus reduce the amount consumed in A. The result will be that total output will go up and that output for the foreign market will go up; but the increase in output for the foreign market will be greater than the total increase in production. Now when the subsidy is raised there will be a gain equal to the rate of divergence on the (relatively small) increase in total output, but in addition there will be a loss equal to the rate of subsidy (i.e. the excess of marginal cost over the price paid by foreign consumers) on the (relatively large) increase in sales in the foreign market. The loss from a further rise in the rate of export subsidy will, therefore, offset the gain when the rate of subsidy on exports is still at a lower rate than the rate of divergence on total production. The export subsidy should be raised nearer to the rate of divergence on total production, the more nearly the expansion of total production approaches the expansion of exports. This will be so the less output for the home market falls off, i.e. the less elastic the home demand and the more elastic the supply.

Finally, there might be a case in which there was an excess of marginal value over marginal cost in the home consumption in A of a commodity which was also exported from A. In this case the appropriate commercial policy would be an export tax. This would divert supplies away from the foreign market for consumption on the home market. It would depress the price in the home market with the result that home production would fall but home consumption would rise. In other words when the rate of export tax was raised, home consumption would increase but the export of the product would fall by a larger amount. There would be a gain equal to the initial rate of divergence on the (relatively small) increase in home consumption, and a loss equal to the rate of export duty on the (relatively large) decrease in exports. In other words, the gain would be offset by the loss from any further rise in the rate of export duty, when the rate of export duty still remained lower than the rate of divergence on home consumption. The export duty should, however, approach more nearly to the rate of divergence on home consumption, the more nearly the increase in home consumption approaches to the decrease in exports—i.e. the less is the decline in home production.

This will be the case, the less elastic is the home supply and the more elastic is the home demand for the product.

In the three cases which we have just outlined there is, therefore, some case for an interference with freedom of trade—an import subsidy to promote home consumption of an import, an export subsidy to promote home production of an export, or an export tax to promote home consumption of an export. But these are not necessarily the ideal policies. If the raising of revenue did not itself lead to any divergences elsewhere between marginal values and costs, the promotion of the home consumption of an import would be best undertaken by a subsidy to consumption; the promotion of the home production of an export by a subsidy on home production; and the promotion of the home consumption of an export by a subsidy on home consumption.

If the divergences in these cases had been excesses of marginal cost over value instead of excesses of marginal value over cost, so that contractions rather than expansions of consumption or production were required, the 'ideal' policies would require taxes rather than subsidies; they would contribute revenue which would enable the general taxes to be reduced rather than requiring the raising of still more general revenue; and they would thus on every count be preferable to the changes in commercial policy which would indirectly have the desired effect in discouraging domestic consumption or production.

But in the cases in which an expansion of home consumption or production is required, the 'ideal' policies would require the payment of subsidies and if the general revenue for these subsidies could not be raised without causing some divergences between marginal values and costs, it would be inevitable to take second-best considerations into account. Each of the three cases just examined needs special consideration from this point of view.

In the case in which it is desired to promote the home consumption of a commodity some part of the home consumption of which is fed by imports, the 'ideal' policy requires a subsidy on home consumption while the appropriate 'commercial' policy takes the form of a subsidy on imports. Is there any reason to believe that a subsidy on imports might be preferable to a subsidy on home consumption? Let us consider the subsidy on home consumption. If this method is adopted, the rate of subsidy should be somewhat less than the rate of divergence between marginal value and cost on the home consumption. The reason for this is clear. Suppose that the rate of subsidy being paid is very nearly equal to the rate of divergence on consumption. Consider the effect now of raising the rate of subsidy still a little higher. There will be some increase in consumption but the gain on it will be negligible since the divergence on consumption has already been almost entirely offset by the subsidy. But the indirect effect of the loss incurred through the adverse effects of raising still more revenue to pay a still higher subsidy may not be negligible. Thus the subsidy on home consumption should stop short of the rate of divergence on home consumption which it is intended to offset.

Now a uniform subsidy on home consumption is equivalent to a subsidy on home production and a subsidy on imports, both at the same rate. The question now arises whether, starting with such a uniform subsidy on home consumption, it might be possible to improve the position still further by subsidizing imports more heavily and home production less heavily. Suppose that the elasticity of supply of exports from the foreign country B is greater than the elasticity of supply of production in the home country A. Consider the consequences in these conditions of paying a somewhat lower rate of subsidy on home production and a somewhat higher rate of subsidy on imports. Since the supply of imports is elastic, a small rise in the rate of subsidy on imports will greatly increase their supply; and since home production is inelastic, a quite large reduction in the subsidy paid to home production will not greatly reduce the supply. Therefore, with a given total payment of subsidy (and therefore with a given disadvantage from the point of view of the ill effects of raising general revenue), a larger stimulus to home consumption can be obtained by paying rather more in subsidy on imports, whose supply is elastic, than on home production, whose supply is inelastic. And since the rate of subsidy from which we start is (*a*) less than the rate of divergence on home consumption and (*b*) uniform for home production and for imports, it follows that (*a*) the increase in home consumption adds to welfare, and (*b*) the shift from home production to imports does no harm. It is only after the rate of subsidy on imports has been raised substantially above the rate of subsidy on home production that any further shift of the subsidy would do great harm by shifting production from a source (home production) on which the subsidy was low and the remaining rate of divergence between marginal value and cost was therefore high on to a source (imports) on which the subsidy was high and the remaining net divergence between marginal value and cost was therefore low. But after a point this sort of situation would exist and the advantage from the net increase in production and so consumption which a further shift of the subsidy would produce would be more than offset by the loss due to the shift of supplies from the low cost home supplies to the higher cost foreign supplies.

It follows that if the supply of exports by B were more elastic than the domestic production in A, there would be an argument in favour of some element of import subsidy in the best possible arrangement for the promotion of consumption in A. And, as we have seen (Chapter XII, pp. 195–6), in the normal case there may be some presumption that the supply of exports from B will be more elastic than the production of the product in A.

We can deal in very much the same manner with the choice between an 'ideal' policy of a subsidy on production in A or a 'commercial' policy of a subsidy on the export by A of some commodity in the production of which in A there is an excess of marginal value over marginal cost. Let us start with some subsidy on production. Since this will have the disadvantages connected with the raising of the revenue necessary to meet the subsidy, the rate of subsidy paid on home production should not be raised to the level which entirely offsets the divergence on home production. A production subsidy is the same as a uniform rate of subsidy on home consumption and on export. The question then arises whether some net advantage could be gained by paying a rather larger subsidy on exports and a rather lower subsidy on home consumption out of the funds raised to pay any given amount in total subsidies. This redistribution of a given total subsidy will give rise to a larger increase in production if the elasticity of demand for exports is greater than the elasticity of demand for home consumption. In this case there will be a net gain because (*a*) the rate of divergence on production is greater than the rate of subsidy so that there is gain from the further expansion of output, and (*b*) the initial rate of subsidy on home consumption is the same as that on exports so that there is no loss at first on the diversion of sales from the home to the foreign market.

Therefore, if the elasticity of demand for exports is greater than the elasticity of demand in the home market, there is some case to be made out in favour of some element of the 'commercial policy' adjustment of an export subsidy. Moreover, as we have seen (Chapter XII, pp. 197–8), in the normal case there is some presumption that the foreign demand for A's exports will be more elastic than the domestic demand in A; and to this extent some element of export subsidy over and above any general subsidy on production may be justified as a means of promoting production in A.

Finally, we have the case in which it is desirable to promote the consumption of an exportable commodity. Here the choice is between an 'ideal' policy of subsidization of home consumption or the 'commercial' policy of a tax on exports which will divert supplies on to the home market. Let us start with a policy of subsidizing home consumption but at a rate of subsidy which falls short of the rate of divergence on home consumption because of the damage done by raising the revenue for the payment of the subsidy. If now a tax is levied on the exports, this will reduce exports but increase home consumption. There will be a gain from the increase in home consumption because the subsidy is not as great as the initial rate of divergence on consumption, so that some net divergence still exists. On the other hand, at first there will be no loss on the reduction of exports because as yet they have so far been untaxed. There is, therefore, in this case an argument for some element of export duty to help to promote the home consumption of the exportable product.[1]

[1] In this chapter we have considered a divergence between marginal value and cost in an industry in A which competes (*a*) with imports into, and (*b*) with exports out of A. It would be quite possible to deal on similar lines with a divergence in an industry in A the output of which was complementary to goods of a kind which were (*a*) imported into, and (*b*) exported out of A. The reader must be left to himself to apply the analysis to any such cases of complementarity between the traded goods and the output of the domestic industry in A.

CHAPTER XV

THE SECOND-BEST ARGUMENT FOR TRADE CONTROL: (4) DUMPING AS A COMPLEX CASE

In the last three chapters we have been examining cases in which there was some argument for a departure from free trade on the grounds that there was a divergence between marginal value and cost in some part of the economy and that a duty or subsidy on imports or exports would help to offset the effects of this divergence. But in each of these three chapters we have confined our attention to only one divergence—in Chapter XII a divergence due to the raising of revenue, in Chapter XIII a divergence in foreign trade due to some pre-existing tax or subsidy on trade, and in Chapter XIV a divergence in some domestic industry which competes with imports or exports. In each of these cases we have assumed that there was no other initial divergence. Such an analysis, it is hoped, may be useful in calling attention to some of the most important considerations which may be relevant in considering arguments for a departure from a free-trade policy.

The assumption of a single divergence between marginal value and cost in the world economy is, of course, a totally unrealistic one. The conclusions reached in the preceding three chapters must, therefore, be applied with the greatest caution. They are only indications of some of the most important factors which may be at work; but they would have to be modified before they could be applied to any particular situation in which there were other important and relevant divergences to be taken into account.

A simple and obvious example will serve to illustrate the point. We argued in the last chapter that if there were an industry in A producing goods which competed with imports from B and in the production of which there was an excess of marginal value over marginal cost, then there might be some argument for the imposition of a duty on imports into A as a means of expanding the industry in A in the interests of world economic efficiency. But this argument relies, of course, upon there not being a similar excess of marginal value over marginal cost in B's export industry. Nothing is gained from the point of view of maximizing world production by shifting output from B to A if there is the same excess of marginal value over marginal cost in B's industry as in A's industry. Nor is this situation at all an improbable one. If the excess of marginal value over marginal cost in A's industry is due to some external economy in that industry, it is not at all improbable that the same industry in B will enjoy the same type of external economy. In such conditions the appropriate type of action would be something which expanded production in both countries, such as a subsidy on production in both countries or a tax on other commodities which competed most closely with the output of this particular product in both countries.[1]

The cases in which there are more than one relevant initial divergence to be taken into account in considering the choice of commercial policies we may call 'complex' cases as opposed to the 'simple' cases in which there is only one divergence. Such complex cases may be considerably less obvious than the one which we have just outlined. Let us give one more example. Suppose as before that in production in a domestic industry in A which competes with imports there is an excess of marginal value over cost; and suppose that there is no similar excess of marginal value over marginal cost in B's corresponding export industry. Then the maximization of production does require that output should be shifted from B's industry to A's industry; and a duty on imports from B into A would have this effect.

But the imposition of the duty on imports from B into A may have many other indirect effects, some of which, because of the existence of other divergences between marginal values and costs, might outweigh the advantages of the import duty in stimulating this particular industry in A. One such case might be where B had a heavily protective policy on all her imports from A. The imposition of a duty by A on imports of, say, blankets from B in order to expand A's blanket industry would cause a reduction in A's imports of blankets from B. This would leave B's balance of payments with A in deficit. There would have to be what we called in Chapter XIII a series of 'tertiary' adjustments in the general level of A's and B's money prices and incomes so as to expand A's other imports from B or to contract B's imports from A. Let us suppose that circumstances are such (the elasticity of demand for imports being much higher in B than in A and the elasticity of supply of exports being much higher in A than in B) that the adjustment of the balance of payments between A and B is brought about mainly by a reduction of B's imports from A rather than by an expansion of A's other imports from B. There would be a loss of economic welfare on all this reduction of imports from A into B equal to the *ad valorem* rate of duty levied on them by B. This tertiary repercussion would certainly reduce the net gain to be reaped by a policy of protection for A's blanket industry and would mean that a lower degree of protection for that industry would be

[1] If, for some reason, the elasticity of supply of production were much greater in A than in B, a duty on imports into A might do some good in that it would stimulate output much more in A than it would contract it in B. But there is, of course, no presumption at all that the elasticity of supply of production (as opposed to the elasticity of supply of exports) will be materially different in A and in B; and indeed it might just as well be greater in B than in A.

justified than would otherwise be the case. If the duties levied by B on imports from A were at a sufficiently high *ad valorem* level, it is possible that the case for protection of A's blanket industry would be completely destroyed.

In order thoroughly to investigate the effects on economic welfare of any change in commercial policy it would, strictly speaking, be necessary to follow through all its primary, secondary, and tertiary effects upon every transaction in the whole world economy in the case of which there was any divergence between marginal values and costs. There are, of course, very many such divergences; and every change in commercial policy will have a very large number of secondary and tertiary repercussions. Every real problem of the kind which we have been examining in the last three chapters is, therefore, undoubtedly a 'complex' rather than a 'simple' case. But it is quite impossible in any given case to follow through all the repercussions throughout the world economy in all markets in which there is a divergence between marginal value and cost. All that can possibly be done is to consider all the most immediate and relevant repercussions in order to assess whether a particular change would be desirable or not on the assumption that the repercussions which it has been impossible not to neglect may just as well tell in the one direction as in the other.

In this chapter we propose to take one very straightforward 'complex' case for analysis simply in order to illustrate the use of our technique of analysis in a case in which we start with two initial divergences between marginal values and costs. We shall deal with the case in which the production of some commodity—say, apples—in A is monopolized and in which the monopoly producer is able to sell the apples at a different price to consumers in A and in B. There will then be two rates of divergence, one between the marginal cost of apples in A and their marginal value to A's consumers (i.e. the price at which they are sold in A) and the other between the marginal cost of apples in A and their marginal value to B's consumers (i.e. the price at which they are sold in B). We wish to know whether in these circumstances there is any case for governmental action to promote or to restrict (i.e. to subsidize or to tax) the export of apples from A to B.

Let us start by considering what will determine the amount of apples sold and the price charged for apples by the monopolistic producer in each of the two markets—the home market in A and the foreign market in B. In order that the monopolist producer may be able successfully to discriminate in the prices which he charges in the two markets we must assume that there is some obstacle—for example, a prohibition on the import of apples into A—which prevents apples from being re-exported back from B to A if the price charged for them in A is much higher than the price charged for them in B.

Now let us suppose that in B A's apples have to compete with apples produced in B. We have already seen that in this case the elasticity of demand for A's apples is likely to be higher in B than in A. (See Chapter XII, pp. 197–8.) For this reason an increase in sales of A's apples is likely to depress prices more if the extra apples are sold in A than if they are exported to B where they can compete with B's own home-produced apples.

TABLE XX

Discriminating Monopoly

Number of A's apples sold in either market	Price in		Total receipts in		Marginal receipts in	
	A	B	A	B	A	B
(*a*)	(*b*)	(*c*)	(*d*) = (*a*) × (*b*)	(*e*) = (*a*) × (*c*)	(*f*)	(*g*)
	$	$	$	$	$	$
6	1·12	1·04	6·72	6·24	—	—
7	1·09	1·03	7·63	7·21	0·91	0·97
8	1·06	1·02	8·48	8·16	0·85	0·95
9	1·03	1·01	9·27	9·09	0·79	0·93
10	1·00	1·00	10·00	10·00	0·73	0·91
11	0·97	0·99	10·67	10·89	0·67	0·89
12	0·94	0·98	11·28	11·76	0·61	0·87
13	0·91	0·97	11·83	12·61	0·55	0·85
14	0·88	0·96	12·32	13·44	0·49	0·83
15	0·85	0·95	12·75	14·25	0·43	0·81
16	0·82	0·94	13·12	15·04	0·37	0·79
17	0·79	0·93	13·43	15·81	0·31	0·77
18	0·76	0·92	13·68	16·56	0·25	0·75
19	0·73	0·91	13·87	17·29	0·19	0·73

The producers of apples in A will distribute their sales of these apples in such a way as to bring it about that they cannot increase their revenue by selling one more apple in A and one less in B or vice versa. This is illustrated in Table XX. In column *a* of the table we show the number of apples sold in either of the two markets. In columns *b* and *c* respectively we show the market price then obtainable for apples in the two markets; thus we suppose that when 10 apples are sold in country A the market price is $1, but when only 9 are put on the market the price rises to $1·03 (column *b*), whereas when 10 apples are put on the market in B the price is also $1, but when only 9 apples are put on the market the price can be raised only to $1·01 (column *c*). It will be observed that we are assuming for the sake of simplicity that when 10 units are sold in either market the price will be the same, namely, $1; but the price can be raised much more easily when the supplies are restricted in A's home market where there is no alternative production to compete with than when supplies of A's apples are restricted on B's market where they have to compete with B's own home production. In fact it will be seen that whereas on A's market the price goes up or down by 3 cents for every unit decrease or increase in supplies, it goes up or down by only 1 cent in B's market for every unit decrease or increase in supplies. In column *d* we give figures of the total amount received by producers in A for the amount sold in A's market; the figures are obtained by multiplying the amount sold in A's market (column *a*) by the price obtained in A's market (column *b*). Similarly, for the figures in column *e* of the total amount sold in B's market. Column *f* then shows the amount which the producers in A would add to their total receipts by selling one more unit in A's market; thus since they would receive $7·63 if they sold 7 units and $8·48 if they sold 8 units in A's market (column *d*), they will add $8·48 minus $7·63 or $0·85 to their total receipts by selling 8 instead of 7 units in A's market; and accordingly $0·85 is shown against the 8th unit in column *f*. Similarly for the figures in column *g* showing the addition to their receipts by selling one more unit in B's market.

Now in order to maximize their profits the producers of apples in A must sell their output in the two markets in such amounts that they add the same to their total receipts by the sale of the last unit in both markets. Thus, suppose that they were producing 25 units and were selling 12 units in A's market and 13 units in B's market. By selling 11 instead of 12 in A's market they would lose only $0·61 in receipts (column *f*), whereas by selling 14 instead of 13 in B's market they would add $0·83 to their receipts (column *g*)—a net gain of $0·21. They could then profitably transfer yet one more unit of sales from A's market (where they would lose $0·67 by giving up the 11th unit of sales) to B's market (where they would gain $0·81 for the 15th unit of sales). And so on, until they were selling 9 units in A's market (where they would now lose $0·79 if they sold yet one less unit) and 16 units in B's market (where they would gain only $0·77 by selling yet one more unit). Out of 25 units they will thus sell 9 units in A's market at a price of $1·03 (column *b*) and 16 units in B's market at a price of $0·94 (column *c*). It will pay them to charge a higher price in A's market than in B's market, simply because the price is more sensitive to variations in supplies in A's market than in B's market; in the position of equilibrium with 25 units of sales it does not pay to sell more than 9 units in A's market although there is a high price of $1·03 there, because further sales would so greatly depress the price of the units which are already being sold on that market, whereas this consideration is much less important in the case of B's market.

Equilibrium will finally be reached by the discriminating producer's monopolist when (i) the distribution of sales between the two markets is such that the marginal receipts from the sale of the last units in each market is the same (the figure in column *f* is equal to the figure in column *g*) and (ii) the total output produced is such that the additional cost incurred in producing one more unit is equal to the marginal receipts that can be obtained by the sale of that extra unit in either market. Thus in the numerical example of Table XX, if the marginal cost of production is \$0·91, 17 units will be produced and 7 sold in A's market at a price of \$1·09 and 10 sold in B's market at a price of \$1, the marginal receipts in both markets in this case being equal to the marginal cost of \$0·91; if the marginal cost were only \$0·85, then 21 units would be produced with 8 sold in A's market at a price of \$1·06 and 13 sold in B's market at a price of \$0·97; and so on.

Let us suppose then that the apple producers in A do constitute a discriminating producer's monopoly of this kind and that they are selling apples at a higher price to home consumers in A (let us say 9 units at \$1·03) and at a lower price to foreign consumers in B (let us say 16 units at \$0·94).[1] What effect will this have upon the optimization of trade and upon the maximization of production, and what measures might be taken to correct any wastes which are involved?

The market price of apples in A is \$1·03 and in B is \$0·94. If there were no other divergences between marginal values and costs in any other section of the world economy, the optimization of trade would require some policy designed to reduce the export of apples from A to B. Consumers in A value one more apple at \$1·03 worth of other tradeable commodities, whereas consumers in B value one more apple at only \$0·94 worth of other tradeable commodities. The transfer of one apple from B's market to A's market in return for \$1 worth of other tradeable products transferred from A's market to B's market would cause A's consumers to gain something worth \$1·03 to them at the sacrifice of something worth only \$1 to them, and would cause B's consumers to gain something worth \$1 to them at the sacrifice of something worth only \$0·94 to them. Both would gain.

The optimization of trade would thus require the imposition of a tax upon the export of apples from A to B in order to divert apples from the low-priced market in B on to the high-priced market in A. But the maximization of production would require exactly the opposite type of commercial policy, namely, a subsidy on exports from A to B. Because of the monopolistic power of A's producer in B's market, the price charged for apples in B's market will be higher than their marginal cost of production in A. In our example the marginal cost of production

[1] The marginal cost of producing these 25 units is \$0·79, i.e. equal to the marginal revenue obtainable in either market.

in A is \$0·79, but the price in B's market is \$0·94. But if B's apple industry is competitive the marginal cost of producing an apple in B will be equal to the price of an apple in B, namely \$0·94. We should then have a situation in which the marginal cost of producing an apple was \$0·79 in A and \$0·94 in B. Let us take blankets as typical of other tradeable products. Then, assuming that there are no divergences between marginal values and costs except in A's apple industry, the price of a blanket will be equal to the marginal cost of a blanket in A and in B and will be the same in A as in B. Let us suppose that the price of a blanket is \$1.

Thus we obtain the following schedule of marginal costs, from which it follows that if productive resources were shifted in A from producing blankets to producing apples and in B from producing apples to producing blankets, the output of one commodity could be increased without the output of the other being decreased. Thus if \$1 worth of factors

Marginal cost of one	In country	
	A	B
Apple	\$0·79	\$0·94
Blanket	\$1·0	\$1·0

of production were shifted from producing blankets to producing apples in A and from producing apples to producing blankets in B, (i) the output of blankets would fall by 1 unit in A and rise by 1 unit in B, so that there would be no net change in their output, but (ii) the output of apples would rise by $\frac{1\cdot00}{0\cdot79}$[1] or by 1·27 in A and would fall by $\frac{1\cdot00}{0\cdot94}$ or by 1·06 in B, giving a net increase in the world supply of 0·21 apples for every \$1 worth of factors so shifted. In the interests of the maximization of production it is, therefore, desirable to encourage the production of apples at the expense of other tradeable products in A, and vice versa in B. The expansion of A's apple industry could be encouraged by a subsidy on A's exports of apples. A tax on the export of apples from A would, of course, have the opposite effect of encouraging apple production in B and of discouraging it in A.

[1] Since it takes \$0·79 worth of factors to produce one more apple, \$1 worth of factors will produce $\frac{1\cdot00}{0\cdot79}$ more apples.

This desirability of a policy for the encouragement of apple production in A in the interests of maximum production is not a universal feature of discriminating monopoly in A. It will be observed from the numerical example just given that the argument depends essentially upon the divergence between the marginal cost of apple production in A ($0·79) and in B ($0·94). But there might be discriminating monopoly without any such divergence. Suppose that (i) the supply of A's apples in B's market makes up only a very small part of the total supply for B, the greater part of which came from B's own production, and (ii) the supply of B's apples to her own market is very sensitive to changes in the price, a very small fall in the price causing a large contraction in B's supply because the marginal cost of apple production in B is not appreciably reduced when the output of apples in B is reduced. Then the producers of apples in A will exert no appreciable influence over the price of apples in B; if they put more on B's market it will have a very small initial effect upon the price because A's producers account for such a small part of B's total supplies, and any small initial effect on the price will be subsequently counteracted by the contraction of B's own production. The consequence will be that the marginal cost of apples in A will be equal to (instead of less than) the price of apples in B, which in turn—if B's apple industry is competitive—will be equal to the marginal cost of apple production in B. This is quite compatible with the exercise by A's monopolized producers of a very considerable monopolistic influence over the price of apples in A. In A's market they may restrict supplies until the price is considerably in excess of the marginal cost of production. In such a case there would be no argument for expanding the production of apples in A in the interests of the maximization of production, although the arguments which we have previously given in favour of increasing the sale of apples in A rather than in B in the interests of the optimization of trade would, of course, still be valid.

Thus if A's producer had no monopolistic power in B's market but only in A's market, there would be no conflict between the maximization of production and the optimization of trade. A tax on the export of apples from A to B would be appropriate in order to encourage the consumption of apples in A rather than in B. We should in fact have the 'simple' case which we examined in the last chapter (pp. 242–3) in which there was an excess of marginal value over marginal cost in the consumption in A of a product some part of the output of which was exported. As we there concluded, there would be some case for an export duty.

But if we revert to the case in which A's producer has a monopolistic power in B's market as well as in A's market, although he exercises a smaller degree of monopoly power in B's market than in A's market, we have a 'complex' case. There are now two initial divergences. There is one (relatively large) excess of marginal value over marginal cost in the case of production in A for sale to consumers in A and another (relatively small) excess of marginal value over marginal cost in the case of production in A for sale to consumers in B. We now have a direct conflict between the type of commercial policy (an export tax) which is required to optimize trade and the type of commercial policy (an export subsidy) which is required to maximize production.

The problem can be handled in the following way. There is a certain divergence between marginal value and cost on what is produced for the home market, and a certain smaller rate of divergence between marginal value and cost on what is produced for the foreign market. An increased tax (or a reduced subsidy) on sales in the foreign market will reduce exports and increase sales at home; but it will reduce exports more than it increases sales at home because the increased tax (or reduced subsidy) on part of the market will discourage production. A rise in the rate of tax (or a reduction in the rate of subsidy) on exports will thus cause a gain in economic welfare equal to the relatively large monopolistic divergence on the relatively small increase in sales on the home market, and it will cause a loss of economic welfare equal to the relatively small monopolistic divergence plus the existing rate of export tax (or minus the existing rate of export subsidy) on the relatively large decrease in sales on the foreign market. The point at which the loss from a further rise in export tax (or reduction in export subsidy) will just balance the gain will be determined by this formula. All one can say in general is that a tax rather than a subsidy will be required if (i) the rate of monopolistic divergence is much greater on the home market than in the foreign market, and (ii) the increase in sales in the home market resulting from a rise in duty is nearly as great as the reduction in sales on the foreign market. Condition i will be fulfilled if the elasticity of demand in the home market is much smaller than the elasticity of demand abroad and condition ii will be met if the elasticity of supply of the product is small so that in any case there will not be much change in the total amount produced for both markets.[1] But if the elasticity of supply were very large and the elasticity of demand in the foreign market were not much bigger than in the home market it would be desirable to subsidize exports. In this case the gain from a further rise in the export subsidy would be equal to the monopolistic divergence in the foreign market less the rate of export subsidy on the relatively large increase in exports and the loss would be equal to the monopolistic divergence in the home market on the relatively small decrease in home

[1] The reader is referred to Section XV of the mathematical supplement to this volume for the precise formula which governs the optimum rate of export duty or subsidy in this case.

sales. If (i) the elasticity of supply was great so that the increase in foreign sales was much bigger than the decrease in home sales, (ii) the monopolistic divergence in the foreign market was not much smaller than the monopolistic divergence in the home market, and (iii) the rate of export subsidy was not already high, it is clear that some further rise in an export subsidy might increase economic welfare.

The preceding analysis shows the conditions in which the taxation or subsidization of the exports of a monopolistic producer who is able to discriminate in the prices charged to foreigners and to home consumers may add to world economic welfare. But this does not, of course, imply that a tax or a subsidy on exports would be the best possible type of policy to choose; it means only that it would be better than nothing. Quite different types of policy—such as a policy which would restore competitive conditions in the domestic industry—might be possible which would cause the home production to be expanded until the marginal cost more nearly approached the price charged to consumers in both the home and the foreign market. We have undertaken the analysis of the above problem merely in order to illustrate the sort of problems which arise in the case of a choice of commercial policies when there are two conflicting initial divergences between marginal value and cost.

CHAPTER XVI

THE STRUCTURAL ARGUMENT FOR TRADE CONTROL

At the end of Chapter IX we concluded that the case for free trade was essentially an argument which related to utopian marginal conditions for economic efficiency, and that it might need modification if we had to deal with a second-best choice between policies or with structural changes or with problems of the distribution of income. In the preceding four chapters we have considered the problems which arise when there are already other existing divergences between marginal values and costs so that we are concerned with a second-best choice. In this chapter we shall assume that there is a utopian marginal situation (in the sense that throughout the world economy there is a policy of 'modified laissez-faire' which has successfully removed all divergences between marginal values and costs) and that there is no problem of distribution (in the sense that the policy-makers give the same distributional weights to all citizens of the world). In these conditions no marginal changes can add to economic welfare either by increasing economic efficiency or by improving the distribution of income.

But nevertheless it may be possible to increase economic efficiency through a large structural change, and it will be our purpose in this chapter to inquire in what circumstances a departure from free trade may be desirable in order to influence the structure of the world economy and so to increase economic efficiency.

In this chapter we shall maintain the assumption which we are making throughout Part II of this volume, namely that there is no movement of factors of production between our two countries A and B. If a structural change takes place in A, this is brought about by moving factors of production within A out of pre-existing industries in A into the new industry in A. It is not brought about by moving factors out of B into the newly formed industry in A. The structural industrial change in A may, of course, affect A's international trade. For example, it may well mean that A ceases to import the products of the newly established industry. In Part III we shall consider the problems of international factor movements and accordingly in Chapter XXVI of Part III we shall supplement the argument of the present chapter by considering the effect of international factor movements upon these problems of structural change.

Let us suppose now that a certain structure of industries exists in our two countries A and B and that all the marginal conditions of economic welfare are observed inside each country and in their relations with each other. The world economy is at the summit of the particular mountain which past history has chosen for it to ascend. The question which we intend to raise in this chapter is in what circumstances State action should be taken in order to change this structure. In what conditions ought country A or B to introduce a new industry into its economy or to drop an existing industry from its economy?

Let us first consider this question in its simplest form. Let us suppose that A is not producing any output of commodity X. We wish to discover in what conditions the authorities in A ought, in the interests of world economic efficiency, to take steps to introduce an industry to produce X in A, on the assumption that the structure of industries in B will and should remain unchanged, i.e. that B is already producing X and will go on producing X.

This is a straightforward application of the general principles considered in Chapter VIII of Part I. To obtain the correct answer it would theoretically be necessary to measure, on the principle of column *d* of Table XII, the total value to consumers of the output of X in A which would be produced in A if the X-industry were set up and operated on the correct marginal principles, and to measure, on the principle of column *f* of Table XII, the cost to society of this output of X in A. These total values and costs to society must, it will be remembered, be measured on the assumption that for every output of X in A the outputs and prices of X in B and of Y, Z, etc., in A and B and the prices of all the factors of production in A and B (reckoned on the assumption that the factors cannot move between A and B) are all adjusted so that in every industry and trade the marginal conditions of economic welfare are observed. Industry X should then be set up in A if the total value to consumers measured in this way exceeds the total cost to society measured in this way. In practice, of course, it will be impossible to make any accurate calculation on these lines; but it is only by consideration of the factors involved in the calculations that an informed 'hunch' can be reached as to the desirability of setting up the new industry.

It may be of interest to consider the relationship between this analysis and the frequently repeated arguments in favour of temporary State assistance for the encouragement of 'infant industries' in a country which does not already possess them. The argument usually runs as follows. The producers in country A have no experience of producing commodity X. If a few firms were set up to produce X, these firms would at first make a loss and therefore it will not pay to set them up. But if they were in fact set up, after a time experience would bring with it the necessary skills and know-how and the industry would turn out to be an economic one for the country to undertake. In such circumstances, it is argued, it would increase real income to give temporary protection to the industry which could be withdrawn as soon as the industry was able to stand on its own feet.

But the analysis developed in Chapter VIII suggests that infancy as such provides no argument even for temporary State support. Growing up from inefficient infancy to effective manhood does not necessarily involve either atmosphere-creating external economies or large indivisible factors of production; and, as we have argued, in the absence of these there is no case for special State support. Consider, for example, a single firm being set up to produce X in A. In the first five years it will be inefficient and will lose, let us say, $20,000 a year or $100,000 in all. Thereafter it will have learnt its job and will cover its total costs of production. This in itself is no argument for the State to pay it a subsidy of $20,000 a year for the first five years. The $100,000 is a capital investment by the firm in learning how to produce the product. The money which the firm spends on machinery to start production uses up the economic resources which produce the machinery and which could otherwise have been used to produce equipment for some other industry. The capital investment should take place in this industry only if the future output from the machinery will enable the firm to earn the current rate of interest on the capital involved. Similarly, the money involved in hiring factors of production not so much to produce a current output of the product as to acquire the skill and know-how to produce in the future takes resources away from other occupations in which they could be producing equipment for other industries. This again is worth while only if the future production is so increased as to enable the current rate of interest to be earned on the $100,000 invested in learning the job. But if this return can in fact be earned by the firm, private enterprise will have an incentive to invest the $100,000 in this way; and there will be no case for a State subsidy.

Infancy as such, therefore, provides no argument for even temporary State support. But atmosphere-creating external economies may be connected with infancy; it may be difficult for one infant to learn without thereby affecting the knowledge of other infants. And these external economies may well justify some temporary State assistance. Thus the loss of $100,000 by the firm which we considered in the preceding paragraph may result in the discovery of technical know-how about the best methods of producing X in the particular physical or social atmosphere in country A; and this knowledge may then be automatically available to all other firms setting up to produce X in A. Or the setting up of the first firm by making one set of workers familiar with mechanical devices may start a general acquaintance with, and interest in, things mechanical which, once it has started, may spread and may perpetuate itself. Again, in this case the single and once-for-all loss of $100,000 by the first firm may alter the conditions of production for all subsequent competitors. Now it may well be that the future profits made by the first firm would not alone be sufficient to earn the current rate of interest on the $100,000, so that no firm would have an incentive to set up the industry. But it may at the same time well be the case that the investment of $100,000 will earn the current rate of return if account is taken of the improvement which it brings to the future operation of the whole industry. In such a case the temporary subsidization of the first firm may be socially desirable; but this would be so not because infants have to learn but because infants teach each other.

Another particular argument which is often employed in favour of State support for new industries in a particular country is for the diversification of the economy of the country. This argument may be combined with the infant-industry argument. Thus it may be argued that once the industries have been established they will be able to stand on their own feet; and the consequent diversification of industry may be mentioned merely as an additional advantage to be obtained from the temporary State support. But, as we shall see, the logic of the diversification argument, unlike the logic of the infant-industry argument, does not imply only temporary State assistance; it may well be used to justify permanent continuing assistance.

The argument itself runs as follows: Country A may at present be producing only one product or one group of products or, more probably, may be employing a very large proportion of her factors of production upon the production of one product or one group of products. But the future is uncertain. At any time conditions of demand in other countries or technical conditions affecting the supply of substitute products in other countries might change in an unforeseen manner so as to cause a heavy decline in the demand for the product on which country A is specializing. But it takes time to set up alternative industries; plans for new investments must be laid, skills must be learned, and new arrangements of many kinds must be made. If disaster unexpectedly overtook the industry in which A specialized, there would intervene a period of acute poverty while A's resources were being shifted into the next most profitable industries. But if a nucleus of those industries already existed, the shift would be much quicker and smoother. Even, therefore, if they need permanent annual subsidization it may be worth while setting them up and maintaining them as an insurance premium against the risk of future disaster to the predominant industry.

The argument, so stated, is no doubt formally correct. The setting up of industry X may mean that uncertainty of future poverty may be reduced for workers in industries Y and Z. Industry X carries with it an atmosphere-creating external economy in so far as uncertainty is a thing which is in itself undesirable. But the application of this argument in practice is peculiarly difficult. It is difficult to assess how much the existence of industry X on a certain scale would in fact relieve distress if disaster did overtake the existing predominant industry; it is difficult to assess the risk that such disaster will occur; and it is difficult to assess the social undesirability of a given risk. Yet all these assessments would have to be made, in addition to all the other difficulties discussed in Chapter VIII in connexion with Table XII, before a rational judgement could be passed. Moreover, alternative methods by which society could insure against the risk would have to be considered in order to see whether they were less costly than the method of setting up immediately industries which if current conditions continued would be socially unprofitable. For example, suppose that the citizens of A rely almost entirely upon the production and export of Y to obtain the purchasing power required to purchase from B commodities X and Z and all the other many commodities required for their health and happiness. The authorities in A could insure against a future collapse of the Y-industry either by taking action to set up X- and Z-industries in A now or by taxing the citizens of A and using the proceeds to build up a capital reserve of B's money. If disaster overtook A's exports of Y to B, this reserve could be used to continue to import from B the necessary supplies of X and Z and other commodities while the new industries were starting up in A. If this method were cheaper than that of the annual subsidies which would otherwise have to be paid to maintain a diversified industry in A, it would be socially preferable to adopt it.

There is one form of atmosphere-creating external economy—what we may call the economies of conglomeration—which may well be of great importance in considering the structure of the international economy. There may be important economies to be derived from the fact that a large number of firms in any one industry, and, indeed, a large number of industries, are all 'conglomerated' close together int he same locality. Communications and transport between the firms producing components for each other will be easier; there will be a pool of skilled labour from which each firm may draw as its own activity fluctuates; know-how, skill, and technical ideas may be more easily spread when all the producers and workers are in easy contact with each other; and so on. For these and many similar reasons the costs of production incurred by any one particular firm may be considerably lower if that firm is in the middle of a developed industrial region than if it is alone and isolated.

Such then are some of the issues involved in making a rational decision whether an industry to produce X should be set up in A. This decision should theoretically depend upon the outcome of calculations of the type discussed in Chapter VIII. But, as we have already observed, it will rarely if ever be possible to make actual calculations of this kind. It may, therefore, be useful as an indication of the sort of things which should be considered in forming any practical hunch as to whether industry X should be set up in A to enumerate the main considerations which would theoretically lie behind the outcome of the type of calculations discussed in Chapter VIII and which should therefore be taken into account in the formation of any practical judgement of an issue of this kind.

In the case which we are at present examining, X is produced and will continue to be produced in B. The question is whether the identical product should also be produced in A. Our problem is, therefore, essentially to decide whether it is cheaper to produce various quantities of the product in B alone or partly in A and partly in B. It is the cost conditions for various outputs which must play the essential role.[1] The following then are the most important cost considerations in deciding whether it is socially desirable that X should be produced in A as well as in B.

(1) We have already observed in Chapter VIII that there will be no case for State action to carry out a structural adjustment unless the industry in question operates under conditions of economies of large-scale production. In our particular case this means that, apart from ensuring that the marginal conditions are correct, no special State action is required to cause industry X to be set up in country A unless this industry enjoys increasing returns to scale. But it does not, of course, follow that X should necessarily be set up in A just because there are increasing returns to scale for X in A. Obviously it would not pay to produce bananas at the North Pole merely because the production of 10 bananas a year would cost only $1,000,000 a banana whereas the production of 5 bananas a year would cost $1,500,000 a banana. But there is a rather more subtle point which must be remembered. If X is produced in A as well as in B, the world consumption of X will require a smaller output of X from B since part now of the demand is satisfied by A. But if the production of X enjoys economies of large-scale production in A, it will probably also enjoy such economies in B. The cost advantage to the world as a whole of producing X on a large scale in A will be offset, in part at least, by the cost disadvantage of producing X on a smaller scale in B.

This point is of great importance. The possibility of producing under conditions of increasing returns to scale is often used as an argument for State action to set up industries in unindustrialized countries. Thus

[1] The demand conditions are not, of course, totally irrelevant since they will affect the quantities which it will be desirable to produce if production is carried on in only one country and if production is carried on in both countries. The size of these quantities will affect the total costs and will affect the difference between total costs and total value to consumers. This influence of demand is illustrated in Appendix 3 (pp. 586–90) by the choice in Figure I between points S (where only one country should produce) and V (where both countries should produce).

it is argued on behalf of the industrialization of unindustrialized countries that it is largely an historical accident that they have no industry; that it needs State action to start up industries; but that if they were once started up and reached a certain size, then, because of the external economies associated with large-scale production, they would be truly economic. But representatives of the older industrialized countries can argue with equal plausibility that it is paradoxical to use the argument of economies of large-scale production—i.e. the argument of economies of conglomeration—for a policy of dispersing industry over a large number of countries; that industries can operate on the largest scale if they are concentrated in a few centres such as those which the existing industrialized regions constitute; and that world prosperity is thus best served if some countries concentrate on industrial production and others on primary production. The argument of increasing returns to scale can thus be used both for and against a policy of the industrialization of unindustrialized countries. Which side is right?

The answer is the unexciting one: sometimes the one side, and sometimes the other; it all depends upon what in Chapter III (pp. 36–37) we have called the relationship between structural and marginal economies of large-scale production. Thus suppose that there is a very large world market for product X and that the increasing returns to scale in X are important but are such that they are fully realized as soon as industry X is of a quite moderate size. In this case when industry X in A is set up on quite a moderate scale the full economies of scale can be enjoyed in A without interfering with the enjoyment of the full economies of scale in B as well, since a sufficient market will be left for B's output for B also to enjoy the full economies of scale. In this case it would be correct to set up the industry in A if it were judged that when it was of quite a moderate size the average cost of production in A would fall as low as the present average cost in B and without taking into account any possibility that it will also raise the average cost in B. But if there were only a small world market for X and if the economies of scale could be enjoyed only if the industry were on a very large scale, then it would not be sufficient to ask whether A could produce a moderate output at an average cost as low as the present cost in B; it would be necessary also to take into account the social loss due to the fact that what was still produced in B would now be produced at a higher average cost.[1] This could be done through the application of the principles of calculation outlined in Chapter VIII; and it is thus clear that whether State action is desirable to set up an industry X in A as well as in B depends not only upon the existence of increasing returns

[1] It will be remembered that we are still analysing the problem on the assumption that X continues to be produced in B as well as in A. The possibility of transferring the industry completely from B to A will be considered below.

to scale in the industry, but also upon the shape of those increasing returns, i.e. upon whether their full operation comes into play quickly as the industry grows to a moderate size or only slowly as the industry grows to a very big size.

(2) The cost calculations which are appropriate in order to discover whether it is sensible to produce X in A as well as in B will, of course, also have to take into account those conditions which are not connected with increasing returns to scale. The first of these is the existence of a suitable physical, social, and political atmosphere for the production. Different combinations of sunshine, rainfall, temperature, humidity, etc., are necessary to produce different products economically. But social and political atmosphere is also relevant. For example, the production of certain things can be carried on economically only where law and order is regularly maintained; for other things this condition may not be so vitally essential.

(3) But the country must possess not only a suitable atmosphere. It must also have an appropriate endowment of the necessary factors of production. We have already considered at length the vital importance of this consideration in international trade. If the production of wheat needs little labour but much land and that of vegetables little land but much labour, it will be cheap to produce wheat in a country with a small population per acre and to produce vegetables in a country with a large population per acre. In the former the relative abundance of land will cause the rent of land to be low and the relative scarcity of labour will cause the wage rate to be high; as a result, wheat production (which needs much of the cheap factor land and little of the expensive factor labour) will be cheap to produce relatively to vegetables (which need much of the expensive factor labour and little of the cheap factor land). The opposite will be the case in the other country. Thus, in so far as this factor alone is concerned, it will be cheaper to produce wheat in the former country and vegetables in the latter.

(4) Finally, we may note the relevance of transport costs. Let us suppose that the X which is produced in A is exactly the same commodity as the X which is produced in B but that it costs something to transport X between A and B. We have then two commodities X-in-A (i.e. X available for consumption in A) and X-in-B (i.e. X available for consumption in B). Now there are two ways of producing each commodity. Thus X-in-A can be produced simply by producing X in A or by producing X in B and transporting it to A. When X is produced only in B, then both X-in-A and X-in-B are produced in B. But A has an advantage in producing X-in-A in being able thereby to avoid the cost of transport of the product. How great this advantage is will depend, of course, upon the cost of transport of a unit of X from B to A in relation to its value. If the transport cost is 10 per cent of the value

of the product, then to this extent A has a 10 per cent cost advantage over B in the production of X-in-A while B has a 10 per cent advantage over A in the production of X-in-B.[1] In so far, therefore, as this factor is important (and outweighs any other considerations of increasing returns to scale, suitable atmosphere, and suitable factor endowments) it will give a reason why production should in each case be undertaken in the country in which the market for the product is situated. If there were no market for X in A (Eskimos do not presumably purchase refrigerators), this would tell in favour of the concentration of the production of X in B; if there were a market for the product in both countries, this would tell in favour of production in both countries.

But the product is not the only thing which can be transported. The raw materials or other intermediate products can be transported from one country to another. Just as the cost of transporting the product will tend to pull the production towards the place in which the product is consumed, so the cost of transporting the raw material will tend to pull the production to the place where the raw material is produced. In any other place the price of the raw material will be raised by the cost of transporting it to that other place, and thus the place at which the raw material is produced will tend to enjoy a lower cost of production.

Which of these pulls is the stronger will depend upon the nature of the product. Some products contain physically practically all of the raw materials which are used in their construction. Thus in so far as the raw cotton used to make a shirt all appears in the shirt itself, no saving of transport of the raw material is achieved by placing textile mills near the source of the raw cotton. This will mean that the cotton will not have to be transported in a raw state from the field to the factory near the consumer. But just as much will have to be transported just as far in a finished form from the factory near the field to the consumer. But other products may not contain much of the raw materials used in their production. Thus the coal needed to smelt iron ore is not contained in the resulting pig iron. To place the smelting works near the coal mine does save the transport of the coal.

But it is not merely a question of the weight of raw material to be transported in the crude form and in the finished product. Cost of transport depends not only upon weight but also upon the bulk, shape, fragility, and other qualities of the commodity. Finished pottery needs to be more carefully packed and handled in transport than crude china clay. On the other hand, weight for weight, iron ore may be a more awkward cargo to handle than pig iron. The true comparison must be between the cost of carrying, from the source of the raw material to the

[1] Thus the 'protective' effect of transport costs is reduced not by a fall in the cost of transport but by a fall in the cost of transport relatively to the cost of production of the products to be transported.

final market, one unit of a product or that amount of the raw material which is necessary for the production of one unit of the product.

Of course there may be more than one raw material used by an industry and more than one product produced by an industry. There will then be separate pulls towards the source of each material and towards the market for each product. In this case the most economical location for the industry from the point of view of the minimization of transport costs will not necessarily be at the source of any one of the materials or at the market for any one of the products. Let us consider a firm that uses raw materials L and M and produces products X and Y, and let us suppose that these materials are used and these products are produced in fixed proportions and that we have chosen our units of measurement so that one unit of M and of L is used, and one unit of Y is produced, for each unit of X produced. Then for each unit of X produced the firm would have a total transport cost equal to the cost of transporting a unit of X to the market for X plus the cost of transporting a unit of Y to the market for Y plus the cost of transporting a unit of L from the source of L plus the cost of transporting a unit of M from the source of M. If these markets and sources of supply were themselves each concentrated at one point, the position of the firm which would minimize transport costs can be visualized from the following sketch:

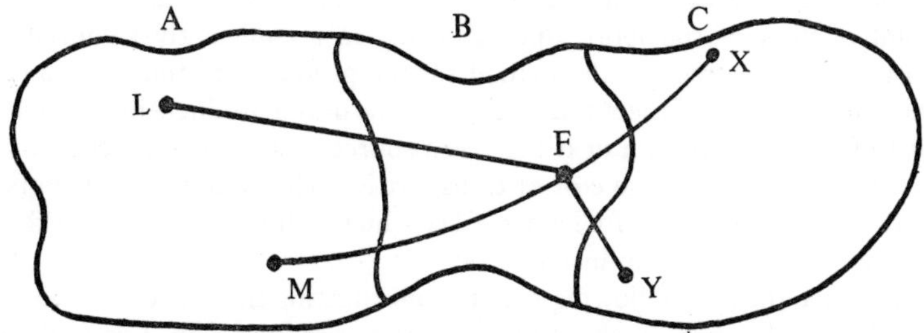

The point F represents the position of the firm in relation to the points L, M, X, and Y which represent the positions of the sources of L and M and the markets for X and Y respectively. The total transport cost involved will be the distance LF multiplied by the cost per mile of transporting a unit of that particular material plus the distance XF multiplied by the cost per mile of transporting a unit of that particular product, and so on. Each point L, M, X, and Y thus exerts a pull towards it of the firm F which is proportional to the cost of transport of the material or product in question.[1] The position of the firm should approach any one particular point more closely, the higher is the cost

[1] In Appendix 4 (pp. 591–5), there is a precise mathematical formulation of the resulting best position for F. Here we must be content with a summary of a few of the main conclusions, which are at least intuitively plausible.

of transport of the material or product in question. If the cost of transport of that particular material or product is sufficiently high, then the firm should be placed actually at the source of that material or at the market for that product. This result, namely the location of the firm actually at one of its material sources or product markets, is the more likely to be the correct one, if that material or product not only has an exceptionally high transport cost but also happens to have its source or market in a position in which it is surrounded on all sides by the other material sources or product markets. For in that case the location of the firm at the particular source or market in question will involve a minimum increase in the distances over which the other materials and products have to be carried.

The relevance of this analysis to our present argument is as follows. Let us for the moment drop the assumption which we are making in this Part that the world is made up of two countries. Let us suppose that there are three countries, A, B, and C as marked in the sketch on p. 263. In such conditions it is clear that the industry might be carried on most economically in B where the raw materials and markets can most conveniently be brought together, even though no raw material source and no product market were actually in B itself.

To revert to our two-country world, it is clear that whether a particular industry can economically be set up in A depends, from the point of view of transport, upon A being in a sufficiently favourable position both as regards the market for the product and the sources of the raw materials. If there is a market for one of the products in A whose cost of transport is high or if there is a source of supply of a necessary raw material in A whose cost of transport is high, these will be factors in the cost calculation of Chapter VIII which will be favourable to the decision to set up the industry in A.

We have then the following four factors affecting the cost calculations which must be made in deciding whether to produce X in A as well as in B: (i) the existence and form of increasing returns to scale in the production of X in A and in B; (ii) the existence of a suitable atmosphere for the production of X in A; (iii) the existence of a suitable factor endowment for the production of X in A; and (iv) the existence of suitable conditions of transport for the product and the materials when X is produced in A. Considerations ii, iii, and iv will all have their appropriate effect in deciding the actions of private producers when they consider whether it is profitable to start to produce in A; it is the modification of these considerations by appropriate attention to consideration i—namely, the effect of increasing returns to scale—which may make it appropriate for the State to intervene to bring about the setting up of the industry in A even though private producers have no incentive to do so.

So far we have considered the case for a structural change in A's economy through the setting up of industry X on the assumption that there was no accompanying structural change in B's economy. But in fact the setting up of the X-industry in A may prove undesirable if B's structure remains unchanged but desirable if B's structure is appropriately changed either by the disappearance of some industry which already exists in B or else by the setting up in B of some new industry. These are cases in which the principles of calculation of the social advantage of the structural change can still be carried out on the lines discussed in Chapter VIII but with the modifications discussed on pp. 130–2 of that chapter. It is necessary to consider (i) the value of introducing A's industry in a world in which B's industry does not exist, (ii) the value of introducing A's industry in a world in which B's industry does exist, and (iii) the value of introducing B's industry in a world in which A's industry does not exist, and comparing these with (iv) the value of maintaining a position in which neither industry exists.

Let us consider first of all the case where industry X in A would produce a product which was a very close substitute for that of industry Y in B. The simplest example of this case would be where X and Y were exactly the same product and where the cost of transporting this product between A and B was very small. To produce X in A and Y in B may not be worth while if the economies of large-scale production were important and the total world market for X and Y were not very large. This would be merely to have two small industries which in the extreme case might, for that reason, be so uneconomic that it would be preferable not to produce X or Y at all. To produce either X in A without Y in B or Y in B without X in A might be worth while; either industry alone might be of a sufficient size to make it economic to produce. But it might be that it was more economic to produce X in A than Y in B, even though for historical reasons in fact Y was being produced in B and X was not being produced in A. Here would be the case in which the calculus used in Chapter VIII would indicate that the industry should be transferred from B to A.

But in this connexion it is important to distinguish between two quite different questions: (i) If one was starting from scratch without either industry in existence, would it be preferable to set up industry X in A or industry Y in B? (ii) Is it worth while transferring an existing industry from B to A? The answer to the former question is more likely to be favourable to the setting up of the industry in A than is the answer to the latter question. There are in fact some pure costs of transfer involved. Thus if the industry already exists in B but not in A, the installation of the industry in A may require a period of infancy during which special costs of initiation in A are necessarily incurred. This is not the case in B. Moreover, in B's industry there may be specialized equipment whose value in alternative industries is very small and certainly very much lower than the cost of replacing or of expanding it. In other words, the resources temporarily tied up in these specialized instruments could not be used to produce much in any other industries, so that for the period during which they can still be used the cost of continuing production in B must be reckoned as very low. The calculations of Chapter VIII must, therefore, be done on a basis which allows for the specially high costs of infancy in A and the specially low costs of senility in B. Such costs of transfer always weight the scales properly somewhat in favour of the *status quo*; it is mere common sense that everyone should start with a prejudice in favour of doing what they are already skilled at doing. Prejudices can, of course, be overdone; and transfers of industry should be made if, but only if, the permanent gain outweighs the initial cost.

Apart from these costs of transfer, whether a product should be produced in A or B or in both depends upon the costs of production in the two different countries and upon the scale of the world demand for the product. Clearly if the total demand for the product is small and if there are important structural economies of scale in its production, it should be produced only in one of the countries, and it should be produced in that country (say, country B) in which the costs of production for a small output are lowest. At a somewhat higher level of demand it might still be best to concentrate the production only in one country, since the level of demand may still not be sufficient to allow both countries to take adequate advantage of the economies of large-scale production; but it is possible that it would now be best to concentrate the production in country A instead of in country B. This might be the case if in country B costs were lower than in country A for small levels of output, but economies of large-scale production were more important in A than in B so that for a somewhat larger output costs were lower in A than in B. For still higher levels of demand it might be most economical to produce in both A and B; economies of scale could be enjoyed in both countries, and increased costs due to scarcities of particular factors of production in each country could be avoided if the industry was not too much expanded in either country. Thus the problem of the most economic geographical structure for the world economy may be an extremely complicated one, taking one shape if the demand is at one level and another shape if demand is at another level.[1]

So much for the case where the setting up of a new industry in A should be combined with the closing down of an industry in B. Let us turn now to the case where the setting up of a new industry in A should

[1] A particular example of the case where the two products are perfect substitutes for each other (i.e. both countries produce the same commodity and there are no costs of transport) is illustrated geometrically in Appendix 3 (pp. 586–90).

be combined with the setting up of a new industry in B as well. Suppose that A were well qualified by her existing atmosphere and factor endowment to produce X but not to produce Y, and suppose that the opposite were the case in B. Suppose further that X and Y were complementary products—X being, let us say, a raw material necessary for the production of Y and having little use for any other purpose—so that it was no use producing X without Y or Y without X. If either A or B undertook the production of both products it might not be worth while doing so, since the costs of producing Y in A or X in B might be prohibitively high. But if A produced X and B produced Y, there might be a net social gain; and if both X and Y are produced under conditions of increasing returns to scale it may require jointly planned State action in the two countries simultaneously in order to achieve the desirable structural adjustment.

This case may not be of very frequent occurrence. It is applicable only when one industry requires a raw material which is produced under conditions of increasing returns to scale and which is not already being produced anywhere for any other purpose; it does not, of course, apply to the case where the institution of a new manufacturing industry requires the development of the existing output of some raw material. But cases may from time to time occur where joint international planning is required to set up simultaneously in two countries two separate parts of a new line of production.

So far we have considered the conditions which may make it desirable to promote a structural change in the distribution of different industries among our two countries A and B. We have so far said nothing about the forms of governmental policy which might be adopted for promoting these changes.

In this connexion we need to distinguish clearly between two rather separate problems: (i) the degree and forms of once-for-all State intervention which may be necessary in order to bring the structural change about, and (ii) the degree and forms of continuing State intervention which may be continuously necessary to maintain or to perfect the change once it has been made.

Let us deal with the second of these two problems first of all. It is possible that once the structural change has been successfully made no further State intervention will be required and that a policy of complete laissez-faire and free trade would thereafter be appropriate. Let us give an example of this. Suppose that the industry or industries to be introduced into A carry with them important external economics of conglomeration. If the scale of production is small in the locality, it is expensive and unprofitable. But if there are a large number of competing firms and industries concentrated close to each other in the region, the whole productive atmosphere will be changed so that costs of production are sufficiently low to make the production economic. Now it is possible that the market in A for the product of the new industry is so great that when it has been set up and is operating on the correct marginal principles it will be on so great a scale that there are no economies of scale to be reaped from a further expansion. The average cost to the firm in the industry would then be the same as the marginal social cost of the product. In these conditions once the structural change had been made it would maintain itself indefinitely and the firms could all produce the correct outputs. Prices would be equal to marginal and to average costs and there would be no divergence between marginal private and social costs. Once the change was made, no continuing governmental intervention would be necessary. In the terminology used in Chapter III (pp. 36–37) there would have been important structural economies of large-scale production, but no marginal economies of large-scale production would remain.

But this is not necessarily the case. It might well be that when firms and industries were all of the correct size in the sense that their marginal social costs equalled the price offered by consumers for their products, there would still be marginal economies of conglomeration to be reaped from the further concentration of industry in the region. Whether or not this would be so would depend solely upon the size of the market for the products of these new firms in A in relation to the scale necessary for the industries concerned to have enjoyed to the full all the possible economies of conglomeration. If these economies have not been fully used up, then it will be true in the new continuing situation that the establishment of yet one more firm would help to bring down the costs of the other existing firms so that the marginal social cost to the industry would still be lower than the marginal private cost to the new firm. There would thus in the absence of special State policy be a divergence in the relevant industry between marginal values and costs. What ought to be done in this case as a continuing act of policy is precisely the question which we have already discussed in Chapter XIV. The ideal policy is to subsidize the industry directly, if one neglects the problems raised by the levying of the revenue necessary to finance the subsidy. If the new industries are still competing with imports, there may be some case for a continuing restriction of imports by tariffs or other measures to aid in the stimulation of the domestic industries. If the new industries are now exporting their products, duties on imports will not help; but, as has been discussed above (p. 242), if there are problems involved in raising the revenue for a straightforward subsidy on output, a case may be made out for some element of export subsidy. These issues, however, are in no way different from those which we have already discussed in Chapter XIV.

The problem is only a little different in the case in which the economies of large-scale production which make the structural change desirable are not external economies of an atmosphere-creating kind, but are internal economies due to the indivisibility of some of the factors of production which must be used in the new industries. Thus the industrial development may require a railway system or a system of electrical generation, which must be built on a considerable scale if they are to be built at all because of the technical indivisibility of the capital investment which is required. When the development has been completed, there will be a problem in the control of monopoly which was not present in the case of external economies which we have examined. The railway system or the electrical generating system, being a single indivisible unit, will have the monopolistic power to raise the prices obtainable for its services by restricting its output of them.

But otherwise the problems of continuing support for these new industries will be essentially the same as those which we have just discussed in the case of external economies. Suppose that by price control or otherwise some arrangement were made to prevent the new monopolistic industry from receiving a price for the sale of its product above the average cost of producing it. If the market for its product were just of the right size, so that the output produced makes a full use but not more than a full use of the indivisible capital equipment (see pp. 32–36 above), then a price equal to the average cost of production will just suffice to pay each factor in the industry a reward equal to the value of its marginal product. But if the demand for the industry's output were rather less than this, a price equal to the average cost of production would not bring in enough revenue to pay rewards to the factors of production as high as the value of their marginal products. There would be an excess of marginal value over marginal cost; and the output would need to be stimulated further. The ideal policy for this would be to add to the regulation that the price received from the consumer must be equal to the average cost of production a subsidy to the output, which would then stimulate output until the marginal social cost were equal to the price charged to consumers. But if there were difficulties involved in raising the revenue required to finance such a subsidy, there might be some argument for an element of import duty or of export subsidy, according to whether the industry competed with imports or produced for export, to stimulate the home production. Once more the arguments are precisely the same as those employed in discussing divergences between marginal values and costs in Chapter XIV.[1]

[1] If the demand for the industry's output were so large as to cause the indivisible equipment to be overworked without making it worth while to duplicate the whole equipment, the charging of a price equal to the average cost of production would mean that the industry was over-expanded, since in this case the marginal cost would be greater than the average cost which is equated to the consumer's price and so to the marginal value of the commodity. The correct policy in this case would be to impose some tax on the output. But since the raising of this tax (unlike the payment of a subsidy) does not

Thus it can be seen that the problem of *structural* change does not provide any new arguments for permanent departures in commercial policy from the free-trade principle other than the arguments examined in Chapter XIV for dealing with divergences between *marginal* values and costs. But problems of structural change may very well provide special arguments for temporary departures from the free-trade principle. Consider once more the possible case of an industry which enjoys important structural economies of conglomeration but for which, when it has once been set up, the freely available market will be sufficiently large to mean that there are no remaining marginal economies of conglomeration. Both before the change (i.e. without the new industries at all) and after the change (i.e. with the new industries producing automatically their marginally ideal outputs) there would be a continuing equilibrium which did not require any State intervention for its maintenance. But there would be no incentive for the private producers to embark upon the structural change since any one producer who set up a new firm alone would lose money by so doing.

In these conditions the structural change may require some State intervention to jolt the economy from the first to the second structural position, although when once the jolt has been administered there is no need for any continuing State aid.

The amount of pressure which must be exercised to give the required jolt will differ from case to case. There may be cases in which there is extremely little friction and practically no cost of growth, so that some moderate inducement held out for a very short time may suffice to bring about a considerable structural change. But normally the costs of growth will be significant. New techniques have to be mastered; the necessary know-how has to be acquired; and labour has to be trained in the necessary skills. The greater are these costs of growth, the greater and more prolonged will be the necessary process of jolting the economy into the new structural shape. We have already argued that pure costs of growth in themselves constitute no argument for State intervention. An infant firm should cover its own costs of growth, unless either of two other conditions are fulfilled: its growth should be subsidized if its own acquisition of the necessary skills, etc., indirectly helps other firms to learn as well, or if a mere increase in its size indirectly decreases costs for other firms. Where these things are combined—that is to say, where firms need time to learn by experience to become economic, where the experience required by one firm helps other firms to become more efficient more quickly, and where other firms are helped merely by an increase in the size of an individual firm—there

involve any problems of putting a further strain on general tax revenues—indeed it relieves that strain—there would be no point in considering an import subsidy or an export tax as an alternative method of restricting home output.

are circumstances in which a structural change may in the end prove self-supporting and repaying, but may need a considerable jolt to be brought into effect.

Any jolt which may be necessary may take one of many forms. If the industries concerned are producing tradeable products, then they will be being imported in the initial situation in which the industries do not exist in country A. In this case the imposition of sufficiently heavy import duties will serve to give the economy a jolt at least in the desired direction. Indeed, if in the new situation some part of country A's supplies of the products in question will be imported, a temporary import duty may be sufficient to give the economy the whole of the jolt necessary to reach the new situation. If, however, the economies of large-scale production cannot be enjoyed until country A has not merely produced supplies sufficient for her own consumption but has embarked upon production for export as well, it may be necessary to add a temporary export subsidy to the temporary import duty in order to bring about the required degree of structural change.

But in extreme cases the domestic cost of production might initially be so high that even the most extreme protective policy would not make production profitable for the first pioneer producers. In this case the jolt could not be given solely by commercial policy through import duties and export subsidies. Some direct subsidy of a temporary character to the domestic industry would be required. And even in those cases in which the jolt could be given by commercial policy, it is not necessarily desirable that it should be given in that form. It could always be given by means of a direct subsidy to the domestic production. This method has obvious advantages. An import duty and export subsidy will cause the prices charged to consumers for the products concerned to be higher in A than in B. So long as they last they will, therefore, interfere with the optimization of trade and thus cause some avoidable loss of economic welfare. On the other hand, the direct subsidization of the domestic production, while it is the obvious way of getting the desired change of production without interfering with the advantage to be reaped from trade, will involve in a much more marked degree the difficulties connected with the raising of the revenue necessary for the finance of the subsidy on production. For this reason some element of the commercial policy weapons of import duty and export subsidy may be permissible. Once again the analogy with the type of analysis developed in Chapter XIV should be clear.

CHAPTER XVII

THE DISTRIBUTIONAL ARGUMENT FOR TRADE CONTROL: (1) THE INTERNATIONAL TERMS OF TRADE

THE basic argument in favour of free trade which we developed in Chapter IX disregarded the effects of trade policy upon the distribution of income. The argument concerned the effect of a free-trade policy upon economic efficiency. Similarly, the various modifications of the free-trade argument which we have examined in Chapters XII–XVI have taken no account of the effect of trade policies upon the distribution of income. They have all been concerned with reasons why free trade may fail to lead to the greatest economic efficiency on the assumption that the same distributional weight is applied to marginal changes in the income of every citizen of the world.

We turn in this and the following chapter to a consideration of the effect of trade policies upon the distribution of income. The argument of Chapter IX has not provided any presumption that free trade will lead to the optimization of distribution and the effect of trade controls upon the distribution of income must, therefore, be considered without any prejudice in favour of a free-trade policy.

Broadly speaking, there are two ways in which trade controls may affect the distribution of income. First, trade controls may affect the terms on which A's products exchange for B's products and may thus affect the distribution of real income as between the citizens of A and the citizens of B. Second, trade controls by affecting the conditions of demand for each country's products may cause the economic position of one group of citizens within A to improve at the expense of another group of citizens within A; and similarly for B. The first of these two types of distributional effect will be examined in this chapter, and the second will be examined in Chapter XVIII.

In this chapter then we are concerned with the effect of trade controls upon the distribution of income between the citizens of A and the citizens of B, and we shall not be concerned with the distribution of income as between groups of citizens within any country. In other words we assume for the time being that the policy-makers allot one single distributional weight to all citizens in A and one single distributional weight to all citizens in B.

Now it is possible that country A by imposing a trade tax can turn the terms of trade in its favour. By taxing exports and discouraging the flow of exports to B, it can make its export products scarce in B's market and can thus induce B's consumers to pay a better price for them. Or by taxing imports and discouraging the purchase of B's export products in A, it can cause a surplus of such products to develop in B and so can lower the price at which they can be procured in B. By cutting down the volume of its trade with B, A can obtain better terms of trade for the trade which still remains. If the terms of trade move sufficiently in A's favour, then A will obtain a greater total amount of B's export products for a smaller total amount of A's export products. In this case A's gain is clear. But if the terms of trade do not improve so much as this, A will obtain a smaller total amount of B's products in return for a smaller amount of her own. In this case we have to ask whether the loss to A from the smaller volume of profitable trade is less than the gain to A from the improvement in the terms on which this smaller volume is conducted.

The position is very comparable to that of the monopolistic seller or monopsonistic purchaser which we have examined above (pp. 16–18). The monopolistic seller, for example, so long as the price which he can obtain for his product is higher than the cost to him of producing it, could improve his position if he could sell more without having to cut his selling price. But being a monopolist, he must appreciably cut his selling price in order to expand the market for his product. He must weigh the gain on the new units of trade from the loss due to the fall in price received on all the existing units of trade. Or the monopsonistic purchaser, so long as the price at which he can buy the product is lower than its value to him, could improve his position if he could purchase more without driving up the price against himself. But, being a monopsonist, his purchases will influence the market, and he can purchase more only at the cost of paying a higher price for all his purchases. He must weigh up the advantage to him of having additional units to consume at the available price against the cost of driving up against himself the price of all the units which he is already purchasing.

Now the individual exporters in country A may be completely competitive; each alone may possess no monopolistic influence over the price receivable for A's apples in country B. And the individual importers in country A may also be completely competitive; each alone may possess no monopsonistic influence over the price payable for B's blankets in B. Yet if A's exporters together supply a large proportion of B's total consumption of apples, the government of A by taxing and so restricting the trade in apples may be able significantly to raise the price which B's consumers will pay for A's apples. Or if A's consumers together account for a large proportion of the total market for B's blankets, A's government by taxing and so restricting the trade in blankets may be able significantly to lower the price at which B's producers will offer their blankets for sale. The analogy with the theory of monopoly or monopsony is complete. A's government can take action to restrict the whole export or import trade of A and can thereby exercise some monopolistic or monopsonistic influence over the price of A's apples in terms of B's blankets.

Whenever A's trade with B is large enough for a restriction of A's sales of apples to B or of A's purchases of blankets from B to raise at all significantly the price of apples in terms of blankets, it will pay the citizens of A for A's government to impose some tax on the trade between A and B. Suppose there is free trade between A and B and that in this position the price of an apple is one blanket. Suppose now that if A's exports of apples to B were increased by 2 per cent—from 100 to 102—the price of an apple would fall 1 per cent from 1·01 to 1 blankets. Then by providing 102 instead of 100 apples A is obtaining 102 × 1 (or 102) instead of 100 × 1·01 (or 101) blankets. In other words, for the last 2 apples provided by A in the free-trade position A's citizens as a whole have obtained only 1 additional blanket. Although the market price of an apple is 1 blanket, the cost to A's citizens as a whole for obtaining the last additional blanket is 2 apples. But in the free-trade position, since the market price of a blanket to citizens of A is only 1 apple, they will be consuming blankets and apples in such amounts that one additional apple has the same value to them as 1 additional blanket. Yet in fact if they consumed 2 more apples at home instead of exporting them they would so turn the terms of trade in their favour that they would have to give up only 1 blanket for the 2 additional apples; and this would clearly improve their welfare. Thus so long as country A as a whole can by restricting trade appreciably turn the terms of trade in its favour there will be some rate of duty which will increase its welfare.

But this does not mean that any and every rate of duty will in such circumstances improve the welfare of the citizens of A. The rate of duty may be too high and thus lead to a loss of welfare. Thus in the above example, the citizens of country A in their trade with B in fact are giving up 2 apples in order to obtain the last additional blanket from B although 1 blanket is worth only 1 apple to them in consumption. In such circumstances their welfare will be increased as a rate of trade tax is imposed which raises the market price ratio in A from 1 apple to 1 blanket up to 2 apples for 1 blanket, which represents the true marginal cost of a blanket to A obtained from foreign trade. In other words, a 100 per cent *ad valorem* import duty would give the best result. Anything below this would leave the market price of a blanket in A lower than its true marginal cost to A in exported apples and would thus still leave some tendency for A to concentrate too much on exporting apples to obtain blankets. But if the tax were imposed at a higher rate (say, at 200 per cent *ad valorem*), then the price of imported blankets in A would be three times as high as in B. This might cause a serious over-correction of the previously existing situation. Whereas in the free-trade position the market price of 1 apple for 1 imported blanket was much below the marginal cost to A of obtaining an imported blanket by exporting apples (namely, a cost of 2 apples for the last blanket imported), now the market price in A of imported blankets in terms of apples might be raised so much above the marginal cost to A of obtaining an imported blanket by exporting apples that there was a serious tendency to concentrate too little on exporting apples in order to obtain blankets. If the duty is too high, there may be more loss from undertrading than there was in the free-trade position from over-trading.

Thus if country A by restricting its trade with B can appreciably improve its real terms of trade with B, it will pay A to abandon the free-trade position. Its welfare will be increased as it raises the rate of trade tax up to some 'optimum' level. As the rate of trade tax is raised beyond this point its welfare will tend to fall again from the maximum level achieved by the optimum rate of trade tax. If the rate of duty is raised sufficiently high, A's welfare will fall actually below the level attained in the free-trade position; and the imposition of the duty will then have made conditions worse than in the free-trade position for A as well as for B.

There is, therefore, an optimum rate of trade tax for A to impose which will cause the terms of trade to turn in A's favour to such an extent that the gain to A from the terms of trade less the loss to A from the restriction in the volume of profitable trade is maximized. This rate of duty will be the one which makes the market price of imported products in A in terms of A's exported product equal to the real marginal cost to A of obtaining one more unit of the imported product by means of trade with B. The *ad valorem* height of this optimum rate of trade tax will be determined solely by the conditions of demand for imports and supply of exports in B, i.e. solely by those conditions in B which determine the extent to which A by restricting her trade with B can turn the terms of trade in her favour.[1]

This is illustrated in Table XXI. We suppose in case i of the table that when A's exports to B increase from 100 to 102 (column *a*) the amount of B's exports which are obtained by A increases from 100 to 101 (column *b*). These figures represent a case in which the elasticity of B's offer of blankets for apples is approximately 2. This can be measured in the following way. In column *c* we show the ratio between the figure in column *a* and the corresponding figure in column *b*. This shows the terms of trade. Thus when A exports 102 apples to B she receives 101 blankets in return; or, in other words, A then pays $\frac{102}{101}$ or, approximately, 1·01 apples for each blanket. The price of blankets in terms of A's apples has risen by 1 per cent. Another way of putting this is to say that

[1] The formulae for the optimum rates of duty are given in Sections XVI and XVII in the mathematical supplement to this volume.

when A exports 102 instead of 100 apples to B, the number of blankets which B pays per apple falls by 1 per cent. A can sell 2 per cent more apples in B only at the cost of a 1 per cent fall in the blanket price of apples; or the elasticity of B's offer of blankets for apples is 2.

TABLE XXI

The Optimum Rate for a General Trade Tax

Number of apples exported from A to B (*a*)	Total number of blankets received in exchange by A (*b*)	Terms of trade or market price of a blanket in B, i.e. number of apples given up by A for each blanket (approximately) (*c*) = (*a*) ÷ (*b*)	Marginal cost to A in terms of apples of an additional blanket imported from B (*d*)	Optimum rate of trade tax in A (approximately) (*e*) = (*d* − *c*) ÷ (*c*)
Case (i). *Elasticity of B's Offer of Blankets for Apples approximately* 2. *Optimum Rate of Trade Tax in A approximately* 100 *per cent*				
				%
100	100	1·00	—	—
102	101	1·01	2	100
Case (ii). *Elasticity of B's Offer approximately* 3. *Optimum Rate of Trade Tax in A approximately* 50 *per cent*				
100·	100	1·000	—	—
101·5	101	1·005	1·5	50
Case (iii). *Elasticity of B's Offer approximately* 5. *Optimum Rate of Trade Tax in A approximately* 25 *per cent*				
100·	100	1·0000	—	—
101·25	101	1·0025	1·25	25

In this case it can be seen that the marginal cost to A of obtaining an additional blanket through trade with B is 2 apples. Thus to obtain 101 instead of 100 blankets, i.e. 1 more blanket (column *b*), A has to export 102 instead of 100 apples, i.e. 2 more apples (column *a*). This marginal cost is shown as 2 in column *d*. In this case the market price of a blanket in country B is approximately 1 apple (i.e. 1·01 in column *c*); but the marginal cost of an imported blanket to A as a community is 2 apples (column *d*). It is necessary, therefore, to impose an *ad valorem* duty of some 100 per cent to bring the market price of a blanket in A into equality with the marginal social cost to A of obtaining a blanket by trade with B.

Cases ii and iii of Table XXI merely illustrate the operation of the same principles when the elasticity of B's offer of blankets is considerably larger. Thus in case ii when A puts 101·5 instead of 100 apples on B's market (column *a*) B offers 101 instead of 100 blankets (column *b*). This represents a ½ per cent fall in the blanket price of apples in B (the number of apples required to purchase a blanket rises by ½ per cent from 1 to 1·005 in column *c*). We have then a situation in which 1½ per cent more of A's apples will be purchased in B (i.e. 101·5 instead of 100) when the price falls by ½ per cent; the elasticity of B's offer is 3. But in this situation the marginal cost of a blanket to A is 1·5 apples (column *d*) because when A imports one more blanket (101 instead of 100 in column *b*) she has to give 1·5 more apples (101·5 instead of 100 in column *c*). We have then a situation in which the market price of blankets in B is approximately 1 (column *c*), whereas the marginal cost to A of importing an additional blanket is in fact 1·5 (column *d*). To make the market price in A correspond to the marginal cost in A, we need an *ad valorem* import duty of 50 per cent (column *e*). And similarly with case iii where the elasticity of B's offer of blankets for apples is about 5, and the optimum rate of trade tax in consequence turns out to be about 25 per cent *ad valorem*.

The essential reason why the government of A may be able to improve the economic welfare of the citizens of A by taxing trade is because when the amount of A's exports which are put on B's market is restricted the amount of B's products which A can receive per unit of her exports may be raised. There are two reasons for this. First, the elasticity of the demand in B for A's exports and, second, the elasticity of the supply in B of A's imports may not be indefinitely great.

In the first place, when more of A's apples are put on B's market, the price of A's apples in terms of B's currency and so in terms of B's other products may have to be lowered in order to induce B's consumers to take more of them. Secondly, when A does put more apples on B's market and obtains more of B's currency for them,[1] she will purchase more of B's exportable blankets with the proceeds of her greater sales. But if the elasticity of B's supply of exports is less than infinite, this

[1] We can confine our present analysis to the cases in which A will obtain more of B's currency for a larger supply of A's own products, i.e. to the case in which the elasticity of B's demand for A's products is greater than one, because it will always pay A to restrict her trade further if B's elasticity of demand for imports is less than unity, so that she can get more of B's products for less of her own. The optimum trade tax can only be at a point at which B's demand has an elasticity greater than one.

will drive up somewhat the price which A's traders will have to pay for B's blankets.

Up to the present we have been analysing the optimum rates of trade taxes upon the assumption that A exported only one product, apples, and imported only one product, blankets, or rather upon the assumption that A imposed only one rate of export duty which covered all her exports at a single *ad valorem* rate and imposed only one rate of import duty which covered all her imports at a single *ad valorem* rate. In such circumstances we have seen that the optimum rate of duty is the same whether A's government operates by means of an import duty or by means of an export duty. The *ad valorem* height of this optimum rate of duty will be the greater, the more quickly the terms of trade would turn against A as more of A's products are put on B's market. But it is only the speed at which the terms of trade would move against A that is relevant. It does not make any difference whether the deterioration in the terms of trade is due to a low elasticity of demand for imports in B (so that the price which B's consumers pay for A's products falls quickly) or whether it is due to a low elasticity of supply of exports in B (so that the price which B's producers charged for their products rises quickly).

But in fact, of course, the government of A can impose export and import taxes at different *ad valorem* rates on different exports and imports. As soon as we allow for this A can gain much more at the expense of B. The government in A can impose an export tax on each particular export at a rate which allows for the particular improvement in the price received for that product which could be achieved by a given restriction on the export of that particular product to B. It can also impose an import duty on each particular import at a rate which allows for the particular improvement in the price at which that product may be bought in B as a result of a given restriction in the amount purchased and imported from B. If A puts high export duties on the products for which the elasticity of demand for imports in B is relatively low, low export duties on products for which the elasticity of demand for imports in B is relatively high, high import duties on the products for which the elasticity of supply of exports is relatively low in B, and low import duties on the products for which the elasticity of supply in B is relatively high, A's citizens will be able to enjoy a maximum advantage from the possible movement of the terms of trade in their favour.

In this case it is, of course, necessary to consider the elasticities of demand for B's imports and the elasticities of supply for B's exports separately. The principles upon which the authorities in A might find the optimum rate of export and import duty for each particular line of import and export are illustrated in Table XXII. Section 1 of the table

TABLE XXII

The Optimum Rates for Particular Import and Export Taxes

1. *Optimum Rates of Import Tax*

Amount of commodity imported into A from B (*a*)	Price at which B will supply the commodity to A (*b*)	Total amount paid by A (*c*) = (*a*) × (*b*)	Marginal cost to A of additional unit of product (*d*)	Optimum rate of import tax (*e*) = (*d* − *b*) ÷ (*b*)
	$	$	$	%
Commodity (i). *Elasticity of Supply in B is* 1. *Optimum Rate of Import Duty in B is* 100 *per cent*				
100	1·00	100	—	—
101	1·01	102	2	100
Commodity (ii). *Elasticity of Supply in B is* 4. *Optimum Rate of Import Duty is* 25 *per cent*				
100	1·0000	100	—	—
101	1·0025	101·25	1·25	25

2. *Optimum Rates of Export Tax*

Amount of commodity exported from A (*a*)	Price at which B will purchase the commodity (*b*)	Total amount received by A (*c*) = (*a*) × (*b*)	Marginal receipts by A from sale of additional unit of commodity (*d*)	Optimum rate of export duty (*e*) = (*b* − *d*) ÷ (*d*)
Commodity (iii). *Elasticity of Demand in B is* 2. *Optimum Rate of Export Duty is* 100 *per cent*				
100	1·000	100	—	—
101	0·995	100·5	0·5	100
Commodity (iv). *Elasticity of Demand in B is* 5. *Optimum Rate of Export Duty is* 25 *per cent*				
100	1·000	100	—	—
101	0·998	100·8	0·8	25

covers the case of two commodities which are imported into A, the elasticity of the supply of exports in B being 1 in the case of commodity i and 4 in the case of commodity ii. Thus when importers in A import 101 instead of 100 units of commodity i (column *a*) the price at which B's exporters will supply it rises from \$1 to \$1·01 (column *b*); or in other words, the elasticity of supply of exports by B is 1 because a 1 per cent increase in the price offered to B's exporters will call forth an increased supply of 1 per cent. From column *c* it can be seen that when A's importers purchase 101 instead of 100 units the total cost to them rises from 100 to 102 (column *c*), so that the last unit imported adds \$2 to the import bill (column *d*), although the market price in B is only about \$1 (column *b*). In other words, a tax of about 100 per cent on imports (column *e*) is required to raise the market price of the commodity in B of about \$1 up to the true marginal cost of the import to A as a community of about \$2.

In the case of commodity ii the elasticity of supply of exports in B is much greater, and the optimum level of A's import tax is therefore much lower. In this case when A's importers increase their purchases by 1 per cent from 100 to 101, the price at which B's exporters will sell rises only by $\frac{1}{4}$ per cent from \$1 to \$1·0025, which represents an elasticity of supply of 4. The marginal cost to A as a community is thus \$1·25 since the total cost of 100 units is \$100 × 1 or \$100 while the total cost of 101 units is \$101 × \$1·0025 or \$101·25. Now in order to raise the market price in B of approximately \$1 (column *b*) to the true marginal social cost of the import to A of \$1·25 (column *d*) it is necessary to impose an import duty at an *ad valorem* rate of approximately 25 per cent.

Commodities iii and iv in Section 2 of Table XXII illustrate the cases of two exports from A to B for which the elasticity of demand in B is relatively low in the one case and high in the other, being 2 in the case of commodity iii and 5 in the case of commodity iv. Thus in the case of commodity iii when A's exporters increase their exports by 1 per cent from 100 to 101 (column *a*) the price offered by B's importers falls by $\frac{1}{2}$ per cent from \$1 to \$0·995 (column *b*), which represents an elasticity of demand in B of 2. As a result the total receipts by A from the sale of the commodity go up from 100 × \$1 or \$100 to \$101 × \$0·995 or \$100·5 (column *c*) so that the addition to A's receipts of foreign exchange due to the sale of the 101st unit of the commodity is \$0·5 (column *d*). In order to maximize the welfare of citizens of A it is necessary that the market price offered for the commodity in A should be equal to the marginal receipts which A in fact obtains from the last unit of export (i.e. the \$0·5 of column *d*) rather than to the market price of the commodity in B (i.e. the \$0·995 of column *b*). To achieve this result it is necessary for the authorities in A to impose an export duty at an *ad valorem* rate of approximately 100 per cent (column *e*) in order to raise a market price in A of approximately $0·5 to a market price in B of approximately $1. And similarly for commodity iv. Here the elasticity of demand for imports in B is much greater so that there is a much smaller fall in the price offered by B's importers as A's exports increase. In consequence the addition to A's receipts of foreign exchange due to the sale of one more unit of the commodity on B's market is much more nearly equal to the price on B's market, and only a relatively low export duty of 25 per cent *ad valorem* is required to raise the marginal receipts to A from the commodity of $0·8 (column *d*) to the market price in B of the commodity of about $1 (column *b*).

Up to this point we have argued on the very unrealistic assumption that while the authorities in A are busy finding the optimum rates of duty to impose on A's trade with B the authorities in B will maintain a free-trade policy. But just as the authorities in A can turn the terms of trade in favour of A if B's government does not intervene, so the authorities in B could turn the terms of trade in favour of B by imposing optimum rates of trade taxes provided that A's government did not intervene. Now if A's government imposes a trade tax and B's government does not do so, this will certainly decrease the welfare of the citizens of B. The effect of the trade tax in A will be to turn the terms of trade against B. The traders in B are still free to trade as they please, since B's government is *ex hypothesi* still adopting a free-trade policy, the only change being that they must trade on less favourable terms with the outside world. The welfare of the representative citizen in B is necessarily lowered. As we have seen above, the welfare of the representative citizen in A will have been increased if the trade taxes in A are at a moderate level so that the turn in the terms of trade in A's favour is more important to A than the reduction in the volume of trade conducted at the improved terms of trade; but the welfare of the representative citizen in A will also have been reduced if the trade taxes in A are excessively high so that A loses more from the restriction in the volume of trade than is gained from the favourable movement in the terms at which the lower volume of trade is conducted.

But suppose now that the government in B also seeks to improve the welfare of B's citizens by imposing trade taxes in order to turn the terms of trade in B's favour. In so far as the terms of trade are concerned, the trade taxes imposed by B's government will tend to offset the trade taxes imposed by A's government. Import duties imposed in A, by restricting the demand for B's export products in A's market, will tend to depress the price at which B's traders sell B's exports to A; and export duties imposed by A will tend to raise the price charged to B's traders for A's exports. A obtains more imports for each unit of exports. But simultaneous import duties imposed in B will tend to reduce the price which A's exporters can obtain for A's exports, and simultaneous export duties imposed by B will tend to raise the price which A's traders must pay over to B's exporters and to B's government for B's exports. The net effect may well be to leave the terms of trade more or less unchanged. In this case it will be certain that the citizens of both countries will lose as a result of the trade taxes in the two countries.

Thus suppose that before and after the imposition of trade taxes of 100 per cent *ad valorem* in the two countries 1 apple from A exchanges for 1 blanket from B. Then after the imposition of the taxes the market price of a blanket in A will be 2 apples, 1 apple being the price paid over to B and 1 apple representing the tax paid over to A's government. In B after the imposition of the taxes the market price of an apple will be 2 blankets, 1 blanket being paid over to A to import an apple and 1 blanket being paid over to B's government in tax. In these circumstances the citizens of A would certainly gain if both trade taxes were removed. They would in fact get 1 more blanket for every additional apple exported, while the market price of 2 apples for a blanket shows that in the taxed position each additional blanket is worth 2 apples to them to consume and costs 2 apples for them to produce for themselves at home. Similarly, the citizens in B would get more apples at a cost of 1 blanket for each additional apple imported, though the market price of 2 blankets for an apple in B shows that in the taxed position each additional apple is worth 2 blankets to them to consume and costs 2 blankets for them to produce for themselves at home. The simultaneous removal of the trade taxes in both countries would enable the citizens in both countries to gain by expanding the volume of profitable trade at unchanged terms of trade.

Trade taxes of a sufficiently moderate degree may therefore best be regarded as a method of transferring wealth from one country to another. A can gain at the expense of B if A imposes taxes of a moderate height and if B refrains from imposing any such taxes. The imposition of trade taxes by A and by B simultaneously is likely to be a mere waste since it represents an attempt to transfer wealth simultaneously from A to B and from B to A in such a way that some net wealth is destroyed in the process. In a rational world trade taxes, which were imposed as a means of controlling the terms of trade, would be employed by A alone or by B alone according to whether it was desired to transfer wealth in the one direction or the other. They would never be simultaneously employed by both.

An alternative method of transferring wealth from B to A would be by the imposition of trade subsidies in B instead of trade taxes in A. The government of B might raise revenue by means, say, of a general income tax and might use the revenue to pay a subsidy on the export of blankets to A or on the import of apples from A. This will turn the terms of trade in A's favour since it will tend to lower the price of B's blankets in A (if B is subsidizing the export of blankets) or to raise the price offered by B's importers to A's exporters of apples (if B is subsidizing the import of apples). In either case the citizens of A will be unequivocally better off. The only change from the point of view of A's economy will be an improvement in the terms at which they can trade their own produce for the produce of the outside world. The change will also be an unequivocal reduction in the welfare of B's citizens. The terms of trade will have moved against B from, say, 1 blanket for 1 apple to, say, 2 blankets to 1 apple. B's citizens would be worse off even if they were free to trade simply at these new and less favourable terms of trade. But the subsidy on trade will cause the market price of apples in B to be reduced to, say, $1\frac{1}{2}$ blankets to 1 apple. If the new terms of trade had deteriorated to 2 blankets to 1 apple and had been fixed at that new level, the citizens of B would have suffered a given loss, even though they had been free to trade at that new level merely up to the point at which the last unit of imported apples was worth 2 blankets to them. But because of the subsidy they will import still more apples until the last apple is worth only $1\frac{1}{2}$ blankets to them, even though the real marginal cost of an imported apple is 2 blankets. Thus they lose both because of the deterioration in the terms of trade and also because, as a result of the subsidy, they over-trade at the new and worsened terms of trade. A trade subsidy, therefore, unequivocally transfers wealth from the subsidizing country to the other country.

Thus a moderate level of taxation of trade imposed by the government of A or any level of subsidies to trade paid by the government of B will make the citizens of A better off and the citizens of B worse off. From the purely nationalistic point of view of the citizens of A this is a desirable development. Indeed, the levels of the optimum rates for trade taxes which we examined at the beginning of this chapter were calculated solely on the basis of this nationalistic point of view of A's government. In our terminology, these optimum rates of duty give the levels at which economic welfare will be maximized on the assumption that the policy-makers allot a positive distributional weight to the citizens of A but a zero weight to the citizens of B.

Let us now consider the problem of trade controls imposed for the purpose of redistributing wealth between the citizens of A and of B not from the nationalistic point of view of either A or of B but from the world point of view. That is to say, we assume that positive distributional weights are allotted by our world policy-makers to the citizens of both countries, although the weight allotted to the citizens of A is not necessarily the same as that allotted to the citizens of B.

If the distributional weights allotted to the two sets of citizens were the same, then—on our assumption that there were no divergences between marginal values and costs in other parts of the economy—there would be no argument in favour of any departure from a policy of free trade. A moderate set of trade taxes imposed by A's government, for example, would transfer income from the citizens of B to the citizens of A. But since the distributional weights allotted to the gainers is, *ex hypothesi*, the same as that allotted to the losers, this redistribution would in itself bring no gain or loss. But the trade taxes would, as we have seen, interfere with both the optimization of trade and the maximization of production, and thus there would result a net loss of economic welfare.

Suppose now that the distributional weight allotted to the citizens of B were somewhat lower than that allotted to the citizens of A. Then some structure of trade taxes by A's government would be appropriate, but these taxes should be imposed at rates which are lower than the purely nationalistic optimum rates which we have examined earlier in this chapter. The truth of this proposition can be seen as follows.

Suppose first that the trade taxes imposed by A were at the purely nationalistic optimum rates. These are rates such that a slightly lower rate would have practically no effect upon A's welfare, since the rate is such that the marginal cost to A as a consumer of obtaining another unit of imports (i.e. the cost after taking into account any deterioration in A's terms of trade) is equal to the marginal value of the imports to A. But the reduction in A's duty would, as we have seen, certainly benefit B which could continue to trade freely but at improved terms of trade. If, therefore, any weight is given to the welfare of B, A's trade taxes should be at a rate lower than the rate which is the optimum rate from A's purely nationalistic point of view.

Suppose now at the other extreme that there was free trade. The imposition of a small rate of trade tax by A would lead to some decrease in the flow of A's exports to B and cause some decrease or increase in the flow of B's exports to A—according as B's demand for A's exports had an elasticity greater or less than unity. Now starting from a free-trade position in which there was no divergence between marginal values and costs, these first small changes in the flow of trade would have no effect upon economic welfare if the distributional weights were the same in A and in B. But the duty would turn the terms of trade in favour of A; that is to say, the decrease in the amount of apples sent from A to B would be smaller than the decrease in the amount of blankets sent from B to A, each valued at its old free-trade prices. So if the distributional weight allotted to A were greater than that allotted to B, there would be some gain in economic welfare.

In other words, if a distributional weight is allotted to the citizens of B which is positive but less than that allotted to the citizens of A, economic welfare would be improved by the imposition of trade taxes by A, provided always that these were not accompanied by trade taxes imposed by B. But these trade taxes should be lower than the optimum rates of duty which would be appropriate if a zero distributional weight were allotted to the citizens of B.[1]

So much for the use of trade taxes by A's government to achieve the best redistribution of income between A's and B's citizens when appropriate weight is given to the interests of both parties. But, as we have already seen, income can be transferred from B to A by a system of trade subsidies financed by B's government even more certainly than by a system of trade taxes levied by A's government. Would it be still better to rely upon a system of subsidization of trade by B rather than upon a system of taxation of trade by A?

The answer to this is that, if we can for the moment neglect the divergences between marginal values and costs which may be introduced in B through the levying of the taxation required to finance the trade subsidies, it is best to rely in equal measure upon trade taxes by A and trade subsidies by B.

Consider the effects of a 10 per cent duty on imports by A, of a 10 per cent subsidy on exports by B, and of the combination of a 5 per cent import duty in A with a 5 per cent export subsidy in B. In all three cases the prices of A's exports (apples) will be the same in A as in B. In the case of a 10 per cent duty on imports by A the price of A's imports (blankets) will be 10 per cent higher in A than in B; production will not be maximized because A will have too large an incentive to produce blankets and B will have too small an incentive to do so; and trade will not be optimized because out of a given world production A will have too small an incentive to consume blankets and B too large an incentive to do so. In the case of a 10 per cent subsidy on exports by B the price of blankets will be 10 per cent lower in A than in B; production will not be maximized because A will have too small and B too large an incentive to produce blankets; and trade will not be optimized because A will have too large and B too small an incentive to consume blankets. In the case of A's import tax production will be too autarkic and trade will not be sufficiently developed; in the case of B's export subsidy production will be concentrated too much on export products and trade will be over-developed.

But in the case of a 5 per cent import duty in A combined with a 5 per cent export subsidy in B, the market price of blankets will be the same in A as in B. The lowering of the price of B's blankets to A's con-

[1] The formula for the correct height of A's trade taxes in this case is discussed in Section XVI of the mathematical supplement to this volume. The reader's attention is drawn to the fact which is there discussed that the relationship between the distributional weights which should be allotted to B and to A will itself vary according as A employs a tax on imports or a tax on exports.

sumers and producers below the price charged to B's consumers and producers by B's 5 per cent export subsidy will be exactly offset by the raising of the price of B's blankets to A's consumers and producers by A's 5 per cent import duty. Thus there will be no interference with either the optimization of trade or the maximization of production.

An import duty in A will transfer income from B to A at the expense of causing trade to be under-developed; an export subsidy in B will transfer income from B to A at the expense of causing trade to be over-developed; but the combination of an equal import duty in A and export subsidy in B will transfer income from B to A without any interference with the optimization of trade or the maximization of production.

But, as can be seen from Chapter XI (pp. 181–3), an import duty in A which is offset by an exactly equal export subsidy in B is exactly equivalent to the raising of some revenue by B's government and its transfer as a gift to A's government. Since the export subsidy paid by B is exactly offset by the import duty raised by A, the price of the traded goods is in no way affected either to A's or to B's producers or consumers. The fiction of export subsidy and import duty could be dropped. There would be exactly the same result if A dropped the import tax and B the export subsidy; and if B's government transferred to A's government an exactly equivalent amount in direct grant. B's government could continue to raise the revenue to pay this grant by exactly the same methods as it had been raising the revenue to pay the export subsidy; and A's government could spend the money received from the grant in exactly the same way as it had previously been spending the same sum raised by its import duty. In other words, a direct transfer of income from the citizens of B to the citizens of A financed by a tax levied by B's government on B's citizens, the proceeds of which are handed over to A's government for the supplementation of the incomes of the citizens of A, is the ideal way of redistributing income internationally, since it interferes neither with the optimization of trade nor with the maximization of production.

But so far we have made no allowance for the divergences between marginal values and marginal costs which may be introduced into B's economy by the taxes imposed to raise the revenue for the payment of the grant to A's government. There are two important implications to be drawn from this for our present purposes.

First, because of these problems connected with the raising of revenue in B, some damage may be done to economic efficiency in B by the transfer of income from A to B. In this case the loss of economic welfare due to the economic inefficiencies introduced into B must be weighed against the gain of economic welfare due to the redistribution of income from B's citizens with their low distributional weights to A's citizens with their high distributional weights. The consequence of this would be that the international redistribution of income should not be carried so far as would have been the case if it had caused no divergences between marginal costs and costs in B.

Second, because of these problems connected with the raising of revenue in B, it may happen, for reasons of the kind discussed in Chapters III and VII, that it is desirable to raise some of the revenue required by B's government to make a grant to A's government by means of the taxation of particular commodities in B. If on these grounds a case could be made out for the levying of a specially high rate of tax on the export of certain commodities from B or on the import of certain commodities into B as its best means of raising the revenue for B's government to make a grant to A's government, then in fact some element of trade taxation by A would by implication be justifiable as a means of redistributing income from B to A. For a tax on B's exports the revenue from which is handed over to A's government is exactly the same as an import duty levied by A; and a tax on B's imports the revenue from which is handed over to A is exactly equivalent to an export duty in A.

But this case can hardly be made out. There is no reason to believe that it will not be best for B's government to raise its revenue mainly by a general income tax rather than by a few special commodity taxes. In so far as special commodity taxes are needed, there is no reason to believe that non-tradeable commodities such as houses may not be among the most appropriate commodities for revenue-raising purposes.

Moreover, in so far as an exportable product (such as blankets) or an importable produce (such as apples) is the most appropriate commodity for B to tax on revenue-raising grounds, there is no presumption whatsoever that the tax should be confined to B's exports or imports of these products rather than to B's total production or consumption of them. Indeed, there is a strong presumption that B's exports or imports should be specially lightly taxed.

Consider the taxation of B's exports of blankets. If the tax is now spread over the whole of B's production of blankets, whether for export or for home consumption, there is likely to be a gain in welfare. The tax being levied on a larger base the rate of tax will be lower, and so the rate of divergence between marginal values and costs will be lower. But there are two reasons why it may very well pay to go somewhat further and to lower the rate of tax on B's exports of blankets and to raise it on B's own consumption of blankets. In the first place, the elasticity of demand for B's blankets in B is likely to be smaller than the elasticity of demand for imports of B's blankets into A, where they may have to compete with blankets produced in A; and on these grounds there is likely to be less interference with economic efficiency if B's consumption of B's blankets is taxed more heavily than A's consumption of B's blankets, as we have already argued in Chapter XII. But, secondly, as the whole purpose of the tax is to transfer income from B to A there are also special distributional reasons for keeping the tax on A's consumption of blankets low.

Exactly similar arguments can be applied to any tax raised by B on an importable product such as apples. Suppose B is taxing the import of apples and changes this into a tax on the consumption of apples. The basis of the tax will be broadened; and the rate of tax, and so the rate of divergence between marginal values and costs, can be lowered. But there may be strong grounds for going rather further and shifting still more of the tax off imported apples and on to apples produced in B. First, B's elasticity of supply of home-produced apples is likely to be lower than A's elasticity of supply of exports of apples which can also be sold on A's market; and thus, as we have argued in Chapter XII, world economic efficiency will require that the rate of tax levied by B on B's own production of apples should be higher than that levied by B on her imports of apples. Secondly, since the whole purpose of the tax is to redistribute income in A's favour, there are special distributional grounds for keeping down the tax on apples produced by A's citizens.

Thus there is very little to be said for B's using special trade taxes to raise revenue to transfer income to A. Even if B should use commodity taxes for this purpose, these will be a presumption against the taxation of B's imports or exports of those commodities. We may conclude, therefore, that if there is sufficient co-operation between the governments of A and B to aim at an agreed redistribution of income, the most efficient means will be to transfer income directly from B's government to A's government on a sufficient scale to bring about the required redistribution. B's government would then be free to tax in whatever way it considered to be the most efficient[1] just as A's government would be free to distribute the revenue to its own citizens in whatever way it considered to be most efficient.

It may be useful to summarize the conclusions of this chapter:

(1) A's government can improve the welfare of A's citizens at the expense of the citizens of B by taxing its imports and exports at moderate rates.

(2) B's government can improve the welfare of A's citizens at the

[1] It would be free even to tax exports to A or imports from A if for some peculiar reason or another it considered these to be the most efficient bases of taxation. But the amount of the transfer which B would have to make to A to obtain a given degree of real redistribution of income between the citizens of A and B would not, of course, be independent of the ways in which B's government chose to raise the revenue. Thus if B's government taxed the import of apples from A and a large part of the burden of the tax fell on A's citizens, then a larger total transfer would have to be made from B to A to obtain any given net improvement in the welfare of A's citizens.

expense of the citizens of B by subsidizing its imports and exports at any rate.

(3) The improvement in distribution obtainable by A's government through trade taxes will be certain only if B's government does not simultaneously impose trade taxes designed to improve the welfare of B's citizens. If both governments so act, the citizens of both countries are quite likely to be worse off than in the free-trade position.

(4) Any agreed degree of redistribution of income between A and B could be achieved by a system of trade taxes in A and of trade subsidies in B.

(5) Apart from the difficulties associated with the raising of the necessary revenue in B, the best system is a system of trade taxes in A matched by exactly equivalent trade subsidies in B or, what comes to exactly the same thing, a direct grant of income from B's government to A's government.

(6) The difficulties connected with the raising of revenue in B may be a good reason for limiting the amount of redistribution that is attempted but are unlikely to justify any modification of the general principle that the payment of a direct grant from B's government to A's government is the best method of redistribution.

CHAPTER XVIII

THE DISTRIBUTIONAL ARGUMENT FOR TRADE CONTROL: (2) THE DOMESTIC DISTRIBUTION OF INCOME

WE turn now to the effect of trade controls upon the distribution of income inside the countries concerned.[1] We shall at first consider this problem on the very much simplified assumptions that there are only two countries, A and B; that there are only two products produced in these two countries, apples being exported from A to B and blankets from B to A; that some blankets are also produced in A and some apples in B; that there are only two factors of production, labour and land, used in the production of both the commodities in both the countries; that there is perfect competition in both countries; that there are constant returns to scale in the production of both products in both countries; and that technical knowledge and productive atmosphere is the same in both countries, so that if the same amount of labour and land were used in A as in B to produce, say, apples, the output of apples would be the same in both countries. We shall consider the effects of modifying these assumptions at the end of this chapter. Meanwhile the analysis of the problem in terms of this much simplified model will enable us to understand some of the principal forces at work.

Let us suppose then that the authorities in A impose a protective duty upon the import of B's blankets into A. We intend to consider the effect of this action upon the distribution of the national income between the wages of labour and the rent of landlords in A and in B.

As will be made clear in later sections of this chapter, the effect of the tax upon the distribution of income between wages and rents in each country will depend basically upon the effect of the tax upon the market prices offered for apples and blankets in the two countries. Thus, suppose that apples are produced mainly with land and with little labour, while blankets need much labour and little land for their production. Then a fall in the market price offered for home-produced blankets relatively to that offered for home-produced apples will represent a fall in the demand for labour relatively to that for land and will thus tend to redistribute income unfavourably to labour and favourably to land. Our first task in this chapter must therefore be to inquire how a duty in A imposed on the import of B's blankets into A will affect the market price offered for blankets relatively to the market price offered for apples in each of the two countries.

[1] This subject is treated more precisely in Section XVIII of the mathematical supplement to this volume.

Now the 'normal' effect of such a tax may be assumed to be to raise the market price of blankets relatively to that of apples in A, and to lower the market price of blankets relatively to that of apples in B. The imposition of the tax on the import of blankets from B into A would not directly affect the price of apples in either country. Its direct effect would presumably be to raise to some extent the market price of blankets in A and to lower to some extent the market price of blankets in B, the gap between the two prices being filled by the duty. The market price of imported blankets in A being higher than before, it would be probable that the amount of imported blankets demanded in A would be reduced; and this reduction in the demand for exports of blankets in B would depress the price of blankets in B. Or, to start at the other end, the price of exported blankets in B being lower than before, it would be probable that a smaller number would be supplied for export; and this reduction in the amount supplied on A's market would tend to raise the price of blankets in A above its previous level. Only if the supply of exported blankets in B was quite insensitive to the price offered for them would the amount supplied to A, and so the market demand price in A, remain unchanged; and in this case there would be no rise in the price of blankets in A, but their price in B would fall by the whole amount of the tax. Similarly, only if the demand for imported blankets in A were totally unaffected by their price would the amount demanded from B remain the same regardless of what happened to the price, in which case the market supply price in B would not be depressed and the market demand price in A would rise by the whole amount of the tax.

Thus we might conclude that the natural direct effect of the tax on imports of blankets into A or on exports of blankets from B would be to raise the market price of blankets in A and to lower it in B. And for this reason it is natural to conclude that the tax will cause the ratio of the market price of blankets to that of apples to rise in A above, and to fall in B below, the pre-tax level. But we cannot legitimately reach this conclusion without taking into account the indirect effects of the further price changes which are necessary to preserve equilibrium in the balance of payments after the imposition of the trade tax.

The imposition of the duty on imports of blankets into A will tend to create a surplus on A's balance of payments. The government of A will receive in A's currency for distribution to A's citizens the revenue from the import duty in A, so that the cost of A's imports in foreign exchange is only the price paid by the importers in A less the import tax. The impact effect of an import duty in A is, therefore, to create a surplus on A's balance of trade by reducing somewhat the volume and the price (excluding tax) payable for A's imports.

The impact effect of A's import duty is to reduce the market price of blankets in B and to raise this market price in A without affecting the price of apples in A or in B. But A's balance of payments is now in surplus. In order to restore equilibrium to the balance of payments the exchange value of B's currency depreciates. This in itself tends to reduce the price of B's blankets in A's currency and to raise the price of A's apples in B's currency, so that in both A and B the ratio of the market price of blankets to that of apples falls. It is possible in certain conditions that this movement of prices which is needed to preserve equilibrium in the balance of payments will go so far that the ratio of the market price of blankets to that of apples will in the end fall in A below the pre-tax level—in which case it must, of course, fall in B even farther below this level.

In order to find out in what conditions this would happen, we will proceed as follows. We will suppose that the market price of blankets relatively to that of apples falls in B by the full amount of the tax, so that the market price of blankets relatively to that of apples remains in A at its pre-tax level. We will then consider what would be the balance in such conditions between A's demand for imports of blankets from B and of B's supply of exports of blankets to A. If A's demand for imported blankets had grown less than B's supply of exported blankets, then the price of blankets would fall still farther in A and in B. We should then end up with the 'abnormal' case in which the final effect of the imposition of the duty on imports of blankets into A would be to reduce the price of blankets relatively to that of apples in A as well as in B.

For this abnormal case to occur two conditions must be fulfilled. First, the marginal propensity to import in A must be small; and, second, the elasticity of demand for imported apples in B must be low.

Let us first consider the marginal propensity to import in A. In the case which we are examining the citizens of A will unquestionably enjoy higher real incomes: their earnings in terms of their own products will not have fallen, and these incomes will be supplemented by the revenue from the import duty, which will be available for their government to distribute to them in one way or another. Having higher incomes in terms of apples they will certainly be better off, since the price of imported blankets is assumed not to have risen in A. Being better off, consumers in A will purchase more goods and services of all sorts. Among other goods, they are likely to increase their purchases of imported blankets. If they greatly increased their purchases of imported blankets when their real incomes rose, this would be an important influence keeping up the price of blankets in terms of apples, and might, indeed, well cause the market price of blankets in A (inclusive of tax) to be higher than before. Only if the proportion of any increase in A's consumers' purchases which takes the form of increased purchases of imported blankets is sufficiently low (i.e. only if the marginal propensity to import in A is sufficiently low) can the market price of blankets in A actually fall below its pre-tax level.

Let us next consider the elasticity of the demand for imported apples in B. The citizens of B will certainly be worse off than before. Their earnings in terms of their own product, blankets, will be unchanged; but *ex hypothesi* the market price of their product, blankets, in B will have fallen relatively to that of their import, apples, by the full amount of the duty, and the earnings of B's citizens are not supplemented by any part of the revenue from the duty. The citizens of B will therefore purchase less apples from A for two reasons: first, because they are worse off and will therefore tend to buy less of everything; and second, because the rise in the price of apples relatively to that of blankets will cause them to shift their consumption somewhat from the more to the less expensive product. Now if the elasticity of demand for imported apples in B were greater than unity, then when the price of apples went up in B the consumers in B would so greatly reduce their demand for imported apples that they would offer a smaller total amount of blankets for them than before. But if the elasticity of demand for imported apples in B were less than unity, the citizens of B would not greatly reduce the volume of their apple imports when the price of apples rose, so that the higher price of apples would outweigh the smaller volume of apple imports and B would offer a greater total amount of blankets for the smaller volume of apple imports.

We can see now that if the marginal propensity to import in A is very small, there may be a very small increase in A's demand for B's blankets, whereas if B's elasticity of demand for imports is very low there may be a considerable increase in B's supply of exported blankets. In this case there would be a further influence depressing the world price of blankets relatively to apples. The net result of the imposition of A's duty on imported blankets would be the 'abnormal' one of reducing the market price of blankets relatively to that of apples within A as well as within B.[1]

If the government in A imposes a duty on the export of apples from A to B instead of a duty on the import of blankets into A from B, essentially the same analysis can be applied, though the monetary mechanism involved is somewhat different. The immediate effect of the export duty on apples is to raise the price of apples in B without altering the price of apples in A or of blankets in A or B. This would cause some reduction in the demand for imported apples in B and this

[1] For a more formal proof of these propositions, see pp. 71–75 of my *A Geometry of International Trade* (London, Allen & Unwin, 1952). This section is based upon Professor L. A. Metzler 'Tariffs, the Terms of Trade, and the Distribution of Income', *Journal of Political Economy*, 1949.

would be likely to cause some decline in the price of apples in A. If this were all that happened, we should have another example of the 'normal' case; the ratio of the price of apples to that of blankets would be raised in B and lowered in A so that the common pre-tax price ratio would be intermediate between these two post-tax price ratios.

In this case this may be the end of the story. No adjustment of the foreign-exchange rate may be needed in this case to restore equilibrium. The price of apples will have risen in B. Importers in B may as a result spend a greater, an unchanged, or a smaller total amount of B's currency (and so of B's blankets) on A's apples, according as the elasticity of demand for imported apples in A is less than, equal to, or greater than unity. If the elasticity of demand for imports in B is very small, when the price of A's apples goes up in B, consumers in B will purchase almost the same quantity and therefore pay a larger total amount for imported apples; and there will be a deficit on B's balance of payments with A. B's currency will have to depreciate in terms of A's currency to restore equilibrium. But if the elasticity of demand for imported apples in B is very great, when their price rises in B, consumers in B will greatly reduce the quantity which they purchase and the total expenditure in B on imports will fall; there will be a surplus on B's balance of trade and the exchange value of B's currency will appreciate.

An appreciation of B's currency will, of course, cause a rise in the price of blankets in A in A's currency and a fall in the price of apples in B in B's currency. In this case then (i.e. where the elasticity of demand for imports in B is high) there will be a further fall in the ratio of the price of apples to that of blankets in A and this price ratio cannot therefore attain the pre-tax level. But in the case in which B's currency has to depreciate in order to restore equilibrium to the balance of payments (i.e. where the elasticity of demand for imports in B is very low), there will in consequence be a fall in the price of blankets in A in A's currency and a rise in the price of apples in B in B's currency.

It is possible in this case that the fall in the relative price of blankets in A due to the depreciation of B's currency will outweigh the previous tendency for the relative price of apples to fall in A because the export duty on apples had reduced B's demand for imported apples. Whether or not there is in the end a net fall in A in the market price of blankets relative to the market price of apples will depend upon the same real factors as we discussed above in the case of an import duty in A. In terms of A's products citizens of A will earn as much as before; these earnings will be supplemented by the distribution to them of the revenue from the export duty. If the market price of blankets relative to that of apples were unchanged by the tax, they would certainly be better off. Being better off they would purchase more blankets, the increase in their purchases of blankets being greater the greater were their marginal propensity to import. If the supply of blankets from B is increased by less than this, then the price of blankets will have to rise in A above its pre-tax relationship with that of apples; but if the supply of blankets from B is increased by more than this, then the relative price of blankets in A may actually fall. Now the supply of blankets from B to A will be increased a lot if the elasticity of demand for imported apples in B is much below unity. The price of apples rises in B because of the export tax in A; if the demand for it is very inelastic in B, then importers in B pay over to A for a somewhat smaller amount of apples a much greater amount of B's money and so of B's blankets, and the supply of B's blankets is thus much increased in A. We can, therefore, reach the conclusion that the imposition of an export tax in A, just like the imposition of an import tax in A, will cause the market price in A of B's blankets actually to fall relatively to the market price in A of A's apples if both the marginal propensity to import blankets in A is low and also the elasticity of demand for imported apples in B are sufficiently low.[1]

We can, therefore, conclude that the 'normal' effect of the imposition of a trade tax by A will be to raise the market price of blankets relatively to apples in A and to lower this ratio in B. But the opposite 'abnormal' case is by no means inconceivable. If the marginal propensity to import blankets in A and the elasticity of demand for apples in B were both sufficiently low, then the effect of the protective duty on blankets in A might be to lower the price offered for home-produced blankets relatively to that offered for home-produced apples in A as well as in B.

Let us for the moment confine ourselves to the normal case in A. As a result of the import duty on blankets in A, the prices which producers of blankets in A can receive for their product goes up relatively to the price which producers of apples in A can receive for their product. This will cause producers in A to shift resources from the production of apples to the production of blankets, since the latter will have become relatively more profitable to produce.

This development will increase the demand for the factors of production which are most important in the production of blankets relatively to the demand for the factors of production which are most important in the production of apples. Let us suppose that in A a higher ratio of labour to land is employed in the blanket industry than in the apple industry. Blankets in A are things which need much labour and little land to produce, whereas apples in A are things which require much land and little labour to produce. In this case the shift of demand produced by the import duty in A away from A's home-produced

[1] The precise condition is that the sum of the marginal propensity to import in A and the price elasticity of demand for imports in B should be less than unity. See p. 74 of my *A Geometry of International Trade*.

apples on to A's home-produced blankets will indirectly represent a shift of demand away from land on to labour. In consequence the rent of land will tend to fall and the wage of labour to rise in A.

If the proportion of labour to land is higher in the blanket industry than in the apple industry, a shift of labour and land from the apple industry to the blanket industry will tend to raise the proportion of land to labour in *both* industries.

The truth of this apparently paradoxical proposition can be seen from the numerical example given in Table XXIII. Suppose that to begin with there is a ratio of 1 to 3 of labour to land in the apple industry where much land (3,000 units) and little labour (1,000 units) are

TABLE XXIII

Factor Proportions in Two Industries

	Apple Industry			*Blanket Industry*		
	Amount of		Proportion of land to labour	Amount of		Proportion of land to labour
	land	labour		land	labour	
Before the movement of factors	3,000	1,000	3·0	1,000	3,000	0·33
After the movement of factors	3,000 −100 =2,900	1,000 −100 =900	3·22	1,000 +100 =1,100	3,000 +100 =3,100	0·35

employed. Suppose that in the blanket industry the reverse is the case and there is a ratio of 3 in 1 of labour to land, since in this industry much labour (3,000 units) and little land (1,000 units) are employed. Both labour and land now move from the apple industry to the blanket industry. We may suppose that they move in some ratio intermediate between that in which they are employed in the apple industry from which they are coming (3 land to 1 labour) and that in which they are employed in the blanket industry to which they are going (1 land to 3 labour). In Table XXIII we suppose that 100 units of land and 100 units of labour move so that the movement is in the intermediate ratio of 1 land to 1 labour.

As a result of this the ratio of land to labour in the apple industry which was $\frac{3000}{1000}$ rises to $\frac{3000-100}{1000-100}$, i.e. from 3 in 1 to 3·22 in 1. The ratio rises because the ratio of land to labour which is subtracted from the industry is lower than the ratio of land to labour already existing in the industry. On the other hand, the ratio of land to labour in the blanket industry which was $\frac{1000}{3000}$ rises to $\frac{1000+100}{3000+100}$, i.e. from 0·33 to 0·35. It rises in this case because the ratio of the land to labour which is added to the industry is greater than the ratio of land to labour originally employed in the industry. Thus as a result of the movement of factors from the land-intensive apple industry to the labour-intensive blanket industry the ratio of land to labour employed will rise in both industries.

Now if there are no increasing returns to scale in either industry, the marginal product of each factor in each industry will depend solely upon the proportions in which the factors are employed in the two industries and not at all upon the scale of production in each industry. But the proportion of labour to land will have fallen in both industries in A. It follows that in both industries the marginal product of labour will have risen (the importance of having one more unit of labour will be greater because labour is now scarce relatively to land) and the marginal product of land will have fallen (it will be less important to have one more unit of land because land has less labour to co-operate with). Whether measured in terms of blankets or of apples, the marginal product of labour will have risen and of land will have fallen.

If there are conditions of competition in both industries, each factor in each industry will be paid a reward equal to the value of its marginal product. In this case it is clear that the real wage rate will have risen, whether it is measured in terms of apples or of blankets, and the real rent rate will have fallen, whether it is measured in terms of apples or of blankets. With constant total amounts of labour and land in the whole economy of A the total wage bill will be unequivocally higher and the total of rents will be unequivocally lower than before.[1]

In the normal case, therefore, in which the protection of the blanket industry in A causes the price of blankets to rise relatively to the price of apples, there will result a redistribution of A's national income in favour of wages (labour being the important factor in the protected

[1] This does not mean to say that the landlords will necessarily be worse off than before. They will certainly earn rents which have a lower purchasing power over both apples and blankets. But in the text we have considered only the earnings from wages and rents. We have not considered the further amelioration of personal incomes that will result from the distribution to the citizens of A of the revenue derived from the import duty (see pp. 158–62 above). If the duty moved the terms of trade much in A's favour and the revenue from the duty were mainly distributed to landlords, they might also be better off than before. But apart from changes in distribution due to the way in which this revenue is distributed, the change is one which unequivocally improves the position of workers vis-à-vis landlords.

blanket industry) and away from rent (land being the important factor in the industry making the exported product, apples). But, as we have seen, protection of the blanket industry might conceivably reduce the price of blankets relatively to apples in A. This would occur if the marginal propensity to import blankets in A and the elasticity of demand for imported apples in B were both sufficiently small.

In this case the effects upon the redistribution of income in A would, of course, be the opposite of those which we have just examined. There would be a net shift of demand in A away from A's home-produced blankets on to A's home-produced apples, and so an indirect shift of demand away from A's labour (which is the important factor in the blanket industry) on to A's land (which is the important factor in the apple industry). Labour and land would be shifted from the blanket industry to the apple industry; and this, being the reverse of the movement illustrated in Table XXIII, would in this case cause the ratio of land employed to labour to fall in both industries. In consequence the marginal product of labour and so the real wage rate would tend to fall in terms of both apples and blankets; and the marginal product of land and so the real rate of rent would tend to rise in terms of both apples and blankets. There would tend to be an unequivocal redistribution of the national income in favour of rents and against wages.

Let us next turn to the position in country B. The restriction of imports of blankets into A will without doubt reduce the price of blankets relatively to the price of apples in B. This will be so even in the 'normal' case in which the import duty in A raises the price of blankets in A, because, as we have seen, in that case the price in A will go up by somewhat less than the whole of the import duty and the price of blankets in B will fall by the remaining part of the import duty. The price of blankets in B will, of course, fall even more markedly in the 'abnormal' case in which the effect of the import duty is to reduce the price of the protected blankets in A relatively to the price of apples. In this case the price of blankets in B will have to fall by the whole of the import duty and, in addition, by the fall in the market price of blankets in A.

Suppose that the production of blankets is labour-intensive in B as well as in A, so that a larger proportion of labour to land is used in the production of blankets than in the production of apples in B. Then the fall in the price offered for blankets relatively to the price offered for apples in B will represent an indirect reduction in the demand for labour relatively to the demand for land in B. There will be an excess supply of labour and an excess demand for land in B. In both the blanket industry and the apple industry in B there will be a tendency to increase the ratio of labour employed to land employed. As more labour is employed per unit of land in both industries in B, the marginal product of labour will tend to fall whether it be measured in terms of apples or of blankets. And as the amount of land employed per unit of labour tends to fall in both industries, the marginal product of land will tend to rise whether it be measured in terms of apples or of blankets. There will be an unequivocal fall in wages and rise in rents.

The above argument is valid on the assumption that the blanket industry is the labour-intensive industry in B as well as in A. Now if for technical reasons it is not possible to vary very much the technical methods of production in either industry, this is likely to be the case. If in one of the countries the apple industry is the sort of industry which requires a much higher proportion of land to labour than the blanket industry, this is likely to be the case in the other country also.

But this is, at least theoretically, not the only possibility. If one of the industries is such that the ratio in which labour and land must be employed is more or less rigidly fixed for technical reasons and if in the other industry it is possible to vary this ratio very widely, then it is quite possible that the apple industry might be the labour-intensive industry in B, even though the blanket industry were the labour-intensive industry in A. Suppose, by way of example, that in both A and B for technical reasons blankets must be made with a relatively invariable proportion of labour and land in their production. Even though labour were to become very cheap and land very expensive, it would not be possible to switch to other methods of production which relied more upon the use of the cheap labour and less upon the use of the expensive land; and vice versa. But suppose that, at the same time, apple production could technically be carried out either by very extensive farming in which little labour was used over a very large number of acres of land or by very intensive farming in which much labour was applied intensively to a very small area of land. If labour were very expensive and land very cheap, the first method of production of apples would be adopted. But if land became very expensive and labour very cheap, producers would turn to the production of the same output of apples by the alternative method which economized in the use of the expensive factor land and which depended mainly upon the employment of the cheap factor labour.

Suppose, then, that in both A and B blankets must be produced by the same relatively fixed proportion of labour to land. But suppose that in both A and B producers have a choice in the production of apples of using different methods of production which involve very different ratios of labour to land. Suppose, further, that A is a country which has a large area of land and a very small population whereas B has a very large population and a very small amount of land. In these conditions, if both countries have blanket industries, both countries must employ a rather similar proportion of labour to land in their blanket industries. In A there will be left over for the apple industry a very large amount of land and very little labour; labour will be scarce and expensive, land plentiful and cheap; apple-farmers in A will adopt methods of extensive apple production which use a high ratio of the cheap factor land; in A the blanket industry will employ a much higher ratio of labour to land than will the apple industry. But in B, after the relatively fixed proportion of labour to land is employed in the blanket industry, there will be left over for the apple industry a very large amount of labour and little land; labour will be plentiful and cheap, land scarce and expensive; apple-farmers in A will farm intensively with much labour on little land; in B the blanket industry will employ a much lower ratio of labour to land than will the apple industry. In A the blanket industry is more labour-intensive than the apple industry; in B it is less labour-intensive than the apple industry.

Now it is not at all incompatible with this that A should export apples and B should export blankets. Conditions of supply and demand in A and B might be such that, in the absence of international trade, apples would be cheaper relatively to blankets in A than in B, so that with the opening of trade A would export apples in return for imported blankets. If then in the free-trade position A imposed a duty on imported blankets, this would, as we have seen, certainly reduce the price of blankets relatively to that of apples in B. Labour and land would be shifted in B from the relatively unprofitable blanket industry to the relatively profitable apple industry. But since in B apple production and not blanket production is the labour-intensive industry, this involves a rise in the demand for labour relatively to the demand for land. In both industries in B there will be some tendency to employ a lower ratio of labour to land; the marginal product of labour will tend to rise and the marginal product of land to fall, whether these marginal products be measured in terms of apples or of blankets. There will be an unequivocal rise in wages and fall in rents.

The above argument leaves us with four possible combinations of circumstances in A and B, which are shown schematically in Table XXIV. (1) In the first and most probable case, the duty on imported blankets in A will have the 'normal' effect of raising the price of blankets in A, and the blanket industry, which is labour-intensive in A, will also be labour-intensive in B. In this case the effect of the duty is to raise wages and to lower rents in A, and to lower wages and to raise rents in B. (2) If the duty still had the normal effect of raising the price of blankets in A but if the blanket industry was land-intensive in B, then the effect of the duty would be once more to raise wages and to lower rents in A, but it would now have the same effect in B as well. (3) If the duty had the abnormal effect of lowering the price of blankets in A as well as in B, and if the blanket industry were labour-intensive in both countries, then the effect would be to lower wages and to raise rents in both countries. (4) Finally, if the duty had the abnormal effect of lowering the price of blankets in A and if the blanket industry was land-

TABLE XXIV

The Effect of a Duty, imposed by A on the Import of Blankets from B, upon the Distribution of Income in A and B

	Blankets in A are labour-intensive and in B are		Effect on the distribution of income in A	B
Normal case: Price of blankets rises in A	labour-intensive	(1)	W_a+	W_a-
	land-intensive	(2)	W_a+	W_b+
Abnormal case: Price of blankets falls in A	labour-intensive	(3)	W_a-	W_a-
	land-intensive	(4)	W_a-	W_b+

(W+ and W− mark a rise or a fall respectively in wages accompanied by a fall or rise in rents. W_a and W_b mean that the change in distribution will be most marked if apples or blankets respectively are most important in the consumption of wage-earners.)

intensive instead of labour-intensive in B, we should have exactly the opposite result from the most probable case (considered under (1) above); wages would fall and rents rise in A, and wages would rise and rents fall in B.

It will be noticed that in the above analysis we have not considered at all whether apples or blankets are the commodities which make up most of the consumption of the workers or of the landlords. Yet it would appear that this point must be relevant. For it must make a difference when, for example, the price of blankets goes up in A as a result of an import duty upon B's blankets, whether blankets are consumed mainly by the workers or by the landlords. If something happens to raise the price of blankets and to lower that of apples, this will surely have one effect upon the distribution of real income if blankets are consumed mainly by the landlords and apples mainly by the workers and quite a different effect if blankets are consumed mainly by workers and apples mainly by landlords.

In fact, in the simple conditions which we are examining this consideration will have no effect at all upon the direction of the change in the distribution of income; but it will affect the degree of change in the distribution of income. The conclusions as to the conditions under which a duty imposed on imported blankets in A will raise or lower wages or rents in A or B remain unaffected as we have summarized them on pp. 300–1 and as they are laid out in Table XXIV by the W+'s and the W—'s. But the degree of the change which will take place in either direction is greatly affected by the relative importance of the two commodities, apples and blankets, in the consumption of the two classes of income recipients, workers, and landlords. This we must now proceed to explain.[1]

Let us start by considering the effect upon the distribution of income between wages and rents in A in the normal case in which the imposition of the import duty in A causes the price of blankets to rise in A. Let us suppose that it causes the price of blankets in terms of apples to rise by 10 per cent in A. As we have seen, if blankets are labour-intensive in their production, this will cause labour to be used in a smaller proportion to land in both industries in A and the marginal product of labour will therefore rise absolutely whether it is measured in terms of apples or of blankets. But it will certainly have gone up more in terms of apples than in terms of blankets. If the marginal product of labour has gone up by 5 per cent in the blanket industry measured in terms of blankets and if the price of blankets has gone up by 10 per cent in terms of apples, then in equilibrium the marginal product of labour in the apple industry in terms of apples must have gone up by 15 per cent.

This is so because if the rise were less in terms of apples labour would be able to earn a higher money wage in the blanket industry than in the apple industry. If the marginal product and so the wage paid to labour had gone up by the same percentage—say, 5 per cent—in terms of the products of the two industries apples and blankets, and if at the same time a blanket had become worth 10 per cent more in terms of apples, the money wage rate in the blanket industry would have gone up by 10 per cent more than the money wage rate in the apple industry. Labour would then move from the apple industry to the blanket industry until it was so scarce in the former and so plentiful in the latter that its marginal product in the former had so risen and in the latter had so fallen that its money wage was the same in the two industries. With a 5 per cent rise in the marginal product and so the wage rate in terms of blankets, and with a 10 per cent rise in the price of blankets in terms of apples, this point of equilibrium would be reached only when the marginal product and so the wage rate had risen by 15 per cent in terms of apples.

[1] The conclusions of the following argument are summarized in Table XXIV by the a and b subscripts to the W+'s and W—'s. See the explanation at the foot of that table.

Similarly, it can be seen that the rise in the price of blankets in A in terms of apples, by leading to an increase in the ratio of land to labour in both industries in A, would cause a fall in the marginal product of land in both industries and so a fall in the rent of land whether it was measured in terms of apples or of blankets. But in this case the fall in the marginal product of land must be greater in the blanket industry than in the apple industry, if equilibrium is to be maintained in the market for land and if there is to be no incentive to transfer land from one industry to the other. If the marginal product of land has fallen by, say, 3 per cent in terms of apples and if the price of blankets has risen by 10 per cent in terms of apples, money rents will be the same in the two industries only if the marginal product of land and so its rent has fallen by 13 per cent in terms of blankets.

We reach, then, a position such as the following:

Percentage Changes in Marginal Products

	Expressed in terms of	
	apples	blankets
Of labour	+15	+ 5
Of land	− 3	−13

Suppose now that labour bought only apples. The real wage rate would be up by 15 per cent in terms of the wage-good apples and real wages would thus be up by 15 per cent. But if labour consumed only blankets, the real wage rate would be up by only 5 per cent. In fact the movement in real wages will be somewhere between these two figures, depending upon the importance of the two commodities in the workers' budget. And, similarly, with the real incomes of landlords. Thus, to take the two extreme cases, if workers consumed only apples and landlords only blankets, there would have been a 15 per cent rise in real wages at the expense of a 13 per cent fall in real rents, whereas if workers consumed only blankets and landlords only apples, there would have been only a 5 per cent rise in real wages and a 3 per cent fall in real rents.

We can deal briefly with the remaining cases. If the import duty in A had the abnormal effect of lowering the price of protected blankets in A, then the ratio of labour to land will rise in both industries in A, and the marginal product of labour will fall and of land will rise in both industries. But since blankets have now fallen in price in terms of apples, to preserve equilibrium in the markets for labour and land the marginal product of labour must have fallen more, and the marginal product of land must have risen less, in terms of apples than in terms of blankets. If apples are consumed only by wage-earners and blankets only by landlords, we should then have the most marked fall in real wages and rise in real rents.

Turning to B, we know that the price of blankets will have fallen in terms of apples. If blankets are labour-intensive, this will have resulted in an increase in the ratio of labour to land in both industries. The marginal product of labour will have fallen and of land will have risen in terms of both products. But since money rewards must be the same for each factor in both industries and since the price of blankets has fallen in terms of apples, the marginal product of labour must have fallen more, and the marginal product of land must have risen less, in terms of apples than in terms of blankets. Once again the change in real wages and real rents will be most marked if wage-earners consume only apples and landlords only blankets.

Finally, if blankets were land-intensive in B, the effect of the fall in the price of blankets would have been to lower the ratio of labour to land in both industries in B. The marginal product of labour would have risen and of land would have fallen in terms of both products. But to preserve equilibrium in the markets for labour and land the marginal product of labour must have risen more, and the marginal product of land must have fallen less, in terms of blankets than in terms of apples. In this case, and only in this case, the change in real wages and real rents will be the most marked if wage-earners consumed only blankets and the landlords only apples.

The preceding analysis relates only to the case of trade taxes. Trade subsidies may, of course, also be used for the purpose of affecting the internal distribution of income. Thus suppose that in B the exported product, blankets, is labour-intensive and that the authorities in B desire to adopt a trade policy which will redistribute income away from the rent of land on to the wages of labour. The imposition by B of a tax on trade would normally expand the demand in B for B's apples which compete with imported apples and contract the demand in B for B's blankets which constitute her export product; and this would increase the demand for, and so the reward paid for, land at the expense of the demand for, and reward paid for, labour in B. In such a case the subsidization of trade would be the appropriate policy if B's government wished to expand the demand for her export product blankets (and so for her labour) at the expense of the product, apples, which competed with imports (and which was made mainly with land).

Suppose, then, that in B a subsidy is paid on the export of blankets to A. The effect of such a subsidy can be analysed in just the same terms as the effect of a duty on the import of blankets into A. The conclusions of such an analysis are set out schematically in Table XXV, which corresponds to the results of the analysis of the effect of an import duty in A which were set out in Table XXIV. The analysis by which the results of Table XXV are reached is exactly analogous to the analysis by which the results of Table XXIV were reached and which we have already explained at length. Here it will suffice to indicate in the briefest outline the main steps necessary to reach the conclusions of Table XXV.

TABLE XXV

The Effect of a Subsidy, paid by B on the Export of Blankets to A, upon the Distribution of Income in B and A

	Blankets in B are labour-intensive, and in A are		Effect on the distribution of income in B	Effect on the distribution of income in A
Normal case: Price of blankets rises in B	labour-intensive	(1)	W_a+	W_a-
	land-intensive	(2)	W_a+	W_b+
Abnormal case: Price of blankets falls in B	labour-intensive	(3)	W_a-	W_a-
	land-intensive	(4)	W_a-	W_b+

(W + and W − mark a rise or a fall respectively in wages accompanied by a fall or a rise respectively in rents. W_a and W_b mean that the change in distribution will be most marked if apples or blankets respectively are most important in the consumption of wage-earners.)

When a subsidy is paid in B on the export of blankets to A, this will in all cases increase the supply of blankets in A and lower their price there. In the normal case, this increase in the demand for B's blankets will raise their price in B and thus cause an increased demand for home-produced blankets relatively to home-produced apples in B. In this case, if blankets are labour-intensive and apples are land-intensive in production in B, this will cause indirectly a rise in the demand for labour and a fall in the demand for land in B. As a result, wages will rise and rents will fall in B; and since in B the market price of blankets has risen relatively to that of apples, the rise in real wages and the fall in real rents will be the more marked, the more important are apples in the consumption of workers and blankets in the consumption of landlords. This explains the signs W_a+ under country B in rows 1 and 2 of Table XXV.

But if the elasticity of demand for imported blankets in A is very low, the price of B's subsidized blankets in A may fall very low indeed relatively to the price of apples in A, and A may export to B a smaller total amount of apples in return for a larger total volume of blankets. The result of this in B will be a heavy reduction in the total available supply of apples; and this may cause the price of apples to rise relatively to that of blankets in B. It will do so unless the demand for apples in B falls off by as much as the supply. There will certainly be some fall in the demand for apples in B because B's citizens will certainly be worse off than before when, as a result of the export subsidy, B has to export a larger volume of blankets to A in order to import a smaller volume of apples. Being worse off than before, citizens in B will spend less on apples and less on blankets. But if they economize mostly on blankets (i.e. if their marginal propensity to spend on imports is low), the demand for apples will remain in excess of the supply and the price of apples will go up in B relatively to the price of blankets. In this abnormal case there will in B be a shift of demand away from home-produced blankets on to home-produced apples. If blankets are labour-intensive and apples are land-intensive in production in B, this will cause rents to rise relatively to wages; and since the market price of apples will have risen in B relatively to the market price of blankets, the fall in real wages and the rise in real rents will be the greater, the greater is the dependence of wage-earners in consumption on apples and the greater is the dependence of landlords in consumption on blankets. This explains the sign W_a— under country B in rows 3 and 4 of Table XXV.

In A, as we have seen, the price of blankets must fall relatively to that of apples as a result of B's export subsidy on blankets. If blankets are labour-intensive and apples are land-intensive in A's production, this will cause wages to fall and rents to rise in A. But since the price of blankets has fallen relatively to that of apples, the fall in real wages and the rise in real rents will be greater, the more wage-earners consume apples and landlords blankets. This accounts for the sign W_a— under country A in rows 1 and 3 of Table XXV.

If, however, blankets are land-intensive and apples labour-intensive in A, the fall in the price offered for blankets in A will cause rents to fall and wages to rise. But since the price of blankets has fallen and that of apples has risen, the rise in real wages and the fall in real rents will in this case be the greater, the more wage-earners consume blankets and landlords apples. This accounts for the sign W_b+ under country A in rows 2 and 4 of Table XXV.

We must now attempt to assess, in the light of the foregoing analysis, how effective trade controls might be as instruments for the redistribution of income within any country. If the country which is using this instrument for this purpose makes up an insignificant part of the whole of the world economy, then the fact that it is taxing its imports or subsidizing its exports will not have any appreciable effect upon the conditions of supply and demand in the relevant markets in the rest of the world. In other words, the country in question will not be able, through its own trade controls, to affect the terms at which it can trade with the rest of the world.

If, for example, country A imposed a duty on imported blankets and the consequential changes in A's imports of blankets and exports of apples had quite negligible effects in B's markets, then there would be no effect upon the relative prices of blankets and apples in B and, in consequence, no effect upon the distribution of income in B. Moreover, the price of blankets relatively to that of apples would rise in A by the full amount of the import duty. The import duty clearly would not have the abnormal effect in A of lowering the price of blankets in A. The effects of the duty upon income distribution would be confined to those shown under country A in the first two rows of Table XXIV. The last two rows would be inapplicable because the 'abnormal' case would be ruled out, and the first two rows under country B would show no changes in distribution because there would be no price changes in B. If blankets were labour-intensive in A and if A made up a very small part of the world economy, then A could effectively cause some redistribution of income in favour of wages by protecting the home production of blankets.

Similarly, if B were a negligibly small part of the total world economy and if her export product, blankets, were labour-intensive in its production in B, the authorities in B could bring about some redistribution of income in B in favour of wages by subsidizing the export of blankets. In this case the export subsidy would have no significant effect upon the prices of blankets or apples in the vast market of A; and its effect would, therefore, be solely to raise the price of blankets relatively to that of apples in B by the full amount of the subsidy. In Table XXV the last two rows could not apply since the 'abnormal' case of a fall in the price of blankets in B could not arise. Moreover, in this case the signs under country A in the first two rows of Table XXV would both have to be zero because the export subsidy in B could not have any effect upon relative prices in A and so would leave the distribution of income in A unaffected. It is clear, therefore, that in such circumstances the authorities in B could always bring about some redistribution of income in favour of wages by subsidizing the export of their labour-intensive product, blankets.

But A and B (who together comprise the whole of the world) cannot simultaneously both make up insignificant parts of the whole world economy. Suppose that blankets are labour-intensive in both A and B and are exported from B to A, and suppose, further, that A is an insignificantly small part of the whole world economy. Then the authorities in A certainly can redistribute A's income in favour of wages by taxing the import of blankets. But in these conditions B can have no significant effect in redistributing income in favour of wages in B by subsidizing blanket exports. A's markets are so small that any absolute change in A's imports of blankets and exports of apples which might be brought about by the export subsidy in B will have a negligible effect upon the total demand for B's home-produced blankets and apples. The relative prices of blankets and apples will be unchanged in B and there will be no appreciable effect upon the distribution of income in B. The only effect of B's export subsidy will be to reduce the price of blankets relatively to apples in A, and thus to cause a redistribution of A's income away from wages and in favour of rents. In such circumstances the authorities always could redistribute income in A in favour of wages by protecting imports. But the authorities in B could not affect their own internal distribution of income by subsidizing exports; all that they could do would be to offset the effect of A's import duty upon the distribution of income in A.[1]

The situation would be very different if both A and B constituted important parts of the total world economy. Let us suppose that they divide the world into two roughly equal parts. Let us suppose, as before, that blankets which are exported from B to A are labour-intensive in both countries and that both countries wish to use trade controls in order to redistribute income in favour of wages. Since our present purpose is merely to illustrate possible conflicts between national policies adopted in A and B, we will confine ourselves to the 'normal' cases in which a duty on imported blankets in A will tend to raise the price of blankets relatively to that of apples in A and where a subsidy on the export of blankets in B will tend to raise the price of blankets relatively to that of apples in B. In other words, we confine our attention to the first rows of Tables XXIV and XXV.

In these circumstances, as can be seen from these two tables, the authorities in A should impose a duty on the import of blankets to A in order to raise the price of blankets and so the wages of labour in A; but this will incidentally cause a fall in the price of blankets and so in the

[1] Incidentally, of course, if B's authorities paid an export subsidy which offset the effect of A's import duty upon the prices of commodities in A, this would represent a direct transfer of purchasing power from B's taxpayers (who raised the revenue for the subsidy) to A's taxpayers (who received the benefit of the revenue from the import duty). This would, of course, redistribute income away from B's citizens in favour of A's citizens. But it would affect the distribution of income within B and within A only in so far as the tax revenue needed to pay the subsidy was levied on the owners of one factor rather than another in B and the revenue received from the import duty was used to benefit the owners of one factor rather than another in A.

wages of labour in B. At the same time the authorities in B should pay a subsidy on the export of blankets to A in order to raise the price of blankets and so the wages of labour in B; but this will incidentally cause a fall in the price of blankets and so in the wages of labour in A. Obviously the two national policies will tend to offset each other in so far as the effect upon the internal distribution of income is concerned. Indeed, if the rate of import duty in A is the same as the rate of export subsidy in B the direct offsetting effect will be exact. An export subsidy by B of 10 per cent will make the price of blankets 10 per cent lower in terms of apples in A than it is in B, while an import duty by A of 10 per cent will make the price of blankets 10 per cent higher in terms of apples in A than it is in B. The combination of the two will leave the price of blankets in terms of apples the same in A as in B. The only result would be a transfer of income from taxpayers in B who were contributing the money to pay the export subsidy to the taxpayers in A whose burdens would be relieved by the raising of the revenue from the import duty.[1]

There may, therefore, be cases when it is literally impossible to achieve desirable redistributions of income within both countries simultaneously merely by the weapon of trade control. But even if these international conflicts of policy did not exist, difficult conflicts of policy might arise even from the narrowest point of view of the distribution of income within one country.

This would happen in country A if only two traded commodities were produced in it—say, an exportable commodity apples and an import-competing product blankets—and if more than two factors of production—say, land, labour, and capital—were involved in the production of each commodity. Suppose that in A blankets were produced with little land but with much labour and capital and apples with much land and little labour and capital. Protection of the blanket industry in A would, as we have seen, normally cause the price of blankets in A to rise relatively to the price of apples. This would cause a net increase in the demand for labour and capital (which are important in the expanding blanket industry and unimportant in the contracting apple industry)—and a net decrease in the demand for land (which is important in the

[1] The tax burden in B and the tax relief in A might be so met as to cause some net redistribution between taxpaying classes in the two countries. See the preceding footnote. Another possibility is that taxpayers in A who are now relieved of some tax payments might spend more (or less) of this additional income on labour-intensive blankets than the reduction in expenditure on labour-intensive blankets by the taxpayers in B who have to reduce their total consumption by an equivalent amount. This might lead to some net rise (or fall) in the price of blankets relatively to apples and so to some redistribution of income in favour of (or against) wages in both countries. But unless the marginal propensities to spend on the two commodities were very different in the two countries this would constitute a very secondary change.

contracting apple industry and unimportant in the expanding blanket industry). There would result a rise in the wages of labour and the profits of capital and a fall in the rent of land. But from the point of view of the distribution of the national income in A it might be desired to raise the wages of labour at the expense of both profits and rents. Yet, in the conditions outlined above, it would be impossible to adopt a trade-control policy which would make wages move in the opposite direction to profits or profits in the same direction as rents.

This difficulty might be overcome if it were possible to find yet another, third, commodity—say, coal—in which there was yet another type of combination of factors—say, a large amount of capital working with little land and labour. A trade-control policy might then be adopted to restrict the demand for the home production of coal, either by taxing exports of it if it were exported or by subsidizing imports of it if the home production competed with imports. The result of a contraction of the production of coal would be a large decrease in the demand for capital relatively to the decrease in the demand for labour and land; it would therefore tend to reduce profits and to raise wages and rents. In such circumstances a moderate expansion in the demand for blankets (which would tend to raise wages and profits and to lower rents) and a moderate decrease in the demand for apples (which would tend to lower rents and to raise wages and profits) combined with a heavy decrease in the demand for coal (which would tend to lower profits and to raise wages and rents) might bring about a rise in wages at the expense of both rents and profits. This possibility is illustrated schematically in Table XXVI.

It can be seen from the above analysis that the greater is the number of traded commodities relatively to the number of factors of production used in their production and the more diverse are the ratios in which the various factors are used in the production of the various commodities, the more probable it is that any desired redistribution of income could be obtained among the various factors by a combination of trade policies which produced an appropriate shift in the demand for the various products. But if many factors are involved the policy would not be a simple one and might involve a very complicated structure of import taxes, import subsidies, export taxes, and export subsidies.

But it must not be forgotten that a redistribution of income between factors of production, however nicely it can itself be controlled, is not the same thing as a redistribution between persons. Landlords as a class may be richer than wage-earners and a redistribution of income from rents to wages may thus generally shift income from the richer to the poorer. But there may well be some small landlords who are individually poorer than some prosperous wage-earners; and in these cases a general shift from rents to wages will increase the inequality of in-

TABLE XXVI

The Effect upon the Distribution of Income between Three Factors of Changes in the Demand for Three Products

		Effect of		
		moderate decrease of demand for land-intensive apples	moderate increase of demand for labour-and-capital-intensive blankets	heavy decrease of demand for capital-intensive coal
Effect upon relative	wages	+	+	+ +
	rents	−	−	+ +
	profits	+	+	− −

dividual incomes. At the best redistribution among factors must be a clumsy instrument for achieving a desired redistribution among individuals.

Trade controls are, therefore, open to a number of far-reaching objections as methods of redistributing the national income.

(i) There is the obvious point that, in this case as in the others which we have examined, trade controls which are imposed solely for redistributive reasons may have adverse effects upon economic efficiency. They are likely to interfere with the maximization of production and the optimization of trade in the ways described in the earlier chapters of this Part.

(ii) They may be in conflict internationally in the sense that it may be impossible to find a set of trade controls which will lead to the desired redistribution of income in A and B simultaneously.

(iii) Where there are many factors and relatively few traded products with relatively similar factor ratios in their production, any scheme of trade controls which will achieve the desired redistribution even in one country may require a most complicated and extensive interference with free-trade price relationships.

(iv) Trade controls are bound to be a somewhat clumsy instrument for redistribution since at the best a redistribution among factors is only an approximation to a desired redistribution among persons.

It remains, therefore, to consider whether there are likely to be alternative and preferable methods of redistribution which are not open to so many objections.

There is one method which is almost bound to be superior to the use of trade controls. Suppose that in A to raise the demand for home-produced blankets and to lower that of home-produced apples will bring about a desired increase in the demand for labour relatively to the demand for land. This, as we have seen, can normally be done by taxing the import of blankets into A and the export of apples from A; but it could even more certainly be done by means of a tax on the total home production of apples and a subsidy on the home production of blankets.

Suppose then that we are asked to choose between (i) a tax on the import of blankets and/or on the export of apples and (ii) a subsidy to blanket production and/or a tax on apple production (combined, if necessary, with production taxes or subsidies on other products produced in A), the rates of subsidy and tax with method ii being so adjusted as to have exactly the same effects upon the prices offered to producers of apples, blankets, and other products in A as the alternative trade taxes which might be used with method i. Since, *ex hypothesi*, the effects on the prices offered to producers will be the same with both methods, the effect on the output of blankets, apples, and other products in A will be the same. Therefore, the effect upon the demand for labour and land in A will be the same; and, therefore, the effect upon the wage rate and the rate of rent will be the same. From the point of view of the effect upon the distribution of income there will thus be nothing to choose between the two methods.

But from the point of view of economic efficiency method ii will almost certainly[1] be preferable to method i. Method ii will be open, in exactly the same way as method i, to objections iii and iv on p. 311. But method ii would not be open at all to objections ii and it would be less open than method i to objection i.

As far as objections iii and iv are concerned, a system of general production taxes and subsidies would operate in exactly the same way as a system of trade controls in achieving a redistribution of income among persons indirectly through a redistribution among factors, this latter being in turn indirectly achieved through a change in the demand prices offered for different home-produced commodities. Objections iii and iv would, therefore, apply equally to both systems.

But objection ii would not apply at all to the system of general

[1] If there were no problems of economic efficiency involved in the raising of revenue, method ii would—as the argument in the text shows—certainly be preferable to method i. But if there are problems of efficiency involved in the raising of revenue, there is something to be said for relying partly on a tax on imports of blankets as well as on a subsidy to blanket production in order to raise the price offered to the home producers of blankets, simply because the import tax raises revenue and the production subsidy needs public expenditure to be financed out of other revenue. To this extent there is some argument for dealing with the problem with some element of tax on the import of blankets.

production taxes and subsidies since the fact that A is taxing the production of her export product apples and subsidizing the production of her import-competing product blankets in order to increase the demand for blankets at the expense of apples in no way stops B from subsidizing the production of her export product blankets and taxing the production of her import-competing product apples with the same object in view. If the production tax on apples and the production subsidy on blankets are sufficiently high in both countries, consumers will be tempted to consume in total more blankets and less apples and the relative demand for blankets and so for labour can be raised simultaneously in both countries. This is a result which, as we have seen, cannot be achieved by a simultaneous import duty on blankets in A and export subsidy on blankets in B.

As for objection i, a system of general production taxes and subsidies in A and B which brought about the same change in the prices offered to the producers of apples, blankets, and other products in A and B (and so the same effect upon internal redistribution) as did a given system of trade taxes and subsidies would have the same effect as those trade taxes and subsidies upon the maximization of production and the optimization of production, but would have a better effect from the point of view of the optimization of trade. A given change in the prices offered to the producers of apples, blankets, and other products in A will bring about the same shifts in the amounts and the uses of productive resources in A in the various occupations, whether the shift be caused by taxes and subsidies on trade or on production. And similarly for B. It follows, therefore, that under both systems, if the price changes are the same, there will be exactly the same changes in the amounts of each factor used in each industry in each country. There cannot, therefore, be any difference between the two results from the points of view of the maximization or the optimization of production.

But the position will be very different in so far as the optimization of trade is concerned. In the case of taxes and subsidies on total production the prices charged to consumers of apples and blankets will be the same in A as in B because there will be no taxes or subsidies imposed merely on the import or export of either commodity. But under a system of trade taxes and subsidies the price charged to the consumer for the same commodity will differ in A and in B by the amount of the net trade tax or subsidy on that commodity. In the former case trade will be optimized and in the latter case it will not.

One simple example will serve to illustrate this point. Suppose that in B the price of apples and of blankets remains unchanged throughout; no policy for trade or for production taxes and subsidies is adopted, and B is sufficiently large relatively to A for A's actions to have an inappreciable effect upon the terms of trade in B. Suppose that A adopts a policy to raise the price offered to producers of blankets, and that this is done (i) by an import duty on blankets, and (ii) by a subsidy to the production of blankets. As we have argued, the effects upon the employment of each factor in each industry in A and so upon the output of each product in A will be the same in both cases. But under (i) the price of blankets to consumers will be high relatively to that of other products (which we will call apples), and for consumers the ratio of the price of blankets to that of apples will be higher in A than in B. Consumers in A will consume many apples and few blankets; this they will do out of their given production by exporting few apples and importing few blankets, even though at the margin one extra blanket is worth more apples to a consumer in A than to a consumer in B. Under (ii) the price ratio will be the same to consumers in both countries. A's consumers will have more imported blankets and will export more of their domestic production of apples; and they will be better off as a result, because before this extension of trade they could always gain more by consuming another blanket (for which they were prepared to pay a high price) than they would lose by exporting to B sufficient apples to purchase an additional blanket in B (an amount of apples for which they themselves were prepared to pay only a relatively low price).

Domestic redistribution through a system of production taxes and subsidies is thus almost bound to be better than domestic redistribution through a system of trade taxes and subsidies: it is compatible for all countries to use the system at the same time, and it interferes less with the optimization of trade. But it may, of course, be possible to do still better. A system of direct taxes on high incomes and subsidies to low incomes would not be open to objections ii, iii, and iv of p. 311 at all, since they would represent a direct redistribution of income among persons which all governments could carry out simultaneously.

As far as objection i is concerned, these methods of redistribution would have no adverse effects upon economic efficiency if it were possible to raise the revenue from those whose incomes were to be reduced by some method (e.g. progressive lump-sum taxes or the State ownership of income-bearing property) which did not cause any divergence between *marginal* values and costs. This may not be practicable; and, as we have seen in Chapters III and VII, for this reason some element of taxation of particular commodities may be desirable as a means of raising revenue for purposes of redistribution as for other purposes. We have already discussed at some length the main problems which arise in this connexion. It may, for example, provide a reason for relying to some extent upon the taxation in A of certain commodities which are elastic in supply, which are consumed mainly by the rich, and whose consumption is complementary with leisure (see Chapter VII). But it is not probable that there will on these grounds be any case for taxing imports more heavily than home production; indeed the presumption is the other way (see Chapter XII). And in any case this is an entirely different consideration than the taxation of imports of blankets in order to stimulate the demand for home-produced blankets and so for domestic labour. The case for trade controls as a means of exerting a direct influence upon the domestic distribution of income is, therefore, a weak one.

PART III. THE CONTROL OF FACTOR MOVEMENTS

PART III. THE CONTROL OF FACTOR MOVEMENTS

CHAPTER XIX

TRADE AND SPECIALIZATION

THROUGHOUT Part II we maintained the assumption that, while products could be traded between countries and while factors of production could move from industry to industry within any country, there was complete immobility of factors of production between countries. The time has now come to remove this assumption, and to examine the various implications of international factor movements.

We shall, however, approach the problem in stages. Until we reach Part IV we shall, of course, continue to assume that there are only two countries, A and B. But in addition to this, in order to isolate certain fundamental relationships between international trade and international factor movements, we shall, until we reach Chapter XXIV, maintain two further important simplifying assumptions. First, we shall assume that in each country domestic economic policies of what we have called 'modified laissez-faire' have been successfully adopted so that each factor is being paid a reward equal to the value of its marginal social net product, and that factors move freely within each country in search of the highest available reward. Thus in each country the same reward will be paid to the same factor in all industries, and this reward will in each case measure the value to society of the additional product produced by having one more unit of that factor in that industry. Secondly, we shall assume that the total world supply of each factor is fixed. For example, we assume that, while labour may migrate from A to B, the total world population remains unchanged. We shall modify these two assumptions in due course when we come to Chapters XXIV–XXIX.

We consider, then, in this Part, what are the modifications which the international movement of factors of production will make to the conclusions reached in Part II. The first question which we shall have to ask and which we shall discuss in Chapters XX–XXIII is whether the free international movement of factors of production would make any significant difference to the position achieved by the free international movement of products. For, as we shall show, it is quite possible to conceive of conditions in which any improvements in economic welfare which could be brought about by a movement of factors of production between A and B could equally well be brought about by a movement of commodities between A and B.

We shall turn to a discussion of this possibility in the next chapter; but before we do so there is one preliminary matter which it is useful to clear up and which we shall discuss in this chapter. As we shall see in the following chapters, one of the most important considerations which will help to determine whether free trade alone is sufficient without factor movements to maximize economic welfare, is whether or not free trade lends to the complete specialization of production in the trading countries. We shall accordingly consider the relationship between freedom of trade and the specialization of production in this chapter before we turn to a direct consideration of the question whether free trade is alone sufficient to maximize welfare.

Now, suppose that for some reason or another trade is prohibited between A and B, so that each country must produce what it wants of each commodity for its own consumption. Suppose, however, that A is better suited to produce apples (for example, because A is rich in land which is important in apple production) and that B is better suited to produce blankets (for example, because B is well endowed with the skilled labour required for their production). Then when trade between them is prohibited blankets will be expensive relatively to apples in A and will be cheap relatively to apples in B.

Let us suppose that in this initial position in which trade is prohibited the price of a blanket is 2 apples in A and 1 apple in B. In other words, the marginal cost of a blanket will be twice as high as that of an apple in A and will be equal to that of an apple in B. Now in order that this should represent a position of equilibrium for the factors of production in A, it must be true that the marginal social net product of any factor of production is twice as high in the apple industry as in the blanket industry in A. Since the price of a blanket is twice that of an apple in A, and since in equilibrium any factor will be paid the price of its marginal product in each industry, the reward paid to any factor of production will be the same in both industries in A, only if the fact that the price of a blanket is twice that of an apple is offset by the fact that the marginal product of each factor in blankets is only half as high as in apples. On the other hand, in B, where the price of an apple is the same as the price of a blanket, any one factor will be earning the same reward in both industries only if its marginal product in terms of blankets is the same as its marginal product in terms of apples.

Suppose that in this situation the prohibition on trade between A and B is removed and the commodities can be freely exchanged between the two countries. Apples will now be exported from A where they are relatively cheap to B where they are relatively expensive, and blankets will be exported from B where they are relatively cheap to A where they are relatively expensive. The apple industry will expand in A and contract in B, while the blanket industry will contract in A and expand in B. Factors of production will move from the blanket industry to the apple industry in A and from the apple industry to the blanket industry in B. This movement may come to an end in any one of three ways.

(1) It may continue until only one of the two commodities is produced in each country, i.e. until A is producing only apples and B only blankets. This is the case of specialization in both countries: A produces no blankets and B produces no apples.

(2) It may continue until one of the countries is producing only one of the commodities but the other country is still producing both, i.e. until A is producing only apples but B is producing both blankets and apples or until B is producing only blankets but A is producing both apples and blankets. This is the case of specialization in one country: either A produces no blankets or B produces no apples.

(3) It may come to an end at a point at which both countries are still producing both commodities. This is the case of no specialization.

Let us consider each of these possibilities in turn. We start with the price of blankets at 2 apples in A and at 1 apple in B. Free trade will tend to lower the price of blankets in A (as more blankets are imported into A and more apples are exported) and for the opposite reasons to raise the price of blankets in B. In the absence of transport costs this will continue until the price of the two products is the same in both countries. Let us suppose that it settles down at $1\frac{1}{2}$ apples for 1 blanket.

In these circumstances land, labour, capital, and other resources will shift from the blanket industry to the apple industry in A, since initially the marginal social net product of each factor is 2 apples and only 1 blanket in A, and 1 blanket is now worth only $1\frac{1}{2}$ apples in the market. Now if only one factor of production, say, labour, were to shift from the blanket industry to the apple industry in A one might expect its marginal social net product to rise in the blanket industry and to fall in the apple industry until at some point the marginal social net product of labour in the apple industry were only $1\frac{1}{2}$ times instead of twice as high as in the blanket industry. At this point there would be no further incentive for further movement of labour because the value of 1 blanket in the market is $1\frac{1}{2}$ apples, which is also equal to the rate at which apples could be produced instead of blankets by moving labour from the blanket industry to the apple industry.

But not only labour will be moving in A from the blanket industry to the apple industry; capital, land, and other resources will also be moving because initially their marginal social net product is also twice as high in apples as in blankets while the market price of blankets has fallen to only $1\frac{1}{2}$ apples. While the movement of labour from the blanket industry to the apple industry in A alone would have caused the marginal social net product of labour to fall in apples and to rise in blankets, the movement of other co-operating factors from the blanket to the apple industry will tend to lower the marginal social net product of labour in blankets again, since labour will have less equipment of capital and other resources to work with there, and will tend to raise the marginal social net product of labour in the apple industry again, since labour will once again enjoy an increase there in the factors with which it has to co-operate. When all factors move together from one industry to another there is no immediate reason for believing that there will be any substantial change in the marginal social net product of any one of them either in the industry which they are leaving or in the industry which they are entering. If this is so, and if the marginal social net product of all factors remains approximately twice as high in the apple industry as in the blanket industry in A, then so long as the price of a blanket is only $1\frac{1}{2}$ times as high as the price of an apple, the movement of factors out of the blanket industry and into the apple industry will continue unabated until A's blanket industry is completely closed down.

The opposite may be happening in B. All factors will be moving from the apple industry to the blanket industry because blankets are now worth $1\frac{1}{2}$ apples in the market whereas the marginal social net product of all factors is no higher in the apple industry than in the blanket industry. But since all factors are moving together from the apple industry to the blanket industry in B there may be no substantial change in the marginal social net product of any one of them in either industry. And if the marginal social net product of every factor remains substantially the same in terms of blankets as in terms of apples in B while the price of a blanket remains $1\frac{1}{2}$ apples in the market, the movement of factors in B will continue until B's apple industry is closed down. At this point A will be producing all the apples and B all the blankets, and they will be exchanging these products at the rate of $1\frac{1}{2}$ apples for a blanket.

Such is the first possibility, when each country specializes completely in the production of one of the two commodities. We must turn now to the second possibility, when only one of the two countries gives up the production of one of the two commodities. Suppose that by the process just described we have reached momentarily the position in which A produces only apples and B only blankets and they are exchanging them at the rate of $1\frac{1}{2}$ apples for a blanket. But suppose, further, (i) that A is a very much smaller country than B in the sense that there is a great deal less land, less labour, less capital, and less of other resources in A than in B, and (ii) that apples are a much more important commodity than blankets in the sense that consumers in both countries spend most of their income on apples and very little of it on blankets. Then the position in which only A produces apples could not continue. A being a small country could produce only a small output of apples, while consumers in both countries, the large as well as the small, wish to spend most of their income on apples; the demand for apples would be greatly in excess of the supply. Similarly, the supply of blankets on which the large country B is concentrating would be greatly in excess of the demand which is low in both countries. The price of blankets could not remain at 1½ apples for 1 blanket but would fall towards 1 apple for 1 blanket, the rate at which it initially started in B before trade was opened up between A and B. At the market price of 1 apple for a blanket B could now once again profitably produce some apples as well as some blankets. A, however, could produce only apples profitably, since the marginal product of her factors in the apple industry is twice as high as in the blanket industry and the market price of the two commodities is the same. In this case we end up with a new equilibrium in which A produces only apples, B produces both blankets and apples, and A exports apples and imports blankets at a price of approximately 1 apple for 1 blanket. This makes it profitable for B to continue to produce both products, but for A to shift all her factors of production out of the blanket industry.

There is a third possibility which we must consider in much greater detail. As factors of production are moved in A from the blanket industry to the apple industry, it is possible that the marginal social net product of all factors will fall in the apple industry and will rise in the blanket industry until the marginal social net product of any factor is only 1½ times instead of twice as high in the apple industry as in the blanket industry in A. Simultaneously, it is possible that as factors of production move from the apple industry to the blanket industry in B the marginal social net product of all factors may fall in the blanket industry and rise in the apple industry in B until it is 1½ times instead of only once as high in the apple industry as in the blanket industry in B. In this case a new equilibrium may be reached in which both A and B are producing both apples and blankets, in which A is exporting some apples and importing some blankets, and in which 1½ apples exchange for 1 blanket.

One reason why this may happen is the existence of some specialized factors in each of the two industries in each of the two countries which cannot be used in the other industry or cannot be moved to the other industry. Thus, suppose that in A in addition to the labour and capital which can be used either in the production of apples or of blankets there is also some land which is good for apple production but of no use for blanket production and some other land which is useful for blanket production but of no use for apple production. Then as labour and capital moves from blanket production to apple production in A the marginal social net product of both these factors of production will fall in the apple industry because more and more of them have to work on an unexpanded amount of the land which is specialized for apple production. Similarly, the marginal social net product of labour and capital will rise in the blanket industry because a smaller and smaller amount of them can work with an unchanged amount of the land which is specialized for blanket production. For this reason the marginal social net product of both labour and capital in A may fall from twice to only $1\frac{1}{2}$ times as much in the apple industry as in the blanket industry even though some of both commodities are still being produced. And the opposite may occur in B as labour and capital move from the apple industry to the blanket industry. Because of other factors which can be used only in the one industry or the other the marginal social net product of labour and capital will rise in terms of apples and fall in terms of blankets until it is $1\frac{1}{2}$ times instead of only once as great in the former as in the latter. At this point both countries will be producing something of both commodities; and the price of a blanket will be $1\frac{1}{2}$ apples.

But an equilibrium may be reached in the free-trade position between A and B, in which both countries continue to produce something of both commodities even if there are no specialized factors of production which can be used only in the one industry or the other. In order to explain how this may happen we will take the following much simplified example. Suppose that apples and blankets are the only two commodities produced; suppose that labour and land are the only two factors used in their production; suppose that A is initially endowed with a great deal of land and little labour, and B with a great deal of labour and little land; and suppose that the production of apples always needs a high proportion of land to labour while the production of blankets always requires a high proportion of labour to land.

Since in A land is plentiful and labour is scarce, we would expect the price of land to be low relatively to the price of labour. For this reason apples would be cheap to produce in A relatively to blankets because apple production makes large demands upon the relatively cheap factor land and small demands upon the relatively expensive factor labour, while the opposite is true in the case of blanket production. In B the position is reversed. Land is scarce and expensive; labour is plentiful and cheap; in consequence apples, which need much land and little labour, are expensive to produce as compared with blankets, which need much labour and little land. Thus, before trade takes place, we find that the price of blankets is 2 apples in A and only 1 apple in B.

If now trade takes place, apples will be exported from A to B and blankets from B to A. In consequence apples will become scarcer and blankets more plentiful in A, and the price of blankets in A will fall from 2 apples towards 1 apple. At the same time as a result of the trade apples will become more plentiful and blankets scarcer in B and the price of blankets will rise from 1 apple towards 2 apples in B. Let us assume as in previous examples that the world price settles midway between the two prices at $1\frac{1}{2}$ apples for a blanket.

The fall in the price of blankets from 2 apples to $1\frac{1}{2}$ apples in A will discourage the production of blankets and encourage the production of apples in A. But as the blanket industry is contracted in A much labour will be released and little land, since blanket production requires much labour and little land; and as the apple industry in A is expanded much land and little labour will be demanded, since apple production requires much land and little labour. As a result there will develop an excess demand over supply for land and an excess supply over demand for labour in A. The rent of land will rise and the wage of labour will fall. This will cause the cost of apple production to rise relatively to that of blanket production. Whereas previously 1 blanket cost the same as 2 apples in A, now as the output of apples is expanded and of blankets is contracted, 1 blanket will come to cost the same as only $1\frac{1}{2}$ apples in A. At this point the incentive for further shifts of resources from the blanket industry to the apple industry in A will have disappeared. At the new world price of $1\frac{1}{2}$ apples for 1 blanket instead of at the old market price of 2 apples for 1 blanket, A will continue to produce both apples and blankets; but she will produce rather more apples and rather less blankets than before. It is this shift of production which, through the mechanism just described, will have caused the cost of apples to rise as their output expands and of blankets to fall as their output contracts, until the price of $1\frac{1}{2}$ apples instead of 2 apples for a blanket corresponds to the new ratio between the costs of production of the two commodities in A.

Conversely in B, the rise in the price of blankets from 1 to $1\frac{1}{2}$ apples will have caused a contraction of apple production and an expansion of blanket production; this will have caused a rise in the demand for labour and a fall in the demand for land; in consequence rents of land will have fallen and the wages of labour will have risen; this will have raised the cost of blankets relatively to that of apples; and at the expanded output of blankets and the contracted output of apples the new price of $1\frac{1}{2}$ apples instead of 1 apple for 1 blanket will correspond to the increase in the cost of blankets relatively to the cost of apples. B also will continue to produce something of both products at the new price.

Such is the market mechanism by which a new equilibrium may be found after the opening up of free trade between A and B in which both countries may continue to produce both commodities. We have shown how the expansion of the apple industry and the contraction of the blanket industry in A will raise the average cost of apples and lower the average cost of blankets in A, because it will lead to an increased demand for land (which is important in apple production) and a decreased demand for labour (which is important in blanket production) and the consequential rise in the price of land and fall in the price of labour will raise costs in the apple industry and lower costs in the blanket industry.

But, as we have already argued, we shall reach a new equilibrium only if the value of the marginal product of each factor, land and labour, is the same in both industries in A. This can be the case only if the marginal product of any one factor in A was twice as high in the apple industry as in the blanket industry when 2 apples exchanged for 1 blanket and will now be only $1\frac{1}{2}$ times as high in the apple industry as in the blanket industry when only $1\frac{1}{2}$ apples exchange for 1 blanket.

What we have still to explain, therefore, is this. How does it come about that, when land and labour move from blanket production to apple production in A, the marginal social net product of each factor in the apple industry falls from being twice to being only $1\frac{1}{2}$ times as high as in the blanket industry? Similarly, how does it come about that, when land and labour move from apple production to blanket production in B, the marginal social net product of each factor in the apple industry rises from being only once to being $1\frac{1}{2}$ times as high as in the blanket industry?

Let us concentrate on what happens in A. The price of a blanket in A was 2 apples, and the marginal social net product of each factor was twice as high in the apple industry as in the blanket industry. The price of a blanket falls to $1\frac{1}{2}$ apples. Land and labour move from the production of blankets to that of apples. How does this cause the marginal social net product of both land and labour to fall much or to rise little in apple production and/or to rise much or to fall little in blanket production until it is only $1\frac{1}{2}$ times as high in terms of apples as in terms of blankets?

In order to understand this development it is necessary to bear in mind the two following propositions.

First, as labour and land both move from the blanket industry to the apple industry in A the proportion of land to labour will fall in both industries. There will, therefore, be a tendency for the marginal social net product of labour to fall absolutely in both industries, because in both industries each worker will be less well equipped with land; and conversely, in both industries there will be a tendency for the marginal social net product of land to rise because in both industries each acre of land will be used by a larger number of workers. The truth of this apparently paradoxical proposition that as labour and land move from the blanket industry to the apple industry the ratio of land to labour will fall in both industries has already been demonstrated in Table XXIII (p. 296). It was there shown that a movement of labour and land from the apple industry to the blanket industry would raise the proportion of land to labour in both industries. We are now concerned merely with the reverse movement in which a shift of labour and land from the blanket industry to the apple industry will lower the ratio of land to labour in both industries.

Second, the other proposition which we need for our argument is to the following effect. When the ratio of land to labour falls in the apple industry, in which land is the important factor and labour the unimportant factor, the marginal product of land is likely to rise a little and of labour to fall a lot. On the other hand, when the ratio of land to labour falls in the blanket industry, in which labour is the important factor and land the unimportant factor, the marginal product of land is likely to rise a lot and of labour to fall a little. In other words, when the marginal product of any factor changes because of a change in the factors employed in the industry, the change—whether it be an increase or a decrease—is likely to be relatively large if the factor in question is unimportant in that industry and is likely to be relatively small if the factor in question is important in that industry.

This proposition is illustrated in the numerical example in Table XXVII. We suppose that the amount of labour in the apple industry remains unchanged at 1,000 units (column *b*) but that the amount of

TABLE XXVII

Variations in the Marginal Products of Two Factors

Amount of land (*a*)	Amount of labour (*b*)	Output of apples (*c*)	Marginal product of land (*d*)	Rent of land (*e*) $= a \times d$	Wages of labour (*f*) $= c - e$	Marginal product of labour (*g*) $= f \div b$
2,999	1,000	7,998	—	—	—	—
3,000	1,000	8,000	2	6,000	2,000	2
3,001	1,000	(i) 8,001·9 (ii) 8,001	1·9 1·0	5,701·9 3,001	2,300 5,000	2·3 5·0

land employed rises from 2,999 to 3,000 to 3,001 (column *a*). We suppose that the corresponding output of apples is as shown in column *c*. From this we can deduce the marginal product of land (column *d*) which is 2 apples for the 3,000th unit of land, since increasing the amount of land by 1 unit from 2,999 to 3,000 has increased the output of apples by 2 units from 7,998 to 8,000. But the marginal product of land falls as more and more land is used with the same amount of labour, so that the increase of land by 1 more unit from 3,000 to 3,001 causes an increase in the output of apples by something less than 2. Here we have assumed two cases. In case i the marginal product falls only slightly to 1·9, and in case ii it falls a lot to 1.

Now if we suppose that there are constant returns to scale we can from the figures in columns *a*, *b*, *c*, and *d* of the example derive the marginal product of the other factor labour. This is done in columns *e*, *f*, and *g*. Now we know that where there are constant returns to scale, the payment to each factor of a reward equal to the value of its marginal product will just absorb the whole of the product, neither more nor less (pp. 34–36). The figures in column *e* of our numerical example show how much the rent of land would absorb if land were paid a reward equal to its marginal product, these figures being derived by multiplying the amount of land in column *a* by its marginal product in column *d*. The difference between the total output of column *c* and the rent of land of column *e* is what is left over to pay in wages of labour, and this is shown in column *f*. But if there are constant returns to scale, this wage bill of column *f* will be just sufficient to pay each worker a reward equal to the value of his marginal product, so that the figure in column *f* divided by the number of workers in column *b* will give the marginal product of labour which is shown in column *g*.

Now it is to be observed that when as in case i the marginal product of land falls by 0·1 of an apple (i.e. from 2 to 1·9), the marginal product of labour rises by 0·3 of an apple (i.e. from 2 to 2·3). Similarly, when as in case ii the marginal product of land falls by 1 (i.e. from 2 to 1), the marginal product of labour rises by 3 (i.e. from 2 to 5). Generally speaking, one can say that where land is three times as important as labour in the sense that the total reward of all the land employed (6,000 apples) is three times as great as the total reward of all the labour employed (2,000 apples), then the proportionate change in the marginal product of labour will be three times as great as the proportionate change in the marginal product of land.[1]

By putting these two propositions together it can be seen how, when both labour and land move from the blanket industry to the apple

[1] Let $A = F(M, L)$ represent the production function for apples where A is the output of apples, and M is the amount of labour and L the amount of land employed. By differentiation $dA = F_m \,.\, dM + F_l\, dL$, where $F_m \left(\equiv \frac{\delta A}{\delta M}\right)$ is the marginal product of labour and F_l the marginal product of land. With constant returns to scale the production function is homogeneous of the first degree, so that $A = F_m \,.\, M + Fl \,.\, L$. Differentiating this equation we have $dA = F_m \,.\, dM + M \,.\, dF_m + Fl \,.\, dL + L \,.\, dFl$. Combining these two expressions for dA we have $M \,.\, dF_m = - L \,.\, dFl$.

This can be expressed as:

$$-\frac{\dfrac{dF_m}{F_m}}{\dfrac{dFl}{Fl}} = \frac{Fl\, L}{F_m\, M}$$

In other words, the ratio between the proportionate change in the marginal product of labour and the proportionate change in the marginal product of land will be equal to the ratio between the total rents and the total wages paid in the industry concerned.

industry in country A, the marginal social net product of each factor in the apple industry falls relatively to its marginal social net product in the blanket industry. As both labour and land move, the ratio of land to labour will fall in both industries; even though the blanket industry gives up more than its normal ratio of land to labour (thus causing some fall in the ratio of the remaining land to labour in the blanket industry), the additional factors received by the apple industry represents a fall in the ratio of land to labour in that industry because the initial ratio of land to labour employed there is so high. As the ratio of land to labour falls in the apple industry the marginal social net product of land in terms of apples rises and of labour falls; but since land is the important factor in this industry, the rise in the marginal social net product of land is small and the fall in the marginal social net product of labour is large. In the blanket industry also the ratio of land to labour employed has fallen, and in consequence the marginal social net product of land has risen and of labour has fallen; but in this industry labour is the important factor, so that the fall in the marginal social net product of labour is small and the rise in the marginal social net product of land is large. We reach, therefore, a state of affairs in which (i) there has been a large fall in the marginal social net product of labour in the apple industry and only a small fall in the blanket industry, and (ii) there has been a small rise in the marginal social net product of land in the apple industry and a large rise in the blanket industry, with the result that for both factors the marginal product will have fallen in the apple industry relatively to the blanket industry.

Thus a new equilibrium may have been reached in A with A continuing to produce some blankets even though the price of a blanket has fallen from, say, 2 to 1½ apples. The shift of labour and land from the blanket industry to the apple industry in A has, by the mechanism just described, caused the marginal product of both factors in A to change from being twice as high in the apple as in the blanket industry to being only 1½ times as high in the apple as in the blanket industry. There will then be no further incentive for either factor to move in either direction because for both of them their new marginal products in the two industries correspond to the new market prices of the two products.[1]

The opposite may have happened in country B. Initially the price of a blanket was 1 apple, and it then rose to 1½ apples. Land and labour in B in consequence move into the blanket industry from the apple industry. This causes a rise in the ratio of land to labour in both industries. As a result the marginal product of land falls in both industries; but it falls little in the apple industry where it is the important factor and

[1] A detailed numerical example of this process of adjustment within A is given in Appendix 5 (pp. 596–9).

much in the blanket industry where it is the unimportant factor. At the same time the marginal product of labour rises in both industries; but it rises much in the apple industry where it is the unimportant factor and little in the blanket industry where it is the important factor. As a result the ratio of the marginal product in the apple industry to the marginal product in the blanket industry rises for both factors from 1 to $1\frac{1}{2}$.

Thus in both countries a new equilibrium is reached in which both countries continue to produce something of both commodities at the same price of $1\frac{1}{2}$ apples for a blanket. But now in both countries for both factors the marginal product in apples is $1\frac{1}{2}$ times the marginal product in blankets. No factor in either country has any further incentive to move, although each country is still producing something of both commodities.

This completes our explanation of the mechanism whereby free trade may lead to a case of no specialization in which countries A and B continue to produce some output of both commodities, apples and blankets, in the free-trade situation.

CHAPTER XX

TRADE AS A SUBSTITUTE FOR FACTOR MOVEMENTS: (1) THE CASE EXPLAINED

WE are now in a position to turn to the main issues to be discussed in this Part. In Part II we considered the trade policies which were necessary to maximize economic welfare. In Chapter IX we saw that the basic argument for free trade was that it would set the marginal conditions which were necessary to ensure economic welfare through the optimization of trade and the maximization of production, on condition that modified laissez-faire policies were adopted within each country so that each factor of production was offered in each industry a reward equal to the value of its marginal social net product and was free, in the search for the highest reward, to move where its marginal product was highest. But the maximization of production which we discussed in Part II was the maximum level of world production which could be reached subject to the limitation that, while every factor was completely free within each country to move in search of the highest reward and so to the point at which its marginal product was the highest, it was completely unable to move from one country to another.

The maximization of production which we were discussing in Part II was therefore a limited one. The best choice of trade policies discussed in that Part could not be aimed at avoiding the possibility that the marginal product of, say, labour might be higher in, say, the apple industry in A than in B. In this case an unqualified maximization of world production would involve the movement of a unit of labour from B (where the marginal product of labour was, say, 1 apple) to A (where it was 2 apples), thus adding a net output of 1 apple to world production.

In this chapter we shall continue the assumption that in each country a policy of modified laissez-faire is adopted domestically so that within each country each factor in each industry is offered a reward equal to the value of its marginal social net product and is free to move to its point of highest reward. We shall suppose also that there is free trade at least in certain commodities between A and B. We wish to inquire how probable it is that in these circumstances situations may still arise in which the marginal product of any one factor in any one industry will remain higher in one country than another so that the full maximization of world production would require the free movement of factors of production not only domestically within each country but also internationally between the trading countries.

Now there are certain conditions in which the need for these international factor movements will in fact never arise, so that complete immobility of factors of production between countries would not in fact interfere at all with the maximization of production. Such a situation would arise if—in addition to the assumption that domestic policy is such that each factor always moves domestically from a job in which the value of its marginal social net product is lower to one in which it is higher—the following five conditions are fulfilled:

(1) First, it must be assumed that there is only a limited number of different factors of production. We will discuss this assumption more precisely later on and in particular in Chapter XXIII. For the time being we will assume that there are only two factors of production, namely land and labour.

(2) Second, the production functions in all industries must be the same in both our countries. This means that if the employment of 100 men and 100 acres of land would produce 100 apples in A, then 100 men and 100 acres of land would produce 100 apples in B. And similarly for any other combination of factors in this or in any other industry: any given combination of factors in any given industry would produce the same output in A as it would in B. In other words the atmosphere for production is the same in both countries.

(3) The production functions must be of a certain kind. We assume that in every industry some labour and some land is needed for production. Moreover, we assume that there are constant returns to scale in all industries in both countries. We have already discussed the meaning of this assumption in Chapter III (see pp. 32–43). It means that if the amounts of labour and of land were both increased by 10 per cent in any industry in either country, then the output of that industry in that country would also be increased by 10 per cent. A further implication of the assumption of constant returns is, as we have seen, that the marginal product of any one factor in any one industry depends solely upon the proportion in which it is employed with other factors and not at all upon the scale of production. We assume that the higher the ratio of labour to land employed in any one industry, the lower will be the marginal product of labour and the higher the marginal product of land (see pp. 37–38).

(4) There must be at least two internationally traded products for which the costs of transport are negligible and which are produced in common in both countries.

(5) Among the internationally traded products which satisfy the conditions laid down immediately above in (4) there must be at least two of which one is always relatively land-intensive and the other always relatively labour-intensive in production. The meaning of these terms is straightforward. To take an example, the production of apples would always be land-intensive and of blankets labour-intensive, if,

given any single wage rate and any single rate of rent at which labour and land were available for employment in either industry, it would always pay to use a higher ratio of land to labour in the production of apples than in that of blankets.

Now, it can be shown that in these conditions free trade in the two products mentioned in (5) will itself bring about a situation in which the marginal product of any one factor of production in any one industry is the same in both country A and country B, even if there is complete immobility of factors of production between A and B. In this case, therefore, there will be no need for any international movement of factors of production in order to achieve the maximization of production.

Suppose then that apples and blankets are produced in both countries, that their costs of transport are negligible, that there is free trade in apples and blankets so that the price of each is the same in both countries, and that apples are always relatively land-intensive and blankets labour-intensive in production. Our first step is to show that the money price of each factor of production must be the same in both countries, i.e. that the money wage rate must be the same in A as in B and the money rate of rent must be the same in A as in B.

It can very readily be seen that free trade between A and B may well tend to make the rewards paid to the factors of production approach more nearly to equality in A and in B than would be the case in the absence of trade between A and B. Thus suppose that A has much land and little labour, and B has much labour and little land. Suppose further that apples require much land and little labour and that blankets require much labour and little land in their production. In the absence of trade the plentiful supply of land and the scarce supply of labour is likely to make land cheap and labour expensive in A; and this will make it cheap to produce apples in A (in which the cheap factor land is important) and expensive to produce blankets in A (in which the expensive factor labour is important). Conversely, in B land (and in consequence apples) will be expensive and labour (and so blankets) will be cheap.

When trade is opened up, B will import A's cheap apples and A will import B's cheap blankets. This will lead to an increased demand for apples produced in A and a decreased demand for blankets produced in A. This will represent indirectly an increased demand for land and a reduced demand for labour in A, so that the rent of land will tend to rise and the wage of labour to fall in A. Conversely in B there will be an increased demand for B's blankets for export to A and a reduced demand for B's apples which are being replaced by imports from A. This will represent a reduced demand for land and an increased demand for labour in B, and rents will tend to fall and wages to rise in B.

Thus the differences between the rewards of the factors in the two countries will tend to close. Rents which were low in A and high in B will tend to rise in A and to fall in B. Wages which were high in A and low in B will tend to fall in A and to rise in B. What we wish to show now is that on the five assumptions enumerated on p. 332 this tendency will go on until the money wage rate is the same in A as in B and the money rate of rent is the same in A as in B.

Consider the equilibrium which is finally reached after free trade has been established between A and B. There will be certain factor prices in B. This will mean that there is a certain cost for each product in B (the cost of each product in B will depend only on the price of the factors because scale of production is assumed to make no difference to costs). Since we are assuming that there is perfect competition in B and that both products are produced in B, the prices of the products in B will be equal to these costs of production. Since we are assuming international trade which is free and costless for apples and blankets, the price of apples and blankets in A will be the same as in B. Since we are assuming that there is perfect competition in A and that both commodities are produced in A, the costs of apples and blankets in A will be the same as their prices in A. It follows, therefore, that the cost of an apple must be the same in A as in B and the cost of a blanket must be the same in A as in B.

Now if the wage rate were the same in A as in B and the rate of rent were the same in A as in B, then the cost of apples would be the same in A as in B, since product costs depend solely on factor prices when scale of production and the geographical location of production are both irrelevant. And similarly, the cost of blankets would in these conditions be the same in A as in B. Thus if factor prices were equal, free trade between A and B in apples and blankets will be compatible with the continued production of both products in both countries, since the cost of production would be the same in both countries. But it is not enough for us to show that if the factor prices were the same in both countries, then the product costs would be the same in both countries. What we have to show is that if the product prices and so the product costs are the same in both countries, then the factor prices must be the same in both countries.

But suppose now that the prices of the factors in B, and so the costs and the prices of the two traded products apples and blankets in A and B, are given at their final free-trade equilibrium levels. Might the wage rate nevertheless remain higher in A than in B? We can see at once that if the wage rate in the free-trade equilibrium position remains higher in A than in B, then the rate of rent must remain lower in A than in B. For, when scale of production and the geographical location of production are irrelevant, costs depend solely on factor prices. If, therefore, the wage rate were higher in A than in B and the rate of rent were not lower in A than in B, the cost of every product would be higher in A than in B. A would import all freely tradable products and would export nothing. Her balance of payments would not be in equilibrium and the prices and costs of all her products would have to fall relatively to the prices and costs of B's products.

Thus if the wage rate does remain higher in A than in B, the rate of rent must remain lower in A than in B. Let us revert to the case in which the wage rate and the rate of rent is the same in A as in B, so that the cost of apples (and of blankets) is the same in A as in B. Suppose then that the wage rate rises and the rate of rent falls in A. If a rise in the wage rate always caused the cost of labour-intensive blankets to rise more than the cost of land-intensive apples, and if a fall in the rate of rent always caused the cost of land-intensive apples to fall more than the cost of labour-intensive blankets, then this rise of the wage rate and fall of the rate of rent in A would raise the cost of A's blankets relatively to that of her apples. But since the prices of B's apples and blankets are unchanged, this rise in the cost of blankets relatively to the cost of apples in A would be incompatible with our free-trade equilibrium. There would be a still further shift of demand away from A's on to B's blankets and away from B's on to A's apples. Thus the forces tending to equalize factor prices would continue to operate until factor prices were actually the same in both countries.

In other words, if we can show that in either country a rise in the wage rate or a fall in the rate of rent will raise the cost of the labour-intensive product (blankets) relatively to that of the land-intensive product (apples), we have completed the proof that on the five assumptions given on p. 332 the price of each factor must be the same in A as in B.

Now it may at first sight appear obvious that a rise in the wage rate in A will cause the cost of the labour-intensive product (blankets) to go up relatively to that of the land-intensive product (apples). This would certainly be the case if it were impossible to substitute labour for land or land for labour in either industry. Suppose that the proportion of the total cost which is made up of wages is 45 per cent in the apple industry and 55 per cent in the blanket industry. Suppose then that the wage rate rises by 10 per cent and that it is impossible for technical reasons to alter the amounts of land or labour used in either industry to produce a unit of product. Then the cost of land will remain the same in both industries and the cost of labour will rise by 10 per cent in both industries. In other words the cost of apples will go up by 4·5 per cent and that of blankets by 5·5 per cent. The cost of the labour-intensive product will necessarily rise relatively to that of the land-intensive product.

But if land and labour can be substituted for each other in the two industries the result is not quite so clear. When the wage rate rises the cost of each product would go up by the rise in the wage rate multiplied by the amount of labour employed, if production were continued with the old methods and the old proportions of labour to land. But in so far as it is technically possible to substitute land for labour (e.g. to produce apples by farming more extensively with less labour but more land), some part of this rise in cost can be avoided. The producer will find that at the higher rate of wages it pays him to take on less of the relatively expensive labour and more of the relatively cheap land, in order to avoid some part of the increase in cost which the higher wage rate would otherwise entail. Suppose that for technical reasons there are greater opportunities available to the blanket-producer than to the apple-producer for the avoidance of increases in cost by the substitution of a relatively cheap for a relatively dear factor. May it not be possible now for a rise in wage rates to cause a greater increase in the cost of the land-intensive apples than of the labour-intensive blankets? True, the blanket-producer loses more than the apple-producer through the rise in wage rates in so far as his wage-bill is a higher proportion of his total

TABLE XXVIII

The Effect upon the Cost of Production of a Rise in the Rate of Wages

	Rate of		Amount of factors required to produce one unit of output		Ratio of labour to land	Cost of		
	wages	rent	labour	land		labour	land	both factors
	$	$	men	acres	men per acre	$	$	$
	(*a*)	(*b*)	(*c*)	(*d*)	(*e*) $= c \div d$	(*f*) $= a \times c$	(*g*) $= b \times d$	(*h*) $= f + g$
				(i) The apple industry				
(1A)	1·0	1·0	45	55	0·82	45	55	100
(2A)	2·0	1·0	45 − 15 = 30	55 + 15 = 70 55 + 30 = 85	0·42 0·35	60	70 85	130 145
(3A)	1·01	1·0	45 − 3 = 42	55 + 3 = 58 55 + 3·03 = 58·03	0·72 0·72	42·42	58 58·03	100·42 100·45
				(ii) The blanket industry				
(1B)	1·0	1·0	55	45	1·22	55	45	100
(2B)	2·0	1·0	55 − 19 = 36	45 + 19 = 64 45 + 38 = 83	0·56 0·43	72	64 83	136 155
(3B)	1·01	1·0	55 − 5 = 50	45 + 5 = 50 45 + 5·05 = 50·05	1·00 1·00	50·5	50 50·05	100·50 100·55

costs; but he can avoid more of this increase in cost than can the apple-producer in so far as he has a greater opportunity of saving cost by shifting from expensive labour to cheap land. May he not be able to save so much more than the apple-producer by such substitution of land for labour that his costs rise less although his product remains the labour-intensive product?

Table XXVIII is designed to show the answer to this question. In row 1A we assume that the wage rate and the rate of rent are both \$1 (columns *a* and *b*); that the apple-producer employs 45 men and 55 acres of land (columns *c* and *d*) or a ratio of 45/55 or 0·82 men per acre (column *e*) to produce 1 apple. This means that he pays \$1 × 45 in wages and \$1 × 55 in rent (columns *f* and *g*), making up a total cost of \$100 for an apple (column *b*). In row 1B we assume that the initial conditions in the blanket industry are exactly the same except that 55 men and 45 acres (instead of 45 men and 55 acres as in the apple industry) are employed to produce 1 blanket. The cost of an apple and the cost of a blanket are initially both \$100; but the blanket industry is labour-intensive relatively to the apple industry. In the blanket industry the number of men per acre is 1·22 (row 1B column *e*) as compared with 0·82 in the apple industry.

Suppose now that the wage rate rises from \$1 to \$2 (rows 2A and 2B, column *a*). What may be the effects upon the cost of production in the two industries? Let us first consider the apple industry (row 2A). We suppose that the rise in the cost of labour causes the apple-farmer to take on less of the more expensive labour to produce 1 apple and to take on more of the land whose price has not gone up to take the place of the dismissed labour. Simply for illustrative purposes we suppose that he reduces his labour force by 15 from 45 to 30 (row 2A, column *c*). We can immediately say that his labour cost per apple will be \$2 × 30 or \$60 (column *f*). But what will have happened to his land cost? This will clearly depend upon the amount of extra land which he must take on to replace the 15 units of labour which he has dismissed. This in turn will depend upon the technical conditions of production in the apple industry. All we can do is to lay down a lower and an upper limit for the amount of extra land which he must take on. These limits are determined in the following manner.

We can regard the large rise in the wage rate from \$1 to \$2 as being made up of a series of, say, 100 small rises from \$1 to \$1·01, from \$1·01 to \$1·02, and so on. In perfect competition the wage rate is equal to the value of the marginal product of labour and the rate of rent is equal to the marginal product of land. It follows that at the outset (row 1A) when the wage rate and the rate of rent are both \$1, he will be employing labour and land in such a ratio (namely 45 men to 55 acres) that the marginal product of labour is equal to the marginal product of land. A this point, therefore, he must replace each unit of labour which he dismisses with 1 extra unit of land in order to continue to produce 1 apple. But as the amount of labour is reduced and the amount of land is increased, the ratio of labour to land will fall; and for this reason, as we have seen (p. 38), the marginal product of labour will rise and that of land will fall. When the wage rate has risen to $1·01, the rate of rent remaining at $1, he will be employing a lower ratio of labour to land such that the marginal product of labour is 1 per cent higher than the marginal product of land. Otherwise the value of the marginal product of each factor would no longer be equal to its price. At this point, therefore, in the process of rising wage rates he must replace each unit of labour dismissed by 1·01 units of land. To keep a constant output of 1 apple he must take on 1·01 land to replace each unit of labour, when the product lost by losing 1 unit of labour is 1·01 as great as the product gained by taking on 1 more unit of land.

Thus as the wage rate rises, the ratio of labour to land falls, and the marginal product of labour rises and of land falls. At each successive stage a larger amount of extra land must be taken on to replace each unit of labour which is dismissed. At the end of the process (row 2A) when the wage of labour ($2) is twice as high as the rent of land ($1), the marginal product of labour will be twice as high as the marginal product of land. At this last stage, therefore, for every unit of labour dismissed 2 extra units of land must be employed.

Now of the 15 units of labour which we are assuming to be dismissed when the wage rate rises from $1 to $2, some part will be replaced at the early stages of the process when only 1 unit of land need be taken on to replace each unit of labour, and some will be replaced at the late stages of the process when 2 units of land must be taken on to replace each unit of labour. Thus the 15 units of labour will in fact be replaced by something between 15 and 30 units of land.

In other words, something between 70 (55 + 15) and 85 (55 + 30) units of land will now be needed (row 2A, column *d*). We can now immediately show the lower and upper limits of the new rent cost of producing 1 apple. These are $1 × 70 and $1 × 85 (row 2A, column *g*). It follows that the total cost of producing an apple will lie between $60 + $70 or $130 and $60 + $85 or $145 (row 2A, column *h*). If the technical conditions in apple production were such that the substitution of land for labour could all take place at an early stage in the process of rising wage rates when the marginal product of land was not much higher than that of labour, then the new cost will be near the lower limit of $130. If, on the other hand, most of the substitution could take place only when the marginal product of labour had risen and that of land had fallen a lot, the new cost would be near the upper limit of $145.

Now these two limits to the rise in the cost of apples which is brought about by the rise of wage rates by $1 can be considered in a slightly different way. After the change 30 units of labour are employed. On these 30 units of labour there will be a rise in wages of $30, since each unit of labour costs $2 instead of $1. Now if the dismissed 15 units of labour could all be replaced at an early stage of the process of rising wage rates by 15 units of land, each costing only $1, then there would be no further rise of cost. But if each unit of labour had to be replaced at the end of the process by 2 units of land each costing $2, there would in fact be no saving at all from the substitution. The rise in cost would be exactly the same as if no substitution were possible, and would be equal to the rise in the wage rate from $1 to $2 on all the 45 units of labour initially employed. The final rise in the cost is, therefore, something in between $30 (which is the rise of the wage rate of $1 on all the labour *finally* employed after the substitution takes place) and $45 (which is the rise of the wage rate of $1 on all the labour *initially* employed). This result is of general validity. When the price of a factor rises, the ultimate increase in cost will be something in between the rise in the price of the factor reckoned on the amount of that factor which is initially employed and the rise in the price of that factor reckoned only on the amount of that factor which is finally employed after other factors have been substituted for it to the maximum extent which is economic in view of the technical conditions of production.

We can now apply exactly the same analysis to the blanket industry (rows 1B and 2B of Table XXVII). When the wage rate rises by $1 from $1 to $2 we assume that the amount of labour which is dismissed is 19 (row 2B, column *c*). The new labour cost of producing 1 blanket is therefore 36 units of labour at the new wage rate of $2 or $72 (column *f*). When 19 units of labour are dismissed, something between 19 and 2 × 19 or 38 units of land must be taken on to replace it (column *d*), so that the new rent cost of producing a blanket is something between $1 × 64 and $1 × 83, i.e. between $64 and $83 (column *g*). Thus the total cost of producing a blanket is something between $72 + $64 or $136 and $72 + $83 or $155 (column *h*). Once again we see that the rise in cost is something between the rise in the wage rate of $1 on the 36 units of labour employed *after* the rise in wage rates and the rise in the wage rate of $1 on the 55 units of labour employed *before* the rise in wage rates.

The numerical example which we have chosen in rows 2A and 2B is so devised that the ratio of labour to land (column *e*) is higher in the blanket industry than in the apple industry both before and after the change in the wage rate. Before the change the number of men per acre was 1·22 in the blanket industry and 0·82 in the apple industry (rows 1B and 1A, column *e*). After the rise in wage rates the number of men per acre is between 0·56 and 0·43 in the blanket industry and between

0·42 and 0·35 in the apple industry (rows 2B and 2A, column *e*). The blanket industry is the labour-intensive industry both before and after the change.

Yet even so, it does not necessarily follow that the cost of blankets will have gone up more than the cost of apples as a result of the rise in wage rates. All that we can say is that the cost of apples has gone up by something between 30 and 45 per cent (row 2A, column *h*) while the cost of blankets has gone up by something between 36 and 55 per cent. If the rise in the cost of apples were near its upper limit of 45 per cent and the rise in the cost of blankets were near its lower limit of 36 per cent, the rise in the cost caused by a rise in wage rates would be higher in the case of apples than in the case of blankets even though blankets were the labour-intensive product both before and after the rise in wage rates.

What is the explanation of this apparent paradox? It rests upon the fact that assumption 5 on p. 332 does not merely require that the blanket industry should be the labour-intensive industry, both at the low wage rate of $1 and at the high wage rate of $2. It requires also that the blanket industry should be the labour-intensive industry at every wage rate in between $1 and $2 as well. We can show that if this requirement is also fulfilled then the cost of blankets must go up more than the cost of apples.

That this is probable can be seen in the following way. If the cost of apples goes up almost by its upper limit of 45 per cent, this, as we have seen, means that as the wage rate begins to rise (from $1 to $1·01, for example) very little substitution of land for labour is profitable. Such substitution becomes profitable on an important scale only when the wage rate has risen nearly to $2 (say to $1·90), at which point, of course, very little can be gained in cost reduction by the substitution. On the other hand, if the cost of blankets goes up by little more than its lower limit of 36 per cent, this means that the greater part of the substitution of land for labour in the blanket industry can profitably take place when the wage rate has risen only a little (say to $1·10) so that great economy results from the substitution. It is, therefore, not unlikely that at a wage rate of, say, $1·10, the blanket industry will be the land-intensive product (since a large substitution of land for labour takes place in the blanket industry at that wage rate), whereas at a wage rate of, say, $1·90 the apple industry will have become the land-intensive industry once again (since a substantial substitution of land for labour takes place in the apple industry at this late stage in the process of rising wage rates).

A more complete proof of the proposition that if the blanket industry is labour-intensive not only at wage rates of $1 and of $2 but at every intermediate wage rate, then the cost of blankets must rise more than the cost of apples, is provided in rows 3A and 3B of Table XXVIII.

We start (rows 1A and 1B) with a wage rate of $1 and with apples the land-intensive and blankets the labour-intensive product. Let us now consider the rise in the wage rate from $1 to $2 as taking place by a series of successive small rises. Now we have assumed (row 2B, column *c*) that when the wage rate rises from $1 to $2 the amount of labour employed to produce 1 blanket will be reduced by 19. This reduction in the labour employed and its replacement by land will in fact take place some of it when the wage has risen to $1·1, some when the wage has risen to $1·2, and so on. In other words, the smaller the rise in the wage rate above $1 the smaller will be the amount of labour which will have been dismissed and replaced by land in the production of a blanket. Let us consider any rise in the wage rate above $1 which is sufficiently small not to reduce the amount of labour still used to produce 1 blanket below the amount of labour initially used to produce 1 apple. Thus we assume, purely for purposes of illustration, that a rise in the wage rate to $1·01 (row 3B, column *a*) will cause the amount of labour employed in producing 1 blanket to be reduced by 5, which means that the smaller amount of labour now used to produce 1 blanket, i.e. 50 units (row 3B, column *c*), still remains higher than the amount of labour used at the old wage rate of $1 to produce 1 apple, i.e. 45 units (row 1A, column *c*).

We can now see at once that this small rise in the wage rate from $1 to $1·01 must have raised the cost of blankets more than the cost of apples. The *upper* limit to the rise in the cost of apples is, as we have seen, the old amount of labour used to produce 1 apple, i.e. 45, multiplied by the rise in the wage rate of $0·01, or $0·45 (row 3A, column *h*).[1] The *lower* limit to the rise in the cost of blankets is, as we have seen, the new amount of labour employed to produce 1 blanket, i.e. 50, multiplied by the rise in the wage rate of $0·01, or $0·50 (row 3B, column *h*). The rise in the cost of blankets must, therefore, be greater than the rise in the cost of apples.

We have shown, therefore, that if blankets are labour-intensive and if we concern ourselves with a rise in the wage rate which is not so large as to cause the new labour component in the production of 1 blanket to fall below the old labour component in the production of 1 apple, then the rise in the wage rate will raise the cost of a blanket relatively

[1] The figures in row 3A are constructed on exactly the same principle as the figures in row 2A. We assume that the amount of labour dismissed from the production of one apple when the wage rate rises to $1·01 is 3 units (column *c*). This must be replaced by something between 3 and 1·01 × 3 units of land (column *d*). The wage cost is therefore 42 × $1·01 (column *f*) and the rent cost is something between 58 × $1 and 58·03 × $1 (column *g*), giving a new total cost of between $100·42 and $100·45 (column *h*). We are concerned only with the highest possible rise in the cost of apples which is $0·45, or the amount of labour employed at the start (45) multiplied by the rise in the wage rate ($0·01).

to that of 1 apple. In other words, if blankets are labour-intensive at any given wage rate, a moderate rise in the wage rate will raise the cost of blankets more than that of apples.

Now assumption 5 on p. 332 requires that blankets should be labour-intensive at every wage rate. It follows, therefore, that at every possible wage rate between $1 and $2 a moderate rise in the wage rate will raise the cost of blankets relatively to that of apples. But suppose that the wage rate rose continuously from $1 to $2. If at every single possible wage rate in between these limits a further moderate increase in the wage rate caused a further rise in the cost of blankets relatively to the cost of apples, then it follows at once that the complete rise of the wage rate from $1 to $2 must have raised the cost of blankets relatively to that of apples.

We have, therefore, shown that if blankets are the labour-intensive product at every single wage rate, then a rise in the wage rate will raise the cost of blankets relatively to that of apples. We could by an exactly similar process of reasoning show that in the same conditions a fall in the rate of rent will lower the cost of apples relatively to that of blankets.

We have now completed the formal proof of the proposition that on the assumptions enumerated on p. 332 free trade in products will be sufficient to equalize the prices of the factors of production. But it may be useful very briefly to recapitulate the stages of the argument.

In the free-trade position there will be certain prices of the factors in B. These factor prices in B will lead to certain costs of each product in B, which are independent of the scale of production in either industry in B. Since both products are produced in B and there is perfect competition in B, the prices of the products in B will be equal to these costs of production. Since there is free and costless trade, the prices of the products will also be at this same level in A. Since both products are produced in A and there is perfect competition in A, the costs of production of these products in A will be equal to these prices which are set by B's costs of production.

If the factor prices were the same in A as in B, then, since scale of production is irrelevant in A as well as in B and the production functions are the same in A as in B, the costs of production of the products would be the same in A as in B, and this would therefore be a situation which was compatible with all the assumptions on p. 332.

But suppose that the wage rate were higher in A than in B, then clearly the rate of rent must be lower in A than in B; otherwise the cost of every product would be higher in A than in B. But, as we have just shown, a rise in the wage rate and a fall in the rate of rent both combine to raise the cost of blankets relatively to that of apples, since blankets are labour-intensive at every given rate of wages and rate of rent. It follows that a higher wage rate and lower rate of rent in A could not leave the costs of both apples and of blankets in A equal to their costs in B. So long as the wage rate remained higher in A than in B, consumers in both countries would have an incentive still further to shift their purchases of blankets from A's producers to B's producers and their purchases of apples from B's producers to A's producers. Equilibrium would not yet have been attained. A difference in the money rate of wages or in the money rate of rent as between A and B must, therefore, be incompatible with one or other of the assumptions enumerated on p. 332.

We can now proceed easily to the conclusion that the marginal product of any one factor (say, labour) will be the same in any one of our two traded products (say, apples) in A and in B. Since the wage rate and the rent rate are the same in both countries and since the conditions of production are the same in both countries, being affected neither by the scale of output in either country nor by productive atmosphere in either country, apples will be produced with the same combination of land and labour in each country. But since the marginal product of labour in the apple industry depends only upon the amount of land with which it co-operates (assumption 3 on p. 332), the marginal product of labour in terms of apples will be the same in A as in B. And, similarly, for the marginal product of labour in terms of blankets and for the marginal product of land in terms of apples or of blankets. The marginal product of each factor in terms of each product will be the same in A as in B.[1]

We have now shown that, on the assumptions listed on p. 332, the money wage rate will be the same in A as in B and the money rate of rent will be the same in A as in B. From this we can also deduce that the marginal product of any one of our two factors (say, labour) will be the same in A as in B, not merely in either of our two special free-trade industries (apples and blankets) but also in every industry which is common to both A and B. Consider house-building, an industry whose product cannot be internationally traded. Once again assumptions 2 and 3 state that the scale of house-building and the atmosphere and locality in which it takes place are irrelevant. All that can be relevant to the costs and technique of production in house-building is, therefore, the price of labour and capital. Since these are the same in both countries, the ratio of labour to land used in house-building will be the same in both countries, since builders will have no more incentive in the one country than in the other to substitute labour for land or vice versa. Moreover, since the scale of operations is irrelevant, the marginal social net product of labour in house-building will depend

[1] An algebraic proof of these propositions is given in Appendix 6 (pp. 600–1). In Appendix 7 (pp. 602–8) there is a detailed numerical example of these propositions which the reader may peruse if he finds elaborate arithmetical illustrations helpful.

solely upon the amount of capital per head with which it can co-operate. But since the amount of capital employed per unit of labour in house-building will be the same in A as in B, the marginal social net product of labour in house-building will be the same in A as in B.

There remain only those industries which are found in one of our two countries but not in the other. Even in these cases the marginal product of any one of our two factors (say, labour) will be the same in both countries in terms of the products which are produced in only one of the countries. Suppose that carpets are produced in A but not in B. If a carpet industry were started in B with the employment of a small amount of labour, this labour would in fact be employed with the same amount of land per unit of labour as in A. Since the money wage rate and the money rate of rent is the same in both countries and since neither the scale nor the locality of production is relevant to the cost per unit of output (assumptions 2 and 3 on p. 332), it will pay the producer who is setting up a carpet industry in B to use exactly the same processes of production as are being used in A. Labour being equipped with the same amount of land per head and scale and locality of production being irrelevant, the marginal product of labour in the carpet industry in B would be the same as it was in A. In other words, if a unit of labour moved from making carpets in A to making carpets in B, its marginal product in terms of carpets would be the same in both countries.

We have, therefore, shown that on the assumptions listed on p. 332 the marginal product of any one factor in terms of any one product—whether that product be traded or not and whether that product be produced in both countries or not—will be the same in A as in B. It follows that the international movement of factors of production cannot be needed for the maximization of production because the movement of any factor from any given industry in A to the same industry in B would leave world output unchanged.

In Chapters XXI, XXII, and XXIII we shall examine in detail each of the assumptions listed on p. 332 in order to see how important it is in reaching the conclusions of the above argument, in what way its removal would modify those conclusions, and whether it is likely to exist in reality. At this point it may be useful to mention one or two assumptions which are sometimes made in the exposition of the above argument but which are not in fact necessary for its validity.

In the first place, as the form of our argument has shown, there is no need to assume that apples and blankets are the only commodities produced. The argument is seen to be generally valid however many commodities are produced in either country. All that is necessary is that there should be at least two commodities which can be traded freely and without cost and which are produced in both countries.

Secondly, we have in fact assumed in our argument that there are only two countries A and B. But this we have done solely because this volume is so constructed that we are examining only a two-country world until we reach Part IV. Our argument would be equally valid if there were three countries A, B, and C between which the two commodities, apples and blankets, could be freely traded and in each of which there was some production of each of these two commodities. The reason for this can be easily seen. The argument which we have developed in the preceding pages to prove that on the assumptions listed on p. 332 the marginal product of any one factor would be the same in A as in B at no point rested upon the absence of a third country C. And an exactly similar argument could be developed to show that if the stated assumptions were simultaneously satisfied between C on the one hand and the rest of the world A-B on the other hand, the real marginal product of any one factor in C would be the same as in A and B.

In fact this result could be reached on even less stringent assumptions. Suppose that the marginal product of any one factor is the same in A as in B because both countries produce some apples and some blankets, and there is free and costless trade between A and B in these products. Then C might be linked to A because both C and A produced some carpets and some drugs, there being free and costless trade between A and C in these two commodities. In this case, with the other assumptions on p. 332 satisfied, the marginal product of any one factor in C would be the same as in A and, therefore, the same also as in B. Or C might be linked to A-B, the rest of the world, because A and C both produced some carpets, there being free and costless trade in carpets between A and C, and because at the same time B and C both produced some drugs, there being free and costless trade in drugs between B and C. The price of carpets and drugs would be fixed relatively to each other regardless of the existence of C because their cost of production would be the same in A as in B, since A and B are linked together through the common production of, and free trade in, apples and blankets. Therefore, free trade between A and C in carpets and between B and C in drugs would fix the prices of carpets and drugs at the same levels as in A and B and would thus cause the price and the marginal product of any one factor in C to be the same as in A and B.

To summarize, the existence of a third country in no way essentially alters the argument. If the third country C produces something of, and trades freely in, the commodities which link A and B, this is obviously the case. But C can be linked also in other ways to A and B. All that is necessary is that C should produce something of both of two commodities (either or both of which may be, but need not be, one of the commodities which link A to B), that something of each of these two commodities should be produced in at least one of the other countries, that there should be free and costless trade in each of these commodities between C and at least one of the other countries in which that commodity is also produced, and that all the products which serve as links between the three countries should stand in an unchanging order of labour-intensiveness in production.

Finally, the conclusion that the marginal product of any one factor should be the same in both countries does not depend upon there being universal free trade between A and B. The argument of the preceding chapters will be seen to depend only upon there being free trade in the two commodities, apples and blankets, which link the two countries together. There may be heavy protection of national production of any other commodities which might otherwise be traded between them.[1] Prohibition of the trade in carpets, for example, will turn carpets into commodities like houses which are in any case non-tradable because of costs of transport; but, as we have already seen (p. 343), the existence of such commodities does not alter our conclusions.

As we have expressed the argument so far, it might be the case not only that the trade in all other commodities was subject to protective duties or to transport costs but also that both the two critical commodities, apples and blankets, were exported from the same country, say from A to B. The argument in fact depends solely upon there being free and costless trade in these two commodities both of which are produced in both countries; it does not depend upon the direction in which they are traded.

But if all other commodities were subject either to trade taxes or to transport costs, there would in fact be no trade in any products except apples and blankets. We have seen that, on the assumptions made on p. 332, the cost of producing any commodity would be the same in A as in B regardless whether in fact it was at the moment being produced or not in any particular country. It would, therefore, always be more profitable for a product to be produced in the country in which it was going to be consumed, than for it to be imported from the other country if there were any tax or transport cost involved in the trade. If, therefore, the two commodities, apples and blankets, in which there was free and costless trade were both produced in A and exported to B, the balance of trade between A and B would be out of equilibrium. A would be exporting both commodities to B and importing nothing from B. This

[1] The above statement must not be taken to imply that heavy protection in all but two commodities will in no way alter the probability of there being an equality between the marginal product of any one factor in the two countries. On the contrary, it will greatly affect the probability of the remaining two commodities in fact continuing to be produced simultaneously in both countries. (On this see pp. 385–90 below.) All that is maintained in the text is that if the other two commodities continue to be produced in both countries, then the protection of the other industries is irrelevant to the conclusion.

is not an impossible situation if the balance of payments between A and B contains autonomous transfer items from A to B which balance the surplus on A's balance of payments. (See Chapter I of Volume I.) But if equilibrium requires that A's balance of trade should balance, then we can add to assumption 4 on p. 332 the requirement that of the internationally traded products there mentioned at least one must be exported from A and at least one exported from B.

CHAPTER XXI

TRADE AS A SUBSTITUTE FOR FACTOR MOVEMENTS: (2) ATMOSPHERE AND SCALE

THE argument of the preceding two chapters has shown that conditions are conceivable in which freedom of trade in commodities would itself lead to a complete equality between the marginal product of one factor in one industry in A and the marginal product of the same factor in the same industry in B. In this case no international movement of factors would be necessary in order to achieve the maximization of world production; whatever policy of control over factor movements is adopted will be quite irrelevant from this point of view.

But this argument has been based upon a number of very special assumptions which were enumerated in Chapter XX on p. 332. In reality it is very probable that some at least of these assumptions will not be even approximately fulfilled; and if that is so, it will no longer follow that trade is a complete substitute for factor movements. Policies of control over factor movements will become very relevant and important.

Accordingly, it is our purpose in this and the two following chapters to modify each of the assumptions made on p. 332 and to examine the extent to which its modification makes it no longer possible to treat freedom of trade as a complete substitute for freedom of factor movements.

Accordingly, in this chapter we shall consider the modification of assumptions 2 and 3 on p. 332. That is to say, we shall examine what difference is made to the proposition that freedom of trade is a complete substitute for freedom of factor movements when we allow costs to be affected by differences in the atmosphere in which, and the scale on which, products are produced in different countries. As we shall see, the analysis of these two cases is fairly straightforward. But the importance in actual fact of an economic conclusion is not to be judged by the degree of complexity of its analysis; and, in fact, the points raised in this chapter may be among the most important reasons for believing that international factor movements are often of the greatest significance.

Let us suppose then that the general atmosphere is more favourable to production in A than in B. This may be due to the fact that the physical climate is more favourable in A or else to the fact that social arrangements and psychological attitudes are more favourable to high productivity in A.

In such conditions a given amount of land, labour, and capital will produce a larger output in A than in B and, in this sense, it is no longer a matter of indifference whether the factors are situated in A or in B. Suppose, then, that the same ratio of labour to land to capital were employed in each industry in A as in B. Suppose, further, that the favourable atmosphere in A were of general application so that it increased the productivity of each factor in each industry in A by, say, 10 per cent above the productivity of the same factor in the same industry in B. In these special circumstances the price and cost of every product could be the same in both countries and each product could be produced in both countries. The only difference would be that the real marginal product and so the real and the money rewards of each factor would be 10 per cent higher in A than in B. Free trade would thus be compatible with a continuing excess of the marginal product of each factor in A over its level in B.

In order, then, that world production should be maximized it would be desirable in such circumstances that the factors of production which can move from B to A—namely, labour and capital—should so move. The reduction in the output of the industry from which they move in B will be smaller than the increase in the output of the same industry in A, when they move into it.

Land, however, is a factor which cannot be moved from B to A. As labour and capital move from B to A, the marginal product of land in B will become smaller and smaller. Land will be becoming less and less scarce in B relatively to labour and capital; it will be less and less intensively used in every industry in B; and the addition to output which could be achieved in B by having yet a little more land would become smaller and smaller. On the other hand, in A the marginal product of land will be rising higher and higher. As labour and capital move into A, the existing amount of land there will become scarcer and scarcer relatively to labour and capital; it will be more and more intensively used; and the addition to output in A which could be achieved by having yet another small additional amount of land in A will become higher and higher. If the movement of labour and capital from B to A is quite free and costless, a new equilibrium will be reached when the marginal products of labour and land have fallen somewhat below their initial high level in A (because more labour and capital will be crowded on to the same amount of land in A) and have risen somewhat above their initial low level in B (because less labour and capital will be combined with the same amount of land in B). Thus the marginal products and rewards of labour and capital will reach an equality at a level intermediate between their initial high level in the country of favourable atmosphere and their initial low level in the country of unfavourable atmosphere.

But in the case of land the initial discrepancy between the rents of land in A and B will become even more marked as a result of the subsequent movement of labour and capital. The marginal product of land will, as we have seen, rise in A, the country in which it was initially high, because of the inflow of labour and capital into A. Conversely, it will fall in B as labour and capital leave B. In the end the rent of land in A will exceed the rent of land in B by an amount which reflects both the initial advantage which land, like every other factor, enjoys from the better atmosphere for production in A and also the subsequent increased scarcity value of land due to the crowding of more and more of the mobile factors on the limited land of A and the desertion of the mobile factors from the unchanged area of land of B. In fact the mobile factors will have moved up to the point at which the advantage of atmosphere for their use in A is just offset by the disadvantage due to the fact that each unit of the mobile factors has to work with less land in A than in B. When this point is reached, no further increase in world production can be obtained by a further movement of labour and capital from B to A. Such a further increase could now be obtained only if land were able to join in the migration.

In the above example we have confined the analysis to the very simple case in which the difference of atmosphere in A and B is such as to provide an equal advantage for every factor in every industry in A over the same factor in the same industry in B. This, of course, may not be so. The atmosphere for the production of one product (say, blankets) may be better in A than in B while the atmosphere for the production of another product (say, apples) may be more favourable in B than in A. Even more significant from our present point of view is the possibility that the atmosphere for the employment of one factor (say, labour) may be better in A than in B and for another factor (say, capital) may be better in B than in A.

In both these types of case the maximization of world production is likely to need a movement of mobile factors of production between the countries. Suppose A not to be very richly endowed with labour as compared with B, but to be a country in which the atmosphere for labour productivity is very specially favourable. Suppose at the same time that A is rather richly endowed with capital as compared with B, but is a country in which the atmosphere for the use of capital is rather unfavourable. It would be obvious that to maximize world production labour should move from B to A and capital from A to B.

Or suppose A to be a country which has a very low ratio of labour to land and B to be a country with a high ratio of labour to land. Suppose, further, that apples required always a high ratio of land to labour in their production and blankets required a high ratio of labour to land. Suppose, finally, that A possessed an atmosphere which was specially favourable to the production of blankets and B an atmosphere specially favourable to the production of apples. Then on grounds of atmosphere B should concentrate on the production of apples and A on blankets. But B's factor endowment is specially suited to produce blankets and A's to produce apples. What is needed is a migration of labour from B to A until A has the high, and B the low, ratio of labour to land so that the country's factor endowments and their atmospheres are both favourable to one line of specialization.

It is not perhaps necessary to go into any detail in the analysis of these possibilities. It should be clear that where there are significant differences of atmosphere for different productions or employments in the two countries, then the maximization of world production may very well need factor movements as well as product movements between the trading countries. Differences in atmosphere between two countries may clearly make it a matter of real importance that certain factors should be employed in the one country rather than in the other.

The same sort of analysis can be applied to the case in which assumption 3 on p. 332 is modified and in which allowance is made for the fact that the scale on which production takes place in any one country may affect the costs of production. Let us suppose that country A is a much bigger country than country B in the sense that A is endowed with more land, more labour, and more capital than B and can, therefore, produce on a larger scale than B. Suppose, further, that there are increasing returns to scale in all industries due either to the fact that there are important indivisibilities in some of the factors employed or else to the fact that a large scale of production creates a favourable atmosphere for production (see pp. 32–43 above). Suppose, finally, that in both countries, internal policies of modified laissez-faire are adopted so as to make the reward paid to each factor of production equal to the value of its marginal social net product.

The *average* product of the factors would, in the conditions assumed above, be higher in the large country A than in the small country B. Other things being equal, the very fact that all lines of production could be carried out on a large scale in A and only on a small scale in B would give A the advantages of large-scale production and would deprive B of these advantages. Output per unit of factors employed would be higher in A than in B.

But it is not at all certain in which country the *marginal* product of the factors would be the higher. Suppose that the increasing returns were of such a kind that very great economies could be obtained by expanding industries in B beyond their small scale in B, but that all such economies were already fully used up long before industries reached the large scale ruling in A. Then the marginal productivity of factors might be considerably higher in B than in A. The addition of a few more factors in B by increasing the scale of operations might enable important new economies of production to be introduced, so that the additional product due to the additional factors might be very great even though the average output per factor was rather low. On the other hand, suppose that the economies of large-scale production were such that they came significantly into play only when industries were already operating on the large scale ruling in A and that a moderate increase in their size above the very small scale ruling in B would not help significantly to improve their efficiency. In this case the marginal as well as the average productivity of factors would be higher in A than in B. But it is clear that when increasing returns are important it would be a pure coincidence to find that the marginal productivity of factors was the same in the large as in the small country.

Once again we have a situation in which freedom of trade between A and B may lead to an equilibrium in which the marginal product of a given factor of production in a given industry is higher in one country than in the other. Free trade will have caused the price of apples to be the same in A as in B and the price of blankets to be the same in A as in B. As in the case examined in Chapter XX, the ratio of labour to land employed in the apple industry may be the same in A as in B, and similarly for the blanket industry. As a result, in each country the ratio of the marginal product of labour in the apple industry to the marginal product of labour in the blanket industry may be equal to the ratio of the marginal product of land in the apple industry to the marginal product of land in the blanket industry, and this may be equal to the ratio between the price of blankets and the price of apples. In this case in the free-trade position there would be a full domestic equilibrium in each country. The value of labour's marginal product in A, and so the wage of labour in A, would be the same in the apple industry and in the blanket industry.

But the absolute levels of labour's marginal product in A and in B would no longer depend solely upon the ratio in which labour and land were employed. The actual marginal product might be higher in A or in B because of increasing returns to scale, according to whether it made more difference to productivity to expand the scale of operations still more in A (where the scale was already large) or in B (where the scale was still small).

Suppose, merely for the sake of illustration, that the marginal product of factors is higher in A than in B. Then the mobile factor, labour, should move from B to A in order to increase world production. As labour moves, the ratio of labour to land will rise in A and fall in B. This in itself will tend to reduce the marginal product of labour in A (each unit of which will have to co-operate with less and less land) and to raise the marginal product of labour in B (each unit of which will become better and better endowed with land). The marginal product of labour in A may at some point begin to fall considerably because the advantages due to a still further increase in the scale of operations in A are offset by the fact that each unit of labour in A has to work with a smaller and smaller equipment of land; and the marginal product of labour in B may begin to rise as any disadvantages due to a still further decrease in the scale of operations in B are offset by the fact that each unit of labour in B has a larger and larger amount of equipment of land with which to work. A point may well be reached at which the marginal product of labour is the same in A and in B; and at this point no further movement of labour is needed for the maximization of production.

So far we have considered only the case in which the advantages of scale relate to all factors in all industries. But this may not be so. Suppose that economies of large scale occur only in the blanket industry. Suppose that A is the large country and therefore has a larger blanket industry than B even though B exports blankets to A. Suppose, further, that the economies of scale are of such a kind that with the same ratio of labour to land in the blanket industry in A and in B the marginal product of both factors in the blanket industry is higher in A than in B. In other words, further expansion brings more additional economies in A's large industry than in B's small industry.

Now if there is free trade, the price of an apple will be the same in both countries and the price of a blanket will be the same in both countries. If the price of a unit of labour were also the same in both countries and the price of a unit of land were the same in both countries, then the cost of an apple would be the same in both countries (since there are no economies of large scale in the production of apples) but the marginal cost of a blanket would be lower in A than in B (because the factor prices are the same but the marginal products of the factors are higher in A than in B).

In such circumstances the blanket industry in A, in which prices were high relative to marginal costs, would expand and would attract resources from the apple industry in A. Conversely, in B prices would be higher relatively to marginal costs in the apple industry, and the apple industry would expand and would draw factors away from the blanket industry. This would enable A to concentrate more fully on the industry, blankets, in which A had special advantages in increasing the scale of production. But if blankets are always labour-intensive and apples land-intensive, the expansion of the blanket industry in A and the contraction of the apple industry in A will represent an increased demand for labour relatively to land in A. The wage of labour will rise and the rent of land fall. A higher ratio of land to labour will therefore be employed in both industries in A. This will go on until the marginal product of land has fallen and the marginal product of labour has risen in both industries in A to correspond to the new rate of rent and the new wage rate in A.

In B the opposite movement will have taken place. The expansion of the apple industry and contraction of the blanket industry will have increased the demand for land relatively to labour; the rent of land will have risen relatively to the wage of labour; in all industries methods of production will be used which employ more labour and less land; and as a result of the employment of a higher ratio of labour to land the marginal product of land will have risen and of labour will have fallen in both industries.

Free trade will thus lead to a situation in which the marginal product of labour in the apple industry will be lower in B than in A; it was the same in both countries before the changes described above took place, but as a result of those changes it has risen in A and fallen in B. Moreover, the marginal product of labour in blankets will also be higher in A than in B, partly because the marginal economies of scale in the blanket industry in A caused it to be higher before the adjustments just described took place but also because these adjustments will themselves have caused a rise in the marginal product of labour in the blanket industry in A and a fall in its marginal product in that industry in B. Thus once again free trade will leave us with a position in which the marginal product of labour will be higher in A than in B, so that a movement of labour from B to A is needed in order to maximize world production.

The maximization of world production would also require a movement of labour from B to A, if the marginal economies of large-scale production had been in the apple industry in B (instead of in the blanket industry in A). But if the marginal economies of large-scale production had been found in the apple industry in A or in the blanket industry in B (instead of in the blanket industry in A), then the maximization of world production would require a movement of labour from A to B.

The general lines of the analysis are exactly the same as that which has just been developed. We start in each case from the position described in Chapter XX in which there are no economies of large-scale production; in which some apples and some blankets are produced in each country; in which there is free and costless trade; and in which, therefore, the ratio of labour to land employed and so the marginal products of labour and of land in any one industry are the same in A and in B. We now modify this free-trade equilibrium by introducing a marginal economy of large-scale production into (i) the apple industry in B, (ii) the blanket industry in B, and (iii) the apple industry in A.

(i) Because of the marginal economy of large-scale production in the apple industry in B, the marginal cost of apples will be lower relatively to their price in B than in A. The consequent expansion of the apple industry and contraction of the blanket industry in B will raise the price of land relatively to labour in B. More labour per unit of land will be used in blanket production in B, and the marginal product of labour in blankets will fall in B. The blanket industry will, however, expand in A at the expense of the apple industry; the wage of labour will therefore rise relatively to the rent of land; more land per unit of labour will be used in A's blanket industry and the marginal product of labour will therefore rise in A's blanket industry. Since the marginal product of labour in the blanket industry was initially the same in A as in B, it will now be higher in A than in B [1] and a migration of labour from B to A will be necessary in order to maximize world production.

(ii) Because of the marginal economy of large-scale production in the blanket industry in B, the marginal cost of blankets will be low relatively to their price in B as compared with A. The blanket industry will expand and the apple industry will contract in B and the opposite movement will take place in A. This will cause a scarcity of labour in B and of land in A. Apples will be produced with a higher ratio of land to labour in B and with a lower ratio of land to labour in A. The marginal product of labour in the apple industry will thus rise in B and fall in A; and since it was initially the same in both countries, it will now be higher in B than in A.[2] Free trade has thus led to a position in which labour must move from A to B in order to maximize world production.

(iii) In the remaining case there are marginal economies of large-scale production in the apple industry in A, so that the marginal cost of apples will be relatively low in A. The apple industry will expand in A and contract in B, and the blanket industry will contract in A and expand in B. This will cause a scarcity of land in A and of labour in B. The ratio of land to labour employed in the blanket industry will fall

[1] The marginal product of labour in the apple industry will also be higher in A than in B in the absence of an international migration of labour. Initially, it is true, it will be higher in B than in A because of the marginal economies of large-scale production in B's apple industry. But as the expansion of B's apple industry and the contraction of A's apple industry proceed, the marginal product of labour will rise in A's apple industry (because of the increasing ratio of land to labour employed in it) and the marginal product of labour will tend to fall in B's apple industry (because of the falling ratio of land to labour there). The movement must go on until the marginal product of labour in the apple industry is higher in A than in B. This must be so because, for the reasons given in the text, the marginal product of labour in the blanket industry will be higher in A than in B, and with the price of apples the same in A as in B and of blankets the same in A as in B, equilibrium will be reached in the labour markets in the two countries only when the marginal product of labour in A exceeds the marginal product of labour in B by the same amount in both industries.

[2] In this case the marginal product of labour will obviously be higher in B than in A in the blanket industry as well as in the apple industry. It will start higher in B because of the marginal economies of large-scale production in B's blanket industry; it will fall in A because of the increase in the ratio of labour to land in A's blanket industry as that industry contracts; and it will rise in B because of the decrease in the ratio of labour to land in B's blanket industry as that industry expands.

in A and rise in B, so that the marginal product of labour in the blanket industry will fall in A and rise in B. Since it was initially the same in both countries it will now be higher in B than in A.[1] Free trade will lead to a situation in which a movement of labour from A to B is needed in order to maximize world production.

All these are cases in which there is some conflict between the products upon which countries should concentrate their resources in order to make the best use of their initial factor endowments and the products upon which they should concentrate in order to make the most of the economies of large-scale production. Thus in case iii discussed immediately above, even when A has developed her apple industry relatively to her blanket industry sufficiently to allow for the facts that she is well endowed with land relatively to labour and that apples are the land-intensive product, there still exist marginal economies of large-scale production in A's apple industry which do not exist in any other industry. If A is to develop her apple industry still further in order to make the most of these economies, then her industries will on the average have too much labour and too little land relatively to her initial endowment with land and labour. She will then produce in all industries with a relatively low ratio of land to labour as compared with the industries of B; and this is itself a source of economic waste.

In order then to achieve the best results it will be necessary to adjust the initial factor endowments of the two countries (in this case by a migration of labour from A to B) to make them correspond to the ratios in which the factors would be wanted in the two countries when each country concentrated on the products in which it enjoyed the highest marginal economies of large-scale production. By this means alone is it possible to make the best of both worlds: to produce those things for which the country's relative factor endowments and also its scale of production are most appropriate.

In these respects differences of atmosphere for production in different countries and differences of economies connected with the scale of production in different countries are very similar. They both provide possible reasons why factor movements must take place in order to match the actual supply of the country's factors with the factors needed by those industries which are most favoured by the country's conditions of atmosphere or of scale of production.

[1] The argument in the text proves that the marginal product of labour will be higher in B than in A in terms of blankets. But by a process of reasoning analogous to that used in the footnote 1 on p. 355 it can be seen that it will also be higher in B than in A in terms of apples.

CHAPTER XXII

TRADE AS A SUBSTITUTE FOR FACTOR MOVEMENT: (3) TRANSPORT COSTS

ASSUMPTION 4 on p. 332 was to the effect that there were at least two commodities each of which was produced in both countries and for each of which the costs of transport between the two countries were negligible. In this chapter we propose to see how far the conclusions of Chapter XX would need to be modified if we made allowance for the fact that costs of transport of the products which were made in both countries could not be neglected in this manner.

Suppose that A is a country well endowed with land and B a country well endowed with labour, and that apples are a product which require much land in their production and blankets a product requiring much labour. Then *either* (i) A can concentrate her plentiful land on apple production and B her plentiful labour on blanket production, the surplus output of A's apples being exchanged for the surplus output of B's blankets *or* (ii) B's labour can migrate to A until the ratio of labour to land is more nearly equal in both countries, in which case each country can efficiently produce both apples and blankets for its own consumption.[1] Thus either the products can be traded or the factors moved for economic efficiency. But solution i requires the movement of apples from A to B and of blankets from B to A. If in fact costs of transport of products cannot be neglected, these transport costs must be counted against this solution. On the other hand, solution ii requires the movement of labour from B to A; and if the cost of movement of labour is appreciable, this must be counted against the adoption of solution ii.

Thus it is clear that when we make allowance for transport costs we need in some sense to balance the cost of transporting products against the cost of movement of factors in order to see whether trade or factor movements constitute the more economic alternative. Accordingly, in the analysis of this chapter we shall have to concern ourselves with costs of factor movements as well as with the costs of transporting commodities in international trade. For this reason, before we examine the effect of transport costs in international trade upon the results of our analysis in Chapter XX, we must make a few introductory remarks about the cost of movement of factors of production.

We can distinguish between the various factors of production according to the ease with which they can move from country to country. Thus 'land', comprising the actual area of a country, cannot be moved from one country to another, or, at any rate, can be moved only at such

[1] See the conclusion of Appendix 7 (p. 608).

prohibitive cost that the question of its movement never arises. In what follows, therefore, we shall assume that land is immobile between countries no matter how great may be the increased rent which it could obtain in the new country and no matter what policy may be adopted for encouraging or discouraging factor movements.

'Labour', on the other hand, can migrate from B to A, but its movement is not likely to be costless. In the first place, there is the actual physical cost of the transport of the worker and his family from the old to the new place of residence. This is a capital cost since a certain lump sum is needed to purchase the necessary transport services; but it can be converted into a recurrent annual cost at the current rate of interest. Thus if the cost of transport were $1,000 and the rate of interest were 5 per cent, the cost of movement can be reckoned as a recurrent future charge of $50 a year. Moreover, if the rate of interest correctly measures the marginal productivity of capital, we can argue that if the cost of transport is $1,000 and the rate of interest is 5 per cent, then the movement of the worker uses up in transport resources which, if used to supplement the country's capital equipment instead, would have added a future annual output worth $50. This sum can then be compared with the increase in the wage earnings of the worker to see whether the increase in annual earnings would cover the annual interest charge on the cost of movement.[1]

But there may also be other less tangible costs of migration. The worker may prefer to remain in his own country speaking his own language and enjoying his old friends and familiar surroundings even though he could increase his net earnings by moving. Such intangible, but no less real, costs of migration can be reckoned only at the valuation which the worker himself sets upon them. This can be discovered only by observing what margin between net earnings in the new country (i.e. after deduction of the physical costs of movement) and earnings in the old country[2] is necessary to induce a man to move when he is free to do so or not to do so and is fully informed of the possibilities open to him. If he will move in expectation of a 20 per cent improvement in his real standard of living, but not for less, we must say that there is a cost of movement to him, equal to 20 per cent of his annual earnings, involved in the intangible elements of disturbance in the move.

'Capital' is also a factor which can move internationally. But the concept of the cost of the international movement of capital is a little more

[1] The interest charge must, of course, be reckoned in perpetuity and the increase in wage earnings only for the remainder of the wage-earner's working life. But this point can be met by reducing both to a present capital value, i.e. by comparing the cost of transport with the present value of the expected increase in wage earnings over the worker's expected working life.

[2] Both must, of course, be reckoned in real terms, i.e. in terms of money corrected for divergences in the cost of living in the two countries. Some of the problems connected with this will be considered below (pp. 367–74).

difficult and subtle. When capital moves from B to A, this means that a saver of money income in B lends the funds to some borrower in A or himself invests the funds in some enterprise in A; and at a later stage the borrower in A transfers interest on the debt to the owner in B or the profits of the enterprise earned in A are directly transferred to the owner of the enterprise in B. Now we are assuming throughout this volume that by the means discussed in Volume I the balance of payments between A and B is kept in equilibrium, with full employment of domestic resources, through price adjustment of one kind or another.[1] This being so, there must be an excess of exports of goods and services from B to A over the imports of goods and services from A to B during the period when the capital sum is being transferred from B to A, in order that there may be, in the terminology of Volume I, a surplus on B's autonomous trade items to offset the autonomous capital transfer from B to A.

There is thus a monetary and a commercial aspect to the international investment of capital. Suppose that a resident in B invests funds in A instead of in B. The monetary aspect takes the form of the saver purchasing foreign money with his savings in order to invest the funds in some foreign concern or enterprise. In the absence of foreign-exchange controls or taxes on the transfer of funds, these transactions have only a very small real cost, consisting solely in the work which the banker or foreign-exchange dealer must undertake in transferring the funds from one currency to another. The other financial costs and charges would be incurred if the funds were invested in an enterprise in B as well as if it were invested in an enterprise in A.

The tangible costs of the monetary transfer of capital are, therefore, very small. There may be certain intangible costs. A resident in B may prefer to invest his funds in B rather than in A even though the degree of risk attached to the investment is the same in both countries and even though the expected yield on the two is the same. But this is not likely to be of very great importance. Money, unlike men, does not find difficulty in learning foreign languages or feel the pangs of separation from its old surroundings; and the owner of capital funds need not himself move with his capital.[2] We can, for practical purposes, treat the real costs of moving monetary funds as likely to be relatively low. But in so

[1] That is to say, either by the mechanism of the 'gold standard' or by variable exchange rates. See Part IV of Volume I.

[2] It is, of course, possible that, while a given investment in A by a resident of A is equally risky as a given investment in B by a resident of B, the same investment in A *by the resident of B* may be more risky than the given investment in B by the resident of B. The authorities in A may be likely, for example, to treat foreign owners of capital less favourably in matters of taxation and the like than their own residents. But this we shall not treat as a real intangible cost of foreign investment by residents of B, but rather as a part of the policy of control over capital movements exercised by the government of A. There is nothing like a threat of uncompensated expropriation of foreign funds to keep foreign funds from flowing in.

far as they exist they can also be reckoned by the margin between the return on capital in the foreign investment over its return in a home investment of similar risk which would be necessary to induce the movement of funds on the part of a well-informed investor. Thus if such an investor will invest $1,000 at home at 5 per cent per annum but will invest it abroad only if he can get at least $5\frac{1}{4}$ per cent per annum, the cost of movement of the $1,000 of funds may be reckoned as being $2·5 a year.

But when we turn to the real aspect of international investment the problem is very different. The investment of funds in a piece of capital equipment, say a machine, in A instead of in B means that B's exports to A must exceed B's imports from A by an amount equal to the value of the machine. It does not necessarily mean that there must be one more machine exported from B to A. It may take that form, in which case we must take into account the additional costs of transport involved in shipping one more machine from B to A. But it might quite well be the case that A was a country which exported, and B a country which imported, machinery. In this case the investment of capital funds in a machine in A instead of in B might well take the form of the export of one less machine from A to B than would otherwise have been the case. In this case we should have to take into account the saving in the costs of transport due to the fact that one less machine was being moved from A to B.

But the surplus in B's balance of trade may be achieved in a quite different form. It may not involve the export of more, or the import of less, capital goods like machinery, but rather the export of more, or import of less, consumption goods like food and clothing. Suppose that the foreign investment takes the form of building an aerodrome in A rather than in B. It is impossible, or at least prohibitively expensive, to export finished aerodromes from one country to another. But labour and other resources which would have built an aerodrome in B may be used instead to grow wheat, and labour and other resources which would have grown wheat in A may be used instead to build an aerodrome. The surplus in B's balance of trade will then be achieved by B exporting the additional output of wheat to A to make up for A's reduced output of wheat or by B ceasing to import from A an amount of wheat equal to the decline in A's output of wheat and making up for this in her own consumption by the increase in her own domestic output of wheat. In this case again we must take into account the costs of transport of wheat between A and B. In the case in which the surplus on B's balance of trade is brought about by an increase in B's exports of wheat this will involve an additional transport cost, and in the case in which it is brought about by a decrease in B's imports of wheat it will involve a net saving in transport costs.

Transport costs are, thus, involved in the real transfer of capital from A to B. But it should be noted that there is just as likely to be a net saving of transport costs as a net increase in transport costs involved in any real capital movement. There will be a transport cost only in so far as the lending country's exports increase, and a transport saving in so far as its imports decrease. In considering the cost of international capital movements we must, therefore, take into account not only the direct costs involved in the international transfer of the monetary funds, but also the increase or decrease in the costs of transport of the products whose increased or decreased flow between A and B provides the real basis for the transfer of capital funds between the two countries.

But when we are considering costs of transport of products as well as of factors there is another reason for distinguishing between the international migration of labour and the international investment of capital. This is due to the fact that labour is not only a factor of production. Men and women not only provide through their work one of the most important factors of production; their economic welfare, obtained through their enjoyment of goods and services and of leisure, constitutes the end of all economic policy. Thus when labour migrates from country B to country A we must remember that there has moved from B to A not only a certain number of units of a certain productive factor but also a certain number of consumers whose satisfaction is the ultimate end of all economic policy.

It is very different with capital movements. When a man migrates from B to A he takes with him not only his hands to grow wheat but also his mouth to consume wheat. When a machine is installed in A rather than in B, the owner of the machine (who has lent the money to the producer in A) may still reside in B and wish to consume in B the goods and services which can be purchased from the income earned by the capital invested in A. After the change has occurred the effect upon B's balance of trade may be very different in the two cases. After a migration of labour from B to A there will be no need for B's balance of trade to be different from what it was before the change, provided that the labour consumed just the equivalent of its wage income in B before the change and consumes just the equivalent of its wage income in A after the change.[1] But after a movement of capital funds from B

[1] This may not be exactly so. The emigrants from B to A may remit back part of their earnings in A in remittances to members of the family whom they have left behind in B. To this extent the effect is the same as the remittance back from A to B of a dividend earned on an investment of capital made in A by a resident of B. But an emigrant from B to A may, on the other hand, take with him the ownership of some property in land or capital; and after the change he may consume in A instead of in B not only the whole of his wage income but also some income from property as well. The essential point is that consumption of the income earned by a factor is normally located wherever the owner of the factor resides and not where the factor is employed, and the factor and its ownership may be geographically divorced in all cases except—slavery apart—in the case of labour.

to A the consumption of the dividend earnings will still take place in B although they are now earned in A and not in B. There must, therefore, develop a surplus on A's balance of trade in products equal in value to the dividend income to be transferred from A to B. This will take the form of increased exports from A to B if the consumption of the dividends in B is of the sort of thing which A exports or of decreased exports of B to A if the consumption in B is concentrated on the sort of things which B exports. In the former case it will involve the additional transport costs of moving the additional products from A to B; and in the latter case it will involve a saving of transport costs on the products no longer exported from B to A. We shall see in what follows that this may constitute an important difference between the theory of the international migration of labour and that of the international investment of capital.

We are now ready to consider the difference which is made to the analysis of Chapter XX when we allow for the costs of transport of products between A and B. Let us suppose that assumption 4 on p. 332 cannot be exactly fulfilled because there are no two products for which the costs of transport are entirely negligible. But let us suppose that apples (exported by A) and blankets (exported by B) are the two commodities which most nearly fulfil the required conditions. That is to say, each is produced in both countries; and of the products which are produced in both countries these two enjoy the lowest transport costs in relation to their value.

Now if it costs something to send apples from A to B and/or to send blankets from B to A, the market price of blankets in terms of apples will be higher in A than in B. For, to the extent that it costs something to send apples from A to B, the price of apples will be higher in B than in A and, to the extent which it costs something to send blankets from B to A, the market price of blankets will be higher in A than in B. Let us assume, as an example, that because of transport costs 1 blanket exchanges for 1·5 apples in A and for only 0·75 apples in B. If, however, the trade in apples and blankets had been absolutely costless, we should have had a common price for each commodity in both markets and 1 blanket would have exchanged for, say, 1 apple in both A and B.

We shall consider this matter by supposing first of all that trade is costless and that 1 blanket exchanges for 1 apple in both countries, and by supposing that then transport costs arise which raise the price of a blanket to 1·5 apples in A and lower the price of a blanket to 0·75 apples in B. We shall proceed by examining the effect upon the marginal productivity of the factors of production in both countries which is likely to occur as a result of this change.

If—as we are assuming—all the other assumptions on p. 332 are fulfilled, then in the first position in which trade is costless the real rewards and the marginal products of each factor will be the same in both countries. This is the result obtained in Chapter XX. But when transport costs are introduced, this no longer remains true. In A the rise in the price of blankets relatively to the price of apples will cause the blanket industry to expand at the expense of a contraction in the apple industry, this being, of course, the natural result of transport costs which will make it economical for A to become rather more self-supporting in blankets and B rather more self-supporting in apples. Conversely, in B the rise in the price of apples relatively to that of blankets will cause an expansion in the output of apples and a contraction in the output of blankets.

But we are assuming that the blanket industry is labour-intensive and the apple industry is land-intensive. This means that in A the contraction of the apple industry releases a lot of land and the expansion of the blanket industry absorbs a lot of labour. As a result land becomes relatively plentiful in A and labour relatively scarce. In all industries the rent of land falls and the wage of labour rises; methods of production are introduced which involve using more land and less labour; and the marginal product of land falls and of labour rises in all industries, as a larger proportion of land to labour is everywhere employed.

Exactly the opposite will be happening in B where the expansion of the land-intensive apple industry and the contraction of the labour-intensive blanket industry will make land scarce relative to labour, will raise the rent of land relatively to the wage of labour, will cause cheap labour to be substituted for expensive land in all industries, and will thus cause the marginal product of land to rise and of labour to fall in all occupations as a higher ratio of labour to land is everywhere used.

As a result of these changes it will no longer be true that the marginal product of labour in A will be the same as the marginal product of labour in B. It was the same before the introduction of transport costs. But, as we have seen, the introduction of transport costs has caused the marginal product of labour to rise in A and to fall in B. The marginal product of labour is, therefore, now higher in A than in B, and the maximization of world production may therefore require an international migration of labour from B to A.

Table XXIX provides a numerical example of what may have happened. We start from the position in which trade is costless (case i of Table XXIX) and we suppose that in this case the marginal product of each factor is 1 apple and 1 blanket in both countries. As a result 1 apple exchanges for 1 blanket in both countries. But then with the introduction of transport costs the apple industry contracts and the blanket industry expands in country A and, in the way which we have just explained, this involves a rise in the ratio of land to labour in both industries in A so that the marginal product of land falls in both industries in A and of labour rises in both industries in A. We assume in our example in Table XXIX that in A the marginal product of land falls from 1 apple to 0·5 apple and from 1 blanket to 0·$\dot{3}$ blanket, and that the marginal product of labour rises from 1 apple to 2 apples and from 1 blanket to 1·$\dot{3}$ blankets.

In this example we have at work the principle stated above and illustrated already in Table XXVII (see pp. 327–8). Since labour is the unimportant factor in the apple industry, we have assumed that the change in the marginal product of labour in that industry is large relatively to the change in the marginal product of land in that industry. Thus the marginal product of land in the apple industry in A is assumed to fall only by 50 per cent (from 1 to 0·5) whereas the marginal product of labour has risen by twice as great a percentage, namely by 100 per cent (from 1 to 2). Similarly, in the blanket industry in A we have assumed twice as large a change in the marginal product of the unimportant factor, land, as in that of the important factor, labour. In fact the marginal product of land has fallen by $66\frac{2}{3}$ per cent (from 1 to 0·$\dot{3}$) while the marginal product of labour has risen only by $33\frac{1}{3}$ per cent (from 1 to 1·$\dot{3}$). In accordance with the argument developed on p. 328 above, this illustration is, therefore, compatible with an initial ratio of land to labour of 2 to 1 in A's apple industry and of 1 to 2 in A's blanket industry in the free-trade position before the introduction of transport costs.

As a result of these changes the price of blankets will have gone up in A in terms of apples. Thus if the marginal product of land in A is 0·5 in the apple industry and 0·$\dot{3}$ in the blanket industry, then, in order that the rent earned by a unit of land in A should be the same in the two industries, 0·5 apples must exchange for 0·$\dot{3}$ blankets, or 1·5 apples for 1 blanket. Similarly for the wage of labour in A. If the marginal product of labour in A is 2 apples and 1·$\dot{3}$ blankets, then for there to be equilibrium in the labour market 2 apples must exchange for 1·$\dot{3}$ blankets, or once again 1·5 apples for 1 blanket.

We have made similar assumptions in the numerical example given for country B. In B the ratio of land to labour employed has fallen in both industries. The marginal product of labour has therefore fallen and of land has risen in both industries. But the marginal product of labour has fallen more in the apple industry where it is the unimportant factor than in the blanket industry where it is the important factor. And the marginal product of land has risen less in the apple industry where it is the important factor than in the blanket industry where it is the unimportant factor. As a consequence, for there to be equilibrium in the markets for land and labour, i.e. for the earnings of any one factor to be

TABLE XXIX

The Relation between Product Prices and Marginal Products in Two Countries

	Country A		Country B	
	Case (i). *No Costs of Transport of Apples or Blankets*			
Apple industry				
Marginal product of land	1	1 apple	1	1 apple
Marginal product of labour	1	exchanges	1	exchanges
Blanket industry				
Marginal product of land	1	for	1	for
Marginal product of labour	1	1 blanket	1	1 blanket
	Case (ii). *Costs of Transport of Apples from A to B and/or of Blankets from B to A*			
Apple industry				
Marginal product of land	0·5	$\frac{0{\cdot}5}{0{\cdot}\dot{3}} = \frac{2{\cdot}0}{1{\cdot}\dot{3}} = 1{\cdot}5$	1·25	$\frac{1{\cdot}25}{1{\cdot}\dot{6}} = \frac{0{\cdot}5}{0{\cdot}\dot{6}} = 0{\cdot}75$
Marginal product of labour	2·0	so that 1·5	0·5	so that 0·75
Blanket industry				
Marginal product of land	$0{\cdot}\dot{3}$	apples exchange	$1{\cdot}\dot{6}$	apples exchange
Marginal product of labour	$1{\cdot}\dot{3}$	for 1 blanket	$0{\cdot}\dot{6}$	for 1 blanket

the same in both industries, a relatively small amount of apples must exchange for a blanket. In fact in our example we find that only 0·75 instead of—as previously—1 apple exchanges for 1 blanket.[1]

As can be seen from Table XXIX, it is now no longer true that the marginal product of any one factor in any one industry will be the same in A as in B. The marginal product of labour, as a result of the costs of transport of apples and blankets between A and B, is now 300 per cent greater in apples and 100 per cent greater in blankets in A than in B. Conversely, the marginal product of land is now 150 per cent greater in apples and 400 per cent greater in blankets in B than in A.

From this it might seem natural to conclude that the maximization of world production obviously requires the movement of labour from

[1] We have taken figures for B which are compatible with the initial ratio of land to labour being 2 to 1 in B's apple industry and 1 to 2 in B's blanket industry, i.e. the same ratios as ruled in A's industries initially in the absence of transport costs.

B to A (it being assumed that land is absolutely immobile) until the difference between the marginal product of labour in B and in A was no longer greater than any cost involved in the migration of an additional unit of labour from B to A. And in one sense this is, of course, the correct conclusion. But it is unfortunately not quite so simple and straightforward a conclusion as it may at first sight appear to be.

The reason for this is that when there are costs involved in the transport of a commodity from one country to another we can no longer argue as if there were only one commodity involved. There are in fact two. An apple-in-A is not the same thing as an apple-in-B if it costs something to move an apple from A to B. When a man longs for an apple to eat in B, it is not much comfort to him to know that they are available at a penny a piece in A. He needs one to eat in B; and to transport it to B may require a great deal of additional work and effort in packing, shipping, and similar services. When we are considering the inducements offered to labour to move from one country to another and the changes in economic welfare which would result from such movements, we must not only consider the difference between the marginal product of labour measured in terms of certain physical commodities in one country and another. We must also make allowance for the fact that the workers concerned will wish to consume their income in one country rather than another, thus causing a certain cost or a certain saving on the transport of the products of those factors.

Let us revert to our numerical example in which, after the introduction of transport costs, a blanket has the price of 1·5 apples in A and of only 0·75 in B. Now this might be the result of different combinations of cost of transport of blankets and apples respectively. To take an extreme example, it might be the result of 100 per cent costs of transport of blankets from B to A combined with zero costs of transport of apples from A to B. Thus if the price of a blanket were \$1 in B and its cost of transport to A were \$1 (i.e. 100 per cent of the value of the blanket in B), then its price in A would be \$2. If, at the same time, the price of an apple were \$1·3̇ in A and, since there are no costs of transport for apples, \$1·3̇ also in B, we would have a state of affairs in which \$2 would buy 1 blanket or 1·5 apples in A and in which \$1 would buy 1 blanket or 0·75 apples in B.

Or to take another example at the other extreme, suppose that the cost of transporting apples from A to B were 100 per cent of their price in A, but that there were no costs of transporting blankets from B to A. Suppose, once again, that the price of a blanket in B were \$1. Then it would also be \$1 in A in the absence of transport costs for blankets. Suppose at the same time that the price of an apple in A were \$0·6̇; then, with 100 per cent transport costs for apples from A to B, it would be $1·3̇ in B. In these circumstances $1 would purchase 1 blanket or 1·5 apples in A; and $1 would purchase 1 blanket or 0·75 apples in B. Again the price of a blanket would be 1·5 apples in A and 0·75 apples in B.

Or these exchange rates between apples and blankets in A and B might be due to some intermediate position in which there were some transport costs for each product. Thus suppose that there were 50 per cent transport costs of blankets from B to A. Then if the price of a blanket were $1 in B, it would be $1·5 in A. If, at the same time, the price of an apple were $1 in A, and the cost of transporting apples from A to B were 33⅓ per cent, then the price of an apple in B would be $1·3̇. In these conditions $1·5 would purchase 1 blanket or 1·5 apples in A and $1 would purchase 1 blanket or 0·75 apple in B. Once again these same rates of exchange between blankets and apples would rule in A and B.[1]

These different combinations of transport costs are shown in Table XXX, which also illustrates the effect which these different combinations of transport cost will have upon the money rewards paid to the two factors in the two countries. The top half of Table XXX merely reproduces the bottom half of Table XXIX for ease of reference. It shows the marginal products of the two factors in the two industries in the two countries which we assume in our numerical example to exist after the introduction of transport costs on such a scale as to cause the number of apples given for a blanket in A (namely 1·5) to be twice as high as the number of apples given for a blanket in B (namely 0·75).

The next two rows—i.e. rows 5 and 6—of Table XXX merely lay out the numerical examples of the effect upon product prices of the various combinations of transport costs which we have discussed in the last few paragraphs. Our starting-point is always to assume a price of $1 for a blanket in B (row 6, column *d*).[2] Now if the price of a blanket is always $1 in B, then the price of an apple in B must be always $1·3̇ (row 5 column *d*), because 0·75 apples must be purchasable with the $1 which is the price of 1 blanket. Now if there are 100 per cent costs of transporting blankets from B to A the price of a blanket in A will be

[1] It is to be observed that it is a 50 per cent cost of transport in one direction plus only a 33⅓ per cent cost in the other which has the same effect on the rates of exchange between the two products as a 100 per cent cost of transport in the one direction plus a zero cost in the other. In fact the number of apples exchanged for a blanket in A will exceed the number exchanged for a blanket in B in a proportion equal to $x + y + xy$, where x represents the proportionate transport costs in the one direction and y the proportionate transport costs in the other direction.

[2] This is our *numeraire*. If in fact the price of a blanket in B were to rise by 10 per cent to $1·1, then every figure in the bottom half of Table XXX would also rise by 10 per cent. There would be no alteration in the relationships between the various product prices and factor rewards; and it is only these relationships which are relevant to the subsequent argument.

\$2 instead of \$1 as it is in B (row 6, column *a*) and if there are no costs of transporting apples from A to B the price of an apple in A will be the same as in B, namely \$1·3̇ (row 5, column *a*). And these costs are compatible with a rate of exchange of 1·5 apples for 1 blanket in A, because in A \$2 will now buy 1·5 apples or 1 blanket. If, however (column *b*), there are 100 per cent transport costs for apples and zero transport costs for blankets, then the price of a blanket will be \$1 in both countries, but the price of an apple in A will be only half its level in B (i.e. \$0·6̇ instead of \$1·3̇). But once again the same amount of money—in this case \$1—is needed in A to purchase 1 blanket or 1·5 apples. If, finally (column *c*), the cost of transport of blankets is 50 per cent, the price of blankets will be \$1·5 in A, and if the cost of transport of apples is 33⅓ per cent the price of an apple in A will be \$1, so once again the same amount of money—in this case \$1·5—is needed in A to purchase 1·5 apples or 1 blanket.

Rows 7 and 8 of Table XXX illustrate the effect of these three possible transport situations upon the money rewards of the two factors of production in A and B. The figures in these two rows are obtained in the following way. Consider the \$0·6̇ which represents the money rate of rent of land in country A (row 7, column *a*). Now we know from

TABLE XXX

The Effect of Transport Costs upon Product Prices and Factor Rewards

		Country A			Country B
Apple industry					
Marginal product of land	(1)	0·5	1·5 apples exchange for 1·0 blanket		1·25 (0·75 apples exchange for 1·0 blanket)
Marginal product of labour	(2)	2·0			0·5
Blanket industry					
Marginal product of land	(3)	0·3̇			1·6̇
Marginal product of labour	(4)	1·3̇			0·6̇
		Case i. 100 per cent cost of transport of blanket	Case ii. 100 per cent cost of transport of apple	Case iii. 50 per cent cost of transport of blanket + 33⅓ per cent cost of transport of apple	Cases i, ii, and iii
		(*a*)	(*b*)	(*c*)	(*d*)
		\$	\$	\$	\$
Price of apple	(5)	1·3̇	0·6̇	1·0	1·3̇
Price of blanket	(6)	2·0	1·0	1·5	1·0
Rent of land	(7)	0·6̇	0·3̇	0·5	1·6̇
Wage of labour	(8)	2·6̇	1·3̇	2·0	0·6̇

the top half of the table that the marginal product of land in A is $0{\cdot}5$ apples or $0{\cdot}\dot{3}$ blankets; and we know from rows 5 and 6 of column *a* that the market price of an apple and of a blanket in A are $\$1{\cdot}\dot{3}$ and \$2 respectively. The value of the marginal product of land in A is, therefore, $0{\cdot}5 \times \$1{\cdot}\dot{3}$ or $\$0{\cdot}\dot{6}$ in the apple industry and $0{\cdot}\dot{3} \times \$2$ or $\$0{\cdot}\dot{6}$ in the blanket industry.[1] Since we assume rewards to be equal to the value of marginal products, this figure of $\$0{\cdot}\dot{6}$ is entered in column *a* as the rent of land in A in these conditions. The other figures in rows 7 and 8 for the values of the different factors in the different industries have been similarly computed.

Now it is to be observed that the money wage of labour is $\$2{\cdot}\dot{6}$ in A when the cost of transport is solely on the goods sent from B to A and only $\$1{\cdot}\dot{3}$ when it falls solely on the goods sent from A to B (row 8 columns *a* and *b*). In both cases the money wage of labour in B is $\$0{\cdot}\dot{6}$. Thus in column *a* the money wage in A is no less than 300 per cent higher than in B, whereas in column *b* it is only 100 per cent higher. To what extent does this correspond to a real difference in the incentive for labour to move from B to A, and to what extent does it imply that the maximization of economic welfare is more urgently in need of such a migration of labour in the former than in the latter case?

In order to answer these questions we must take into account two further considerations. (i) Do the migrating workers intend to consume their income in A or in B? (ii) Do they intend to spend their income mainly on apples or on blankets? It will be seen from what follows that these two questions are as relevant to our analysis as the question already raised, namely: (iii) Does the cost of transport fall mainly on the exports of products from A to B or mainly on the export of products from B to A? We shall now proceed to examine the last four rows of Table XXX under various combinations of answers to these three questions.[2]

Let us first take the cases where the migrating workers intend to consume the whole of their income in B, the country from which they are emigrating. It may be rather unrealistic to assume this of labour,

[1] It is not, of course, accidental that both these figures work out at the same sum, namely $\$0{\cdot}\dot{6}$. To be compatible with a position of equilibrium, the arithmetical example has been so selected that the ratio between the marginal product of land in apples and in blankets $\left(\frac{0\cdot5}{0\cdot\dot{3}}\right)$ is the same as the assumed rate of exchange between apples and blankets $\left(\frac{1\cdot5}{1\cdot0}\right)$. Also the ratio between the price of blankets and the price of apples $\left(\frac{2\cdot0}{1\cdot\dot{3}}\right)$ in A corresponds to the rate of exchange $\left(\frac{1\cdot5}{1\cdot0}\right)$ between the two products. It follows at once that $0{\cdot}5 \times 1{\cdot}\dot{3} = 0{\cdot}\dot{3} \times 2{\cdot}0$.

[2] Since each of the three questions may be answered in two ways we have in fact 2^3 or 8 possible cases.

since it would mean that the workers who migrated from B to A remitted back to relatives in B the whole of their earnings in A. But, nevertheless, we shall examine this case for two reasons. First, the migrant workers may wish to remit part of their earnings in A back to relatives in B, and it may be a helpful exercise to examine the effects of the extreme case of this, where all earnings are remitted in this way. Secondly, many of the points examined in this consideration of labour migration will be found to be directly applicable to the analysis of international capital movements. The consideration of the case in which all earnings are remitted back to B is directly relevant to the examination of the case in which an owner of capital resides in B but invests his capital in A and wishes to consume his interest, profits, or dividends in B.

Now in this case in which the migrating workers intend to consume in B what they earn in A it will be irrelevant to our problem whether they are interested mainly in the consumption of apples or of blankets. The price of both of these is given in B—\$1 in the case of blankets and $\$1\cdot\dot{3}$ in the case of apples (rows 5 and 6 of column *d*). The workers will, therefore, be interested solely in the excess of the money income which they can earn in A over their earnings in B and the comparison of this with the cost of their movement from B to A.

But whether the costs of transport are mainly on the transport of blankets from B to A (column *a*) or on the transport of apples from A to B (column *b*) is now clearly very important to the workers who are considering migration. In the former case a worker by migrating will increase his money earnings by \$2 (i.e. from $\$0\cdot\dot{6}$ to $\$2\cdot\dot{6}$), whereas in the latter case he will increase his earnings by only $\$0\cdot\dot{6}$ (i.e. from $\$0\cdot\dot{6}$ to $\$1\cdot\dot{3}$). He will be induced to move in the former case if the costs of movement of the factor on an annual basis[1] are less than \$2 and in the latter case only if they are less than $\$0\cdot\dot{6}$.

Now it can be shown that these are the appropriate incentives from the point of view of economic welfare. Consider first of all the case in which the transport costs fall solely on the transport of blankets from B to A (column *a* of Table XXX); and let us ask the question whether a worker by migrating could improve his own consumption standards without reducing the consumption standards of any other individual in A or B. The abstraction from the blanket industry in B of one unit of labour would cause a reduction in the output of blankets-in-B of $0\cdot\dot{6}$, since that is the marginal product of labour in B. Its employment in the blanket industry in A would increase the output of blankets-in-A by $1\cdot\dot{3}$. In order that consumers in A should be equally well off, the exports of blankets from B to A can be reduced by $1\cdot\dot{3}$. This will have a double effect. First, the amount of blankets available for consumption in B are

[1] See p. 358 above.

directly increased by $0\cdot\dot{6}$, since production is down by $0\cdot\dot{6}$ but exports are down by $1\cdot\dot{3}$. Second, there is a saving on the transport of blankets from B to A of an amount equal in value to the $1\cdot\dot{3}$ blankets no longer sent from B to A, since we are assuming 100 per cent costs of transport. This releases from transport work factors of production in B which can produce another $1\cdot\dot{3}$ blankets. There is, therefore, a net increase in the amount of blankets available for consumption in B by the worker who has migrated to A of $0\cdot\dot{6} + 1\cdot\dot{3}$ or 2 blankets. Since blankets are priced at $\$1$, this is equivalent to an increased consumption of $\$2$. And this is in fact the increase in the earnings of the worker in A over his earnings in B (i.e. $\$2\cdot\dot{6} - \$0\cdot\dot{6}$). If, therefore, the movement of the worker from B to A itself costs factors whose earning power in B is less than $\$2$, the migration will be in the social interests of the maximization of production as well as in the private interest of the owner.[1]

We can now consider the case in which the migrating workers, as before, consume their earnings in B, but in which the cost of transport is now solely on apples sent from A to B. As we have seen, a worker will now have an incentive to move only if the cost of movement is less than $\$0\cdot\dot{6}$, i.e. less than the increase in his earnings from $\$0\cdot\dot{6}$ in B to $\$1\cdot\dot{3}$ in A.

Once again it can be seen that these private incentives fit in with the maximization of production. If a worker does move from the blanket industry in B to the blanket industry in A, this will cause a reduction of $0\cdot\dot{6}$ blankets-in-B and an increase of $1\cdot\dot{3}$ blankets-in-A. But since in this case there are no costs of transport of blankets, this means that the worker could have $0\cdot\dot{6}$ more blankets in B ($1\cdot\dot{3} - 0\cdot\dot{6}$) without anyone in A or B having any less of any other product. But $0\cdot\dot{6}$ blankets in B are worth $\$0\cdot\dot{6}$. It is, therefore, in the interests of the maximization of production that the worker should move if the cost of moving is less than the equivalent of $\$0\cdot\dot{6}$ in B. And this corresponds to the private incentive provided by the $\$0\cdot\dot{6}$ excess of the wage offered to labour in A ($\$1\cdot\dot{3}$) over the wage offered in B ($\$0\cdot\dot{6}$).[2]

Let us now turn to the more normal case in which workers migrating

[1] The above analysis has been conducted solely in terms of blankets. But exactly the same results would have been obtained if it had been done in terms of apples. Thus the transfer of a unit of labour from the apple industry in B to the apple industry in A would reduce the output of apples-in-B by $0\cdot5$ and increase the output of apples-in-A by 2. But since in this case there are no costs of transport of apples, this would mean that there would be a net additional supply of apples in B of $2 - 0\cdot5$ or $1\cdot5$ available for the owners of the transferred factor. The price of an apple in B is $\$1\cdot\dot{3}$ so that the value of $1\cdot5$ additional apples is $1\cdot5 \times \$1\cdot\dot{3}$ or $\$2$. This once again is in fact equal to the difference in earnings due to the transfer of the factor which earns $\$0\cdot\dot{6}$ in B and $\$2\cdot\dot{6}$ in A.

[2] The reader is left to himself to do the analysis in terms of apples and to see that this once more comes to the same result, when account is taken of the additional transport cost which is now involved in transporting to B the larger output of apples in A for consumption in B.

from B to A intend to consume their new incomes in A and not in B. Whether the cost of transport of products falls on apples or on blankets can now be seen to be irrelevant to the private incentives which are offered to movement. In the case in which the cost of transport falls solely on blankets, labour can raise its earnings to $\$2\cdot\dot{6}$ but the cost of living will be $\$1\cdot\dot{3}$ an apple and \$2 a blanket (column *a*). In the case in which the cost of transport falls solely on apples, labour can raise its earning to $\$1\cdot\dot{3}$ which is only one half of $\$2\cdot\dot{6}$, but in this case the cost of living will be only half as high ($\$0\cdot\dot{6}$ instead of $\$1\cdot\dot{3}$ for an apple and \$1 instead of \$2 for a blanket). If labour is interested in real earnings, we need consider only the change in the marginal product of labour due to the change; and, as the top half of Table XXX shows, this will raise the real reward of labour in terms of apples by 300 per cent (i.e. from a marginal product of 0·5 to one of 2 apples) and in terms of blankets by 100 per cent (i.e. from a marginal product of $0\cdot\dot{6}$ to one of $1\cdot\dot{3}$ blankets).

But it is equally clear from this that a very relevant consideration indeed will be whether labour consumes mainly apples (in which case its real income will rise by 300 per cent) or blankets (in which case its real income will rise by only 100 per cent). Labour will have an incentive to move in the former case if the cost of movement is anything less than three-quarters of its prospective earnings in A and in the latter case only if the cost of movement is less than half of its new earnings in A.

Moreover, this clearly corresponds to the requirements of the maximization of production. A worker by moving from the apple industry in B to the apple industry in A can obtain 2 instead of 0·5 apples. If he consumes only apples and if the cost of movement of labour takes up factors in A which produce less than 1·5 apples (i.e. three-quarters of the value of labour's wage in A),[1] then this unit of labour by moving can have more to consume without anyone else having less. And an exactly similar analysis can be undertaken for the case in which labour consumes only blankets, in which case the movement should take place only if the cost of moving labour was less than half of the wage earned by labour in A. Thus, once again, private incentives correspond to the social requirements for the maximization of production.

We can now summarize the conclusions which we have reached.

First, in all the cases which we have examined we have found that labour will have an incentive to migrate when, but only when, its movement is required for the maximization of production. This result

[1] It will be seen that whereas in the former case (p. 371) we assessed the real cost of the factor's movement in terms of factors employed in B, in this case we are assessing it in terms of factors employed in A. We are doing this solely for convenience. In other words, we assume that 'transport facilities' are produced in both countries without cost of transport of transport facilities from country to country. Any lack of reality in this assumption probably does not essentially affect the conclusions.

is not really surprising. We have throughout been examining cases in which (i) every factor in every industry in every country is paid a reward equal to the value of its marginal social net product, (ii) every owner of every factor must pay the marginal cost of movement of that factor, and (iii) every owner of every factor is well informed of the prospects of earnings of that factor in every industry in every country. It was really a foregone conclusion that in such circumstances private incentives should coincide with the social requirements for the maximization of production. But it may nevertheless have been worth while seeing how this general principle works out in the case of a factor movement when costs of transport of products and costs of movement of factors are involved.

Second, the existence of costs of transport of products between A and B will tend to keep up the marginal product of labour in the country (A) in which labour is scarce relative to other factors and to keep down the marginal product of labour in the country (B) in which labour is plentiful relative to other factors. There will, therefore, be a private and social advantage in the migration of labour from B to A if the cost of the migration is not too great.

Third, in considering whether the cost of migration is too high to make the migration desirable it is necessary to take into account the following three points:

(i) How far the cost of transport of products which causes the need for migration falls on the transport of products from A to B and how far on the transport of products from B to A;

(ii) How far the migrating workers will wish to remit their new earnings in A back to B for consumption by their families in B; and

(iii) How far the earnings of the migrating workers are likely to be spent on the sort of product which A exports or on the sort of product which B exports.

Fourth, if labour which migrates to A remits most of its earnings back to B, then the desirability of migration from B to A will be greatest if there is little cost of transport on products (apples) moving from A to B and most cost of transport on products (blankets) moving from B to A. The reason for this is clear. The remission of earnings from A to B means that A's exports must be expanded and B's exports contracted. The less, therefore, is the cost of transporting A's apples to B and the greater is the cost of transporting B's blankets to A, the greater is the saving in transport cost due to the remission of earnings, and the more worth while it is to migrate to A to earn the larger wage for remission to B. In so far as earnings are not remitted from A to B there is no need to generate an export surplus for A by any expansion of A's exports of apples or any contraction of B's exports of blankets. In this case it makes no difference whether the transport costs which are the cause of the whole problem fall on the movement of apples from A to B or on the movement of blankets from B to A.

Fifth, in so far as the migrating labour does not remit its earnings in A back to its families in B, the desirability of migration will be greater if labour wishes to spend its earnings in A on the product (apples) in which labour is the unimportant factor of production rather than on the labour-intensive product (blankets). The cost of transporting apples and blankets between A and B will have kept the price of labour up in A and down in B. Productive methods will be rather land-intensive in A and labour-intensive in B. This will have kept up the marginal product of labour especially high in the apple industry in A and will have kept the marginal product of labour especially low in the apple industry in B, since labour is the unimportant factor in the apple industry in both countries (see pp. 327–8 above). Labour will, therefore, get a much greater advantage in moving if it is interested in its real wage rate measured in terms of apples rather than in terms of blankets. This consideration becomes less and less relevant as labour wishes to remit more and more of its earnings back to its families in B. If these families consume mainly apples in B, it is true that the workers by moving from B to A can greatly increase their earnings in terms of apples, but against this must be set the cost of moving the apples from the producers in A to their families in B. If these families consume mainly blankets in B, it is true that the workers by moving from B to A can only slightly increase their earnings in terms of blankets, but against this must be set the fact that these blankets can be remitted back to the workers' families in B merely by transporting less blankets from B to A with a consequential saving of transport costs. These two sets of considerations balance each other, so that in so far as the workers in A remit their earnings back to B for consumption in B it is irrelevant whether the consumers in B wish to spend them on the land-intensive product (apples) or on the labour-intensive product (blankets).

We are now in a position very briefly to consider the effect of transport costs upon the need for international capital investment. The above conclusions which we have just summarized in the case of international movements of labour can all be more or less directly applied to the international movement of capital by an exactly similar process of analysis which there is no need to repeat. In the conditions which we are assuming there will necessarily be a coincidence between the private incentives to move capital internationally and the movements which are required to maximize world production. The existence of costs of movement for products in international trade will mean that in the absence of international capital movements the marginal product of capital will remain higher in those countries which are originally endowed with little capital relatively to other factors of production than in those countries which are originally endowed with much capital relatively to other factors of production. If as is normal the earnings on capital in the country in which it is newly invested are remitted back to be consumed by owners resident in the country from which the capital has come, then the desirability of capital movement will be greatest if the transport costs which are the basic cause of the problem are on the export of goods from the creditor to the debtor country rather than on the export of goods from the debtor to the creditor country, since the transfer of dividends must involve an increase in the debtor's exports and a contraction in the creditor's exports. In so far, however, as the owners of the capital move with the capital from the creditor to the debtor country and spend the earnings on the capital in the debtor country, the desirability of movement will be at its greatest if the owners of the capital wish to spend their earnings in the debtor country on products which require little capital for their production rather than on capital-intensive products. For it is in terms of the former group of products that the marginal product of capital will be especially high in A and especially low in B.

There is, however, one additional consideration (see pp. 360–1 above) which we must take into account in the case of international capital movements and which is not relevant in the case of the international migration of labour. The remission of wages or of dividends earned in A back to B for expenditure in B involves the generation of an excess of exports over imports on A's balance of trade. In the above analysis we have shown that for this reason, if earnings in A are going to be remitted back to B then the movement of the factor from B to A (whether it be a migration of labour from B to A or an investment of capital in A by owners of capital in B) will be the more desirable the greater the cost of transport of B's products to A and the smaller the cost of transport of A's products to B.

Now the movement itself of capital funds from B to A can represent an effective transfer of real capital from B to A only if it is accompanied by the generation of an excess of exports over imports on B's balance of trade. In this respect the movement of capital from B to A differs from the movement of labour from B to A, which can of course take place without the generation of any corresponding excess of B's exports over B's imports.

In so far as the movement of capital from B to A takes the form of an increased demand in A and a decreased demand in B for capital purposes for products of a kind which are exported from A to B, the surplus on B's balance of trade will take the form of a reduction in B's import from A of these products; and in so far as the transport of these products from A to B is costly, the movement of capital will itself involve a saving of transport costs and will be so much the more desirable. In other words, we may conclude that the more the transfer of capital funds from B to A on the real side is likely to be accompanied by a reduction in A's exports to B and the more the costs of transport between A and B (which are the cause of the whole problem) fall on A's exports to B rather than on B's exports to A, the more likely is it that it will be desirable for capital to move from B to A.

Conversely, if real capital development in A rather than in B means an increased demand in A and decreased demand in B for products of a kind which are exported from B to A, the real transfer of the capital funds from B to A will involve an expansion of B's exports rather than a contraction of B's imports. In so far as the costs of transport are heavy on B's exports, this will make the movement of capital from B to A less desirable than would otherwise be the case.

It is to be observed that the considerations raised in the two preceding paragraphs do not themselves lead to any modification of our general conclusion that in the conditions otherwise assumed in this chapter the private incentives for the international movement of factors of production will coincide with those which are needed for the maximization of world production. A's exportable products will be cheaper in A than in B by the cost of transporting them from A to B. If these products are those which are most needed for schemes for capital development, then the fact that goods needed for capital construction are cheaper in A than in B will give an additional incentive to undertake such construction in A rather than in B to an extent which just reflects the saving in transport costs if the construction were placed in A rather than in B. Similarly, B's exportable products will be more expensive in A than in B; and if they are the products which are most needed for a work of capital construction, this will provide an incentive not to undertake the development in A. The strength of this incentive will exactly correspond to the additional cost of transporting from B the products which are required for any scheme of capital development in A.

Subject to this important distinction between the considerations determining the desirability of an international movement of capital and those determining the desirability of an international migration of labour, exactly the same analysis can be applied to the effect of transport costs upon international investment as has been applied earlier in this chapter to its effect upon international migration. In both cases the existence of transport costs for the products of the factors of production will tend to cause the marginal product of a factor to remain higher in that country which is initially not well endowed with the factor in question. Whether the factor will or should move will then depend upon whether the cost of movement of the factor is greater or less than the excess of its marginal product in the country to which it might move. On examination whether this is likely to be so or not is found to be a more complicated problem than might at first be expected. It is, however, apparent that in order to maximize world production factors *may* have to move internationally; and there is reason to believe that, if the assumptions made on p. 373 are fulfilled, private incentives to move will coincide with the social requirements for the maximization of world production, so that a policy of permitting the free and uncontrolled movement of factors between countries will achieve the correct results.

CHAPTER XXIII

TRADE AS A SUBSTITUTE FOR FACTOR MOVEMENTS: (4) NUMBER OF FACTORS, SPECIALIZATION, AND FACTOR-SUBSTITUTIONS

IN the two preceding chapters we have examined three of the most obvious and important reasons why, even in conditions of free trade, the maximization of world production may require the movement of factors of production from one country to another. Thus if the atmosphere for production is more favourable in A than in B, the maximization of production may require the movement of labour from B to A. Or if there are marginal economies for labour in a large scale of production and A is a large economy, the maximization of world production may require the movement of labour from A to B. Or if there are heavy costs involved in transporting the labour-intensive product from B to A but only small costs involved in transporting labour itself from B to A, once again the maximization of world production may involve the migration of the labour itself rather than the trade in its product. All these are essentially simple and obvious points. But they are none the less important for that. They probably in fact in the real world constitute the main reasons why free trade is not sufficient alone without international movements of factors to maximize world production.

We turn now in this chapter to certain other conditions which may make factor movements necessary even though there are no differences in productive atmospheres, no economies of scale, and no transport costs for products. These conditions are a little more difficult to analyse, but they are not necessarily more important in their influence in the real world.

In assumption 1 on p. 332 we stated that for trade alone to bring the marginal physical product of each factor into equality in both the trading countries it was necessary that the number of factors of production should be strictly limited. In the argument which we used in Chapter XX we assumed that there were only two factors of production (namely land and labour). We argued that if, in these circumstances, there were at least two products (namely apples and blankets) which were produced in both countries and which were traded freely and without cost between the two countries, then the marginal product of land would be the same in A as in B and the marginal product of labour would be the same in A as in B.

Let us now suppose that there are only two products, apples and blankets, which are produced in both countries and which are the subject of free and costless international trade; but suppose that there are three factors of production, land, labour, and capital. It now no longer follows that the marginal product of each factor will be the same in A as in B. Let us start from the position with two factors which we examined in Chapter XX. Apple production is land-intensive and blanket production labour-intensive; A has a higher ratio of land to labour than B; both A and B produce both apples and blankets, but A imports some of her home consumption of blankets from B and B imports some part of her home consumption of apples from A; and for the reasons given in Chapter XX the marginal product of land is the same in A as in B in terms of apples and of blankets, and similarly with the marginal product of labour.

We start then with the situation in which A's land-intensive industry (apple production) is expanded through the export of apples to B and B's labour-intensive industry (blanket production) is expanded through the export of blankets to A. As a result the ratio of land to labour is the same in the apple industry in A as in B and the same in the blanket industry in A as in B, although A possesses over the average of both industries a higher ratio of land to labour. In the absence of economies or diseconomies of scale, of differences in productive atmosphere, *and of any third factor of production*, the marginal product of land depends solely upon the proportion with which it is used with labour and vice versa. Since the ratio of land to labour is the same in each industry in A as in B, the marginal product of each factor in each industry will be the same in A as in B. Such in brief is the basic argument of Chapter XX.

Let us now introduce a third factor, capital, into this simple model; and let us suppose that A is much richer in capital than B, so that the ratio of capital to land and the ratio of capital to labour is much higher in A than in B. We have supposed that the apple industry is always land-intensive as compared with the blanket industry in the sense that at any given rate of rent and rate of wages a higher ratio of land to labour will be employed in the apple than in the blanket industry, so that if wages and rents were the only elements in cost a higher proportion of the costs would always go to the rent of land in apple production than in blanket production. Suppose that the capital-intensivity of the apple industry and the blanket industry differed very little in the sense that at any given rates of rent of land, wages of labour, and interest on capital the proportion of the cost of production which represented interest on capital would be much the same in both industries. Since capital is so plentiful in A relatively to other factors, we would expect the price of capital (the rate of interest) to be much lower in A than in B. In both industries, apples and blankets, in A much capital would be used relatively to the land and labour employed, because capital was so cheap. In B, on the contrary, little capital would be used relatively to the land and labour employed, because capital is expensive. As a result of this the marginal product of capital will be low in both industries in A (because each unit of capital has relatively little land and labour to co-operate with it), but the marginal products of land and labour will both be high (because in each industry land and labour are both very well provided with capital equipment). In B, on the other hand, the marginal product of capital will be high in both industries (because each unit of capital has much land and labour to co-operate with it) and the marginal products of land and labour will be low (because each unit of land and labour has little capital equipment to work with).

There is, of course, no reason to believe that the introduction of capital into the two economies will, in the absence of further adjustments, leave the costs of apples relatively to the cost of blankets the same in A as in B. If, for example, capital were a somewhat more important factor of production in the blanket industry than in the apple industry, then the introduction of the new factor, capital, might reduce the cost of blankets relatively to that of apples very considerably in A (where much capital is introduced) and only slightly in B (where little capital is introduced). The cost of blankets relatively to that of apples will, therefore, be lower in A than in B unless there is some further adjustment.

Such an adjustment will, however, be brought about by free trade in apples and blankets. Consumers will buy more of their blankets and less of their apples in A where the cost and so the price of blankets is now low relatively to that of apples. For similar reasons they will buy more of their apples and less of their blankets in B. Since apples are markedly land-intensive and blankets markedly labour-intensive, this will cause an increased demand for labour and a reduced demand for land in A, and so a further rise in the wage rate and some decline in the rate of rent in A. Similarly in B, where the demand for land-intensive apples has risen and for labour-intensive blankets has fallen, there will be some furthur rise in the rate of rent but some decline in the rate of wages. This will tend to raise the cost of labour-intensive blankets relatively to that of land-intensive apples in A and to lower it in B. This movement will go on until costs and so prices are once more the same in A as in B.

In the final equilibrium we shall have reached a situation of the following kind.

First, the rate of wages will be much higher in A than in B. It will have been raised much more in A than in B by the fact that the co-operating factor, capital, is much more plentiful in A than in B; and this tendency will have been intensified by the subsequent expansion of A's, and contraction of B's, labour-intensive blanket industry.

Second, the rate of rent will probably be somewhat higher in A than in B. As in the case of labour, the rate of rent will have been raised much more in A than in B because of the plentiful supply of the co-operating factor, capital. But this tendency will have been mitigated by the subsequent contraction of A's, and expansion of B's, land-intensive apple industry.

Third, the rate of interest will be lower in A than in B. The basic reason for this is that capital will be plentiful in both of A's industries and scarce in both of B's industries, so that the marginal product of capital will be low throughout A's economy and high throughout B's economy. This discrepancy will continue in spite of some partial offset due to the subsequent expansion of A's, and contraction of B's, capital-intensive blanket industry. But this offset will be only very partial because the blanket industry is much more markedly labour-intensive than capital-intensive and the apple industry is much more markedly land-*dis*intensive than capital-*dis*intensive. Thus, the equalization of the costs of blankets and of apples in A and B will be brought about rather through a further rise in wage rates in A relatively to wage rates in B and through some secondary decline in the rate of rent in A relatively to the rate of rent in B than through a rise in the rate of interest in A relatively to the rate of interest in B. In these circumstances free trade would leave the rate of interest in B higher than in A and would leave the rate of wages (certainly) and the rate of rent (probably) higher in A than in B.

The position would be very different if there were a third commodity, say cars, which was freely traded between A and B, produced in both countries, and very capital-intensive in production. Let us take a very simple example. Let us suppose that apples are unequivocally land-intensive, blankets unequivocally labour-intensive, and cars unequivocally capital-intensive. By this we mean that at any given rate of rent, rate of wages, and rate of interest the ratios of land to labour and of land to capital would be much higher in the apple industry than in either the blanket or the car industry; the ratios of labour to land and of labour to capital would be much higher in the blanket industry than in the apple industry or the car industry; and the ratios of capital to land and of capital to labour would be much higher in the car industry than in the apple or blanket industry. There would now once more be strong forces exerted by free trade in these three commodities to equalize the marginal products of the three factors in the two countries.

Thus suppose that in this situation the rate of interest were much lower and the rates of wages and rents were much higher in A than in B. Cars, which are capital-intensive, would now be much cheaper to produce in A than in B; but apples, which are land-intensive, and blankets, which are labour-intensive, would be much more expensive to produce in A than in B. Free trade would then lead to the expansion of A's car industry and the contraction of her apple and blanket industries; and this would raise the demand for capital and reduce the demand for land and labour in A with the result that the rate of interest in A would rise towards its level in B and the rates of rent and of wages in A would fall towards their levels in B. The opposite would be happening in B, where the car industry would be contracting and the apple and blanket industries expanding, so that the rate of interest would be falling and the rates of rent and wages rising. As a result of these changes a new equilibrium may be reached in which each of the three products is being produced in both countries with the same factor ratios in any one industry in both countries and so with the same marginal product for each factor in both countries.

When we are dealing with situations in which there are many factors of production, important complications may be introduced by special relations of complementarity between two or more factors. Let us take an example. Suppose that there are four factors—land, unskilled labour, skilled labour, and capital. Suppose, as before, that the car industry is very capital-intensive. But suppose further that skilled labour is very complementary with capital equipment in the manufacture of cars; it is not much use in making cars to have capital equipment without the skilled labour to operate it or to have skilled labour without the machinery for it to work on. Suppose now that trade is opened up between A and B. The car industry will expand in A and contract in B, because interest on capital is the main element in its cost and capital is plentiful and cheap in A and is scarce and expensive in B. But this will mean an accompanying expansion in A and contraction in B in the demand for skilled labour. If skilled labour were not especially plentiful or scarce in A or in B before trade was opened up, the wages of skilled labour might be much the same in A as in B before trade was opened up. The opening up of trade will now bring the rate of interest on capital in A more nearly into equality with the rate of interest on capital in B, because the expansion of the car industry in A will increase the demand for capital in A and the contraction of the car industry in B will decrease the demand for capital in B. But this will cause an accompanying increase in the car industry in A for the subsidiary complementary factor, skilled labour, and an accompanying decrease of this factor in B's car industry. For this reason the wages of skilled labour will be bid up in A and will be reduced in B; and the reward earned by this factor may, as a result of trade, become less equal in A and in B than before. In this case in order to maximize world production there would, of course, be a strong need for skilled labour to migrate from B to A to co-operate with the plentiful supply of capital in A's car industry.

This tendency of free trade to make some factor prices less equal in A and in B than before might be overcome if there were yet some other industry, say the production of drugs, which required the use of much skilled labour relatively to capital and other factors and which could be freely traded between A and B. In this case as the car industry developed in A and tended thus to drive up the wages of skilled labour in A above their level in B, the drug industry would expand in B and contract in A, because its main element of cost—the wages of skilled labour—was tending to be higher in A than in B. If this industry were of a sufficient size previously in A, it might be possible for its migration to B to release so much skilled labour in A for A's car industry and to mop up so much skilled labour in B from B's car industry, that the wages of skilled labour would remain equal in the two countries, while free trade in cars at the same time brought the rate of interest into equality.

Now these forces which are at work tending to make the marginal products and the rewards of the various factors the same in both countries will, of course, exert their full influence and make marginal products fully equal only if the relevant industries continue to exist in both countries. We may illustrate this point from the example which we have just given in the previous paragraph. Suppose that the drug industry were a very small one indeed in consumer's demand both in A and in B so that throughout the world very few resources were in fact committed to it. Now it would remain true that when trade was opened up between A and B the expansion of the car industry in A and its contraction in B would tend to drive up the demand for skilled labour in A and to depress it in B, with the result that the wages of skilled labour became more unequal than before; and it would remain true that at first this tendency would be offset by the contraction of A's drug industry with the consequential release of skilled labour to A's car industry and the expansion of B's drug industry with the consequential mopping up of the skilled labour released from B's contracting car industry. But if the drug industry in A is very small, the point will soon come when it has been closed down completely and there is no more skilled labour to be released to A's car industry from this source. From this point on, when the vital industry (in this case the drug industry) has become completely specialized in B, the process of continued expansion of A's car industry and contraction of B's car industry will lead to a driving up of the wage rate of skilled labour in A and a reduction of the wage rate of skilled labour in B.

We have already explained in Chapter XIX how in the simple case in which A exports only apples to B and B exports only blankets to A, the opening up of trade between them may lead to the complete specialization of production of one of the two products in one of the two countries. Thus suppose that (i) A were a very much smaller country than B in the sense that A possessed much less of both factors—land and labour—than B, (ii) that apples were a much more important product in consumption than blankets in the sense that consumers in both A and B spent a much larger proportion of their incomes on apples than on blankets, and (iii) that there were great discrepancies in factor endowments in A and in B in the sense that the ratio of all land to all labour is much higher in A than in B. Then when trade is first opened up between A and B, A will start by exporting apples to B and B will start by exporting blankets to A, since land-intensive apples will be cheap to produce in A which is relatively well endowed with land, and labour-intensive blankets will be cheap to produce in B which is relatively well endowed with labour. This process will start to bring the marginal products and the rewards of the factors into equality in A and B by the process described in Chapter XX. The expansion of A's apple industry and the contraction of her blanket industry will be raising the demand for the plentiful land and reducing the demand for the scarce labour in A, and vice versa in B.

But before the change has been anything like on a sufficient scale to close entirely the gap between the marginal products of the two factors in the two countries, A's blanket industry may have been entirely closed down. A's blanket industry will be very small because (i) A is very small as compared with B, and (ii) even within A only a small proportion of the national income was spent on blankets. The shift of all the resources out of A's blanket industry into her apple industry will not make a great deal of difference to the factor ratios in A's blanket industry, because even in the pre-trade position A's blanket industry was small relatively to A's apple industry.[1] Thus the shift of all the resources previously employed in A's blanket industry into A's apple industry would have only a very small effect in raising the marginal product of land and in lowering the marginal product of labour in A, because it would only slightly increase the ratio of labour to land in A's apple industry.

In B the fall in the marginal product of land and the rise in the marginal product of labour which would follow upon the complete closing down of A's blanket industry would also be small. Since A's blanket industry was small to begin with, its closing down would necessitate only a small expansion of B's blanket industry to meet the

[1] Suppose that A's blanket industry employed 200 labour and 100 land and A's apple industry employed 1,000 labour and 2,000 land in the pre-trade position, so that A's blanket industry is four times as labour-intensive as A's apple industry, the ratio of labour to land being 2 in the former and 0·5 in the latter. Even if all the blanket industry's resources were transferred to the apple industry the labour to land ratio would rise only from 0·5 $\left(\text{i.e. } \frac{1000}{2000}\right)$ to 0·57 $\left(\text{i.e. } \frac{1200}{2100}\right)$, because the blanket industry is so small relatively to the apple industry.

demand in A; and this would be small relatively to the resources already employed in B's blanket industry, because A is assumed to be a small country relatively to B. The amount of apples exported to B by A to pay for the new exports of blankets from B to A would be small because A's demand for blankets is assumed to be small. In consequence the contraction of B's apple industry would be very small in proportion to the absolute size of that industry both because B's industry is large relatively to A's initially and also because the apple industry in both countries is large relatively to the blanket industry. Thus even when blanket production is closed down completely in A, the factor proportions in B's industries will be very little changed, because the size of B's blanket industry will have been increased only by a small percentage and her apple industry will have been decreased only by a small percentage, so that the demand for labour relatively to the demand for land will have been increased only very slightly.

If A and B started with very different factor endowments in the pre-trade position and so with very different marginal products for the factors, there will remain large disparities in these marginal products even when A's blanket industry has been completely closed down. Wages will have fallen little in A and will have risen still less in B; and rents will have risen little in A and will have fallen still less in B. Moreover, as soon as A's blanket industry is completely closed down free trade can no longer exert any influence equalizing factor prices because it can no longer cause A to produce more apples for export and less blankets for home production (thus raising rents and lowering wages in A); and for this very reason it cannot lead B to produce more blankets to replace a further reduction in A's home output of blankets and thus it cannot cause any further rise in the demand for labour relatively to the demand for land in B.

We have already argued in Chapter XX that if there are only two factors, land and labour, then it is not necessary for the full equalization of factor prices that there should be more than two commodities, say apples and blankets, in which trade should be free and costless and each of which should be produced in both countries. A policy of import duties and protection in regard to other commodities would be quite compatible with the maintenance of factor-price equalization. But because of the possibility of specialization of production that is not the same thing as saying that factor prices are just as likely to be equalized if free trade is permitted in two commodities as they are if free trade is permitted in three, four, or more commodities. Indeed, it can be seen that the more commodities are subject to trade taxes the more likely it is that there will be complete specialization in the commodities in which free trade is permitted.

Table XXXI is designed to illustrate this point. We suppose that there are three products, apples, blankets, and cars, and two factors, land and labour; and we suppose that in the fully free-trade position the amounts of the factors used in the industries in A and B are as shown in Table XXXI. We assume that apples are the most land-intensive product and blankets the most labour-intensive, with cars in an intermediate position; and we assume that free trade in the three commodities has led to a situation in which the ratio of land to labour in the apple industry is the same in A as in B, and similarly with the other two industries. The figures in the table, ignoring for the moment those in brackets, are compatible with these assumptions. Thus the ratios of labour to land in apple production in A $\left(\frac{200}{400}\right)$ and in B $\left(\frac{100}{200}\right)$ are both equal to $\frac{1}{2}$; the similar ratios in blanket production in A $\left(\frac{2000}{1000}\right)$ and in B $\left(\frac{4000}{2000}\right)$ are both equal to 2; and these ratios in the car industry in A $\left(\frac{1600}{1600}\right)$ and in B $\left(\frac{800}{800}\right)$ are both at the intermediate level of 1. In these conditions the marginal product of each factor will be the same in A as in B in any one industry, since each factor in the same industry will be working with the same proportion of the other factor in both countries. Marginal products will be equalized, and free trade will have maximized world production.

Now country A is the country with a relatively high total supply of land per head of working population, i.e. 3,000 units of land to 3,800 units of labour, whereas country B has the lower ratio of 3,000 units of land to 4,900 units of population. But in each industry the land to labour ratio is the same in A as in B because A has more resources in the land-intensive apple industry and in the intermediate car industry (in both these cases the A-industry is twice as big as the B-industry), whereas B has more resources in the labour-intensive blanket industry (which is twice as large in B as in A). If the demands for the various products are much the same in A as in B, then presumably in these conditions A will be exporting apples and cars to B in return for the export of blankets by B to A.

Now in these conditions we have free trade in three products, all of which are produced in both countries, and this is more than sufficient to ensure equal factor proportions in each industry and so equal marginal products for each factor in both countries. Let us then see what happens if the intermediate industry producing cars is protected in country B. This means that at ruling prices and costs B will now have to make all her cars for herself and A will have to make only those cars

TABLE XXXI

Protection and Specialization. Three Products and Two Factors

		Industries making			All industries (d)
		apples (a)	blankets (b)	cars (c)	
Country A					
Amount of land	(1)	400 (+ 66⅔)	1,000 (+33⅓)	1,600 (−100)	3,000
Amount of labour	(2)	200 (+33⅓)	2,000 (+66⅔)	1,600 (−100)	3,800
Country B					
Amount of land	(3)	200 (−66⅔)	2,000 (−33⅓)	800 (+100)	3,000
Amount of labour	(4)	100 (−33⅓)	4,000 (−66⅔)	800 (+100)	4,900
Both countries					
Amount of land	(5)	600	3,000	2,400	6,000
Amount of labour	(6)	300	6,000	2,400	8,700

which she needs for her own consumption. B's car industry will have to expand and A's to contract. Let us suppose at first that the demand for cars is in any case higher in A than in B, so that all that is needed is an expansion of land and of labour used by car production by 100 units each in B (from 800 to 900 units) and a similar contraction of both factors in A's car industry by 100 units each (from 1,600 to 1,500). These adjustments are shown in the figures in brackets in column *c* of the table.

Now in this case the policy of protection of B's car industry will have no significant effect upon costs or factor rewards. It will merely mean that rather more of the world's car industry is localized in B, while rather more of the world's apple and blanket industries are localized in A. But world costs, outputs, and consumptions will all be unchanged. The consequential shifts in the other industries which will have this result are shown in the figures in brackets in columns *a* and *b* of the table.

The reason why this is possible is that the factor proportions used in the car industry are intermediate between those used in the apple and blanket industries. Thus the land drawn into B's car industry can be taken mainly from B's land-intensive apple industry (66⅔ from apples and 33⅓ from blankets), while the labour drawn into B's car industry can be taken mainly from B's labour-intensive blanket industry (66⅔ from blankets and 33⅓ from apples). As a result the factor ratios need not change in any of the three industries in B, even though the car industry expands and the other two contract.

Similarly in A, the land released from the car industry can go mainly into the apple industry and the labour released from the car industry can go mainly into the blanket industry, with the result that the factor ratios remain unchanged in all three of A's industries as well. Thus the marginal product of each factor in terms of each product in each country remains unaltered. Moreover, as the figures in brackets in the table show, the world demand and supply for each product remains in equilibrium because, as can be seen, the expansion of the apple industry in A exactly equals its contraction in B, the expansion of the blanket industry in A exactly equals its contraction in B, and the contraction of the car industry in A exactly equals its expansion in B.

In this case the policy of protecting B's car industry has had a perfectly trivial result. In fact the figures as adjusted by the figures in brackets were just as likely as the unadjusted figures to have resulted from a free-trade policy in the first place. If we started with the adjusted figures which show the position when B devotes 900 units of both factors to produce all her cars for herself and then allowed free trade to develop, there would be no forces tending to shift car production to A. Since factor ratios are the same in any one industry in both countries, costs of each product will be the same in both countries and there will be no factors shifting demand away from any of A's products on to B's or vice versa.

The reason why the figures in Table XXXI as adjusted by the figures in brackets are compatible with a continuation of equal factor ratios for each industry in both countries is, of course, because we have only two factors, land and labour, and are still left with two products, apples and blankets, which are freely traded between A and B and which are produced in both countries. But this might not be the result of a policy of protection of B's car industry. Suppose now that B prohibited the import of cars and that B's demand for cars was about the same in size as A's demand for cars. In this case the number of units of each factor employed in B's car industry would have to expand by, say, 400 from 800 to 1,200; and the number employed in A's car industry would have to contract by, say, 400 from 1,600 to 1,200. Now at first for each 100 units by which the employment of the factors rises in B's car industry and falls in A's car industry we can make an adjustment exactly similar to those shown in brackets in Table XXXI; and so long as this goes on there will merely be a trivial relocalization of industries with costs, factor rewards, consumption, and so on all remaining unchanged.

But after the third such adjustment (that is to say when the number of units of land and labour employed in A's car industry have fallen by 300 from 1,600 to 1,300 and in B's car industry have risen by 300 from 800 to 1,100), this type of adjustment can go no further. The reason is that B's apple industry will now have closed down; it will have lost $3 \times 66\frac{2}{3}$ or 200 units of land and $3 \times 33\frac{1}{3}$ or 100 units of labour (i.e. all the land and labour which it initially employed).

If there is another adjustment decreasing both factors by 100 in A's car industry and increasing both factors by 100 in B's car industry, the process will now be different in an essential manner. In A it is true that the land released can still go as to $66\frac{2}{3}$ units to the apple industry and as to $33\frac{1}{3}$ units to the blanket industry, and the labour can still go as to $33\frac{1}{3}$ units to the apple industry and as to $66\frac{2}{3}$ units to the blanket industry, leaving factor ratios unchanged in every industry in A. But in B now all the 100 units of land and the 100 units of labour required for the further expansion of the car industry must come out of the blanket industry. But since the blanket industry starts with a ratio of 1 land to 2 labour, the subtraction of an equal amount of land and labour will lower the ratio of land to labour. The marginal product of land will thus rise and of wages will fall in B below their level in A.

We started with three products, apples, blankets, and cars, in which there was free trade and which were produced in both countries. This was more than sufficient to ensure equality of marginal products for two factors. All that was required for that purpose was two products which satisfied this requirement. But the protection of B's car industry removed two of the three products from satisfying the necessary conditions: it removed cars because cars were no longer freely traded and it removed apples because apples no longer continued to be produced in B as well as in A. This happened because A was previously financing a considerable part of her heavy imports of blankets from B by the sale of her cars to B. When A's exports of cars to B were cut off, she had to develop her other export, apples, to B in order to find the means to continue to finance her import of blankets from B. But in our example the apple industry is small relatively to the other industries; and A can develop her export of apples to the point of having completely eliminated B's production of apples before A has developed sufficient exports to replace the loss of her export of cars to B. From this point onwards the further development of B's car industry to replace the cars previously imported from A can take place only by the contraction of B's blanket industry and the reduction of B's export of blankets to A. But this necessarily leads to a higher and higher ratio of labour to land in B's blanket industry as B's resources go off into her less labour-intensive car industry. There is now only one product, blankets, in which there is free trade and which at the same time is produced both in A and B; and now in this industry the ratio of land to labour is lower in B than in A, so that the marginal product of labour is now higher in A than in B. The protection of B's car industry has led to the specialization of apple production in A with the result that marginal products are no longer equal in the two countries; and the maximization of world production requires the migration of some labour from B to A in search of the highest marginal product. The probability that marginal products will be equalized by free trade is increased by increasing the number of products which can be freely traded, because this reduces the likelihood of specialization of production in one country of products which form a vital link in the process which leads to the equalization of marginal products.

There is yet one more important condition which must be fulfilled if free trade is necessarily to lead to the equalization of factor prices. The various products must be consistently land-intensive, labour-intensive, capital-intensive, and so on. Consider the simple case in which there are only two factors, land and labour, producing only two products, apples and blankets. Suppose that for technical reasons it is necessary always to employ a more or less fixed ratio of land to labour in the production of blankets, but that apples can be produced by extensive farming with little labour and much land or by intensive farming with little land and much labour. In these conditions if the rate of rent were very low and the wage rate very high, apples would be produced with a great deal of land and very little labour, while blankets would continue to be produced with the more or less rigidly fixed ratio of land to labour; the apple industry would employ a higher ratio of land to labour than the blanket industry. But if now the rate of rent were very high and the rate of wages very low, apples would be produced with a great deal of labour and very little land, while the ratio of labour to land would have risen only very little in the blanket industry; the apple industry would now have become the labour-intensive industry.

Suppose that in these conditions we start from a position in which A has an endowment of much land and little labour while B has little land and much labour. If trade is prohibited between A and B, land will be very plentiful and the rate of rent therefore low, while labour will be very scarce and the wage rate very high in A. The opposite will be true in B, where land will be scarce and the rate of rent high and labour will be plentiful and the rate of wages low. In these conditions a much larger ratio of land to labour will be used in A's apple industry than in B's apple industry, and a slightly higher ratio of land to labour will be used in A's blanket industry than in B's blanket industry. In both industries the ratio of land to labour will be higher in A than in B. In consequence, the marginal product of land in terms of both apples and blankets will be lower in A than in B, and the marginal product of labour in terms of both products will be higher in A than in B.

But in these conditions it is not at all certain whether before trade is opened up between A and B the price of apples relatively to the price of blankets will be lower in A or in B. In A the cost of apples will be low because the rate of rent is low and apples are the land-intensive product in A where apple-farming is extensive in character; but in B the cost of apples will be low because the rate of wages is low and apples are the labour-intensive product in B where apple-farming is intensive in character. It would not be at all impossible for the price of apples relatively to the price of blankets to be the same in A as in B in this pre-trade situation; and in this case the opening up of possibilities of trade between A and B would have no effect at all. There would be no profitability in exporting apples from A and blankets from B or vice versa. But the marginal product of labour would continue to be much lower in B than in A, and the maximization of world production would therefore require a migration of labour from B to A.

It would, however, be the most improbable coincidence if in the absence of all trade between A and B the price and cost of apples in terms of blankets happened to be precisely the same in both countries. Let us suppose that this is not the case, but that in the pre-trade position the cost of apples is slightly lower relatively to that of blankets in A than in B. When trade is opened up, apples will then be exported from A to B and blankets from B to A.

The effect in A will be an expansion of demand for the home production of A's land-intensive product, apples, and a contraction of the demand for the home production of her labour-intensive product, blankets. This will tend to raise the rate of rent and to lower the rate of wages in A. In B there will be an expansion of the demand for the home production of B's land-intensive product, blankets, and a contraction of the demand for the home production of her labour-intensive product, apples. Just as in A this will tend to raise the rate of rent and to lower the rate of wages in B. But this movement of factor prices, which is in the same direction in B as in A, will have the opposite effect on the costs of the two products in the two countries. In A the rise in rents and fall in wages will tend to raise the cost of A's land-intensive product, which is apples, in terms of A's labour-intensive product, which is blankets. In B the rise in rents and fall in wages will tend to raise the cost of B's land-intensive product, which is blankets, in terms of B's labour-intensive product, which is apples. Free trade will therefore cause the price of apples to rise in A and to fall in B until a new equilibrium is reached. In this new free-trade equilibrium rents will be higher than before in both A and B and wages will be lower than before in both countries. But there is no reason at all to believe that the marginal products of the factors will be more nearly equal in the two countries; they may be less nearly equal than before. Much less is there reason to believe that free trade will have made the marginal product of each factor in each industry the same in A as in B. The maximization of world production will require the migration of labour from B (where it is plentiful, cheap, used in a high ratio with land, and having therefore a low marginal product) to A (where it is in the opposite situation).

It is difficult to express precisely the conditions which must be fulfilled when there are many products and many factors of production, in order that free trade alone should lead to the equalization of the marginal product of each factor in each industry in the two countries. But we can indicate some of the most important influences which will be at work by summarizing the various points made in this chapter.

First, free trade is the more likely to lead to the equalization of marginal products, the less difference there is in the original factor endowments in the trading countries. In this case the relative scarcities and so the marginal products will not differ too much in the original situation, and free trade will have less work to do in bringing about their complete equalization.

Second, the fewer are the number of factors of production in each country, the smaller will be the number of jobs which free trade will be called upon to do in equalizing marginal products.

Third, the greater are the number of products produced in each country, the larger will be the potential number of channels through which free trade can do its work of equalizing the marginal products of the factors.

Fourth, the larger are the number of products for which a policy of free trade is adopted in both countries, the larger will be the number of actual channels through which free trade can exert its influence.

Fifth, the larger are the differences in the proportions in which the various factors are used in the production of the various products, the greater will be the leverage which free trade can exert upon the relative demands for the various factors in the two countries.

Finally, the more consistent are the differences in the proportions in which the various factors are used in the production of the various products, the more likely is this leverage to be exerted in a way which will bring factor prices into equality in the trading countries.

CHAPTER XXIV

THE SECOND-BEST ARGUMENT FOR FACTOR CONTROLS

We have now expressed the case for freedom of international movements of factors of production. We have shown that, for the reasons explained in Chapters XXI–XXIII, freedom of commodity trade between A and B will not necessarily cause the marginal product of any given factor to be the same in both countries. The marginal product of labour, for example, may remain higher in A than in B; and in this case the maximization of world production would require the movement of labour from B to A, so long as the cost of such migration were less than the excess of the marginal product of labour in A over its marginal product in B. If factors are free to move internationally, are everywhere offered rewards equal to the value of their marginal products, and must meet their own costs of movement, then freedom of factor movements will tend to maximize world production through movement from countries of low to countries of high marginal productivity.

But this case for the freedom of factor movements is subject to a number of exceptions, just as the case for freedom of trade in commodities (expounded in Chapter IX) was found to be subject to a number of exceptions (discussed in Chapters XII–XVIII). Indeed the analogy between the two problems is a very close one. The argument for freedom of factor movements, just like the argument for freedom of commodity trade, is that it is one of the necessary marginal conditions for utopian efficiency. Just as in the case of the argument for freedom of trade, the conditions in which some degree of control over factor movements may be desirable in the interests of economic welfare fall into three groups.

In the first place, control over factor movements may be desirable because we are not dealing with a *utopian* but with a *second-best* situation. It may not be always desirable that a factor should move from A to B simply because its reward in B is higher than its reward in A; for there may be divergences between marginal social values and costs in either or both economies, so that rewards do not correspond to marginal products throughout the world economy.

In the second place, control over factor movements may be desirable to bring about a large structural as opposed to a small marginal change in the world economy. Factor movements will automatically and freely take place from countries of low to countries of high productivity only if the *marginal* product of the factor is higher in the latter than in the former. If the greater productivity in the latter were to depend upon a large movement of factors to enable a *structural* change to take place in the world economy, it is not necessarily true that freedom of movement in a competitive economy would bring about the change.

Finally, control over factor movements may be desirable as a means of influencing the distribution of income. The argument for free factor movements which, by implication at least, we have been examining in the preceding chapters of this Part has been based solely upon the fact that a movement of a factor from a country of low to a country of high productivity will enable a greater total output to be produced with a given amount of effort. It will increase economic *efficiency*. But it may also have effects upon economic *equity*, i.e. upon the distribution of income between the world's citizens, and these distributional effects must be taken into account before final judgement is passed upon the desirability of the movement.

In this and the three following chapters we shall consider these three groups of argument for some positive control over the international movement of factors of production. Our discussion will not be as detailed or as lengthy as the corresponding discussion in Chapters XII–XVIII of the exceptions to the free-trade rule. To a large extent our present problem is the application of exactly the same technique as that used in those earlier chapters, and it would be unnecessarily tedious to repeat it with the same degree of elaboration in its second application to this analogous problem.

In this chapter, then, we shall start by considering the second-best argument for controls over international factor movements.

Theoretically, there might be a problem in the control of factor movements analogous to that discussed in Chapter XIII (on the Partial Freeing of Trade) in the case of trade policy. In that chapter we argued that it might not be desirable to reduce an import duty on the import of one commodity (say, wheat) into A from B if there was in existence a high and unchanged duty on the import of some other closely substitutable commodity (say, oats) into A from B. For while there would be an addition to economic welfare due to the fact that more wheat was moved from A to B (the extent of this primary gain in welfare depending upon the height of the wheat duty, i.e. upon the extent of the divergence between the selling value of the wheat in A and its supply cost in B), there would simultaneously be a decrease in economic welfare due to the reduction in the amount of the substitute oats which would be imported into A from B (the extent of this secondary loss in welfare depending upon the height of the oat duty, i.e. the excess of its selling value in A over its supply cost in B). If the oat duty were higher than the wheat duty and if the two commodities were very close substitutes for each other so that the increase in wheat imports was almost completely offset by the decrease in oat imports, the secondary loss might well outweigh the primary gain.

The present analogy to this analysis would be as follows. Suppose that the marginal product of both of two factors (say, skilled labour and unskilled labour) was higher in A than in B so that the maximization of world production would require the migration of both types of labour from B to A. But suppose that the authorities in A impose some obstacle on the movement of both types of labour into A. Suppose, further, that in A's industries these two types of labour are good substitutes for each other, it being possible to produce in two different ways, the one of which requires skilled labour and the other unskilled labour. In these circumstances the removal of the obstacle to the migration of one type of labour (say, skilled labour) from B to A without any modification of the existing obstacle to the migration of unskilled labour from B to A might do more harm than good. The movement of skilled labour into A would increase economic welfare to an amount dependent upon the excess of the marginal product of skilled labour in A over its marginal product in B. But the consequent cheapening of skilled labour in A would reduce the demand for competing unskilled labour there. If this reduced the flow of unskilled labour from B to A, there would be a secondary loss of economic welfare to an extent dependent upon the excess of the marginal product of unskilled labour in A over its marginal product in B. If the degree of restriction on the immigration of unskilled labour had initially been much more severe than on the immigration of skilled labour, the excess of the marginal product of labour in A over its marginal product in B would be considerably greater in the case of unskilled labour (whose migration is now reduced) than in the case of skilled labour (whose migration is increased). If at the same time the two types of labour were very good substitutes for each other and an increased immigration of skilled labour caused a large decreased demand for unskilled immigrants, the primary gain due to relaxation of the obstacle to the immigration of skilled labour might be more than offset by the secondary loss due to the reduced immigration of unskilled labour.

This case, though theoretically conceivable, is likely in fact to be of only minor importance. One reason for this is that the broad categories of factors whose movements are likely to be subject to governmental controls are much less likely to be close substitutes for each other than are the categories of commodity imports which may be subject to separate import controls. Capital and labour, for example, are less likely to be close substitutes for each other than are two cereals which may be subject to distinct import duties. Indeed, it is very possible that two groups of factors whose movements are subject to distinct controls will actually be complementary to each other. A reduction in the price at which labour can be hired may well lead to an increase in the demand for capital to co-operate with the increased amount of labour; and a reduction in the price at which skilled labour can be employed may well lead to an increased demand for unskilled labour to complement the labour force. In this case there would, of course, be no argument for the maintenance of any restriction on the immigration of skilled labour into A. On the contrary, if there were any existing restriction on the migration of unskilled labour into A and so some excess of the marginal product of unskilled labour in A over its level in B, there would be an argument for some degree of artificial encouragement to the migration of skilled labour into A, since this might cause a secondary increase in the migration of unskilled labour into A on which there would be a gain in economic welfare.

But there is a second and much more important reason why these considerations are likely to be of much less importance in the case of factor movements than they are in the case of commodity trade. Factor movements, if they are controlled at all by national governments, are likely to be controlled by means of quantitative regulations rather than by means of taxes. For example, immigration of labour will probably be controlled by a quantitative quota which lays down the number of migrants of a particular description who may enter the country concerned in any one year; or the export of capital is likely to be regulated by an exchange control which regulates quantitatively the amount of capital which may be lent abroad. It would be unusual for the immigration of labour to be controlled simply by a tax on immigrants or the export of capital simply by a tax on exported capital.

If controls over factor movements are of this quantitative kind, the arguments examined in the previous paragraphs for the control over factor movements become irrelevant. It cannot be argued that an immigration quota for skilled labour should not be enlarged because of the simultaneous existence of an unchanged quota restriction upon the immigration of competing unskilled labour. It may still be true that the removal of the restriction on the immigration of skilled labour into A, by making the supplies of this factor more abundant in A, may reduce the demand for unskilled immigrants in A. But this reduction in the demand for such labour in A will not reduce the scale of its immigration which is limited by a quantitative quota, unless the reduction in demand is so extensive that the reward offered for unskilled labour in A falls down to the level offered for it in B. But in this case there is no excess of the value of the labour in A over its cost in B and there is no secondary loss in welfare connected with any reduced migration from B to A.

Similarly, if skilled labour is complementary with unskilled labour in A, a removal of a restriction on the migration of skilled labour into A may increase the demand for unskilled immigrants into A. But if the number of unskilled workers who may migrate into A is fixed by quota, there can be no secondary gain because there cannot be any secondary increase in the volume of immigration of unskilled workers. Where the control over the immigration of unskilled workers into A takes the form of a quantitative quota, there can be no argument for the maintenance of a restriction on the immigration of skilled workers in order to stimulate indirectly the immigration of competing unskilled workers or for an artificial encouragement of the immigration of skilled workers in order to stimulate indirectly the immigration of complementary unskilled workers. Any partial reduction of barriers or of artificial encouragements to factor movements will make a primary contribution to economic welfare without any secondary loss where the only other divergences between marginal values and costs is due to the existence of other quantitative quota controls over other international factor movements. In this case there is no need to modify the general rule in favour of even partial steps towards freedom of factor movements.

For the reasons which we have just given, it may in the real world be relatively unimportant to consider the secondary effects of a change in the amount of one *factor* which moves from B to A upon the amount of another *factor* which moves from B to A. But it may be important to consider the effect upon economic welfare of the secondary effects of a primary change in the amount of a *factor* which moves from B to A upon the amount of some *product* which moves from B to A. Suppose that blankets are a very labour-intensive product and that labour is scarce and expensive in A and plentiful and cheap in B. In such circumstances the real wage of labour is likely to be higher in A than in B and the price of blankets is likely to be higher in A than in B.

Now in a very essential respect blankets and labour must be regarded as substitutes for each other in the international transactions between A and B. Economic efficiency can be increased either by the import of more of B's blankets into A (which will indirectly reduce the demand for labour in A and increase the demand for labour in B) or else by the migration of labour from B to A (which will indirectly increase the supply of blankets in A and reduce the supply of blankets in B).

But these two movements are not always perfect substitutes for each other. Suppose, for example, that B had some atmospheric advantage in the production of blankets. Then it would be better for the labour to stay in B and produce the blankets there for export to A than that the labour should move to A to produce the blankets there. This would show itself in the price relationships in A and in B. If, because of the difference in atmospheres, labour was much more productive in the blanket industry in B than in A, then while the wage of labour might be somewhat higher in A than in B (say, 20 per cent higher in A than in B) the cost and so the price of blankets might be much higher (say, 100 per cent higher) in A than in B.[1]

Suppose that in these conditions labour is prevented by a quota restriction from moving from B to A, although the wage rate is 20 per cent higher in A than in B: and suppose that blankets when they are imported into B from A are subject to a 100 per cent *ad valorem* duty. There is an excess of marginal value in A over marginal cost in B of 20 per cent in the case of a migration of labour from B to A and of 100 per cent in the case of an expansion of A's imports of B's blankets. Now the primary effect of an enlargement of the quota for the migration of labour from B to A would be to raise economic welfare because of the 20 per cent divergence between the wage in B and in A. But the consequent increase in the output of blankets in A and decrease in the output of blankets in B might cause a secondary reduction in the export of blankets from B to A on which a 100 per cent loss of economic welfare would be experienced. This secondary loss might outweigh the primary gain. There may be a case for controlling factor movements on the grounds that they will cause secondary changes in the trade in products for which they are close substitutes and on which there is a large divergence between marginal values and costs.[2]

The second-best argument for controls over factor movements may also be important, when we consider the analogy with the argument for trade controls presented in Chapter XIV. It was there argued that it is sometimes desirable to control the movement of goods between A and B on the grounds that there are divergences between marginal values and costs within A's or B's economy. For example, suppose that B is exporting to A some commodity in the case of which there is a very large divergence between marginal values and costs in B but a very small or

[1] Another reason why it might be better to make the blankets in B rather than move the labour to A would be if the cost of transport of blankets were low and of labour were high. This also would show itself in the price relationships. Suppose that the wage of labour and the price of blankets were both 50 per cent higher in A than in B; that the cost of transport of blankets was zero; and that the cost of movement of labour was equal to 20 per cent of the wage rate in B. Then after allowing for costs of movement the excess of the marginal value of blankets in A over their marginal cost in B would be 50 per cent, but the excess of the marginal value of labour in A over the marginal cost of acquiring it in B and moving it to A would be only 50 — 20 or 30 per cent.

[2] In the case in which the factor movements are controlled quantitatively there can be no reverse case for a control over the trade in products in order to avoid secondary changes in the international movement of factors which are close substitutes for the products primarily concerned. In terms of our example a reduction in A's 100 per cent duty on the import of B's blankets might indirectly reduce the demand for labour and so the wage rate in A. But it would not reduce the amount of labour migration from B to A (which is subject to a quantitative restriction) until the wage rate in A had been reduced to the wage rate in B; and in this case there would be no loss of economic welfare from this secondary repercussion, since there would no longer be any excess of the marginal value of labour in A over its marginal cost in B.

zero divergence in A. Then in the interests of economic efficiency it might be desirable to restrict the export of the product from B or its import into A. A small reduction in the supplies in A would not appreciably affect welfare, since in A the marginal cost of the product is equal to its marginal value; but an equal small increase in the supplies available in B would appreciably increase economic welfare, since in B the marginal value of the product considerably exceeds its marginal cost.

Now there may well be many analogies to this sort of trade-policy problem in the case of factor movements as well. Consider the position of one particular factor—say, skilled labour of a particular kind—in A and B. There are a number of reasons why in either or both countries there may be a considerable divergence between the marginal social net product of this labour and the reward it actually receives, i.e. between its marginal social value and cost. These causes of divergence fall into the familiar categories.

First, there may well be external economies associated with marginal increases in the employment of this factor in either or both countries. For example, if B were a country in which the employment of skilled labour were on rather a small scale, some building up of this labour force might lead to a general diffusion of more skilled techniques throughout the labour force of the country. There might in this way be a considerable marginal external economy associated with the increased employment of this skilled labour in B. At the same time if A were already highly industrialized and equipped with a large skilled labour force, the marginal external economies associated with a further expansion of that force might be quite small.

A second reason why there might be a higher excess of marginal value over marginal cost for a particular type of skilled labour in B than in A might be due to a difference in the organization of the labour market in the two countries. Suppose, for example, that the employers are fewer in number or more monopolistically organized in B than in A, so that employers in B by restricting the amount of labour which they employ have a monopsonist's power of keeping down the wage rate. If in A the individual employers are more competitive, because they are greater in number or less monopolistically organized, and if at the same time the workers in A are more highly organized, then the individual employer in A may have no appreciable effect upon the wage rate by expanding the volume of his employment. In such a case employers in B will cease to employ more of this labour at a point at which the wage rate is still considerably below the value of the labour's marginal product; but employers in A would employ labour until the wage rate paid was practically as high as the value of the marginal product. The divergence between marginal social value and cost in this labour market would be much higher in B than in A.

A third reason for divergences between the marginal product and the net wage of the skilled labour in question might be the levying of taxes on the incomes of the wage-earners concerned. Thus if the marginal rate of tax on the skilled labour were much higher in B than in A, this also would be a reason why the divergence between marginal values and costs in this particular labour market should be higher in B than in A.

Now if for these or any other reason the wage offered to labour is lower relatively to the marginal product of labour in B than it is in A, then there will be an uneconomic tendency to employ this labour in A rather than in B. Even though the marginal product of this labour is higher in B than in A the reward offered for the labour might be lower in B than in A. In such circumstances, if the cost of movement of the labour were small, there might be some tendency for the labour to migrate from B to A instead of moving from A to B, as it should do in order to maximize world production. In this case it would be desirable in the interests of economic efficiency not merely to restrain the movement of the labour from B to A but also to take some positive measures to stimulate such movement from A to B.

If there is some cost of movement between A and B, the possibilities are a little more complicated, though the principles involved are exactly the same. This is illustrated in Table XXXII. Throughout that table we assume that the wage rate in A is \$100 and the value of the marginal product of labour is \$110, which means that there is a 10 per cent excess of marginal value over marginal cost in the labour market in A. Throughout the table we also assume that the divergence between marginal value and cost in the labour market in B is greater than in A and is in fact always 30 per cent. (The figure in column *b* of the table is always 30 per cent above the corresponding figure in column *a*.)

In case i (the top half of the table), we assume that there is only a small cost of movement of the labour from A to B or from B to A, namely \$5.[1] We can now see in columns (*c*) and (*d*) that there are five possible situations in so far as migration policy is concerned.

(1) If the marginal product of the labour in B is greater than \$136·5, the wage paid in B will be greater than \$105, since there is always a 30 per cent divergence in B and $\$105 \times 1{\cdot}3 = \$136{\cdot}5$. In this case labour will in fact move from A to B because the wage in B, being greater than \$105, will exceed the wage in A (\$100) by more than the cost of movement (\$5). In this case also the labour should move from A to B because its marginal product in B (which is more than \$136·5) exceeds its marginal product in A (\$110) by more than the cost of

[1] This cost must be reckoned as the interest and sinking fund over the worker's future working life of the capital cost involved in the move. See p. 358 above.

movement ($5). No interference with the direction of migration is required.

(2) If the value of the marginal product of the labour in B is between $136·5 and $123·5, the wage paid in B will be between $105 and $95. In this case labour will in fact move in neither direction. The wage paid in A is $100. At anything lower than a wage of $105 in B it will not pay labour to spend $5 on moving from A to B; and at any higher than a wage of $95 in B it will not pay labour to spend $5 on moving from B to A. Labour will not move. But it should still move from A to B,

TABLE XXXII

Domestic Divergences and International Factor Movements

Wage rate in A is $100 and in B is (*a*)	Value of marginal production in A is 1·1 times the wage rate or $110 and in B is 1·3 times the wage rate or (*b*)	Labour will move (*c*)	Labour should move (*d*)
	Case (i). *Cost of Movement is* $5		
$	$	from A to B	from A to B
105·0	136·5		
		in neither direction	
95·0	123·5		
		from B to A	
88·5	115·0		
			in neither direction
80·75	105·0		
			from B to A
0	0		
	Case (ii). *Cost of Movement is* $50		
		from A to B	from A to B
150	195		
		in neither direction	
123	160		
			in neither direction
50	65		
		from B to A	
46	60		
			from B to A
0	0		

since the marginal product of labour in B (which is above $123·5) still exceeds the marginal product of the labour in A ($110) by more than the cost of movement ($5). A policy for the artificial stimulation of migration from A to B is now required.

(3) Suppose now that the marginal product of labour in B falls between $123·5 and $115, so that the wage in B lies between $95 and $88·5. Labour will now move from B to A since the wage in A ($100) exceeds the wage in B (which is below $95) by more than the cost of movement. But in fact the labour should move in the opposite direction, from A to B, since the marginal product of labour in B (which is above $115) exceeds the marginal product in A ($110) by more than the cost of movement ($5). It would now be desirable not merely to stimulate the movement of A's labour into B but also to restrict the movement of B's labour into A.

(4) Suppose the marginal product in B to be between $115 and $105. Then labour should not move in either direction since the difference between the marginal product in A ($110) and in B (between $115 and $105) would not cover the cost of movement in either direction. But since the wage of labour in B will be below $95 (i.e. between $88·5 and $80·75) labour will want to move from B to A. This emigration from B would need to be directly restrained.

(5) If the marginal product in B is below $105 then labour should move from B to A, and labour will have a still greater incentive to move in that direction. No direct control is required to alter the direction of the migration.

In the second half of Table XXXII (case ii of the table) we examine the possibilities when the cost of movement is very much greater, namely $50. As will be seen from columns *c* and *d*, the pattern of possible situations is in one respect different from that of case i examined in the first half of the table. But the principles are exactly the same, and the detailed working is left to the reader to consider for himself.

The result is that we start once more with a range (when the marginal product in B is above $195) when labour will and should move from A to B. No policy is required to affect the direction of the flow of migration. We go on, as before, to a second range (when the marginal product in B is between $195 and $160) when labour will no longer have any incentive to move from A to B although in the interests of economic efficiency it should do so. The third range is now one (with the marginal product in B between $160 and $65) in which there neither is nor should be any incentive to move in either direction, so that no positive migration policy is required. It is in this respect that the situations in case ii with heavy costs of movement differ from those in case i with low costs of movement. We now have a middle range in which there neither is nor should be any incentive to move, instead of a middle range in which there is an incentive to move from B to A although economic efficiency requires a movement from A to B. We then have, as in the former case, a fourth range (with the marginal product in B between $65 and $60) in which labour will wish to move from B to A but should not do so, and a fifth range (with the marginal product in B less than $60) in which labour will and should wish to move from B to A. In this fourth range some restriction of the migration of labour from B to A would be justified,[1] while in the fifth range once more no positive migration policy is required to alter the direction of the movement of labour.

[1] Throughout this chapter phrases such as 'the restriction of migration would be justified' must be taken to refer only to the effects of migration policy upon economic welfare. Such conclusions may need qualification on non-economic grounds. Thus it may be argued that in the interests of personal freedom individuals should not be constrained to reside in or prohibited from residing in any particular country. For this reason, it may well be argued, the encouragements or discouragements to the movements of labour which are required in the interests of world economic efficiency should be provided in the form of subsidies to or taxes on labour movements, rather than in the form of direct quantitative controls.

Moreover, there is another important non-economic reason why these conclusions may need modification. For sociological reasons it may be desirable to limit the speed with which one community absorbs immigrants of an alien race and culture. Such considerations might provide a reason for limiting migration more strictly than would be justified on the economic grounds expressed in this chapter. In so far as free trade in commodities or the free movement of other factors such as capital are substitutes for the free movement of labour in achieving economic efficiency (cf. Chapters XIX–XXIII), any such non-economic arguments against extensive population movements would reinforce the arguments for the freeing of commodity trade and of the international movement of other factors as alternative means of promoting the efficient use of the world's resources.

CHAPTER XXV

DOMESTIC FISCAL POLICIES AND INTERNATIONAL MOVEMENTS OF LABOUR AND CAPITAL

In this chapter we propose to illustrate the second-best argument for factor controls of which we gave a general outline in the preceding chapter by means of a more detailed consideration of one particular problem. We shall suppose that countries A and B both have domestic fiscal policies which are designed to bring about some redistribution of income domestically within each country. To what extent and in what ways is the existence of such domestic fiscal policies likely to modify the general argument in favour of the freedom of international factor movements?

Before we can start to answer this question we must first consider the problem of double taxation. A distinction must be drawn between a factor of production and the owner of that factor of production or, perhaps more accurately, the person who enjoys the income earned by the services of the factor in question.

In the case of labour this distinction is of relatively little importance. If a worker works at a particular job in a particular region and earns an income from that work, then the same individual is likely to enjoy that income in the same place. This is, of course, not necessarily or universally true. The most obvious exception to it might occur in the case of slavery. The owner of a unit of labour (i.e. the slave owner) and the unit of labour itself (i.e. the slave) are no longer identical. The slave owner may live in country A and put his slaves to work in country B.

In such a case the problem of double taxation might arise. We are supposing that the authorities in both A and B have income tax systems whereby incomes of all kinds are taxed on a certain scale. Is the income produced by the slave in B but enjoyed by the slave owner in A to be taxed by the government of B or by the government of A? If it is taxed by both, then there is a case of double taxation. If it is taxed by B's government, then the principle of taxation in the country of origin of the income is observed. If it is taxed by A's government, then the principle of taxation in the country of residence of the income-receiver is observed.

Even if we rule out the case of slavery, it is still possible for the problem of the double taxation of wages to arise. A man may, for example, be resident normally and for the greater part of the year in A, but may go to B for a short stay where he earns some income which he takes back with him to spend in A. It is even possible for a man to earn income in B without ever leaving A, as in the case of a man who can give advice by post or telephone, thus earning an income in a region other than that in which he resides. Another example of a somewhat different kind is where a man migrates from B to A leaving his family in B. If he then remits a large part of his earnings in A back to his family in B, there is once more a distinction between the country in which the income is earned and the country in which it is enjoyed. All such cases can give rise to the problem of double taxation—whether the income should be subject to tax by the government of the one country or of the other or by both.

In the case of labour, however, by far the most normal case is for the worker and his family to enjoy the income which he earns in the same country as that in which he earns it. The problem of double taxation does not then arise; there is clearly only one national tax authority which can levy a tax upon the income in question. In what follows we shall therefore neglect all problems of double taxation in the case of the wages of labour.

But when we turn to other factors of production the position is very different. A landowner need not reside in the same country as his land nor need an owner of stocks and shares invest his money in concerns which operate within his own country. Indeed, a typical case of an international movement of capital is where an owner of capital resident in A invests his capital in B without himself emigrating from A to B. In the case of such factors as land and capital, therefore, the problem of double taxation arises in a way which cannot be neglected.

Let us suppose that someone resident in A owns some capital which is invested in B. So far as the problem of double taxation is concerned there are now four possible cases.

(1) It may be that the government of A levies tax on all income enjoyed by the residents of A, while the government of B levies tax on all income originating in B.[1] In this case the income on the capital in question will be subject to A's income tax and to B's income tax. This is the case of double taxation. It may act as an important deterrent to the international movement of capital from countries of low to countries of high marginal productivity of capital. A resident in A who considers investing capital in B because the productivity of capital in B is higher than in A must either pay tax twice on his dividends or himself be prepared to migrate from A to B.[2]

[1] In some cases a country will levy tax on all income which is enjoyed by its residents as well as on all income originating in its territory. This is, of course, a special case which is included in the above category.

[2] Migration with his capital will not, of course, solve his problem if B's government taxes income enjoyed in B as well as income originating in B and if he does not take all his capital with him. For he would then be taxed in A and

If it cost the owners of capital nothing to migrate from one country to another and if there were no real or imaginary amenities involved in residing in one country rather than in another, owners would tend to move with their capital from countries of low to countries of high productivity of capital.[1] But it does cost something for owners of capital to migrate and there are advantages to people in residing in one country rather than another. It is not merely that people may have a very real preference for living in the country in which they were born and bred, in which their friends and relatives also reside, and in which their own language is spoken. There may be more tangible economic advantages. Thus, to take an extreme example, suppose that capital must be invested in some parched and arid desert or in some bleak sub-arctic region in order to exploit some mineral resource which is located in either of these places. If the owner of the capital who lends it to the enterprise concerned must reside there with his capital, he may not only find the climate intolerable but the cost of living excessively high, since some goods (e.g. performances of operas and ballets) may be unobtainable and others (e.g. goods whose cost of transport from manufacturing areas is very high) obtainable only at very great cost. It is important economically that the owner of capital should be free to reside in a region different from that in which his capital is invested; and in so far as double taxation tends to tie the owner geographically to his property, it introduces an important inefficiency into the economic system.

(2) A second possibility is that the governments of both A and B levy tax on all income originating in their countries but avoid levying tax on income originating in a foreign country but enjoyed by residents of their own country. In this case a resident of A who owns capital invested in B would be subject only to B's tax and not to A's. From the point of view of the incentive to invest capital where its productivity is highest this would be likely to be an improvement on the case of double taxation discussed in (1). A man who moves his capital from A to B in search of a higher yield would no longer be deterred by the fact that he would have to pay tax twice over. If the rate of tax in B were the same as the rate of tax in A and if the cost of moving the capital were negligible, this system would give the correct incentives. If the gross yield on capital were higher in B than in A, a resident of A would improve his net income by moving his capital from A to B. But the rate of tax in B may differ from the rate of tax in A. If the tax rate is higher

in B on the income on the property which he left behind in A. But if he must take all his property with him he will be deprived of an important opportunity of spreading his risks by investing in a number of different concerns in different countries.

[1] This, of course, is subject to the fact that if there are marked differences in national tax rates they and their capital will tend to be drawn uneconomically towards the countries where tax rates are lowest.

in B than in A, there will still be some uneconomic fiscal disincentive against shifting capital from A to B, even when its product is somewhat higher in B than in A, though this uneconomic disincentive will not be so marked as in the case of double taxation. If the rate of tax is lower in B than in A, then there will be some uneconomic fiscal incentive to shift capital from A to B, even when its yield is not higher in B than in A. Indeed, in this case a system of double taxation might conceivably be preferable from the point of view of economic efficiency, because this might prevent an export of capital from A to B solely because the tax rate is lower in B than in A and even though the productivity of capital were higher in A than in B. We can sum up the case in which both governments tax according to the origin of the income by saying that it would leave the owners of capital with no special fiscal incentive or disincentive to choose a particular country of residence. They could choose the residence which really suited their tastes best because their tax payment would not depend upon it, and in this respect the system would be an efficient one. But, on the other hand, there would be an inefficient tendency to invest their capital in those countries in which the rate of tax was lowest, and this would introduce an economic inefficiency into the system.

(3) Another possibility is that each government adopts the principle of taxing all incomes enjoyed by the residents of its own territory without levying tax on income originating in its own territory but accruing to residents in a foreign country. In this case a resident in A who owns capital invested in B will pay tax on the income to A's government at the rate of tax levied by A's income tax law. From the point of view of the incentive to invest capital where its yield is highest this system normally has advantages over both the system of double taxation and of taxation according to the country of origin of the income. For the rate of tax levied now depends upon the residence of the owner and not at all upon the country in which the capital is invested. If the movement of capital from A to B would bring in a larger gross (pre-tax) yield, it will also bring in a larger net (post-tax) yield, since if the owner continues to reside in A the rate of tax will not depend upon the country in which the investment takes place.

There are theoretically two possible cases in which this principle would provide the ideal set of incentives for the location of capital investments. In the first place, if the cost of movement of capital from A to B were zero, then the capital would move whenever its net yield was higher in B than in A; and since its net yield would be higher in B if and only if its gross yield were higher in B, it would always in fact move when it should move and would not move when it should not move. Secondly, if the tax schedule in A were of the poll tax variety (see p. 50) so that no additional tax were paid on any increase in income, the increase in the net yield (i.e. after tax) would be equal to the increase in the gross yield (i.e. before tax) due to the movement of the capital; and the capital would therefore be moved if the increase in its gross yield (i.e. in its marginal product) were less than the cost of moving it.

But if the cost of movement of capital were not zero and the marginal rate of tax were not zero, the capital would not always move when it ought to do so. Suppose, as is illustrated in the following figures, that

	Gross yield or marginal product	Net yield after tax of 40%	Increase in gross yield	Increase in net yield
	$	$	$	$
In A . .	100	60	—	—
In B . .	150	90	50	30

a given amount of capital has a marginal product with a value of $100 in A and of $150 in B. Then the capital should, in the interests of economic efficiency, move from A to B if the cost of its movement is less than $50, which is the increase in product due to its movement. But with a tax rate of 40 per cent on income enjoyed in A the net yield will rise as a result of moving the capital from A to B only by $30 (from $60 to $90). If the cost of moving the capital were above $30 but under $50, we should have a situation in which it would not pay to move the capital although, in the interests of economic efficiency, it ought to be moved.

In these conditions it is conceivable that the principle of levying tax according to the country of origin of the income might have a better effect from the point of view of economic efficiency. Suppose that in the numerical illustration which we have just given the income were subject to A's tax of 40 per cent if the capital were invested in A but to B's tax of only 26⅔ per cent if the capital were invested in B. Then we should have the situation shown in the following figures:

	Gross yield or marginal product	Net yield after tax of 40% in A or 26⅔% in B	Increase in gross yield	Increase in net yield
	$	$	$	$
In A . .	100	60	—	—
In B . .	150	110	50	50

The total amount deducted in tax would be the same (namely $40), whichever country the capital was invested in; from the point of view of the investor the tax would correspond to a poll tax; and the increase in net yield would correspond to the increase in gross yield. But this would, of course, be a very special case. The incentive to move the capital from A to B would be increased only if the rate of tax on capital originating in B was lower than that originating in A. And even then it would be entirely fortuitous if this difference happened to be of just the correct size. It might be insufficient to give an incentive for the capital to move; or it might, on the other hand, be so great that the total tax payable was lower in B than in A, in which case it might give an incentive to move to B some capital for which the cost of movement exceeded any increase in yield and which, therefore, ought not to be moved either.

Generally speaking, we can say that if the cost of movement of the capital is small or if the national tax systems approach those of poll taxes, then the levying of taxes according to the country of residence of the recipient of the income will be ideal from the point of view of the most efficient location of factors concerned. But it would, of course, not be ideal from the point of view of the choice of residence of the owners of the factors. Owners of capital would have some tendency to take up residence in the countries in which the tax rate was lowest. They might invest their capital in the country where its productivity was really highest; but they would not necessarily reside and spend their incomes in the country where the amenities of the country and the goods and services which they would secure with this income really suited them best. They would tend to be drawn towards the country in which the rate of tax was lowest.

In this connexion it is important to realize that it is not always possible to divide the country of the capital and of the capitalist so readily as has been assumed in the above exposition. In the case of an investor who plays no direct part in the concern in which his money is invested this division is quite possible. A rentier in A can own bonds of a concern which operates in B as easily as the bonds of a concern which operates in A. But with the entrepreneur, i.e. the capitalist who is actively engaged in operating in business, the case is quite different. A man who has risked his own capital in a business which he is actively engaged in managing cannot be readily separated geographically from his capital. If national tax systems are based upon the taxation of the incomes received by the residents in their countries, then entrepreneurs will have an inducement to reside in the country of lowest tax rates; and they must bring their capital with them to set up businesses in the same country. To this extent the principle of taxation according to the residence of the income earners as well as the principle of taxation according to the origin of the income will give an incentive for risk capital to move to the country of lowest tax rates.

(4) A final, though perhaps unlikely, possibility is that while the

authorities in A exempt from tax all income originating outside A even though it is enjoyed in A, the authorities in B exempt from tax all income enjoyed outside B even though it originates in B. In this case a resident of A who owned capital invested in B would escape tax altogether. Such a system would, of course, give an uneconomic incentive for capital to be invested in B and for owners of capital to migrate to A.

The effect upon international capital movements of different national fiscal systems for the domestic redistribution of income will clearly depend upon which of these four possible situations exists in so far as the problem of double taxation is concerned. In what follows we shall assume that double taxation (case 1) and the complete avoidance of tax (case 4) is avoided by international agreement to adhere either to the principle of taxing a factor's income in the country of origin (case 2) or to the principle of taxing the income in the country of residence of its owner (case 3). We do this primarily in order to avoid undue prolixity in our analysis; the reader must work out for himself the modifications of the analysis which would be necessary if either case 1 or case 4 were in fact applicable.

In the above paragraphs we have discussed, at least by implication, some of the arguments for and against the two principles of taxation according to the country of origin and according to the country of enjoyment of income. But there is one distributional argument which has not so far appeared. Suppose that A is a net creditor and B a net debtor country, i.e. that on balance owners of capital resident in A hold capital invested in B. If the principle of origin of income is adopted it will be B's government which receives the revenue raised on the income which is transferred from B to A. But if the principle of enjoyment of income is adopted, then A's government will receive the revenue involved. A change from the one system to the other would thus involve a net shift of revenue from B's government to A's government. This would involve a redistribution of world income which would be desirable if the distributional weight to be applied to A's citizens were higher than that to be applied to B's citizens. But if, as may perhaps be the more probable case, the distributional weight applied to the citizens of the debtor country is higher than that applied to the citizens of the creditor country, then on these distributional grounds the principle of taxation according to origin of income would have an advantage.

On somewhat different distributional grounds the advantage may seem to lie with the principle of taxation according to the country of enjoyment of income. A national tax system will achieve greater equity among the national citizens if citizens with the same real income are taxed at the same rate. This goal would be more easily attained with the adoption of the principle of taxation according to the country of enjoyment of income. In such a case the national taxing authority need draw up only a single schedule taxing each individual according to the total income which he enjoys from all sources. But if the principle of taxation according to the country of origin of income were adopted, one citizen might be taxed at one rate because his income originated in one country while another citizen was taxed at a different rate though his income was the same, merely because it originated in another country.[1]

With these introductory remarks about the different effects of national tax systems which are based on the principle of taxing income enjoyed in the country and those based on the principle of taxing income originating in the country, we may now pass to the main topic of this chapter. What will be the effect upon international movements of labour and capital of national fiscal policies designed to redistribute income within each of our countries A and B?

In order to focus attention upon the problems which arise specifically because A and B are separate countries with separate fiscal policies, let us suppose at first that the two countries form two regions of one single country with a single government and a single budgetary system designed for the redistribution of income from the richer to the poorer citizens of this single country. We will examine some of the implications of such a unitary fiscal system and in particular we will inquire into the implications of this system upon the movements of the factors of production between the two regions, A and B, of this single State. We will then suppose that these two regions are divided into two distinct nations, A and B, which have to be quite separate and self-supporting in their own distinct fiscal policies; and we will then inquire what is the difference which this separation of budgetary systems may have upon the incentive for factors of production to move between them.

Suppose then that the country AB has a single fiscal system designed to redistribute income from rich to poor within AB. There is a single general income tax within the country such that any individual who

[1] In fact it is only persons and not factors (i.e. the owners of machines and not the machines themselves) who can make sacrifices, pay taxes, be the subjects of equitable or inequitable treatment, or have their welfare increased or decreased. It seems logical therefore to assess taxes on the recipients of income. This is certainly the case where there is only one tax system. But where there are two systems there is a choice of illogicalities. Is it more illogical to tax at different rates two citizens of A who have the same income generated in A and in B or to tax at different rates a citizen of A and a citizen of B who have the same income generated in B? But while it may not be more logical it is certainly technically easier to make sure of taxing all recipients of income enjoyed in A at the same rate than it is to tax all recipients of income generated in B at the same rate. If B's tax is progressive, this involves the authorities in B assessing the whole income received by a resident of A. In fact taxes levied in B on income originating in B but enjoyed in A are not likely to be assessed on a scale which is progressive according to the income of the recipients in A, but, like a profits tax, at a flat rate on all such income.

lives anywhere within AB will pay a given amount in income tax, this amount depending upon the size of his income but not upon where he lives or where he earns his income. The revenue from this income is used to pay social security benefits or to finance other social services, the amount of benefit received by any citizen depending once more upon the size of his income but not upon where he lives within the country AB.

Now if each individual received in benefits the same amount which he paid in taxes—what we may call the pure benefit principle—there would clearly be no interference with economic incentives in so far as economic efficiency was concerned. Each individual could still choose the most productive region of the country to earn his income and the most economic region to spend his income without any distortion from this pattern through the fiscal system, because what he sacrificed in tax would be equal to what he gained in benefit, regardless of where he earned or he lived.

But this would not necessarily continue to be the case if the fiscal system redistributed net income and benefits from the rich to the poor, if, that is to say, the rich man paid more in tax than he received in State benefits and the poor man received more in State benefits than he paid in tax. Theoretically such a fiscal redistribution of income could take place without any net effect upon economic incentives if the income tax was made up of a system of progressive poll taxes and the social benefits were made up of a system of progressive poll subsidies. (See p. 50.) In other words, it would be possible to redistribute income by fiscal policies without affecting incentives if the tax levied on potentially richer citizens were greater than that levied on potentially poorer citizens and the benefit received by potentially richer citizens was less than that received by potentially poorer citizens without either of them being given the opportunity to avoid tax or to attract more benefit by earning less. But, as we have seen in Chapter III, such a system, though theoretically conceivable, is an administrative impossibility.

If the fiscal system in AB is redistributive between rich and poor, it will in fact impose a marginal burden on the rich and confer a marginal benefit on the poor. A rich man by earning more will incur a larger net burden (in the sense of an excess of tax payment over benefit received) and the poor by earning less will attract some additional net fiscal advantage (in the sense of receiving a larger excess of benefit over tax payment). Such a tax system in AB will have two important implications from our present point of view.

First, it must be realized that the mere fact that the fiscal system of AB is a unified one in the sense in which we have described it above does not mean that the redistributive fiscal system exerts no adverse effect upon the movement of the factors of production to their most economic position within AB. Thus suppose that some factor of production—say, a particular type of skilled labour—can earn \$100 within region A and \$200 within region B of the single country. But suppose that the fiscal system is such that a citizen earning \$100 must pay an excess of taxes over benefits of \$20 whereas a citizen earning \$200 must pay an excess of taxes over benefits of \$50. Then by moving from region A to region B the value of the skilled labour's marginal product would rise by \$100 from \$100 to \$200; but the skilled labour's net income would rise by only \$70 from \$80 (i.e. \$100 less net taxes of \$20) to \$150 (i.e. \$200 less net taxes of \$50). If the cost of movement were zero, this would not matter. The worker concerned could by moving increase his net income after paying taxes so long as his gross earnings were greater in the new region. But with a marginal tax system he would increase his net income by less than the value of his pre-tax earnings, i.e. by less than the value of his marginal product. In our example his product would rise by \$100 but his net income by only \$70. If there is some cost involved in the movement from A to B, the fiscal system might discourage him from moving even though economic efficiency would require his movement. Thus, in our example, if the cost of movement were \$80, he ought to move (since his product would rise by \$100 which is more than sufficient to cover the cost of movement) but he would have no incentive to move (since his net earnings would rise by only \$70 which is less than the cost of movement).

This is, of course, only a particular regional example of the general principle that a marginal system of taxation will have some adverse effects upon economic incentives. Exactly the same sort of consideration would arise if the skilled worker in our example were considering improving his income from \$100 to \$200 not by moving from one region to another within AB but by working harder, by moving into another occupation, or by training for a still greater skill. The value of his marginal net product would rise by \$100 in each of these cases, but with the given fiscal system his net income would rise by only \$70. In each case the extra effort or expense might be more than compensated by \$100 but less than compensated by \$70. There would be some blunting of all these economic incentives.

There is a second implication of the unified fiscal system in AB which is relevant for our present purpose. The fiscal system is quite neutral between the regions A and B in the sense that a citizen with a given income would bear the same net tax burden whether he resided in A or in B. But this would not imply that the one region would not in a sense be subsidizing the other. It might so happen that because of differences in immobile factors (like land or other natural resources) or in atmospheres for production it would be economic for some industries to be concentrated in region A and for others to be concentrated in region B; and it might well follow from this that certain mobile factors ought therefore to move into A and others into B, so that the mobile factors matched the immobile factors. Suppose that as a result of this it so happened that the industries which required a very large proportion of capital and highly skilled labour to unskilled labour ought properly, purely on efficiency grounds, to be concentrated in A, whereas the industries which required a large proportion of unskilled labour were concentrated in B. Then a large proportion of the high incomes per head would be concentrated in A and a large proportion of the low incomes per head in B. The redistributive tax system would in fact mean that much revenue was on balance levied on the rich citizens of A and used to pay out benefits to the poorer citizens of B. In this sense, merely because of the geographical distribution of rich and poor individuals, region A would be subsidizing region B. Each system would in fact be self-financing only if either there were no element of redistribution involved in the unified tax system (i.e. if the pure benefit principle were involved so that each citizen received in benefits exactly as much as he paid in taxes) or else if by chance it so happened that the average income per head[1] in region A was the same as in region B. But we cannot rely upon the distribution of incomes being uniformly spread over AB in this manner.

Suppose now that this system of uniform fiscal arrangements throughout AB is interrupted by its division into two separate countries A and B each of whose budgets must be self-supporting. When the division first takes place A, the country in which there is a relatively high average income, will have an excess of tax revenue over payments of social security benefits, while B, with the lower average income, will have an excess of expenditure on benefits over tax revenue. In order that each may now be fiscally self-supporting, in A the rates of tax must be lowered and/or the rates of benefits raised and in B the rates of tax must be raised and/or the rates of benefit lowered. What effect will this have upon the incentive for factors of production to move between A and B? In considering this problem we must distinguish between at least three different influences which may be at work. (i) There may be differences in A and B, which are perfectly justifiable on grounds of economic efficiency, between the ratios of 'rich' to 'poor' factors employed in the two regions. (ii) There may in A or in B be a discrepancy between the ratio of 'rich' to 'poor' factors which ought to exist on grounds of economic efficiency and the ratio of 'rich' to 'poor' factors which does in fact exist. (iii) There may be differences in the degree of redistribution of incomes which the two governments of A and of B respectively may attempt to bring about through their fiscal

[1] And, to be accurate, its dispersion about that average.

policies. We will consider these different points in turn by examining cases in which each of these influences is in turn isolated.

Let us start off then by considering influence (i). In order to isolate its effect we assume that the governments of A and B both desire to carry out the same sort of policy of redistribution of incomes and that initially the mobile factors (labour and capital) are distributed in the most economic way between A and B, so that the value of the marginal product of labour (or of capital) is initially the same in A as in B. But because of differences in the immobile factors or in the productive atmosphere in the two countries we assume that a higher proportion of the well-paid factors are concentrated in A and of the lower-paid factors in B. For this reason the average income is higher in A than in B.

The separation of the two fiscal systems will now mean that net tax rates can be lowered in A and must be raised in B. The almost inevitable result is that the net marginal tax burden is lowered for all factors of production in A and is raised for all factors of production in B. Every mobile factor of production will now have some incentive to move from the poor country B to the rich country A and this incentive for movement will be a wholly undesirable one from the point of view of economic efficiency. Highly skilled and rich labour will have an incentive to move from B to A because there are more rich people and less poor people in A, and therefore in order to give a certain benefit to each poor person a lower rate of tax is required on each rich person in A than in B. Unskilled and poorly paid labour will have an incentive to move from B to A because there are less poor people and more rich people in A, so that a given rate of net tax on each rich person raises sufficient revenue to give a higher rate of benefit to each poor person in A than in B.

A similar uneconomic incentive will be at work as regards international capital movements if the tax systems in A and B are both devised on the principle of taxing income in the country in which the income has its source. Since marginal net tax rates will be higher in B than in A there will be an incentive for capital to move uneconomically from B to A. But if the tax systems are based upon the country of residence of the recipient of the income there will be no incentive to move capital as such uneconomically from B to A, but there will be an uneconomic incentive for capitalists and entrepreneurs to move from B to A.

The extent to which there will for this reason be an uneconomic incentive to move from B to A will depend upon the cost of movement. If this cost is low, quite small differences in net tax rates due to these differences in the appropriate industrial structures of A and B might cause a serious inefficiency in pushing mobile resources into A from B. If the cost of movement is high, then quite appreciable differences in tax rates might appear without in fact leading to any appreciable movement of factors and so without leading to any very appreciable degree of economic inefficiency. In any case it is clear which way this first influence—namely, differences in industrial structure leading to natural differences in average levels of income between A and B—tends to operate. A uniform fiscal system covering both A and B and involving a transfer of revenue from A to B would not in itself introduce any adverse geographical incentive effects. But the separation of fiscal responsibilities between the two countries would introduce an uneconomic incentive for factors to move from the poor country B to the rich country A. Some control over the movement of all mobile factors from B to A would be justifiable on these grounds.[1]

The second influence which we proposed to examine (p. 414) was the result of the separation of fiscal systems between A and B in a situation in which initially there was an uneconomic distribution of the mobile factors of production between A and B. We assume, therefore, once again that the two governments have the same desires to redistribute income by means of fiscal policy. Unlike the previous case, however, we now assume that there is no natural and economic tendency for the richer factors to be concentrated in A and the poorer in B. But at the same time we assume that in fact B is initially overcrowded with the mobile factors labour and capital relatively to its productive atmosphere and its endowment in land and other immobile factors, with the result that income per head is on the average initially higher in A than in B. In such circumstances economic efficiency demands that the mobile factors should be left with an incentive to move from B, the country of lower marginal productivity, to A, the country of higher marginal productivity. Now if the costs of movement were nil, this incentive would still remain under a unified fiscal system under which each individual was taxed according to his income regardless of where he resided or earned his income; each individual could still increase his net income by moving from B, where his gross earnings were lower, to A, where his gross earnings would be higher. But, as we have seen, the unified fiscal system would somewhat blunt this inducement, since an individual by moving from B to A would not succeed in increasing his net income by as much as his gross earnings, since some part of the increase in the latter would be removed by the marginal rate of tax on his earnings. If movement from B to A involved some cost, this blunting of the incentive to move might be sufficient to prevent the movement.

In such circumstances the division of A and B into two separate self-supporting fiscal units might restore the incentive to move from B to A. Since the marginal productivity of factors is at the moment lower in B

[1] Numerical examples of the cases analysed in this and the following paragraphs will be found in Appendix 8 (pp. 609–14).

than A, B will be on the average poorer than A. In order to restore equilibrium to each national budget, the rate of tax must be raised in B and lowered in A and the rate of social security benefit must be lowered in B and raised in A. The increment of net income which can be retained by moving from B to A will now be increased, because by moving from B to A the factor now moves from a region in which tax rates are high and benefits low into a region in which tax rates are low and benefits high. The factor may now have an incentive to move which it did not have under the unified fiscal system.[1]

Finally, there is the third possible influence (p. 414) which we must take into account when the fiscal systems of A and B are sharply divided. Suppose now that there is no reason to believe that either A or B should or will in fact have a greater concentration of richer factors of production. But there may be different social philosophies in the two regions. Suppose that after the separation of fiscal systems the government of B carries the fiscal policy of redistribution further than the government of A, levying higher net tax rates on the higher incomes and paying higher net benefits to the poorer citizens. This will obviously introduce an uneconomic incentive for the factors which earn the higher incomes to move from B to A and for factors which earn the lower incomes to move from A to B.[2] This is an obvious influence, which does not require any elaborate analysis. But it is not for that reason unimportant. In fact, differences in social philosophy in different countries as between those which lay great stress upon the welfare state and the redistribution of income and those which lay much less stress upon such policies may well be one of the most potent forces at work in the modern world causing free movements of factors between nations to lead to uneconomic results.

[1] In this case, as in the previous case, it is of course necessary to distinguish between the movement of capital as such and the movement of the capitalist and entrepreneur. If in each country tax is raised on income originating within the country there will be an increased incentive for the capital to be moved from B, the country of heavy net taxation, to A, the country of low net taxation; but the incentive for the capitalist himself to move will remain blunted by the fact that under the tax schedule of the country in which his capital is situated he does not himself reap the whole of the net increase in his income which he may obtain by moving himself from the one country to the other. If, however, in each country the tax is raised on the income receivers resident in the country, the capitalist and entrepreneur will now have an incentive to move to A to avoid the higher tax rates of B, but the incentive to move capital as such will remain blunted by the fact that under the tax schedule of whichever country the owner does choose for his residence he will not enjoy all the increase in the income which he could earn by moving his capital from the region of low productivity to that of higher productivity.

[2] Once more the distinction between the movement of capital and capitalists must be drawn. If persons are taxed according to residence, then it will be the richer capitalists and entrepreneurs who are uneconomically induced to move from B to A. But if profits are taxed according to their geographical origin, then it will be capital itself which may be induced to move.

Let us now summarize the ways in which independent fiscal policies for the redistribution of incomes within A and B may give rise to valid arguments in favour of the control of international factor movements in the interests of economic efficiency.

In the first place, they may give rise to an uneconomic movement of all mobile factors—labour and capital—from a country which has a natural concentration of those factors whose marginal products are low to a country which has a natural concentration of the high-earning factors. In such a case there would be a valid case for putting some obstacles in the way of the migration of labour and of the movement of capital or of capitalists (according as to whether national tax systems were based on the origin of income or the residence of income earners) from the naturally poor to the naturally rich countries or indeed of promoting the flow of labour and capital in the opposite direction. As we have seen, this will be particularly important if the costs of movement of the factors concerned is not great.

Secondly, independent national fiscal policies may give rise to a much greater degree of redistributive finance in the one country than the other. In this case there may well be a valid argument for restricting the movement of the richer factors from the egalitarian state to the other or indeed for promoting its movement in the opposite direction, and an argument for restricting the movement of the poorer factors into the egalitarian state out of the other and even for promoting its movement in the opposite direction.

Both these problems would be avoided if the governments of the countries concerned developed some form of unified fiscal system, whereby rich factors the world over were taxed in order to redistribute income to all the poorer factors. This would, of course, involve the transfer of income from the richer to the poorer countries.[1] But in so far as it were achieved it would remove all fiscal incentives for the uneconomic movement of the mobile factors out of naturally poor regions; and since there would be only one universal tax and benefit schedule, it would also prevent any tendency for all the richer factors to be attracted to one country and all the poorer to another.

[1] This policy of fiscal unification must be clearly distinguished from the much more radical policy of making transfers from the poorer (B) to the richer country (A) on such a scale that net income per head is made uniform throughout AB regardless of the differences in productivity of different factors. Such a system would, of course, remove all economic incentives to move. All that is proposed above is a system whereby an individual with a given income pays the same net tax or receives the same net social benefit regardless of where he lives. This, after a given degree of redistribution, would of course still leave a country in which there was some concentration of less productive factors somewhat poorer per head than a country in which there was some concentration of more productive factors. It would merely mitigate such inequalities. The complete equalization of net incomes regardless of all differences in productivity would, of course, remove every incentive to increase productivity by moving.

But a universal system of fiscal redistribution would, as we have seen, somewhat blunt the incentive for any given factor to move from places of low to places of high productivity. If costs of movement were nil, even this argument against a unified fiscal system would be invalid. But if costs of movement were appreciable, the problem would arise whether any steps could be taken to promote movement to places of higher productivity when the marginal burden of net taxation was seriously blunting the incentive for them. This is merely the geographical aspect of the much wider problem of reconciling a progressive fiscal system with the maintenance of incentives for each individual economic agent to take all the various steps possible—of which geographical movement is only one—to increase his earnings.

CHAPTER XXVI

THE STRUCTURAL ARGUMENT FOR FACTOR CONTROLS

We explained in Chapter VIII how a structural change in an economy might be desirable even though there was no marginal incentive for it. As we saw in that chapter, this could be so only if there were some economies of large-scale production. In that case the production of a product might be socially repaying if it were undertaken on a large scale, even though the production of only a very few units on a small scale would involve such high costs that the production would not be economic. Such economies of large-scale production, as we saw, might be due either to the technical indivisibility of capital equipment so that the production of only one plant had to be on a large scale in order to be economic or it might be due to favourable atmosphere-creating external economies which were associated with a growth in the number of small competing plants. In either case State action might be required in order to establish the new line of production.

In Chapter XVI we applied this analysis to the problem of international trade. That is to say, we examined the conditions in which a particular line of production would not be repaying in a particular country if it were undertaken on a very small scale but might be repaying if it were established there on a large scale. This led us to consider the conditions in which it would be legitimate from the point of view of world economic efficiency for the government of a particular country to take special steps—whether by commercial-policy measures or otherwise—to introduce new industries into its economy.

But the analysis of Chapter XVI was undertaken on the assumption which was maintained throughout Part II of this volume, namely that the factors of production in each country were fixed in amount and would not move from the one to the other. In this chapter it is our task to inquire what difference would be made to the analysis of Chapter XVI if we removed the assumption that the factors cannot move between countries. Instead we assume that the factors move from one country to another whenever the marginal conditions for economic efficiency require that they should do so, i.e. whenever the marginal product of the factor in one country exceeds its marginal product in the other by more than the cost of movement. Suppose that the question arises of taking special action to establish a new industry in A. Is it more likely to be in the world interest to do so if labour and capital can move freely into A from B or out of A into B than if no such factor movements are possible?

The formal difference in the analysis of Chapter XVI which results from the removal of the assumption that all factors are immobile can easily be explained. We explained in Chapter VIII the only way which is theorctically satisfactory to assess whether a new industry should be established or not. The total value to consumers of any given level of output must be calculated by taking the price which would be paid for the first unit of output, adding to this the price which would be paid for the second unit of output, adding to this the price which would be paid for the third unit of output, and so on. The cost to society of the same output must be calculated by taking the price of the factors which would be required to produce the first unit of output, adding to this the price of the additional factors that would be required to produce a second unit of output, adding to that the price of the additional factors needed to produce yet a third unit of output, and so on. If for any output the social value so measured exceeds the social cost so measured, then the industry ought to be established.

This is the type of analysis which must be applied in any case to the problem whether a particular industry ought to be set up in A or not. If we are assuming (as in Chapter XVI) that the factors of production cannot move between A and B, then these calculations of the social values and costs must be undertaken on the assumption that the prices of the factors and of the products behave in A as the industry is developed in the way in which they would behave if there were a fixed and unalterable supply of each factor in A. If we are assuming (as in this chapter) that each factor of production moves from A to B (or vice versa) whenever its marginal product and so its price in B exceeds its price in A (or vice versa) by more than the cost of movement, then the calculations of the social values and costs of different levels of output as outlined in the preceding paragraph must proceed on the assumption that, as the output of the new product is expanded in A, the prices of the factors and of the product behave in A as they would behave if the factors moved into and out of A on this marginally optimum principle.

Formally that is all that need be said on the theoretical issue raised in this chapter; but it will be helpful perhaps to add one or two illustrations of the sort of difference that may in fact be introduced into the calculations in particular cases through the possibility of international factor movements. This is so for two reasons. First, such illustrations may be useful in helping to understand the analysis itself. But, secondly, the theoretically correct procedure for estimating whether a particular industry should be introduced into an economy is, as we have observed in Chapter XVI, most unlikely to prove to be a practical procedure. All that the policy-makers can hope to do is to form a reasonably well-informed 'hunch' in each particular case. But in order that the hunch should be reasonably well informed, it is necessary that the main factors which will affect the theoretically correct answer should be borne in mind; and that this may be so, it is useful to have considered some particular applications of the theoretically correct procedure.

Let us suppose, therefore, that A is a country which has natural resources and atmosphere which are well suited to the industrial production of certain products; that these lines of production require a high ratio of labour and capital to land for economical operation and are also subject to important economies of large-scale production; and that country A has itself initially only a very small population and a very meagre capital equipment.

Let us now consider the calculation of the social cost involved in setting up this industry in these conditions in A, first on the assumption that labour and capital cannot move into A from B and secondly on the assumption that these factors can move into A. On the assumption of no international factor movements the calculation of the social costs will give a high figure for the following reasons. On the first units of output the cost of the factors required will be high because with a small scale of output productivity will be low and a large amount of factors will be required to produce each unit of output. On the later units of output the cost of the factors required to produce more output will also be high, but for a different reason. Since the scale of production is now greater, productivity will have risen and not so large an increase in the amount of the factors will now be needed in order to add another unit to the output. But the price of the additional factors will now be very high. The expansion of the output of the new product will have taken up large amounts of the factors, labour and capital, which are important in the new industry but of which the country has only a small supply. This may have appreciably reduced the amount of these factors available to the other industries of the country before the new industry has grown to a really economic size. The marginal product of these factors in the other industries in A will have risen because of their scarcity; their price will thus be high; and the cost of further additions to the new industry will now be high because the price of the factors on which it most relies is high. And this is a correct estimation of the social cost. Since in our present case the factors for A's new industry can come only from A's other industries, the real cost of putting more of them into the new industry is the loss of output due to their withdrawal from the existing industries. That is to say, it is measured by their high marginal product in these other industries, i.e. by the high price which the new industry must pay for them to attract them from A's other industries.

The case might be very different if these factors could move into A from B and thus be attracted into A's new industry from the whole range of existing industries in B. This is likely to be particularly important if these particular factors which are most essential for the new industry in A are plentiful in B though they are very scarce in A. Then as A's new industry develops and the price of these factors is driven up in A they will be able to come into A from B. Quite a large absolute migration of these factors into A—enough to expand A's new industry to an economic level—may not cause much rise in their price, because it represents only a small proportionate decline in the supply available for B's industries and so only a small percentage rise in their marginal product in B. The social cost of A's new industry may then turn out to be relatively small; the cost of the additional factors will be low because their price will be low and this will truly represent a low social cost because the marginal product lost in the other industries when they come into A from B will be low.

The effect upon the cost calculation of the possibility of the migration of factors from B to A, which we have outlined above, is a fairly obvious one. There is, however, a rather less obvious but rather similar possible effect upon the calculation of the social value of the output of the new industry. Suppose that the product which is to be newly produced in A is itself costly to transport between A and B. When none of it is being produced in A, some supplies may be imported from B and consumed in A. But the price in A will be very high, because the cost of its transport from B is very heavy. In consequence the amount consumed in A will be small and its marginal value to consumers in A will be great. When the industry has been established in A, its output in A may replace the imported supplies. If the output were still further increased, its price in A would have to fall very greatly in order still further to expand the market for it. The market in A would be further increased only by a reduction in price which induced consumers in A to purchase more of it; and the market for A's output in B could only start to develop when the price in A had fallen below the price in B by an amount equal to the heavy cost of transporting it from A to B. In other words, as the output was increased in A the marginal value of the new product in A and so its price would decline.

But the extent to which the price would decline in A as A's output was expanded would depend upon whether or not the factors of production could move from B to A to help with the building up of the new industry in A. If factors of production do move into A from B, then the decline in the marginal value and so in the price of the new product in A will be less rapid and will go less far than it would do if labour and capital could not move into A from B. If the factors used in A's new industry are gained wholly by a subtraction of these factors from existing industries in A, then there is no expansion of the total market for goods and services in A. Wages which were earned in other industries in A are now earned in the new industry in A. But if the factors used in A's new industry come from B, they represent a net addition to the labour and capital which is earning income in A. In this latter case the market for the new product in A will be expanded together with the markets for other products in A. For this reason the marginal value and price of the product in A will tend to be maintained above the level which it would otherwise have attained.

There are two qualifications which it is necessary to add to this conclusion.

In the first place, the movement of factors from B to A will tend to expand the demand for A's product in A only in so far as the factors which move from B to A carry their consumption with them. (See pp. 361–2 above.) In so far as labourers migrate from B to A, earn income in A, but then remit the income so earned back to their families in B, this will not, of course, increase the market for A's goods at the expense of B's goods. This may not be important in the case of labour. But capitalists resident in B may well invest their capital in A's new industry instead of in industries in B and yet bring the income from the investment back for consumption in B. In this case the movement of the factor from B to A does not, of course, expand the market for the new product in A.

The second qualification to the above analysis which we must introduce concerns the cost of transport of the new product between A and B. It is only in so far as the product costs something to transport between the two countries that the movement of the factors from B to A will expand the market for the product made in A. If the product costs nothing to transport, then it would make no difference whether income were consumed in A or in B; in either case the supply of the product would be bought for consumption from that source, whether in A or in B, in which its cost of production was cheapest regardless of the distance of the source of supply from the point of consumption. A movement of income from B to A would not therefore cause any increase in the demand for A's output as opposed to B's output. But if it costs something to transport the product from B to A the position will be different. If the cost of production in B exceeded the cost of production in A by less than the cost of transporting the product from A to B, then a unit of income spent in B will be spent on B's product; and if the cost of production in B was lower than the cost of production in A by less than the cost of transporting the product from B to A, then a unit of income spent in A will be spent on A's product. If, therefore, the cost of production in B relative to the cost of production in A fell between these two limits, a movement of expenditure from B to A would shift the demand from B's product on to A's product.

Thus it remains true that in so far as a shift of factors from B to A carries the consumption of the owners of the factors with it and in so far as it costs something to transport the new product between A and B, the social value of a new line of production in A is likely to be greater if the factors of production required in that production can move into A from B than it would be if the factors could not move. Moreover, as we have already seen, the possibility of factor movements is likely to keep down the total social costs of production in A. We may conclude, therefore, that in the case which we are examining the possibility of international factor movements is likely to increase the strength of the case for establishing the new industry in A.

For these reasons it may be repaying to develop A industrially if labour and capital are able to move into A, in conditions in which the development would not be worth while if such factor movements were impossible. But once again, as we have already seen in the case in which factor movements are ruled out (pp. 259–60 above), it must not be forgotten that if A gains through economies of large-scale operation when her industries are developed, B may lose through diseconomies of small-scale operation when her industries are contracted. If the amount of the factors and so the scale of operations is initially very small in A, then A may gain a lot through the economies of large-scale when factors move into A. If at the same time the amount of the factors and the scale of operations were very large indeed in B, then B may not lose much—indeed, may not lose at all—through the contraction in her industries which will result from the movement of labour and capital from B into A. Even after this contraction the scale of operations in B may be so large that the economies of large-scale operation can still be enjoyed. But if the scale of operations in B is initially not so large as this, then a movement of factors out of B may cause appreciable diseconomies in B. In this connexion it must be remembered that just as the possibility of a movement of factors into A is likely to mean that new industrial development in A represents a net expansion of all markets in A and therefore a net gain in economies of large-scale production, so the movement of factors out of B adds to the chance that the new development in A will cause a net loss of economies of large-scale production in B. Whether the possibility of movement of factors from B to A ultimately much enhances the probability that economic development in A is in the world interest will depend, therefore, upon whether or not the scale of operations in B relatively to the scale which is needed to give the full advantages of mass production is such that a contraction in B will not do much damage there.

All this would be taken into account by the theoretically desirable calculation which we outlined above (p. 421). We argued that as the development of the new industry took place in A the price of the additional factors required at each stage to add yet another unit of output in A's new industry would be kept down if it were possible to attract these factors out of B's industries as well as out of A's existing industries. But suppose that as B's industries contract because of their loss of factors to A's industries, there is an appreciable loss of economies of large scale in B's industries. Then the marginal social net product of B's factors in B's industries will become much higher; the employment of another factor in B's industries because of the external or internal economies in B's industries will have a very large effect on the output of B's industries. If, as we are assuming, a policy of modified laissez-faire were adopted in B's economy, the price paid to B's factors in B would be equal to the value of their marginal social net product in B's industries. If there were an important loss of economies of large scale through the contraction of B's industries, then the price of B's factors would rise rapidly as factors were drawn away from B. This would mean a more rapid rise in the price of the factors employed in A's developing industry, and would thus exercise its due effect in raising the calculation of the cost of establishing the new industry in A.

The theoretical calculation would thus take account of any adverse effects upon productivity of a contraction in the scale of operations in B consequent upon an expansion of operations in A. But in practical life it would never be possible to make the calculation in its theoretically perfect form. This is simply one of the many factors which must be borne in mind in forming a hunch about the desirability of the establishment of some new industry or industries in A. How far would the possibility of movement of factors from A to B (i) increase the scale of operations in A so as to make the new industries productive without (ii) decreasing the scale of operations in B so as seriously to diminish the productivity of B's industries?

If the initial scale of operations in B is large relatively to the scale required to enjoy the economies of large-scale production, and if A's economy is initially very small and restricted, then the possibility of factor movements from B to A may well make socially repaying the development of industries in A, which would not otherwise be worth while undertaking. A might be even better suited than B from the point of view of atmosphere and natural resources for industrial production, while A had a small population and B a very large population. A moderately large working force might be necessary to reap for industry the basic economies of large-scale production. In such a case there would be a strong argument in the interests of world economic efficiency for a considerable migration from B to A.

Even more striking examples may be found in the case of the international movement of capital. There are certain basic services, like roads, railways, ports, water control, etc., which require considerable sums of capital investment, which must be undertaken on a considerable scale if at all, and which, being a *sine qua non* for many other forms of economic activity, may pay a considerable social dividend if they are carried out on the necessary minimum scale. In an undeveloped economy with few capital resources, the development of these basic capital projects may be out of the question unless they are financed, in part at least, by the inflow of capital funds from other countries which are richer in capital and which could spare the capital without threatening their own industries with the diseconomies of small-scale production.

Yet these movements of labour and capital which may be socially repaying may not at first be privately profitable. The first migrants from B to A might find that they could earn less in A than in B; and it would not be until large numbers had migrated from B to A that the scale of industry would be sufficiently great for it to be sufficiently productive for it to be able to offer wages in A which competed with those earned in B. A small migration might be privately unprofitable, though a large migration might in the end prove very repaying. Or in the case of capital, the investment of funds in building in A a first small road might (even if some toll system could be devised to levy a charge on those who made use of the road) prove quite uneconomic. But as part of a network of roads and railways which covered the country, it might be a profitable project.

In such cases the movement of factors from B to A may never start if it is left to the owners of individual units of labour and capital to consult their own private interest at the margin. But a movement of factors organized on some considerable scale might prove repaying. Some special temporary encouragement to the international movement of factors might in these circumstances be justifiable in order to help to give the economic structure a jolt of the kind which we have discussed at length at the end of Chapter XVI.

CHAPTER XXVII

THE DISTRIBUTIONAL ARGUMENT FOR FACTOR CONTROLS[1]

WE must next consider the effect which a movement of a factor of production between A and B may have on the distribution of income, because there may be a case for the control of factor movements on the grounds that free movement will lead to a less desirable distribution of income, even though it leads to a more efficient economic position.

Let us suppose that for one reason or another the value of the marginal social net product of labour is higher in country A than in country B, that labour in both countries is paid a reward equal to the value of its marginal social net product, and that the cost of migration of labour from B to A is zero. In these conditions labour will have an incentive to move from B to A in search of the higher reward in A. Moreover, such a movement is in the interests of economic efficiency, because the marginal product of labour is higher in A than in B so that by a movement of labour from B to A total world output can be increased.

Now since in our example labour is paid a reward equal to the value of its marginal product in both A and B, any labour which moves from B to A will increase its own income exactly by the value of the change in total world output. There will be exactly as much left over as before for all the other citizens of A and B. But there may in fact be some redistribution of this given income among these other individuals as a result of the repercussions in the market from the changes due to the migration of labour from B to A. These possible repercussions upon the distribution of income must be examined under two heads: first, the effect upon the distribution of income internationally between the pre-existing citizens of the country of immigration on the one hand and the remaining citizens of the country of emigration on the other; and second, the effect upon the distribution of income domestically within either country between wages and other incomes.

The first of these two effects of migration from B to A—namely the redistribution of income between the pre-existing citizens of A and the remaining citizens of B—can be measured directly by any change in the real terms of trade between A and B which may result from the movement of labour. Thus if as a result of the change the price of

[1] Much of the argument of this chapter is expressed in mathematical form in Section XIX of the mathematical supplement to this volume, which covers the effects of migration upon the relative prices of A's and of B's exports. This is the basic relationship explaining the distributional effects of migration.

A's export product, apples, falls relatively to the price of B's export product, blankets, then the remaining citizens in B will be able to trade on more favourable terms with the pre-existing citizens of A, and will gain at their expense. Moreover, as will become clear in the subsequent argument, the distribution of income within each country between wages on the one hand and profits, rents, etc., on the other will itself in many cases be indirectly affected by changes in the terms of trade between the country's import and export products. Accordingly, we shall in this chapter put the first emphasis upon an examination of the effect which a movement of labour from B to A will have upon the terms of trade between A's apples and B's blankets, and we shall then in the course of the argument derive from this the effects upon the domestic distribution of income in the two countries.

Now it is not possible to say unequivocally what the effect upon the terms of trade will be. It can be shown that in some circumstances the movement of labour will cause the terms of trade to move in A's favour and that in other circumstances it will cause them to move in B's favour. In order to sort out the different circumstances in which these two different effects are likely to occur it is necessary to consider the effect which the movement of labour from B to A is likely to have, first, on the general level of world demand for B's export product (blankets) relatively to A's export product (apples) and, second, on the world supply of blankets relatively to that of apples. If the change is likely to cause the demand for blankets to rise relatively to that of apples and at the same time is likely to cause the supply of apples to rise relatively to that of blankets, then the price of blankets will rise relatively to that of apples and the terms of trade will turn in favour of B; and vice versa.

We are assuming that labour moves from B to A because the marginal product of labour (and so the wage rate) is higher in A than in B. The movement of labour will thus lead to an increase in total world production, since less output is lost in B than is gained in A. The real income of all citizens of the world together will be greater. Whether or not the change will cause a net increase in the demand for blankets relatively to that for apples will therefore depend primarily upon whether blankets are the sort of commodity on which people spend a large part of any increase in their real income and upon whether apples are the sort of commodity on which people spend a very small part of any increase in their real income.[1] If when people obtain larger incomes they wish to buy many more blankets but very few more apples, then on the demand side the movement of labour from a position of low productivity in B to a position of high productivity in A would be

[1] In technical terms, this depends upon whether the income elasticity of demand for blankets is high and for apples is low.

likely to expand the demand for blankets relatively to that of apples, and thus move the terms of trade in favour of B's export product. This would tend to make the remaining citizens of B gain at the expense of the pre-existing citizens of A. The opposite would be the case if apples rather than blankets were the commodity which people wished to purchase in greater amounts as their incomes rose.

This analysis on the demand side may be complicated by the fact that, while the total world income will rise as a result of the movement of labour, there is likely—as we shall see at a later stage of the argument—also to be some redistribution of income between groups within each country. Thus while the total world income will rise, there may well be some groups whose incomes will fall. Because of differences of social habits or because of differences in the average level of real income from which they start, one group of persons may react differently from another in adjusting their expenditure on goods and services to a change in the level of their incomes. All that one can say is that the price offered by consumers for blankets is the more likely to rise relatively to the price offered by them for apples, (i) the greater the proportion of any increase in their incomes which will be spent on blankets by those groups which gain from the change, and (ii) the smaller the proportion of any fall in their incomes which will be met by economies in the purchase of blankets by those groups which lose from the change.

But whether or not the terms of trade will turn in favour of blankets—and so of B—will depend not only upon whether the change causes the demand for blankets to rise relatively to that for apples. The change might cause the demand for blankets to rise relatively to that for apples; and yet nevertheless the price of blankets might fall relatively to the price of apples if the change caused the world production of blankets to increase very much relatively to the world production of apples. We must, therefore, consider the effect of a movement of labour from B to A upon the output of A's export product (apples) and of B's export product (blankets).

We can express the two possibilities very crudely in the following way. (i) Suppose that labour could be used only to produce blankets and land only to produce apples. A movement of labour from B, where its productivity is low, to A, where its productivity is high, would in this case mean an increase in the world output of blankets without any change in the world output of apples. The terms of trade would tend to turn against blankets and in favour of apples. This would mean a movement of the terms of trade in favour of the country which was the importer of the commodity (blankets) which the moving factor of production (labour) specialized in producing. (ii) Suppose, to take the other extreme, that labour and land can be usefully employed in producing both products, but that for one reason or another only apples are produced in A and only blankets in B. Then a movement of labour from B to A will increase the world output of apples and reduce the world output of blankets. On the supply side apples will become more plentiful and blankets more scarce; and the terms of trade will tend to move against apples and against A. Thus in considering the effect upon the terms of trade of a movement of labour from B to A we shall have to consider carefully to what extent in each type of situation it is one of the factors, and to what extent it is one of the countries, which is specialized in producing each product.

In order to carry out this examination, we must distinguish between the possible reasons for the initial divergence between the marginal product of labour in A and in B (and so the difference between the real wage rate in the two countries) which gives rise to the migration of labour from B to A.

In an earlier chapter of this Part (Chapter XX) we outlined certain conditions the fulfilment of which would mean that trade in the products of the factors would alone be sufficient to ensure that the marginal product of any one factor was the same in both trading countries even in the absence of international movements of the factors themselves. We then showed (Chapters XXI–XXIII) how the absence of any one of these conditions might well lead to circumstances in which the marginal product of any given factor remained at different levels in A and in B in spite of the free flow of commodity trade between the two countries. As the following discussion will show, in order to determine the effect on the terms of trade between apples and blankets of a movement of labour from a position of low productivity in B to a position of high productivity in A, we must distinguish between the various reasons why the trade in apples and blankets between A and B has not itself been sufficient to make the marginal product of labour in B as high as the marginal product of labour in A.

Let us start by considering the case in which the reason why the marginal product of labour is higher in A than in B even after the development of free trade between A and B is that there are different productive atmospheres in the two countries.[1] Let us suppose that A and B are roughly of the same size, that apples and blankets are items of roughly the same importance in consumers' expenditures throughout the world, and that there is not an excessive discrepancy between the initial endowments of the two countries with the factors of production, land and labour. A is somewhat better endowed with land and B somewhat better endowed with labour. In this case the development of trade between A and B might be expected to bring the marginal product of any one factor into equality in the two countries. Before trade

[1] This reason for differences in marginal products in the two trading countries has been considered in Chapter XXI (pp. 348–51).

the ratio of land to labour in either industry might be expected to be somewhat higher in A where land is plentiful than in B where labour is plentiful; in consequence the marginal product of labour and so the real wage rate would be higher in A than in B and that of land would be lower in A than in B. The land-intensive product, apples, would be cheap in A and the labour-intensive product, blankets, would be cheap in B; trade would develop between A and B; the expansion of the labour-intensive blanket industry in B would absorb mainly labour while the expansion of the land-intensive apple industry in A would absorb mainly land; and by this mechanism the ratio of land to labour in either industry would be brought into equality in both countries, while both A and B continued to produce something of both commodities, apples and blankets.

Normally this might be expected to bring the marginal product of labour in A into equality with the marginal product of labour in B, since the ratio of land to labour in either industry would now be the same in both countries. Let us suppose that the mechanism works exactly as explained above but that there is a more favourable atmosphere for production in A of all commodities by all factors. That is to say, we suppose that any given combination of land and labour in the apple industry will produce, say, 100 per cent more apples in A than in B; and any given combination of land and labour in the blanket industry will also produce 100 per cent more blankets in A than in B. The mechanism of trade in products might still make the ratio of land to labour employed in A's apple industry equal to the ratio of land to labour employed in B's apple industry; and similarly for the two blanket industries. But this would not now mean that the marginal product of labour was the same in A as in B; each factor in each industry would, because of the difference in productive atmosphere, have a marginal product which was 100 per cent higher in A than in B.

Now suppose that some labour moves from B to A in search of the higher marginal product and so the higher real wage rate in A. It is exactly as if when 100 workers emigrated from B, 200 workers arrived for immigration into A: each worker becomes 100 per cent more productive merely by moving from B to A. In other words, the movement of labour from B to A is equivalent to an increase in the total supply of labour to the world economy. What will be the effect of this upon the world supply of blankets and apples?

The change will represent an increase in the ease of producing the labour-intensive product, blankets, relatively to the ease of producing the land-intensive product, apples. Let us consider first the extreme form of labour-intensiveness and land-intensiveness of production. Suppose that blankets must always be produced by labour and by labour alone (the ratio of land to labour in blanket production is zero) and that apples must always be produced by land and by land alone (the ratio of land to labour in apple production is infinitely large). Then when labour moves from B to A, it moves necessarily out of blanket production in B into blanket production in A. But since, because of the better productive atmosphere in A, it will produce 100 per cent more blankets in A than it did in B, the world supply of blankets will increase. But since no land has moved between A and B, there will be no change in the supply of apples. The world supply of blankets will have increased relatively to the world supply of apples; and as far as the supply side of the problem is concerned there will be a tendency for the price of blankets to fall relatively to that of apples, and the terms of trade will tend to move against B and in favour of A.

It is easy to infer also from this how the movement of labour from B to A will have affected the distribution of income within A and B. If labour makes blankets and only blankets and if land makes apples and only apples, then the movement of the terms of trade against blankets and in favour of apples will represent a fall in the real income of labour in both countries with a counterbalancing rise in the real income derived from rents.

Now the same underlying forces will be at work in the less extreme cases of labour-intensiveness and land-intensiveness of production. Suppose next that both land and labour are used in producing apples and that both land and labour are used in producing blankets; that the ratio of land to labour in apple production is fixed and invariable (land and labour cannot be substituted for each other at all) and is the same in A as in B; that, similarly, the ratio of land to labour in blanket production is fixed at the same level in both countries; but that the fixed ratio of land to labour is higher in the apple industry than in the blanket industry. Finally, we assume that all land is 100 per cent more productive in all uses in A than in B and all labour is 100 per cent more productive in all uses in A than in B. Then it can be shown that a movement of labour from B to A will increase the world supply of blankets and reduce the world supply of apples. This is illustrated numerically in Table XXXIII.

In all the cases throughout the table we are examining the effects of an emigration of 12 workers from B (rows 2, 4, and 6 of column *b*) and the immigration of these 12 workers into A (rows 1, 3, and 5 of column *b*). We also assume that in both countries A and B 1 unit of labour is always employed with 2 units of land in the land-intensive apple industry and that 2 units of labour are always used with 1 unit of land in the labour-intensive blanket industry. Our problem is to determine how many of the 12 workers who migrate from B to A will come out of B's apple industry and B's blanket industry; and how many of them will find their way into A's apple industry and into A's blanket industry.

We start off in case i by seeing what would happen if half the labour came out of B's and went into A's apple industry and the other half of the labour came out of B's and went into A's blanket industry. Thus we assume that 6 units of labour come out of B's apple industry (row 2, column *c*) and 6 units out of B's blanket industry (row 2, column *e*), while 6 units of labour go into each of A's industries (row 1, columns *c* and *e*). But since 2 units of land are used with each unit of labour in

TABLE XXXIII

Migration of Labour from B to A and the World Supply of Apples and Blankets

	Country	Supply of labour	Factors employed in apple industry		Factors employed in blanket industry		Demand for land
			labour	land	labour	land	
	(*a*)	(*b*) (= *c* + *e*)	(*c*)	(*d*)	(*e*)	(*f*)	(*g*) (= *d* + *f*)
	Case (i). *Migration of labour from B's to A's apple industry and from B's to A's blanket industry*						
(1)	A	+12	+6	+12	+6	+3	+15
(2)	B	−12	−6	−12	−6	−3	−15
	Case (ii). *Migration of labour from B's to A's blanket industry*						
(3)	A	+12	Nil	Nil	+12	+6	+6
(4)	B	−12	Nil	Nil	−12	−6	−6
	Case (iii). *Migration of labour from B to A. Final equilibrium*						
(5)	A	+12	−4	−8	+16	+8	Nil
(6)	B	−12	+4	+8	−16	−8	Nil

the apple industry and $\frac{1}{2}$ unit of land with each unit of labour in the blanket industry, this will lead to an increased demand for land in A of 12 units in the apple industry (row 1, column *d*) and of 3 units in the blanket industry (row 1, column *f*), a total increase in the demand for land in both industries in A of 15 units. At the same time in B 12 units of land will be released from B's apple industry (row 2, column *d*) and 3 units from B's blanket industry (row 2, column *f*), a total reduction in the demand for land in B of 15 units (row 2, column *g*). Clearly there can be no equilibrium in this case. There is no change in the supplies of land in either country. There is, therefore, an excess demand for land of 15 units in A and an excess supply of land of 15 units in B. Rents will rise continuously in A and fall continuously in B so long as this goes on. The cost of the land-intensive apples will therefore rise in A and fall in B relatively to the cost of blankets. With free trade between A and B people will buy their apples in B and their blankets in A; A's blanket industry will expand at the expense of her apple industry; and the opposite will happen in B. Clearly the expansion of A's apple industry and the contraction of B's apple industry will both be less than is assumed in case i.

We try then in case ii the possibility that there is no expansion in A's apple industry or contraction in B's apple industry. We assume that all the 12 units of labour which emigrate from B move out of B's blanket industry (row 4, column *e*) and all the 12 units of labour which immigrate into A enter A's blanket industry. As a result there is now a reduction of 6 units in the demand for land in B to match the reduced employment of labour in B's blanket industry (row 4, columns *f* and *g*) and an increase of 6 units in the demand for land in A to match the increased employment of labour in A's blanket industry (row 3, columns *f* and *g*). The situation is better than in case i. There is now an excess demand for land in A of only 6 instead of 15 units, and there is an excess supply of land in B of only 6 instead of 15 units. But there is still no equilibrium. The excess demand for land in A, though smaller, will still cause rents to rise in A; and the excess supply of land in B will still cause rents to fall in B. The cost of apples relatively to that of blankets will still rise in A and fall in B, and consumers in both countries will therefore still shift their demand from A's apples to B's apples. It is clear therefore that a final equilibrium will be reached after the shift of labour from B to A only if there is some net contraction of A's apple industry and some net expansion of B's apple industry.

The final equilibrium will be as shown in case iii. Suppose that 16 units of labour move into A's blanket industry (row 5, column *e*), 4 units of which come from A's apple industry (row 5, column *c*), and the remaining 12 from the net increase in A's labour force (row 5, column *b*). There will now be no net increase or decrease in the demand for land in A since there will be a reduction in the amount of land required in A's apple industry of 8 units, i.e. of twice the loss of labour from that industry (row 5, column *d*), and an increase in the amount of land required in A's blanket industry of 8 units, i.e. of half the gain of labour in that industry (row 5, column *f*). In B the amount of labour in the blanket industry is reduced by 16 units (row 6, column *e*), of which 12 emigrate to A (row 6, column *b*) and the remaining 4 move into B's apple industry (row 6, column *c*). This will be accompanied by an increased demand for land in B's apple industry of 8 units, or twice the increased number of units of labour employed there (row 6, column *d*), matched by an equal decrease in the demand for land in B's blanket industry of 8 units, or half the reduced number of units of labour employed there (row 6, column *f*), so that there is no net increase or decrease in the total demand for land in B.

We are now in a position to consider the effect of this movement of labour from B to A upon the world supplies of apples and blankets. It can be seen that, as far as the amounts of factors used are concerned, the expansion of A's blanket industry (columns *e* and *f*, row 5) is exactly equal to the contraction of B's blanket industry (columns *e* and *f*, row 6). A's blanket industry is employing 16 more units of labour and 8 more units of land, while B's blanket industry is employing 16 less units of labour and 8 less units of land. But since the productive atmosphere is twice as favourable in A as in B, the world output of blankets will have risen as a result of the change. By a similar reasoning it can be shown that the world output of apples will have fallen. The expansion, in terms of factors of production employed, in B's apple industry is equal to the contraction in A's apple industry; but as the productive atmosphere in A is once again twice as favourable as in B, this will involve a net reduction in the world output of apples. Since world blanket production will have risen and world apple production will have fallen, there will be a strong tendency on the supply side turning the terms of trade against blankets and so against the country which exports the labour-intensive product, blankets.[1]

From the fact that the terms of trade will move against blankets and in favour of apples, we can conclude that there will also be some redistribution of income within A and B away from wages towards rents. We can see this best by asking what would happen if the wage rate and the rate of rent remained unchanged in each country when the price of apples rose and the price of blankets fell (i.e. when the terms of trade moved against blankets). Individual producers in each country would have an incentive to hire more labour and land to produce more apples (where the rise in price would have given rise to high profits) and to dismiss labour and land from the production of blankets (where the fall in price would have given rise to losses). But these attempts to expand

[1] In our particular example this happens to be B; but so far as the essential analysis goes, it might just as well be A. The essential argument is simply that if the productive atmosphere is much better in one country than another, the mobile factor will move to the better atmosphere. This will lead to an increase in the relative supply of the product which the mobile factor is specially fitted to produce. This will tend to turn the terms of trade against that product and so against the country which is a net exporter of that product.

land-intensive apple production would give rise to a large increase in the demand for land and to only a small increase in the demand for labour, while the attempt to contract the labour-intensive blanket industry would release much labour and little land. There would be a scarcity of land and an excess supply of labour; rents would rise and wages would fall; and this rise in rents and fall in wages would in fact go on until the cost of the land-intensive apples had risen to meet their higher selling price and until the cost of the labour-intensive blankets had fallen to meet their lower selling price. But as a result of this process which would operate in both countries there would be a redistribution of income away from labour (apart, of course, from the labour which by migrating from B to A had increased its income) to rents.

The above analysis does not yet allow for the fact that in both the apple industry and the blanket industry labour and land may be substituted for each other; the ratio of land to labour in each industry will probably not in fact be rigidly fixed by technical factors; when labour becomes cheaper relatively to land it may be economic to substitute the cheaper labour for the more expensive land in both industries. It is relatively simple to modify the above argument in such a way as to allow for this possibility; and the result is not to alter the kind of effect which a movement of labour from B to A will have upon the distribution of income between A and B and within A and B, but merely to reduce the magnitude of these changes. The terms of trade will still move against blankets, but less markedly than before; and wage rates will still fall in both countries relatively to rates of rent, but by a smaller amount than before. This can be shown in the following way.

It would pay producers to substitute labour for land, or land for labour, only if the wage rate had changed relatively to the rate of rent. If the wage rate had fallen relatively to the rate of rent it would pay producers to produce each commodity with a larger amount of the cheap factor, labour, and a smaller amount of the expensive factor, land. But if the wage rate and the rate of rent had remained unchanged, each individual producer of each product would have no incentive to produce by any methods other than those which he was previously employing. Let us see then what would happen if as a result of the movement of labour from B to A there were no changes in the rates of wages or of rents previously ruling in the two countries.

In this case the proportions in which the factors were used in the two industries would not change. The analysis would be exactly the same as that which we have just conducted for the case in which the factor proportions are fixed for technical reasons. The movement of labour from A to B would cause the world output of blankets to rise more in A than it fell in B and would cause the world output of apples to fall more in A than it rose in B; it would thus lead to a rise in the world supply of blankets and a fall in the world supply of apples; this would cause the price of blankets to fall and the price of apples to rise on the world market; this would cause producers all over the world to try to produce more apples and less blankets; but this would increase the world demand for land relatively to that of labour, so that in effect we cannot assume that rates of wages and rents remain unchanged. The rate of wages will fall and of rents will rise.

It will be observed that the argument in the preceding paragraph remains unaffected whether we are assuming that the factor proportions are fixed because they are rigidly fixed by technical factors or whether they are constant only so long as rates of wages and rents remain unchanged so that there is no incentive to alter them. In both cases we can show by the argument in the preceding paragraph that the price of blankets will in fact rise, that the price of apples will in fact fall, that the rate of rents in both countries will in fact rise, and that the rate of wages in both countries will in fact fall.

But from this point onwards the analysis of the case of technically fixed factor proportions differs from that of the case of variable factor proportions. As the wage rate falls and the rate of rent rises, producers will produce both commodities with more labour and less land if they are able technically to substitute the one factor for the other. This will be an additional factor helping to maintain the demand for labour and helping to damp down the demand for land. The rate of wages will not therefore fall as much as it would otherwise have done and the rate of rents will not therefore rise as much as it would otherwise have done.

Moreover, the fact that more labour can be used per acre of land in both the apple industry and the blanket industry will enable producers effectively to shift from producing blankets to producing apples when the price of the former falls and of the latter rises. Producers, as in the previous case, dismiss much labour and little land from the unprofitable blanket industry and absorb little labour and much land into the profitable apple industry. This excess demand for land and excess supply of labour does not now simply lead to a rise of rents and a fall of wage rates until it is profitable for producers to be content with the previous output of apples and blankets. On the contrary, the apple industry can now effectively be expanded and the blanket industry effectively contracted; and the consequential excess demand for land and excess supply of labour can be removed by a rise in rents and a fall in wages sufficient to cause all producers in all industries to produce with rather more labour and rather less land. Since the fall in the price of blankets and the rise in the price of apples can now itself cause an effective secondary expansion of the apple industry and contraction of the blanket industry, the final decrease in the world supply of apples will not be as large as in the case in which factor proportions were rigidly fixed. For this reason the fall in the price of blankets relatively to that of apples will itself not be as great as in the case of fixed factor proportions.

We can conclude therefore that the movement of labour from B to A in search of a higher reward in A which is due solely to the existence of a better all-round productive atmosphere in A will (i) cause the terms of trade to move against the labour-intensive product (blankets) and so against the citizens of the country which exports this labour-intensive product, and (ii) cause the workers in both countries which have not moved between B and A to lose income to the owners of land in both countries. But both these distributional effects will be the smaller, the easier it is technically to substitute one factor for another in the two industries. They will also, of course, be the smaller, the easier it is for consumers to substitute the one product for the other in their consumption. If blankets fall in price relatively to apples and this causes consumers to shift on a large scale from the purchase of apples to that of blankets, the effect will be to mitigate the fall in the price of blankets. All the distributional effects of such a price change would then also be moderated.

We have so far analysed the effect upon the domestic and international distribution of income of a movement of labour from a country of low marginal productivity, B, to one of high marginal productivity, A, when the difference in marginal productivity is due solely to a more favourable productive atmosphere in A. But exactly the same type of analysis is applicable when the higher marginal productivity of labour in A is due to the existence of a third factor—say, capital[1]—or to increasing returns to scale.[2] Suppose there to be a situation such as that described in Chapter XX where all the conditions enumerated on p. 332 are fulfilled and, as a result, the development of free trade between A and B has itself led to an equality between the marginal product of labour in A and in B. Suppose that in such a situation the amounts of land and labour in country A were suddenly halved but that the average and marginal productivities of land and labour in A were simultaneously doubled. Everything would remain unchanged—output, trade, product prices, etc.—except that every unit of land and of labour in A would have twice as high a productivity and twice as high a reward as before.

Now this increase in the overall productivity of land and labour in A might be due to a better productive atmosphere in A, in which case we should have the situation which we have just analysed at some

[1] This reason for a continuing divergence in marginal productivities even after the development of free trade in products has been discussed in Chapter XXIII (pp. 378–83).

[2] This reason for differing marginal productivities has been considered in Chapter XXI (pp. 351–6).

length in the preceding paragraphs. But the higher all-round productivity of land and labour in A might equally well be due to the fact that in A both the apple and the blanket industries were much more plentifully supplied with some third factor, capital, so that both labour and land were more productive in A than in B. Or it might be due to the facts that A was a much larger economy than B and that there were important economies of large-scale production in both the apple industry and the blanket industry, so that both industries being on a much larger scale in A than in B the productivity of both land and labour were higher in both industries in A than in B. In both these cases even after free trade in products had led to an equality of product prices in A and B the marginal product of labour and of land would remain higher in A than in B; labour would move from B to A; and the effect of this movement upon the domestic and international distribution of income would be exactly similar to those which we have already analysed in the case of differences in marginal productivities due to differences in productive atmosphere.

Our analysis of the case in which the productive atmosphere was more favourable in A than in B rested upon the assumption that any combination of land and labour in any industry would be, say, 100 per cent more productive in A than in B. This was in at least three ways an example of a very generalized productive advantage in A: first, it meant that the marginal and the average product of each factor were equally affected; second, it meant that labour was as much affected as land; and, third, it meant that the favourable productive advantage was as marked in A's apple industry as in A's blanket industry. It is only if the productive advantages which may be reaped in A from an abundant supply of a third factor like capital or from a large scale of output also have these very generalized favourable effects that the previous analysis can be directly applied to them.

In fact, of course, it is improbable that a productive advantage in A—whether derived from a more favourable atmosphere, more abundant supplies of a third factor, or a larger scale of operations—will have these generalized effects. Thus to have a large supply of capital to work with may do much more to raise the productivity of labour than it does to raise the productivity of land; or it may do much more to raise the productivity of land and labour in the blanket industry than it does to raise their productivity in the apple industry. Or, to take another example, the psychological atmosphere in A may be one which is very congenial to hard and effective effort by workers, but may leave the productivity of land much the same; on the other hand, the climatic atmosphere might be specially favourable for the production of apples in A, leaving the conditions for blanket production much the same in the two countries. Similarly, a large scale of operations may give advantages in one industry but not in another, or may give advantages to one factor and not to another: the blanket industry might give chances of large-scale economics while the apple industry did not; or a large labour force might give opportunities for the spread and growth of technical knowledge, while no net advantage per acre is to be gained simply from having a large rather than a small number of acres.

It is, therefore, important to see how the conclusions of the previous analysis would be modified if the productive advantage in A were concentrated either on one factor to the exclusion of the other or on one industry to the exclusion of the other. We shall accordingly consider briefly the four cases in which there is a productive advantage in A which makes (1) all land, (2) all labour, (3) land and labour in the blanket industry, and (4) land and labour in the apple industry, more productive in A than in B.

(1) Suppose, then, that the economies of A and B are in equilibrium, freely trading with each other, and with all the conditions enumerated on p. 332 fulfilled so that the marginal product of each factor is the same in A as in B. Suppose then that the productivity of land in A is doubled and the amount of land in A is halved. Everything remains unchanged except that the marginal product and the rent per acre of land is doubled in A. We are now in a position of equilibrium which differs from the previous one solely by the fact that land has a productive advantage in A. The marginal product of land will be higher in A than in B; but land is immobile and cannot move from B to A in search of this higher reward. The marginal product of labour will remain unchanged at the same level in A and in B. Labour will have no incentive to move. Our present problem, of the effect of a movement of labour from B to A on the distribution of income, just does not arise.

(2) Suppose that we start once more from an equilibrium position in which, because of the fulfilment of the conditions enumerated on p. 332, the marginal product of each factor is the same in A as in B. Suppose, however, that this time the productivity of labour in A is doubled and the amount of labour in A is halved. The immediate effect upon the economy will be to leave everything unchanged except that the productivity and the real wage of a unit of labour in A will be doubled. But this case is not the end of the story. Since labour is the mobile factor, there will now be a movement of labour from B to A in search of the higher reward. But the analysis of the effects of this movement upon the distribution of income will differ in no material respect from that which we have already carried out at length to cover the case of a favourable productive atmosphere for both factors in A. In the case now under consideration the productivity of labour in any given situation is twice as high in A as in B, while the productivity of land in any given situation is the same in A as in B. But, since land is immobile

between A and B, it makes no difference at all to any relevant factor if A had, say, only 50 acres of land with a productivity of 100 per acre instead of 100 acres of land with a productivity of 50 per acre. We can therefore treat the present case as if A had only half as much land as she has but the productivity of both land and labour were twice as high in A as in B. The method of analysis of the effects of a movement of labour from B to A will thus be exactly the same as in the case of a general productive advantage in A, which we have already analysed at length.

(3) Let us turn next to the case where A has a productive advantage over B for both factors in the blanket industry but not in the apple industry. As we shall show, the effects of a movement of labour from B to A are likely to have the same sort of distributional effects as they do in the more general case where A's productive advantage applies to both industries; the terms of trade are likely to be turned against the country which produces blankets, and domestically in both countries the rate of wages is likely to fall relatively to the rate of rent. But this case needs some elaboration of the previous argument.

Let us deal with the problem by assuming yet once more that we start with a position of equilibrium in which all the conditions enumerated on p. 332 are fulfilled and in which, therefore, the marginal product of labour in terms of apples or of blankets is the same in A as in B. Suppose that in this situation productivity were doubled in A's blanket industry without any change in productivity in B's blanket industry. The immediate effect of this would be to cause the cost of blankets to fall relatively to the cost of apples in A without any similar change in B. Consumers in A and B would start to buy their blankets in A rather than in B and their apples in B rather than in A. The blanket industry would be expanded and the apple industry contracted in A. This would represent indirectly a net increase in the demand for labour in A to produce the labour-intensive product, blankets, and a net fall in the demand for land in A as the land-intensive apple industry was contracted. Wages would rise in A relatively to rents; a higher ratio of land to labour than before would be employed in A in both industries.

In B the opposite would have happened. The contraction of the blanket industry and expansion of the apple industry would have caused a net increase in the demand for land and decrease in the demand for labour. Wages would have fallen relatively to rents; and in both industries in B the ratio of land to labour employed would be reduced somewhat.

Let us now compare the position in A and in B of the apple industry, which has no special productive advantage in either country. Before A's blanket industry had enjoyed any productive advantage the real rate of wages had been the same in A as in B and the real rate of rent had been the same in A as in B. It would therefore have paid apple farmers in A to use the same ratio of land to labour in apple production as was used by the competing apple producers in B. But, as we have seen, as a result of the change in productivity in A's blanket industry, the ratio of land to labour has risen in A's apple industry and fallen in B's apple industry. Since there has been no change in productive advantages in the two apple industries, this means that the marginal product of labour will have risen in A's apple industry and fallen in B's apple industry. The marginal product of labour in terms of apples will therefore now be higher in A than in B. But as there is free trade between A and B the price of blankets in terms of apples will be the same in A as in B. If the marginal product of labour and so the real wage of labour is higher in terms of apples in A than in B, it must therefore also be higher in terms of blankets in A than in B. Labour will therefore move from B to A in search of the higher reward in A.

It is the effect of this movement of labour upon the distribution of income which we have to consider.[1] Its general effects will be the same as those considered in the more general case discussed on pp. 431–9 above. The movement of labour from B will mean the loss in B of a factor which is specially useful in producing blankets; the arrival of the labour in A will mean the gain in A of a factor which is specially useful in producing blankets; and since the productivity of labour is higher in A than in B for the reasons just described, the most obvious effect of the movement of labour on the supply side will be an increase in the relative supply of blankets. This will give rise to a tendency for the terms of trade to move further against labour-intensive blankets and in favour of the land-intensive apples. This in turn will give rise to some general lowering of wages and raising of rents in both countries.

The influence of the movement of labour from B to A is, in fact, very like that illustrated in case iii of Table XXXIII. The movement of labour from B to A will cause a relative scarcity of labour and plenty of land in B and may thus well involve some expansion of B's apple industry to absorb the land released by the contraction of B's blanket industry. Similarly the arrival of the labour in A will cause a relative scarcity of land and surplus of labour in A, and may thus well involve some contraction of A's apple industry to release the land required in

[1] In other words, we want to know not whether a high productivity of A's blanket industry will turn the terms of trade against blankets (and so against the exporters of blankets) simply by increasing the world supply of blankets. Of course, it will do so. We are concerned only with a subsequent possible secondary movement of the terms of trade against blankets. After the increased productivity in A's blanket industry, free trade in products without any factor movements will have led to a new equilibrium with presumably a lower world price of blankets. Our question is whether any movement of labour from B to A which may then occur will cause a further movement of the terms of trade against blankets.

A's expanding blanket industry. Now if in both A and B the ratio of land to labour was rigidly fixed at 2 in the apple industry and at $\frac{1}{2}$ in the blanket industry, the numerical example given in case iii of Table XXXIII would exactly cover the present case. As we saw in our discussion of that table (p. 436), as far as the amounts of factors were concerned there would be a contraction in A's apple industry which exactly equalled the expansion of B's apple industry, and there would be an expansion of A's blanket industry which exactly offset the contraction of B's blanket industry. Since in our present case A's apple industry has no productive advantage over B's, this would leave the world output of apples unchanged. But since A's blanket industry has a productive advantage over B's, the world output of blankets would be increased. The relative supply of blankets being larger, the movement of labour would have tended to turn the terms of trade against blankets.

We cannot in our present problem apply exactly the analysis of case iii of Table XXXIII because in our present problem the ratio of land to labour in the blanket (or in the apple) industry will not be the same in A as in B. As we have seen, the expansion of A's blanket industry, and so of the demand for A's labour, due to the productive advantage enjoyed by A's blanket industry, will have caused the ratio of land to labour to be higher in each of A's industries than in the corresponding industry in B. But this in itself will not have removed the fundamental tendency which we are now examining. So long as the blanket industry is the labour-intensive industry in B (i.e. so long as the ratio of land to labour is higher in B's apple industry than in B's blanket industry), the emigration of labour from B will cause mainly a reduction in the output of blankets in B. And so long as the blanket industry is also the labour-intensive industry in A (i.e. so long as the ratio of land to labour is higher in A's apple industry than in B's apple industry), the immigration of labour into A will cause mainly an increase in the output of blankets in A. But since A's blanket industry has a productive advantage over B's, the increased output of blankets in A will be greater than the decreased output of blankets in B. The main effect of the movement of labour will thus be to increase the output of blankets.[1]

For this reason the terms of trade are likely to be turned against blankets and thus to be turned against the country which exports blankets. In our present case the exporter of blankets may be A or B. If B is the country which is richly endowed with labour and only sparsely endowed with land, B would have a factor endowment which suited her to concentrate on the production of the labour-intensive product, blankets, and to import apples in return for blanket exports. But in our present case A at the same time has some special productive

[1] The reader is referred to Section XIX of the mathematical supplement for a formal proof of this assertion.

advantage (due to something other than her factor endowment) in the blanket industry. If this special productive advantage outweighs the inappropriate factor endowment of A, then it may be A which exports blankets. Thus when the terms of trade are turned against blankets by the movement of labour from B to A, the movement will be to the advantage of the pre-existing citizens of A if B is the exporter of blankets and of the remaining citizens of B if A is the exporter of blankets.

But in both cases the movement of the terms of trade against blankets will tend to depress the wages of labour (which is the important factor of production in the production of blankets in both countries) and to raise the rent of land (which is the important factor in the production of apples in both countries). Thus the movement of labour from B to A by increasine thg relative world supply of blankets and moving the terms of trade against blankets will cause some shift from wages to rents inside both countries.

(4) Let us next consider the case where A has some productive advantage over B in the land-intensive apple industry but not in the labour-intensive blanket industry. Let us start once more with a situation in which all the conditions enumerated on p. 332 are fulfilled, so that free trade between A and B has led to an equilibrium in which the marginal product of each factor in each industry is the same in A as in B. Suppose that A's apple industry then obtains some special productive advantage. The cost of apples relatively to the cost of blankets would fall in A below the existing level in B. World demand would shift on to A's apples and B's blankets. The expansion of A's apple industry and contraction of A's blanket industry would raise the demand for land and reduce the demand for labour in A and thus raise rents and lower wage rates in A. Conversely, in B the expansion of the blanket industry and contraction of the apple industry would raise wage rates and lower the rate of rents. This movement would go on until the rise of rents and fall of wages in A had so raised the cost of apples relatively to the cost of blankets in A, while the fall of rents and rise of wages in B had so lowered the cost of apples relatively to the cost of blankets in B that the cost ratio was once more the same in both countries in spite of the productive advantage in A's apple industry.

Now the rise in rents and fall in wages in A will have caused employers in A in both industries to take on more labour and less land, i.e. to employ less land per unit of labour. In B the opposite will have happened. The fall in rents and rise in wages will have induced employers to employ more land per worker. Let us consider the blanket industry in both countries, remembering that in our present case this industry has no special productive advantage in either country. Before we allowed for the expansion of A's apple industry the marginal product of each factor in the blanket industry was the same in A as in B. The ratio of the amount of land employed to the amount of labour employed would in those circumstances be the same in A's as in B's blanket industry. But, as we have seen, a productive advantage in A's apple industry will have lowered the ratio of land to labour in A's blanket industry and will have raised the ratio of land to labour in B's blanket industry. The ratio of land to labour will therefore be lower in A's than in B's blanket industry. In consequence, the marginal product of land will be higher in A's than in B's blanket industry but the marginal product of labour will be higher in B's than in A's blanket industry. Since we are assuming free trade, the price of apples in terms of blankets will be the same in both countries. Thus if the marginal product of labour (and so the real wage rate) is higher in B than in A in terms of blankets, it will also be higher in B than in A in terms of apples.

Thus we reach the conclusion that a productive advantage in A's apple industry would cause the marginal product of labour to be higher in B than in A. It could not, therefore, be the cause of a movement of labour from B to A, but only of a movement of labour from A to B. If we wish to continue to consider movements of labour from B to A, we must assume that it is B's and not A's apple industry which enjoys the productive advantage. In that case we can employ the argument of the preceding two paragraphs merely with the transposition of countries A and B to reach the conclusion that a productive advantage in B's apple industry will cause the marginal product of labour to be higher in A than in B.

Suppose that as a result of this some labour moves from B to A. As before, since blankets are the labour-intensive product in both countries, this will cause the output of blankets to fall in B and to rise in A. This will release land in B which can be used for the expansion of B's apple industry; and it will absorb some land in A's blanket industry which will lead to a contraction of A's apple industry. Now once more we have a situation very like that discussed in connexion with case iii of Table XXXIII. Since the marginal product of labour is higher in both industries in A than in B, the movement of labour from B to A is likely to lead to an increase in the supply of the labour-intensive product (blankets) relatively to that of the land-intensive product (apples).

This will tend to turn the terms of trade in favour of apples. This will be to the advantage of the country which is the net exporter of apples, which will be A if the initial advantage of A in its good endowment of land outweighs the other special productive advantage in B's apple industry and will be B if A's factor endowment is less marked than B's special productive advantage. In either case the movement of the terms of trade in favour of the land-intensive product, apples, and against the labour-intensive product, blankets, will tend to raise rents and to depress wages in both countries, and will thus lead in both A and B to some redistribution of income in favour of rents.

So much for the cases in which the marginal product of labour is higher in A than in B because some lines of production in one country enjoy a special productive advantage—due to a favourable productive atmosphere, to increasing returns to scale, or to a third factor of production which is specially useful in one industry. We can summarize the results by saying that where all of A's economic activity or all of A's labour or all of A's labour-intensive industries (i.e. blankets) or all of B's land-intensive industries (i.e. apples) have a productive advantage, the marginal product of labour will tend to be higher in A than in B; and in these cases the movement of labour from B to A will tend to increase the relative world supply of blankets, to turn the terms of trade against blankets, and to redistribute income in favour, first, of the country which exports apples and, second, in both countries in favour of rents.

In all the above cases we assumed that both blankets and apples were produced in both countries. Let us now turn to the cases in which, as before, for some reason or another the marginal product of labour is higher in A than in B so that labour has some incentive to move from B to A but in which, unlike the previous cases, for some reason or another at least one of the countries does not go in for the production of one of the products at all. In other words, we wish to examine the effects upon the distribution of income of a movement of labour from a point of low productivity in B to a point of high productivity in A when at least one of the countries is completely specialized on the production of one of the two products.

We will start with the very simple but very important case in which, for some reason or another which for our present purposes we need not specify, A produces only apples and no blankets and B produces only blankets and no apples. The value of the marginal product of labour might well be higher in A than in B.[1] Suppose that as a result of this some labour moved from B to A. The effect upon the international and

[1] One reason for this might be as follows. Suppose that A has a great deal of land and practically no labour at all and B has a great deal of labour and practically no land at all. This state of affairs might well be the cause of A's complete specialization on the production of apples—since A's factor endowment is hopelessly inappropriate for a labour-intensive blanket industry—and for B's complete specialization on the production of blankets—since B's factor endowment is hopelessly inappropriate for a land-intensive apple industry. But in terms of apples the marginal product of labour in A might still be very high because of the great shortage of labour in A and in terms of blankets the marginal product of labour in B might be very low because of the great surplus of labour in B. But unless the world demand for apples were very low and for blankets were high relative to their supplies, the value of an apple in terms of blankets would not necessarily be especially low. In this case the value of labour's marginal product would be much higher in A than in B.

the domestic distributions of income would be clear and unequivocal.

As far as the international terms of trade are concerned, this movement of labour from B to A would necessarily mean a reduction in the output of B's product (blankets) and an increase in the output of A's product (apples). As far as the supply side is concerned, there would be a movement of the terms of trade against apples and so against the pre-existing citizens of A and in favour of the remaining citizens of B.

As far as the domestic distributions of income were concerned, there would be a movement in favour of wage rates in B and in favour of rates of rent in A. In B the emigration of labour out of the blanket industry will reduce the ratio of labour to land in that industry and thus raise the marginal product (and so the wage rate) of the remaining labour there and lower the marginal product (and so the rate of rent) of B's land. In A the immigration of labour into the apple industry will increase the ratio of labour to land employed and thus lower the wage rate of the pre-existing labour in A and raise the rate of rent on land there.

This we may call the case of pure specialization. But there are two other 'mixed' cases which we must examine. It may be (1) that A produces only apples while B produces both apples and blankets, or (2) that B produces only blankets while A produces both apples and blankets. These are mixed cases, because, in the former case for example, in country A all productive resources are specialized on apple production, whereas in country B land will be specially important for the production of the land-intensive product apples and labour specially important for the production of the labour-intensive product blankets.

(1) Let us first consider the case where A produces only apples, but B produces both apples and blankets. This case (as we have seen in Chapter XIX, pp. 322–3) might arise where apples are land-intensive, blankets are labour-intensive, A is very well supplied with land and very badly supplied with labour, B is very well supplied with labour and very badly supplied with land, but either A is a much smaller country than B or else apples are a much more important product in consumption than are blankets. As far as the factor endowments are concerned, it would be suitable for A to make only apples and B only blankets. But if this were so, the world would be starved of apples either because A is such a small country or else because apples were such an important product. In this case equilibrium would be found only with the price of apples sufficiently high in terms of blankets that B was tempted—in spite of her scarcity of land and consequential high rents of land—to use some of her factors to produce apples. But A with her very plentiful supply of land and scarcity of labour would produce apples by much more extensive farming methods than B; the ratio of land to labour would be

higher in A's apple industry than in B's; the marginal product of labour and so the wage of labour would therefore be higher in A than in B; and labour would have an incentive to move from B to A.

When the labour moves into A, it will cause an increase in A's output of apples. When the labour moves out of B it will cause a decline primarily in the output of B's labour-intensive product, blankets. It is not so likely to cause a decline in the output of B's land-intensive product, apples. Indeed, if the ratio of land to labour is much higher in B's apple industry than in her blanket industry and if it is not easy to alter the ratio of land to labour much in these two industries, the contraction of B's blanket industry (as labour moves out of it to emigrate to A) will leave land unemployed in B and this will give rise to some positive expansion of B's apple industry.[1] Thus the apple output will go up in A (and perhaps in B also), while the output of blankets will fall in B. The world supply of apples will rise relatively to that of blankets. The terms of trade will move against apples and so against A, the exporter of apples. In A there will be a higher ratio of labour to land in the only existing industry, the apple industry, so that there will be some redistribution of A's national income in favour of rents. In B the terms of trade will have moved in favour of B's labour-intensive product (blankets) and against B's land-intensive product (apples) with the result that there will be some redistribution of income in B in favour of wages. Thus the general effects of the movement of labour from B to A upon the distribution of income between the two countries and within each country will be in the same direction as in the case of pure specialization when A produces only apples and B only blankets.

(2) Suppose that conditions are the same as those which we have just discussed except that B is a very much smaller country than A and that blankets are a much more important item in consumers' expenditures than apples. Since A is very well endowed with land and very badly endowed with labour and the opposite is the case in B, from the point of view of factor endowments alone it would be appropriate for A to specialize on the production of apples and B on that of blankets. But in this case there would be a world shortage of blankets because B could not alone produce enough. The world price of blankets would rise sufficiently to encourage A to produce some blankets in spite of the scarcity of labour and high wage rates in A. But because of this scarcity of labour in A the wage rate would be higher in A than in B, and blankets would be produced with a higher ratio of land to labour in A than in B. The marginal product of labour would be higher in A than in B.

When labour moved from B to A there would be a reduction in B's output of blankets. When the labour moved into A there would be an increase in the output of the labour-intensive product, blankets, in A.

[1] This case is illustrated by row 6 of Table XXXIII.

Now in so far as the ratio of labour to land was higher in the blanket industry than in the apple industry in A and in so far as it was difficult to increase the ratio of labour to land in these industries, the expansion of the blanket industry in A would involve an actual contraction of the apple industry in A, because the employment of the newly immigrated labour in A's blanket industry would involve the employment of some more land in that industry and this land would be found (without any further great increase in the labour needing to be absorbed) only by a contraction of the apple industry in A.

As a result there would be a net decrease in the world supply of apples and a net increase in the world supply of blankets (the increased output of blankets in A being greater than the decreased output of blankets in B both because the marginal product of labour is higher in A's blanket industry than in B's and also because of the shift of resources from A's apple industry to A's blanket industry). In consequence the terms of trade would move against blankets and so against B which, since it produces only blankets, must be the exporter of blankets. Moreover, inside B there would be a redistribution of income in favour of wages, since a higher ratio of land to labour would be used in B's only industry, the blanket industry. In A the terms of trade would have moved against the labour-intensive product blankets, so that there would be some redistribution of income in A against wages and in favour of rents.

In this case, therefore, the effect of the movement of labour from B to A upon the domestic distribution of income within each country would be in the same general direction as in the case of pure specialization—namely, a shift in favour of rents in A and in favour of wages in B. But the effect upon the international distribution of income would now be in a different direction; the terms of trade would move in favour of apples and so in favour of A, whereas in the case in which A specialized only on apples the terms of trade were found to move in favour of blankets and so of B.[1]

[1] In all our examples A stands for the country which is relatively well endowed with land and apples for the land-intensive product; and vice versa for B and for blankets. It will be observed that our examples do not cover the cases in which A produces only blankets or B produces only apples. As far as factor endowments are concerned such cases could obviously not arise. But it is possible that while A's factor endowments were such as to make her best suited for apple production, yet she might enjoy a productive atmosphere which made her best suited for blanket production. In extreme cases the productive atmosphere might be so important that, for example, A produced only blankets in spite of the fact that A was initially well endowed with land and badly endowed with labour. Such cases are not covered either by the preceding discussion in this chapter of differences in productive atmosphere (where we have assumed that both countries produce something of both products) or by the preceding discussion of cases of specialization due to extreme differences in factor endowments. The reader is left to work out for himself, with the help of the formulæ given at the end of Section XIX of the mathematical supplement, the cases where specialization occurs due to differences in productive atmospheres which outweigh the influence of differences in factor endowment.

We turn now to the examination of another reason why, even in conditions of complete free and costless trade in products between A and B, the marginal product of labour may still be higher in A than in B so that labour will have an incentive to move from B to A. We suppose, as before, that A is much better endowed with land and that B is much better endowed with labour. But we now drop the assumption that apples are always the land-intensive and blankets the labour-intensive product. Let us suppose that in the production of blankets it is for technical reasons difficult to substitute land for labour or labour for land; whatever the rent of land or the wage of labour more or less the same ratio of land to labour must be used in blanket production. But suppose at the same time that very great technical possibilities exist for varying the way in which apples are produced. If land is expensive and labour cheap, apples will be produced by intensive farming techniques which employ very little land and much labour; whereas if land is cheap and labour expensive, apples will be produced by extensive farming techniques mainly with land and with the employment of very little labour.

Now in this case[1] the plentiful supply of land and the scarcity of labour in A may cause rents to be very low and wages to be very high in A, while the opposite factor endowments in B will cause rents to be very high and wages very low. In A, therefore, apples will be produced by land-intensive methods and the ratio of land to labour will be higher in the apple industry than in the blanket industry. In B apples will be produced by labour-intensive methods and the ratio of land to labour will be higher in the blanket industry than in the apple industry. In A apples will be cheap relative to blankets because land is cheap and apples are the land-intensive product; in B apples will be cheap relative to blankets because labour is cheap and apples are the labour-intensive industry. In such circumstances it is quite possible for the price of apples relatively to the price of blankets to be the same in both countries as a result of free trade between them in their two products, for both countries to continue to produce something of both products, and yet for the wage rate to be much higher in A than in B and for the rate of rent to be much higher in B than in A.

In such a case the marginal product of labour will be higher in A (where each unit of labour works with a large amount of land in the apple industry) than in B (where each unit of labour works with very little land in the apple industry). Labour will therefore have an incentive to move from B to A. When it does so, its emigration from B will cause mainly a contraction in the output of the product, apples, which is labour-intensive in B. There may have to be some actual expansion in B's land-intensive product, blankets, to absorb the land released from

[1] This case has been considered in Chapter XXIII, pp. 390–1.

B's contracting apple industry. On the other hand, the immigration of the labour into A will cause an expansion primarily of the product, blankets, which is labour-intensive in A. There may have to be some contraction in A's land-intensive product, apples, in order to release the land which is being drawn into A's expanding blanket industry. Clearly the world supply of blankets will expand relatively to the world supply of apples. The terms of trade will tend to move against blankets and so against whichever of the two countries happens to be the exporter of blankets.

Within B the movement of the terms of trade against blankets will be a movement against B's land-intensive industry and will thus tend to some domestic redistribution of income against rents of land and in favour of the wages of labour. Within A the movement of the terms of trade against blankets will be a movement against A's labour-intensive industry and will thus lead to some domestic redistribution in favour of rents and against wages.[1]

There remains for discussion one further case in which in spite of free trade in products between A and B the marginal product of labour may be higher in A than in B. As we have already seen,[2] if it costs something to transport the land-intensive product, apples, which is exported from A to B and/or to transport the labour-intensive product, blankets, which is exported from B to A, there will be some impediment to the development of trade between the two countries. As a result the price of apples relatively to the price of blankets will remain higher in B than in A. In consequence the apple industry will be contracted in A and expanded in B, and the blanket industry will be contracted in B and expanded in A, relatively to the free-trade position without transport costs. As a result of this the demand for land will be contracted in A and expanded in B, and the demand for labour will be contracted in B and expanded in A, relatively to the free-trade position without transport costs. In consequence the marginal product of land and the rate of rent will remain lower in A than in B, while the marginal product of labour and the real rate of wages will remain lower in B than in A. Labour will have some incentive to move from B to A, provided that the cost of movement of labour does not outweigh the advantage in real wages so obtained.

The price of apples in B must exceed the price of apples in A by the cost of transport from A to B; and, similarly, the price of blankets in A

[1] It can easily be seen by a similar process of reasoning that if it was the blanket industry in which the substitutability between factors was very great and the apple industry in which it was very low, then once more labour would move from B to A; and when it did so, the terms of trade would now be turned against apples and so against the country which exported apples. But once more within A there would be a shift to rents and within B a shift to wages.

[2] This case has been discussed in Chapter XXII.

must exceed their price in B by the cost of transport. Those relationships cannot be upset by the movement of labour from B to A. But this does not, of course, mean that the terms of trade between apples and blankets may not be affected in both countries by the movement of labour. If, for example, the price of apples rose in both countries by 10 per cent and the price of blankets fell by 10 per cent in both countries, the terms of trade would in both countries move 20 per cent against blankets, but the same percentage margins as before between the price of apples in A and in B and of blankets in B and in A would exist to cover the cost of transport.

Now there is some reason to believe that the movement of labour from B to A will in these circumstances tend to increase the world supply of blankets relatively to the world supply of apples. The wage rate is higher in A than in B and the rate of rent higher in B than in A; in both industries therefore it will pay to economize labour in A and to economize land in B; in each industry therefore the ratio of land to labour employed will be higher in A than in B; in terms of both products, therefore, the marginal product of labour will be higher in A than in B. The situation is, therefore, very comparable, so far as marginal changes are concerned, to the case (examined on pp. 431–9 above) where the productivity of labour is higher in both industries in A than in B. In that case we found that a shift of labour from B to A would tend to increase the world supply of the labour-intensive product, blankets, relatively to that of the land-intensive product, apples. The emigration of labour from B would tend to decrease the supply of the labour-intensive product in B and, by releasing land from that industry in B, to cause an increase in the supply of the land-intensive product, apples, in B. Conversely, the immigration of labour into A would tend to increase the supply of the labour-intensive product, blankets, in A and, by absorbing some land into that industry, to decrease the output of the land-intensive product, apples, in A. But since the productivity of labour is marginally greater in A than in B, these changes in output would be greater in A than in B. In consequence the world output of blankets would tend to rise relatively to that of apples and the terms of trade to move therefore against blankets. In so far as this happened, there would tend to be some redistribution of income in favour of the pre-existing citizens of A and against the remaining citizens of B. Moreover, within both countries there would tend to be some shift of income in favour of land which is most important in the production of apples, in whose favour the terms of trade had moved, and against labour which was most important in the production of blankets against which the terms of trade had moved.

This tendency might, however, be reinforced or offset by another factor which is peculiar to the present case. In Chapter XXII we have seen that the real increase in economic efficiency to be gained in this case by the movement of labour from B to A is the saving of resources which is achieved through the reduction in transport costs due to the fact that not so many apples will now be carried from A to B nor so many blankets from B to A. We are in fact dealing with three industries —the apple industry, the blanket industry, and the transport industry. Now if the transport industry is very labour-intensive, transport services will presumably be being supplied by B. The fall in the demand for transport services will thus tend to reduce their price. This will represent a further movement in the terms of trade against one of B's export industries, transport services, and it will also release labour rather than land, thus further reducing wage rates relatively to rents in both countries and further lowering the price of B's other export, blankets, relatively to A's export, apples. If, however, transport services were land-intensive and supplied by A, the fall in the demand for such services would directly reduce the price offered for this export of A, would release land rather than labour, lower rents relatively to wages, and apple prices relatively to blanket prices. In this case it would work in the other direction.

We have now considered a large number of possible cases in which the migration of labour from B to A may have different effects upon the prices of the products and of the factors. But these all can be regarded as a playing of the changes on two main forces:

(1) Where country A is specialized entirely on one product and B on another, a movement of labour from B to A will increase the world supply of A's product and decrease the world supply of B's product. The terms of trade will move in favour of B. Within A there will be a redistribution of income away from wages, since the ratio of labour to other factors has gone up in A's industry; and within B there will be a redistribution of income in favour of wages, since the ratio of labour to other factors has fallen in B's industry.

(2) Where the countries are not specialized but where labour is specially well suited to produce one product (blankets), then the movement of labour from B where its marginal product is low to A where its marginal product is high will tend to increase the world supply of the labour-intensive product relatively to the supply of other products. The terms of trade will move against the country which exports the labour-intensive product. In this case in both countries there will be some redistribution of income against labour, since in both countries there has been a movement of prices against the labour-intensive product.

Now controls might be imposed on international factor movements as a means of increasing economic welfare in order to redistribute income either internationally or domestically in favour of those persons to whom a high distributional weight has been allotted. In the remaining pages of this chapter we intend to consider some of the problems which would arise in using controls over factor movements for this purpose. It would be tedious to consider once more all the possible cases. Solely in order to illustrate some of the issues, we shall confine ourselves exclusively to the case of complete specialization, where A produces only apples and B only blankets, and where in consequence a migration of labour from B to A will turn the terms of trade against B and will redistribute income in B in favour of wages and in A to the disadvantage of wages.

Suppose that in both countries a higher distributional weight is given by the policy-makers to wages than to rents. Then the authorities in B would have some incentive to subsidize or otherwise to encourage emigration because this would not only help to turn the terms of trade in B's favour but also to redistribute B's income in favour of wages.

But the authorities in A would, of course, have exactly the same sort of reasons for taxing or otherwise impeding the immigration of labour into A, since such immigration would turn the terms of trade against A and would redistribute income within A against wages. There would thus be a direct conflict of policies.

In so far as the motives of the two governments were to turn the terms of trade in favour of their own citizens, this conflict of interest is, of course, inevitable. But in so far as the migration policies are devised in the interests of the domestic redistribution of income the conflict is not inevitable. If both governments act by taxing landlords in order to subsidize wage-earners instead of by subsidizing emigration in the case of B and taxing immigration in the case of A, there need be no conflict of policies. Both can simultaneously succeed in their objectives.

Suppose, however, that both governments do try to influence the domestic distribution of income by encouraging emigration (in B's case) and discouraging immigration (in A's case). Suppose that B's government subsidizes emigration and A's government taxes immigration. A's tax might just cancel the effect of B's subsidy in so far as the effect upon the movement of labour was concerned. There would be no net effect upon movement, and thus no net effect upon the distribution of income in either country. The only effect would be that B's government would be paying out a subsidy which A's government would be collecting in tax; and indirectly B's citizens would be subsidizing A's citizens.

This example shows incidentally how much stronger in such a conflict of national policies is the bargaining position of the country which wishes to stop the movement than is that of the country which wishes to encourage the movement. This same principle is as true of the control of trade as it is of the control of factor movements. Suppose that

B's government had wished for some reason to promote the export of its blankets to A, while A's government had wished to discourage the import of B's blankets into A. For every dollar paid in export subsidy by B, A's government can raise an import duty of a dollar. This will exactly offset the effect of the subsidy on the promotion of trade and will result simply in B's government paying money over to A's government. This is a game which A's government is bound to win.[1] She can merrily impose any tax on the import of B's blankets or immigration of B's labour which is needed to offset any level of subsidy given by B, and she can equally cheerfully then raise her taxes still further in order to exert a net discouragement upon the movement of goods or of men which she wishes to avoid.

For this reason, in any conflict of national policies for the control of international factor movements, it is the negative policies of hindrance and prohibition of such movements which are likely to be most evident. In so far as the domestic distribution of national incomes is concerned, if the national objective is more often to aim at a high ratio of capital to labour than at a high ratio of labour to capital, we should expect to find as a general rule prohibitions or restrictions on the immigration of labour and on the export of capital rather than prohibitions and restrictions on the emigration of labour and on the import of capital.

An important argument against the use of controls over factor movements as a means of influencing the domestic distribution of income is thus that it may often lead to futile conflicts of national policies which might have been avoided if more direct measures had been taken to redistribute income domestically.

But there is another important argument against the use of controls over factor movements for the purpose of influencing the domestic or the international distribution of income. Controls used for this purpose only are very likely to lead to economic inefficiency. Thus, in the example used above, the government of B may subsidize the emigration of labour from B in order to move the terms of trade in favour of B and/or to redistribute income from rent and profits to wages in B. But on the units of labour which move only because of the subsidy, the marginal product of labour will in fact be lower in A than in B. There is a loss of world production on the units of labour which are artificially encouraged to move from B to A. Alternatively, in the absence of a migration policy on the part of the government of B, the government of

[1] We have put the argument solely in terms of the ease of offsetting subsidies by taxes. But it is also true if the national policies take the form of quantitative controls rather than of taxes and subsidies. If, for example, A's government ruled that no blankets from B or workers from B were to be allowed to enter A's territory and if at the same time B's government ruled that not less than 1,000,000 blankets and 100,000 workers must leave its territory for A each year, it is pretty clear which side would win the administrative battle.

A may restrict the immigration of labour into A with the object of moving the terms of trade in favour of A and/or influencing the domestic distribution of income in favour of labour in A. But on the units of labour which, in the absence of this artificial obstacle, would have moved from B to A there is a loss of world production, since the marginal product of labour will continue to be higher in A than in B.

From the world point of view the sensible arrangement would be to abandon the use of national controls over international factor movements simply for the purpose of influencing the domestic distribution of income. Domestic or international policies designed for the direct levying of taxes on those whose distributional weight is low in order to subsidize the incomes of those whose distributional weight is high would avoid both the economic inefficiency and the conflict of national policies which are associated with the use of controls over international factor movements for this purpose. It is true that such progressive fiscal policies carry with them their own disincentives. This we have already discussed at some length (see Chapter III). But unless there are some very special considerations on the other side there is always a presumption that the direct method will do less harm than an indirect method, since the latter in order to achieve a given degree of redistribution will probably involve an unnecessarily large element of disturbance from the point of view of economic efficiency.

CHAPTER XXVIII

THE WORLD SUPPLY OF LABOUR AND CAPITAL

UP to this point throughout Parts II and III of this volume we have tacitly assumed that the given rate of growth of world population and the given rate of accumulation of capital throughout the world are unaffected by the economic policies which are adopted for the control of trade or for the control of international factor movements. We have examined the arguments for and against controls over international trade and over international factor movements on the grounds that they will affect economic efficiency and on the grounds that they will affect the distribution of income, and we have done this in terms of marginal changes and of structural changes and in terms of utopian and of second-best solutions. But throughout these discussions we have assumed that at any given time the total combined population of A and of B and the total combined stock of capital in A and in B will be unaffected in size by the commercial policies and the policies affecting the international movement of factors which the governments of these two countries have chosen to adopt.

Now these assumptions are not necessarily at all realistic, and we have already seen in Chapter VI how economic welfare may be affected by changes in the size of the population and in the supply of capital. We must therefore consider the effect which different international economic policies may have upon economic welfare through changes in the total world supply of labour and capital. There is, of course, a certain illogicality in having postponed the discussion of the whole of this topic until this point. The choice of commercial policies may exert as important an influence on the world supply of labour and capital as is exerted by the imposition or removal of controls over the international movements of these factors. The logical arrangement would, therefore, have been to have discussed at the end of Part II the arguments for trade controls on the grounds that they might improve the supplies of labour and capital and to have discussed at this point the arguments for controls over international factor movements which may be brought forward on the same grounds. But these subjects are so closely interrelated that it seems sensible to discuss them together.

Now there are two logically distinct types of question which may be raised by this discussion.

(1) In the first place, a change in international economic policies—i.e. a change in the controls exerted in A or in B over international trade or over international factor movements—may change conditions

in such a way that the optimum size of the population or the optimum rate of savings is altered without necessarily altering the actual size of the population or the actual rate of new savings. In so far as this is so, the analysis which we have carried out in Parts II and III will not for this reason need any modification; our underlying assumption that these international economic policies do not affect the total world supply of the factors of production remains true. But in a case in which a change in international economic policies does itself change the optimum size of the population or the optimum rate of savings it may be desirable for the authorities in A or in B as a result of a change in their international economic policies to alter their domestic demographic or investment policies so as to bring their rates of population and capital growth into line with the new optima, that is to say, to alter their demographic or investment policies in such a way as to make the best possible use of the new conditions created by the change in international economic policies.

(2) But a change in international economic policies may so change conditions as to affect the size of the actual population or the actual rate of savings in A and B, without necessarily affecting the optimum size of the population or the optimum rate of savings. In this case our underlying assumption in Parts II and III that there were certain given supplies of labour and capital in the world is falsified. These factor supplies are themselves now affected by the changes in international economic policies and we must make some allowance for these consequential changes in the total supplies of labour and capital before we reach a final judgement about the desirability of any one of these changes in international economic policy from the point of view of economic welfare.

In this chapter questions of the first of these two types will be neglected for two reasons. In the first place, it would be impossible to treat them adequately without a much more exhaustive treatment of the theories of optimum population and optimum savings which were merely sketched in Chapter VI. This more exhaustive treatment cannot be undertaken in this volume. But, secondly, the fact that a change in international economic policies may affect the optimum supply of population or savings may, as we have stated, affect the domestic policies which governments should adopt in order to bring their supplies of labour and capital into line with these new optima. But it does not modify the rest of the analysis of Parts II and III of this volume. That will happen only in so far as a change in economic policies causes a change in the actual supply of factors of production and thus falsifies the tacit assumption which we have so far made that these total supplies are unaffected by changes in international economic policies. For both these reasons the discussion of the effects of changed conditions (including changes in international economic policies) upon the optimum supplies of factors of production will not be pursued in this volume. But we must say something about the effect of changes in international economic policies upon the actual supply of the factors.

It would be quite impossible to attempt to cover this subject exhaustively and to discuss all the possible combinations of effect upon the supplies of labour and of capital which different changes in commercial policies and in controls over international migration and international investment might have on various combinations of assumptions about the relevant determining factors. All that we can possibly do is to give one or two particular examples merely in order to illustrate the type of analysis which is relevant to deal with this class of problem.

Accordingly, we shall proceed to give some examples of each of the following possible relationships:

(1) the effect of a change in trade controls upon the world population;
(2) the effect of a change in the control over international capital movements upon the world population;
(3) the effect of a change in controls over international migration upon the world population;
(4) the effect of a change in trade controls upon the supply of savings;
(5) the effect of a change in controls over international capital movements upon the supply of savings; and
(6) the effects of a change in controls over international migration upon the supply of savings.

Let us start with an example of a case in which a change in commercial policy might affect the actual size of the population. Suppose that country A removes some barriers to international trade, that this increases the demand for B's products, and that this raises real income per head of the initial population in B.

The effect will depend in the first place upon the distributional policy adopted in B. If there is a more or less equal distribution of income in B, everyone's real income will go up when real income per head goes up in B. If, however, owners of factors received rewards which were dependent upon the size of the marginal products, then the income of one class, e.g. wage-earners, might conceivably go down if (cf. Chapter XVIII) the change were such as to cause a sharp reduction in the demand for labour-intensive products in B. In this case, of course, the incomes of another class, e.g. property owners, would go up so much the more.

The effect of the change of commercial policy will depend, in the second place, upon how each class of citizens reacts to a change in their real incomes. A rise in the standard of living will lead to an increase of numbers if, in the case of the group of citizens concerned, there is a

Malthusian pressure of numbers upon the means of subsistence. On the other hand, as is now well known, it is possible that a rise in the standard of living will reduce fertility and so reduce numbers.

We cannot examine all the possibilities. We shall take as a simple illustration the case in which (i) there is a more or less egalitarian distributional policy in B so that the standard of living of all citizens is raised by the change in commerical policy, and (ii) there is in B a Malthusian pressure of population upon the means of subsistence. The effect of the commercial policy change will now be to raise the standard of living in B temporarily above the physical subsistence level. Population in B will therefore grow and this growth will continue until the pressure of population is once again great enough to reduce the standard of living to the same physical subsistence level. If this basic physical subsistence level is lower than what we have called the welfare subsistence level, the net result will merely be that there is a larger number of persons living in distressful conditions. The sum total of misery will have been permanently increased. Against this must be set the consideration that during this process of population growth the standard of living will have been raised and there will have been, in the early stages at least of the change, a reduction in the degree of distress in the population.

The change may also have had some permanent effect upon the welfare of the citizens of A. The greater freedom of trade may have raised real incomes in A as well as in B, provided that (see Chapter XVII) the reduction in A's trade barriers has not turned the terms of trade against A to such an extent that the gain in economic efficiency due to the removal of the barrier to trade has not been thereby completely offset. Moreover, the growth of numbers in B may lead to an absolute increase in the demand for imports in B and so for A's exports and thus tend to turn the terms of trade once more in A's favour. If this were so, then the citizens of A might permanently gain from the change, provided of course that there was not a similar pressure of population growth in A upon the basic means of subsistence so that A's population did not also grow without restraint as a result of a temporarily raised standard of living in A.

Let us continue with the assumption that B is a country in which there is a Malthusian pressure of population upon the means of subsistence, that there is a more or less fully egalitarian system for the distribution of income within B, and that in A there is no Malthusian pressure of population upon the means of subsistence. We have just examined how a movement towards a greater freedom of trade might in such circumstances lead to an increase in world population which in turn might seriously modify some of the arguments used in Part II in favour of freeing trade. We can now turn to an examination of the effect of a greater freedom of movement of factors of production between A and B upon world population in such conditions and of the modifications which may for that reason have to be introduced into some of the arguments for freer factor movements which have already been developed in this Part.

Now if there is a very heavy Malthusian pressure of population upon resources in B, labour is likely to be very plentiful relatively to capital in B, so that the marginal product of labour (and so the wage rate) will be low and the marginal product of capital (and so the rate of interest) will be high in B. In the absence of a similar Malthusian pressure in A, the marginal product of labour (and the wage rate) will probably be lower in B than in A and the marginal product of capital (and so the rate of interest) will be higher in B than in A. A removal of obstacles to the international movement of capital would, therefore, probably lead to a flow of capital from A to B; and a removal of obstacles to the international migration would tend to a flow of labour from B to A. These movements of factors in search of higher rewards would also represent a movement from points of lower to points of higher marginal productivity. On the general grounds discussed in the preceding chapters of this Part they should, therefore, be encouraged on grounds of economic efficiency.

But in the conditions which we are now examining this conclusion might need to be modified because of the effects of the factor movements upon population growth. Consider the movement of capital from A to B. Suppose that both in A and in B all capital which is owned by citizens of A is paid a reward equal to the value of its marginal product. When a first unit of capital moves from A to B, its owners in A will receive a reward equal to the value of its marginal product. There will be some rise in the average standard of living in A, since the income from this capital is raised; but there will be no change in the average standard of living in B, since the new capital obtains the whole of its marginal product in B so that exactly as much as before is available to the citizens of B as a whole. The movement of capital from A to B will make capital relatively to labour more plentiful in B; it may, therefore, raise the marginal product of labour and reduce the marginal product of capital in B, and thus cause some shift in the distribution of income inside B against capitalists and in favour of workers. But the total real income available to the citizens of B will be unchanged and this redistribution of income within B can be offset by B's egalitarian fiscal policies.

As further units of capital flow from A to B the picture is modified. Once again the new units of capital owned in A and invested in B, if they receive a reward equal to their marginal product, will leave the same total real income available to the owners of existing factors in B. But now some of the owners of existing factors in B will be citizens of A who have already invested capital in B. Any effect which the further flow of capital from A to B now has in redistributing income earned in B from profits to wages will now for this reason lead to some redistribution of income from citizens of A in favour of citizens of B. The standard of living in B will thus tend to be raised.

But if there is a Malthusian population pressure and an egalitarian fiscal policy in B, this rise in the average standard of living in B will be only temporary. It will lead to an increase of population which will continue until the standard of living in B has fallen again to the physical subsistence level. The final effect in B will be simply that there is a larger instead of a smaller population living in absolute distress and misery. This adverse effect upon welfare in B through population growth in B would have to be taken into account before any final judgement was reached about the effect of free factor movements upon world welfare.

From the point of view of world economic welfare it would not justify any complete prohibition of investment in B by the citizens of A. For, as we have seen, the first instalments of capital invested in B will bring a higher return to the citizens of A (who are not subject to a Malthusian pressure of population) without affecting the standard of living in B. But it will justify calling a halt to further flows of capital from A to B at some point before the marginal product of capital in B has been reduced as low as its level in A. Consider the point reached when so much capital has moved from A to B that the marginal product of capital in B is now only slightly higher than in A. A further flow of capital from A to B will enable that capital to earn a little more in B than in A, and to this extent there will be some very small gain to the citizens of A who own this capital. But it will cause a reduction in the return to capital already invested in B by the citizens of A; and this loss to the citizens of A might more than offset any gain to the citizens of A on additional capital sent from A to B. Thus there would be a net loss to the citizens of A. It is true that this would be rather more than made up by the immediate gains of income by the citizens of B; but if any such temporary gain in B will in fact merely lead to a larger permanent mass of distressful population in B, there will be a net loss from the point of view of world welfare in allowing the last units of capital to flow from A to B.[1]

[1] The above argument has proceeded upon the tacit assumption that the movement of capital from A to B will not affect the commodity terms of trade between A's and B's export products. But, following the argument of Chapter XXVII, the movement of capital from A to B would turn the terms of trade against A if the factors were specialized and the movement of capital therefore led to an increase in the world supply of capital-intensive products, and against B if the countries were specialized and the movement of capital therefore increased the world supply of B's exportable products. The more nearly the situation approaches towards the former of these two conditions, the stronger

Let us consider next the effect, in the conditions which we are examining, of removing any obstacles to the migration of labour from B to A. The basic effect of this is all too clear. The opening up of A to immigrants from B will temporarily remove the checks to B's population growth. The growth of numbers will now proceed so long as the standard of living enjoyed by an immigrant in A is above the physical subsistence level. When A has been sufficiently overpopulated by immigration from B for the standard of living of the immigrant into A to be reduced to this basic subsistence level, the Malthusian checks to population growth in B will be restored. The result will be that, taking the world—A and B—as a whole, there will be a much larger mass of distressful population of B-origin than before. A temporary alleviation of distress will have resulted in a permanently greater mass of distress.[1]

If this were the whole of the story, the control of migration from B to A would clearly be in the interests of world economic welfare. And this would be the end of the story if an egalitarian fiscal policy is adopted in A, so that the newcomers from B enjoy a standard of living of the average level in A. In this case the growth of numbers in B would continue until the whole of A's and of B's population was reduced to the distress of the physical subsistence level.

But the position would be different if the authorities in A, while admitting immigrants from B, did not share with these newcomers the income earned by the factors owned by the pre-existing citizens of A. In this case the pre-existing citizens of A would be better off as a result of the movement of labour from B to A. If labour received a reward equal to the value of its marginal product in A, then the first immigrants from B would receive the whole of their product there, and the citizens of A would have exactly as much for themselves as before. The increased labour supply in A would tend to lower wage rates and raise the rate of interest and the rent of land in A; but this redistribution of income between the pre-existing citizens of A could be offset by a suitable distributional fiscal policy in A. But as more immigrants come

---

is the argument in the text for some restriction on the export of capital from A to B. The fact that such capital movements will turn the terms of trade against A will reduce the gain which A can enjoy from the capital movement; and in B it will merely increase the opportunities for a rapid increase in the population.

[1] In the world as a whole there will be more persons of B-origin than before. There may be in the end either a smaller or a larger population in B itself. If factors are specialized on products (in the sense discussed in Chapter XXVII), then the movement of labour to A will have tended to turn the terms of trade against B's labour-intensive export products. This will tend to reduce the real income of any given population in B, and B would be unable to support so large a number of persons as before. If, however, countries are specialized on products, then the movement of labour from B to A would turn the terms of trade against A's and in favour of B's products, and this would enable B ultimately to support a larger population at the physical subsistence level.

from B, the situation is somewhat different. Once again the new immigrants get just their marginal product. But the accompanying redistribution of income in A away from wages to incomes from property represents now in part a redistribution from the previous immigrants of B-origin to the pre-existing citizens of A. These citizens do thus enjoy a net gain from the immigration, though they will have to cope with the problem of the redistribution of income among their own numbers as between wages and incomes from property.[1]

It follows that if the authorities in A leave the immigrants from B out of their distributional fiscal policies (i) the pre-existing citizens of A will gain instead of losing by admitting immigrants from the land of Malthusian pressure, and (ii) the population of B-origin, whether in A or in B, will not be able to grow to such large numbers as is the case if the authorities in A share out the income of the pre-existing citizens of A between all residents in A. On both these grounds the argument for the control of migration from B to A becomes somewhat weaker on purely economic grounds, though it must be remembered that there are serious non-economic problems involved in the maintenance of a two-nation community in A of well-to-do citizens of indigenous origin and of abjectly poor citizens of foreign origin.

We can turn now to some examples of the ways in which a change in international economic policies may affect the actual world supply of capital. For this purpose let us suppose that some obstacle to commodity trade between A and B or to the movement of labour or capital between A and B is removed. What effect will this have upon the level of savings in A and in B?

Suppose that this removal of an obstacle to international trade or factor movements is of a kind which leads to greater economic efficiency. There will then be an increase in the general level of real income in the world. When real income rises, people are likely to use part of the increase in order to consume more and part of the increase in order to save more. A removal of international barriers to international trade or factor movements which does effectively raise the general level of real income in the world is thus likely to cause some increase in the level of world savings. And if, for the reasons discussed in Chapter VI

[1] This argument is based on the tacit assumption that the movement of population from B to A does not change the commodity terms of trade between the exports of A and the exports of B. If factors are specialized on products (see Chapter XXVII), then the movement of population from B to A will turn the terms of trade against B's labour-intensive products. The welfare of A's pre-existing citizens will be further increased and the ability of B to supply an increased population will fall. On both grounds the argument for the restriction of migration from B to A is further weakened. If, however, countries are specialized on products, the movement of labour from B to A will turn the terms of trade in favour of B. This will increase B's ability to keep up the supply of new population and will reduce any net gain enjoyed by the pre-existing citizens of A. The argument for a restriction on the migration will be reinforced.

(p. 100), it is probable that world savings are initially below the optimum level, then this incidental effect of a removal of international controls will also be favourable from the point of view of economic welfare. It must be brought into the final calculation.

The main relationship, so far as the world supply of capital is concerned, is thus simple and direct. Any change in international economic policies which raises real income is likely incidentally also to raise the level of world savings, and—since savings are more likely to be below than above the optimum level—this is favourable to economic welfare.

But the actual rate of savings depends not only upon the level of real income but also upon the distribution of real income. Our general proposition needs, therefore, to be modified in order to take account of the possible repercussions of the primary change in international economic policies not only upon the level of the world's real income, but also upon the distribution of that income both between countries and between classes within countries and so upon the total level of world savings.

Let us consider first the effect of a change in international economic policies upon the distribution of income between countries, i.e. upon the terms of trade between A and B, and so upon the total supply of world savings. Now, as we have seen (Chapter XVII), a removal of a trade tax by A or of a trade subsidy by B will turn the terms of trade in favour of B, and vice versa. Moreover, as we have seen (Chapter XXVII), the removal of an obstacle to the movement of population from B to A will turn the terms of trade in favour of B if the two countries are specialized on the production of certain products but against B's labour-intensive export products if the factors of production are specialized on the production of certain commodities. Similarly, the removal of an obstacle to the movement of capital from A to B will turn the terms of trade against B if the countries are specialized on the production of certain commodities but against A's capital-intensive export products if the factors are specialized on the production of certain products.

Let us suppose, simply by way of example, that the change in international economic policy is of a kind which turns the terms of trade in favour of B and that real income per head is lower in B than in A. Now it is possible that the higher is real income per head the greater will be the proportion of any increase in real income which is saved and not devoted to internal consumption. If this were so, the marginal propensity to save would be lower in B than in A. Now the more the terms of trade moved in B's favour, the greater would be the proportion of any increase in the world's real income which accrued to citizens of B as opposed to citizens of A; and in the case under examination the more this happened, the less would be the proportion of the increase n world income which was saved. Indeed, a case might possibly arise in which the terms of trade moved so much in B's favour, that real income per head actually fell in A so that B enjoyed more than the whole of the net increase in world income. In such a case, if the marginal propensity to save were much greater in A than in B, the net fall in savings in A (due to a small fall in A's income) might actually be greater than the rise in savings in B (due to a large rise in B's income). In this case the rise in world income, because of the repercussions upon its distribution between A and B, would have led to a fall in world savings; and this would be a disadvantage to be set in the final calculation against the other advantages of the initial change in international economic policies from the point of view of world economic welfare.

Exactly similar considerations arise when we take into account the possible effects of a change in international economic policies upon the distribution of income within countries. Thus the removal of an obstacle to the export of its labour-intensive exports by B is likely, as we have seen (Chapter XVIII), to cause an increase in the demand for labour relatively to other factors in B and so to a redistribution of income in favour of wages and against rent and profit in B. The removal of an obstacle to the import of capital into B from A is also, as we have seen (Chapter XXVII), likely to have a similar result in B, since it will reduce the ratio of labour to other factors in B and cannot do anything directly to increase the supply of labour-intensive products. On the other hand, the removal of an obstacle to the migration of labour from B to A will reduce the ratio of labour to other factors in B (which in itself would also tend to redistribute income in favour of wages in B), but it might also increase the world supply of labour-intensive products if the labour were specialized on the same products in A as it was previously in B (in which case the terms of trade might turn against these labour-intensive products and so against labour in B). In any case it is clear that the change in international economic policy may well cause a change in the distribution of income within the countries concerned. Suppose that by one or other of the mechanisms outlined above it were to cause a redistribution of income in favour of wages in B; that wage-earners were poorer than the owners of land and capital; and that for that reason wage-earners saved a smaller proportion of any increase in their incomes than did the owners of land and capital. In this case the initial change in international economic policy would be associated with such a change in the distribution of income within B that the increase in world savings resulting from any increase in world income would be much reduced.

From the above considerations it is clear that there may well be a sharp conflict between the contributions which some change in international economic policy makes to economic welfare through its effect upon the distribution of income and through its effect upon the supply of capital. Consider a change in international economic policy which in itself represents a movement towards greater economic efficiency and so makes a contribution to economic welfare. World income is thereby raised. Now if at the same time the change causes a redistribution of income from rich countries to poor countries or from rich classes to poor classes within countries, its direct positive contribution to economic efficiency will be reinforced by an indirect positive contribution to economic equity. But unfortunately the greater the redistribution from rich countries to poor countries, or from rich citizens to poor citizens within a country, the smaller the part of the increased world income which will be added to world savings. What is desirable on distributional grounds may well be undesirable in its effects upon the world supply of savings, and vice versa.

Up to this point we have conducted this analysis upon the tacit assumption that we can properly confine our attention to the effect of a change in international economic policy upon the world level of savings without differentiating between the level of savings in A and the level of savings in B. If there were no real or artificial obstacles to the movement of capital between A and B, this would be a perfectly satisfactory procedure. But if there is some cost of moving capital from A to B, we cannot leave the argument at this point. For now savings made in A are likely to be invested in real capital development in A and savings made in B are likely to be invested in real capital development in B.

Suppose B to be a country with much population and little capital as compared with the position in A. The marginal social net product of capital may now well be considerably higher in B than in A. Capital accumulation is more productive in B than in A. A given increase in savings in B is, therefore, more desirable than a given increase in savings in A, simply because what is saved in A is likely to be invested in A and because of the real or artificial cost of capital movement is not so likely to be invested in B in spite of the higher yield in B.

In such circumstances the total contribution of any change in international economic policy to world economic welfare must be judged not only by its effect upon world savings but also by its effect upon savings in A and in B separately. Thus as between two policies which raised world savings by the same amount, the one which raised savings in B the more markedly would be *pro tanto* preferable.

This consideration leads to certain important modifications of the conclusions previously reached. Consider a change of international economic policy (for example, the removal of import duties in A) which raises real income, but simultaneously so moves the terms of trade in B's favour as to leave the citizens of A worse off than before. Now if the standard of living is lower in B than in A so that a lower distributional weight is allotted to income in A than to income in B, this change may be desirable in that it will raise real income and improve its distribution. We argued above that it might, however, be counted undesirable in so far as the poorer citizens of B saved very much less than the richer citizens of A, so that the redistribution of income actually led to a fall in the level of world savings.

But in this case the level of savings will have risen in B (where income has risen) and will have fallen in A (where income has fallen). If B's savings are likely to be invested in B and A's savings in A, and if there are obstacles to the movement of capital from A to B, any adverse effect of the redistribution of income in favour of B upon the total level of world savings will be offset in part at least by the fact that the savings which are made are now more likely to be invested in B where capital is scarce than in A where capital is plentiful.

Indeed, it is possible that any change in international economic policy which by raising real income in B raises the level of real savings in B, may break a vicious spiral of poverty in B. The making of savings in B may be the only way in which capital accumulation can be stimulated in B, if there are obstacles in the way of the movement of capital from A to B. Now savings in B may be low because income per head in B is low; income per head in B may be low because output in B is low; output in B may be low because capital equipment is scarce in B; and capital equipment may be scarce in B because funds cannot readily be borrowed from A and domestic savings are low in B. Anything which gives a favourable jolt to real income per head and so to savings in B may help to break this vicious circle and initiate a self-generating process of development.[1] If the change in international economic policy raised real income and savings in B in circumstances in which such a jolt in B would break a vicious spiral of poverty of this kind and would set off a cumulative process of growth and development, then the ultimate effect upon the total of world savings (i.e. after taking into account the ever-growing level of savings in B resulting from the ever-expanding level of real income in B) might be favourable, even though the immediate effect of the change were to make savings fall more in A than they rose in B.

We have so far been concerned with the effects which a change in international economic policy may have upon the supply of saving through its effects upon the size of the incomes from which different classes of person make their savings. This probably constitutes the most

[1] The change is likely to generate a cumulative process of continuing development if a small increase of income causes a large increase of savings and if a small increase in the stock of capital equipment causes a large increase in production and so in real income. If these two relationships are unfavourable an initial jolt upwards in real income will not serve to break the vicious circle of poverty.

important set of influences. But savings may also be influenced by changes in the rate of interest which savers may obtain upon their savings. If income remains unchanged but the rate of interest rises, some persons may save more now that the future return on a given sacrifice of current consumption is raised. On the other hand it is possible that some people are saving in order to attain a given income from capital or a given capital sum at some future date; and such persons need not now save so much in order to achieve their fixed ultimate objective.

It is, therefore, uncertain whether a rise in the rate of interest will lead to a rise or to a fall or to no significant change in the current level of savings. But it may have some effect one way or the other. Now changes in international economic policies of the kind which we have examined in Parts II and III of this volume may have some effects upon the rate of interest and so upon the level of savings in A and B. The most obvious example of this is the removal of an obstacle to the movement of capital from A to B. This will open up to savers in A new possibilities of profitable investment in B and is thus likely to be the direct cause of some rise in the rate of interest which savers in A can obtain on their savings. To borrowers in B the change is likely to represent a reduction in the rate of interest, since they can now borrow more freely on the capital market in A, which is relatively well provided with capital. This will mean that savers in B will no longer be able to obtain so favourable a rate of interest on what they lend to borrowers in B. This fall in the rate of interest facing savers in B and rise in the rate of interest facing savers in A may cause some changes in the supply of savings in the two countries.

Changes in international economic policies might also have some less direct effects upon the rate of interest in the two countries. Thus the removal of trade barriers between A and B might lead to a net increase in the demand for A's capital-intensive exports and for B's labour-intensive exports. This would probably lead to some increase in A and decrease in B in the demand for capital and so in the rate of interest. Or a movement of population from B to A, if factors were specialized on products, would lead to a relative increase in the world supply of labour-intensive products, thus to a movement in the terms of trade against such products in both countries, thus to a decrease in the demand for labour relatively to capital and land in both countries, and thus to a rise in the rate of interest in both countries; or if the countries were specialized on the products, the movement of labour from B to A by increasing in A and decreasing in B the ratio of labour to capital and land in the production of each country's specialities would tend to raise the rate of interest in A and to lower it in B. Finally, as we have seen in the preceding paragraph, the removal of an obstacle on the movement of capital from A to B would have a direct effect upon the rate of interest available to savers in the two countries. But in addition to this the movement of capital from A to B might have some further indirect effects upon the rate of interest in the two countries. If factors are specialized on products, the movement of capital from A to B would cause an increase in the world supply of capital-intensive products, a movement in the terms of trade against such products, and thus some fall in the demand for capital and so in the rate of interest in both countries. On the other hand, if the countries are specialized on products, the movement of capital from A to B by making capital scarcer in A's special industries and more plentiful in B's special industries would tend to raise the rate of interest in A and to lower it in B.

There are, therefore, many possible repercussions of changes in international economic policies upon the rate of interest and so upon the supply of savings. But it is uncertain whether changes in the rate of interest will have much effect upon savings, and these different influences pull in different directions. It is not possible to go beyond these illustrations of the sort of analysis which is appropriate for this general class of problem. Each particular instance must be treated on its own merits.

CHAPTER XXIX

CAPITAL MOVEMENTS AND THE MAINTENANCE OF INTERNAL AND EXTERNAL BALANCE

WE have in the earlier chapters of this Part discussed various reasons why it may be desirable to exercise some control over international movements of factors of production—including controls over capital movements—in the interests of world economic welfare. But throughout this discussion we have assumed that there was no problem of internal or external balance, or rather that full employment was preserved and the balance of payments was kept in equilibrium by price adjustments of the kind discussed in Part IV of Volume I of this work. We considered in Volume I—particularly in Chapters XVII, XX, and XXII—a number of the problems of the control of international capital movements from the points of view both of the exchange-control techniques which are necessary in order to make such controls effective and also of the usefulness of such controls in easing adjustments of international balances of payments.

Now it so happens that the arguments for controls over capital movements on balance-of-payments grounds in some cases reinforce, but in other cases clash with, arguments for such controls on grounds of economic welfare. It is the purpose of this chapter to consider the extent to which these two types of argument reinforce or clash with each other.

Let us start with the clearest case of a clash between the two sets of considerations. Suppose that B is a country which is very rich in capital compared with the rest of the world A, but has a serious deficit on its balance of payments with A. The fact that B is relatively rich in capital will probably mean that the yield on capital in B is much lower than in A, and this may give a strong incentive for owners of capital in B to invest it in A. If the market yields on capital in the two countries correspond to their marginal social net products in the two countries, then, as we have already seen, world economic efficiency requires the movement of the capital from B where its productivity is low to A where its productivity is high. But if B is a deficit country, this movement of capital from B to A will cause a disequilibrium in the balance of payments between A and B. An exchange control over the capital exports from B to A might be a simple way of getting rid of the balance-of-payments problem.

Now there is no reason at all in the nature of things why a country which is rich in domestic supplies of capital should not be in deficit on its balance of payments.[1] If a capitally-rich country has a sufficiently inflationary domestic financial policy, it may have an excessive demand for imports and may consume at home too many of the goods which would otherwise have been available for export. Or if a capitally-rich country has fixed an exchange rate for its currency at so appreciated a value that its money prices and costs are much too high relatively to the money prices and costs of products in the rest of the world, the rest of the world may buy little from it and sell excessive amounts of goods to it. There is nothing to prevent a country which is rich in capital from being in deficit on its balance of payments on current account; and if then it allows a free flow of lending abroad, its balance of payments will be doubly in deficit.

In such a case there is an obvious conflict between considerations of the balance of payments and considerations of economic welfare; but there is really little doubt which set of considerations should give place to the other in a case of this kind. If world conditions are such (see Chapter XVI of Volume I) that adjustments of income and prices can be expected to be reasonably effective in adjusting the balance of payments, then the capitally-rich country should by a deflation of its money income, prices, and costs and/or by a depreciation of the foreign-exchange value of its currency generate such a surplus on its balance of current payments that it can finance the free flow of capital from it to the rest of the world. Economic welfare in these conditions requires that there should be a surplus on this country's balance of payments on current account in order to enable real capital to move from the country of low to the country of high productivity. There is a tendency in the modern world to believe that international capital movements should be controlled so as to conform to the existing balances of payments on current account of the various deficit and surplus countries. It is much more nearly true to argue that the price mechanism should be used to adjust balances of payments on current account to the free flow of capital funds between countries.[2]

Now this basic argument against the use of controls over capital movements on balance-of-payments as opposed to economic-welfare

[1] The United Kingdom in the years after 1945 was in balance-of-payments difficulties but was also very rich in capital in comparison with most of the rest of the world.

[2] This is literally true, of course, only on the assumption that the free flow of capital funds does represent a flow of capital from a country in which its marginal social net product is low to one in which it is high. If it does not do so—for any of the reasons discussed earlier in this Part or because it represents a political flight of 'hot money' (see Chapter XXII of Volume I)—then the conclusion must be modified. But if capital controls are then introduced, the essential reason is not to protect the balance of payments (a political flight of 'hot money' from a surplus country which is poor in capital to a deficit country which was rich in capital would also be obnoxious) but to steer capital into the most productive uses.

grounds applies not only to the use of exchange controls which directly prohibit or limit such movements, but also to other less rigid forms of control. In particular it applies to the use of 'tied loans' as a method of diminishing the adverse effects of international capital movements upon the balance of payments. It is possible for the authorities in our capitally-rich but deficit country, B, to make regulations which are designed to ensure that if a lender in B lends to a borrower in A, then the borrower in A will spend the loan on capital goods produced in B. Such regulations may take either of two forms; they may attempt to tie the finance to the goods or to tie the goods to the finance. Thus it may be laid down that a lender in B can lend to a borrower in A, if the borrower in A spends the money on goods produced in B; or it may be laid down that when an exporter in B sells goods to an importer in A, the exporter in B may lend to the importer in A the money necessary to finance the trade. Either type of regulation is designed to ensure that loans are made only in circumstances in which they automatically generate additional exports which will prevent them from leading to an additional strain on the balance of payments.

It may be argued against such systems of 'tied loans' that either they are largely ineffective in achieving their objective, in which case they are merely a bureaucratic nuisance which should be removed as quickly as possible, or else in effecting their objective as far as the balance of payments is concerned they introduce an element of economic inefficiency and are therefore inimical to economic welfare. We must examine both parts of this indictment.

The apparent assurance given by a system of 'tied loans' that an additional loan will generate additional exports may be altogether illusory. Suppose the situation is such that in the absence of any control an investor in A would have borrowed funds in B in order to spend the money on the purchase of capital equipment produced in A; but suppose that a 'tied-loan' regulation merely states that the borrower in A must spend the borrowed money on B's products. Then the borrower in A may with the loan purchase in B some products which have little or nothing to do with A's investment project and which would in any case have been imported into A by A's regular importers. The borrower in A imports these products into A, sells them in A for A's currency, and uses this currency to spend on the capital equipment made in A which he wants for his investment project. In the end the loan from B to A has been associated with no net increase in B's exports to A. The products of B which the investor in A does purchase are not additional exports; they merely replace exports from B which some other importer in B would have purchased if the 'tied loan' had not been made.

Or suppose that an investor in A is determined in any case to purchase some equipment in B for use in an investment project in A. Suppose further that if the investor in A is permitted to do so, he would borrow the necessary capital funds in B where the rate of interest is lower; but if this is not allowed, he will borrow the necessary capital funds in A even though the rate of interest which he must pay will then be somewhat higher. A 'tied-loan' regulation would in this case have no effect on trade whatsoever. The investor in A is going to purchase the equipment from B in any case whether the loan from B to A is permitted or prohibited.

In either of these two cases—either because the 'tied' exports from B to A would have taken place anyhow or else because they merely replace other 'untied' exports—a 'tied-loan' regulation is in fact ineffective. In so far as this is the situation the regulation should not be applied. It will involve some bureaucratic cost and inconvenience without achieving its purpose.

But if it is effective—and it may, of course, be effective—it will reduce economic efficiency. Suppose that the rate of interest is 4 per cent in B and 5 per cent in A, and that these rates correspond to the true marginal social net product of capital in the two countries. Then it is in the interests of world productivity that savings in B should be invested in capital development in A, since capital will add more to output in A than in B. But suppose that at the same time the cost of transporting capital equipment between A and B is very high indeed—for example, capital development takes the form of using local labour to build roads or dams which cannot readily be constructed in one country and transported to the other. Then the process of moving capital from B to A will involve the following types of adjustment. In B labour is used to produce consumption goods instead of capital equipment; more consumption goods are sent from B to A or less are sent from A to B; in A labour which was previously producing consumption goods is now released through the higher imports of such goods into A or the reduced export of such goods from A and is used instead to produce capital equipment in A; and the excess of B's exports over her imports of consumption goods is matched, as far as her balance of payments is concerned, by the fact that savings in B which were previously lent to investors in B to spend on capital developments in B are now lent to investors in A to spend on capital developments in A.

A 'tied-loan' from B to A which meant that the money lent to A had to be spent on capital equipment made in B would be a wasteful method of transferring capital from B to A because it would involve excessively high costs of transport of capital goods from B to A. Greater efficiency would be achieved by the alternative method of allowing the free flow of capital funds from B where the yield is low to A where the yield is high, and then allowing a price adjustment (i.e. a depreciation of B's exchange rate or a fall in B's prices and costs relatively to A's) until B's consumption goods undercut A's consumption goods sufficiently to generate the required surplus on B's balance of trade. If B is rich in capital but—either because of transport costs or because of natural differences in cost of production—A is the efficient producer of the capital equipment, an effective 'tied loan' would be a source of economic inefficiency. And if these conditions were not fulfilled, it would be ineffective.

So far we have not brought into consideration the possible effect which controls imposed upon capital movements upon balance-of-payments grounds may have upon the terms of trade between the two countries and so upon the distribution of world income between the two countries. If the control of capital movements does turn the terms of trade and so redistribute income in favour of the country to whose citizens the policy-makers have allotted a high distributional weight, then this in itself will make some contribution to economic welfare which must be set against the loss of economic efficiency.

Now just as there is no necessary connexion between capitally-poor countries and deficit countries, so there is also no necessary connexion between countries with low real incomes per head on the one hand and deficit or capitally-poor countries on the other. In fact a country may be found in any one of the following eight types:

	Capitally-rich (R) or capitally-poor (P)	Surplus (S) or deficit (D) on the balance of payments	High (H) or low (L) real income per head
1	R	S	H
2	R	S	L
3	R	D	H
4	R	D	L
5	P	S	H
6	P	S	L
7	P	D	H
8	P	D	L

There is likely, of course, to be some correlation between capitally-rich countries and countries with a high level of real income. For if two countries were otherwise in the same position (i.e. if they had similar populations, natural resources, and productive atmospheres), the one with the larger stock of capital would have a larger output and so a higher standard of living. But it is by no means certain that a country which is rich in capital (in the sense that capital is so plentiful relatively to other factors of production that its marginal social net product is very low) will have a high standard of living. Consider a country which has very few and poor natural resources, an unfavourable productive atmosphere, and an excessively large population. As far as these elements are concerned, it will have a low standard of living. And its standard might well remain low even though it was plentifully endowed with capital. The marginal product of capital would fall quickly to a low level as more and more capital was applied in a bad productive atmosphere to very poor natural resources. The country would be capitally-rich but with a low standard of living.

Let us consider the lines of utopian policy which ought to be adopted in such a case in which one country, say, country B, is capitally-rich but has a low standard of living. Because it is capitally-rich it ought to export capital to A; capital invested in A will produce more in co-operation with A's good natural resources and in A's good atmosphere; and thus, if the proper distribution of world income is assured by some other independent means, the inhabitants of B would be better off if they received the income which their capital would produce in A instead of the income which it would produce in B. As the standard of living is much lower in B than in A, presumably a higher distributional weight should be allotted to income in B than in A; and a utopian solution to the problem of distribution would involve the raising of revenue by A's government from A's rich citizens, its payment to B's government, and its redistribution by B's government to B's poor citizens. In the utopian solution these grants would be paid on whatever scale was necessary so to raise B's income and to lower A's income that the distributional weights to be allotted to the two classes of income were now judged to have become equal.

In such a system capital would flow from B to A in search of the higher yield obtainable on capital in A, but direct grants would be paid by A's government to B's government in order to redistribute income. As far as the balance of payments between A and B is concerned the direct income grants from A to B would tend to offset the flow of capital funds from B to A. But if the offset were not complete and B was still in balance-of-payments deficit, then in a utopian solution the price mechanism would be used to remove B's deficit; for example, B's currency would be depreciated until B's exports had been so stimulated and her imports so contracted that her balance of payments was in balance once more.

As we have seen in Volume I, this process of price adjustment might very well cause some shift in the terms of trade against B. If this were to happen, then the standard of living in B would fall relatively to that in A. In the utopian solution this would naturally lead to some increase in the income grants transferred from A to B, which would themselves somewhat mitigate the balance-of-payments problem and so the deterioration in the terms of trade. In any case a final solution would be found in which the three following conditions were simultaneously fulfilled:

(1) capital was flowing from B to A on a scale sufficient to equalize the marginal products of capital in A and B;
(2) relative prices were adjusted (e.g. through changes in the exchange rate between A's and B's currency) until there was a balance in the payments between the two countries; and
(3) income grants were made from A to B on a scale sufficient to equalize the distributional weights allotted to A's and B's income.

It may seem a rather pointless arrangement for capital funds to be transferred from B to A and simultaneously for income grants to be transferred from A to B. Why not reduce the flow of capital from B to A by an amount equal to the income grants, from A to B and then abolish those income grants? If this were done there need be no immediate reaction upon any significant economic quantity. The citizens of B could maintain their present standard of living by reducing their savings by an amount exactly equal to the reduction in the income grants previously paid to them, and they could reduce the amount they lent abroad by the same amount. The citizens of A could increase their savings for the finance of that part of their investment which was previously financed by borrowing from B, and their consumption could be maintained at its previous level in spite of this increase in their savings, because there would be an exactly equal reduction in the amount which they would have to pay in tax to finance the income grants to B. Thus a system of governmental controls which (i) limited the export of capital from B to A by an amount equal to the income grants that would otherwise be payable, (ii) ensured that the whole of the reduction in receipt of income grants in B was met by a fall in savings and no part by a fall in consumption in B, and (iii) ensured that the whole of the reduced taxation in A previously necessary to finance the income grants to B was now added to savings in A and no part of it was spent on consumption in A, would achieve exactly the same results as the utopian solution outlined above;[1] but this new solution would clearly be quite unnecessarily complicated from an administrative point of view. As is so often the case in economic policy, a separate direct approach to each separate problem provides the simplest total solution. Let capital move freely to the point of highest yield; let exchange rates be adjusted to maintain external balance; and let there be a system of direct taxes and subsidies on income to obtain any desired distribution of income.

But the utopian solution may for very obvious reasons be politically

[1] The only difference would be that with the new solution the future interest and dividends on the capital previously flowing from B to A would accrue to citizens of A instead of, as previously, to citizens of B; but with a truly utopian solution this would make no real difference, since the actual distribution of world income in the future would not depend upon the actual ownership of assets but simply upon the distributional weights allotted to citizens of A and B respectively. A larger income from interest for A-citizens would be offset by a more extensive policy for redistribution from A to B.

quite out of the question, involving as it does a system of international direct income grants. In this case it is impossible to neglect the effect upon the terms of trade of the price-adjustment methods of restoring external balance. Consider once again a country, say B, which is capitally-rich, which is in deficit, and which has a relatively low standard of living. To allow a free movement of capital funds out of B will intensify B's deficit; the cure of B's deficit by price adjustment (e.g. by a depreciation of the currency of the deficit country) may turn the terms of trade against B; and this would reduce B's standard of living relatively to that of the rest of the world, A. Some control over the export of capital would itself reduce B's deficit, would thus reduce the degree of price adjustment necessary to restore external balance, and thereby mitigate the deterioraton in the terms of trade against B, the country with the higher distributional weight. There would be some argument on distributional grounds for some restriction on capital movements out of B.

It is to be observed that this argument for some restriction of capital movements from B to A is closely analogous to the argument developed in Chapter XVII of this volume for some restriction of imports into a country in order to turn the terms of trade in favour of that country. In both cases there is some restriction of B's purchases of A's currency, in the one case for the finance of imports from A and in the other for the finance of capital movements to A. Both may have a direct effect in improving from B's point of view the terms on which the particular transactions that are still permitted are conducted. In the one case, if A's elasticity of supply of the exports concerned is not infinite, the imports which are still allowed into B will be purchased in A at a lower price because they are purchased in smaller volume. In the other case, if A's elasticity of demand for capital loans from B is not infinite, the loans which are still made to A will earn a higher rate of interest in A simply because less capital is offered by B on A's capital market. Both actions will also improve B's balance of payments and thus enable B to maintain a more appreciated foreign-exchange value for its currency, and this may cause some general movement in the terms of trade in favour of B.[1]

[1] It would be a nice exercise in the economic analysis of 'second-best' solutions to examine how far B should rely on import controls and how far on controls over capital movements as the instrument for achieving a given improvement in her terms of trade and so in her standard of living. Suppose that B is relying solely on import controls and that she then relaxes her import controls somewhat and imposes new controls over capital movements to an extent sufficient to offset any adverse effect upon her terms of trade to the degree required to keep her standard of living at the same level. There will be a divergence between marginal social value and cost on the newly permitted imports equal to the *ad valorem* incidence of the ruling import restriction. But there will initially be no divergence between the marginal social value and cost on the restricted capital movements, since initially the flow of capital was

There is, however, one important difference between the method of import restriction and the method of control over capital movements. In the case of import restriction there will be some improvement in the terms of trade for B which will then be permanent and unchanged, so far as the effect of the import restrictions are concerned. In the case of a restriction of capital movements, we have so far examined only the effect on the terms of trade during the period in which capital is flowing from B to A. But there will in this case be further consequential effects upon the terms of trade when the capital is used in country A. As we have seen in Chapter XXVII, if the countries are specialized on the production of commodities, then the movement of capital from B to A will ultimately cause the world output of B-products to be lower and the world output of A-products to be higher than would otherwise have been the case. This will tend to turn the terms of trade against B. Capital controls would then shift the terms of trade in favour of B while the capital was being transferred, but would shift the terms of trade in favour of B in the future periods when the capital was being used in A instead of in B.[1]

But, as has been shown in Chapter XXVII, if it is the factors rather than the countries which are specialized on producing particular products, then the use of capital in A (where its marginal product is high) rather than in B (where its marginal product is low) would tend to increase the world output of capital-intensive products relatively to other products. And since B is capitally-rich, these would be the export products of B. This relative increase in the world supply of the type of products which B exports would tend to turn the terms of trade against

---

unrestricted and its marginal social net product would be no higher in A than in B. There would thus be a net gain in economic efficiency. But as the shift from import controls to capital controls developed, the *ad valorem* incidence of the import controls would diminish, and the gain in economic efficiency from their further reduction would thus diminish. At the same time, a divergence would appear between marginal social values and costs in the lending of funds from B to A, since the restriction on such lending would cause the yield on capital to become lower in B and/or higher in A. At some point the gain in economic efficiency due to a further reduction in B's import restrictions would be just offset by the loss in economic efficiency due to that amount of extra reduction in capital movements from B to A which was just necessary to offset the adverse effect on B's terms of trade to the degree required to maintain B's standard of living unchanged. This would be the optimum combination of restriction from A's point of view. B's standards would be maintained at a given level with the minimum adverse effect upon world economic efficiency. This problem will not be further pursued here. The interested reader is left to work out the optimum point for himself on the principles developed in earlier chapters in this volume.

[1] This was assumed to be the case in the formula given in the footnote on p. 300 of Volume I, where each country was assumed to be producing only one product—or rather where it was assumed to be possible to treat each country's products as constituting one homogeneous group whose prices always moved together.

B when the capital was used in A rather than in B. In this case the restriction of capital exports from B to A would tend not only to improve B's terms of trade during the period when the capital was being transferred from B to A, but also in subsequent periods when the capital was being employed to produce in B rather than in A.

It is clear, therefore, that there may be a case in some situations for the control of capital movements as a means of influencing the terms of trade. But this is essentially a case for increasing economic welfare by a better distribution of world income rather than a case for the use of capital controls as a means of restoring equilibrium to the balance of payments.

So far in this chapter we have tacitly assumed that there have been no difficulties in maintaining internal balance within both our countries, A and B. We shall turn now to the examination of certain problems which arise when governments find difficulty in maintaining internal balance and in reconciling internal balance with the maintenance of external balance in the payments between the two countries. Do cases then arise in which capital controls might both be useful to help maintain external balance and also be compatible with the maximization of economic welfare?

Let us first consider the case where there is an uncontrolled slump in A. (Cf. Chapters V and VI of Volume I.) Demand falls in A; this causes a reduction of prices, output, and employment in A; there is some reduction in A's demand for B's products; the balance of trade moves unfavourably to B; and the reduction in A's demand for B's products communicates the slump in expenditure, prices, output, and employment to B's economy. But suppose that in B the authorities adopt a financial policy for internal balance, that is to say that by fiscal measures (reductions of taxation or increases in government expenditure) or by monetary measures (by increasing the supplies of money and so reducing interest rates and stimulating private expenditure on capital development) they so restimulate the demand for B's products as to prevent any net fall in national income and employment in B. The result of this will, of course, be to raise B's demand for imports and thus to impose on B's balance of payments with A a still heavier strain than would have occurred if no financial policy for internal balance had been adopted in B.

In this case in which a slump occurs in A's economy but successful full-employment measures are taken by B, there will probably develop a serious deficit in B's balance of payments. As we have seen in Volume I, there are essentially four types of measure which B's authorities can take in an attempt to remove this deficit on B's balance of payments without giving up full employment in B and without any reflation of national income in A.

(1) The authorities in B might carry out a deflation of money incomes in B, but combine this with a very flexible reduction of money wage rates and other money costs, so that the deflation took the form of an equal downward movement of money incomes, prices, and costs in B. In this case full employment might be preserved and the fall in B's money prices and costs relatively to A's might serve to restore B's balance of payments.

(2) The authorities in B might maintain money incomes, prices, and costs in B at the pre-slump level by means of their internal financial policy, and they might meet the strain on B's balance of payments by allowing the foreign-exchange value of B's currency to depreciate. This would be an alternative way of making B's products cheap relatively to A's and might serve to restore B's balance of payments.

(3) The authorities in B might impose controls over imports into B and put B's balance of payments into equilibrium by a direct limitation of imports to correspond to the amount of foreign currency available for their finance.

(4) If capital is being lent by people or institutions in B to borrowers in A, the authorities in B might ease the strain on the balance of payments by restricting, through an exchange control, this movement of capital from B to A.[1]

Our present problem is to consider whether in the conditions which we are assuming there is any special reason from the point of view of economic welfare for laying emphasis on method 4 rather than on methods 1, 2, or 3. We may start by eliminating method 1 from our consideration. This we can do on two grounds. In the first place, in modern conditions method 1 is probably impracticable. Usually the only practicable way to get money wage rates and other costs down is to restrict demand and cause such a reduction in output and employment that the deflationary pressure in the labour market causes wage rates to fall. But this is to give up the objective of maintaining full employment in B. Method 1 can be used only if there is a very unusual degree of downward flexibility of wage rates. But, in the second place, from our present point of view there is little to choose between method 1 (if it

[1] There remains, of course, one further way of coping with the balance-of-payments problem. B's authorities might acquire from A's authorities special funds of A's currency to continue to finance B's balance-of-payments deficit with A. This use of what in Volume I we have called 'accommodating finance' may for our present purpose be regarded simply as a special form of method 4 discussed in the text. From our present welfare point of view we want to know whether in the situation under discussion there is any special argument for meeting the problem of external balance by a governmental policy which reduces the net flow of capital from B to A. From this point of view it is largely irrelevant whether this is done by restricting the autonomous outflow of funds from B to A or by offsetting this autonomous outflow by an accommodating inflow of capital funds. In both cases the situation is met by a net reduction in the movement of capital from B to A.

were practicable to get money wage rates and other money costs down without serious unemployment) and method 2. Both are ways of getting B's money incomes, prices, and costs down relatively to A's. If we confine our present discussion to method 2, what will be said for and against method 2 from the point of view of economic welfare can very easily be applied to method 1, if method 1 were in fact a feasible alternative.

Let us start then by comparing methods 2 and 3 from the point of view of economic welfare. It is to be observed that both are methods which will deal with the deficit on B's balance of payments by improving B's balance of trade. Method 2 will expand B's exports (i.e. A's imports) as well as contracting B's imports (i.e. A's exports), while method 3 will operate essentially only by contracting B's imports. But if the deficit is to be removed by either the one method or the other there will be the same final result on the net balance between B's imports and exports. This improvement in B's balance of trade will exert some deflationary pressure in A. The restriction of B's imports under method 3 will have an obvious effect in restricting the market for A's products. The reduction in B's prices relatively to A's under method 2 will have the same effect either by making it easier for B's exports to replace A's import-competing products in A's domestic markets or else by making it easier for B's import-competing products to replace A's export products in B's domestic markets. But since the appropriate use of either method will have the same net effect in expanding B's exports and/or restricting her imports, the choice between the two will not in itself make any significant difference to the level to which income, output, and employment will be further reduced in A.

But with a given level of output and employment in A world economic efficiency should be greater under method 2 than under method 3. For method 2 is compatible with the maintenance of free trade in products and so with the optimization of trade and the maximization of production (given the level of employment in A) while method 3 will necessarily restrict the volume of trade.[1] Method 2 is thus preferable to method 3 on grounds of economic efficiency. It is true, of course, as we have seen in Chapter XVII of this volume, that the use of method 3 by restricting imports into B is likely to cause the terms of trade to be more favourable to B than would have been the case if method 2 had been adopted. But from the point of view of world economic welfare this is most unlikely in itself to constitute a distributional argument in favour of the use of method 3. On the contrary, it probably constitutes an additional

[1] It is assumed, of course, in the above argument that import restriction is not required in B in order to optimize trade or to maximize production on grounds discussed in Part II of this volume. If import restriction is required on these grounds, the imports should have been suitably restricted before the slump in A occurred.

argument against the use of method 3. The slump in A combined with the maintenance of full employment in B is itself likely to impoverish A relatively to B for two reasons. First, the decline in employment and production will reduce real output and so real income per head in A. Secondly, the slump in A is likely in itself to cause the prices of A's products to fall relatively to the prices of B's products and so to turn the terms of trade in B's favour. Before the slump, if B was a poorer country than A and the distributional weight allotted to incomes in B was therefore higher than the distributional weight allotted to incomes in A, there may have been some distributional argument in favour of some restriction of imports into B in order to turn the terms of trade in B's favour. But since the slump in A will itself have lowered real incomes in A relatively to real incomes in B, the distributional argument for the restriction of imports into B will probably be less strong after, than it was before, the slump in A. The depreciation of B's currency under method 2 may serve largely merely to counteract the improvement which the slump has brought about in B's terms of trade. There remains the fact that the reduction in output in A will have reduced real income in A relatively to real income in B.

Let us turn to a comparison of methods 2 and 3 (the depreciation of B's exchange rate or the restriction of B's imports from A) with method 4 (the restriction of capital movements from B to A). There are two strong arguments in favour of the use of method 4 in the conditions which we are at present examining.

In the first place, as we have already argued, methods 2 and 3 are methods which put B's balance of payments into equilibrium by improving B's balance of trade; and this by contracting the market in A for A's import-competing products and in B for A's exports will intensify the slump and so the reduction in employment and output in A. Method 4 operates by restricting capital transfers from B to A, and this is unlikely to cause any direct intensification of the slump in A, where the problem is not a shortage of capital funds but a failure to stimulate expenditure on capital development and on consumption to a degree sufficient to maintain full employment. Method 4 is compatible with a higher level of output in A than are methods 2 and 3.

But in the second place, if there is a slump and mass unemployment in A the rate of interest and the market yield on capital in A does not truly measure a shortage of real capital in A. Full employment in B may have been maintained by an expansive monetary policy which has led to a reduction in interest rates in B from, say, 5 per cent to 2 per cent per annum. The slump may have developed in A because of a failure in A to adopt a similar expansive monetary policy in A. The rate of interest in A has remained, say, at 5 per cent, whereas it would have had to be reduced to 2 per cent in order so to stimulate capital development in A as to avoid the general slump in the demand for goods and services in A.

Now the decline in interest rates in B from 5 to 2 per cent and the maintenance of interest rates in A at 5 per cent may have greatly increased the incentive to move capital funds from B to A. But this movement of capital funds corresponds to no real need of the economic situation. When there is full employment in A and B, then—in the absence of an increase in the rate of savings in the world—real capital development can be increased in A only if capital development is reduced in B, if the factors so released in B are used to produce extra goods for export to A or to produce goods which replace imports from A, and if the factors so released in A's import-competing industries or in A's export industries are used to produce more capital equipment in A. But when there is general unemployment in A, an expansive monetary policy in A which reduces the rate of interest in A can stimulate capital development in A which is undertaken by the unemployed resources in A without any reduction in other investment or consumption in A or in B. The generation of a surplus on B's balance of trade to correspond to the financial flow of capital funds from B to A is totally unnecessary for the expansion of capital development in A.

Indeed, as we have just seen, the expansion of B's exports or contraction of B's imports in order to generate a surplus on B's balance of trade to cover a movement of capital funds into A may simply intensify the general slump in A. This further contraction in the total market for A's products will tend to make A's industries less profitable; and at any given rate of interest in A this is likely to cause an actual reduction of capital development in A's industries. For this reason when there is full employment in B and a general slump in A there is a very strong welfare reason for dealing with B's balance-of-payments deficit by restricting the flow of capital funds from B to A. This method, as compared with methods 2 or 3 which operate by expanding B's exports or restricting her imports, is likely to help to maintain output and capital development in A. The movement of capital from B to A is not needed as a means for expanding real capital investment in A. In these conditions the movement of capital from a point of low market yield in B is not required for the maximization of world production. Indeed, it is likely to be detrimental to it. There are strong welfare arguments in favour of using the method of restriction of net capital movements from B to A as a means of defending B's balance of trade against the effects of a slump in A when full employment is maintained by financial policy in B.

The restriction of capital movements from B to A is, of course, itself only a second-best measure. A still better policy would be for the authorities in A themselves to adopt a domestic financial policy for internal balance so that the fall in income and growth of unemployment was prevented in A as well as in B. In this case the particular welfare arguments for the control of capital movements which we have just examined would no longer be relevant. If resources are fully employed in A and in B and the yield on capital remains higher in A than in B, then the maximization of world production does require the shift of real capital from B to A, and this does require the generation of a surplus on B's balance of trade in real products in order to transfer the capital in real terms from B to A.

But in this case there remains one possible set of conditions which deserves further attention. Suppose that we start with A and B in full internal and external balance and with a yield on capital of 5 per cent in both countries. Suppose then that some general world deflationary influence develops and that a fall in income and employment in both countries is threatened. Suppose further that the slump in B is prevented, as in our previous example, by the adoption of an expansive monetary policy in B, whereby monetary supplies in B are increased until the rate of interest in B has fallen from 5 to 2 per cent. At this lower rate of interest sufficient new expenditure on capital development is stimulated in B to offset the effects of the initial spontaneous deflationary disturbance. Suppose that in A too a financial policy for internal balance is developed; but in this case monetary policy is not used and the rate of interest in A remains at 5 per cent. The authorities in A use the weapon of fiscal policy; they reduce tax rates so as to increase the net spendable incomes of private citizens and thus induce them to increase their demands for consumption goods on a scale sufficient to offset the initial spontaneous deflationary disturbance.

The fact that the authorities in B have used the weapon of monetary policy and have reduced interest rates from 5 per cent to 2 per cent, while the authorities in A have used the weapon of fiscal policy and have maintained the rate of interest at 5 per cent, may greatly increase the incentive to move capital funds from B to A. In order to preserve equilibrium in B's balance of payments it may therefore be necessary either to depreciate B's currency in order to generate a corresponding excess of B's exports over her imports or else to restrict the flow of capital funds from B to A. Should the method of restriction of capital movements from B to A be used in these circumstances in the interests of world economic efficiency?

The authorities in B have in fact chosen to offset the spontaneous deflationary tendency by a method which tends to maintain the level of savings at a relatively high rate, whereas the authorities in A have chosen to meet the spontaneous deflationary disturbance by a method which tends to stimulate consumption expenditure rather than expenditure on capital development and which keeps the community's savings at a relatively low level. The expansion of monetary supplies in

B and the reduction in the rate of interest there may possibly have some effect in inducing people to save less and to spend more on consumption goods, but it will also have an effect in stimulating the borrowing of funds at the low rate of 2 per cent for expenditure on projects of capital development which would not have been undertaken at the higher rate of 5 per cent. Out of the given stabilized total income in B perhaps a little less will be saved and a little more will be spent on consumption; but a main effect of the fall in interest rates will be to keep up the level of expenditure on capital development as a means of counteracting the threatened slump. But in A the rate of interest is maintained at 5 per cent and the main influence of the reduction in rates of tax will be to give private citizens a larger tax-free income to stimulate their expenditure on consumption goods. It is true, of course, that private individuals having a larger tax-free income and being able to earn as before 5 per cent on their savings will save more money; but this will all be needed to finance the budget deficit which is caused by the reduction in taxes and which the government must finance by borrowing; and the budget deficit is being used to finance the current consumption of the public authorities. Indeed, the reduction in tax and the consequent increase in the budget deficit must be sufficient to cause private consumption in A to rise by an amount equal to any initial decline in capital development in A due to the spontaneous deflationary disturbance. The community's savings in A—i.e. private savings less the budget deficit or public dissavings—will have been reduced in A.

If savings and the rate of capital development are high in B and low in A, then the yield on further capital development will be low in B and will be high in A. In this case it would at first sight seem desirable that the plentiful savings which are made in B should in part be invested in A, since the real social yield on capital in B is low (2 per cent), simply because new capital is plentiful in B, and in A is high (5 per cent), simply because new capital is scarce in A. And this would in fact be the case if we could assume that the total supply of savings would be unaffected by allowing the capital to flow from B to A. There is a higher marginal efficiency of capital in A than in B, and an increased rate of domestic investment in A matched by a lower rate of domestic investment in B and an increase in B's foreign investment and a decrease in A's foreign investment (i.e. an increased surplus on B's balance of trade) would be in the interests of the most efficient use of a given volume of world savings.

But in the conditions which we have outlined we cannot assume that the world supply of savings is unaffected by the movement of capital funds from B to A. Such a movement of funds will require the generation (e.g. through a depreciation of the foreign-exchange value of B's currency) of a surplus on B's balance of trade. This in itself will, as we have seen, exercise an inflationary pressure in B (since it will represent a larger market for B's exports or for B's import-competing products) and will exercise a deflationary pressure in A (since it will represent a smaller market for A's import-competing products or for A's exports). If B offsets this inflationary pressure by a restrictive monetary policy leading to higher interest rates and so to a restriction of B's domestic expenditure on capital developments, and if A offsets this deflationary pressure by an easier fiscal policy leading to a still further increase in tax-free incomes and so in expenditure on consumption in A, then the final net effect of the free flow of capital funds will be a reduction in domestic investment in B and an increase in consumption in A. The world supply of savings will be reduced by an amount equal to the flow of capital from B to A.

It is at this point that consideration of the optimum level for world savings must be brought into the picture. If the authorities in both A and B always maintained savings at an optimum level, each would have to use a judicious combination of monetary and fiscal policy to combat a threatened slump. Each would have to rely more on an expansive monetary policy and so a stimulation to investment if the country's savings tended to fall below the optimum level and more on a fiscal policy and the stimulation of consumption through tax reductions if savings tended to rise above the optimum level. If both operated in this way, then free capital movements between A and B would be desirable as the authorities in both countries developed their policies for combating the threat of a world depression; for in this case the rate of interest in each country would measure the marginal efficiency of capital in each country at given optimum rates of savings.

But suppose savings are at the optimum level before the threat of a world slump, and suppose then that in B the slump was offset solely by an expansive monetary policy and in A solely by a fiscal stimulation of consumption, and suppose further that the balance of trade between A and B is adjusted by means of exchange-rate variations to fit in with the flow of capital between A and B. In these circumstances any increased flow of capital from B to A which took place because the rate of interest was maintained in A while it had been lowered in B would tend to reduce the total of world savings. In the interests of maintaining the supply of savings at a better level it might be desirable to restrict the flow of capital from B to A.

There might also be some special argument for the use of controls over capital movements from B to A which does not depend upon the maintenance of the total supply of world savings, if in the conditions discussed above the world deflationary tendency was itself merely a temporary phenomenon. We have seen that in these circumstances capital funds will tend to flow from B (where interest rates are lowered by monetary policy) to A (where interest rates are maintained because consumption is stimulated by fiscal policy) and that if this flow of capital is freely allowed B's prices and costs must be lowered relatively to A's prices and costs to generate a surplus on B's balance of payments to correspond with this flow of capital. But, as we have seen in Volume I, the generation of a surplus on the balance of trade by price adjustment of this kind may be more difficult in the short run than in the long run. It takes time for changes in relative prices to cause appropriate changes in trade channels while traders become aware of the new price relationships and their implications, while new trading connexions are built up, and while new capital equipment is installed in the particular industries which need to expand and while old capital equipment is wearing out in the particular industries which need to contract as a result of these new price relationships. If the world deflationary influence is only a passing one, then, when it is over, the authorities in country B will presumably restrict monetary supplies and raise interest rates again, while the authorities in A will restore tax rates and maintain the same rate of interest as before. When this happens, the special inducement to move capital funds from B to A will have passed; the surplus on B's balance of trade will no longer be necessary; the painful and slow process of building up a surplus on B's balance of trade will have to be put into reverse; and the old trade channels, trading connexions, and industrial structure will—perhaps equally painfully and slowly—need to be restored. If B is to use monetary policy and A fiscal policy to deal with a *temporary* threat of world slump, then there may be some argument for a *temporary* restriction on capital movements from B to A.[1]

Exactly the reverse arguments can be used if there is a threat of world inflation and boom which B meets by a contraction of monetary supplies, a rise in the rate of interest, and so a curb on investment in B, and which A meets by a rise in tax rates, a reduction in private consumption, a budget surplus, and so some increase in savings in A. Interest rates will rise in B but not in A. Capital funds will tend to be attracted to B from A. This will require the generation of a surplus on A's balance of trade with B through a depreciation of A's exchange rate. This will cause some deflationary pressure in B and further inflationary pressure in A. B will meet this by a relaxation of monetary policy and some reduction in the rise of interest rates in B. A will meet it by a still severer fiscal policy, i.e. by a further cut in consumption in A and increase in savings in A. Total savings will rise and may rise above the optimum level, unless the flow of capital from A to B is restricted.

[1] Or, of course, for a *temporary* movement of offsetting accommodating funds from A to B. This may well be preferable to the apparatus of capital controls which would be needed to restrict the flow of funds from B to A.

Moreover, if the world inflationary threat is only temporary, the painful process of generating a surplus on A's balance of trade may have to give place to the equally painful reverse process after a short period of time. On both these grounds some curb on the flow of capital from A to B might be in the interests of economic welfare as well as serving directly to maintain equilibrium in the balance of payments.

There is one other possible case which is worth examining. Suppose again that both A and B are threatened with a world inflationary tendency and both take domestic measures to offset the inflationary disturbance. Suppose, as before, that the authorities in B curb the boom in part at least by means of a contractionist monetary policy. Interest rates are raised and expenditures on capital developments of all kinds are curbed. Suppose that the authorities in A also fight the inflationary pressure mainly by curbing expenditures on capital development in A. Suppose, however, that they do not employ a contractionist monetary policy for this purpose, but impose a system of direct controls over the amount of capital development. The rate of interest is not raised in A; but building operations and the purchase of machinery are restricted by licence, new issues of shares on the capital market are subject to official approval, and so on. In both countries the boom is prevented by curbing expenditure on projects for capital development; but in B the rate of interest is raised and in A the rate of interest remains unchanged. There will thus be an incentive to move capital funds from A to B in search of the higher yields in B. In B the rate of interest will correspond to the marginal efficiency of capital; additional capital projects which will earn less than 5 per cent will not be undertaken because it now costs 5 per cent to finance them. In A, on the other hand, the rate of interest will no longer correspond to the marginal efficiency of capital; entrepreneurs will have an incentive to undertake all projects which will earn more than the low current rate of interest of, say, 2 per cent, but they will be prevented by the direct controls from embarking on any projects which will earn less than, say, 5 per cent. The social yield on additional projects of capital development is in fact no lower in A than in B. Economic efficiency does not, therefore, require a movement of real capital from A to B. A free flow of capital funds from A to B in search of the higher market rate of interest in B may well put a strain on A's balance of payments; and in such circumstances the control of capital movements from A to B to protect A's balance of payments would correspond to the basic requirements of world economic efficiency.

We have now seen that there may be certain cases in which problems connected with the maintenance of internal balance within A and B may justify on grounds of economic welfare the use of restrictions on capital movements between A and B as one of the instruments for preserving external balance between them. As we have seen, such a situation may arise, (i) if A fails to prevent a slump while B does effectively do so, or (ii) if A prevents a boom or slump mainly by fiscal policy and B mainly by monetary policy, or (iii) if in the interests of internal balance A curbs expenditure on capital development mainly by a system of direct controls while B uses the instrument of a high rate of interest. But suppose that none of these problems arise. The authorities in A and B both use domestic financial policy effectively to prevent booms and slump, both avoid direct controls over expenditures, and both use a mixture of monetary policy and fiscal policy which is devised to maintain an optimum rate of savings. The control of capital movements between them is even so sometimes recommended on grounds which are connected with the financial problems involved in the maintenance of the balance of payments between them.

If the authorities in A and B employ their domestic financial policies for the maintenance of internal balance, they cannot maintain external balance by deflating and inflating domestically on the gold-standard principles for the maintenance of external balance. If at the same time they avoid direct controls over their imports and exports on the general free-trade grounds examined in Part II of this volume, then, in the absence of controls over capital movements,[1] they must use the method of variable exchange rates to preserve external balance. Up to this point we have not given any very precise meaning to the idea of internal balance, and to do so at all completely would be out of place in this volume. But let us suppose that while serious inflations and deflations are avoided in both countries, the problem of maintaining internal balance is not precisely the same in both countries. Suppose, for example, that in B there is a more highly developed trade-union organization among wage-earners and that therefore at any given level of unemployment there is a stronger upward pressure on money wage rates in B than in A. As a result of this the avoidance of inflationary pressure may be rather less complete in B than in A. In both countries total domestic expenditure is so controlled as to maintain the same moderate level of unemployment, but money wage rates rise in B at a rate, say, 1 per cent greater per annum than in A. As a result of this, money costs and money prices of products rise in B at a rate 1 per cent per annum higher than in A. To take the simplest example, prices are constant in A, but rise in B at 1 per cent per annum. External balance between A and B will in the absence of other factors require that the value of B's currency should continually depreciate in terms of A's currency at a rate of 1 per cent per annum in order to keep B's prices and costs in line with A's prices and costs.

It is sometimes argued that in such circumstances a perpetual control

[1] Or of the use of accommodating finance on an unlimited scale.

over capital movements from B to A must be maintained. Otherwise, so it is argued, people will foresee that there is a continuing depreciation of B's currency in prospect and they will therefore continually move funds from B to A in order to speculate on the depreciation of B's currency. Suppose that the rate of interest is the same in B and in A, say 5 per cent per annum; and suppose that B's currency is the pound and A's the dollar and that this year's rate of exchange is \$4 to £1. Then if £100 is invested in B, it will be worth £105 next year at the 5 per cent rate of interest ruling in B. But if the £100 is exchanged at \$4 to the pound into \$400 this year, it will be worth next year \$420 at the rate of interest of 5 per cent ruling in A, and this \$420 can be exchanged next year at next year's rate of exchange of \$3·96 to the pound into £106 (approximately). Thus the £100 invested in B will earn 5 per cent; but if it is moved to A, invested there for one year, and then brought back to B it will earn 6 per cent. But, so the argument runs, the rate of interest inside A and B is the same—namely 5 per cent. This means that the marginal product of real capital is the same in A and B; and thus the extra 1 per cent inducement to shift funds from B to A to take advantage of the depreciation of B's exchange rate does not correspond to the true welfare requirements for the attainment of world economic efficiency.

There is, however, a simple error in this argument. Suppose that the real marginal productivity of capital is the same in A as in B, namely 5 per cent. This means that if 100 units of goods are not consumed in B this year but are added to the capital stock, then 105 such goods will be available for consumption next year; and similarly in A. We will call this the real rate of return on capital. Now if money prices are constant in A, then the money rate of interest which will be required in A in order to avoid booms or slumps will also be 5 per cent per annum. At this rate the cost of borrowing money capital in A will just correspond to the return which can be earned on the real investment financed by those capital funds.

But if the general level of money prices in B is rising at 1 per cent per annum the situation will be different in that country. If 100 units of goods are not consumed there, and if the real rate of return on capital there is 5 per cent, then 105 units of goods will be available for consumption next year. But since the money prices of those goods will be 1 per cent higher next year than this year, the money rate of return on this investment will be approximately 6 per cent. £100 worth of goods are given up this year, and £105 worth of goods are available next year at the same price level; but as the price of a unit of goods will have risen from £1 to £1·01, the money value of these goods will now be 105 × £1·01 or, approximately, £106. If the real rate of return on capital is 5 per cent and prices are rising by 1 per cent per annum, then the money rate of return on capital will be approximately 6 per cent; and in order that internal balance may continue to be maintained in B (i.e. in order that a still higher rate of inflation should be avoided) the money rate of interest in B must be 6 per cent. If it were only 5 per cent, entrepreneurs would have an incentive still further to expand their rate of expenditure on capital development in B, borrowing money at 5 per cent and investing it in additional projects which would earn a money rate of return of 6 per cent.

If, therefore, A and B are in the same real position with a real rate of return on capital of 5 per cent in both countries, but if at the same time there is the purely monetary difference that the general level of prices will rise in B by 1 per cent per annum and will remain constant in A, then two things follow. First, to preserve external balance B's currency must depreciate by 1 per cent per annum which will itself give an additional incentive of 1 per cent per annum to invest funds in A rather than in B in order to take advantage of the exchange-rate profit. But, secondly, in order to preserve internal balance the money rate of interest must be 6 per cent in B and only 5 per cent in A, and this will give an additional incentive of 1 per cent to invest funds in B rather than in A. These two incentives will cancel out. The final money returns on investment in the two countries will be the same when the real rate of return on capital is the same. There is no need to impose controls over capital movements on grounds of economic efficiency.

The argument which we have just examined and rejected may take a rather more complicated form. But once again it is fallacious. Suppose now that the authorities in B are just as successful as the authorities in A in preventing inflations and deflations in the sense that domestic financial policies are used in both countries to an extent which keeps the general level of prices constant in both countries. But suppose now that there is some real change going on in the world which is shifting demand away from the type of goods which B produces on to the type of goods which A produces. For example, output per head in both countries is growing as capital is accumulated and as technical improvements take place; consumers in both countries are becoming richer and richer; but B produces the sort of necessities which poor men most want to buy, and A produces the luxuries on which people spend a larger and larger proportion of their incomes as they become richer and richer. This continuing shift of demand away from B's products on to A's products will tend to put B's balance of payments into deficit. To correct this the price of B's products must continually be reduced relatively to A's products to tempt consumers back on to B's products on a scale sufficient to keep the value of B's imports and of her exports in line with each other. In other words, there is a force at work which requires a continuing movement of the terms of trade against B at a rate of, say, 1 per cent per annum.

In the conditions which we are assuming in which the money price of B's products is constant in terms of B's currency and the money price of A's products is constant in terms of A's currency, this will require a continuing depreciation of B's currency in terms of A's currency of 1 per cent per annum. Once again in so far as this continuing depreciation of B's currency is foreseen, there will be a 1 per cent per annum extra inducement to invest capital in A rather than in B in order to make a profit on the appreciation of A's money in terms of B's money.

Once again it may be argued that world economic efficiency requires that this speculative inducement to move capital from B to A should be offset. Suppose that the real rate of return on capital is 5 per cent both in A and in B, in the sense that 100 units of A-products not consumed in A and invested in A will produce 105 units of A-products next year and that 100 units of B-products not consumed in B and invested in B will produce 105 units of B-products next year. Since in the present case the price of A-products is constant in terms of A's currency and of B-products is constant in terms of B's currency, the money rates of interest must also be 5 per cent both in A and in B in order to preserve internal balance in both countries, that is to say, in order to give entrepreneurs in these two countries no incentive to borrow at a higher (or lower) rate in order to expand (or contract) their rate of money expenditure on new capital developments. In this case the real rate of return on capital is 5 per cent in both countries, but there is an additional 1 per cent incentive to move capital funds from B to A because while the money rate of interest is 5 per cent in both countries there is a 1 per cent exchange-rate profit to be obtained by shifting funds out of B's currency into A's currency. Apparently the incentive to move capital from B to A no longer corresponds to the fact that the real rate of return on capital is the same in both countries.

But this argument also contains a simple error. It is true that if the money rates of interest are maintained in A and B at the 5 per cent level which is required in both countries to maintain internal balance, there will be a 1 per cent inducement from the exchange-rate variation to move capital funds from B to A. But in this case the movement of real capital from B to A is required in the interests of world economic efficiency. If 100 units of B-products priced at £1 each this year are set aside from consumption this year and invested in B, they will produce 105 units of B-products next year, the real rate of return on capital in B being 5 per cent. But at the current rate of exchange of $4 to £1, these 100 units of B-products are worth 100 units of A-products priced at $4 each this year. This means that the marginal value to consumers this year of one unit of B-products (priced at £1) is the same as the marginal value to consumers this year of one unit of A-products (priced at $4), because they have the same price in a free competitive market. Consumers would therefore make the same sacrifice this year if instead of giving up the consumption of 100 units of B-products they gave up the consumption of 100 units of A-products, which, if they were invested in A, would produce 105 units of A-products next year. For the same sacrifice by consumers this year, consumers can obtain either 105 B-products or 105 A-products next year. But next year the terms of trade are going to change 1 per cent against B-products; that is to say, next year 105 A-products are going to have the same marginal value to consumers as 106 B-products. There is a 1 per cent advantage to consumers in having next year the 105 A-products (which are the sort of thing which is becoming relatively scarcer) rather than 105 B-products (which are the sort of thing which is becoming relatively more plentiful). The 1 per cent additional profit to be gained from moving capital funds from B to A to take advantage of the expected depreciation of B's currency in this case truly represents the fact that A-products are going to become more valuable relatively to B-products so that, although the real rate of physical return on capital invested in A is no higher than that on capital invested in B, it is an advantage to society that the capital should be invested in such a way as to produce this given real return in the form of A-products which are going to become progressively more valuable at the margin to consumers.

By means of the type of analysis used in the examination of these two particular simplified cases, it can be seen that speculation in the future course of exchange rates in a free foreign-exchange market in itself presents no argument at all for the control of capital movements on grounds of economic efficiency. If full employment is preserved in both countries by a use of monetary policy which keeps the money rate of interest, after adjustment for the rate of increase or decrease in the general level of prices, in line with the real return on capital in each country, and if the future course of prices and of exchange rates is correctly foreseen by the speculators, the movement of capital funds between the two countries should correspond to the requirements of world economic efficiency. It is, of course, quite a different matter if speculation on the future of the exchange rate is not of this character, if in the terminology used in Chapter XVII of Volume I speculation is perverse, deficient, or excessive. There may be reasons for the control of speculative movements of capital on grounds of economic efficiency, if for political or psychological reasons speculators are moving funds in a direction or in an amount which in no way corresponds to the movements which well-informed competitive speculators would undertake in their own interests. But well-informed competitive speculation in foreign exchange markets helps to make capital movements correspond to the requirements of economic efficiency.

It may be of interest to conclude this discussion by showing how the speculative inducement to shift funds from B to A which we examined in the second case discussed above would show itself under the 'gold-standard' mechanism with a fixed rate of exchange between A's and B's currency. Suppose as before that a gradual shift of world demand away from B's products on to A's products is in process so that to maintain equilibrium in a free world market for both products the price of B's products must fall at a rate of 1 per cent per annum in terms of A's products. The rate of exchange between A's and B's currency being fixed, this means that either the price of B's products must fall in terms of B's currency or else the price of A's products must rise in terms of A's currency. Let us suppose that the adjustment is shared between the two countries, as we have suggested in Volume I that it should be.[1] Money prices, incomes, and costs fall by ½ per cent per annum in B and rise by ½ per cent per annum in A, and there is sufficient flexibility of money wage rates and other costs in both countries to enable this to take place smoothly. Suppose further, as we did before, that the real rate of return on capital is 5 per cent in both A and B in the sense that 100 units of A-products (or B-products) invested in industry in A (or in B) would produce 105 units of A-products (or of B-products) next year.

In these circumstances in order to preserve equilibrium in the market for capital funds in B, the money rate of interest in B must be only 4½ per cent per annum. A borrower of £100 this year could buy 100 units of B-products at a present price of £1 a unit, could invest them in B, and could thus end up with 105 units of such goods next year. But as the price of these goods would now be ½ per cent less than before (i.e. only £0·995 instead of £1), these 105 goods would be worth only 105 × £0·995 or, approximately, £104½. The money rate of return on the investment would be only 4½ per cent because of the fall in prices. Conversely, in A the real rate of return on capital is also 5 per cent; but the rise by ½ per cent per annum in the general level of money prices in A would mean that 5½ per cent could be earned on money invested in real capital development in A. The money rate of interest would have to be correspondingly higher in A in order to preserve equilibrium in the capital market in A.

We should therefore be in a position in which the money rate of interest was 4½ per cent in B and 5½ per cent in A with a fixed rate of exchange between the two currencies. People would therefore have once more a 1 per cent incentive to move capital funds from B to A; and this would correspond to the real requirements of world economic efficiency because, although the real rate of return on capital is the same in both countries, to the consumers of finished products the value of a given amount of goods produced by capital in A is continually rising relatively to the value of a given amount of goods produced by capital in B.

[1] See Condition 2 of Chapter XVI of Volume I.

PART IV. MULTILATERAL TRADE

PART IV. MULTILATERAL TRADE

CHAPTER XXX

THE CASE FOR MULTILATERAL FREEDOM OF TRADE AND FACTOR MOVEMENTS

UP to this point in this volume we have proceeded on the assumption that there were only two trading countries, A and B. This has enabled us to consider a large number of the issues which arise in trying to decide whether, on grounds of economic welfare, there is a case for governmental control of international movements of products or of factors of production.

But there is one important type of question which the assumption of a two-country world automatically excludes from discussion, namely, questions concerning discrimination between countries. To discuss problems of this kind we must introduce at least one more country, C. We can then ask questions of the following type. Given that the authorities in A are controlling imports on one ground or another, should they, as a means of increasing economic welfare, control imports from B (or C) more vigorously than imports from C (or B)? Or does the maximization of economic welfare require that any control over imports into A should be non-discriminatory as between the two alternative sources of supply, A and B?[1] Similar questions can obviously be raised about the desirability of discrimination in the control of exports or in the control of the immigration or emigration of factors of production.

Now, as we saw in Chapter IX in discussing a two-country world, the essence of the argument for free trade was that by facilitating the optimization of trade and the maximization of production it provided some of the *utopian marginal* conditions necessary for the achievement of economic *efficiency*. This basic argument is not significantly affected by the introduction of further countries into the world trading system. The thesis which we shall maintain in this chapter is essentially the same, namely that in a three-country world the following proposition is still true. If a policy of modified laissez-faire is adopted domestically so that inside every country prices are equal to marginal social values and to marginal social costs, then free trade between the countries will ensure (i) that it is not possible to make one consumer in one of the

[1] The precise criterion by which one can attempt to measure whether a given type of control is discriminatory in its effects has been discussed at some length in Chapter XXVIII of Volume I of this work. We shall not repeat that discussion in this volume.

countries better off by making marginal alterations in the amounts of the various products which are traded between the countries without making some other consumer in some country worse off, and (ii) that it is not possible to produce more of one product in the world as a whole by making marginal changes in the distribution of the industry concerned among the various countries without reducing the world output of some other product.

In essence there is no difference in the analysis which was required in Chapter IX to establish these two propositions for a two-country world and the analysis which will be required to establish them in this chapter for a three-country world. But there is one interesting implication of the analysis which it is useful to bear in mind in the case of a three-country world. As we shall see, it will normally be impossible to achieve the two objectives mentioned in the preceding paragraph by trade between the three countries which in any significant sense is bilaterally balanced. Normally country A will have to have an excess of exports to, say, country B which will be balanced by A's excess of imports from country C, if world trade is to be optimized and world production to be maximized. We shall conduct the following analysis in such a way as to observe the implications of a free-trade policy in a three-country world upon the bilateral balance of trade between each pair of countries.

The proposition that free trade will optimize trade and maximize production in a many-country world, just as it was shown to do in a two-country world in Chapter IX, is intuitively so obvious that it scarcely needs a formal proof. In a free-trade world each freely tradeable product (*a*pples, *b*lankets, *c*oal, *d*rugs, *e*ggs, etc.) must have the same price in every trading country (A, B, C, D, E, etc.). Otherwise it would pay merchants to move the product concerned from the lower to the higher priced market. Suppose then that there is a general policy of free trade, so that the price of each tradeable product is the same in every country. Let us for convenience choose units of the various products in such a way that in the free-trade position the price of a unit of each product is the same, say \$1.[1] We proceed then to inquire whether, in this situation, it is possible either (i) to alter the consumptions of the various consumers of the given outputs of the various products in such a way that one consumer is better off without any other being worse off, or (ii) whether it is possible to alter the outputs of the various products in the various countries in such a way that the world output of one product is increased without any reduction in the world output of any other product.

[1] That is to say, we simply define a unit of apples as that amount of apples—whether it be an ounce, a pound, 5¼ pounds, or half-a-ton—which is bought and sold for \$1 in the free-trade equilibrium. And similarly with the other products.

Let us start then with the optimization of trade. We need to know whether it is possible to take one unit of one product (say an apple) from a consumer in one country (say A), to exchange this apple by any means in any or all of the other countries leaving the consumer concerned equally well off at each such exchange, and yet to bring back in the end to A an amount of some other product which will more than make up to the consumer in A for the loss of 1 apple. It is clear that in our free-trade world this is impossible. Suppose 1 apple is exported from A to B and exchanged in B for blankets. Since the prices of an apple and of a blanket in B are both \$1 and since prices measure marginal values to consumers in B, only 1 blanket can be received in exchange if B's consumers are to be left as well off as before. Now if this 1 blanket were brought back to A, it would only just compensate the consumers in A for the loss of the 1 apple, since in A also the price of an apple is the same as the price of a blanket so that the marginal value of a blanket is the same as that of an apple. But suppose that the blanket received from B's consumers were exported to C and there exchanged for another product, say coal. Since the price and the marginal value of a blanket is the same as that of a unit of coal in C, 1 unit of coal can be exchanged for 1 blanket in C without making C's consumers worse off. If this unit of coal were then given to A's consumers, it would only just make up for the loss of 1 apple by them. Clearly whatever is the product of which we choose in the first place to export \$1 worth and whatever is the country from which we choose to export it and whatever series of exchanges in other countries for other products we choose to make, we can never bring back to the first country more than \$1 worth of any other product, if we are to avoid making any consumer in any other country worse off. And \$1 worth of any other product is in the original country only just sufficient to compensate the consumers for the loss of \$1 worth of the original product. Trade is in fact already optimized by the free-trade policy.

An exactly similar process of reasoning will show that in our many-country world free trade will also have served to maximize production. Suppose that in our free-trade world in any one country (say A) one more unit of any one product (say apples) is produced. The resources used in A to produce 1 more apple must come from the production of some other product (say blankets); and since in A the marginal social cost of every product is the same, namely \$1, it follows that if 1 more apple is produced 1 less blanket will be produced in A. Let us then consider any other country (say B) and suppose that it increases its output of blankets by 1 unit to make up for the reduction in A's output of 1 blanket. If in B the resources used to produce this extra blanket come from the apple industry, then, because the price and therefore the marginal cost of an apple is the same as that of a blanket in B, 1 less apple will be produced in B. But this is as great as the original increase in the output of apples in A, so that there is as yet no net increase in world output. But suppose that the resources for increased blanket production in B come from a reduction in the output of any third product (say coal). The world output of coal will then be reduced by 1 unit, since the marginal cost of a unit of coal equals the marginal cost of 1 blanket in B. Suppose that this reduction in the output of coal in B is counterbalanced by an increase in the output of coal by 1 unit in any other third country (say C). Then if the resources for this expansion of coal output in C come from the apple industry, it will cause a reduction in the output of 1 apple in C, since the marginal cost of an apple is equal to the marginal cost of a unit of coal in C. But this would exactly offset the original increase in A's output of 1 apple. There would be no net increase in world production. It is clear that by whatever series of industrial adjustments between whatever pairs of commodities and in whatever countries one likes to choose one will never be able to keep all other outputs constant and yet to increase the output of one product in the free-trade conditions which we are assuming. The marginal condition for the maximization of production is achieved in the free-trade equilibrium position.

We have thus shown that in a many-country world, just as in the two-country world of Chapter IX, a policy of free trade will lead to the optimization of trade and the maximization of production, if within each country a policy is pursued which equates prices to marginal social costs and to marginal social values. But it is important to observe that if the forces of free trade are allowed to operate in a many-country world, there is likely to result some element of multilateralism in international trade and payments. In other words the advantages of free trade in a many-country world cannot be reaped in the absence of a system which enables country A, for example, to finance its purchases from, say, C by means of its sales to, say B.

It is perhaps worth while noticing that in order that multilateralism should become an issue in international trade it is necessary not merely that there should be more than two trading countries (if only A and B existed, trade would obviously have to be bilateral), but also that there should be more than two tradeable products. Suppose there are only two tradeable products, apples and blankets. Suppose that A exports $1,000 worth of apples. If her balance of trade is to balance she must, therefore, import $1,000 worth of blankets. Consider A's relationship with any other country—say C—to whom A is exporting any part of her apples. Suppose A is exporting $200 worth of apples to C. Then C must be an importer of apples and an exporter of blankets. She must be exporting $200 worth of blankets to finance her purchase of $200 apples from A. But, since we are ignoring transport costs, there is no reason why A should not purchase these $200 of blankets from C as part of A's total expenditure of $1,000 on imports of blankets. In other words, A's trade with C can be bilaterally balanced without any distortion even of free-trade market conditions.

In a world in which there are only two tradeable products, apples and blankets, there will be no trade between any two countries both of which export apples and import blankets or both of which export blankets and import apples. The trading world can in this case be divided into two quite separate groups, within each of which no trade will take place: on the one hand, the countries which export apples and import blankets, and, on the other hand, the countries which import apples and export blankets. In the absence of transport costs it is a matter of indifference which particular exporter of apples supplies which particular importer of apples; and similarly with blankets. All trade can, therefore, be bilaterally balanced, each $1 worth of apples moving from a particular apple-exporting country to a particular apple-importing country being exactly matched by a $1 worth of blankets moving from the latter to the former country.[1]

In order that there should be a real need for multilateralism in international trade it is necessary that there should be at least three products as well as at least three countries. An example of such a trading situation is shown in Table XXXIV. We suppose that A is a country with very special advantages in the production of apples or else a very specially low demand for apples, so that in the absence of trade the price of apples would be very low in comparison with the price of the other tradeable products (blankets and coal) in A. A therefore exports 300 apples (row 1, column *a*) and imports 200 blankets and 100 units of coal (row 1, columns *b* and *c*). We assume that A's productive disadvantage or the strength of her own needs is less marked in the case of coal than in the case of blankets, so that in the free-trade position she

[1] There is a careless tendency to use the terms 'bilateral' and 'discriminatory' as if they had the same meaning. The fact that all trade in two commodities between any number of countries can always be cleared bilaterally, shows how different the meaning of the term 'bilateralism' is from that of 'discrimination', because trade in two commodities between three countries certainly may be conducted on discriminatory or on non-discriminatory lines. Suppose A to be an exporter of apples and an importer of blankets and both B and C to be an exporter of blankets and an importer of apples. The trade may be freely conducted all round and, therefore, automatically conducted on a non-discriminatory basis. A may impose a duty on imports of blankets from C without imposing a duty on similar imports from B. This is certainly discriminatory. This will discourage A's trade with C and thus encourage A's trade with B. C will export less blankets to A and therefore import less apples from A. B, to fill the void in A's market created by the reduction of supplies from C, will export more blankets to A and will import more apples from A. The price of blankets relatively to apples will be higher in B than in C. But in both these cases—the full non-discriminatory free-trade case and the case where A puts a discriminatory duty on the imports of C's products—the trade between A and B and the trade between A and C will be bilaterally balanced.

imports blankets in greatest amount but also imports some coal; and she covers these imports by large-scale exports of apples. We assume that B is a country with a most marked productive advantage or a most markedly low domestic demand in the case of blankets. She exports 600 blankets in order to finance her imports of 400 apples and 200 coal (row 2 of the table). In other words, her productive disadvantage or the strength of her own domestic demand is rather more marked in the case of apples than in that of coal, so that her apple imports are heavier than her coal imports.

TABLE XXXIV

Multilateral Trade

		Volumes and values of imports (+) and exports (−) in a free-trade situation in which the price of an apple = price of a blanket = price of a unit of coal = $1		
		apples (*a*)	blankets (*b*)	coal (*c*)
Countries				
A	(1)	−300	+200	+100
B	(2)	+400	−600	+200
C	(3)	−100	+400	−300

C, on the other hand, we assume to be a country which imports only one of the three products (namely blankets) and exports something of both of the other two (apples and coal). In other words, we are assuming that the most marked feature of C's economy in the pre-trade position was a productive disadvantage or a high domestic demand in the case of blankets, to obtain which she exports something of both the other commodities. But her productive advantage or the low level of her own demand is somewhat greater in the case of coal than in that of apples, so that coal constitutes her larger export (row 3).

Now the pattern of trade which we have depicted in Table XXXIV is a multilateral one, in which A has an excess of exports to B, B has an excess of exports to C, and C has an excess of exports to A. Thus A is exporting 300 apples, all of which go to B since B is the only importer of apples; she is importing 200 blankets, all of which come from B since B is the only exporter of blankets; and this excess of exports over imports in A's trade with B is balanced by imports of 100 coal, all of which comes from C since C is the only exporter of coal. Thus A has an export surplus of 100 in her trade with B, matched by an import surplus of 100 in her trade with C. Similarly, it can be seen that B has an export surplus of 100 in her trade with C, matched by the 100 import surplus in her trade with A. Since we now have three products it is possible for each country to trade with each other country without any country simultaneously importing and exporting the same product; and in the particular case which we have chosen, A has an excess of exports of 100 to B, B an excess of exports of 100 to C, and C an excess of exports of 100 to A.

It is important to realize that this multilateral trade pattern could be balanced bilaterally if one of our three countries simultaneously imported and exported one of the products. This is shown in the following diagrams where *a* represents apples, *b* blankets, and *c* coal. Diagram i

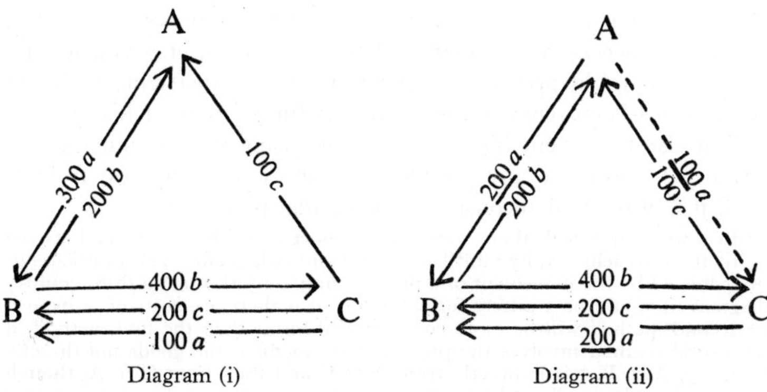

Diagram (i)
Diagram (ii)

merely reproduces the figures in Table XXXIV, where A is exporting 300 apples to B and importing 200 blankets from B and 100 coal from C; and so on. From this diagram it can readily be seen that A has an export surplus with B (to whom she exports 300 *a* and from whom she imports 200 *b*). Similarly, B can be seen to have an export surplus with C (to whom she sends 400 *b* and from whom she receives 100 *a* and 200 *c*); and C can be seen to have an export surplus with A (to whom she sends 100 *c* without receiving anything from A).

Now diagram ii shows that each of these trades would become bilaterally balanced by one simple change, namely if A sent 100 of her apples to C instead of to B, and if C then sent 100 more apples to B. In other words, each trade would be bilaterally balanced if a flow of 100 apples were sent from A to B not directly but indirectly *via* C.[1]

Such a rearrangement of the trading pattern can be said to give a

[1] The changed trade flows which are necessary for this purpose are shown in italics in diagram ii.

bilateral solution only in the most formal sense of the word bilateral. In real terms there is clearly little essential difference between (i) an arrangement whereby C earns A's currency by selling coal to A, transfers A's currency to B in payment of an import surplus into C from B, and thus enables B to purchase an import surplus of apples from A, and (ii) an arrangement whereby C buys an extra amount of A's apples with the proceeds of her coal exports to A, sells these extra apples together with her own exports to B, and thus obtains sufficient of B's currency to finance her own excess imports from B. Arrangement (i) may be described as a multilateral payments arrangement and (ii) as a multilateral trading arrangement. They both tend to essentially the same results. But if a truly bilateral balance of trade is for some reason desired, it is important to institute controls over trade and payments which simultaneously exclude both of these possible types of multilateral arrangement. Thus, in our example, if it were desired to impose a real bilateral balance of trade between the three countries A, B, and C, it would be necessary not only to institute a control of payments of a kind which would prevent B's exporters from transferring their net earnings of C's currency to residents of A (in payment of B's debts to A), but also to prevent B's exporters from using their earnings of C's currency to purchase any product (in our example, apples) from C itself, if C was simultaneously importing that product from A.[1]

[1] In a world in which there were no transport costs the difference between multilateralism achieved by multilateral payments (diagram i) and multilateralism achieved by the movement of a product indirectly through a third country (diagram ii) would be a purely formal one. But if there are costs of transport, the second method will be more costly in real terms than the first method, if the second method involves the physical movement of the goods not directly from, say, A to B, but indirectly from A to C and then from C to A, though the second method will not be more costly in transport costs if it merely means that the goods have got to pass from the ownership of citizens of A to that of citizens of C and thus indirectly into the ownership of citizens of B. Which of these things is implied will depend upon the forms of bilateral payments controls which are instituted. If, for example, B's or C's control lays it down that B's exporters to C can spend their earnings of C's currency only on products exported from C to B, then the physical transport of apples from A to B *via* C is involved. If, however, the control merely says that B's earnings of C's currency may be spent only on the import into B of products owned by residents of C, then diagram ii on p. 505 merely implies that A's apples should be sold to residents of C and by them to residents of B and then transported direct from A to B. Thus the advantage of a system of free multilateral payments (diagram i) over that of a bilateral balancing of payments with a multilateral exchange of goods (diagram ii) is that the former will avoid wasteful transport costs which may be inevitable under the latter system. Of course if there are transport costs a country may naturally in conditions of free trade simultaneously import and export the same product. Thus an extensive country with a fertile wheat-growing area in its eastern border and a heavily concentrated industrial area on its western border might naturally export wheat over its eastern border and import wheat over its western border and thus save the cost of moving wheat from its eastern to its western districts. But such a situation has nothing to do with bilateralism or multilateralism. Such a natural pattern of trade might just as well appear to make the country's trade more multilateral or more bilateral.

We are now in a position to understand the sort of loss to economic efficiency which a forced bilateralism in international trade may involve. From diagram ii it can be seen that the true bilateral balancing of trade is likely to imply some restriction on B's imports of apples from A, on C's imports of blankets from B, and on A's imports of coal from C. This is likely to raise the price of coal relatively to that of apples in A (where apples are more plentiful because of reduced export of A's apples to B and coal is more scarce because of reduced imports from C), and for similar reasons to raise the price of apples relatively to that of blankets in B and the price of blankets relatively to that of coal in C. We assume that in the free-trade position each product had a price of \$1. In the bilateral trade position the influences which we have just noted might have changed the prices just mentioned in the following way:

	Price of apples	Price of blankets	Price of coal
A .	\$0·9	—	\$1·1
B .	\$1·1	\$0·9	—
C .	—	\$1·1	\$0·9

In this case trade would not be optimized or production maximized. If 1 unit of coal were exported from C to A, $\frac{1 \cdot 1}{0 \cdot 9}$ or 1·2 apples could be taken from A's consumers without making them worse off since the marginal value of a unit of coal in A is \$1·1 and that of an apple only \$0·9. If 1·2 apples were taken to B, $1 \cdot 2 \times \frac{1 \cdot 1}{0 \cdot 9}$ or 1·49 blankets could be taken from B without leaving consumers in B worse off, because 1·2 apples in B have a marginal value to consumers of 1·2 × \$1·1 while 1 blanket has a marginal value of only \$0·9. But if these 1·49 blankets were brought into C they would have a marginal value of 1·49 × \$1·1 or \$1·64, whereas the initial export of a unit of coal from C to A meant a loss to C's consumers of only 1 × \$0·9 or \$0·9. In other words, C's consumers could be made better off without any other consumers being made worse off by an interchange of existing products. Trade would not be optimized in the bilaterally balanced trade position.

Similarly, production would not be maximized. Suppose C produced 1 less blanket and transferred the resources so released into her coal industry. Then she would produce $\frac{1 \cdot 1}{0 \cdot 9}$ or 1·2 more units of coal, since the marginal cost of a unit of coal in C is \$0·9 and of a blanket is \$1·1. But if in A 1·2 less unit of coal is produced to set against the increased output of coal in C, $1 \cdot 2 \times \frac{1 \cdot 1}{0 \cdot 9}$ or 1·49 more apples could be produced since the marginal cost of an apple is only \$0·9 and of a unit of coal is \$1·1 in A. If now in B 1·49 less apples are produced to set against the increased output of apples in A, $1{\cdot}49 \times \frac{1{\cdot}1}{0{\cdot}9}$ or 1·64 more blankets could be produced since the marginal cost of apples is \$1·1 and of blankets is only \$0·9 in B. Thus there could be an increased output of 1·64 blankets in B to set against a reduced output of only 1 blanket in C without the world output of any other product being reduced. In the bilaterally balanced trade position world production is not maximized.

We have now shown how in a many-country world as in a two-country world free trade—if domestic policies of modified laissez-faire are successfully adopted—will lead to the fulfilment of the marginal conditions necessary for the optimization of trade and the maximization of production. We have also seen how, if we are dealing with a many-product as well as a many-country world, this free-trade policy will most probably involve a multilateral trade pattern. Any effective interference with this multilateralism would necessitate an abandonment of the free-trade policy and would thus probably be incompatible with the optimization of trade and the maximization of production.

It may be useful at this point to digress for a little from our main point (i.e. the question whether the existence of many countries modifies the arguments given in Chapter IX in favour of a free-trade policy), in order to examine the process whereby adjustment may be made between countries in a many-product many-country world. Suppose that, as in Table XXXIV, A is an exporter of apples to B and an importer of blankets from B. Suppose, then, that A's demand for blankets rises and for apples falls. If A and B were the only two countries and apples and blankets the only two products, then the price of blankets would have to go up and the price of apples down (i.e. the terms of trade would have to move against A) until A had thereby been tempted to import so many fewer blankets from B and B had been tempted to import so many more apples from A that A's balance of trade was in equilibrium again.

But the existence of more products and of more countries may greatly help to ease this process of adjustment. Suppose that there is a third country C which is trading in some product which is a fairly good substitute for A's apples and in some product which is a fairly good substitute for B's blankets. Then the fall in the price of A's apples resulting from the reduced demand for them in A may cause C to export less to A or B or to import more from A or B of products which are good substitutes for A's apples, thus keeping up the demand for A's apples in A or in B. And, similarly, the rise in the price of B's blankets caused by the increased demand for them in A may cause C to export more or to import less of some products which are good substitutes for B's blankets, thus keeping down the demand for B's blankets in A or in B. In our example in Table XXXIV C exports apples to B and imports blankets from B. The shift in demand from apples to blankets in A may be partially met by a reduced export of apples from C to B and a reduced import of blankets into C from B. Indeed, in an extreme case C might swing from being a net exporter to a net importer of apples or of other products which are close substitutes for apples or (what is less likely in our particular numerical example) from being a net importer to a net exporter of blankets or of other substitutes for blankets.

Similarly, the existence of a third product—coal—may ease the adjustment. An increased demand in A for imports of blankets from B will put some initial strain on A's balance of payments and thus will cause A's prices and costs to fall relatively to B's prices and costs, either through the gold-standard mechanism of a deflation in A and inflation in B or else through the mechanism of a variable exchange rate and a depreciation of A's currency in terms of B's. Now if both A and B are trading in a third product, coal, this will tend to lower the cost of home-produced coal relatively to the foreign-market price of coal for A and to raise the cost of home-produced coal relatively to the foreign-market price of coal for B. A will tend to import less or to export more coal and B will tend to import more or to export less coal. Part of the readjustment of A's and B's balance of trade may therefore come about through the international market for coal. In the particular example which we have given in Table XXXIV A and B both import coal from C. The increased demand in A for blankets from B will put A's balance of payment in deficit and B's in surplus. Part of the readjustment may then come about through A buying less and B more coal from C. Indeed, in our particular example, it is possible that A might swing from being a net importer to being a net exporter of coal. The existence of a large range of products and a variety of trading countries may thus introduce many indirect ways of correcting an initial disturbance in the trade in any particular products between any particular countries.

It is important to recognize one particular form which the multilateral principle may take in the transfer of capital from one country to another. Suppose that A is a country which is particularly rich in capital in the sense that the marginal social net product of capital is very low in A, and that C is a country which is particularly poor in capital in the sense that the marginal social net product is very high in C. Then the maximization of production will involve the movement of capital funds from A where the (social) yield on capital is low to C where the (social) yield on capital is high; and this, as we have seen, means that A must generate a surplus and C a deficit on their balances of trade in order to enable the flow of funds from A to C to be matched by a movement of real resources from A to C.

Now it may well be that this adjustment of the balance of trade should take place through a third country B. This would be particularly obvious if B happened to be the country which had the productive atmosphere or the factor endowment which was particularly well suited to produce the capital goods which C needed for her capital development projects. C's import surplus would then be generated by the purchase in B of these capital goods out of the funds borrowed by C from A. B would then have to import more or export less of something else to regain her balance-of-payments equilibrium, and A would have to export more or import less to generate her export surplus. If initially there was a large trade between A and B of a kind which could fairly easily be expanded or contracted, then the most economic form of this adjustment would be an expansion of A's exports to B and/or a contraction of B's exports to A.

In other words the marginal conditions for economic efficiency require that capital funds moving from one country to another should not be tied to expenditure in any particular country. If there is a natural flow of funds from A where yields are low to C where yields are high and if it at the same time B produces most economically those goods which C will need during her process of capital development,[1] then the funds raised in A should be spendable by C on B's products.

Loans can in fact be tied in either of two ways. Either the money loan may be tied to the goods or the exports may be tied to the money loan. The authorities in one country, say A, may rule that borrowers in C can borrow funds from A only if these funds are spent on particular products purchased in A rather than in B, even though the cost of these products is higher in A than in B. This would be a method whereby a country which was rich in capital could use that richness in capital to increase the demand for its own products; and this is in fact the more usual form of tied loans. But theoretically the authorities in a country which was very well suited to produce products specially needed for developmental purposes, say country B, might rule that importers of these products in any other country, say C, were allowed to purchase

[1] In the text we assumed that B produced most cheaply the capital goods required in C. But it may be that C produces these products (e.g. irrigation works) herself with her own local resources. Then the transfer of real resources to C must take the form of C's labour being used to produce capital works in C instead of goods for export or instead of goods which are now replaced by additional imports into C. If B is the country which can best go without the goods which C was previously exporting or can best produce the goods which are newly imported into C to take the place of the goods formerly produced in C by the resources now employed on the capital works in C, then once again the most economic form of the transfer of real resources from A to C may involve A exporting more to, and importing less from B, so that B can import less from or export more to C.

them only if they borrowed the funds for the purpose in B rather than in A, even though the cost of borrowing were higher in B than in A. This would be a means of keeping up the demand for foreign loans in B and so for maintaining the rate of interest obtainable by B's lenders to C's borrowers. Either form of tied loan would mean that resources were used in a less efficient manner than is possible if the country with the lowest yield on capital provides the capital funds for C's development while the country with the lowest cost of production provides the real products for C's development.

So much for the case for free multilateral trading. Before we close this chapter it may be worth pointing out that there is a similar case for a free multilateral movement of factors of production, if there are many countries and many factors of production.[1] Consider the position illustrated in Table XXXV. We assume that there are four factors of production, land, capital, skilled labour and unskilled labour[2] and that

TABLE XXXV

Multilateral Factor Movements

	Land	Capital	Skilled Labour	Unskilled Labour
Country A	1,000	1,100 +100	900 −100	1,000
B	1,000	1,000	1,100 +100	900 −100
C	1,000	900 −100	1,000	1,100 +100
Total	3,000	3,000	3,000	3,000

[1] The problem differs, of course, essentially from that of free multilateral trading. In the case of trade the value of each country's total imports must (after allowance for other autonomous elements in the balance of payments) be equal to the value of its total exports. There is, of course, no such balance-of-payments condition in the case of multilateral factor movements; it is not necessary that the value of A's annual export of capital should be matched by an immigration of labour of equal value.

[2] In our trade example we needed only three countries and three products, apples, blankets, and coal to illustrate our problems of multilateralism. In this factor example we need three countries and four factors, land, capital, skilled labour, and unskilled labour. The apparent paradox is resolved when we consider that in the trade case we were thinking of the best way of applying three transportable products (apples, blankets, and coal) to an immobile set of consumers within each country, while in this case we are considering how best to apply three mobile factors (capital, skilled labour, and unskilled labour) to an immobile amount of land within each country.

the world as a whole is endowed with 3,000 units of each of these factors. Let us suppose further that for the reasons discussed in Chapters XXI–XXIII free trade in the products of the factors does not suffice to equalize the marginal product of each factor in all the trading countries. The maximization of world production involves the international movement of the factors of production from countries of low to countries of high marginal productivity. Let us suppose further that land is immobile and that the maximization of production requires that factor proportions should be the same in every country. Then if we start with an initial endowment of factors such as that given in Table XXXV, production can be maximized only if 100 units of capital move from A to C, 100 units of skilled labour from B to A, and 100 units of unskilled labour from C to B.

This is a possible example of a purely multilateral movement of factors which is needed for the maximization of world production. But since in the case of factor movements there is no balance-of-payments requirement that the inflow of factors into any country should equal the outflow from that country, there is no logical restriction on the patterns of flows of factors which may be desirable in order to maximize production. One country might have to face an outflow (or an inflow) of all the mobile factors simultaneously. But it is clear that in a world of many factors and many countries the optimum pattern of factor movements may involve many 'multilateral' flows.

CHAPTER XXXI

THE PARTIAL FREEING OF TRADE : (1) UNILATERAL TARIFF REDUCTIONS

In this chapter we intend to discuss certain problems connected with the unilateral reduction of barriers to trade by the authorities in one country in a world in which there are a number of other countries whose authorities maintain an existing structure of trade barriers unchanged. For the sake of simplicity we will suppose that there are only three countries in the world, A (the country whose authorities make a unilateral reduction in its trade barriers) and B and C (the other countries of the world whose authorities maintain unchanged an existing structure of barriers to their trade with A and with each other).

For many purposes a unilateral reduction by A's authorities of barriers to trade with B and C can be treated by the methods which were developed in Part II in the consideration of a two-country world. A can be regarded as one of the two countries and B-C, i.e. the rest of the world, as the other of the two countries. Thus if we are concerned with the effect of the reduction of a duty on imports into A from B and C upon the distribution of income between A on the one hand and B-C on the other or upon the distribution of income within A or B and C, we can use with little or no modification the analysis developed in Chapters XVII and XVIII in Part I.

Thus a reduction of A's barriers to trade with B and C is likely to increase the demand in A for the products of B and C and/or to increase in B and C the supply of the products of A. The price at which traders in B and C will be willing to supply exports to A is likely to be somewhat raised and the price at which they will be willing to take imports from A is likely to be somewhat lowered. The terms of trade will turn against A. There will be some redistribution of real income from the citizens of A to the citizens of B and C.

The reduction by A's authorities of a barrier to trade with B and C is likely to cause some change in the relative prices which producers in A can obtain for the products which compete with imports in A and for the products which are exported from A. The more normal case is perhaps where a larger flow of imports on to A's domestic market and a larger flow of exports out of A's domestic market will cause the price offered to A's producers for products which compete with imports to fall relatively to the price offered for exportable products. In this case there will within A be some redistribution of income away from the factors which are specially adapted to produce import-competing products and in favour of the factors which are specially adapted to produce exportable products.[1]

If the effects of a unilateral reduction of trade barriers by A upon economic welfare are to be finally assessed, these effects upon the international and domestic redistributions of income must be taken into account. But as they do not differ essentially from those discussed in our previous discussion of the two-country world, we shall neglect them in this chapter. It is our present intention to consider certain special features of the efficiency, as opposed to the equity, aspects of a unilateral reduction of trade barriers—features which are essentially due to the fact that there are more than two countries each of which has its own apparatus of trade controls.

Accordingly we will assume that the same distributional weights are allotted to marginal changes of income for all recipients of income in all countries. Welfare is unaffected by any small redistribution of a given world income. We are concerned only with the effect of the unilateral reduction of A's trade barriers upon the size of world income. We shall also assume that within each country there are no divergences between marginal social values and costs. On the other hand each country maintains non-discriminatory import duties on its imports from the other two countries. Thus while there are no divergences between marginal values and costs in production in any one country for consumption in that same country, marginal value does exceed marginal cost when production is undertaken in one country for consumption in another.[2] We can therefore proceed upon the basis that anything which leads to a shift from domestic trade to international trade will help to increase economic welfare, because (i) marginal values are no higher than marginal costs in respect of the domestic trade which is lost, (ii) marginal values are higher than marginal costs in respect of the

[1] From Chapter XVIII (pp. 291–295) it can be seen that if the elasticity of demand for imports from A in the rest of the world (i.e. B-C) were sufficiently low, the terms of trade might move so much against A that even in A's own domestic market the price offered for A's exportable products fell relatively to the price offered for A's import-competing products. In this case the effect upon the distribution of income within A would be the opposite to that mentioned in the text.

[2] This unreal assumption greatly simplifies our argument. But the basic form of the argument would remain even if this assumption were removed. We shall be arguing that anything which helps to increase trade between B and C at the expense of trade within B or within C will help to raise economic welfare because marginal values are no greater than marginal costs in the case of domestic trade whereas they are greater than marginal costs by the amount of the import duty in the case of international trade. But even if marginal values do exceed marginal costs in the case of domestic trade, the basic argument remains unchanged so long as the import duties are the cause of additional divergences between marginal values and costs which affect international but not domestic trade. So long as the rate of divergence between marginal values and marginal costs is likely for this reason to be higher in international than in domestic trade, the basic arguments of this chapter remain valid.

international trade which is encouraged, and (iii) distributional weights are the same for all recipients of income, so that any redistribution of income which incidentally takes place has no effect upon economic welfare.

Let us suppose that in these conditions the authorities in A reduce their non-discriminatory duties on imports from B and C, the authorities in B and C keeping their non-discriminatory duties on imports unchanged. The immediate effect of this will be to lead to a larger quantity of imports into A from B and C. The preservation of equilibrium in A's balance of payments will mean that some further readjustments must take place in A's trade. The strain on A's balance of payments due to the freer inflow of imports into A will cause the prices of A's products to fall relatively to the prices of the products of B and C either through a depreciation of the foreign-exchange value of A's currency or through a flow of gold from A to B and to C with consequential deflation of prices in A and inflation of prices in B and C. These changes will somewhat restrain the increase of imports into A and will stimulate A's exports to B and C. In the normal case the ultimate effect of the reduction of A's tariff will be an increase in the volume of A's imports from B and C, and an increase in the volume of A's exports to B and C in payment for the larger volume of imports purchased at rather worse terms of trade.[1]

Now there will be a gain in economic welfare on what—modifying somewhat the terminology employed in Chapter XIII—may be called the 'primary' increase in trade, namely, the increased imports and exports of A caused by the reduction of A's trade barriers. This gain will be large if:

(i) the elasticities of demand in A for imports from B and C and in B and C for imports from A are large, so that there is a large increase in these two volumes of international trade;

(ii) the rate of duty in A on the imports which are now more freely admitted into A was itself at a high initial level so that there was a large divergence between marginal value and marginal cost in the case of this expanded import trade; and

(iii) the rates of duty in B and C on the type of A's exports which are expanded to keep A's balance of payments in balance are also high, so that there is a large divergence between marginal value and marginal cost in the case of A's increased exports.

[1] For the reasons discussed in Chapter XVIII (pp. 291–295) it is possible that if the elasticity of demand for A's exports in B and C is sufficiently low the final result of the reduction in A's tariff will be an increase in the volume of A's exports to B and C in payment for a *decreased* volume of A's imports from B and C, acquired at very much worse terms of trade. In this case all that is said in the rest of this chapter about the indirect effects upon welfare of the *increase* in A's imports would have to be reversed and related to the indirect effects upon welfare of the *decrease* in A's imports. The reader is left to do this for himself.

But this primary gain in economic welfare may be reinforced by a secondary gain in economic welfare due to an indirect encouragement to the trade between B and C on which also there is a divergence between marginal values and costs due to import duties imposed on each other's product by the authorities in B and C. Alternatively, the gain in economic welfare due to the primary increase in A's trade with B and C might in part or in whole be offset by a secondary loss in economic welfare due to the indirect effects of the primary change in discouraging trade between B and C on which there is a divergence between marginal values and costs. What we must next consider is the way in which the change in A's import duty may affect trade between B and C.

If the authorities in A make a general non-discriminatory reduction in A's duties on all imports from all countries, the strong presumption is that A's imports will be increased both from B and from C. There is also a strong probability that the increase in A's exports which will have to take place to keep A's balance of payments in equilibrium will take the form partly of an increase in exports to B and partly of an increase in exports to C. Accordingly, we shall proceed as follows. We shall consider in some detail the possible 'secondary' effects[1] upon the desire of B's citizens to trade with C of an increase in A's imports from B and of an increase in A's exports to B. We can then allow for the fact that there are corresponding possible secondary effects of A's increased trade with C upon the desire of C's citizens to trade with B. The secondary changes in trade between B and C, whose effect upon economic welfare we must take into account in making a final assessment of the desirability of A's unilateral tariff reduction, will be the result of these two sets of forces in B and in C.

Let us then first consider the effect upon the incentives of B's citizens to trade with C of A's increased demand for imports from B. We will enumerate the conditions in which there is most likely to be a reduction in B's trade with C. Suppose that the products which A imports in greater quantity from B and of which there is now a greater scarcity in B are close substitutes in B for products which B exports to C. There will then be some reduction in the volume of B's exports to C.

This is most obviously the case when the products which B now sells in greater quantity to A are identically the same as products which B sells also to C; then the increased demand in A for these products (due to the reduction in A's tariff on them) will divert B's supplies from C's market to A's market. But the same is true if the products which B sells to A are only close substitutes either in B's consumption or in B's production with the products which B sells to C. When A's demand for certain of B's products is increased because of the reduction in A's duty

[1] For the meaning of the term 'secondary' in this context the reader is referred to Chapter XIII, p. 203.

on them, the price of these products in B's market will be driven up. This will divert the demand of consumers in B away from these products on to any close substitutes for these products; and if B's exports to C are among the close substitutes for these products, there will be an increased consumption in B itself of products which were previously exported to C and thus there will be a reduction in B's exports to C. The rise in the price in B of the products which are now in greater demand in A will at the same time encourage the production in B of these products at the expense of other products which employ the sort of factors of production which are needed to produce the additional exports for A's market (i.e. at the expense of products which are good substitutes in production in B for the products exported to A). Now if B's exports to C are among those products which require for their manufacture the same factors as are required for the manufacture of B's exports to A, then there will once again be a reduction in the supply of B's exports to C when A's demand for B's exports is raised.

Another case in which an increased import into A from B might reduce B's trade with C would be where the products imported into A were in B's consumption or production complementary with products imported into B from C. A imports more cups from B; there is a shortage of cups in B so that B's citizens require less saucers, which happen to be imported from C. Then an increase in A's demand for B's cups causes a reduction in B's demand for C's saucers. Or A imports more mutton from B; there is in consequence an increased production in B of sheep and so of wool, which B imports from C. Once again an increase in A's demand for B's mutton causes a reduction in B's demand for C's wool.

Similar considerations will determine the effect of A's increased exports to B upon the desire of B's citizens to trade with C. If A's exports to B are good substitutes in B's consumption or production for things which B imports from C, then there is likely to be a secondary reduction in B's imports from C. A exports more apples to B; and as a result the price of apples falls in B. B's consumers shift to the consumption of apples away from the consumption of pears which are a close substitute for apples in their consumption and which happen to be imported from C. Or else B's producers shift from the production of apples in B to the production of cherries in B (which can be produced easily on the land previously used to produce apples), thus reducing the demand for imported cherries from C.

A secondary reduction in B's trade with C would also take place if A's exports to B were complementary in B's consumption or production with products which B exports to C. Thus A exports more ink to B, which encourages writing in B, so that B's citizens consume more pens which were previously being exported from B to C. Or A exports more coke to B, so that less coke is produced in B. In consequence less gas is produced in B for export to C.

Such are the relationships in B between the products which A trades with B and the products which B trades with C which are most likely to cause an increase in B's trade with A to lead to a decrease in B's trade with C. But the relationships might just as well be reversed, in which case an increase in A's trade with B would lead to an increase in B's trade with C. If A's imports from B are good substitutes in B for the things which B imports from C or are complementary in B with the products which B exports to C, then an increase in A's imports from B would stimulate B's trade with C. Similarly, if A's exports to B are good substitutes in B for the things which B exports to C or are complementary in B with the products which B imports from C, then an increase in A's exports to B will stimulate B's trade with C.

If we remember that similar relationships are possible between A's increased trade with C and the willingness of C's citizens to trade with B, that B's imports from C are the same as C's exports to B, and that B's exports to C are C's imports from B, we can generalize the relationship in the following way. A primary increase in A's imports from B and C and her exports to B and C is the more likely to cause a secondary decrease in the trade between B and C:

(i) if A's imports are good substitutes in B or are complementary in C with the products which are exported from B to C;
(ii) if A's imports are complementary in B or are good substitutes in C with the products which are exported from C to B;
(iii) if A's exports are good substitutes in B or complementary in C with the products which are exported from C to B; and
(iv) if A's exports are complementary in B or good substitutes in C with the products which are exported from B to C.

In so far as the relationships are of this kind a primary increase in the foreign trade of A will lead to a secondary contraction in the trade between B and C, and in so far as they are the opposite to this a primary increase in A's foreign trade will lead to a secondary expansion in the trade between B and C.[1]

Let us first of all consider the case where the four relationships just mentioned are of a kind to cause negligible net secondary effects in the trade between B and C. In such a case a unilateral reduction of A's

[1] In the rest of this chapter we shall neglect the possible need for tertiary adjustments in trade due to the fact that even though A's balance of payments is in equilibrium, the result of the changes may be to leave B in deficit and C in surplus in its balance of payments. There may then have to follow some fall of B's prices relatively to C's which will reduce C's export trade and B's import trade and increase C's import trade and B's export trade. The welfare effects of these adjustments ought to be taken into account in the final sum. But they are perhaps unlikely to affect the issue very much one way or the other. See the argument developed in Chapter XIII (pp. 217–223).

duties is bound to be favourable to economic welfare. It will cause a primary increase in trade on which there is an excess of marginal values over marginal costs (because of the trade taxes) without any adverse secondary repercussions. Indeed, in the interests of world economic welfare A's authorities would have not merely to remove their barriers on imports but even to subsidize A's imports from B and C. The reason for this is the existence of import duties in B and C on their imports from A. If A increases a subsidy on imports from B and C, this is to encourage further a trade on which there is already some loss of economic welfare, because the existing rate of subsidy on A's imports from B and C means that the marginal value of the imports in A's market is already lower than their marginal cost in B's and C's markets. But the increase in imports into A must be paid for by increased exports from A to B and C; in so far as these products are subject to import duties in B and C there will be a gain of economic welfare in this expansion of A's export trade. If the terms of trade remained unchanged, so that to preserve equilibrium in the balance of payments the increase in the volume of A's exports to B and C had to be equal at current prices to the increase in the volume of A's imports from B and C, then the loss of welfare on an increase in subsidized imports into A would only be as great as the gain of welfare on the corresponding increase in taxed exports from A if the rate of excess of marginal cost over marginal value in the case of the imports were as great as the rate of excess of marginal value over marginal cost in the case of the exports. In other words, the rate of subsidy on imports would have to be raised as high as the rate of tax on exports in order to maximize welfare. The real rate of tax on trade between A and the rest of the world is a compound of A's tax on the trade and the tax imposed by the rest of the world on the trade. The nearest approach to free trade, in the absence of action by the authorities in the rest of the world, is that A's authorities should pay a subsidy which just offsets the tax imposed by the other authorities.

Now suppose that the four relationships discussed on p. 518 are such that the secondary repercussion of an increase in A's foreign trade is to stimulate the taxed trade between B and C. *A fortiori* it can now be argued that a unilateral reduction of A's duties is desirable in the interests of world economic welfare. Indeed, A's imports ought now to be subsidized at a rate which not merely offsets the duty raised in B and C on imports from A but which was even higher than this, because of the indirect secondary advantages to be gained in the expansion of trade between B and C resulting from a further expansion of A's trade with B and C.

It follows from all this that rather special conditions must be fulfilled for it to be true that a unilateral reduction of A's import duties is not desirable on grounds of world economic efficiency. For this to be so the four relationships discussed on p. 518 must clearly be of a kind which cause there to be a secondary contraction of the trade between B and C; and the loss from this secondary contraction of trade between B and C must be sufficiently great to outweigh the gain in economic welfare to be derived not only from the increased imports of A from B and C but also from the increased exports of A to B and C. This is the more likely to be the case:

(i) the more nearly the four conditions discussed on p. 518 conform to those required to cause a secondary contraction of trade between B and C;

(ii) the higher is the *ad valorem* rate of duty levied in B and C on the sort of products which they import from each other (i.e. the larger the loss in economic welfare on each unit of secondary trade which is lost);

(iii) the lower the rate of the import duty in A which is in the process of reduction (i.e. the smaller the gain in economic welfare on each unit of primary import trade which is gained); and

(iv) finally—what is not always remembered—the lower the rates of the import duties levied in B and C on the sort of goods which they import from A (i.e. the smaller the gain in economic welfare on each unit of primary export trade which is gained).[1]

[1] Dr. S. A. Ozga of the London School of Economics has by means of a rather different technique of analysis also reached the conclusion that even a non-discriminating reduction of duties by one country in a many-country world may represent a movement away from, rather than towards, the free-trade position.

CHAPTER XXXII

THE PARTIAL FREEING OF TRADE: (2) DISCRIMINATORY AND PREFERENTIAL TARIFF REDUCTIONS

IN the preceding chapter we discussed the effect upon economic welfare of a unilateral non-discriminatory reduction in A's import duties when the rest of the world is made up not of one country but of a number of other countries, B, C, etc. In this chapter we wish to discuss the effect upon economic welfare of a unilateral discriminatory reduction in A's duties on, say, imports from B without a corresponding reduction in duties on imports from the rest of the world—which may be constituted either of a single third country C or of a number of other countries, C, D, E, etc. This analysis can, however, readily be extended to cover the case where A's discriminatory reduction in duties on imports from B is accompanied by a discriminatory reduction of B's duties on imports from A. In other words, the analysis can be applied to the problem of the formation of a preferential trading area or, in the extreme case, a full customs union between a limited number of trading countries.

In order to isolate certain particular issues for examination we shall make three basic assumptions in this chapter. First, we assume that the distributional weight attached by the policy-makers to the income of each citizen is the same for every citizen regardless of the country in which he resides or the source of his income. In other words, we shall be concerned with the problem of economic efficiency and not of economic equity; and we shall be looking at it from an international point of view and not from the point of view of the interests solely of the countries which give each other preferential treatment or of any other limited group of countries.

Second, we shall assume that within each country a policy of modified laissez-faire is successfully adopted so that there are no divergences between marginal social values and marginal social costs in the domestic trade of any country. This means that no marginal changes in domestic trade which are caused by any change in duties on international trade will add anything to, or subtract anything from, total economic welfare. Changes in domestic trade may be omitted from our calculus of gain and loss.

Third, we shall assume that there are taxes but no subsidies on various parts of the trade in products between the various countries. This means that anything which leads to an expansion of these elements of international trade will add to economic welfare, whereas anything which causes these elements of international trade to contract will reduce economic welfare.

Let us start with the simplest possible case of a three-country world in which the authorities in A make a small reduction in A's duties on certain imports from B without any change in the level of A's duties levied on imports from C. We want to know whether, on the three basic assumptions mentioned in the last paragraph, this is likely to lead to an increase or to a decrease in economic welfare.

The analysis which is necessary to answer this question is merely a particular application of the analysis which we have already carried out at great length in Chapter XIII. Accordingly in this chapter we shall not develop the analysis in great detail, but will merely refer to the ways in which the analysis may be applied in the present three-country case. As was pointed out in Chapter XIII, we may take it for granted that the reduction in the duty on A's imports of, say, blankets from B will cause a primary increase in economic welfare because it will increase the amount of blankets sent from B to A on which there is an excess of marginal value over marginal cost equal to the existing rate of tax on the trade. This primary gain will be the greater, (i) the greater is the expansion in the volume of trade caused by the reduction in the duty (i.e. the greater are the elasticities of A's demand for imported blankets and of B's supply of exported blankets), and (ii) the greater is the initial rate of duty on the trade and so the greater is the initial excess of marginal value over marginal cost in this trade.

But, as was argued in Chapter XIII, there may be important secondary repercussions on the flows of international trade resulting from the primary increase in the export of blankets from B to A. These possibilities may be enumerated under the following eight heads.

(1) A's imported blankets may compete very closely in A's markets with some other imports of A, in which case there will be some secondary reduction in A's imports of these competing products.

(2) A's imported blankets may be complementary in A's markets with some other imports of A, in which case there will be some secondary increase in A's imports of these complementary products.

(3) A's imported blankets may compete in A's markets with products which A exports, in which case there will be some secondary increase in the export of these products from A.

(4) A's imported blankets may be complementary in A's markets with products which A exports, in which case there will be some secondary reduction in the amount of these products which A exports.

(5) B's exported blankets may compete in B's markets with other products which B exports, in which case there will be some secondary reduction in B's exports of these other products.

(6) B's exported blankets may be complementary in B's markets

with other products which B exports, in which case there will be some secondary increase in B's exports of these other products.

(7) B's exported blankets may compete in B's markets with some products which B imports, in which case there will be some secondary increase in B's imports of these competing products.

(8) B's exported blankets may be complementary in B's markets with some products which B imports, in which case there will be some secondary decrease in B's imports of these complementary products.

Now there is only one formal difference between the analysis of the problem discussed in Chapter XIII and the analysis of the problem under discussion in this chapter. In the former case all the secondary repercussions on A's trade (items 1–4 above) were necessarily secondary repercussions on A's imports from B or on A's exports to B; but in the present case these secondary repercussions on A's trade may be secondary repercussions on A's imports from C as well as from B or on A's exports to C as well as to B. Similarly, the secondary repercussions on B's trade (items 5–8) may now fall upon B's import or export trade with C as well as upon her import or export trade with A. But the principle is exactly the same. We must add to the gain of economic welfare from the primary increase of trade any secondary gain due to a secondary increase in A's or B's import or export trade either with each other or with C and we must deduct any secondary loss due to a secondary decrease in A's or B's import or export trade either with each other or with C.

But the fact that we are now dealing with a reduction of a duty by A which applies to B's products and not to C's products may considerably affect the type of secondary repercussion which will in fact take place in A's and B's trade. If A imports, as she may well do, some of the product concerned from C as well as from B, then A's imports from C may be practically perfect substitutes for A's imports from B. If, then, A's authorities reduce a duty on imports of B's products without reducing the corresponding duty on the import of identical or very closely substitutable products from C, a large part of the effect of the tariff reduction will be merely to divert A's imports from purchase in C's to purchase in B's market. There would be a large element of secondary import trade destruction in A (item 1 in the list on p. 522).

Exactly similar considerations may be applied to B's exports. B may well export the same product to C as well as to A. The reduction in A's import duty on B's products without any corresponding reduction in C's import duty on B's product might well have a major effect in diverting B's exports away from sale in C's markets to sale in A's markets. In so far as this is likely to be the normal case it much increases the chance that the main secondary repercussion in B will be one of secondary export trade destruction (item 5 in the list on p. 522).

Now it is not possible to lay down any *a priori* principle on these matters. Each case needs special consideration to determine its probable secondary repercussions. It might be that a reduction in the United Kingdom's duty on French wines (all other duties, including duties on other wines, remaining constant) would have a marked effect by increasing the total supply of wine in the United Kingdom in shifting consumers in the United Kingdom away from the consumption of whiskey on to that of wine, thus releasing more whiskey for export from the United Kingdom to the United States. And it might at the same time be the case that in France the export of additional quantities of wine made wine scarcer in France and caused the French consumer to shift to the consumption of beer, thus stimulating the import of German beer into France. In this case the secondary gains from the United Kingdom's additional exports of whiskey (item 3) and from France's additional imports of beer (item 7 in the list on pp. 522–523) would have to be taken into account.

But a more probable and direct reaction might be that the lowered duty on French wines, while it caused some net increase in the consumption of wine in the United Kingdom, to a very large extent merely caused people to purchase French wines instead of, say, German wines. In France it may very well be that wines are sold to the United States as well as to the United Kingdom. A reduction in the duty in the United Kingdom market may induce the French wine merchants to increase their total export of wine to some extent; but a more marked effect may be that they now have an inducement to sell their wines in the United Kingdom rather than in the United States. In this case there might be a marked secondary loss of economic welfare due to the secondary decrease in the United Kingdom's imports of German wine (item 1) and the second decrease in France's exports of wine to the United States (item 5 on the list on p. 522).

Consider a three-country world made up of countries A, B, and C, in which A reduces a duty on blankets from B without reducing her duties on any other products. Then in order to get the extreme case of secondary import trade destruction which we have just examined we must assume that A imports blankets from C as well as from B. And in order to get the extreme case of secondary export trade destruction we must simultaneously assume that B exports blankets to C as well as to A. In this case C would be importing blankets from B and exporting them to A, which might appear improbable. Indeed, it would be an impossible situation if C were a single country with no problems of transport cost. But if we allow for the fact that C, the rest of the world, may stand for many countries or at least for many regions between which there are important and differing costs of transport, the proposition is not so unrealistic. Indeed, if the United Kingdom is an importer of wines it is most probable that she will import some from other countries (say, Germany) as well as from France; and if France is an exporter of wines, it is most probable that she will export them to other countries (such as the United States) as well as to the United Kingdom.

But this consideration does suggest one important way in which the secondary loss of economic welfare due to this secondary destruction of import trade in A and of export trade in B may itself in turn be mitigated by a series of secondary secondary repercussions. To revert to the particular example which we have just used, if the United Kingdom reduces discriminatorily a duty on French wines, this may divert United Kingdom imports away from German wines on to French wines; and it may divert French wine exports away from the United States to the United Kingdom market. But this leaves the United States citizens short of wine and the German wine merchants looking for markets for wine. The obvious result may be a secondary secondary stimulation of the export of wine from Germany to the United States.[1] We would then have:

(1) an increased sale of French wine to the United Kingdom;
(2) a decreased sale of German wine to the United Kingdom;
(3) a decreased sale of French wine to the United States; and
(4) an increased sale of German wine to the United States.

If all the trade flows are subject to duties, then there is a gain on elements 1 and 4 above and a loss on elements 2 and 3. The amount of gain and loss will depend upon the size of the change of trade in each of these four cases and upon the rate of divergence between marginal value and cost (i.e. the rate of duty levied) in each case. But it is quite clear that the change might lead to a net loss of economic welfare.

Let us take a case in which there is likely to be a large net loss of economic welfare. Suppose that there are no initial duties in the trade between Germany and the United States, which are merely different regions of one large pre-existing free-trade area—our single country C. Then there is no gain from any series of marginal increments in the trade between Germany and the United States, because there is no

[1] While this is the most probable form of the secondary secondary reaction it is by no means the only possible one. The United States might be exporting some commodity to Germany (say, beer) which both in Germany and the United States was a close substitute for wine. The shortage of wine in the United States might encourage the consumption of beer there and so reduce the United States exports of beer, and the glut of wine in Germany might discourage the consumption and import of beer there. In this case the secondary secondary repercussion might take the form of a *reduction* in the flow of beer from the United States to Germany instead of an *increased* flow of wine from Germany to the United States. If this were so and if the beer were subject to an export duty in the United States or an import duty in Germany, it would lead to a secondary secondary loss of economic welfare, since there would be a reduction of the trade in beer in which, because of the duty, the marginal value in Germany exceeded the marginal cost in the United States.

divergence between marginal costs and values in such trade. There is no gain from element 4 above. But suppose at the same time that the reduction in the United Kingdom's duty on French wine causes a little, but very little, expansion in the total export of French wines or in the total import of wine into the United Kingdom. It causes primarily a shift of United Kingdom imports from German to French wines and of French exports from the United States to the United Kingdom market. Then each of elements 2 and 3 above taken separately is almost as large as element 1. The secondary destruction of trade is almost twice as large as the primary creation of trade, since for each additional bottle of wine sent from France to the United Kingdom, one less is sent from France to the United States and one less from Germany to the United Kingdom. If the initial rates of duty, and so the rates of divergence between marginal values and costs, were the same on all these three channels of trade, the secondary loss of economic welfare would be almost twice as large as the primary gain.

But in other cases the discriminatory reduction of the United Kingdom's duty on French wines might well increase total economic welfare. This would be the case where there was quite a large increase in the total import of wine into the United Kingdom (because the reduced duty on imported French wine made it compete much better with home-made drinks in the United Kingdom) and quite a large increase in the total export of wine from France (because the reduced difficulty of selling in the United Kingdom market expanded the domestic production or restricted the domestic consumption of wine in France). In this case element 1 on p. 525 would be considerably greater than element 2 or 3 taken separately. Suppose at the same time that the reduced sale of French wine in the United States is almost entirely replaced by an increased sale of German wine in the United States (element 4 on p. 525 is almost as great as element 3), and that there are duties on the trade between the United States and Germany of about the same level as between the other countries. Then the gain from element 4 would almost offset the loss from element 3; and the gain from element 1 would be much greater than the loss from element 2. There might be a substantial net gain.[1]

[1] In order to make a complete account of the effects of the reduction of a particular duty by one country upon economic welfare, one ought properly to take into account the tertiary changes in the flows of trade. It is almost certain that the combined primary and secondary changes will leave some countries with a deficit and some with a surplus on the balance of payments. The deficit countries will then have to reduce their money prices, costs, and incomes relatively to those of the surplus countries either by a depreciation of the exchange value of the currencies of the deficit countries in terms of those of the surplus countries or by an internal deflation in the deficit and inflation in the surplus countries. This will expand the exports and contract the imports of the deficit countries. Allowance should be made for the effect of these adjustments on economic welfare, since to the extent that the trade is taxed and therefore

All this analysis can be applied very directly to the case of a mutual preferential reduction of duties on the trade between the members of a limited group of countries. Suppose that the authorities of countries A, B, and C all agree to reduce their import duties on each other's products without any reduction of the duties which they levy on imports from outside countries D, E, and F. Is such an arrangement likely to lead to a net improvement or a net worsening of world economic efficiency? The following is a list of the considerations which will determine the answer to this question.

(1) First, there is more likely to be a net increase in economic welfare if the initial rates of duty (and so the initial excesses of marginal values over marginal costs) were high in the case of the trade between A, B, and C which is now allowed to flow with greater freedom.

(2) Second, there is more likely to be a net increase in economic welfare if the elasticities of the demands for the imports on which the duties are reduced are very high in each of the members of the preferential group, A, B, and C, provided that these high elasticities of demand for imports are due to the fact that these imports compete closely with other home-produced products in these member countries, A, B, and C. In such a case there is likely to be a relatively large expansion in the volume of trade in these commodities between the member countries A, B, and C without anything like so large a diversion of imports into A, B, and C away from purchases in the outside world on to purchases from within the preferential area. But if the elasticities of demands for imports of the products on which the duties are reduced are high in the member countries A, B, and C simply because they compete largely with similar imports from outside countries D, E, and F, then the large primary expansion of the trade between A, B, and C will be offset by an almost equally large secondary reduction in imports into A, B, and C from D, E, and F.

(3) Third, in a similar way there is more likely to be a net increase in economic welfare if in the case of the products on which the duties are reduced the elasticities of supply of exports from countries A, B, and C to each other are high, provided that this is due to the fact that these products compete with other lines of home production in A, B,

---

subject to an excess of marginal value over marginal cost the expansion of the exports of the deficit countries will increase economic welfare and the contraction of the exports of the deficit countries will reduce economic welfare. But there is no reason to believe that these tertiary adjustments will have a very significant effect upon economic welfare unless there is special reason to think *either* (i) that in the adjustment of the balances of payments the expansion of the exports of the deficit countries will be of a different order of magnitude than the contraction of their imports, *or else* (ii) that the rates of duty and so the rates of divergence between marginal values and costs which apply to the exports of the deficit countries are very different from the rates which apply to their imports. (See Chapter XIII, pp. 218–223.)

and C and not merely to the fact that they can now be sold in smaller volume in the other export markets of D, E, and F.

(4) Fourth, there is more likely to be a net increase in economic welfare if the rates of duty (and so the excess of marginal values over marginal costs) are low in the case of the trade between A, B, or C on the one hand and D, E, or F on the other hand in the products on which A, B, and C have reduced their duties to each other. For, as we have seen, there is in the case of these products likely to be some diversion of imports to A, B, and C away from sources of supply in D, E, and F on to sources of supply within A, B, and C; and there is likely to be some diversion of exports from A, B, and C away from sales to D, E, and F towards sales within A, B, and C. On this diverted trade there will be a loss of welfare; but the loss will be the smaller, the smaller is the rate of duty and so the excess of marginal value over marginal cost in this trade.

(5) There is more likely to be a net increase in economic welfare if each member of the preferential group, A, B, C, reduces its duties on the import of those products of which the other members of the group are its principal suppliers and/or for which it provides the principal outlet for the exports of the other members. In this case there will be only a small amount of trade between A, B, and C on the one hand and D, E, and F on the other which is capable of being directly diverted from the preferential tariff reductions within A, B, and C.

(6) There is more likely to be a net increase in economic welfare if the elasticity of demand for imports in D, E, and F and the elasticity of supply of exports from D, E, and F is low in the case of those products on which A, B, and C reduce their duties on a preferential basis. An inelasticity of the supply of exports or of the demand for imports of these products in D, E, and F will mean that there is not so great a reduction in the amount of the trade in the products between A, B, C on the one hand and D, E, F on the other. There will thus be less loss from secondary trade destruction.

(7) There is more likely to be a net increase in economic welfare if the rates of duty are high on the trade between D, E, and F in the case of those products on which A, B, and C grant each other preferential reductions of duty. For, as we have seen (p. 525), any secondary reduction in the trade in these products between A, B, C on the one hand and D, E, F on the other is likely to cause a secondary secondary increase in the trade in these products between D, E, and F. The higher are the rates of duty on this trade (i.e. the greater the excess of marginal values over marginal costs in this trade), the greater the contribution to economic welfare caused by any given stimulation of this trade.

The arguments which are developed in the preceding paragraphs strictly apply only to the effects of small marginal changes in rates of duty. If the seven conditions listed above are favourable, this means that, given the initial rates of all duties and the other relevant circumstances, a small marginal reduction of the duties under examination would increase rather than decrease economic welfare. But the analysis can be extended to cover the case of large structural changes in trade taxes.

Let us consider the most extreme example of this, namely the formation of a complete customs union between our countries A, B, and C. Starting from a given structure of duties, including substantial duties on the trade between A, B, and C, these three countries decide totally to remove all duties on the trade between themselves without altering at all the duties levied on imports from other countries, D, E, and F.[1]

This large change in the structure of their import duties can be examined as if it took place by a number of successive small changes. Suppose A, B, and C all had duties initially of 100 per cent on all the products which they imported from each other. They then abolish these duties, all other duties remaining unchanged. The effect of this on economic welfare can be regarded as the sum of the effects of 100 successive marginal adjustments, in the first of which all these duties were reduced from 100 to 99 per cent, in the second of which they were reduced from 99 to 98 per cent, and so on until the duties have disappeared.

Now if the seven conditions mentioned on pp. 527–528 are initially favourable, then the early stages in this successive reduction in the duties on trade between A, B, and C will add to economic welfare; and if the seven conditions remain favourable throughout the process of removal of the duties, the final full customs union will increase economic welfare. Conversely the seven conditions may be initially unfavourable and may remain unfavourable throughout the successive stages of reductions of duties by A, B, and C. In such a case the formation of the customs union clearly reduces economic welfare.

[1] The arrangement described in the text might perhaps be more appropriately described as a 'free-trade area' rather than as a 'customs union', since A, B, and C are not assumed to have drawn up a common tariff schedule for their imports from the outside countries, D, E, and F. The free-trade area has its own peculiar administrative problems. Thus suppose that initially A has a 50 per cent and B only a 10 per cent duty on imports of, say, drugs, which are a principal export of D. If A and B remove all duties on trade between themselves and leave their duties on imports from D unchanged, then drugs could be imported into B for a 10 per cent duty and from B to A without duty. Unless transport costs were heavy, there would be a strong tendency for importers of drugs in A to purchase them from D *via* B and thus pay an import duty of only 10 per cent instead of 50 per cent on them. Unless further steps are taken or unless transport costs are heavy for these indirect flows of trade, the formation of a free-trade area would tend in effect to reduce the effective rates of duty on imports into the area from outside to the lowest import duty imposed by an individual member of the area on the import of that class of product. This sort of difficulty means that in fact the rules of the free-trade area would not be able to extend the free movement of trade to all products moving between the member countries, but would have to confine it to the free movement between the member countries of products which had been manufactured in those countries.

But there are two rather more complicated cases. First, it might be that initially the seven conditions were unfavourable, so that the early stages of tariff reductions reduced economic welfare; but it is possible that in the later stages the conditions would be favourable, so that the later stages would raise economic welfare again. Now whether or not the formation of a complete customs union would cause a net rise or a net fall in economic welfare in this case would clearly depend upon whether the improvement in economic welfare during the last stages of tariff reduction outweighed the deterioration in economic welfare during the first stages of the process. Second, it is possible that the early stages of tariff reduction would lead to some rise in economic welfare while the later stages would lead to some fall. In this case, to judge the desirability of the complete customs union, one would have to balance the gain from the early stages of tariff reduction against the loss from the later stages.

Now there is very good reason for believing that the first of these two cases is a most improbable one, whereas the second is a very likely case. The reason for this is simple. The reduction of duties on the trade between A, B, and C will cause a direct primary increase in that trade. On this there is a gain in economic welfare. But this primary gain depends upon two factors—the amount of the increase in the trade which is caused by the tariff reduction and the rate of excess of marginal value over marginal cost (i.e. the *ad valorem* rate of duty) on that trade. Now the further we have gone through the stages of reduction of duties on the trade between A, B, and C, the lower will be the existing *ad valorem* rates of duty and so the excesses of marginal value over marginal cost in respect of the primary trade created by further tariff reductions. But there is no such reason why in the later stages of the process any secondary loss should be lower than in the early stages. A secondary loss may result, as we have seen, because A, B, and C may divert their import demands away from the products of D, E, and F when the duties on purchasing among themselves are reduced and may divert their exports away from D, E, and F's markets on to each other's markets when entry into their own markets is made easier. The loss on this diversion of trade in turn depends upon two things—the volume of trade so diverted and the rate of excess of marginal value over marginal cost in respect of the trade. This rate of excess is equal to the *ad valorem* rate of import and export duties in A, B, and C on the one hand and in D, E, and F on the other hand on the trade between these two groups. But *ex hypothesi* these rates are unchanged. Thus as the stages of tariff reduction proceed the gain of economic welfare on any given amount of primary trade creation becomes smaller and smaller, while the loss of economic welfare on any given amount of secondary trade destruction remains unchanged. There is thus very good reason to believe that the earliest stages of the process of tariff reductions in the direction of a customs union will be much more useful in raising (or much less pernicious in reducing) economic welfare than the later stages. A very normal outcome may be that the first stages in the process raise, while the last stages in the process lower, economic welfare.

A very simple illustration may help to make this argument clear, though the reader is asked to remember that the argument is of much wider scope than the following example, which takes a very special simple case merely to illustrate the principle.

Suppose (i) that the United Kingdom is the only consumer of wines, (ii) the consumption of wine in the United Kingdom is quite inelastic so that the total amount consumed is fixed, (iii) the United Kingdom, France, and Germany all produce identically the same wines under conditions of increasing cost, and (iv) that the United Kingdom protects her wine-producing industry by means of a 100 per cent *ad valorem* duty on imports from France and Germany. The United Kingdom then by a process of successive small reductions removes the duty on wines imported from France without altering the duty on wines imported from Germany. It will be noted that we have set a problem in which the gain in economic welfare can be simply measured by the reduction in the cost of producing a given fixed world output of wine. Moreover, we have only to consider two elements: (i) the primary gain due to the fact that French wine production may expand at the expense of the United Kingdom production, which at the margin will be more costly than the French by the amount of the duty on imports of French wines into the United Kingdom; and (ii) the secondary loss due to the fact that the French wine production may expand at the expense of the German, which at the margin will be cheaper to produce than the French by the excess of the United Kingdom duty on German wine over the United Kingdom duty on French wine.

Suppose that the conditions of supply (the elasticities of supply) of wine in Germany and the United Kingdom are such that when the French wine producers are enabled by the reduction of the duty to replace German and United Kingdom producers in the United Kingdom market, the German and United Kingdom production is reduced by the same amount. In other words, when the French put two more bottles on the market the Germans and the United Kingdom producers each put on one less.

Consider now the starting point for the United Kingdom's preferential tariff reduction in favour of France. If United Kingdom production of wine at the margin costs \$100, the French and German production at the margin will cost \$50 in both cases, since \$50 with a 100 per cent *ad valorem* import duty is just equal to the marginal cost of $100 of the domestic wine in the United Kingdom. If now a small reduction in duty enables France to produce two more bottles, one at the expense of German and one at the expense of United Kingdom production, there will be a net saving of cost. One bottle will be produced in France at $50 instead of in the United Kingdom at $100, and on this there is a saving of $50 of cost. The other bottle will be produced in France at $50 instead of in Germany at $50 and on this there is no gain or loss. At the starting point there is therefore pure gain offset by no loss. This is illustrated in row 1 of Table XXXVI.

Suppose now that the United Kingdom duty on French wine has already been reduced to 50 per cent, the duty on German wine remaining at 100 per cent. The production of wine in the United Kingdom and Germany will have been restricted at the expense of an expansion of French production; the marginal cost will have fallen in the United Kingdom and Germany and will have risen in France. These changes in marginal costs must be such that the marginal costs in the United Kingdom must still be 100 per cent higher than in Germany (since there is still a 100 per cent duty on the import of German wine) and they must now be 50 per cent higher than in France (since there is now a 50 per cent duty on the import of French wine). Row 2 of Table XXXVI gives a possible example where the price of wine in the United Kingdom (owing to increased French competition) has fallen to $90 with the marginal cost in Germany having fallen to $45 and in France having risen to $60. Now a further small reduction of duty would still increase economic welfare. If such a reduction enabled two more bottles to be produced in France, one at the expense of United Kingdom and the other at the expense of German production, there would be a saving of cost of $30 on the bottle which was produced in France at a cost of $60 instead of in the United Kingdom at a cost of $90, and against this it would be necessary to set a loss of only $15 on the bottle which was produced in France at $60 instead of in Germany at $45.

Row 3, however, shows a case where the duty on French wine has already been reduced so far (namely to 10 per cent) that any further reduction in it would cause a net loss of economic welfare. The price and marginal cost in the United Kingdom has now fallen to $77 because of the increased competition of French wines; the price and cost in Germany has fallen to $38·5 (since $38·5 plus a duty of 100 per cent is equal to the United Kingdom price of $77); and the price and marginal cost in France has risen to $70 (since $70 plus a duty of 10 per cent is equal to the United Kingdom price of $77). If now a further reduction of the duty on French wines enabled the French to produce two more bottles, one at the expense of the United Kingdom and one at the expense of Germany, there would be a net increase in the total

TABLE XXXVI

A Discriminatory Tariff Reduction

	Ad valorem rate of duty imposed in the United Kingdom on imports of wine from		Domestic price and marginal cost of wine in		
	Germany	France	United Kingdom	Germany	France
	%	%	$	$	$
(1)	100	100	100	50	50
(2)	100	50	90	45	60
(3)	100	10	77	38·5	70
(4)	100	0	75	37·5	75

cost of producing the given output of wine. One more would be produced at $70 in France instead of at $77 in the United Kingdom, a saving of $7; but one more would also be produced in France at $70 instead of in Germany at $38·5, an increase in cost of $31·5. The use of the world's resources would be made less economic by reason of the tariff reduction.

Row 4 of the table simply shows how when the duty on French wines has been wholly removed, there must be a net gain in raising it somewhat again. The price in the United Kingdom is now $75; it must therefore be $37·5 in Germany (on whose wines there is a 100 per cent duty) and $75 in France as well as in the United Kingdom. If the final small reduction in duty to zero increased French output by two bottles at the expense of one bottle in the United Kingdom and one bottle in Germany, then it caused a pure loss offset by no gain. One bottle was produced in France at $75 instead of in the United Kingdom at $75, i.e. without gain or loss; but one bottle was produced in France at $75 instead of in Germany at $37·5, a loss of $37·5.

These considerations suggest that there is more likely to be a case for a partial reduction rather than for a complete elimination of duties on a preferential basis, provided, of course, that in neither case are rates of duties raised against the trade with outsiders when the preferential reductions of duties are made among the member countries. There is, however, one way in which this argument for a system of partial preferences rather than for a full customs union may need to be modified. It has been pointed out[1] that when countries form a full customs union they must automatically reduce all duties on all trade with their partners to zero, whereas in the formation of a partial preferential group they can pick and choose the products on which they will make the tariff reductions as well as the extent to which they will reduce each duty. Now the example which we have just used of the import of German and French wines into the United Kingdom will help to show the distinction between a preferential tariff reduction which is in effect primarily a protective device (which may, therefore, be expected to reduce economic efficiency) and one which is primarily a movement towards free trade (which may be expected to raise economic efficiency). If the main effect of the reduction of the duty in the United Kingdom on French wines is to enable the French producers to undercut the previously protected producers in the United Kingdom, then the reduction of duty will be a significant move towards the most efficient free-trade position in which the low-cost French producers would largely replace the high-cost producers in the United Kingdom. But if the main effect of the reduction in the United Kingdom duty was to enable the French producers who enjoyed the preferential treatment in the United Kingdom to undercut the German producers who did not enjoy this preference, then the preferential tariff reduction would represent in the main a method of protecting the relatively high-cost French industry against competition from the relatively low-cost German industry in the United Kingdom market. Suppose that in return for such a preferential treatment of French wines in the United Kingdom market, the French government agrees to reduce a duty preferentially on some particular United Kingdom product which competes in the French market with similar German products rather than with French products. Then the mutual preferential arrangement between France and the United Kingdom would be essentially an arrangement for increasing the protection of certain industries in the two countries against German competition.

The argument on pp. 531–533 must, therefore, not be taken to represent a straightforward argument in favour of partial preferential arrangements as opposed to a customs union. The argument is more limited in scope. It states merely that if there is a choice between (*a*) a partial preferential reduction of certain duties, and (*b*) the total removal of those same duties on the same discriminatory basis as between countries, then there is a greater chance that course *a* will raise economic welfare than course *b*.[2]

[1] Professor Jacob Viner, *The Customs Union Issue* (New York, Carnegie Endowment for International Peace, 1950), pp. 50–1.

[2] Note that the argument does not maintain that course *a* will do more good than course *b*. On the contrary, circumstances can be imagined in which the

It is of some interest to examine a little more thoroughly this choice of products on which countries might give each other preferential tariff reductions. The first point to note is that any preferential tariff reduction which causes a secondary destruction of trade with outside countries is likely to help to turn the terms of trade in favour of the countries forming the preferential group. Thus suppose that when the United Kingdom reduces a duty on French wines there is a substantial reduction in the United Kingdom's demand for German wines (secondary import trade destruction in the United Kingdom). The reduced demand for German wines will probably cause some reduction in the price at which such wines are sold to the United Kingdom and there will thus be some movement in the terms of trade of the Anglo-French area with Germany. Or suppose that when the United Kingdom reduces its duty on French wines there is a substantial reduction in the amount of wine which the French producers are prepared to continue to send to the United States (secondary export trade destruction in France). The reduced supply of French wines in the United States will probably cause some rise in the price which can be charged for them in that market, and there is thus likely to be some improvement in the terms on which the Anglo-French area can trade with the United States. And conversely any secondary repercussions of a preferential tariff arrangement which caused the members to increase either their demand for imports from the outside world or their exports to the outside world would be liable either to raise the price of what they bought from the outside world or else to lower the price of what they sold to the outside world, and thus to cause a deterioration in their terms of trade with the outside world.

But while trade destruction, whether it be of imports or of exports, is likely to move the terms of trade in favour of the members of the preferential area, secondary import trade destruction and secondary export trade destruction may have very different effects upon the balance of payments of the countries forming the preferential area. Thus, suppose that as a result of a preferential reduction of a duty on French wines the United Kingdom reduces its imports of German wines significantly (secondary import trade destruction). Then the amount spent by the United Kingdom on imports of German products will be reduced, and to this extent there will be an improvement in the balance of payments of the Anglo-French area with the outside world. But suppose that the reduction in the United Kingdom duty on French wines causes the French wine exporters to sell significantly less in the United States

later stages of tariff reduction as well as the earlier stages will raise economic welfare. In this case course *b* will do more good than course *a*. But what is true is that the early stages of preferential tariff reduction are likely to do more good (or less harm) than the later stages.

(secondary export trade destruction). Then, provided that the elasticity of demand for imports of French wines in the United States is greater than unity, the value of French exports to the United States will go down, and the balance of payments of the Anglo-French area with the rest of the world will deteriorate.[1]

If, therefore, a group of countries wish to form a preferential area for the purpose of extending the protection of their own domestic industries, they are most likely to select for preferential tariff reductions those imports from each other of which important supplies are simultaneously imported from the outside world. This is likely to protect the industries of the area from the outside competition of these products, to induce the outside world to trade these products on terms which are more favourable to the members of the preferential area, and by reducing the total expenditure on imports from the outside world to improve the balance of trade of the preferential area with the outside world.

The formation of a preferential area or a full customs union between A, B, and C may therefore turn the terms of trade favourably to ABC and against the outside countries DEF by reducing the demand in ABC for the products of DEF or by reducing the supply in DEF for the products of ABC. But there is a second way in which the formation of a preferential arrangement between A, B, and C—particularly if it takes the form of a full customs union—may improve the terms of trade of ABC; it is likely to increase the bargaining power in trade negotiations of the members of the preferential area with outside countries. Thus, consider the possibility of one member of the area, say A, obtaining a trade concession from an outside country, say D, before the formation of the customs union between A, B, and C. The authorities in A may threaten to raise an import duty on some export of D to A unless the authorities in D grant some concession to A's trade with D. This threat may be of little importance if D can find alternative markets for her exports in other countries. Now if B and C are important alternative markets for D's exports, a joint threat by A, B, and C that the whole ABC customs union will raise its import duty on D's exports unless D makes some concession would clearly be of very much greater weight than a similar threat by A alone.

Similarly with A's exports to D. The authorities in A might threaten D with the imposition of a duty on A's exports to D unless the authorities in D granted some concession on A's trade with D. Even if the export in question is a product which it is essential for D to import, the threat may not be a very grave one if D can import it from other sources

[1] If the elasticity of demand for imports of French wines in the United States is less than unity, then the United States will pay a greater total amount of money for a smaller quantity of imports. In this case secondary export trade destruction will also improve the balance of trade of the preferential area with the outside world.

of supply. Now if B and C were important alternative sources of supply of the import for D, then a threat by the combined customs union ABC to impose a tax on the export of the product in question to D would be a much more serious matter for D and would be much more likely than a threat by A alone to wring some trade concession out of D.

Thus by increasing the bargaining power of the independent constituent members, the formation of a customs union may be the means of inducing outside countries to reduce duties on imports from the constituent members of the customs union (thus raising the price available for their products in the outside world) or to reduce duties on exports of the outside world to the constituent members of the customs union (thus lowering the price payable by them for imports from the outside world).

Moreover, the governments of A, B, and C in combination need have much less hesitation than any one of them alone in raising a duty on imports from D. If A raised a duty on imports from D, exporters in D would be free to sell the products to B and C instead. But if A, B, and C simultaneously raise a duty on the same product, D's alternative markets are much more restricted and there is therefore a much greater chance that D's exporters will have to cut the price at which they sell the product to A, B, and C. Similarly, if A alone imposed an export duty on a product sold to D, D could purchase from B or C instead. But if A, B, and C simultaneously tax the export of this product to D, it is much less easy for D to obtain alternative supplies, and it is, therefore, more probable that importers in D will have to be willing to pay a higher price for imports of the products.

In all these ways the formation of a full customs union between A, B, and C, by enabling them to carry out a single joint commercial policy *vis-à-vis* the rest of the world, is likely to enable them to turn the terms of trade with the rest of the world in their favour. Thus the formation of a preferential area or of a full customs union is likely to do something to redistribute income away from the rest of the world and in favour of the citizens of the preferential area, first, simply by reason of the secondary import or export trade destruction which it may occasion even if the duties levied on trade with outsiders remain unchanged and, second, by increasing the bargaining power of the area *vis-à-vis* the rest of the world so that it can more freely raise its own duties on trade with the outside world and can induce outsiders to reduce their duties on their trade with the area.[1] Whether or not this redistribution in favour

[1] The increased bargaining power of the preferential area will improve the area's terms of trade whether it results in an increase in the duties levied by the area on its trade with outsiders or in a decrease in the duties levied by outsiders on their trade with the area. But from the point of view of efficiency as opposed to equity the two results will, of course, be very different. The former result will raise duties and restrict trade between the area and the outside world; the

of the citizens of the preferential area is to be counted as increasing or decreasing economic welfare will depend upon whether a higher distributional weight should be allotted to the citizens of the preferential area or to those of the outside world.

---

latter result will lower duties and expand trade. They will have opposite effects upon efficiency, there being a strong presumption that the former will reduce and the latter will raise world economic efficiency.

CHAPTER XXXIII

THE PARTIAL REMOVAL OF CONTROLS OVER FACTOR MOVEMENTS

In principle the type of analysis which has been developed in the two preceding chapters to cover the case of partial reductions in barriers to trade in products can be applied to the case of partial reductions in barriers to the international movement of factors of production.

Thus suppose that there are three countries A, B, and C. Suppose that A is very specially rich in land, B in labour, and C in capital. Normally there might be a flow of labour from B to A and to C, and of capital from C to A and to B. But suppose that some barriers had been imposed on these international movements of labour and capital. In such a situation there would be an excess of the marginal value over the marginal cost of labour in the countries of immigration A and C; artificial obstacles to the international movement of labour would keep the wage rate in the countries in which labour was scarce (A and C) above the wage rate in the country in which it was plentiful (B) by more than the real cost of movement, and so the value of the marginal product of labour in A and in C would exceed the value of the marginal product of that labour in B by more than the cost of movement. Economic efficiency would require a larger movement of labour from B into A and C.

Similarly, any artificial obstacle to the movement of capital from C into A and B would mean that the value of the marginal product of capital in A and in B exceeded the value of its marginal product in C by more than the real cost of movement. The maximization of production would require a greater movement of capital from C into A and B.

Now suppose that the authorities in A (but not the authorities in B or C) remove the artificial obstacles to the movement of labour and capital into A. The increased migration of labour from B into A may be in part at the expense of the migration of labour from B to C; and as there is an excess of marginal value over marginal cost in the case of the movement of labour from B to C this will represent a loss of economic welfare which must be set against the gain in economic welfare due to the increased movement of labour from B to A. And similarly, the removal of obstacles in A to the inward movement of capital funds from outside will cause an increased movement of capital from C into A, part of which might be at the expense of a movement of funds from C into B. Since there is an excess of marginal value over marginal cost in the case of capital moving into B from C, the reduction in this movement will cause a loss of economic welfare which must be set against the gain in economic welfare due to the increased flow of capital from C to A.

Now whether the net gain exceeds the net loss in economic welfare in such cases depends upon the same principles as those which have already been discussed in the case of commodity trade in Chapter XXXI (p. 520). There is more likely to be a net gain in economic welfare, (i) the more the flow of labour and capital into A is at the expense of the labour in B (the country of emigration) and of the capital in C (the country which is the lender of capital) and the less it represents a diversion of labour from immigration into C and of capital from investment in B, (ii) the more severe are the initial obstacles to the inward movement of labour and capital into A and so the greater are the excesses of the marginal products of labour and capital in A over their levels in the countries from which they are flowing, and (iii) the less severe are the initial obstacles to the movements of labour and capital between B and C, and the smaller therefore are the excesses of marginal values over marginal costs in the cases of those international factor movements which are likely to suffer a secondary reduction as the result of the removal of A's obstacles.

The above example has been given in the form of a reduction of a barrier in A against the inward movement of factors of production. But while a barrier to the immigration of labour is a usual feature of the real world, in the case of capital the more normal case to find is an exchange or other control which prevents the outward movement of capital. But the above analysis can readily be applied to an outward as well as to an inward movement of a factor.

Thus suppose that B is specially poor in capital and that normally capital funds would flow into B from A and C. But suppose that both A and C impose obstacles to this movement. If then A removes her obstacles to the export of capital, more capital will flow from A to B. But some of this may be offset by a reduced flow of capital from C to B. The loss of economic welfare on this secondary reduction in the flow of capital from C to B must be set against the gain of economic welfare due to the primary increase of capital flow from A to B. The problem is clearly of exactly the same general character as that which we have just examined.

The cases which we have just outlined are cases in which A (but not B or C) adopts a policy of making a general non-discriminatory reduction of barriers to factor movements. Let us next consider a case where A makes a discriminatory reduction of a barrier to a factor movement. To take one simple case, suppose that the authorities in A remove an obstacle to the immigration of labour from B without relaxing an obstacle which exists to the movement of labour from C into

A. We can now enumerate eight possible types of secondary adjustment of international factor movements, which correspond to the eight possible types of reaction enumerated for the case of commodity trade on pp. 522–523.

(1) Labour from B may within A be a close substitute for labour from C, in which case the admittance of more labour from B may reduce the labour flowing from C to A.

(2) Labour from B may be complementary in use within A with capital which flows into A from C, in which case the increase in the B-labour force in A may lead to an increased flow of capital from C to A.

(3) Labour from B may in A's industries be a close substitute for skilled A-labour, which is moving from A to C, in which case the increased supply of B-labour in A will increase the rate of flow of skilled labour from A to C.

(4) Labour from B may be complementary in use in A's industries with capital, which is moving from A to C, in which case the increased supply of B-labour in A will decrease the flow of capital from A to C.

(5) Labour in B may be flowing to C as well as to A, in which case the increased flow to A may reduce the flow to C.

(6) Labour in B may in B's industries be complementary with capital which is flowing from B to C, in which case the decreased supply of labour in B will increase the amount of B's capital available to move to C.

(7) Labour in B may in B's industries be competitive with skilled labour which is flowing into B from C, in which case the greater scarcity of B's labour in B will increase the rate of flow of C's skilled labour into B.

(8) Labour in B may be complementary in B's industries with the use of capital which is flowing in from C, in which case the greater scarcity of labour in B will reduce the rate of flow of C's capital into B.

Any one of these types of secondary repercussion is possible as a consequence of a discriminatory reduction of an obstacle to the migration of labour into A from B. Now if there are obstacles in the way of the movements of labour and capital between C on the one hand and A and B on the other hand, then there will be an excess of marginal values over marginal costs in the case of such movements of factors. Any secondary repercussion, therefore, which results in a reduced flow of factors into or out of C (cases 1, 4, 5, and 8 above) will cause a secondary loss of economic welfare which must be set against the primary gain in economic welfare due to the increased migration of labour from B to A. On the other hand any secondary repercussion (cases 2, 3, 6, and 7) which represents an increased flow of factors into or out of C will represent a further increase in economic welfare which must be added to the improvement in economic welfare due to the primary increase in the migration of labour from B to A.[1]

The formal analysis in the case of partial adjustments of barriers to the international movement of factors of production in a many-country world is thus seen to be exactly similar to that which has been applied in the two preceding chapters to the partial adjustment of barriers to commodity trade. But while the formal analysis is exactly similar it is likely in reality to be very much less important in the case of factor movements than in the case of trade in products. The reason for this is simple. Most controls over factor movements take the form of quantitative controls—e.g. immigration quotas which permit a given number of persons to migrate from one country to another each year or exchange controls which permit a given amount of capital funds to flow from one country to another each year.

Now where obstacles to movement take the form of quantitative controls, secondary adjustments are likely to be negligible or at least very much less important than if the obstacles took the form of taxes over international transactions. We have already made reference to this point (see p. 202); but it may be so important in the case of factor controls which is now under examination that it may be worth while giving one or two illustrations of the application of the principle to our present problem.

Suppose then that labour normally flows from B where it is plentiful to A and to C where it is scarce. But suppose that these flows are controlled by a quota in C on the number of persons allowed to migrate into C and a quota in A on the number of persons allowed to migrate into A. Suppose then that the authorities in A expand or even remove A's quota. More labour moves each year from B to A. This makes labour scarcer in B and raises the value of the marginal product of labour and so the wage of labour in B. Now if there were a fixed *ad valorem* rate of tax on the migration of labour from B to C, this would mean that less labour moved from B to C since the rise in the wage rate in B would mean that the excess of the wage rate in C above the wage rate in B was no longer sufficient to offset the tax on the movement of labour from B to C.

But if there is merely a quota on the numbers which may move from B to C, the rise in the wage rate in B will, as before, reduce the excess of the wage rate in C over the wage rate in B; but, so long as the wage

[1] In the case of factor movements we do not have to bother about possible tertiary adjustments. In the case of commodity trade further general tertiary adjustments in trade flows might be necessary to keep balances of payments in equilibrium. But there is no need at all for the value of inflowing factors to be equal to the value of outflowing factors. There is no balance-of-payments problem in this case, and therefore no need for further tertiary adjustments—though there may be what we have called secondary secondary adjustments (see p. 217).

rate in C remains in excess of the wage rate in B (allowing for any real costs of movement), the immigration quota in C will be filled and the amount of labour moving from B to C will remain unchanged. There will be no secondary reduction in international migration and thus no secondary loss of economic welfare.

It is true, of course, that if the newly permitted migration from B into A is on a sufficient scale, the marginal product of labour and so the wage-rate in B may be driven up to the level ruling in C. In this case the numbers migrating from B to C will suffer a secondary reduction. But this will not happen until the marginal product of labour in B has risen as high as its marginal product in C (allowing for any real costs of movement), in which case there will be no remaining excess of marginal value over marginal cost in the case of the flow of labour from B to C. Its reduction will therefore cause no loss of economic welfare, so that we can conclude that if the movement of labour from B to C is itself controlled by a quantitative quota, there can be no secondary loss of economic welfare to set against the primary gain due to the increased migration from B to A.

Let us take another example from a discriminatory removal of a factor control. Suppose that A is very short of labour and that there would normally be migration from B and C into A. Suppose further that A has a quota on immigration from B and a quota on immigration from C. Suppose then that the authorities remove the quota restriction on immigration from B without enlarging the quota on migration from C. The increased amount of labour in A may reduce the marginal product and so the wage of labour in A. But so long as the wage rate in A remains higher than the wage rate in C (allowing for real costs of transport) the quota of permitted immigrants from C will be filled. There will be no secondary reduction of the flow of labour from C to A. If, however, the flow of labour from B to A is on such a scale that the wage rate in A falls to the level of the wage rate in C, then the quota of permitted immigrants from C to A may no longer be filled. But in this case there is no remaining excess of marginal value over marginal cost in the case of the flow of labour from C to A, and therefore no secondary loss from any secondary reduction in the volume of this particular flow of migrant labour.

The reader must not rush to the conclusion that if all controls take the form of quantitative quotas there can be no secondary loss of economic welfare. Suppose, as before, that B has much labour and that there is normally a flow of labour from B to A and to C. Suppose that A has a quota on immigration and B a larger quota on emigration and C has no migration controls at all. Then the immigration into C is fixed by the excess of B's emigration quota over A's immigration quota. If A then removes her quota and more labour moves from B to A, the whole of this must be at the expense of the emigration from B to C, since B's total emigration is fixed. There will be a loss on the secondary reduction of migration from B to C to set against the gain on the primary increase of migration from B to A. In this case, however, there is still likely to be a net gain. Since migration into C is free, labour will be attracted to move into A instead of into C only if the wage rate in A is above that in C. Thus so long as labour chooses to move into A instead of into C because of the removal of the obstacle to movement into A, there will be a net gain in economic welfare. It is equivalent to an equal movement of labour from C (where the marginal product of labour is lower) to A (where it is higher).

It must be left to the reader to consider the various cases outlined in this chapter and to decide for himself what forms of quantitative controls over factor movements would in fact mean that there were no secondary losses of economic welfare. But it is always true that if controls take the form of quantitative quotas, the effect of a partial removal of a control will be different from what it would have been if the controls had been equally severe but had taken the form of *ad valorem* taxes. Where a control takes the form of a direct quantitative limit set to the very flow of factors which might otherwise have been subject to a secondary adjustment, then there can be no secondary losses (or gains) of economic welfare. In this case only the gains from the primary increases in the international movement of factors need be taken into account.

CHAPTER XXXIV

DISCRIMINATION, THE BALANCE OF PAYMENTS, AND ECONOMIC WELFARE

WE can apply the analysis which we have used in Chapter XXXII to deal with a problem which we left unsolved in the last chapter of Volume I of this work.[1] We discussed the use of direct quantitative controls over imports as a means of keeping balances of payments in equilibrium in Part V of Volume I; and in Chapters XXVIII–XXXI of Part VI of that volume we considered the question whether such direct controls, if they are employed at all, should be imposed upon a discriminatory or upon a non-discriminatory basis. We argued that if two deficit countries—D_1 and D_2—are both going to put their balances of payments into equilibrium by restricting their imports, there was much to be said for the principle that they should each restrict their imports from any surplus country—S—more severely than they restrict their imports from each other. If D_1 restricts its imports from S, this directly reduces D_1's deficit and S's surplus and thus helps to restore equilibrium to world balances of payments. But if D_1 restricts its imports from D_2, this reduces D_1's deficit only at the expense of an increase in the deficit of D_2 which will have lost export markets in D_1. This will not do anything directly to improve the world's balance of payments; it will merely restrict the volume of trade between the deficit countries.

We examined in Chapter XXX of Volume I the systems of discrimination in the imposition of import controls on balance-of-payments grounds, which would be calculated to restore equilibrium to all balances of payments with the smallest possible reduction in the total volume of world trade. But this criterion of the minimum reduction in the volume of world trade cannot be accepted as an appropriate criterion for economic welfare. Some elements of trade may carry with them much more economic welfare per unit of trade than other elements do. The maximization of economic welfare demands that, if direct controls are going to be used to keep balances of payments in equilibrium, the import restrictions should be based upon the principle of the minimum reduction in the total volume of world trade after

[1] Many of the points which are made in this chapter are formulated more precisely in Section XX of the mathematical supplement to this volume. The analysis which is developed in this chapter is essentially only a translation into my own terminology of the analysis carried out by Professor J. M. Fleming in his article 'On Making the Best of Balance of Payments Restrictions on Imports', *Economic Journal*, March 1951. As I have stated in the preface to this volume, it was largely as a result of studying this article that I adopted the method used in this volume for dealing with problems of the second-best and for combining considerations of economic efficiency with considerations of economic equity.

weighting each particular unit of trade by its net contribution to economic welfare.

Now we can use the techniques which we have developed in this volume to help to find the answer to this problem.

Accordingly, let us consider the following situation. The world is made up of a number of countries A, B, C, D, etc. In each of these the general level of money wage rates and so of costs and prices is fixed in terms of the currency of the country concerned. In each of them also the authorities have adopted domestic financial policies for internal balance, so that the general level of employment and production and hence also of money incomes is fixed in each country. The rates of exchange between the national currencies are fixed.

In such circumstances in the absence of import restrictions there would almost certainly be important deficits and surpluses in the balances of payments of some at least of the countries. The fixed wage rates, fixed rates of exchange, and the domestic financial policies for internal balance would mean that disequilibria in the balances of payments could not be removed either by means of adjustments of total money demand or by means of adjustments of relative prices in the different countries. Unless by some miraculous coincidence all the foreign exchange rates corresponded exactly—and in spite of any spontaneous changes in the underlying conditions continued to correspond exactly—to the requirements of domestic prices and incomes, some countries whose prices and incomes were too low would have surpluses on their balances of payments and other countries whose prices and incomes were too high would have deficits.

We suppose that the deficit countries have all removed these deficits by means of import restrictions. For the moment we do not assume that they have chosen any particular principle of discrimination or non-discrimination in their import restrictions for this purpose. All that we assume is that each country has imposed import restrictions of one kind or another with sufficient severity to ensure that, after taking into account any loss of export markets due to the import restrictions imposed by other countries, its balance of payments is in equilibrium. Starting from any such position with world balances of payments maintained in equilibrium by any given network of import restrictions, we shall then ask whether any marginal adjustments can be made to this system of import restrictions in such a way as to keep all balances of payments in equilibrium but to raise economic welfare at the same time. In this way we shall hope to discover some of the principles upon which a system of import restrictions should be constructed if it is to keep balances of payments effectively in equilibrium, but at the same time is to do as little harm as possible from the point of view of economic welfare.

For the first stages of this analysis we shall make four further assumptions, the last three of which will, however, be removed in the course of the analysis.

First, we assume that within each country there is a policy of modified laissez-faire, so that for all transactions within each country there is no divergence between marginal social values and marginal social costs. Domestic market prices in each country measure both marginal social values and marginal social costs of the products concerned. This assumption we shall maintain throughout our analysis.[1]

We can measure the degree of severity of any given import restriction by means of the excess of the price of the product in the importing country over its price in the exporting country. Thus suppose that in the absence of transport costs a particular product sells for $100 in A and for $140 in B. This would be the result of a 40 per cent *ad valorem* rate of duty on the import of the product into B from A or of some other restriction on the import of the product from A into B with a protective effect equivalent to that of a 40 per cent *ad valorem* rate of import duty.[2] In what follows we shall call this *ad valorem* rate of excess of the price in the importing country over the price in the exporting country the protective incidence of the import restriction. Since we are assuming that price measures marginal social cost in the exporting country and that price measures marginal social value in the importing country, the protective incidence of any import restriction is equal to the rate of divergence between marginal social value and marginal social cost in the import transactions concerned.

Second, we shall assume at first not only that price is equal to marginal social cost in the exporting country, but also that marginal social costs are constant in the exporting countries. In other words we assume an infinitely large elasticity of supply of each export product. A rise or fall in the foreign demand for any particular export product of A would not affect the marginal cost of supplying the export in A and thus would not lead to any change in the price at which A's exporters are prepared to supply the product. We make this assumption solely for ease of exposition. We shall remove it in due course.

[1] The analysis could be developed further by modifications of this assumption on the lines of the analysis developed above in Chapter XIV. But the reader must be left to do this for himself.

[2] We assume for our present problem that the trade is restricted by the authorities in the importing country, not by the authorities in the exporting country. The revenue from the import duty or from fees charged for the issue of import licences (see Volume I, pp. 276–9) is assumed to accrue to the authorities in the importing country. The result is that, in terms of the example given in the text, the consumers in B pay $140 for the imported product, of which $40 accrues to the budget of the authorities in B and $100 is paid over to the exporters of the product in A. As far as this element in B's imports is concerned the strain on B's balance of payments is only the $100 paid over to A's exporters and not the $140 spent on the imports by B's consumers.

Third, we shall at first assume that policy-makers have allotted the same distributional weights to the incomes of every citizen of the world. The result of this assumption is that the contribution to world economic welfare of a small marginal increase in any particular flow of trade is to be measured by the cost price of the increment of trade weighted by the *ad valorem* rate of divergence between its marginal value in the importing country and its marginal cost in the exporting country. For, since incomes in the importing and exporting countries are given the same distributional weights, the marginal value in the importing country can be compared directly with the marginal cost in the exporting country in the calculation of the contribution of the trade to economic welfare. Since, as we have seen, the divergence between marginal value in the importing country and marginal cost in the exporting country is itself measured by the protective incidence of the import restriction concerned, we can now measure the contribution to economic welfare of any marginal increase in any particular flow of trade as the cost price of that increment of trade multiplied by the protective incidence of any import restriction to which it is being subjected.

This assumption that the same distributional weights are allotted to all citizens of the world will be modified in the course of this analysis. We shall not allow for differences in the distributional weights allotted to different classes of citizens within any one country. But we shall allow for the fact that it may be desired to give the incomes of the citizens of country A a different weight from that given to the incomes of the citizens of country B; and we shall ask what modifications in the ideal system of import restrictions would be required as a result of making allowance for such differences in distributional weights.

Fourth, we shall at first assume that a change in the amount of any product which is allowed to be imported from A to B has no secondary repercussions (as that term is defined on p. 203 of Chapter XIII above) upon the conditions of supply or demand for any other imports or exports of A or of B. This in effect means that we are assuming that the amount of any product which exporters in A would be willing to export will depend solely upon the price which they are offered for these particular exports. It is not affected by any changes in the amount of other imported or exported products available on A's markets as a result of a change in A's or in B's system of import restrictions. Similarly, in the importing country B we are in effect assuming that the amount which consumers will want to purchase of any imported product depends solely upon the price charged to them for that product, and not at all upon the degree to which the availability in B's markets of other goods which are imported or exported by B has been altered by changes in the import controls exercised by B or by other countries over the trade in these other products. This assumption also we shall remove in the course of our analysis, when we come to ask how far any otherwise acceptable scheme of import restriction needs modification when we allow for such secondary repercussions from the adjustment of any one import restriction.

We suppose then that our countries start with some system of import restrictions which are sufficiently severe to keep each country's balance of payments in equilibrium but which are otherwise not subject to any other limitation. We shall now ask on what principles we can find out whether any modifications in this initial set of import restrictions can be found such as to permit an increase in total economic welfare while balances of payments remain in equilibrium. This can best be done by considering the possibilities of four types of adjustment of the existing system of import restrictions.

(1) First consider any country which is importing two or more products from any one other country, one at least of which products is subject to an import restriction. For example, suppose that B is importing products X and Y from A, and that X is subject to an import restriction by B with a protective incidence of 50 per cent whereas Y is subject to an import restriction by B with a protective incidence of only 10 per cent. Choose units of X and Y such that a unit of X and a unit of Y both have a (constant) supply price of $1 in A. Suppose then that the authorities in B restrict imports of Y by another unit and increase the imports of X by one unit. There will be no change in A's or in B's balance of trade; the only change is that $1 which was being paid by B to A for the import of Y is now being paid for imports of X. But the unit of Y which is now no longer imported had a marginal value of $1·1 to consumers in B (i.e. the cost price of $1 in A raised by the 10 per cent protective incidence of the import restriction on Y); and on the other hand the unit of X which is now newly allowed to reach B's market has a marginal value of $1·5 to consumers in B (i.e. the cost price of $1 in A raised by the 50 per cent protective incidence of the import restriction on X). Clearly there is a net gain in the welfare of the citizens of B; and at the same time there is no loss to the citizens in A who in both cases give up something which has a marginal cost to them of $1. From this there can be deduced the first simple rule for the ideal system of import restrictions. If any country is importing a number of products from any other country and is submitting any of them to import restrictions, it should relax the severity of the restrictions on those imports for which the protective incidence of its restrictions is high and it should increase the severity of the restrictions on those imports for which the protective incidence of its restrictions is low, until all products coming from the same country are in fact subject to import restrictions of the same protective incidence.

(2) Consider next two countries, say A and B, each of which is

restricting its imports from the other. Suppose now that the authorities in A relax their restrictions on imports from B so that A's importers can pay \$1 more to B's exporters; and suppose that the authorities in B simultaneously relax their restrictions on imports from A so that B's importers can pay \$1 more to A's exporters. There has once again been no change in any country's balance of trade; the only change in this case is that for both A and B both imports and exports have simultaneously risen by \$1. But there will now be an increase in economic welfare for both countries. A exports—i.e. her consumers have to give up the consumption of—\$1 worth of A's products; but in return A imports—i.e. her consumers can add to their consumption—an amount of B's products which costs \$1 in B, but which because of the protective incidence of A's import restriction has a marginal value of, say, \$1·4 to A's consumers. In other words on the additional \$1 worth of trade between A and B there is a gain to A's consumers equal to \$1 multiplied by the protective incidence of A's existing restrictions on imports from B. Similarly, for B's consumers on the additional \$1 worth of trade there is a gain equal to \$1 multiplied by the protective incidence of B's existing import restrictions on imports from A.

Thus we reach our second rule for building up the ideal system of import restrictions. If two countries are restricting imports from each other, then they should simultaneously relax their import restrictions on each other's products until one of them has completely removed its restrictions on imports from the other.

(3) The second rule which we have just explained can very easily be extended to cover a similar triangular reduction of import restrictions. Suppose that C is restricting imports from B, B is restricting imports from A, and A is restricting imports from C. Suppose then that the authorities in C permit an additional \$1 worth of B's products to be imported; B's authorities permit an additional \$1 worth of A's products to be imported; and A's authorities permit an additional \$1 worth of C's products to be imported. No country's balance of payments is upset. In the case of B, for example, imports from A go up by \$1 but at the same time exports to C go up by \$1; and similarly for the balance of payments of A and of C. At the same time economic welfare is increased for each country. In the case of B, for example, consumers in B have to go without \$1 worth of B's products which are now exported to C. But in return they have available for consumption an additional amount of A's products which has a marginal cost of \$1 in A but a marginal value of more than \$1 in B because of the protective incidence of the restriction imposed by B on imports from A. There is thus a net gain in economic welfare for B's citizens; and similarly for the citizens of A and of C.

Our third rule may therefore be formulated as follows. If there are any three countries A, B, and C such that C is restricting imports from B, B from A, and A from C, then they should all relax their restrictions on imports from each other simultaneously in such a way that each country's balance of payments remains in equilibrium until one of the countries has completely removed its restrictions on imports from the other two countries.

(4) Suppose that rules 2 and 3 are both being fulfilled. In these conditions consider any three countries A, B, and C. Suppose that we find that C is restricting imports from B and that B is restricting imports from A. Then B cannot be restricting imports from C, since if it were doing so we should have two countries, B and C, which were simultaneously restricting imports from each other and rule 2 would be broken. Nor can A be restricting imports from B, since if it were doing so A and B would simultaneously be restricting imports from each other and rule 2 would be broken. Nor can A be restricting imports from C, since if this were so C would be restricting from B, B from A, and A from C, and rule 3 would be broken. It follows that if C is restricting imports from B and B is restricting imports from A, the only other restriction on trade which is compatible with rules 2 and 3 is a restriction of C's imports from A. What we must examine under the present rule 4 is the best relationship between the protective incidences of C's restrictions on imports from B, B's restrictions on imports from A, and C's restrictions on imports from A.

This can be done by means of the following diagram. Suppose that the authorities in C were to relax their restrictions on imports from B so that an additional $1 worth of B's products were imported into C. If at the same time they were to tighten up their restrictions on imports from A so that C's traders spent $1 less on A's products, C's balance of payments would be unaffected. She would be spending $1 more on imports from B, but $1 less on imports from A.

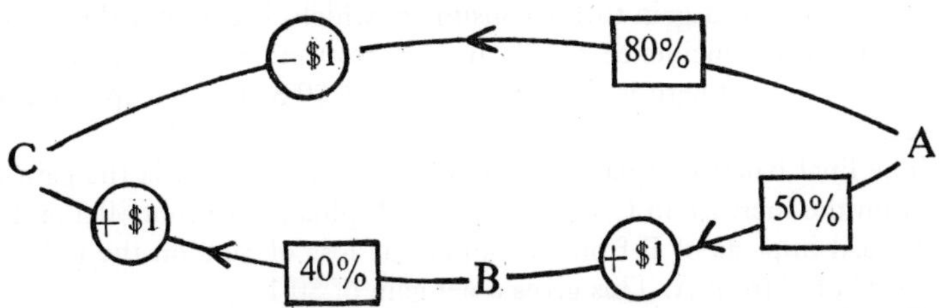

The lines with arrows show the trade flows which are subject to restrictions imposed by the authorities in the importing country, the arrow showing the direction of movement of the products on which restrictions are imposed. The figures in circles represent the effects on the values at cost price of these trade flows of changes in import restrictions in C and B. The figures in squares show the protective incidence of the import restrictions to which each flow of trade is subject.

But the change in C's arrangements for restricting imports would now have put B's balance of payments into surplus (since B is selling $1 worth more products to C), and it would have put A's balance of payments into deficit (since A is selling $1 worth less products to C). This disequilibrium can, however, be very simply corrected if B's authorities relax their restrictions on imports from A so that B imports $1 worth more products from A.

Accordingly, in the diagram on p. 551 we illustrate the case where C imports $1 worth less from A and $1 worth more from B and B simultaneously imports $1 worth more from A. This leaves each country's balance of payments unchanged. We have now to ask in what circumstances a change of this sort will lead to an increase in economic welfare. This question can be answered in the following way.

Consider the reduction in the imports of A's products into C. Here there is a reduction of trade of $1 worth of a product which has a marginal cost in A of $1; but because C's restriction on imports from A has a protective incidence of 80 per cent, this product was worth $1·8 to C's consumers. The reduction of this trade means that A's consumers have an additional unit of their own products which they value at $1 while C's consumers have one less unit of A's products which they value at $1·8. Since we are allotting the same distributional weights to incomes in A and in C we may call this a net loss of $0·8 in economic welfare.

Consider next the increase of $1 worth in C's imports from B. In this case B loses goods worth $1 to her consumers but C's consumers gain a product which, because C's restrictions on imports from B has a protective incidence of 40 per cent, is worth $1·4 to C's consumers. This represents a net gain in economic welfare of $0·4. Finally, consider the increased import into B of $1 worth of A's products. This means a loss to A's consumers of a unit of A's products which is worth $1 to them, and a gain to B's consumers which, because of the 50 per cent protective incidence of B's import restriction, is worth $1·5 to B's consumers. There is therefore a gain of $0·5 in this expansion of trade.

The final balance of gain on the whole rearrangement is the gain of $0·4 on the increase in C's imports from B plus the gain of $0·5 on the increased imports of B from A, minus the loss of $0·8 on the reduced imports of C from A. This gives a net gain of $0·1.

We can thus conclude that C should reduce her imports from A and increase her imports from B, thus enabling B to increase her imports from A, so long as the protective incidence of C's restrictions on imports from A is less than the sum of the protective incidences of C's restrictions on imports from B and of B's restrictions on imports from A. We can express this in an alternative way. C should discriminate in her import restrictions against A and in favour of B until the excess of the protective incidence of C's restrictions on A's products over the protective incidence of C's restrictions on B's products (i.e. the degree of C's discrimination against A) is equal to the protective incidence of B's restrictions on imports from A. This is rule 4 for the adjustment of import restrictions.

Now rules 2, 3, and 4 will leave us with all our countries arranged in an order of strength of their balance-of-payments position such that a weaker country will always be restricting imports from a stronger country and that a stronger country will never be restricting imports from a weaker country. Moreover, rule 4 will mean that if we take any three countries and arrange them in their proper order in our scale of strength or weakness in the balance-of-payments position, the restrictions which the weakest country of the three will impose on imports from the strongest of the three will have a protective incidence which is equal to the sum of the protective incidences of the restrictions which the weakest country imposes on the intermediate country and which the intermediate country imposes on the strongest country.

The following diagram gives a numerical example of a possible pattern of ideal discrimination which will result from the application of the

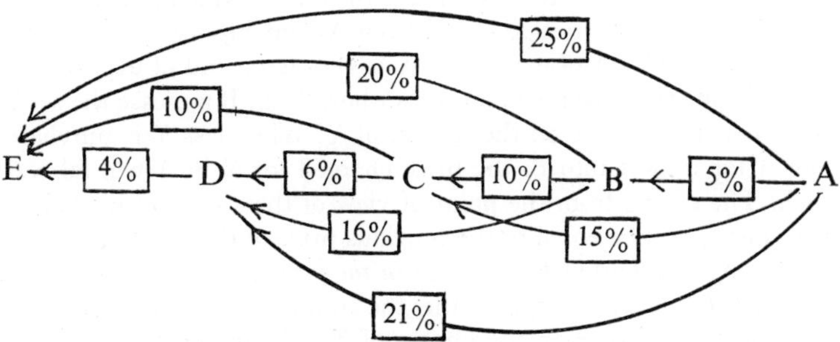

rules 2, 3, and 4 to the import restrictions between five countries A, B, C, D, and E. We suppose that A represents the country which turns out to be strongest in the balance-of-payments list; B turns out to be second in strength in the balance-of-payments list; and so on through the alphabet. The lines, arrows, and percentages in the squares all have the same meaning as in the case of the diagram on p. 551. It will be seen that if any three countries are selected, rules 2, 3, and 4 all apply to the relations between them. That is to say, a weaker country will be restricting imports from a stronger, but it will not be true that at the same time the stronger is restricting imports from the weaker (rule 2); the weakest country of any three will be restricting imports from the intermediate country and the intermediate country will be restricting imports from the strongest, but it will not be true that simultaneously the strongest is restricting imports from the weakest (rule 3); and, finally, in the case of any three countries the protective incidence of the restrictions imposed by the weakest country on imports from the strongest country is equal to the sum of the protective incidences of the restrictions imposed by the weakest country on imports from the intermediate country and of the restrictions imposed by the intermediate country on imports from the strongest country (rule 4).

Such would be the principles of discrimination which would be found in an ideal system of import restriction on the very simple assumptions on which we have so far been examining the problem. We shall now proceed to see in what ways these principles of discrimination would need to be altered if we removed the last three of the four assumptions enumerated on pp. 547–548 above, namely if we remove the assumptions (1) that elasticities of supply of exports are in all cases infinite, (2) that the same distributional weights are allotted to incomes in all countries, and (3) that there are no secondary repercussions upon the supply or demand for imports or exports as a result of primary changes made by the authorities in the volume of any one line of trade which is subject to import restriction.

Let us start then by removing the assumption that all elasticities of supply of exports are infinite. Consider the case in which B is importing both of two commodities X and Y from A, and suppose that the elasticity of supply by A of exports of X is very large and of exports of Y is very small. Suppose now that the authorities in B increase the severity of their restrictions on the import of Y. When less Y is purchased from A for import into B, the price charged for Y in A will fall very much. The saving from the point of view of the strain on B's balance of payments will be equal to the previous price of the units of Y which are no longer imported *plus the fall in the price of the units of Y which continue to be imported.* Suppose that the authorities in B simultaneously relax their restrictions on the import of X. The increased demand for X in A's markets will tend to raise the price of X; but if the elasticity of supply of exports of X is large there will not be any great rise in price. The extra strain on B's balance of payments will be equal to the new price of the units of X newly imported in B *plus the rise in the price on all the units of X already being imported.* But if the elasticity of supply of exports is low in the case of Y and high in the case of X, the saving on B's balance of payments due to the fall in the price of Y will be great while the strain on B's balance of payments due to the rise in the price of X will be small. In other words, if B reduces the volume of her imports of Y very slightly she will be able to finance a very large increase in the volume of imports of X. This constitutes from the point of view of economic welfare a sound argument in favour of relaxing restrictions on imports of X by more than would otherwise be the case at the expense of tightening up the restrictions on imports of Y by more than would otherwise be the case. Rule 1 (p. 549) accordingly needs modification in the sense that if B is importing a number of products from A the protective incidence of the import restrictions should be heavier in the case of the products whose supply to B is inelastic than in the case of the products whose supply to B is elastic.

Rules 2 (p. 549) and 3 (p. 550) do not require any modification solely because elasticities of supply of export may be different in different cases. Both these rules deal with cases in which the import restrictions on a number of products can all be relaxed simultaneously; and no restrictions need at the same time be increased in severity. Differing elasticities of supply will mean that different elements in a general all-round relaxation of restrictions will make different contributions to an increase in economic welfare; but each relaxation will still serve to make some contribution to economic welfare. Differences in elasticities of supply will require some modification of the principles on which an ideal system of import restriction should be based only in the cases in which it is a question of relaxing some restriction at the expense of tightening up some other restriction.

Rule 4, however, as well as rule 1 does fall into this category and therefore needs some modification. This rule deals with the case where C is restricting imports from A and from B, and B is restricting imports from A. We want to know to what extent C should tighten up its restrictions on imports from A and relax its restrictions on imports from B, thus enabling B to relax its restrictions on imports from A. On the assumption that all elasticities of supply were infinite we reached the conclusions (pp. 552–553) that C should discriminate against imports from A until the protective incidence of C's restrictions on imports from A was equal to the sum of the protective incidences of C's restrictions on imports from B and of B's restrictions on imports from A.

But suppose now that the elasticity of supply of exports by A to C was very high, but that the elasticities of supply of exports by A to B and of exports by B to C were very small. When C restricted her imports from A more severely, she would reduce her expenditure on imports by little more than the price of the products no longer imported from A; for since the elasticity of supply of exports by A to C is very high there would be very little saving through a fall in the price charged by A to C for these products. On the other hand, when C relaxed her restrictions on imports from B, this would greatly drive up the price charged by B to C since B's elasticity of supply is small. C could therefore afford to permit only a very small increase in the volume of imports from B, or else she would run into balance-of-payments difficulties. At the same time B, enjoying a given improvement in her balance of payments through the increased value of her sales to C, could permit only a very small increase in the volume of her imports from A; for since the elasticity of supply of A's exports to B is low, a small increase in B's purchases from A will drive up the price of these products against B. If, therefore, the elasticity of supply were high in the case of exports from A to C but low in the case of exports from A to B and from B to C, a relatively large reduction in the volume of C's imports from A would be required to make possible only a relatively small increase in the volume of C's imports from B and of B's imports from A. In such circumstances an increase in the degree to which C discriminates against imports from A would have less desirable effects than if all elasticities of supply were infinite. Rule 4 accordingly needs modification to the effect that the protective incidence of C's restrictions on imports from A should be less than (or greater than) the sum of the protective incidences of C's restrictions on imports from B and of B's restrictions on imports from A according as the elasticity of supply of exports is greater (or less) in the case of A's exports to C than in the case of A's exports to B and B's exports to C.

Let us turn now to the modifications in rules 1–4 which may be required because different distributional weights are allotted to the incomes of citizens in different countries. If the elasticities of supply of exports are infinite, rules 1, 2, and 3 will require no modification merely because the distributional weights are different for different countries. Rule 1 concerns the choice of imports by B from A. If elasticities of supply in A are infinite, it makes no difference to A's welfare whether B spends $1 more on X and $1 less on Y or not. Such a change in expenditure will increase B's welfare, however, if the protective incidence differs in the case of X and Y, since $1 spent on X in A may buy something which is of more value to B's consumers than acquiring $1 worth of Y from A. No comparison of the welfare of B's citizens with A's citizens is required. Rule 1 accordingly needs no modification.

Rules 2 and 3 both deal with cases in which, if elasticities of supply are infinite, an all-round relaxation of restrictions enables the citizens in every country to gain simultaneously. Each country gains by exporting only $1 worth more of its own products and obtaining in exchange an additional amount of imports which while they cost only $1 in the country of export are worth more than $1 in the country of import. There is no problem here of comparing a loss in one country with a gain in another and the rules need no modification simply because different distributional weights are allotted to different countries.

But rule 4 does now require some modification. Consider the adjustments of C's and B's import restrictions which are illustrated on the diagram on p. 551. C imports $1 less of A's products which are worth

\$1·8 to C's consumers and imports \$1 more of B's products which are worth \$1·4 to C's consumers—a net loss to C of \$0·4. B exports \$1 more of her own products which are worth only \$1 to her consumers but imports \$1 more of A's products which are worth \$1·5 to B's consumers—a net gain to B of \$0·5. A exports \$1 less of her own products to C which are worth \$1 to A's own consumers and she exports \$1 more of her own products to B which are also worth \$1 to A's own consumers—an unchanged situation for A. From this it is seen that an increase in the degree of C's discrimination against A's products and in favour of B's products will (i) leave A's welfare unchanged, (ii) increase B's welfare, and (iii) reduce C's welfare as soon as the protective incidence of C's restrictions on imports from A is greater than that of C's restriction on imports from B. If the same distributional weights are allotted to C and to B, then C's discrimination should go to the point described in rule 4 as it is expressed on p. 552. But if a higher distributional weight is allotted to C than to B, C's discrimination against A should be less than the rule as stated on p. 552 requires, because a reduction in the degree of discrimination will *inter alia* help to redistribute income away from B and in favour of C. On the other hand, if a lower distributional weight is allotted to C than to B, C should discriminate against A and in favour of B to a greater extent than the rule on p. 552 requires.

So far we have considered the modifications which must be made to rules 1, 2, 3, and 4 if different distributional weights are allotted to the different countries only on the assumption that the elasticities of supply of exports are infinite. Quite a new set of interrelationships must be brought into consideration if the elasticities of supply of exports are different in different cases and at the same time different distributional weights are allotted to the different countries. The reason for this is perhaps best illustrated by considering rule 2, which states that, if B is restricting imports from A and A is simultaneously restricting imports from B, both countries should relax their restrictions until one set of restrictions has been completely abolished. But suppose that the elasticity of supply of exports from A to B is much lower than the elasticity of supply of exports from B to A. Then an increase in A's expenditure on B's products will cause only a small rise in the price charged by B to A; A will obtain a large increase in the volume of B's products and pay only a slightly higher price for them. But an increase in B's expenditure on A's products will cause a large rise in the price charged by A to B; B will obtain only a small increase in the volume of A's products, paying a much higher price for them. In other words, in such a case the general relaxation of restrictions will turn the terms of trade against B, since the price of B's exports will rise only a little but the price of A's exports will rise a lot. The net result may be that

B is made worse off than before at the expense of A enjoying more than the whole of the net gain in economic efficiency due to the movement towards freer trade. Now if a much higher distributional weight were allotted to B than to A, economic welfare might be raised by maintaining the import restrictions at a level which meant that some restrictions will still be maintained both by A on B's exports and by B on A's exports. In this case rule 2 would need modification.

Now we cannot go through all the possible modifications of the four rules which might be brought about by this combination of unequal elasticities of supply and unequal distributional weights.[1] But the broad principle of the necessary modifications is simple. Products whose elasticity of supply for export is unusually low and which are exported from countries with an unusually low distributional weight should be subject to exceptionally severe restriction, and possibly should even be subject to restriction in cases where the rules would otherwise require the complete absence of restriction. Their severer restriction will tend to turn the terms of trade against the exporting country and thus to redistribute income away from countries with low distributional weights.

There remains the task of modifying the assumption that a change in the amount of a particular product which the authorities in a particular importing country allow to be imported from a particular exporting country will have no secondary repercussions upon the demand for imports or the supply of exports in either the importing or exporting country.

This may not be the case. Suppose the authorities in C are restricting the import of V from B and relax this import restriction so that a little more V is exported from B and imported into C. As we have already argued in Chapter XIII, pp. 207–215, there are the following possible types of secondary repercussion:

(1) V may in C be a close substitute for (or complement to) W which is also imported into C, in which case there will be a secondary decrease (or increase) in C's demand for imports of W.

(2) V may in C be a close substitute for (or complement to) X which is exported from C, in which case there will be a secondary increase (or decrease) in C's supply of exports of X.

(3) V may in B be a close substitute for (or complement to) Y which is also exported from B, in which case there will be a secondary decrease (or increase) in B's supply of exports of Y.

(4) V may in B be a close substitute for (or complement to) Z which is imported into B, in which case there will be a secondary increase (or decrease) in B's demand for imports of Z.

[1] These modifications are expressed in a complete form in Section XX of the mathematical supplement to this volume.

We will now consider each of these four possible types of secondary repercussion in turn in order to see which of them are favourable and which unfavourable to economic welfare in the conditions of the balance-of-payments problem which we are examining.

For the purposes of this discussion we will assume that countries, arranged in a descending order of strength of their balance of payments positions, are A, B, C, D, E.

(1) Suppose that in the importing country C a relaxation of import restrictions on some import, V, from B causes C's demand for some other substitute import, W, to fall. If C is importing W from a stronger country than C (say, A or B), then the decreased demand for W in C will not reduce the amount of W imported, since imports of W from stronger countries will be restricted by quantitative restrictions. It will not, therefore, affect the amount or the value of C's imports of W. The only effect will be a change in the price paid by C's consumers of W. Such a secondary repercussion will have no effect either upon any balance of payments or upon welfare.

But suppose that C imports the substitute import W from weaker countries than C (say, from D or E) and that therefore C does not impose any import restrictions on these imports. Then the fall in C's demand for these products will reduce the exports of these weaker countries D and E and they in turn, in order to maintain an equilibrium in their balances of payments, will have to restrict imports more severely from A, B, or C. These severer restrictions of imports by D and E will involve reductions in economic welfare for which our calculations have not yet made any allowance.

We can, therefore, conclude that a relaxation of a particular import restriction by C will make a smaller contribution to economic welfare than we have so far realized if the imports primarily affected are close substitutes in C for imports from weaker countries on which C is not imposing any import restriction. Conversely, it can be seen that such a relaxation of an import restriction by C will make a larger contribution to economic welfare than we have so far realized if the imports primarily affected, are close complements in C to imports from the weaker countries, D and E.

(2) Let us next consider the case in which the imports V which are allowed into C in larger quantity are close substitutes in C for some product X which C exports. The relaxation of C's import restriction will in this case lower the price at which C is prepared to export X. Suppose that C exports X to stronger countries, A and B, which are not imposing import restrictions on products bought from C. Then the increased supply of exports of X offered by C to A and B will improve C's balance of trade with A and B and will worsen A's and B's balance of trade with C, provided always that the elasticity of demand for

imports of X into A and B is greater than unity.[1] Now this will mean that C can relax some other restrictions on some other imports from A and B without worsening the balance-of-payments position. The primary relaxation of C's import restrictions will thus make a larger final contribution to economic welfare than we have so far realized.

Suppose, however, that C exports to weaker countries such as D and E her exportable product X which is now available in greater quantity for export because of the import into C of more of the substitute product V. D and E will be restricting the volume of their imports of X from C, so that there will be no automatic increase in the volume of X exported by C to these countries. But the increase in the supply of X available for export from C will lower the price at which X is offered by C to D and E. This will improve the balance of payments of D and E and enable them in turn to relax some of their restrictions on imports from C. This also will lead to an improvement in economic welfare for which we have as yet made no allowance.

We may therefore conclude that a relaxation of an import restriction by C must be given a greater weight in any final calculation of the final effects upon economic welfare if the import concerned is a very close substitute in C for any products which C exports to any other countries. Conversely, the relaxation of a particular import restriction by C must be given an exceptionally low value in any calculation of its final contribution to economic welfare if the import concerned is a close complement in C to products exported by C, so that the amount of these products available for export from C is reduced.

(3) Consider next the possibility that the product which C imports in greater quantity is a close substitute in the exporting country B for another product Y which B also exports. The result will be a reduction in B's exports of Y. Now if B exports Y to stronger countries, such as A, which have imposed no restrictions on their imports from B, and if the elasticity of demand for imports of Y in A is greater than unity, then the reduction in the amount of Y available for export from B to A will worsen B's balance of trade with A. This will mean that B must increase the severity of her import restrictions on A's products; and this will lead to a loss of economic welfare for which we have so far made no allowance.

Suppose, however, that B exports Y to weaker countries, D and E. In this case the reduction in the availability of supplies of Y for export from B will not reduce the amount of Y exported from B to A. It will raise the price which exporters in B must receive in order to make the

[1] We shall maintain this assumption throughout the rest of this chapter. If the elasticity of demand for imports is less than unity, then in the case of each part of the following analysis which deals with the effects of changes in the supply of exports by any one country to a stronger country the conclusion must be reversed. The reader is left to do this for himself.

same amount of Y as before available for export. But since imports of Y into D and E are restricted quantitatively this will not reduce the amount imported; it will merely raise the price paid over to B's exporters more nearly up to the price offered for the given supplies by consumers in D and E. But the higher price which must now be paid by D and E for B's exports of Y will put D and E into balance-of-payments difficulties, and they will have to increase the severity of their restrictions on imports from C, B, and A. This will lead to a secondary fall in economic welfare for which we have not yet made any allowance.

We can therefore conclude that in so far as relaxation of an import restriction by C causes an increased import into C of a product which in the exporting country B is a close substitute for other exports of B, there will be a secondary loss of economic welfare for which we have not yet made any allowance. Conversely if the product imported in greater quantity by C were a close complement in B to other exports of B, which were therefore released in greater quantities for export by B, there would be a secondary gain of economic welfare for which we have so far made no allowance.

(4) Finally, consider the case where the product V which is exported in greater quantity from B to C is in B a close substitute for one of B's imports, Z, with the result that there is a secondary increase in B's demand for imports of Z. Now if Z is imported into B from a stronger country such as A, it will be subject to import restriction in B. There will in consequence be no secondary increase in the amount or value of B's imports of Z from A. There will in this case be no significant secondary repercussion. But suppose that Z is imported into B from weaker countries, C, D, and E, and is therefore not subject to import restriction in B. Then the increased demand in B for imports of Z from C, D, and E will improve the balance of payments of C, D, and E and will enable them to relax their restrictions on imports from B. This will lead to a secondary increase in economic welfare for which we have so far made no allowance.

We can, therefore, conclude that if C relaxes a restriction on an import which in the exporting country B is a close substitute for a product which is imported from countries which are weaker than B, then there is a secondary gain from C's relaxation for which we have as yet made no allowance. And conversely, if the product on which C relaxes her restriction is in the exporting country B a complement to some product which is imported from countries weaker than B.

Now in the devising of rules 1, 2, 3, and 4 (pp. 549–552) for the construction of an ideal pattern of import restrictions we proceeded to consider four types of adjustment of import restrictions which would enable balances of payments to be kept in equilibrium but would at the same time enable economic welfare to be raised. The only general conclusion that can be reached is that in considering each of these types of readjustment of import restrictions each of the four main possible types of secondary repercussion upon economic welfare which we have just described ought to be taken into account. Those particular readjustments which will have large favourable secondary effects should be preferred to those readjustments which will have large unfavourable secondary effects upon economic welfare.

It would be too complicated and tedious to attempt to make a systematic survey of the application of all these possible secondary effects to each of the four types of adjustment discussed above in the formation of each of the four rules (pp. 549–552). The reader must be left to make any particular applications in which he may be interested for the study of any particular problem.

There is, however, one application of rather general interest which it may be worth while making here. Consider rule 2 (p. 549) which states that if A and B are both restricting imports from each other, both should relax their import restrictions simultaneously until one set of restrictions is totally removed. There may be secondary repercussions which invalidate this rule. Suppose that A and B are rather strong countries. Suppose further that A's imports from B compete in A closely with A's imports from a very weak country, D, and that B's imports from A compete with B's imports from a weak country E. Then the mutual relaxation of A's and B's restrictions on imports from each other might greatly reduce their demand for the exports of D and E. Now D and E would then have to restrict their imports from A and B either directly or else by restricting their imports from C who in turn would have to restrict her imports from A and B. Now if D and E are very weak countries the protective incidence of D's and E's restrictions on imports from A and B (or the sum of the protective incidences of D's and E's restrictions on imports from C and of C's restrictions on imports from A and B) might be very high, so that the loss of welfare from the reduced trade of D and E might be considerably greater than the increase in welfare on the increased trade between A and B.

This effect might be reinforced if the products which A would export to B are substitutes in A for products which A exports to D or E and if the products which B would export to A are substitutes in B for products which B exports to D or E. Then the increase in the trade between A and B might divert A's and B's exports away from sale in D's and E's markets and thus raise the price to D and E of their restricted imports from A and B. This would make it necessary for D and E to intensify still further their restrictions on imports from A and B.

If both these types of repercussion were important, it might well be that the process of mutual disarmament in import restrictions between two strong countries like A and B should not be carried to the point at which one of them is no longer restricting imports from the other. Thus if we make allowance for the secondary repercussions which we have been discussing in the last part of this chapter we may be led to the conclusion not only that the relative severity of different particular restrictions on imports may have to be different from what they would otherwise be. It may also be necessary to alter the pattern of restrictions and to introduce some restrictions on some flows of trade which would otherwise have been submitted to no restriction.

CHAPTER XXXV

SUMMARY AND CONCLUSIONS

We have now reached the end of two long volumes on the *Theory of International Economic Policy*. At the close of Volume I we expressed the tentative conclusion that there were no insuperable difficulties of a purely economic character to prevent international balances of payments from being kept in equilibrium without the extensive use of direct controls over international trade and payments. But we pointed out that if it were desired to establish such a free system of international payments, a number of important and difficult conditions would have to be fulfilled.

First, the main trading countries would have to adopt reasonably successful domestic policies for internal balance, so as to avoid the stresses and strains that are thrown on to international balances of payments by serious domestic inflations and deflations.

Second, within each of the main trading countries there must be a reasonable degree of price flexibility so that prices of particular products rise as the demand for them exceeds the supply, and fall as supply exceeds demand. In particular, money wage rates must not be too rigidly fixed; but within a domestic financial policy for internal balance they must be capable of some adjustment according as demand exceeds supply or supply exceeds demand in each particular labour market.

Third, the rates of exchange between the various national currencies must be allowed to fluctuate. For if the general level of domestic prices, costs, and incomes is the result of domestic financial policies aimed primarily at the maintenance of internal balance, alterations in the rates of foreign exchange provide the only form of price adjustment which is available for the maintenance of external balance.

Fourth, for a system of free exchange rates to be able to work smoothly there must be an adequate volume of well-informed speculative funds or of international monetary reserves to take the first shock of strain on any national currency, while a change in its foreign-exchange value is having the desired permanent effect upon the channels of international trade. This in the modern world probably means that there must be a system of national and international exchange equalization funds endowed with adequate initial reserves of foreign currencies.

Fifth, the channels of international trade must be free to adjust themselves to changes in relative prices in different sections of a fairly free international market. Variations in exchange rates will bring balances of payments into adjustment only if the price changes which they cause are allowed to react readily upon the volumes of imports and exports of the countries which are affected. In other words if balances of payments are to be kept in equilibrium without resort to quantitative controls over trade and payments, there must not be a host of tariffs and other controls imposed upon international trade for other reasons.

In this volume we have conducted an extensive inquiry into these other reasons why it may be desired to impose controls over the international trade in products or over the international movement of factors of production. If these welfare arguments for direct controls of products and factors in international markets should be found to justify a very extensive apparatus of barriers to trade and factor movements, then it might be necessary to modify the provisional conclusions of Volume I and to argue that in a world in which there was going to be an extensive network of barriers to international trade imposed on 'welfare' grounds it might well be necessary to use direct controls also for the purpose of maintaining equilibrium in balances of payments.

Let us then briefly summarize and comment upon the arguments for controls in international markets which we have examined in this volume. We will start by considering four basic types of arguments in favour of controls over international trade.

(1) First, there is what we have called the 'second-best' argument. As we have seen, there are strong theoretical reasons why in many cases one particular tariff or other trade control should not be removed so long as some other particular tariff or trade control or domestic duty or other divergence between marginal values and costs remains in operation. The maintenance of one particular divergence between marginal values and costs may help to offset the evil effects of another divergence. Welfare might be improved if both were removed; but if one is going to be kept, it may be better that both should be kept.

There can be no question about the validity of this argument. Yet as a precept for practical policy, the present author at least does not find it very compelling. The interrelationships between the different relevant variables in the economic system are so complex that it is not really possible to apply this principle of the 'second best' to each particular adjustment of trade policy. Yet there remains a general presumption that a removal of a trade barrier will have good rather than bad effects. What we have called the 'primary' effect is always to the good. Moreover, any 'secondary' adverse effects must be due to the existence of other divergences between marginal values and costs. The presumption should always rather be in favour of taking steps to reduce these other divergences rather than of maintaining a particular barrier to offset the effect of these other divergences. It must always be remembered that the lowering of any one particular barrier will generally increase the chances that good rather than evil will come out of the lowering of any other barrier to trade.

Indeed, the only practical type of 'welfare' policy would seem to be one in which efforts were made domestically to move as nearly as possible towards policies of what we have called 'modified laissez-faire' and internationally to remove barriers to trade. The chief concession to be made to the principle of the second best in the choice of international commercial policies is that attempts to remove barriers to international trade should be as general in scope as possible and should concentrate particularly on the reduction of the highest duties and of those other barriers which have the highest protective incidence.

(2) Secondly, we have seen that the imposition of trade barriers may affect the international terms of trade and thus help to redistribute income from a richer to a poorer country. To the present author this argument also seems to be rather unconvincing as a guide to economic policy—certainly if it is used as an argument against any general international agreement for all countries to reduce or to remove obstacles to international trade. For if all countries are free to impose barriers to trade each may attempt to turn the terms of trade in its favour. A probable outcome of this is that the terms of trade may not be very greatly affected—the obstacles imposed by one country offsetting the effect on the terms of trade of the obstacles imposed by another; and in this case all countries will lose from a reduction in the volume of trade. A general agreement to reduce obstacles all round would then be to the benefit of each country.

It is, of course, possible that even after each country has freely retaliated against each other in its attempts to improve its terms of trade one country may remain better off than in the free-trade position, having gained more from a movement in the terms of trade in its favour than it has lost from the general restriction in the volume of its trade. Such might be the case of a country which, because it constituted the principal import market for important exports of other countries or because its exports supplied a very large proportion of the world demand for some essential product, possessed an exceptionally favourable bargaining position in international commerce. But there is no *a priori* reason to believe that the poor countries will possess exceptionally strong, and the rich countries exceptionally weak, bargaining power. If any country is left in the end as a net gainer from national freedom to restrict trade, it may just as well be a rich country gaining at the expense of the poor as a poor country gaining at the expense of the rich.

In answer to this it may perhaps be suggested that by international agreement a moderate protective policy designed to move the terms of trade in its favour should be permitted only to the poor country and should be denied to the rich. The present author would certainly agree that on grounds of a better distribution of income there is a special obligation on the part of rich countries to take the lead in removing obstacles to trade. Such a removal of duties by a rich country will lead to greater economic efficiency (unless, of course, there is some cogent 'second-best' argument against the removal of these duties) and to a better distribution of income, since it will help to improve the terms of trade of other countries. But it is another matter to advocate the agreed retention of protective policies by poorer countries for the express purpose of maintaining the terms of trade in their favour. If sufficient international co-operation is possible for the richer countries to agree to give up protective policies while the poorer countries can retain their protective systems, perhaps it would be possible to go one step further. A better final solution could almost certainly be found by a system of free trade combined with the payment of direct grants-in-aid by the richer to the poorer countries, since such a system would achieve the desired redistribution without the introduction of the inefficiencies introduced by otherwise undesirable protective policies in the poorer countries. It is to be hoped that the working out of equitable systems for the shouldering by many countries of a common burden (such as the cost of defence of the countries of the North Atlantic Treaty Organization) or for the finance of world economic development (such as technical assistance and economic aid programmes) contain the embryo of this better solution.

(3) Third, a protective policy may be used by one country in order to redistribute income inside that country in favour of the factors of production which are specially suited for employment in the protected industries. This to the present author is the least compelling of all the serious arguments for a protective policy. The domestic distribution of income raises many difficult problems. It is always difficult to obtain a desired distribution without serious interference with economic incentives; and certainly the effects upon domestic distribution of a protective policy must not be forgotten. But it is almost certainly always possible to find other means of redistributing income domestically which do less damage—or at any rate not markedly more damage—to world economic efficiency than an otherwise undesirable protective policy. To sacrifice any possibilities of general international agreement for the all-round reduction of obstacles to trade merely in order to maintain the possibility of using a protective policy as an instrument of domestic redistribution would indeed be a short-sighted act.

(4) The final basic argument for some system of control over international trade is the structural argument. This, in the opinion of the present author, is much the most difficult argument to assess. Because of the existence of important economies of large-scale production—whether these be due to important indivisibilities of certain factors of

production or to important external economies of an atmosphere-creating kind—it may be that if the structure of industries in a country were quite different from what it now is the change would represent a true increase in world economic efficiency. Yet some artificial encouragement by the governments concerned may be a necessary condition for the achievement of the change. Now it is possible to argue that such encouragement in many cases should take the form of the direct subsidization of the new industries rather than of their protection by import duties or quantitative restrictions on imports. This may well be so, but it does not meet the basic difficulty.

The basic problem arises because of the extreme difficulty of predicting in advance which structural changes are economically desirable and which are not. If the new industries must be encouraged by State action against the competition of imports from industries already established in other countries (and it is a relatively secondary although important consideration whether this is done by heavy subsidization of the new industry or by preventing the import of the old products), the problem arises who should be the judge of the desirability of such action. If the national governments concerned are completely free to judge for themselves, then a coach and horses can be driven through any general agreement to restrict barriers to international trade. For any element of protection could be advocated on general 'structural' grounds.

It remains to be seen whether it will ever be politically feasible to reach agreement whereby important structural changes are in some degree regarded as a question of common international concern. There are, however, two obvious economic factors which might enter as bargaining elements into any such agreement. In the first place, the developing countries may need to protect their infant industries, but they will desire to avoid retaliation by the adoption of protective policies by the developed countries. In the second place, the developing countries often have low incomes per head while the developed countries have relatively high incomes per head, so that the sharing by the latter of the financial burden of structural change in the former might be in the best interests of the distribution of income. The developed countries can offer an undertaking not to retaliate in their commercial policies and to play some part in the finance of structural change in the undeveloped countries, if the latter will confine their protective policies to schemes of structural change which are jointly agreed to be promising economically. But the great technical puzzle remains—how to tell whether a structural change will be economically efficient or not.

We can turn now to some general comments upon the arguments which we have examined in this volume for the maintenance of a system of controls over the international movements of factors of production, that is to say over the international migration of labour and over the international investment of capital. In the case of factor movements we have exactly the same basic types of argument for controls as in the case of international trade. There are 'second-best' arguments to the effect that a particular factor movement should be controlled because in other sections of the domestic or international economy there are divergences between marginal values and costs which the control over the factor movement helps to offset. There are arguments based upon the fact that an international factor movement will affect the international or the domestic distribution of income and for this reason should be artificially encouraged or hindered. Finally, there are arguments to the effect that an international factor movement is required for the promotion of a desirable structural change, and therefore needs to be artificially stimulated or controlled.

We will not comment at any length on these general arguments for factor controls. In this respect the problem of factor controls does not differ in any essential respect from that of trade controls; and the comments which have just been made at some length on the application of each of these four types of argument to trade controls can be applied without any essential change to the problem of international factor controls.

But in the case of international factor movements we have found two rather special forms of argument in favour of controls, and these arguments deserve a special mention in this summary of conclusions.

In the first place, if in any countries there are demographic conditions leading to a rapid and uncontrolled increase of population there may be strong arguments for the prevention of the free migration of labour from such countries into the other countries where the rate of population increase is better controlled. If population increase is really uncontrolled in the countries of emigration, there might be no end to the movement of labour in conditions of unrestricted migration until all the countries of immigration were also severely over-populated. Freedom of international migration demands some control of domestic births in the countries of emigration so that it does not lead to an unlimited expansion in the total world population.

Secondly, in the case of the international movement of labour and of capital we have placed special stress upon one aspect of the 'second-best' argument. If different countries have different domestic policies for the distribution of income and property, there may be a very special reason for exercising some control over the international movement of labour and capital. Suppose that in one country great stress is laid on policies for equality and relatively little on efficiency, while in another country in the formation of economic policies much stress is laid on free incentives for efficiency and relatively little on equality. Then factors which are most capable of earning high rewards will move to the latter country, and factors which are most in need of the comforts of the welfare state will move to the former. These movements may be quite uneconomic. There is for this reason much truth in the idea that either countries must keep roughly in step in their welfare policies or else, while trade in products may be free, international factor movements must be subject to some degree of control.

For the reasons briefly summarized in this chapter the author of this volume would conclude that the many theoretically valid arguments for policies of control over international trade and factor movements which have been presented in this volume do not in fact amount to a conclusive case for the wholesale abandonment of a liberal international economic policy. To those who, like the author of this work, would like to see the rebuilding of a liberal international economic order the arguments developed in this work will point to three rather different general conclusions.

The first general conclusion is that the restoration of greater freedom for international trade and factor movements can be made meaningful only by means of international agreements which cut rather deeply into domestic economic arrangements. One cannot hope to see the abandonment of protective devices except in the framework of an all-round international agreement, since unilateral action is quite likely to cause the free-trade country to lose more from a deterioration in its terms of trade than it gains from the expansion of trade. But as soon as any attempt is made to limit protective devices, a whole host of domestic economic arrangements must be brought under examination. Tariffs and quantitative import restrictions are not the only means for protecting domestic industries. Subsidies, domestic taxes, domestic price and quantity controls, nationalization schemes—all can be used for similar purposes. Yet all of these instruments may be perfectly legitimate instruments of policy for the attainment of certain other perfectly legitimate objectives. Among these objectives the use of such instruments for purposes of structural change—for what is commonly now known as economic development—is one, but only one, notable example. If a more liberal international economy is to be established by international agreement, one must search for a working compromise between the need effectively to curb protective devices and the need to give national governments freedom to adopt effective domestic economic policies for the attainment of legitimate domestic objectives.

The second general conclusion to be drawn from the analysis of these two volumes is that no effective compromise of the kind just mentioned can be attained except among a group of countries which adopt reasonably similar objectives for their domestic policies and employ reasonably similar 'price-mechanism' instruments for their attainment. It would be tedious at this point to recapitulate all the passages in these two volumes which could be called in evidence to support this view. It must suffice to draw attention to a few of the most obvious examples.

Direct controls over trade and payments will certainly need to be employed as a major instrument for maintaining equilibrium in balances of payments, unless all the major countries adopt effective domestic financial policies for the maintenance of internal balance and unless they have sufficiently flexible domestic price systems for variations in foreign-exchange rates to be able to exercise a decisive influence on the flows of international trade. In the choice of domestic financial policies for the maintenance of internal balance it may be important for countries to adopt, broadly speaking, the same type of policies; for if one country chooses to control an inflationary pressure mainly by monetary policy and higher interest rates while another country does so by the maintenance of low interest rates but heavy taxation and a large budgetary surplus, this may cause an uneconomic and large-scale movement of capital from the latter to the former. Second-best arguments for some controls over international trade and factor movements may remain very powerful—for example, to offset the evil effects of certain domestic monopolies—unless domestic policies are generally designed to reduce or to remove domestic divergences between marginal values and costs just as international economic policies are designed to remove such divergences in international markets. Examples such as these could be repeated almost without number. The main point should, however, by this time be sufficiently obvious to need no further development.

A third major conclusion which can be drawn from the analysis of these two volumes is that in modern conditions it is really not possible to achieve a liberal international economic order merely by free trade between sovereign nations; something more positive in the way of international economic institutions (if not of supranational economic authorities) is required for this purpose. This conclusion is closely connected with the two arguments which we have just developed. The mere negative act of outlawing or limiting the use of protective devices in the modern world requires the international supervision, if not the supranational policing, of a number of economic arrangements which are primarily of domestic concern. Moreover, if it be true that a liberal economic order in the modern world can be built successfully only if national governments will avoid certain types of domestic policy, the need for some degree of continuing intergovernmental discussion or supra-governmental control of certain domestic policies is obvious.

But the need is really more positive than this. There are certain functions in the modern world which, in a liberal economic order, demand positive international or supranational action. It is very difficult to draw the line between the negative act of avoiding certain types of domestic policy and the positive act of adopting domestic policies which are appropriate for the international economy. Some of the examples which we have already given of the requirements for appropriate domestic policies are themselves potent arguments for organizing action to some extent internationally. The co-ordination of domestic financial policies for the maintenance of internal balance is a good case in point.

There are, however, some fields of economic policy in which in the modern world it is desirable that still more positive action should be organized internationally. Three examples will perhaps suffice to make this point. We have already argued that if protective policies are to be abandoned as instruments for influencing the distribution of income between countries it is desirable that more positive international action should be organized for this purpose. We have also already drawn attention to the fact that structural change and economic development is in fact a matter of common concern to so-called developed and to so-called undeveloped countries; it is a matter which by its very nature must be the subject of governmental planning; and it is therefore a problem which calls for positive international treatment. Lastly, we may refer to the need for a large number of countries to plan their defence programmes jointly; this brings with it the need to consider jointly the sharing between the countries of the burden of defence expenditures, the location on economic and strategic grounds of certain basic industries, and the sources from which current supplies should be purchased for current defence programmes.

The restoration of a liberal economic order in the modern world is not therefore a negative act of mere laissez-faire. It requires a considerable development of international, if not of supranational, economic organization. It requires also a careful selection of domestic economic policies which, while they are effective for the attainment within the various countries of the major aims of economic policy, are not incompatible with the type of international economic order which we have been discussing in this chapter. To discover whether there are any general principles upon which such domestic policies could be constructed would be a major purpose of any *Theory of Domestic Economic Policy*.

APPENDIX 1

A NUMERICAL EXAMPLE OF THE MEANING OF AN OPTIMUM POPULATION

Note to Chapter VI

IN Table XXXVII we give an hypothetical example of an economy in which, with all other conditions remaining unchanged, the population grows in the way shown in column *a*. The population starts at 5, grows to 6, to 7, and so on until it finally reaches 22.[1] The ratio of working to non-working population is assumed to remain constant at every stage of growth, because at each stage we allow sufficient time to elapse for the age distribution of the population to reach the normal distribution which corresponds to a given and unchanged condition of mortality at every age.

In column *c* we record the output per head at every size of the population. Output per head is at first assumed to rise; for example, with a population of 6 it is only 85 units of output, but with a population of 7 it rises to 90 units of output per head. This is so because there are some increasing returns to scale in the economy. With a very small population the total market for the products of the community is too small to allow a full use of the potential economies of mass production in industry. But as population increases the rate of rise of output per head falls off, until with a population of 12 output per head has started to decline again as population rises. This occurs because after a point the market will have grown to a size which has enabled a large part of all potential economies of large-scale production to have been used, so that the disadvantages of having to employ more and more labour with only a constant total amount of land and capital will begin to outweigh the advantages of producing on a larger scale. As the population grows beyond this point, further economies of large-scale production will become less and less important and further crowding of a population on to a fixed amount of land and other resources will become more and more important, so that output per head will decline faster and faster.

In column *b* of the table total output is shown. This is obtained simply by multiplying the population (column *a*) by product per head (column *c*). In column *d* we show the marginal product of labour. When the population increases from 5 to 6 (column *a*), total output

[1] To make the example more realistic, the reader can suppose that 5 or 6 units of population mean populations of 5,000,000 and 6,000,000, and so on. This would make no essential difference to the argument. The small figures are used in this note solely for convenience.

TABLE XXXVII

The Optimum Population

Population (*a*)	Total product (*b*) = (*a*) × (*c*)	Product per head (*c*)	Marginal product (*d*)	Savings per head $(e) = \frac{100}{(a)}$	Consumption per head (*f*) = (*c*) − (*e*)
5	395	79	—	20	59
6	510	85	115	$16\frac{2}{3}$	$68\frac{1}{3}$
7	630	90	120	$14\frac{2}{7}$	$75\frac{5}{7}$
8	752	94	122	$12\frac{1}{2}$	$81\frac{1}{2}$
9	873	97	121	$11\frac{1}{9}$	$85\frac{8}{9}$
10	990	99	117	10	89
11	1,100	100	110	$9\frac{1}{11}$	$90\frac{10}{11}$
Maximum consumption per head. The per-caput optimum					
12	1,188	99	88	$8\frac{1}{3}$	$90\frac{2}{3}$
13	1,261	97	73	$7\frac{9}{13}$	$89\frac{4}{13}$
Welfare subsistence (60) without redistribution. The efficiency optimum					
14	1,316	94	55	$7\frac{1}{7}$	$86\frac{6}{7}$
Physical subsistence (40) without redistribution					
15	1,350	90	34	$6\frac{2}{3}$	$83\frac{1}{3}$
The maximization of welfare. The total-welfare optimum					
16	1,360	85	10	$6\frac{1}{4}$	$78\frac{3}{4}$
17	1,343	79	−17	$5\frac{15}{17}$	$73\frac{2}{17}$
18	1,296	72	−47	$5\frac{5}{9}$	$66\frac{4}{9}$
Welfare subsistence (60) with redistribution					
19	1,216	64	−80	$5\frac{5}{19}$	$58\frac{14}{19}$
20	1,100	55	−116	5	50
21	945	45	−155	$4\frac{16}{21}$	$40\frac{5}{21}$
Physical subsistence (40) with redistribution					
22	748	34	−197	$4\frac{6}{11}$	$29\frac{5}{11}$

rises from 395 to 510 (column *b*). This is a rise of 115, which measures the addition to total output due to having a population of 6 instead of a population of 5. This is recorded in column *d* as the marginal product of the 6th unit of population. The other figures in column *d* are obtained in a similar manner. It will be observed from column *d* that the marginal product is at first high and rising because an addition to population calls into play important economies of scale so that the net additional output due to an increase in population is very large. But after a point the marginal product declines rapidly because more and more labour is applied to a constant amount of the other factors. Indeed, in the example given in Table XXXVII at a population of 17 the marginal product of labour actually becomes a negative figure; in other words, at this point there is, as it were, such overcrowding that workers merely get into each other's way and total output is reduced rather than increased by any further growth of numbers.

The figures in column (*c*) relate to output per head. But if any part of output is currently saved, consumption per head is less than output per head, and it is upon consumption per head that welfare depends. Suppose that 100 units of output are to be saved in any case. Then savings per head are given by 100 divided by the numbers in the population; and these figures are shown in column *e*. Consumption per head equals output per head minus savings per head, i.e. the difference between the figures in columns *c* and *e* which is shown in column *f*.

It will be observed from columns *d* and *f* that the consumption per head (column *f*) is rising so long as the marginal product (column *d*) is higher than consumption per head (column *f*). So long as an additional man adds more to total output than the existing average consumption, he will help to raise the average consumption without affecting the total amount of output which is set aside for saving. Similarly, as soon as the marginal product has fallen below the average consumption, the average consumption will be declining as population increases. Consumption per head will therefore be at a maximum—we shall have achieved what we have called the per-caput optimum for the population—when the marginal product of labour is equal to the level of consumption per worker. So long as the marginal product exceeds the average consumption, the average consumption will be raised by a further growth of numbers; and as soon as the marginal product is lower than the average consumption, the average consumption will be brought down by a further growth of numbers. It can be seen in our example that this per-caput optimum will be found somewhere between 11 and 12 units of population.

Now suppose that what we have called the welfare subsistence level for a worker's real income is 60 units of output. That is to say, with any real income less than 60 it would from the economic point of view be better if the man had not been born. So long as the marginal product of labour exceeds this figure it would be possible for an additional worker and his family to obtain a net enjoyment from life (by consuming as much as but no more than his own marginal product) without making anyone else in the community worse off. As soon as the marginal product falls below this welfare subsistence level of 60 it is impossible for an additional worker and his family to obtain a net enjoyment from life without making some other member of the community worse off. We define therefore the position at which the marginal product of labour is equal to the welfare subsistence income as the point of the efficiency optimum for the population. This point in our numerical example lies between 13 and 14 units of population.

This is not to say that total welfare could not be increased by a further growth of population beyond the point at which the marginal product of labour is equal to the welfare subsistence income. From the formula in the text (p. 91) we can see that the total-welfare optimum will be reached when the ratio between the total utility and the marginal utility of income to the representative citizen is equal to the excess of the average consumption over the marginal product of a worker. If we suppose that the total utility of a citizen is 50 times as great as the addition to his utility which would be brought about by having one more unit of real product to consume, then in our numerical example the total-welfare optimum is reached at a population of between 15 and 16. With a population of 15 the excess of the average level of consumption (column *f*) over the marginal product (column *d*) is $83\frac{1}{3} - 34$ or $49\frac{1}{3}$, while at a population of 16 it is $78\frac{3}{4} - 10$ or $68\frac{3}{4}$. At some point in between this, excess of average consumption over marginal product will be equal to 50, the assumed ratio of total utility to marginal utility of consumption to the representative citizen.

If the population then grows still further, a point will be reached at which consumption per worker falls to the level of the welfare subsistence income. At a welfare subsistence income of 60 this point is reached in our numerical example when the population is between 18 and 19. This is the point at which, with an equal distribution of income, it would just be worth while for each member of the community to exist. Beyond this figure, from the point of view of economic welfare alone, it would be better if the community did not exist at all rather than that it should exist indefinitely in this over-populated state.

So much for the points of population size which depend upon the welfare subsistence level of consumption. Suppose, however, that there is a lower level of real consumption of 40 which is just sufficient to maintain body and soul together for the worker and his family. Then there are two other significant population points, the first between 14 and 15 units of population at which the marginal product of labour has fallen to this physical subsistence level of 40 and the second between 21 and 22 units of labour at which consumption per worker has fallen to this basic physical subsistence level. The former would be the point at which Malthusian pressure of population upon resources would make further population increase impossible, if all the elements in the population which were responsible for the growth of numbers had to maintain themselves solely on wage incomes which equalled the value of their marginal product. The latter would be the point at which further population growth would be impossible if those who were responsible for the growth of numbers received an equal share with everyone else of all income whether it was derived from wages or from the ownership of land and capital.

APPENDIX 2

A NUMERICAL AND GEOMETRICAL REPRESENTATION OF SOME BARTER DEALS

Note to Chapter XI

IN Table XXXVIII some numerical examples are given of the price relationships which may result from the various types of barter deal, which are discussed on pp. 178–183 of Chapter XI.

Suppose first, in row 1 of Table XXXVIII, the two State-trading organizations barter 100 blankets for $200 (columns *a* and *b*), giving a barter price of $2 a blanket (column *c*). Suppose further that when $200 worth of A-products are abstracted from A's market and made available for sale on B's market and when 100 blankets are abstracted from B's market and made available for sale on A's market, the free market price of blankets in A and in B will both be $2 (columns *d* and *e*). Then we have a barter deal which is the same as the position which would be brought about by free trade. The price in A's market and in B's market being the same as the barter price at which blankets are being sold for dollars between the two countries, neither the importers in A nor the exporters in B would have any incentive to alter the flow of trade. Moreover, since the barter price is the same as the market price in both countries, neither of the two State-trading monopolies would be making a profit or a loss (columns *f* and *g*).

Row 2 illustrates the case in which the barter deal is such as to cause the market price in B to be the same as the barter price (columns *c* and *e* are the same) but to raise the market price in A above the barter price (column *d* is above column *c*). As between rows 1 and 2 the amount of blankets exported from B to A has remained constant at 100 but the State trading-organization in A has struck a successful bargain and is giving only half as many dollars for them ($100 instead of $200). This means that in B's market the amount of A-products available relatively to blankets has been reduced; blankets have become less valuable relatively to A-products, so that the market price of blankets in B has fallen from $2 to $1 (column *e*). On the other hand, in A A-products have become more plentiful because less are being exported to B and have therefore become more plentiful relatively to blankets, of which the same supply is being imported. The market price of blankets has therefore risen in A from $2 to $3 (column *d*). In these circumstances the State import monopoly in A will be making a profit of $200, i.e. the difference between the market price in A of $3 and the barter price of $1 on 100 blankets (column *f*), whereas the State export monopoly in B will make neither a profit nor a loss (column *g*).

TABLE XXXVIII

Some State-trading Barter Deals

Barter deal corresponding to		The barter deal		Price of blanket in terms of $			Trading profit (+) or loss (−)	
		$ given by A	Blankets given by B	Barter price	Market price in A	Market price in B	in A	in B
		a	*b*	$c = a \div b$	*d*	*e*	$f = b(d - c)$	$g = b(c - e)$
		$	No.	$	$	$	$	$
1. Free trade in A and B		200	100	2	2	2	Nil	Nil
2. Free trade in B. $200 import duty in A		100	100	1	3	1	+200	Nil
3. *Either* $75 import subsidies in A with $75 export tax in B, *or* free trade in A and B with $75 transferred from A to B		225	75	3	2	2	−75	+75
4. *Either* $150 import duty in A with $150 export subsidy in B, *or* free trade in A and B with $150 transferred from B to A		150	150	1	2	2	+150	−150
5. *Either* $100 import duty in A with $400 export subsidy in B, *or* $300 export subsidy in B with $100 transferred from B to A	Over-trading	200	200	1	1½	3	+100	−400
6. *Either* $125 import subsidy in A with $187½ export subsidy in B, *or* $312½ export subsidy in B with $125 transferred from A to B	Over-trading	250	125	2	1	3½	−125	−187½
7. *Either* $180 import subsidy in A with $45 export duty in B, *or* $135 import subsidy in A with $45 transferred from A to B	Over-trading	270	90	3	1	2½	−180	+45
8. *Either* $187½ import duty in A with $62½ export subsidy in B, *or* $125 import duty in A with $62½ transferred from B to A	Under-trading	125	125	1	2½	1½	+187½	−62½
9. *Either* $112½ import duty in A with $75 export duty in B, *or* $187½ import duty in A with $75 transferred from A to B	Under-trading	150	75	2	3½	1	+112½	+75
10. *Either* $30 import subsidy in A with $120 export duty in B, *or* $80 export duty in B with $30 transferred from A to B	Under-trading	180	60	3	2½	1	−30	+120

This situation will correspond to one in which there is free trade in B;[1] exporters in B would have no incentive to alter the amount of trade, since the market price of blankets in B does not differ from the barter price obtainable from A. But importers in A would have an incentive to increase the import of blankets since the market price in A is higher than the barter price at which they are obtainable from B. This, in a regime of competitive trade, could be prevented by an import tax in A which would raise the barter price of $1 to the market price of $3, raising in revenue the $200 which, with the State-trading regime, accrues as a profit to the trading monopoly in A.

Row 3 illustrates a barter deal which results in the market price in A being the same as the market price in B but both market prices being below the barter price. As between row 1 and row 3 it will be seen that B is giving up less blankets (only 75 instead of 100) while A is giving more A-products in return ($225 worth instead of only $200 worth). Clearly the deal is a good one for B. Her consumers will enjoy more blankets (since she is exporting less of them) and at the same time more A-products (since she is receiving more dollars to spend on their import). There is no reason to believe, therefore, that the one class of commodity will have become more or less plentiful relatively to the other, since both have increased in supply simultaneously. We assume, therefore, that the market price of blankets in B remains unchanged at $2 (rows 1 and 3, column *e*). Similarly, in A the supplies of both commodities will have fallen because less blankets are being imported and more A-products are being exported. Once again these changes might be such as to keep the *relative* scarcity of the two products unchanged in A. We assume this to be so, so that the market price ratio between the two products remains $2 in A as well (rows 1 and 3, column *d*).[2]

[1] The fact that consumers in B will pay 100 blankets for dollar goods when the price of dollar goods is ½ a blanket per unit of dollar goods (row 1) and will also pay the same total amount of 100 blankets for dollar goods when the price of dollar goods has risen to 1 blanket per unit of dollar goods (row 2) implies that over this range the price elasticity of demand for dollar goods in B is equal to unity. If it were greater (or less) than unity then the number of blankets in column *b* of the table will have to fall (or rise) between row 1 and row 2 of the table.

[2] It would, of course, be a coincidence if the increase in the supplies of the two products in B which kept the relative prices in B constant were exactly the same as the decrease in the supplies of the two products in A which kept the relative prices in A constant. This is the assumption of the table which is made for convenience. But the validity of our argument does not depend upon this assumption. Suppose that a barter of $225 for 75 blankets instead of $200 for 100 blankets kept the price of blankets unchanged at $2 in B but caused some relative scarcity of blankets in A and raised the market price there to $2½. Then some small adjustment of the new deal whereby A gave up dollars for blankets and B blankets for dollars (say, a deal of $240 for 80) would increase the relative scarcity of blankets in B so that their price rose to, say, $2¼ and would reduce the relative scarcity of blankets in A so that their price fell to, say, $2¼. We should then have instead of row 3 in the table a deal of $240 for 80 blankets with a barter price of $3 and market prices of $2¼ in both countries,

As a result of this deal the trading monopoly in A will make a loss of $75 on the deal, and the trading monopoly in B will make an exactly similar gain of $75. This is a position in which in a competitive regime exporters in B would want to export more if they could sell blankets acquired at the market price of $2 in B at a barter price of $3 in the international market; but this could be prevented by an export duty in B which would raise the $75 margin between the barter price and the market price in B. Similarly, importers in A in a competitive regime could be induced to purchase the blankets at the barter price of $3 for resale in A at $2 by an import subsidy costing $75. Or another way of bringing about exactly the same result would be for A's government to raise $75 by an income tax, not for the payment of an import subsidy, but for direct transfer to B's government, which would refrain from imposing an export duty, but would use instead the $75 received from A's government for the reduction of the income tax in B. Traders in A and B would then have no incentive to change the volume of trade shown in row 3 of the table, since the price obtainable for blankets in A's market is already exactly the same as the price payable in B's market.

Row 4 shows merely the reverse of row 3. In this case B is exporting more blankets and A is paying a smaller total amount for them than in the free-trade position of row 1. If we assume that the quantities involved are such as to keep the relative scarcities of the two commodities the same in both markets as before the change, then the market prices in A and B remain unchanged at $2, but the barter price falls to $1. The position is now equivalent to a competitive regime with an import duty which raises $150 in A combined with an export subsidy of the same amount in B. This is also equivalent to a fully free-trade regime with a transfer of $150 from B to A.

Row 1 shows the position in which all three prices in columns *c*, *d*, and *e* are the same. Row 2 shows the position in which one of the market prices and the barter price are the same, but the other market price is different. Rows 3 and 4 show the position in which the two market prices are the same but the barter price is different. Rows 5–10 complete the picture by showing the six possible cases in which all three prices are different. If we denote the three prices in the three price columns by *c*, *d*, and *e*, rows 5–10 show the cases in which the three prices in ascending order of height are in the orders *cde*, *dce*, *dec*, *ced*, *ecd*, *edc*.

Here we must be content to explain the position illustrated in one of these rows and leave the reader to analyse the others for himself

in which case the trading monopoly in A would make a loss of $60 and the trading monopoly in B a gain of $60. The argument of the text could be based on this amended version, if desired.

on the same lines. If the deal in row 5 is compared with the free-trade position of row 1, it will be seen that A is now in the favourable position of paying the same total amount of dollars ($200) for a larger number of blankets (200 instead of 100). This causes blankets to become scarce relatively to other products in B and plentiful relatively to other products in A. The market price of blankets, therefore, rises from $2 to $3 in B and falls from $2 to $1½ in A. But both market prices still remain higher than the barter price of $1. As a result the import monopoly in A makes a profit of $100 (the difference between the market price in A of $1½ and the barter price of $1 on 200 blankets) while the trading monopoly in B makes a loss of $400 (the difference between the market price of $3 and the barter price of $1 on 200 blankets). In a competitive regime private exporters would have an incentive to cut down exports since they would be losing on the present exports which would be buying at $3 in B to sell at a barter price of only $1 in the international market. This could be offset by an export subsidy costing $400. Similarly the importers in A would have an incentive to increase their imports which cost a $1 barter price in the international market but can be sold for $1½ in A. This could be offset by an import duty in A raising $100 in revenue.

Of the $400 trading loss or export subsidy in B, $100 does not in fact lower the price to consumers in A but is offset by the $100 trading profit or import duty in A and thus accrues directly to the government in A. Exactly the same result would thus be brought about if the government in B paid out only $300 in trading loss or export subsidy, thus lowering the price of blankets only to the market price of $1½ in A, and used the remaining $100 of the revenue which it had been raising to cover its trading loss or export subsidy for the purpose of making a direct transfer of $100 to A's government. The government in A could then allow the sale of blankets in A at the world barter price and could use the $100 received from B instead of the $100 profit previously made on the import trade for the purpose of reducing the income tax in A.

It will be observed that rows 5, 6, and 7 are all cases in which the market price in B is greater than the market price in A. They are, therefore, all cases of over-trading, in the sense that—in the absence of other divergences between marginal values and costs—the consumers in both countries could be made better off by revising the deal in such a way that B sent rather less blankets to A and received rather less dollars from A, since blankets are scarcer relatively to A-products in B than in A. Conversely, rows 8, 9, and 10 are all cases of under-trading, in which blankets are scarcer relatively to A-products in A than in B, so that the market price of blankets is higher in A than in B and consumers in both countries could be made better off if rather more blankets were sent from B to A and rather more A-products from A to B.[1]

If we suppose that two State trading monopolies will never be content with bargains which leave it possible for both of them to be better off simultaneously, we can rule out barter deals such as those in rows 2, 5, 6, 7, 8, 9, and 10 of Table XXXVIII and confine our attention to those of the kind illustrated in rows 1, 3, and 4 of the table, where the market price in A is equal to the market price in B.

The figure on p. 584 shows the relationships on which the numerical example in Table XXXVIII has been constructed. Along the *OY*-axis we measure the number of blankets exported from B to A and along the *OX*-axis the total amount of dollars paid for them. Every point in the quadrant *XOY* thus represents a possible barter deal. We assume a system of trade-indifference curves for A and B[2] which are shown on the diagram. The line *K–K′* represents the contract curve, i.e. the locus of the points at which an A-trade-indifference curve is tangential to a B-trade-indifference curve. In the diagram we have assumed that the slope of these trade-indifference curves is the same (namely $2 for 1 blanket) at all points on the contract curve. This would in fact mean that the mere transfer of purchasing power from A to B or vice versa would cause no change in the price ratio between blankets and dollars, but that the consumers who received the transfer would purchase exactly those goods which were no longer purchased by the consumers who made the transfer of purchasing power. Or another way of putting this assumption is that the marginal propensity to spend on imports in the two countries adds up to unity. If the sum of the marginal propensities to import in the two countries added up to less than one we should have to draw the diagram in such a way that as we moved up the *K–K′* curve from south-east to north-west the slopes of the indifference curves became steeper and steeper.[3] We make the assumption that these slopes remain constant solely for numerical simplicity; the introduction of the more complicated assumption would not invalidate the arguments based on Table XXXVIII. The basic change would be that the two market prices in row 3 would have to be somewhat greater than $2, and in row 4 somewhat less than $2.

The numerical examples in Table XXXVIII are all based upon three different barter prices of $1, $2, and $3 respectively (column *c* of the table). These are shown in the diagram by the three price lines passing through the origin, the steepest price line representing a barter price

[1] The plausibility of these conclusions is reinforced by observing that the over-trading cases of rows 5, 6, and 7 are all cases in which the losses on (or subsidies paid to) trade exceed the profits (or duties), while the under-trading cases are all ones in which net monopoly profits are made (or a net revenue is raised from trade taxes).

[2] See pp. 12–18 of my *A Geometry of International Trade* (London, Allen & Unwin, 1952).

[3] See pp. 85–6 of my *A Geometry of International Trade*.

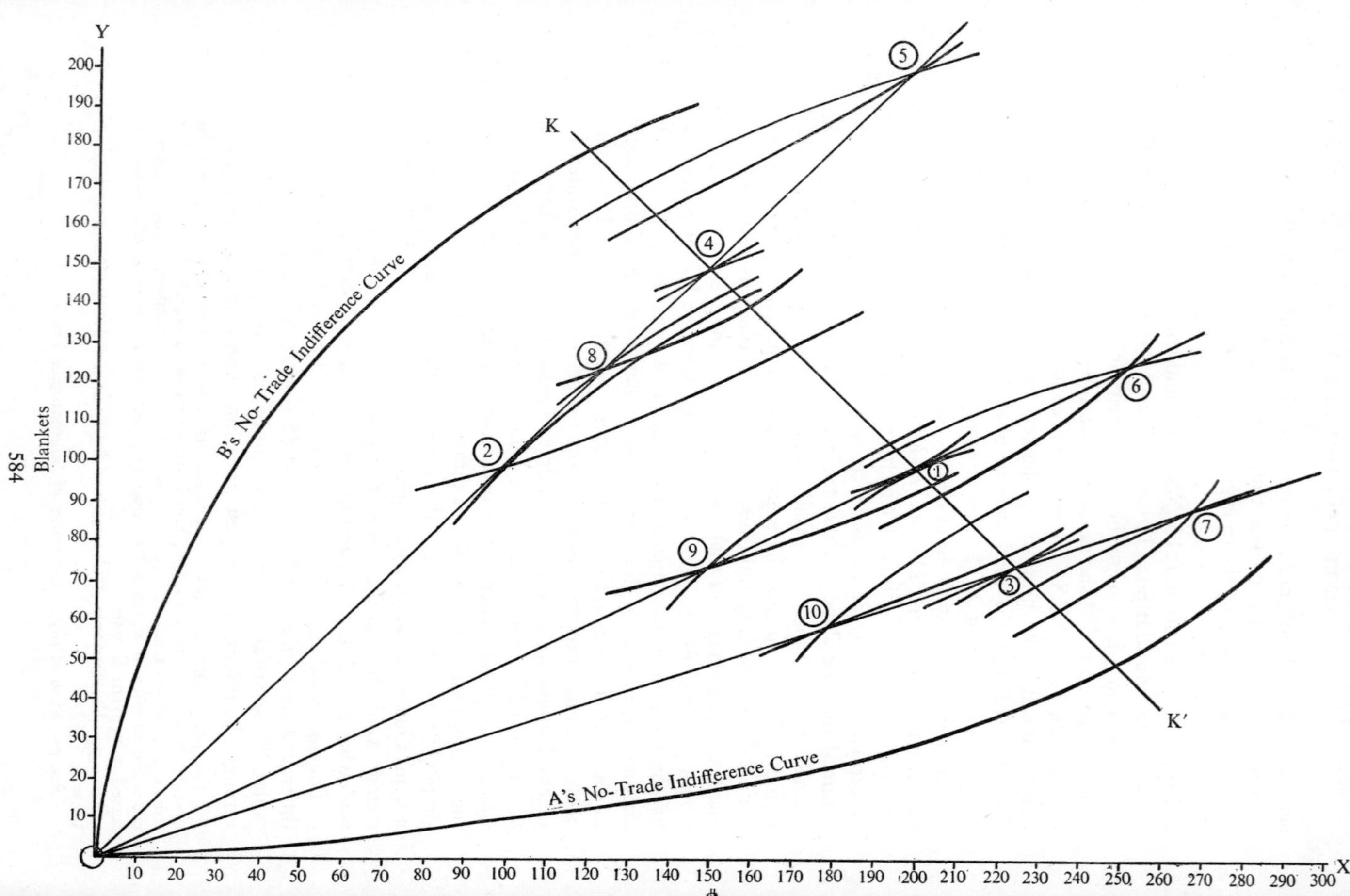

Y
X
K
K′
Blankets
B's No-Trade Indifference Curve
A's No-Trade Indifference Curve
1
2
3
4
5
6
7
8
9
10
200
190
180
170
160
150
140
130
120
110
100
90
80
70
60
50
40
30
20
10
10
20
30
40
50
60
70
80
90
100
110
120
130
140
150
160
170
180
190
200
210
220
230
240
250
260
270
280
290
300

of $1 and so on. The ten positions shown in each of the ten rows of Table XXXVIII are given corresponding numbers in the diagram. The two trade-indifference curves which pass through any one of these numbered points have slopes which correspond to the market prices given for the two countries in columns *d* and *e* of the corresponding row of the table. Thus through point 10 in the diagram the B-trade-indifference curve has a slope of 1 in 1, and the A-trade-indifference curve a slope of 1 in 2½, which corresponds to market prices for blankets of $1 and $2½ respectively.

Inspection of the diagram will reveal the fact that the indifference-maps assumed for A and B obey all the normal rules. They are negatively inclined, concave, and do not intersect. Moreover there is an absence of inferior goods in the sense that if any vertical line is drawn up from the *OX*-axis or any horizontal line is drawn away to the right from the *OY*-axis, the A-indifference curves will have a steeper and steeper slope, and the B-indifference curves a less and less steep slope, as we move along the line.[1]

It is also clear from the diagram that all the barter deals in Table XXXVIII are advantageous to both A and B. The position of A's and B's trade-indifference curves which pass through the origin *O* show that A will gain from any bargain which is more favourable to her than $250 for 50 blankets and that B will gain from any bargain more favourable to her than $120 for 180 blankets.

If we assume that any bargain which will be struck by the two State-trading monopolies will be one which does not permit both of them to become better off simultaneously by striking another bargain, we are confined to the barter deals on the contract curve *K–K′* in the figure.

[1] See pp. 14–16 of my *A Geometry of International Trade.*

APPENDIX 3

A GEOMETRICAL ILLUSTRATION OF THE CHOICE BETWEEN TWO LOCATIONS IN THE ABSENCE OF TRANSPORT COSTS

First Note to Chapter XVI

We assume that there are two countries A and B in which a particular product might be produced, that there are no costs of transporting the product between A and B, and that all the marginal conditions (see Chapters IV and V) are fulfilled for all industries in both countries. Our problem is simply to discover where the product should be produced so as to minimize its cost of production and how this is affected by the scale of the total output.

Draw a curve M_a as in Figure I measuring the output in A along the O_aX_a axis and the marginal cost of production in A up the Y_a axis, so that the area $CDEO_a$ measures the total cost of producing the output O_aE in A. Draw a similar curve for country B, but in this case measure the output in B along the O_bX_b axis from right to left, as in Figure II, so that the area $FGHO_b$ measures the total cost of producing an output O_bH in B. Place the axis O_bY_b of Figure II on O_aY_a of Figure I so that O_b coincides with O_a and then draw the origin O_b away from O_a to the right of O_a as in Figure III. Then the length O_aO_b measures the total output of the product. If we take any point K on O_aO_b, then O_aK represents the output in A and O_bK the output in B. At this point the marginal cost in A is KI and in B is KJ. Since the marginal cost in B is lower than in A, it will save cost to reduce output in A and increase it in B by moving K towards O_a; and indeed in the particular situation shown in Figure III costs could continue to be saved by moving K towards O_a until K coincided with O_a and the whole output was produced in B. The point P in Figure III represents a division of the output O_aO_b between A and B such as to make the marginal cost of production in A and B both equal to PL. But this is in fact not a position of minimum but one of maximum cost. A small shift of P to the left will bring us to a position similar to that at K, where a further shift to the left will reduce total costs. Indeed by shifting P to the left until it coincides with O_a and the whole product is produced in B, will save an amount equal to CLQ in total costs. Similarly by shifting P to the right until it coincides with O_b and the whole production is carried on in A, will save total costs equal to FLR. Clearly the output O_aO_b shown in Figure III should be produced solely in A or solely in B; it should be produced in A rather than B if $FLR > CLQ$, and vice versa. If the product is produced solely in A,

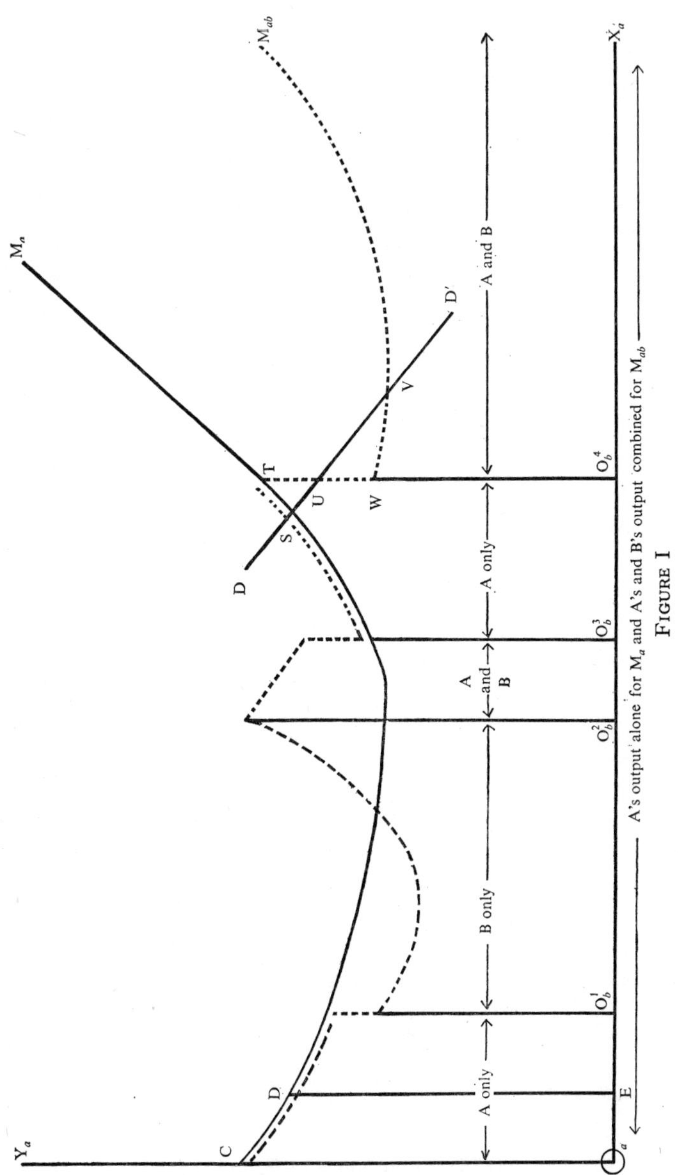

Y_a
M_a
M_{ab}
C
D
E
O_a
X_a
O_b^1
O_b^2
O_b^3
O_b^4
D
D′
S
T
U
V
W
A only
B only
A and B
A only
A and B
A's output alone for M_a and A's and B's output combined for M_{ab}

FIGURE I

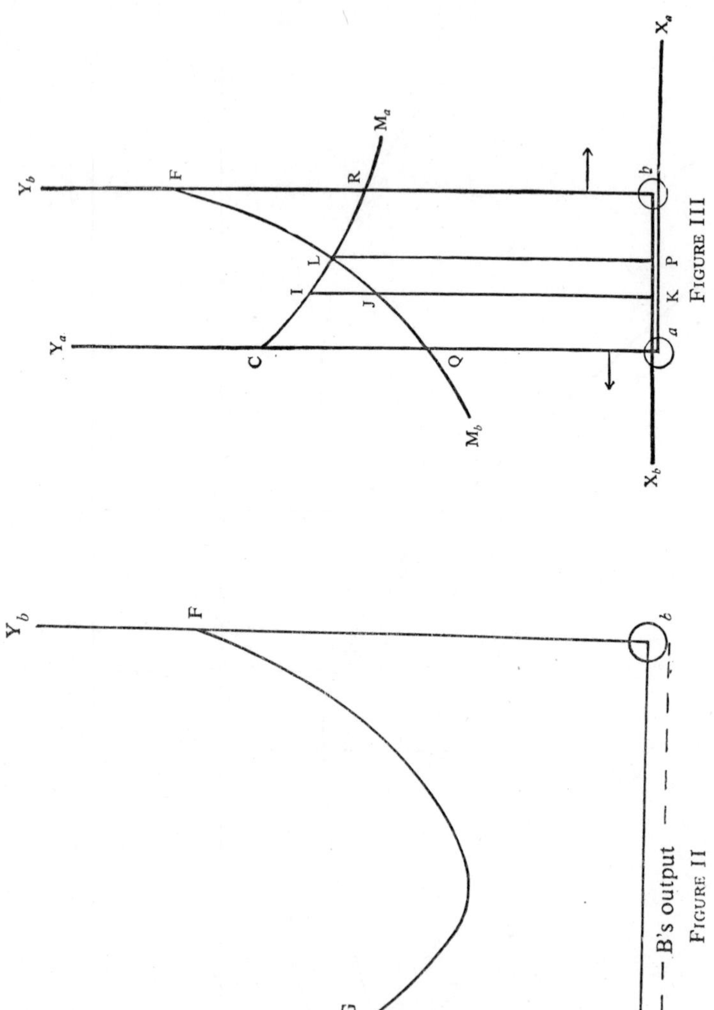

FIGURE II

FIGURE III

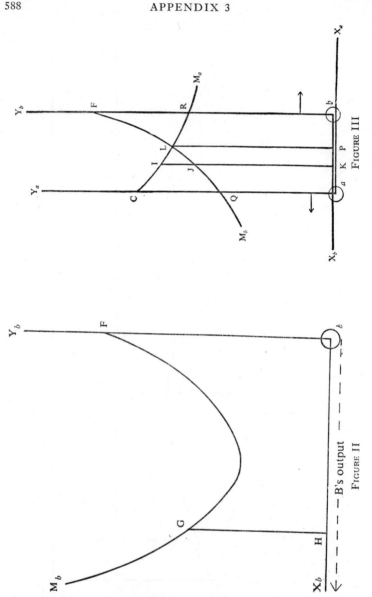

then the marginal cost of production is O_bR, and if solely in B, the marginal cost of production is O_aQ.

In Figure IV we show a position in which it might be economic to produce some of the product in both countries. The point of inter-

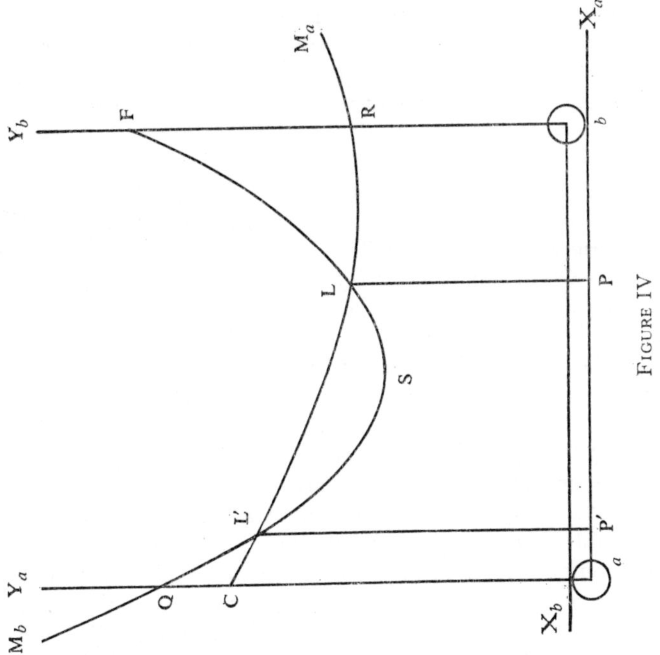

FIGURE IV

section between M_a and M_b at L is again a point of maximum cost (as it was in Figure III) and a movement of P to the right to coincide with O_b would save total costs equal to FLR. A movement of P to the left to P' would save costs equal to $L'SL$; but any movement of P further to the left (i.e. transferring output from A to B) would now raise total costs since M_b lies above M_a. In Figure IV we have to choose between a division of the output O_aO_b either at P' where A produces O_aP' and B produces O_bP' or at O_b where A produces the whole output. The former will be preferable to the latter if $FLR < L'SL$, and vice versa. In the former case the marginal cost of production will be $P'L'$ and in the latter case it will be O_bR.

By this means one can construct a curve showing the marginal cost of producing the product in A or B or in both according as each productive possibility gives the lowest total costs for each level of output. This is shown in the curve marked M_{ab} in Figure I and is derived in the following way.[1] Place O_aY_a of Figure I on O_bY_b of Figure II with O_a on O_b; draw O_b gently to the right. At first the M_a curve lies wholly below the M_b curve and it is clearly cheaper to produce in A alone, and

[1] The reader may trace the *Ma* curve of Figure I and the *Mb* curve of Figure II on two separate pieces of tracing paper, and thus observe for himself the derivation of the curve *Mab* in Figure I according to the indications given in the text.

the marginal cost will be the marginal cost in A. After a time the marginal cost in B, if B were producing the whole output, will be below the marginal cost in A if A were producing no output (Q is below C as in Figure III), but the total cost will still remain a minimum if all production is concentrated in A ($FLR > CLQ$ in Figure III). But as O_b moves further to the right CLQ grows more quickly than FLR in Figure III and it becomes economical to shift all production from A to B and the marginal cost is now the marginal cost in B (O_aQ in Figure III) instead of that in A (O_bR in Figure III). This critical point is reached at O^1_b in Figure I. As O_b moves further to the right the point Q in Figure III moves up towards C and finally moves above C. At this point it becomes economical to share the output between A and B as at the point P' in Figure IV. O^2_b in Figure I marks the critical point at which C moves from below to above Q in Figure III; and from this point onwards the height of M_{ab} in Figure I is the height of M_a and M_b at their point of intersection at L' in Figure IV. Between the points O^2_b and O^3_b in Figure I the area FLR is $< L'SL$ in Figure IV and it saves costs to divide the output at P'. But as O_b moves further to the right $L'SL$ diminishes in size and at the point O^3_b in Figure I FLR becomes $> L'SL$ in Figure IV. It saves cost now to produce only in A at a marginal cost of O_bR in Figure IV. But now as O_b moves further to the right a point is reached at which the area FLR in Figure IV begins rapidly to fall as M_a rises and R rises towards F. O^4_b in Figure I marks the point at which FLR has fallen once more to an area less than $L'SL$ and it pays once more to divide output at a point corresponding to P' in Figure IV; and the height of the M_{ab} curve will once more be equal to $L'P'$. From this point onwards it will always pay to produce in both countries at once. Indeed, a point will soon be reached at which the points L and R both coincide at F in Figure IV and from this point onwards the M_a and M_b curves will have only one point of intersection of the type of L' in Figure IV, which will clearly mark the most economic division of production.

The curve M_{ab} of Figure I thus measures the marginal-cost curve for the product allowing always for the location of production which minimizes costs. What that location should be depends upon the scale of the demand. The correct total output and the answer to the question where productive plants should be situated can be read off from the point at which the demand curve for the product from all sources cuts the M_{ab} curve of Figure I.[1]

[1] As can be seen from the demand curve DD' in Figure I, there may be more than one such point of intersection. In Figure I the points S and V are points of local optima and the point U is one of local pessimum. If output is increased beyond S total costs of SUT will be incurred in excess of consumers' surplus. But beyond U total consumers' surplus of UWV will be reaped in excess of costs. The point V should be preferred to S, if UWV is $> SUT$, and vice versa.

APPENDIX 4

AN ALGEBRAIC ANALYSIS OF THE EFFECT OF TRANSPORT COSTS UPON LOCATION

Second Note to Chapter XVI

CONSIDER any point O on a map and measure distances North and East from O along the axes ON and OE. Consider the location of a firm F which is found at a point E_f to the East of O and N_f to the North of O. Suppose that the firm F purchases a raw material from a source A which is to be found at a point E_a to the East of O and N_a to the North of O. Then from the following diagram it can be seen that (i) the distance by which F is North of A is measured by $N_f - N_a$ (which will be negative if F is South of A), (ii) the distance by which F is East of A is measured by $E_f - E_a$ (which will be negative if F is West of A), and (iii) the distance between A and F is equal to $\sqrt{(N_f - N_a)^2 + (E_f - E_a)^2}$.

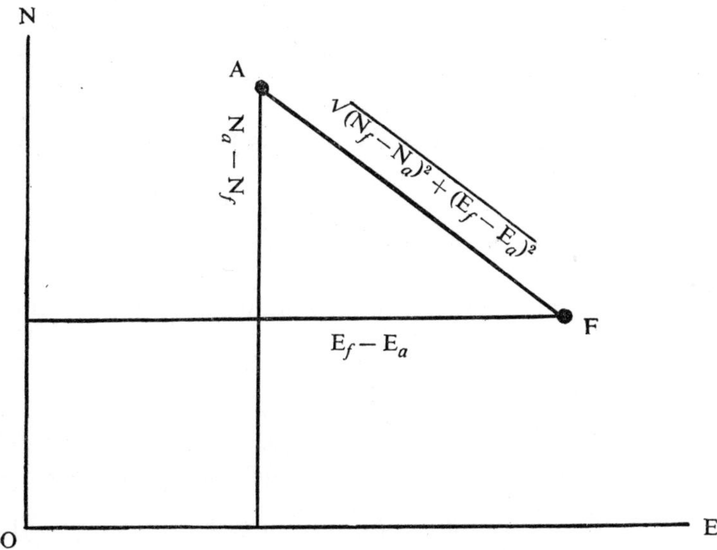

Suppose that an amount of the raw material purchased from A which is necessary for the production of one unit of F's output costs a per unit of distance to transport. Then the production of a unit of output will involve a cost upon the transport of the raw material of $a\sqrt{(N_f - N_a)^2 + (E_f - E_a)^2}$. Similarly, if there were other materials which must be purchased from other places, B, C, D, etc., we should obtain other expressions of exactly the same form for the cost of transport of these products in which the firm F would be involved if it produced one more unit of output.

Exactly similar expressions can be used for the cost of bringing the products of the firm to their markets. In the preceding argument if A is taken as the position of the market for F's product,

$$\sqrt{(N_f - N_a)^2 + (E_f - E_a)^2}$$

now measures the distance of F from the market for its product and $a\sqrt{(N_f - N_a)^2 + (E_f - E_a)^2}$ the cost of carrying a unit of the product to the market. Similarly, B, C, D, etc., can represent the markets in which other by-products must be sold and b, c, d, etc., can represent the cost of transport per unit of distance for an amount of each of these by-products which would be produced when one more unit of the main product is produced. Then expressions exactly similar to those given above can be used to express the cost of carrying the products to market.

The total transport cost directly and indirectly involved in producing one more unit of product (T) can then be represented by the sum of all these transport costs:

$$T = a\sqrt{(N_f - N_a)^2 + (E_f - E_a)^2} + b\sqrt{(N_f - N_b)^2 + (E_f - E_b)^2} + \text{etc.}$$

This transport cost will be reduced to a minimum when T can no longer be lowered by a shift of F to or from the North or a shift to or from the East. A shift of F to the North or to the South will lower transport costs according as:

$$\frac{\delta T}{\delta N_f} \equiv a\frac{N_f - N_a}{\sqrt{(N_f - N_a)^2 + (E_f - E_a)^2}} + b\frac{N_f - N_b}{\sqrt{(N_f - N_b)^2 + (E_f - E_b)^2}} + \ldots \lesseqgtr 0 \quad \ldots (1)$$

Similarly, a shift of F to the East or to the West will lower transport costs if

$$\frac{\delta T}{\delta E_f} \equiv a\frac{E_f - E_a}{\sqrt{(N_f - N_a)^2 + (E_f - E_a)^2}} + b\frac{E_f - E_b}{\sqrt{(N_f - N_b)^2 + (E_f - E_b)^2}} + \ldots \lesseqgtr 0 \quad \ldots (2)$$

We can write these two conditions in the following alternative forms:

$$\frac{\delta T}{\delta N_f} \equiv a\frac{n_a}{d_a} + b\frac{n_b}{d_b} + \ldots \lesseqgtr 0 \quad \ldots (1a)$$

and

$$\frac{\delta T}{\delta E_f} \equiv a\frac{e_a}{d_a} + b\frac{e_b}{d_b} + \ldots \lesseqgtr 0 \quad \ldots (2a)$$

where n_a measures the distance by which F is North of A (n_a is negative if F is South of A), e_a measures the distance by which F is East of A (e_a is negative if F is West of A), and d_a measures the distance between F and A.

From these two conditions we can make the following deductions:

(i) The position for F which will minimize transport costs will be one in which no small shift North, South, East, or West could further reduce such costs. In this case $\frac{\delta T}{\delta N_f}$ and $\frac{\delta T}{\delta E_f}$ will both be equal to zero. If we write the two expressions for $\frac{\delta T}{\delta N_f}$ and $\frac{\delta T}{E_f}$ at (1) and (2) above equal to zero, we then get two simultaneous equations for N_f and E_f in terms of N_a, N_b, etc., E_a, E_b, etc., and a, b, etc. The solution of these two simultaneous equations will thus give the best location for F (N_f, E_f) in terms of the locations of its sources of materials and markets (N_a, E_a; N_b, E_b; etc.) and of the cost of transport per unit of distance for each of its materials and products (a, b, etc.).

(ii) The above provides a formal solution of the problem. But the solution of these equations may provide difficulty except by a simple process of trial and error. Our two conditions in the form given at 1*a* and 2*a* above do, however, provide a very simple formula for answering the following type of question. Suppose we are considering the location of the firm F at a given point; should we be able to economize transport costs by shifting the firm a little to the North or South or a little to the East or West? In order to see whether the position of the firm should be shifted a little North or South we can use condition 1*a* in the following way. Take the cost of transport of the first material (a), multiply it by the distance by which the proposed position for F is North of A (or by minus the distance by which the proposed position for F is South of A), and divide it by the distance between A and the proposed position for F. Do this for all materials and products. If the sum of the resulting terms is positive, then a more Southerly position for the firm should be chosen, and vice versa. A similar procedure with condition 2*a* will show whether a rather more Easterly or Westerly position should be chosen for the firm.

(iii) It follows immediately from the preceding application of condition 1*a* that the best position for the firm cannot be in such a Northerly position that all its sources of materials and all the markets for its products lie to the South of it. In this case all the n's in condition 1*a* would be positive, so that the expression for $\frac{\delta T}{\delta N_f}$ would be > 0, and the firm should come South. Similarly, the best position cannot be one which leaves all sources of materials and markets for products to the North, East, or West of the firm.

(iv) From condition 1*a* one can see that $\frac{\delta^2 T}{\delta N_f \delta a} = \frac{n_a}{d_a}$. Since d_a is always positive, $\frac{\delta^2 T}{\delta N_f \delta a}$ will be $\gtrless 0$ according as $n_a \gtrless 0$, i.e. according as $N_f \gtrless N_a$. This means that a rise in the cost of transport for any one particular raw material (a) will increase the saving in transport cost (or decrease the dissaving in transport cost) by a Northerly movement of the firm if the firm is South of the source of the raw material or of the market for the product in question, and by a Southerly movement of the firm if the firm is North of the source of the raw material or of the market for the product in question. Suppose that initially the firm is in the optimum position, so that $\frac{\delta T}{\delta N_f} = 0$. Suppose then that a increases slightly, $\frac{\delta T}{\delta N_f}$ will then become positive or negative according as n_a is $\gtrless 0$, i.e. as $N_f \gtrless N_a$. In other words, when a increases slightly, the optimum position of the firm is shifted North or South towards the position of the source of the raw material or of the market for the product in question. By a similar analysis of condition 2*a* it could be shown that an increase in the cost of transport a would shift the optimum position of the firm East or West towards the position of the source of the raw material or of the market for the product in question. In other words, a high cost of transport along a particular route pulls the optimum position of the firm towards the source or market in question.

(v) If one particular cost of transport is sufficiently high, it may exert such a pull on the optimum position for the firm that the firm ought to be placed actually at that raw material source or product market. This can be shown in the following manner. Suppose that the firm did happen to lie directly North or South of a particular raw material source A, i.e. that $E_f = E_a$. Then from condition 1 it follows that

$$\frac{\delta T}{\delta N_f} = + a + b \frac{N_f - N_b}{\sqrt{(N_f - N_b)^2 + (E_f - E_b)^2}} + \quad . \quad .$$

if $N_f > N_a$ and

$$\frac{\delta T}{\delta N_f} = - a + b \frac{N_f - N_b}{\sqrt{(N_f - N_b)^2 + (E_f - E_b)^2}} + \quad . \quad .$$

if $N_f < N_a$. If follows that when $N_f > N_a$, $\frac{\delta T}{\delta N_f} \gtrless 0$ according as

$$a \gtrless - b \frac{N_f - N_b}{\sqrt{(N_f - N_b)^2 + (E_f - E_b)^2}} - \quad . \quad . \quad .$$

This means that if a is sufficiently large, then as long as the firm is North of A it would save transport costs for it to be moved South. Similarly, when $N_f < N_a$, $\frac{\delta T}{\delta N_f} \gtrless 0$ according as

$$a \lessgtr b \frac{N_f - N_b}{\sqrt{(N_f - N_b)^2 + (E_f - E_b)^2}} + \quad . \quad . \quad .$$

Or, in other words, if a is sufficiently large, then as long as the firm is South of A it would save transport costs for it to be moved North.

By an exactly similar process of reasoning it can be shown that if the firm happened to lie directly East or West of A, so that $N_f = N_a$, then if a were sufficiently large the optimum position of the firm would be neither East nor West of A but on A.

From this we may conclude that if a is sufficiently large, then the optimum position of the firm is at A. We can also see a little more clearly how large a must be to exert a sufficient pull to bring the optimum position of the firm F actually to A. It can be seen from the above argument that for this to be so both of the following conditions must be fulfilled:

$$(1)\ a > \left|\left(b \frac{N_a - N_b}{\sqrt{(N_a - N_b)^2 + (E_a - E_b)^2}} + c \frac{N_a - N_c}{\sqrt{(N_a - N_c)^2 + (E_a - E_c)^2}} + \ldots\right)\right|$$

$$(2)\ a > \left|\left(b \frac{E_a - E_b}{\sqrt{(N_a - N_b)^2 + (E_a - E_b)^2}} + c \frac{E_a - E_c}{\sqrt{(N_a - N_c)^2 + (E_a - E_c)^2}} + \ldots\right)\right|$$

Now the term $\dfrac{N_a - N_b}{\sqrt{(N_a - N_b)^2 + (E_a - E_b)^2}}$ can be expressed as $\dfrac{1}{\sqrt{1 + \left(\dfrac{E_a - E_b}{N_a - N_b}\right)^2}}$ which is a positive or negative fraction according as $N_a \gtrless N_b$. And, similarly, for the other terms in the above four conditions. It follows at once that if $a > b + c + \ldots$ (i.e. if the a-component in the cost of transport is higher than the sum of all the other separate components) then the optimum position for the firm is at A. Consider an extreme case for the first of the two conditions enumerated above, namely, where all the points B, C, etc., lie directly North of A, so that $E_a = E_b = E_c$, etc., and $N_a < N_b$, $N_a < N_c$, etc. Then the first of the above conditions becomes $a > b + c +$ etc. Now if any of the points B or C, etc., lie at all to the East or West of A, then the relevant term b or c in condition 1 above is reduced by being multiplied by a fraction; or if any of the points B or C lie South of A, then the term b or c in condition 1 above becomes negative. In either case the condition that $a > b + c +$ etc. becomes unnecessarily stringent. In other words, even if all the points A, B, C, etc., lie on the same straight line with A at the extreme end, the firm should be placed at A if $a > b + c$ + etc. But the more dispersed the points B, C, etc., are around A (North, South, East, and West of it) the less large need a be relatively to b, c, etc., in order that the best position for the firm should be at A.

APPENDIX 5

A NUMERICAL EXAMPLE OF THE CASE OF NO SPECIALIZATION IN COUNTRY A

Note to Chapter XIX

IN Table XXXIX[1] we give an example of the process of adjustment whereby, when in country A the price of a blanket falls from 2 apples to 1½ apples, land and labour move from the blanket industry to the apple industry and the marginal product of both factors which was initially twice as high in the apple industry as in the blanket industry thereby falls to being only 1½ times as high in the apple industry as in the blanket industry.

We start with 3,000 land and 1,000 labour in the apple industry, giving a ratio of 3 to 1 of land to labour in this industry; and we suppose that in this situation the marginal product of both factors is 2 apples. In the blanket industry we start with 1,000 land and 3,000 labour, a ratio of 0·333 land to labour, and we suppose that in these circumstances the marginal product of both factors is 1 blanket. This gives in the case of both factors a figure of 2 apples to 1 blanket as the ratio of the marginal product in the apple industry to the marginal product in the blanket industry.

We suppose now that the price of blankets in the market falls from 2 apples to 1½ apples. In the first stage of adjustment we suppose that labour remains immobile but that land is shifted from the blanket industry to the apple industry on a scale sufficient to reduce the ratio of the marginal product of land in apples to the marginal product of land in blankets from 2 to 1½ (column *k*). We suppose that a shift of 300 units of land will bring this about. This shift raises the ratio of land to labour in the apple industry from 3 to 3·3 (column *c*), thus causing the marginal social net product of land in apples to fall (column *d*) and the marginal social net product of labour in apples to rise (column *e*). But the fall in the first case is very much smaller (from 2 to 1·95) than the rise in the second case (from 2 to 2·15) because land is the important factor in the apple industry. In the blanket industry the ratio of land to

[1] The figures in this table have been calculated from the two production functions $A = 3{\cdot}51\, La^{0{\cdot}75}\, Ma^{0{\cdot}25}$ and $B = 1{\cdot}755\, Lb^{0{\cdot}25}\, Mb^{0{\cdot}75}$ where A = output of apples, B = output of blankets, La and Ma = amount of land and labour respectively used in the apple industry and Lb and Mb = amount of land and labour respectively used in the blanket industry. These functions imply constant returns to scale in both industries, and they mean that the ratio of the total rent of land to the total wages of labour will be always 3 to 1 in the apple industry and 1 to 3 in the blanket industry. Moreover, with initial values of La = 3,000, Ma = 1,000, Lb = 1,000, and Mb = 3,000 these functions give marginal products for both La and Ma of 2 and for both Lb and Mb of 1, so that we start with 2 apples exchanging for 1 blanket.

TABLE XXXIX

The Effect of International Trade on Two Industries in One Country in the absence of Complete Specialization

	Apple industry					Blanket industry						
	Amount of		Proportion of land to labour	Marginal product of		Amount of		Proportion of land to labour	Marginal product of		Ratio of marginal product in apple industry to marginal product in blanket industry in case of	
	land (*a*)	labour (*b*)	(*c*) $= a \div b$	land (*d*)	labour (*e*)	land (*f*)	labour (*g*)	(*h*) $= f \div g$	land (*i*)	labour (*j*)	land (*k*) $= d \div i$	labour (*l*) $= e \div j$
Initial position	3,000	1,000	3	2	2	1,000	3,000	0·333	1	1	2	2
Stages of adjustment												
1	3,300	1,000	3·3	1·95	2·15	700	3,000	0·233	1·308	0·914	1·5	2·34
2	3,300	1,650	2·0	2·21	1·477	700	2,350	0·298	1·087	0·971	2·03	1·5
3	3,520	1,650	2·134	2·175	1·55	480	2,350	0·204	1·45	0·884	1·5	1·754
4	3,520	1,950	1·805	2·27	1·367	480	2,050	0·234	1·305	0·914	1·74	1·5
Final position	3,656	2,170	1·686	2·31	1·30	344	1,830	0·188	1·537	0·868	1·5	1·5

labour has fallen from 0·333 to 0·233 (column *h*) and this has caused a large rise in the marginal product of land from 1 to 1·308 and only a small fall in the marginal product of labour from 1 to 0·914 (columns *i* and *j*), because in this case labour is the important factor. The net result is that in the case of land the marginal product in apples has fallen to only 1½ times its marginal product in blankets, since the marginal product in apples has fallen and in blankets has risen (column *k*); but in the case of labour the ratio of the marginal products in the two industries has actually risen from 2 to 2·34 because the marginal product has risen in the apple industry where labour has more land to use than before and has fallen in the blanket industry where there is now less land.

In the second stage of the adjustment we assume that land now remains immobile but that 650 units of labour move from the blanket industry to the apple industry, i.e. on a scale sufficient to bring the ratio of its marginal product in apples to that in blankets down from 2·34 to 1·5, the new equilibrium level (column *l*). This movement of labour is on a sufficient scale to bring the ratio of land to labour in the apple industry down to 2 (column *c*), i.e. not only below the existing level of 3·3 but also below the initial figure of 3. As a result the marginal product of land rises to 2·21 apples (column *d*) but the marginal product of labour falls much more to 1·477 apples (column *e*). In the blanket industry the ratio of land to labour has risen again somewhat, but only to 0·298 (column *h*) and not as high as the initial level of 0·333. As a result the marginal product of land falls again to 1·087 (column *i*) and of labour rises again to 0·971 (column *j*), though in neither case do they move right back to the initial level of 1. As a result of these changes, the ratio of the marginal product in apples to the marginal product in blankets has fallen to 1½ in the case of labour (column *l*) but has risen above 1½ to 2·03 in the case of land (column *k*), since the movement of labour from blankets to apples has raised the marginal product of land in apples and has lowered it in blankets.

It is thus once more the turn of land to move from the blanket industry to the apple industry. In the third stage of adjustment 220 units of land so move. As a result there is a slight fall in the marginal product of land in apples (from 2·21 to 2·175, column *d*) and a very marked rise in the marginal product of land in blankets (from 1·087 to 1·45 in column *i*), so that the ratio between the marginal product of land in apples and blankets is once more 1½ (column *k*). But now in the case of labour the rise in the marginal product in apples and the fall in blankets due to the fact that there is more land to work with in the apple industry and less in the blanket industry has raised the ratio of the marginal product in the apple industry to the marginal product in the blanket industry to 1·754 (column *l*). It is now labour's turn to move once more and in stage 4 the ratio between the marginal product in the apple industry and the blanket industry is lowered to 1·5 for labour but raised again to 1·74 for land. Then land moves again; and so on.

This continues until we reach the final equilibrium shown in the last row of the table. At this point 656 units of land and 1,170 units of labour have moved from the blanket industry to the apple industry. The ratio of land to labour in the apple industry has fallen from 3 to 1·686 (column *c*); as a consequence the marginal product of land which is the important factor in this industry has risen by the moderate amount of 0·31 to 2·31 (column *d*), but the marginal product of the unimportant factor labour has fallen by the much larger amount of 0·70 to 1·30 (column *e*). In the blanket industry the ratio of land to labour has also fallen from 0·333 to 0·188 (column *h*); and as a consequence the marginal product of the unimportant factor land has risen by the very substantial amount of 0·537 to 1·537 (column *i*) whereas the marginal product of the important factor labour has fallen by the much smaller amount of 0·132 to 0·868 (column *j*). As a result of this the ratio of the marginal product in apples to the marginal product in blankets is 1½ for both factors (columns *k* and *l*).

A new equilibrium has thus been reached in A, in which at a price of 1½ apples for 1 blanket both products will continue to be produced in the country. There will be no further incentive for either factor to move in either direction because for both of them the ratio between their marginal products in the two industries corresponds to the market prices of the two products.

APPENDIX 6

AN ALGEBRAIC PROOF OF THE EQUALIZATION OF FACTOR PRICES

First Note to Chapter XX

If we assume constant returns, the scale of output makes no difference to costs. We can then, regardless of the total amount of product A or product B which is produced, write:

$$\left.\begin{aligned} L_aR + M_aW &= p_a \\ \text{and } L_bR + M_bW &= p_b \end{aligned}\right\} \quad . \quad . \quad . \quad . \quad (1)$$

as expressions showing the money prices p_a and p_b of a unit of A and B respectively to be equal to the money rate of rent (R) times the amount of land (L_a or L_b) used in the production of one unit of the product A or B plus the money rate of wages (W) times the amount of labour or manpower (M_a or M_b) used in the production of one unit of the product. This will be so because, in equilibrium, money prices equal money costs. Moreover, because we are assuming constant returns to scale, the payment of rent R and wages W at rates equal to the value of the marginal products of land and labour in the two industries will just absorb the whole of the product produced (see pp. 32–36), so that the equilibrium between money prices and costs shown in equations (1) is compatible with an equilibrium between rewards to the two factors and the value of their marginal products. We shall make use of this fact in equations (4) below.

Differentiating equations (1) we have:

$$\left.\begin{aligned} L_adR + RdL_a + M_adW + WdM_a &= dp_a \\ \text{and } L_bdR + RdL_b + M_bdW + WdM_b &= dp_b \end{aligned}\right\} \quad . \quad . \quad (2)$$

If we write the output of A as a function of the amounts of land and labour (L_a and M_a) used to produce that output and then differentiate, and if we proceed in a similar manner for B, we obtain:

$$\left.\begin{aligned} dA &= dL_a\frac{\delta A}{\delta L_a} + dM_a\frac{\delta A}{\delta M_a} \\ dB &= dL_b\frac{\delta B}{\delta L_b} + dM_b\frac{\delta B}{\delta M_b} \end{aligned}\right\} \quad . \quad . \quad . \quad (3)$$

Finally, since in competitive equilibrium rates of rent and rates of wages will be equal to the value of the marginal products of land and labour in the two industries, we can write:

$$\left.\begin{aligned} R &= \frac{\delta A}{\delta L_a}p_a = \frac{\delta B}{\delta L_b}p_b \\ \text{and } W &= \frac{\delta A}{\delta M_a}p_a = \frac{\delta B}{\delta M_b}p_b \end{aligned}\right\} \quad . \quad . \quad . \quad (4)$$

We can now simplify equations (2) in the following manner. In those equations we are concerned with the change in price of a constant single unit of each commodity, the change in price occurring because of a change in rates of rent and wages which cause a substitution between land and labour for the production of the constant single unit of output. We can, therefore, write $dA = dB = 0$ in equations (3) and then combining equations (3) and (4) we obtain:

$$dL_aR + dM_aW = 0$$
$$\text{and } dL_bR + dM_bW = 0$$

If we put these restrictions on equations (2) and write $dp_a = 0$—i.e. assume that the rise in the rate of rent (dR) is just sufficient to offset the fall in the rate of wages (dW) in so far as the cost of A is concerned—we obtain the two following equations:

$$L_adR + M_adW = 0$$
$$\text{and } L_bdR + M_bdW = dp_b$$

If, finally, we eliminate dR from these two equations, we obtain:

$$\frac{dp_b}{dW} = 1 - \frac{M_a}{L_a} \cdot \frac{L_b}{M_b}$$

If this expression is positive, it means that a fall in the wage rate which is compensated by a rise in the rate of rent on a scale just sufficient to leave the cost of A unchanged will lower the cost and so the price of B. This will be so, if

$$\frac{M_a}{L_a} \cdot \frac{L_b}{M_b} < 1, \text{ i.e. if } \frac{L_a}{M_a} > \frac{L_b}{M_b}$$

i.e. if A is the land-intensive and B the labour-intensive product.

The above proof is true only for a small change in the money wage rate. But so long as the production of A remains relatively land-intensive, a succession of small falls in the money wage rate, each of which is compensated by a rise in the money rate of land which is sufficient to keep the money cost of A constant, will cause a succession of rises in the price of B. If, therefore, A is always land-intensive, a large fall in the money wage rate which is compensated by a rise in the money rate of rent sufficiently large to keep the money price of A constant, will necessarily cause a rise in the money price of B.[1]

[1] Professor A. P. Lerner has devised a convincing geometrical proof of the above proposition. See his *Essays in Economic Analysis* (London, Macmillan, 1953), pp. 67–84.

APPENDIX 7

A NUMERICAL EXAMPLE OF THE EQUALIZATION OF FACTOR PRICES

Second Note to Chapter XX

IN this note we propose to work, in some detail, through an arithmetical example of a case in which freedom of international trade and freedom of international factor movements are complete substitutes for each other—a case in which either free trade alone or free factor movements alone would suffice to bring about a complete equality of the marginal product of each factor in each industry in each country. Essentially the present note will add nothing new to the argument of Chapter XX. Indeed, in at least one important respect the argument of the present note will be seen to be more restricted in its scope than that of Chapter XX.

But there may nevertheless be something to gain from an example of the way in which, in appropriate conditions, either a freeing of trade or a freeing of factor movements may bring international equality to marginal products, if we start from a situation in which the marginal product of any one factor is not the same in the two countries. In Chapter XX we enumerated and explained the conditions which must be satisfied for this to be the case. In this note we shall see an example of the way in which the sizes of the various industries in the two countries and the factor proportions in the various industries in the two countries will change as the transition is made from inequality to equality of marginal products either by the mechanism of free trade or by the mechanism of free factor movements.

We start, then, with all the assumptions which we have made on p. 332, but we add the additional simplifying assumption that only two products, apples and blankets, are made in the whole world economy. Thus we have two countries A and B, each country producing two but only two products, apples and blankets, each product being produced by two but only two factors, land and labour. The production function for each product is supposed to be the same in country A as in country B; and in the case of each industry there are constant returns to scale. There is free and costless trade in apples and blankets between A and B, and the production of apples is always land-intensive and of blankets labour-intensive.

A numerical example based on these assumptions is shown in Table XL. This table is based upon certain production functions. Thus it can be seen, for example, that in country A in the original position $66\frac{2}{3}$ units of labour and 150 units of land combine to produce

2,175 units of apples, the marginal product of labour being then 13·05 units of apples and that of land 8·70 units. Before we use this table to illustrate the argument of Chapter XX, it may be useful to say something about the particular production functions which are used in the table.

(1) These production functions depict constant returns to scale. This can be seen from the table in two ways. First, as between position ii and position iii it will be seen that in the apple industry in A both the amount of labour and the amount of land have gone up by 20 per cent (from 100 to 120 in the case of labour and from 150 to 180 in the case of land) and in consequence the amount of output has also gone up by 20 per cent (from 2,500 to 3,000). Second, in the case of constant returns we have already seen (pp. 32–36) that the payment to each factor of a reward equal to the value of its marginal product will absorb exactly as much as the total output. We have throughout the table assumed marginal products for the factors which satisfy this constant-returns requirement. Thus in the apple industry in A in the original position if $66\frac{2}{3}$ units of labour were paid their marginal product of 13·05 this would make up a wage bill of $66\frac{2}{3} \times 13{\cdot}05$ or 870; and similarly the rent bill would be $150 \times 8{\cdot}7$ or 1,305; and 870 plus 1,305 equals 2,175, which is equal to the total output.

(2) The marginal product of any one factor in any one industry is assumed to depend solely upon the proportion in which it is used with the other factor. Thus between position i and position ii the ratio of labour to land in the apple industry in country A is assumed to rise from $\frac{66\frac{2}{3}}{150}$ to $\frac{100}{150}$; and as a result the marginal product of labour is assumed to fall (from 13·05 to 10) and the marginal product of land is assumed to rise (from 8·7 to 10). But between position ii and position iii the ratio of labour to land in the apple industry in A does not alter although the total amounts of both factors used increases $(\frac{100}{150} = \frac{120}{180})$, with the result that the marginal product of both factors in this industry remains unchanged.

(3) The apple industry is assumed throughout to be land-intensive and the blanket industry to be labour-intensive. This is shown in our numerical example in the following way. The marginal products of each factor varies in such a way that in the apple industry in every situation in each country labour receives 40 per cent of the product, whereas in the blanket industry it always receives 80 per cent of the product. Thus in position i in the apple industry labour receives $66\frac{2}{3} \times 13{\cdot}05$ or 870 out of a total product of 2,175, which is a proportion of 40 per cent; and in position ii it receives 100×10 or 1,000 out of a total product of 2,500, which is once more a proportion of 40 per cent. Now if the amount of labour employed in the blanket industry

receives always 80 per cent of the product and in the apple industry 40 per cent of the product, it is clear that at any given rate of wages and rent of land which is charged to both industries the ratio of labour to land must be higher in the blanket industry than in the apple industry.[1]

We are now in a position to consider the analysis which is illustrated by Table XL. In position i in that table—the original position—we assume that there is no trade and no factor movement between countries A and B. Country A has in all 200 units of labour and 200 units of land, and country B 400 units of labour and 200 units of land. These factors are used in each country to produce the apples and the blankets needed in that country. We assume that within each country the conditions of maximum production are fulfilled. That is to say (i) the marginal social net product of each factor is the same in every firm in either industry in either country (output cannot be increased by moving any factor from one firm to another within an industry within a country) and (ii) in each country the ratio of the marginal social net product of labour to that of land is the same in all industries (output cannot be increased by moving labour from one industry to another and land in the opposite direction). It can be seen from Table XL that this second condition is satisfied in the numerical example given in position i. Thus in country A the ratio of the marginal product of labour to that of land is 13·05 : 8·7 in the apple industry and 10·85 : 7·23 in the blanket industry, and both of these ratios is equal to 1·5 : 1.

But while output is maximized within each country in the original position in Table XL world output is not maximized. Country A starts with a relatively low proportion of labour to land (200 to 200) while country B starts with a relatively high proportion of labour to land (400 to 200). For this reason in country A both apples and blankets have to be produced by means which involve a low ratio of labour to land in both industries; but in country B methods of production have to be used which involve great economies of land relatively to labour. Thus in the original position the ratio of labour to land in the apple industry is only 0·44 to 1 in A but is 0·88 to 1 in B, whereas in the blanket industry it is only 2·66 to 1 in A but 5·33 to 1 in B.

Labour will thus be scarce and land plentiful in both industries in A relatively to B. The marginal product of labour will therefore be high in A and low in B, whereas the marginal product of land will be low in A and high in B. In both industries it is important to have more

[1] The numerical examples in Table XL are in fact calculated from the following formulae $A = 19{\cdot}6\ M_a^{0{\cdot}4}\ L_a^{0{\cdot}6}$
and $B = 16{\cdot}49\ M_b^{0{\cdot}8}\ L_b^{0{\cdot}2}$
where A = output of apples, M_a the amount of manpower, and L_a the amount of land used in their production; and similarly, for B, the output of blankets. These formulae will be found to have all the characteristics mentioned in the text.

TABLE XL

The Equalization of Factor Prices

		Country A: Amounts of factors and output	Country A: Marginal product	Country B: Amounts of factors and output	Country B: Marginal product	Both countries. Amounts of factors and output
		(i) Original Position				
Apple industry	Labour	66⅔	13·05*	133⅓	8·32*	200
	Land	150	8·70*	150	11·10*	300
	Output	2,175	—	2,773	—	4,949
Blanket industry	Labour	133⅓	10·85*	266⅔	9·44*	400
	Land	50	7·23*	50	12·59*	100
	Output	1,807	—	3,147	—	4,954
Both industries	Labour	200	—	400	—	600
	Land	200	—	200	—	400
		(ii) Adjustment through International Migration				
Apple industry	Labour	100	10	100	10	200
	Land	150	10	150	10	300
	Output	2,500	—	2,500	—	5,000
Blanket industry	Labour	200	10	200	10	400
	Land	50	10	50	10	100
	Output	2,500	—	2,500	—	5,000
Both industries	Labour	300	—	300	—	600
	Land	200	—	200	—	400
		(iii) Adjustment through International Trade				
Apple industry	Labour	120	10	80	10	200
	Land	180	10	120	10	300
	Output	3,000	—	2,000	—	5,000
Blanket industry	Labour	80	10	320	10	400
	Land	20	10	80	10	100
	Output	1,000	—	4,000	—	5,000
Both industries	Labour	200	—	400	—	600
	Land	200	—	200	—	400

* Note that (i) $\frac{13{\cdot}05}{8{\cdot}70} = \frac{10{\cdot}85}{7{\cdot}23} = 1{\cdot}5$ and $\frac{8{\cdot}32}{11{\cdot}10} = \frac{9{\cdot}44}{12{\cdot}59} = 0{\cdot}75$

and (ii) $\frac{13{\cdot}05}{10{\cdot}85} = \frac{8{\cdot}70}{7{\cdot}23} = 1{\cdot}2$ and $\frac{8{\cdot}32}{9{\cdot}44} = \frac{11{\cdot}10}{12{\cdot}59} = 0{\cdot}88$

labour in A and unimportant to have more land; and the opposite is true in B. Thus in the numerical example given in Table XL the marginal product of labour is higher in A than B in both industries; in the apple industry it is 13·05 in A against 8·32 in B and in the blanket industry it is 10·85 in A against 9·44 in B. With land it is the other way round; the marginal product is lower in both industries in A than in B (8·70 against 11·1 in the case of apples and 7·23 against 12·59 in the case of blankets).

World production could clearly be increased by a movement of labour from B to A since the output lost in B by the loss of a unit of labour (the marginal product of labour in B) would be less than the output gained in A by the gain of a unit of labour there (the marginal product of labour in A). This is what we suppose to happen in the adjustment shown in position ii. The movement of 33⅓ units of labour from B's apple industry to A's apple industry and of 66⅔ units of labour from B's blanket industry to A's blanket industry will make the ratios between the factors employed in any one industry the same in both countries; it is now 0·66 to 1 for the apple industry in both countries and 4 to 1 for the blanket industry in both countries.

As a result of this movement the ratio of labour to land has gone up in both industries in A; labour has become more plentiful and land has become relatively scarcer. The marginal product of labour has therefore fallen in both industries in A (from 13·05 to 10 in the apple industry and from 10·85 to 10 in the blanket industry). The opposite has happened in A to the marginal product of land which has become relatively scarcer in both industries; the marginal product of land has accordingly risen from 8·7 to 10 in the apple industry and from 7·23 to 10 in the blanket industry. In B, on the other hand, labour has become scarcer and land relatively more plentiful; the marginal product of labour has accordingly risen in both industries (from 8·32 to 10 in the apple industry and from 9·44 to 10 in the blanket industry); and the marginal product of land has fallen (from 11·1 to 10 in the apple industry and from 12·59 to 10 in the blanket industry). In position ii the marginal product of labour is the same in A and B and the marginal product of land is the same in A and B; world production is now maximized, because it is no longer possible to increase total output by a further international movement of factors.

In the numerical example given in Table XL the result of the movement of labour from B to A has been to increase the world output of apples from 4,949 units to 5,000 units, and of blankets from 4,954 to 5,000 units.

Let us now return to position i and assume that there is now no international movement of factors of production but a completely free and costless movement of the products apples and blankets between the two countries. In our numerical example apples are taken to represent an industry which requires a relatively high proportion of land per man employed and blankets an industry in which labour is much more important. Thus in both A and B the ratio of labour to land is higher in the blanket industry than in the apple industry; in A in the apple industry it is 0·44 to 1 and in the blanket industry 2·66 to 1, and in B in the apple industry it is 0·88 to 1 and in the blanket industry 5·33 to 1. Now in A labour is scarce, its marginal product is high, and its wage rate will therefore tend to be higher. On the other hand land is plentiful, its marginal product is low, and its reward will therefore tend to be low. This means that in A it will be relatively cheap to produce apples (where the expensive factor labour is not so important but the relatively cheap factor land is very important) and expensive to produce blankets (where great reliance must be put upon the expensive factor labour). Conversely, in B blankets will be cheap to produce and apples expensive.[1] Thus free trade will lead to an export of apples from A to B and an export of blankets from B to A. The apple industry will expand in A and contract in B; and the opposite will happen to the blanket industry.

By this means we may ultimately reach an equilibrium like that shown in position iii of Table XL. The total amounts of the factors in each country have not changed; as in position i there are 200 units of labour and 200 units of land in A and 400 units of labour and 200 units of land in B. But both labour and land have been shifted from the blanket industry to the apple industry in A and in the opposite direction in B. This has enabled the production of each commodity to be carried on with the same ratio of labour to land in both countries. For example, in the apple industry now the ratio of labour to land in A has risen from 0·44 to 0·66 $\left(\text{i.e. from } \frac{66\frac{2}{3}}{150} \text{ to } \frac{120}{180}\right)$ and in B has fallen from 0·88 to 0·66 $\left(\text{i.e. from } \frac{133\frac{1}{3}}{150} \text{ to } \frac{80}{120}\right)$. The marginal products of each factor have in this way become equal in each country, because each is now used in the same ratio with the other factor in each country. So far as world output is concerned, position iii is as good as position ii, and no further

[1] In our numerical example the marginal products of factors in the apple industry in A are, in physical terms, 20 per cent greater than in the blanket industry (i.e. 13·05 ÷ 10·85 = 8·70 ÷ 7·23 = 1·20). In other words, for equilibrium within A the price of a unit of apples in A must be 20 per cent *below* the price of a unit of blankets. In B the marginal products of factors are 12 per cent lower in physical terms in the apple industry than in the blanket industry (8·32 ÷ 9·44 = 11·10 ÷ 12·59 = 0·88), so that for equilibrium in B the price of a unit of apples must be 12 per cent *above* the price of a unit of blankets. Otherwise money rewards to any factor in any country would be different as between the two industries.

improvement could be achieved by a movement of factors from one country to another.

In other words, position i is an inefficient position because labour has to be used in an inefficiently high ratio to land in B, and because land has to be used in an inefficiently high ratio to labour in A. This could theoretically be rectified in either of three ways. First, the labour could move from B where it is plentiful to A where it is scarce. Secondly, the land might move from A where it is plentiful to B where it is scarce.[1] Thirdly, A might concentrate on the production of the commodities in which it was economically efficient to use a high ratio of land and B on the production of the commodities in which it was economically efficient to use a high ratio of labour, and they might then exchange the products which their original factor endowments made them best suited to produce.

[1] Of course, if 'land' stands for immovable natural resources this solution is ruled out. But if the second factor were movable (e.g. if it were capital) the question would arise whether the capital should move to the labour or the labour to the capital. With our simple assumptions it would be immaterial which factor moved.

APPENDIX 8

A NUMERICAL EXAMPLE OF THE EFFECT OF FISCAL POLICIES UPON INTERNATIONAL FACTOR MOVEMENTS

Note to Chapter XXV

In Table XLI we give a simple numerical example of the three main points raised in the discussion in Chapter XXV of the effect of domestic fiscal policies on the incentives for factors of production to move between countries. To illustrate these points we have confined our attention to one very simple form of progressive fiscal system. We assume that in every case a flat percentage rate of income tax is raised on all incomes of rich and poor alike, but that the whole of the revenue so raised is used to finance the payment to every individual of the same absolute benefits, whether in the form of direct money grants (like cash paid in family allowances) or in the form of real services (like educational or health services provided on the same scale to every citizen, rich or poor). This naturally has the effect of redistributing income from rich to poor. For example, suppose that a community were made up of one rich man with an income of \$1,000 and one poor man with an income of \$200; suppose that a flat rate of tax of 10 per cent is imposed on all incomes so that a revenue of \$120 is raised (\$100 from the rich man and \$20 from the poor man); and suppose that this revenue of \$120 is used to pay social benefits of \$60 to each of the two citizens. Then the rich man's net income is reduced from \$1,000 to \$960 (he loses \$100 in tax and gains \$60 in benefits); and the poor man's income is raised from \$200 to \$240 (he loses \$20 in tax and gains \$60 in benefits). The degree of redistribution can be increased by raising the rate of tax and using the increased revenue to pay more generous social benefits.

We assume throughout our example (rows 1, 2, 3, and 4, columns *a* and *b* of Table XLI) that in A there are two rich factors (A_1 and A_2) with earnings of \$400 each and one poor factor (A_3) earning \$100, and also that \$30 is always paid in social benefits to each factor.

In case i (rows 5, 6, 7, 8, and 9 of the table) we assume that the composition of the factors in country B is such that B has only one rich factor (B_1) and two poor factors (B_2 and B_3); but there is no difference between the marginal product and so the earnings of any one rich factor in A and in B (a rich factor earns \$400 in both countries) or between the earnings of any one poor factor in A and in B (a poor factor earns \$100 in both countries). There is an economic distribution of factors between the two countries, since any given factor has the

TABLE XLI

Domestic Fiscal Policies and International Factor Movements

		Earnings	Benefits	Tax payments: with consolidated budget for AB	Tax payments: with separate budgets for A and B	Net income: with consolidated budget for AB	Net income: with separate budgets for A and B
		$	$	$	$	$	$
		(a)	(b)	(c)	(d)	(e) = (a) + (b) − (c)	(f) = (a) + (b) − (d)
				Country A. All Cases			
				(Rate of tax 12%)	(Rate of tax 10%)		
A_1	(1)	400	30	48	40	382	390
A_2	(2)	400	30	48	40	382	390
A_3	(3)	100	30	12	10	118	120
Total A	(4)	900	90	108	90	882	900
				Country B. Case (i). *B has high proportion of low-earning factors*			
				(Rate of tax 12%)	(Rate of tax 15%)		
B_1	(5)	400	30	48	60	382	370
B_2	(6)	100	30	12	15	118	115
B_3	(7)	100	30	12	15	118	115
Total B	(8)	600	90	72	90	618	600
Total AB	(9)	1,500	180	180	180	1,500	1,500
				Country B. Case (ii). *B's factors have low marginal products*			
				(Rate of tax 12%)	(Rate of tax 15%)		
B_1	(10)	266⅔	30	32	40	264⅔	256⅔
B_2	(11)	266⅔	30	32	40	264⅔	256⅔
B_3	(12)	66⅔	30	8	10	88⅔	86⅔
Total B	(13)	600	90	72	90	618	600
Total AB	(14)	1,500	180	180	180	1,500	1,500
				Country B. Case (iii). *B has a more highly progressive fiscal system*			
					(Rate of tax 20%)		
B_1	(15)	400	60		80		380
B_2	(16)	400	60		80		380
B_3	(17)	100	60		20		140
Total B	(18)	900	180		180		900
Total AB	(19)	1,800	270		270		1,800

same marginal product in both countries. We assume further in case i (column *b*) that the scale of social benefits in B is the same as in A, every factor receiving in both cases $30 in such benefits.

We have now to consider the problem of raising the revenue required to pay these benefits. In columns *c* and *e* of the table we suppose that A and B are amalgamated into a single country with a single uniform rate of tax. Since the total income of AB is \$1,500 (\$900 earned in A and \$600 in B) and since the total benefits to be paid are \$180 (\$90 in A and \$90 in B) a tax rate of 12 per cent is required. (\$180 = 12 per cent of \$1,500). In column *c*, rows 1–9, we show the amounts paid in tax at a uniform rate of tax of 12 per cent. In column *e* we can then see the net income which comes to each factor in each country after deducting tax payments (column *c*) but adding benefits (column *b*) to earnings (column *a*). It will be observed that the effect is that the rich factor's income is reduced to \$382 and the poor factor's income is raised to \$118 in both countries. There has been a redistribution of income from rich to poor factors and, as can be seen from the table, this involves the transfer of \$18 from the rich country A to the poor country B. In A net incomes in column *e* have fallen to \$882, or \$18 below the \$900 earnings in A shown in column *a*. In B, on the contrary, net incomes have risen to \$618 from the initial earnings of \$600. But after the change the rich factor continues to receive the same amount whether it is situated in A or in B and the poor factor continues to receive the same amount whether it is situated in A or in B. There is no uneconomic incentive introduced for movements of factors between the two countries.

But the case is different if, as in columns *d* and *f*, we assume that A and B are now separate countries which must have their own separate budgets. A has earnings of \$900 and needs to finance social benefits of \$90; she needs therefore a tax rate of only 10 per cent. But B has earnings of \$600 from which to finance benefits of \$90; and she therefore requires a tax rate of 15 per cent. In column *d* accordingly we show what the tax payments would be with a tax rate of 10 per cent in A and of 15 per cent in B. From this we can in the same way as before calculate the net incomes which each factor will enjoy after deducting these revised tax payments (column *d*) from the sum of each factor's earnings and social benefits (columns *a* and *b*). The results are shown in column *f*. It can now be seen that the policy of equal social benefits in the two countries has caused the net income of the rich factor to be lower in B than in A and the net income of the poor factor to be lower in B than in A. There will now be some incentive for all mobile factors to move from B to A; and this will be uneconomic since in fact the marginal product (column *a*) of any given factor is as high in B as it is in A.

We turn now to case ii. The position in A we assume to be unchanged, as in rows 1–4 of the table. The position in B, however (rows 10–14), is quite different. The total earnings of B are not changed; they were \$600 in case i (row 8, column *a*) and they are once more \$600 in case ii (row 13, column *a*), as opposed to the earnings of A of \$900 (row 4, column *a*). But the reason for B's relative poverty is now quite different. In case i B was poor because she had only one rich factor and two poor factors; but in case ii B, like A, has two rich factors (B_1 and B_2 in rows 10 and 11) and only one poor factor (B_3 in row 12). But now, for example, because of an unfavourable productive atmosphere in B, each factor is one-third less productive in B than in A. A rich factor which would produce a product worth \$400 in A produces a product worth only \$266⅔ in B; and a poor factor which would produce a product worth \$100 in A produces a product worth only \$66⅔ in B. Provided that the costs of movement do not outweigh these differences in productivity both factors ought to move from B to A. In fact the rich factors will have an incentive to move from B to A unless the cost of movement exceeds the resulting increase in their productivity of \$133⅓ (i.e. \$400 minus \$266⅔); and, similarly, the poor factor will have an incentive to move unless the cost of its movement exceeds the increase in its productivity of \$33⅓ (i.e. \$100 minus \$66⅔).

Let us now consider the effect upon these incentives of the introduction of fiscal policies for the redistribution of income. We assume as before that in both countries (column *b*) \$30 is spent on social benefits for each factor and that the funds are raised by a proportionate income tax. In columns *c* and *e* we assume that A and B form one consolidated country with a single fiscal system. The total income of AB as before is \$1,500 and the total benefits to be paid in AB are also \$180 as before. A uniform tax rate of 12 per cent is needed to raise the required revenue. In column *c*, rows 10–14, we show the effect of this on B in the case which we are now examining. From this we can deduce in column *e* the net incomes which remain to the factors after deducting tax payments from their earnings and social benefits. It is to be observed that the net result is to blunt the incentive to move from B to A. A rich factor's marginal product in A (\$400) exceeds its marginal product in B (\$266⅔) by \$133⅓; and before the introduction of the redistributive fiscal policy in AB it would have moved if the cost of movement had been less than this. After the introduction of the fiscal policy its net income in A (\$382) exceeds its net income in B (\$264⅔) by only \$117⅓. It will move from B to A only if the cost of movement is below \$117⅓, although it ought to move so long as this cost is less than \$133⅓. And similarly with the poor factor. The difference between its product in A (\$100) and its product in B (\$66⅔) is \$33⅓; but now the difference between its net income in A (\$118) and its net income in B (\$88⅔) is only \$29⅓. To this extent its incentive to move is uneconomically blunted. If there were no cost of movement, this would not matter. Each factor's net income will remain higher in A than in B so long as its earnings in A are higher than in B; and if the factor moves from B to A as long as its net income is at all higher in A than in B, this blunting of the incentive does not matter. But if there is a cost of transport—for instance, of \$120 for the rich factor or \$30 for the poor factor in our example—the factor may be discouraged from moving when it is really economic for it to do so.

But the position is changed if (as in column *f* of case ii) each country has to be responsible for its own separate budget. In this case, as in the similar position in case i, the rate of tax in A can be reduced to 10 per cent in order to finance \$90 in social benefits out of total earnings of \$900; but the rate of tax in B must be raised to 15 per cent in order to finance the same expenditure on social benefits out of earnings of only \$600. The resulting tax payments in B are shown in column *d*, rows 10–12; and the resulting net incomes in B are shown in column *f*, rows 10–12.

It is clear that the incentives to move from B to A have now been fully restored. A rich factor's net income in A is now \$390 instead of only \$382 (row 1, columns *e* and *f*); whereas in B it is now only \$$256\frac{2}{3}$ instead of as much as \$$264\frac{2}{3}$ (row 10, columns *e* and *f*). Its net income in A now once more exceeds its net income in B by \$$133\frac{1}{3}$ (\$390 minus \$$256\frac{2}{3}$), which corresponds exactly to the extent to which its marginal product in A (\$400) exceeds its marginal product in B (\$$266\frac{2}{3}$). And the same is true of the poor factor. Its net income in A (\$120) now once more exceeds its net income in B (\$$86\frac{2}{3}$) by \$$33\frac{1}{3}$, which corresponds to the excess of its marginal product in A over its marginal product in B. The correct incentives to move have been restored.[1]

Finally in case iii of the table we illustrate the case where A and B are otherwise similar countries, but have separate and divergent fiscal policies for the redistribution of income. Thus in case iii B's factor composition and earnings are exactly the same as A's; the figures in column *a*, rows 1–3, are reproduced in column *a*, rows 15–17. But the government of B wishes to go further than the government of A in using fiscal policy for the redistribution of income. Social benefits of \$60 are paid to each factor in B (column *b*, rows 15–17), while only \$30 is paid in A (column *b*, rows 1–3). The result is, of course, that whereas A need levy a tax of only 10 per cent on all earnings, B must levy a tax of 20 per cent on all earnings in order to finance her payment of social benefits. The tax payments made under these two scales in A and B are shown in column *d*, rows 1–3, and rows 15–17. From this the net incomes remaining to the factors in A and B are deduced in column *f*, rows 1–3, and rows 15–17.

In both countries the net incomes of the rich factors have been

[1] But this has, of course, been at the expense of a less equal distribution of income. As a result of the separation of national budgets, the net income of the rich factor which was already higher in A than in B has gone up further in A (from \$382 to \$390) and has gone down further in B (from \$$264\frac{2}{3}$ to \$$256\frac{2}{3}$). And similarly with the poor factor. It was already receiving less in B than in A, and its net income has been lowered in B and raised in A.

reduced below their earnings of $400 and the net incomes of the poor factors have been raised above their earnings of $100. But the process has gone further in B than in A with the result that the net income of the rich factor is now lower in B ($380) than in A ($390), while the net income of the poor factor is higher in B ($140) than in A ($120). This might give an incentive for the rich factors to move from B to A and for the poor factor to move from A to B. But these movements would be uneconomic, since the marginal product of any one factor is in fact the same in both countries.

INDEX

PRINTED IN GREAT BRITAIN BY
HAZELL WATSON & VINEY LTD
AYLESBURY AND LONDON